The Ultimate OS/2® Programmer's Manual

John Mueller

McGraw-Hill

New York   San Francisco   Washington, D.C.   Auckland   Bogotá
Caracas   Lisbon   London   Madrid   Mexico City   Milan
Montreal   New Delhi   San Juan   Singapore
Sydney   Tokyo   Toronto

Library of Congress Cataloging-in-Publication Data

Mueller, John, 1958–
    The ultimate OS/2 programmer's manual / by John Mueller.
        p.   cm.
    Includes index.
    ISBN 0-07-043971-0   ISBN 0-07-043972-9
    1. OS/2. (Computer file)   2. Operating systems (Computers)
I. Title.
QA76.76.O63M843   1994
005.4'469—dc20   93-43685
                                                              CIP

pbk 1 2 3 4 5 6 7 8 9   DOH/DOH   9 9 8 7 6 5 4
hc   1 2 3 4 5 6 7 8 9   DOH/DOH   9 9 8 7 6 5 4

ISBN 0-07-043971-0   ISBN 0-07-043972-9

The sponsoring editor of this book was Brad Schepp, the editor was John C. Baker, and the production supervisor was Katherine G. Brown. This book was set in Souvenir Light. It was composed in Blue Ridge Summit, Pa.

Printed and bound by R.R. Donnelley & Sons Company.

For more information on other McGraw-Hill materials, in the United States please call 1-800-822-8158. In other countries contact your local McGraw-Hill representative.   WK2

Contents

Appendices

This book is dedicated to Heather, Aaron, and Jason
for all the joy and happiness they bring to my life.
May your choice in careers be as rewarding as mine is for me.

Introduction

The *Ultimate OS/2 Programmer's Manual* is a complete reference guide to programming in the OS/2 environment. This includes OS/2 function calls; EGA, VGA, and Super VGA displays; and an update on the newest OS/2 2.1 additions. The *Ultimate OS/2 Programmer's Manual* covers both OS/2 full-screen and Presentation Manager programming. It also contains a full description of many of the functions that you need for device driver programming and tells you how to make the most of the memory available in this environment.

This book provides a solid foundation for low-level programming in any language by explaining how particular OS/2 functions work. Especially helpful are the discussions of three currently undocumented OS/2 function groups: KBD, MOU, and VIO. It also provides much heavier coverage of the DOSDevIOCtl function than most books on the market. This makes *The Ultimate OS/2 Programmer's Manual* unique because it does not force you to learn about OS/2 using a language you might not know. It simply provides the tools you need to create dazzling applications.

 # Who should use this book

Both beginners and experienced programmers can benefit from *The Ultimate OS/2 Programmer's Manual*. For beginners, this book explains how OS/2 works, how to use the OS/2 service routines, how to access ROM and OS/2 functions, and what each function does. For experienced programmers, this book provides a handy reference to the many OS/2 and ROM functions available from any language.

You should be familiar with a programming language to benefit the most from this book. I tested all program examples in this book using Borland Turbo Assembler and Borland C++ 3.1. I used the standard Borland debugger in most cases. If you use any other vendors' implementation of C or assembler, you might have to change the program examples in this book slightly to make them work properly.

 # What this book will do

This book provides three types of information necessary for programming an IBM-compatible computer. First, this book will explain how to make maximum use of the OS/2 environment when writing programs. Second, this book shows equivalent programs written in two of the most popular programming languages. Third, this book shows how to mix the different languages to create a single program. For example, you could write part of a program to access the ROM BIOS using assembly language and design a user interface with C. Not only does this book show you how programs in different languages work, but it shows you how to integrate different languages together within the OS/2 environment.

Why use Borland compilers?

Although competing language compilers might offer more features or convenience than the Borland compilers for OS/2, I chose to use Borland compilers for compatibility reasons. Only Borland offers a

complete range of compatible language compilers that can work together. (Microsoft used to provide this capability but dropped all OS/2 support in recent versions of their compiler.) Thus, you can write part of your program in assembly language for speed and direct access to hardware interrupts and functions, and mix your assembly language routines with the more structured C or Pascal languages.

In addition, the Borland C compiler closely adheres to the ANSI C language standards. This means that you can write code using the Borland C compiler and port it over to a completely different machine. Using compilers that follow language standards ensures that this book will always provide relevant, accurate information no matter what new changes appear in future compiler versions.

⇨ Equipment used

Every program in this book is tested on at least two different machines. The first machine includes a Hauppauge 80386 motherboard, 80387 math coprocessor, ATI VGA Wonder card, Logitech MouseMan bus mouse, and a Samtron VGA monitor. The second machine includes a Hauppauge 80486 motherboard, Video Seven VRAM II ERGO card, Logitech MouseMan serial mouse, a MultiSync 3D monitor, a Hitachi 1503S CD-ROM drive, and a Creative Labs Sound Blaster board. The software used includes Borland compilers along with OS/2 2.1. I made every effort to ensure that the program examples work on any computer configuration. However, given the ever changing state of computer equipment and software, this is not possible to verify.

If you experience any problems, try running the same program on a different computer. If the problem disappears, then you know that your computer equipment is at fault. If the problem persists, write to me in care of the publisher and let me know so that I can verify the problem and find a way around it for the next edition of this book. You also can contact me on CompuServe at 75300,576. I really would appreciate hearing any comments (both positive and negative) or suggestions you might have.

⇨ **What this book contains**

Each chapter of *The Ultimate OS/2 Programmer's Manual* discusses a particular aspect of OS/2 programming in more detail. Where possible, program examples include both assembler and C. Many of the low level programming examples require extensive use of assembly language.

✳ **Chapter 1: Visiting the OS/2 command line and Workplace Shell**   This chapter provides the you with three different types of information. First, it tells you how to automate and enhance the OS/2 command-line (character-mode) interface. This includes REXX programming and batch files. Second, this chapter tells you how to manipulate the Workplace Shell and use the graphical user interface to their advantage. This is an important section considering that many programmers come from a character-mode background and might not feel comfortable with a graphical user interface. Using the graphical user interface also means creating test suites using a combination of REXX and the Workplace Shell. Finally, we explore the Developer Connection for OS/2. This is a CD-ROM containing a plethora of programming tools and other aids. The Developer Connection for OS/2 provides you with complete access to most of IBMs beta software so that you always get advanced notice of new technology before it occurs.

✳ **Chapter 2: Processor commands and interfaces**   This chapter provides detailed explanations for the different microprocessors used in the IBM computer family. The chapter covers the 8088/8086, 80286, 80386, and 80486 along with their respective math coprocessors: 8087, 80287, and 80387. It also covers the new Pentium processor from Intel. This might be the only book on your shelf that contains such extensive information on such a wide variety of Intel processors.

✳ **Chapter 3: Video API**   Chapter 3 describes the video application programming interface (API) provided by OS/2. This chapter views programming from the business application viewpoint. Because OS/2 does not allow direct hardware manipulation by "ring 3" applications, the programmer must use the tools supplied by the operating system.

This chapter also assumes that you want to program for the Workplace Shell. (The text will note whether the you can use a particular call for character and graphics mode applications.) There are two main areas addressed by this chapter: drawing functions and window message functions. The programmer needs to know how to use both to program in OS/2. In addition to these two main topics, the chapter also will discuss how to use fonts within an application. This includes determining which fonts the application can access as well as other topics of interest.

✳ **Chapter 4: Keyboard and mouse API**   As with chapter 3, chapter 4 assumes that you need to write application programs. This means that the application runs at ring 3 and cannot access the keyboard or mouse directly. The keyboard sections of the chapter assume that the programmer is writing for the character-mode interface. The mouse sections assume that the programmer is writing for the Workplace Shell. In both cases, the chapter does address the needs for programmers creating device drivers and other ring 2 applications. For example, it is very likely that someone writing a device driver will need to use the OS/2 DOSDevIOCtl functions to access the keyboard and/or mouse.

✳ **Chapter 5: Parallel/serial port API**   This chapter assumes that you want to write a low-level routine that might or might not appear as part of an application. There is one section for each port type. The DOSDevIOCtl function provides you with very low-level access to the port. This usually happens when the developer needs to create a device driver or other ring 2 application. However, you can use these function calls even if you want to create an application program running at ring 3.

✳ **Chapter 6: Disk API**   This chapter covers the three levels of support provided by OS/2 for disk operations. The first layer is the disk operating system level. Ring 2 and character mode applications use this part of the API. The next two sections assume that you want to create a Workplace Shell application. The first section covers standard disk operations in a virtual setting. The second section covers physical disk operations.

✳ **Chapter 7: Multimedia API**   Version 2.1 of OS/2 introduces multimedia extensions that are similar to those found in Windows NT and Windows 3.1. This chapter covers the use of those extensions when used to create REXX applications. Chapter 7 is an extension of the REXX section of chapter 1. It takes a Workplace Shell application approach. Most of the coding samples will concentrate on the sound board and CD-ROM drive because these are the two components most programmers need to include in their applications. You can create any of these applications without buying additional multimedia kits; everything used in this chapter comes with a standard OS/2 installation.

✳ **Chapter 8: Memory management**   Chapter 8 takes a very low-level look at OS/2 memory management. Anyone creating an OS/2 program could benefit from the material in this chapter. It covers memory allocation, protection, virtual memory, and segmentation types. The approach taken for this chapter is the general OS/2 application. It will provide an equal number of application, device driver, and low-level programming examples. At least one of the applications includes the Workplace Shell and shows how to circumvent any problems with that environment.

⇨ Using Hungarian-style notation

There are several programming conventions used throughout this book that might or might not help you in your programming endeavors. Both the programming examples and the text use these conventions to make it easier to see what task a function or variable performs at a glance. An understanding of these conventions will help you receive more information from the examples in this book and from many programming books in general. In addition, these same concepts are equally applicable to C and assembly code. Many developers contributed to the form of these conventions by discussing them at conferences and on bulletin board systems (BBS).

The first stage of development for this system was started by Charles Simonyi of Microsoft Corporation. He called his system Hungarian Notation, and that is what most people call their systems today.

There are many places that you can obtain a copy of his work, including many BBS. This book uses a derivative of that original work as outlined in the following paragraphs. You can use this derivative within your REXX and OS/2 programs to enhance readability. There are four reasons why you should use these naming conventions in your programs.

> Mnemonic value—This allows the programmer to remember the name of a variable easily, which is an important consideration for team projects.

> Suggestive value—You might not be the only one modifying your code. If you are working on a team project, others in the team will most likely at least look at the code you have written. Using these conventions will help others understand what you mean when using a specific convention.

> Consistency—A programmer's ability often is viewed as not only how efficiently they program or how well the programs they create function but how easily another programmer can read their code. Using these conventions will help you maintain uniform code from one project to another. Other programmers can anticipate the value or function of a section of code simply by the conventions you use.

> Speed of decision—In the business world, the speed at which you can create and modify code often will determine the level of success of a particular venture. Using consistent code reduces the time that you spend trying to decide what someone meant when creating a variable or function. This reduction in decision time will increase the amount of time you have available for productive work.

⇨ Function naming conventions

The following rules will help you understand the conventions used to name functions throughout the book:

> All functions will show their return type. Because C is a strongly typed language, this is a very easy task. Even though assembler is not strongly typed, the examples in this book will

make every effort to provide a return type. We will show the return type using a standard qualifier. A listing of these standard qualifiers appears in the section on variable naming conventions.

➤ All function names contained within an application are typed in lowercase. All library functions appear in a mixture of upper- and lowercase with the initial character capitalized. This saves other programmers the time and effort of looking for an unfamiliar function within your code when it really is part of the C library and vice versa.

➤ In many cases, a function converts one value to another value. To differentiate these functions from functions that perform a more generalized task, type the input value, then a 2, then the output value. For example, if you were to create a function for converting a value from the frequency domain to the time domain, you probably would name the function Freq2Time.

➤ Always define a function using only one or two standard qualifiers. The tendency of some programmers is to use so many qualifiers to define a function name that the intent of using this practice is circumvented. The purpose of the function becomes difficult to determine because of the number of qualifiers.

➤ It is always convenient to quickly find where a keyword appears within the source code. To help in this, always capitalize keywords like FOR and SWITCH.

Using these five rules will make it much easier to determine the purpose and origin of the functions you use within a program.

➡ Variable naming conventions

Variables are one of the hardest parts of a program to understand. Unlike functions and procedures, variables are not defined in the manual anywhere and few programs have published data dictionaries. As a result, there often is a lot of confusion that exists about the exact meaning of a variable. There are several ways that you can

make it easier to understand the variables that you use within a program. The following rules are meant as guidelines and are used throughout this book:

> ➤ Always prefix a variable with a single lowercase letter indicating its type. In most cases, this is the first letter of the variable type, so it is easy to remember what letter to use. The following examples show the most common prefixes. This does not include some of the more esoteric OS/2 prefixes, but it should provide you with everything you need for the majority of the material in this book:
> - a   Array
> - ab   Anchor block
> - b   Byte (8-bits)
> - bm   Bitmap
> - c   Count
> - ch   Single-byte character
> - d   Difference between two instances of a type
> - dc   Device context
> - e   Element of an array
> - env   Environment
> - f   Flag
> - fn   Function (not a pointer, but the actual function reference)
> - gr   Group
> - h   Handle
> - hh   Huge handle
> - hp   Huge pointer (32-bit)
> - ht   Help table
> - i   Index (used with a variable)
> - ib   Index byte (an address offset)
> - id   Identifier
> - l   Long (32-bits)
> - lp   Far pointer (32-bit)
> - mq   Message queue
> - mt   Menu table
> - n   Numeric
> - np   Near pointer (16-bit)
> - o   Object
> - p   Pointer

- pal   Palette
- ps   Presentation space
- rcl   Rectangle (normally coordinates in an array structure)
- sb   Segment base
- st   Pascal-type string (length of string in first byte)
- sz   C-type null terminated string
- u   Unsigned (always used with the b, l, or s identifiers)
- v   Never use, someone could confuse it with VOID
- w   Word
- wnd   Window

➤ A standard qualifier can help someone see the purpose of a variable almost instantly. For example, using the Clr qualifier tells the viewer that this variable is used in some way with color. You can even combine the qualifiers to amplify their effect and describe how the variable is used. For example cClrCrs is a character variable that determines the color of the cursor on the display. Using one to three of these qualifiers usually is sufficient to describe the purpose of a variable. The following standard qualifiers are examples of the more common types:

- Ar   Array
- Attr   Attribute
- B   Bottom
- Clr   Color
- Col   Column
- Crs   Cursor
- Dbf   Database file
- F   First
- File   File
- Fld   Field
- L   Last/Left
- Msg   Message
- Name   Name
- R   Right
- Ret   Return value
- Scr   Screen
- Str   String
- T   Top
- X   Row
- Y   Column

➤ An optional "pointer reference:"
- 1,2,3   State pointer references as in cSavClr1, cSavClr2, etc.
- Max   Strict upper limit as in nFldMax, maximum number of Fields
- Min   Strict lower limit as in nRecMin, minimum number of Records

⇨ A note on function names

In some of the tables throughout this book, long function names have been broken and hyphenated. When using these functions, you should spell the names solid, without the hyphen.

1

Visiting the OS/2 command line and Workplace Shell

T HIS chapter provides you with three different types of application specific information. Each piece of information helps you to program more efficiently and with less effort without buying a lot of third-party products that your company might not want to support. Learning to use the tools supplied with a product might seem mundane or unimportant, but these tools can help you realize significant gains in programming speed and accuracy. This is an important consideration in any production programming environment. We're not talking about the obvious tools like the compiler and editor that you need to program, but the ancillary tools supplied with OS/2 that many programmers ignore as too insignificant.

The first section of the chapter tells you how to automate and enhance the OS/2 command-line (character-mode) interface. This includes REXX programming and batch files. You can extend the REXX character mode interface to the Workplace Shell (WPS) using PMREXX. Many programmers already are familiar with DOS-style batch files; OS/2 adds a few twists to batch file programming that you might find interesting. While many people think that REXX is simply another batch file language, it provides much more in the hands of an experienced programmer. The Developer Connection for OS/2 includes many enhanced REXX programming tools that you can use to create fully functional Presentation Manager (PM) applications; you do not need the Developer Connection to run these applications. Using both tools helps you completely automate your programming environment and might even provide an alternative to C++ or assembly language programming in some instances.

NOTE   I'll simply refer to The Developer Connection for OS/2 as the Developer Connection from this point on. The Developer Connection is a subscription service that you can order from IBM to keep you informed of the latest OS/2 developments and tools. You can order this service by calling 1-800-6-DEVCON. Annual service rates start at $200. The subscription currently includes four CD-ROM updates per year along with the *Developer Connection News* newsletter.

The second section of this chapter tells you how to manipulate the Workplace Shell (WPS) and use the graphical user interface to your

advantage. This is an important section considering that many programmers come from a character-mode background and might not feel comfortable with a graphical user interface. Using the graphical user interface also means creating test suites using a combination of REXX and the WPS (or the PMATE utility supplied with the Developer Connection). Make sure you install PMREXX support during your OS/2 installation. This allows you to extend REXX to the Workplace Shell. In addition, many of the examples will require you to use the advanced tools provided with the Developer Connection.

Finally, we explore the Developer Connection. The Developer Connection is a replacement for IBM's Profession Developer Kit (PDK) with a few exceptions and a lot of additions. Unlike the PDK, the Developer Connection is not a one time service; it is a subscription service that keeps you constantly up-to-date on the latest OS/2 developments. This is a CD-ROM and newsletter combination that contains a plethora of programming tools and other aids. The Developer Connection is not simply a compiler (Developer Connection provides a compiler only if IBM has one in the beta test cycle) or beta testing platform; it contains full documentation for many areas of OS/2 that you might find difficult to obtain using other methods. In addition, it provides a complete copy of any OS/2 beta test components (up to and including the entire operating system) and many programming tools that you can use with or without your favorite C/C++ compiler. Even if you decide to use a third-party compiler, many of the tools in the Developer Connection will help you reduce your programming time significantly. (This is especially true if you plan to perform any multimedia programming within OS/2.)

 Using OS/2 CMD files to automate your work

The OS/2 CMD file is equivalent to the DOS BAT file; both allow you to automate tasks at the command line. Anything that you can do with a DOS batch file you can do with an OS/2 CMD file. The two environments are so alike that you can run many of your DOS batch files under the OS/2 environment with little more change than the

file extension. This means that you conceivably could move many of your DOS batch files into the OS/2 environment with little or no change. Of course, you will want to modify the files to take advantage of OS/2 features.

There are a few additional commands provided for the OS/2 batch programming environment. While you can emulate many of these extra commands in the DOS environment, the OS/2 environment is more convenient. The SetLocal and EndLocal commands are one example of these enhancements. (There is both a command and function version of these commands.) You no longer need to rely on esoteric methods for preserving the user's original drive, directory, and environment. These commands allow you to save and restore these important characteristics using simple one-line commands. Table 1-1 provides a complete list of the OS/2 batch file commands.

Table 1-1   **The OS/2 CMD command summary**

Command	Description
Call	This command allows you to call another batch file from within the current batch file. Use it to nest batch files. The Call command essentially allows you to create modularized programs using batch files.
CMD	Use this command to create another copy of the OS/2 command processor.
Command	Use this command to create another copy of the DOS command processor.
Echo	There are two states associated with this command. You can either send the current command to the display using Echo On or remove it from the display using Echo Off. Using Echo Off within the CMD file allows you to hide the details of a process from the user.
EndLocal	Use this command to restore the drive, directory, and environment variables in effect when you last issued a SetLocal command.
Exit	This command allows you to leave the current command processor and return to the previous command processor (if any). You return to the WPS if there is no previous command processor in effect.
ExtProc	You can use this command to define your own batch pocessor. This allows you to use any special commands required to accomplish the work you need to do in a batch environment. CMD.EXE transfers control to your batch file if the ExtProc command appears as the first line in the batch file.

Command	Description
For	The For command allows you to perform repetitive work within a batch file. It works much like any other loop command except that the entire structure appears on one line.
Goto	Use this command to transfer control from the current point in the batch file to any label within the batch file. It works much like the BASIC Goto command.
If	The If command allows you to perform conditional processing of a particular command. If the specified condition is true, then the command gets processed; otherwise, it doesn't. There are three conditions you can test for: the existence of a particular file, an error level returned by an application, or the equivalence of two strings.
Pause	You can use this command to stop batch file processing until the user presses a key. This command is handy for displaying messages on screen and allowing the user time to read them.
ProtShell	Use this command to specify the user command-line interface program and the OS/2 command processor. OS/2 uses a default of CMD.EXE for this command.
REM	This command allows you to place remarks in your batch files.
SetLocal	You can use this command to save the current drive, directory, and environment variables. This allows you to define a local environment without changing the original settings. Use the EndLocal command to restore the saved settings. You cannot nest SetLocal commands; OS/2 saves only the most recent settings for you.
Shell	Use this command to specify the DOS command processor. OS/2 uses a default of COMMAND.COM.
Shift	This command provides the means for using more than 10 variables within a batch file (of course, only 10 are visible at any time). You can shift only to the left. In other words, parameter 1 becomes parameter 0. OS/2 does not allow for reverse shifting; any parameters that scrolled off the left side of the parameter list are unrecoverable.

As you can see, there are minor differences between the OS/2 and DOS environments. This means that you can refer to one of the many DOS batch file programming books on the market for additional ideas. My personal favorite in this category is *Enhanced Batch File Programming* (2nd Edition) by Dan Gookin (ISBN 0-8306-3854-7).

⇨ Using REXX to create utility programs and other aids

Anyone who uses an operating system for very long will find it not only convenient, but essential to automate some of the tasks that they perform. Rather than mechanically reproduce the same set of keystrokes repeatedly, it is a lot faster to record them once and let the computer do the repetitive work.

While OS/2 does provide a batch language, there are two reasons that REXX is a much better solution for automating repetitive tasks. First, REXX is a lot more powerful than the native batch language. Its flexibility will allow you to do a lot more with less effort. In some ways, you can think of REXX as the batch enhancers used by many DOS users. Second, the REXX file extension of CMD will allow you to separate OS/2 specific batch files from DOS batch files on the same drive.

⇨ Understanding REXX command files

To use REXX, you must end the filename of your batch file with the CMD extension and provide a comment as the first line. When you type the name of a file with the CMD extension at the OS/2 prompt, it looks at the file, determines that it is a REXX batch program, then executes the instructions using the REXX interpreter. Every REXX file can contain one or more of the following elements:

> ➤ Comments
> ➤ Strings
> ➤ Instructions
> ➤ OS/2 commands
> ➤ Assignments
> ➤ Labels
> ➤ Internal functions

Each element within a REXX program allows you to perform a specific task. The following sections describe these elements in further detail.

⇨ Comments

Comments provide the means for documenting your batch file. Documentation consists of your name, the date that you created the batch file, the purpose of the batch file, notes on why you added some sections to the batch file or performed some specific task, and a listing of any modifications that you make to the batch file. Many people feel that documenting their batch files is a waste of time and effort, only to find out later that they can't figure out why they wrote a batch file the way that they did. Comments always take some amount of time to write correctly, but the dividends to you later more than make up for the expenditure today.

⇨ Strings

Strings allow you to tell the person using your batch file something or ask for a piece of information. You also can use strings to dress up the appearance of your program. Any time you want to send text to the display, you use a string to do it.

A string always appears within a set of single or double quotes. For example, both "Hello World" and 'Hello World' are strings. In most cases, the choice of using either a single or double quote is up to you. When the REXX interpreter sees the quote, it stops interpreting what you've written and simply displays it.

You occasionally will need to display a quote within a string. If you need to display a single quote, then enclose your string with double quotes as follows: "Jack liked Mary's new car." Sometimes you'll need to display double quotes in conjunction with a single quote. In these cases, just use two double quotes together. For example, the string "Mary heard Jack's brother say ""Boy, do you have a nice car."" displays as: Mary heard Jack's brother say "Boy, do you have a nice car."

 # Instructions

Instructions are REXX specific commands and control structures. This is the way that you tell REXX how you want it to perform a specific task. For example, if you want REXX to display something on screen you can use the SAY command as follows: SAY "Something." I cover commands and control structures as part of the Macro Language description in the following paragraphs.

 # OS/2 commands

Allowing you to execute OS/2 commands is one of the main reasons to use REXX. Once you get the information that you need from the person using your batch file, tell them what the batch file is going to do, and tell REXX how you want it to perform a specific task, you'll execute one or more OS/2 commands. I show you how to integrate OS/2 commands with the REXX macro language in the programming section of this chapter.

 # Assignments

Sometimes, you'll need to keep track of a specific piece of information during the execution of the batch file. REXX allows you to do this by assigning the piece of information to a variable. The variable acts like a box that you store the piece of information in until you need it again. Just like any other box, you can take the old piece of information out and put a new piece of information in. For example, you can store the value of an arithmetic expression in a variable as follows: Sum = 1 + 2. The variable Sum now contains a value of 3. If you make another assignment later, REXX will replace the value of 3 with a new value. You'll see some practical examples of using assignments in the programming section of this chapter.

Labels

Labels act as street signs in your batch file. If you want REXX to stop performing a specific task, you can tell it to go to another part of the

batch files. Labels provide the means for telling REXX where to go; it simply looks for the right street sign.

Internal functions

REXX provides you with shortcut methods for performing some tasks. Internal functions allow you to take one or more pieces of information and use them to find out something else. For example, if you want REXX to figure out the maximum of three numbers, you would use the MAX function as follows: MAX(Number1, Number2, Number3). REXX provides you with over 50 built-in functions. I discuss some of the more important functions as part of the following section.

⇨ Using the REXX macro language

There are three essential parts to any REXX program: control structures, commands, and functions. A control structure tells REXX how to execute your program. In essence, it is a map that REXX follows from the start of your program to the end. A command is an instruction that you want REXX to perform. For example, you can tell REXX to display some information on screen or retrieve information from the keyboard. A function allows you to take a shortcut to finding out specific pieces of information. In many ways, a function in REXX is just like a function in your spreadsheet. You provide REXX with one or more pieces of information, and it provides the information you're looking for as output.

These three parts of REXX combine to form a macro language. In many ways, this macro language is no different from the macros that you create for your word processor or spreadsheet. The only real difference is that REXX works with the operating system, not a specific application.

⇨ Boolean operators

There is one element of the macro language that crosses boundaries into just about every area of REXX programming. Boolean operators

help REXX evaluate a given set of conditions and perform a specific task based on what it finds. There are only two values returned by Boolean operators: 1 for true and 0 for false.

* **AND operator (&)**   The AND operator allows you to perform a logical union of two expressions. You are in effect saying, if expression 1 is true & (and) expression 2 is true, then return a value of true. If either expression is false, then the entire expression is false.

* **Comparisons > < =**   REXX allows you to compare to values. For example, if you wanted to see if one value was greater than another, you would type: Var1 > Var2. Likewise, if you wanted to see if one value is less than another, you would type: Var1 < Var2. The output of these comparisons is 1 for true or 0 for false.

* **NOT Operator (¬ or \)**   You use the NOT operator to reverse the condition of an evaluation. For example, if you said \(1 = 1), then REXX would evaluate the expression as false, even though 1 does indeed equal 1.

* **OR Operator (|)**   The OR operator allows you to perform a logical intersection of two expressions. You are saying, if expression 1 is true | (or) expression 2 is true, then return a value of true. The only time you receive an output of false is when both expressions are false.

⇨ Control structures

There are three basic forms of control structure supported by REXX. The conditional statement allows you to perform an action based on whether or not an expression is true or false. There is only one action to perform. Think of a conditional statement like a light switch in your home. You can either turn the light on or off depending on the position of the switch. The IF..THEN..ELSE control structure is the conditional statement for REXX.

REXX also supports a switch statement. In this case, you select one action from a group of actions based on a specific condition. Think of a switch statement like the soda machine at work. You insert a coin, press one out of a group of switches, and receive a specific kind of

SELECT WHEN *Expression1* **THEN** *Statement1* **[WHEN** *Expression2* **THEN** *Statement2...*] **[OTHERWISE** *Statementn*] **END** The SELECT..WHEN..OTHERWISE switch is the best control structure to use when there is more than one possible choice that the user could make. REXX looks at *Expression1* first. If this expression is true, then it executes the statement following the first THEN clause. If the expression isn't true, REXX evaluates the second and following expressions. If REXX can't find any true expressions, then it looks for the OTHERWISE clause and executes any statements appearing after it. Once it executes one of the THEN clause statements, REXX exits the control structure. You need to supply only one WHEN clause with this control structure. The second and preceding WHEN clauses are optional. The OTHERWISE clause is optional as well. However, if you don't provide an OTHERWISE clause, REXX will exit the control structure without doing anything if it doesn't find a true expression. The following example shows how you could use the SELECT..WHEN..OTHERWISE switch:

```
SAY "Type your age and press Enter."
PULL Age
SELECT
    WHEN Age < 13
        THEN SAY "You are a child."
    WHEN (Age > 12) & (Age < 20)
        THEN SAY "You are a teenager."
    OTHERWISE
        SAY "You are an adult."
END
```

Notice that you must always end a SELECT..WHEN..OTHERWISE control structure with an END clause. This is the only way that REXX knows that you finished the switch. Also, notice that the OTHERWISE clause does not require a THEN clause. If you add a THEN clause, REXX will exit your program with an error.

Like the IF..THEN..ELSE control structure, REXX allows you to combine the SELECT..WHEN..OTHERWISE switch with the DO..END control structure. This allows you to follow a THEN clause with more than one statement.

soda in return. The switch statement in REXX is the SELECT..WHEN..OTHERWISE control structure.

The final control structure is the loop statement. A loop statement allows you to perform one section of code one or more times based on a counter variable. For example, say that you wanted to get three candy bars from the machine at work. First, you'd place some money in the slot, then you'd pull the appropriate switch and retrieve your candy bar. To get three candy bars, you'd perform this sequence of steps three times. There are several loop statements for REXX including the DO..LOOP, DO UNTIL.., DO WHILE.., and DO FOREVER control structures.

You can "nest" these control structures to perform more elaborate sequences of instructions. Nesting structures is the process of placing one control structure within another. Each structure still is its own unique element, but they work together to produce a specific result.

✳ **DO** *Number Statements* **[LEAVE] END** This form of the DO..END loop is the most basic form of the control structure that you'll ever use. REXX executes the instructions within the control structure the number of times specified by number. The only way to exit the structure prematurely is to add a LEAVE clause. The LEAVE clause is an optional part of this control structure. The following example shows how to use the DO..END loop:

```
SAY "Enter a number."
PULL Counter
LastCount = 1
DO Counter
    SAY LastCount
    LastCount = LastCount + 1
    SAY "Do you want to count some more?"
    PULL Answer
    IF Answer = "NO"
        THEN LEAVE
END
```

Notice that you must add an END clause to the end of this control structure. Otherwise, REXX will not know when the control structure ends. This example also shows one way to use the LEAVE clause. Notice that unless the user enters NO when asked if they want to count some more, that REXX continues to process the loop.

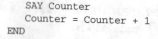
✳ **DO *Variable = Number1* TO *Number2* Statements [LEAVE] END** In some cases, you can increase program execution speed and reduce memory requirements by combining a counter variable with an output variable. This form of the DO..END loop allows you to do both with a little careful planning. It is like the previous form of the control structure in all other respects. The following example shows you how to use this form of the DO..END loop:

```
DO Counter = 1 TO 10
    SAY Counter
END
```

✳ **DO WHILE *Expression* Statements [LEAVE] END** You won't always know how many times to execute a loop. Sometimes, the number of executions depends on conditions that you can't control when you write the batch file. The DO WHILE..END loop checks an expression before it executes the statements within the control structure. It continues to execute the instructions while the expression is true. As soon as the expression becomes false, the control structure exits and REXX continues execution at the statement following the END clause. The following example shows how to use the DO WHILE..END loop:

```
SAY "Enter a filename you want to display."
PULL ListFile
DO WHILE \(ListFile = "")
    type ListFile
    SAY "Enter a filename you want to display."
    PULL ListFile
END
```

✳ **DO UNTIL *Expression* Statements [LEAVE] END** The DO UNTIL..END loop evaluates an expression after it executes a set of statements. This assures that a loop will always execute at least once, no matter what happens. The DO UNTIL..END loop continues to execute a set of instructions until the expression that you specify becomes true. The following example shows how to use the DO UNTIL..END loop:

```
Counter = 1
DO UNTIL Counter = 1 /* Loop executes at least once. */
    SAY Counter
END
DO UNTIL Counter = 10
```

```
    SAY Counter
    Counter = Counter + 1
END
```

✳ **DO FOREVER Statements LEAVE END.** There a reasons to use the DO FOREVER..END loop. This loop execute until the user manages to break out of it. As a should always include a LEAVE clause as part of the co control structure.

✳ **IF *Expression* THEN *Statement* [ELSE *Statement*]** IF..THEN..ELSE control structure is one of the most co structures that you'll need when creating a REXX progr Essentially, this control structure says that, if the expres REXX will perform the statement appearing after the T The ELSE clause is optional, which is why it appears in the heading of this section. REXX automatically perform statement appearing after this clause if the expression i following example shows how you would use the IF..TH control structure:

```
IF Var1 > 5
    THEN SAY "Input was greater than 5"
    ELSE SAY "Input was less than or equal to 5"
```

You can use this control structure with a DO..END cont you need to perform more than one statement after the ELSE clauses. The following example shows how you w two structures together:

```
SAY "Type your age and press Enter."
PULL Age
IF Age > 18
    THEN
        DO
        SAY "You are over 18."
        SAY "What would you like to drink?"
        PARSE PULL DrinkName
        SAY "Fixing you a " DrinkName
        END
    ELSE
        DO
        SAY "You are not over 18."
        SAY "I can't fix you a drink."
        END
```

⇨ Commands

Many people have trouble keeping commands and functions separate when creating a program. The key to remember is that a function always returns a value but might not do any other work. A command always performs some type of work but never returns a value. REXX offers a wide assortment of commands that help you control the batch file environment.

❋ **ADDRESS [*Environment* [*Expression*]] [[*Value*] *Expression 1*]**
This command allows you to redirect the current input stream (the statements in your REXX application) to another application. For example, you could direct the stream to an editor or other application and perform macro-like functions.

There are two ways to use this command. The first method is to place the name of the application that you want to use along with whatever command that you want that application to perform. For example, ADDRESS CMD DIR *.* invokes the command processor and asks it to get a list of files in the current directory. The input stream immediately returns to the REXX application. The second method involves using only the application name with the command. For example, ADDRESS DOIT redirects the input stream to an application called DOIT until you cancel the redirection. Every statement in your REXX application gets sent to the new application. You cancel the redirection with the next ADDRESS command. Use ADDRESS by itself if you want to set the input stream back to the REXX application.

❋ **ARG [*Template*]**   The ARG command is the same as the PARSE UPPER ARG command. You use it to retrieve the argument strings sent to a program or internal routine and assign them to variables. For example, if your application contains the statement CALL MYPROC ('String 1', 1) and you placed the command ARG STRING1 NUM1 at the beginning of the subroutine, then STRING1 would contain 'String 1' and NUM1 would contain '1'.

❋ **CALL *Name* [*Expression*]**   One of the simplest forms of this command is to call a subfunction from within a main procedure or

function. In many cases, it is more convenient to break your program into small pieces. Each piece performs a specific part of a more complex task. For example, you could create a single routine for error trapping or displaying information on screen. The following example shows a simple method of using the CALL command:

```
/* This is the main procedure.  It displays a message to the
   viewer, then requests some information.  If the user doesn't
   supply the information, the main procedure calls an error
   handling function to request the information again. */

Who=""                 /* Initialize the variable. */
DO WHILE Who = ""      /* Do until user provides a response. */
    SAY "Hello! I am REXX"
    SAY "What is your name?"
    PARSE PULL Who
    IF Who = ""        /* Did the user provide a response? */
        THEN CALL Error   /* If not, call error handling function. */
        ELSE SAY "Hello" Who
END
EXIT

/* This is the error handling function.  It displays an error
   message, then returns so the main procedure can ask the user to
   provide the requested information. */

Error:
SAY "Please type your name!"
RETURN
```

There are a few interesting points about this program. First, the error routine uses a label for identification. Notice that the function name is followed by a colon. Second, the function ends with a RETURN command, not the EXIT command. You want to return to the main procedure once the user presses the enter key. Using EXIT would simply return you to the OS/2 prompt.

❋ **CALL <OFF ¦ ON> <ERROR ¦ FAILURE ¦ HALT ¦ NOTREADY > [NAME *TrapName*]**   This version of the CALL command works much like the version discussed in the previous section. The big difference is that you use this version for error-trapping routines. The ON keyword tells REXX to call a specific procedure should a given event occur (ERROR, FAILURE, HALT, or NOTREADY). The optional NAME keyword tells REXX what subroutine to call when the event occurs. You can use the OFF keyword to turn off error trapping for a specific event.

❋ **DROP [*VariableName*]** Use this command to unassign one or more variables. You separate each variable with a space or comma. The DROP command allows you to assign a list of variables to one variable. Calling DROP with the variable enclosed in parenthesis unassigns all the variables in the list without unassigning the variable that holds the list.

❋ **EXIT [*Expression*]** Allows you to exit from the current program back to the calling program. In most cases, the calling program is the OS/2 command processor. The optional expression variable allows you to return a string to the calling procedure or application.

❋ **INTERPRET *Expression*** REXX allows you to build a command within a string using concatenation or any other legal means. You can execute the command using the INTERPRET command. For example, if you had a statement that contained SOMESTR = 'ADDRESS CMD DIR *.*' and added the statement INTERPRET SOMESTR, then you would see a list of files in the current directory.

❋ **ITERATE [*VariableName*]** This command allows you to increment the value of a variable. If you do not include a variable name, then it increments the value of the variable used to call the command. For example, the statement IF I = 2 THEN ITERATE would result in an increase in the value of I. This command normally appears within loops and provides a means for altering program flow.

❋ **NOP** The NOP command stands for no operation. Use this command when you don't want to do anything at all. For example, if you use a SWITCH control structure to select from a set of conditions, one condition could be to do nothing.

❋ **NUMERIC DIGITS [*Expression*] or NUMERIC FORM < SCIENTIFIC ¦ ENGINEERING ¦ [VALUE] *Expression* > or NUMERIC FUZZ [*Expression*]** Use this command to format numeric data and to determine the accuracy of numeric manipulations. There are three forms of this command. The DIGITS keyword allows you to define the number of digits of accuracy used for calculations. Each additional digit increases accuracy but reduces application speed and increases memory requirements. You need to

determine a reasonable level between accuracy and efficiency for each application that you create. In most cases, the default level of 9 digits provides sufficient accuracy.

The FORM keyword allows you to define how REXX displays numeric data using exponential notation. The SCIENTIFIC and ENGINEERING keywords are self explanatory. The VALUE keyword allows you to supply an expression that must evaluate to either scientific or engineering. The default setting for this command is scientific.

The FUZZ keyword allows you to specify how many digits are ignored when you perform a comparison between two numbers. For example, if you set the fuzz factor to 1 and compared 101 with 100, REXX would consider them equal. This allows you to perform comparisons between numbers that might vary slightly from one another due to rounding errors. The FUZZ setting defaults to 0. You must specify a whole number that is less than the number specified in the DIGITS setting.

* **OPTIONS** *Expression* The OPTIONS command allows you to pass directives to the language processor. There are four keywords recognized by the language processor: ETMODE, NOETMODE, EXMODE, and NOEXMODE. The ETMODE keyword turns on support for the double-byte character set (DBCS). This provides support for foreign languages in your application. Using the NOETMODE keyword turns this support off. The EXMODE keyword tells the language processor to handle DBCS data in a logical manner when it appears in instructions, operators, and functions. The NOEXMODE keyword turns off this support.

* **PARSE [UPPER]** < ARG ¦ PULL ¦ SOURCE ¦ VALUE **[*Expression*] WITH** ¦ **VAR** *Name* ¦ **VERSION** > *TemplateList*
The PARSE command looks complex but performs fairly routine tasks. The UPPER keyword converts all input to uppercase. In addition, there are six different functions that you can perform with the PULL command. The ARG keyword is discussed under the ARG command.

The PARSE PULL command accepts input from the keyboard until the user presses Enter. It places the input into the specified variable. PARSE PULL allows you to enter characters in either upper- or lower case, there is no loss of formatting.

Use the SOURCE keyword to determine the source of the program that you are running. The string always begins with OS/2 followed by one of the keywords COMMAND, FUNCTION or SUBROUTINE. The program name, complete with path, is the last part of the string.

The VALUE keyword allows you to parse the result of a function and format it for output. The first part of the expression contains the name of a REXX function. You follow this with the WITH keyword. Finally, you supply a set of variables and strings that PARSE uses to format the output. For example, you could add the statement PARSE VALUE TIME() WITH Hours ':' Minutes ':' Seconds to your program. Hours, Minutes, and Seconds are three variables that contain the output of the TIME() function. The colon separating the variables would appear as part of the output.

The PARSE VAR command allows you to perform complex variable manipulations. You specify the name of a variable that you want to parse and follow it with the name of a variable to receive the parsed data. The contents of the original variable do not change unless you specify it as the third variable in the command. For example, if you used the statement PARSE VAR SomeStr FirstWord SomeStr, then SomeStr would contain everything but the first word and FirstWord would contain only the first word of a string when the statement executed.

Use the VERSION keyword to determine the version of the REXX interpreter. It returns a string containing the word REXXSAA, followed by the version number and the release date.

✳ **PULL** *Variable*   The PULL command acts much like the PARSE PULL command. It places a value typed at the keyboard into a variable. Unlike the PARSE PULL command, PULL converts all characters to uppercase. This is a good feature to use when you want to use the keyboard input as part of an expression for a control structure.

✳ **PUSH [*Expression*]**   The PUSH command works essentially the same as it does in other languages. In this case, you push the contents of an expression onto a LIFO queue. If you don't provide an expression, the queue contains a blank line. Every PUSH command adds one line to the queue. You use the QUEUED command to determine the number of strings that the queue contains.

* **QUEUE [*Expression*]**   The QUEUE command works essentially the same as it does in other languages. In this case, you push the contents of an expression onto a FIFO queue. If you don't provide an expression, the queue contains a blank line. Every QUEUE command adds one line to the queue. You use the QUEUED command to determine the number of strings that the queue contains.

* **RETURN [*Expression*]**   Allows you to return from the current procedure to the calling procedure. This is the command that you use to return from a subfunction to the function that called it. You also could use this command at the end of the program, but the EXIT command allows you to quickly recognize the program ending point. You optionally can add a string to the RETURN command. REXX passes the string to the calling procedure.

* **SAY *Expression***   The SAY command allows you to output the contents of an expression to the display. The expression can contain variables, math expressions, or strings.

* **SIGNAL [*LabelName* ¦ VALUE *Expression* ¦ OFF [ERROR ¦ FAILURE ¦ HALT ¦ NOVALUE ¦ SYNTAX ¦ NOTREADY] ¦ ON [ERROR ¦ FAILURE ¦ HALT ¦ NOVALUE ¦ SYNTAX ¦ NOTREADY] [NAME *TrapName*]]**   The Signal command provides a means for changing the program flow. There are four different ways to use this command. The first method uses the value contained in *LabelName* to go to a specific label within the program. This acts much like a jump command in other languages. The second method works much like the first. The VALUE option allows you to change program flow based on an expression. You do not need to include the word VALUE on the command line to make this option work properly, but it does improve readability.

   The ON and OFF keywords work hand-in-hand to allow you to trap specific conditions. The OFF keyword turns off trapping for the specified condition, while the ON turns it on. The optional NAME parameter of the ON keyword allows you to set a destination for error trapping. If you do not specify the NAME parameter and a label name in the *TrapName* variable, then the ON keyword acts much like the OFF keyword—it turns off error trapping for the specific event.

❋ **TRACE [*Number* ┆ *String* ┆ *Symbol* ┆ VALUE *Expression* [ALL ┆ COMMANDS ┆ ERROR ┆ FAILURE ┆ INTERMEDIATES ┆ LABELS ┆ NORMAL ┆ OFF ┆ RESULTS ┆ ?]]**   Use this command to debug your REXX applications. It allows you to keep constant watch over specific variables, expressions, and events. There are several ways to use this command. The *Number* variable contains a whole number. This option works only when an interactive debug is active. Using a positive number forces REXX to skip that number of clauses in the current application. A negative number not only forces REXX to skip the clauses, but inhibits all debugging as well.

The *String* or *Expression* variable contains a numeric option, alphabetic option, or a null value. The *Symbol* option contains the same information except that it contains a constant value. The numeric options are the same as the *Numeric* variable description. The alphabetic options refer to one of the following options described in the following paragraphs: ALL, COMMANDS, ERROR, FAILURE, INTERMEDIATES, LABELS, NORMAL, OFF, and RESULTS. The null value doesn't do anything with the current trace.

The ALL option tells REXX to trace all clauses in the application. The COMMANDS options traces only clauses containing commands. It also displays any return codes. Use the ERROR option if you need to trace only error conditions. This option takes effect only after the error occurs. The FAILURE and NORMAL options allow you to trace all host commands after a failure occurs. Use the INTERMEDIATES option to trace all clauses before REXX executes them. It also provides the intermediate results of all expressions and substituted names. The LABELS option allows you to trace on the labels within an application. This works much like the call stack option of many debuggers. It is especially useful for tracking the path taken by the application to obtain a particular result. The OFF option turns off all tracing. The RESULTS option traces all clauses before and after execution by REXX. This allows you to see both the input and output of a clause. It also displays the values assigned to all PULL, PARSE, and ARG instructions.

The prefix option (?) allows you to reverse the trace conditions. You can use it with any of the letter options. For example, if you set

interactive trace on, then use a prefix option, REXX turns interactive trace off. This option is convenient when you need to switch between two trace states in an application and don't want to repeat a complex set of instructions each time.

Functions

Functions always return a value. As a result, you normally set a variable equal to the value of the function. For example, if you wanted to find out the absolute value of a number, you could use the ABS function as follows: AbsVal = ABS(SomeNumber). Notice that there is no space between the left parenthesis and the function name. As an alternative to sending the output of a function to a variable, you can send it directly to the display using the SAY command.

✳ **ABBREV(*String, Variable* [, *Length*])**   Use this function to check whether the contents of *Variable* match the starting characters contained in *String*. For example, if *Variable* contained "Some" and *String* contained "Something", the REXX would return a 1 to signify success. REXX returns a 0 for unsuccessful attempts. *Length* contains a number that specifies how many letters must match. For example, if *Variable* contained "Somt", String contained "Something", and *Length* contained 3, then REXX would return a 1 to signify that they matched, even though the fourth letters do not match. If the value in *Length* exceeds the number of letters in *Variable*, then this function fails every time. Likewise, if *Length* contains a *0* and *Variable* contains a null string, then the function always succeeds.

✳ **ABS(*Number*)**   Returns the absolute value of a number. Essentially, this makes negative numbers positive. Positive numbers remain unchanged.

✳ **ADDRESS()**   Returns the name of the current environment. This is the place where all commands in the current file get processed. The default environment is CMD.

✳ **ARG([*Number* [, *Option*]])**   The ARG function returns the number of arguments passed to a procedure if you call it by itself. If you add a value to *Number*, then the function returns the value of

that argument. Specifying a nonexistent argument returns a null string. There are two options that you can specify in the *Option* parameter. E (for exists) returns a 1 if the argument exists. For example, if the user called the function with three parameters and the second parameter was blank, then the exists option would return a 0. Likewise, if you checked for the existence of a nonexistent parameter (say, parameter 4 when the user supplied only three), the REXX returns a 0. O (for omitted) returns a 1 if the argument does not exist.

✳ **BEEP(*Frequency, Duration*)**   This function allows you to send a specific frequency to the speaker for a specified time. The frequency entry contains the frequency in Hertz. The duration entry determines how long you will hear the tone in milliseconds. For example, BEEP(1000, 250) sends a 1000 Hz signal to the speaker for a quarter of a second. The following example shows how you could enhance the error trapping routine of a previous example using the BEEP function:

```
/* This is the error handling function.  It displays an error
   message, then returns so the main procedure can ask the user to
   provide the requested information. */

Error:
BEEP(1000,250)
SAY "Please type your name!"
RETURN
```

✳ **B2X(*String*)**   Use this function to convert a binary string to a hexadecimal string. The string must include either ones or zeros. You can include spaces at four-digit intervals to aid in readability; do not include leading or trailing spaces.

✳ **BITAND(*String1* [, [*String2*] [, *PadCharacter*]])**   The BITAND function compares two strings bit-by-bit using a logical AND. If you do not supply *String2*, then BITAND uses either a null string or the pad character (when supplied) for comparison. Normally, BITAND compares *String1* and *String2*, then returns a string with a length of the longer string. It simply appends the characters of the longer string to the result if you don't supply a pad character. Otherwise, it uses the pad character for any comparisons when it runs out of characters from either of the two initial strings.

✳ **BITOR(*String1* [, [*String2*] [, *PadCharacter*]])** The BITOR function compares two strings bit-by-bit using a logical OR. If you do not supply *String2*, then BITOR uses either a null string or the pad character (when supplied) for comparison. Normally, BITOR compares *String1* and *String2*, then returns a string with a length of the longer string. It simply appends the characters of the longer string to the result if you don't supply a pad character. Otherwise, it uses the pad character for any comparisons when it runs out of characters from either of the two initial strings.

✳ **BITXOR(*String1* [, [*String2*] [, *PadCharacter*]])** The BITXOR function compares two strings bit-by-bit using a logical exclusive OR. If you do not supply *String2*, then BITXOR uses either a null string or the pad character (when supplied) for comparison. Normally, BITXOR compares *String1* and *String2*, then returns a string with a length of the longer string. It simply appends the characters of the longer string to the result if you don't supply a pad character. Otherwise, it uses the pad character for any comparisons when it runs out of characters from either of the two initial strings.

✳ **C2D(*String* [, *Number*])** This function converts a character string to a decimal number. *String* contains the value you want to convert. If you add an X suffix, then REXX treats the string as a hexadecimal number. Otherwise, it treats the string as an ASCII value. Number determines the number of characters in string used for the conversion.

✳ **C2X(*String*)** Use this function to convert a string to its hexadecimal representation. If you input an ASCII character string, then each character is converted individually. Adding an X to the end of the string forces REXX to treat the string as a hexadecimal number. The function converts the hexadecimal string representation to a true hexadecimal number.

✳ **CENTER(*String, Length,* [*Pad*])** This function returns a string of *Length* with *String* centered within it. You can use the CENTER function to dress up your displays. The standard padding character (the character used to center the string) is a blank. However, you can specify any ASCII character using the optional Pad entry. The following example shows how you would use the CENTER function:

```
Answer = 0
DO WHILE \(Answer=3)
  SAY CENTER("This is my menu",80) /* Center heading on screen */
  SAY
  SAY "1. Do Something"
  SAY "2. Do Something Else"
  SAY "3. Quit"
  SAY "Enter your selection"
  PULL Answer
  SELECT
    WHEN Answer = 1
      THEN SAY "Did Something"
    WHEN Answer = 2
      THEN SAY "Did Something Else"
    OTHERWISE
      SAY "Good-bye"
  END
END
```

※ **CHARIN(*Name* [, [*Start*] [, *Length*]])**   You can use CHARIN to input characters from any source. *Name* contains the name of the input source. The default input source is the keyboard (STDIN). The function allows you to specify a starting point for persistent input sources such as files. This allows you to start reading from a point other than the beginning of the file or other persistent source. The default setting is to read from position zero. You also can specify the length of the input stream by proving a value for *Length*.

※ **CHAROUT(*Name* [, [*String*] [, *Start*]])**   You can use CHAROUT to output characters to any output. *Name* contains the name of the output; *String* contains the value that you want to output. The default output is the display (STDOUT). The function allows you to specify a starting point for persistent outputs such as files. This allows you to start writing to a point other than the beginning of the file or other persistent source. The default setting is to write starting at position zero. This function always returns 0 for a successful write; otherwise, it returns the number of characters that it couldn't write.

※ **CHARS([*Name*])**   This function returns the number of characters left in the input stream. It works with input streams like files, but not STDIN (the keyboard) or other indeterminate devices.

※ **COMPARE(*String1*, *String2* [, *PadCharacter*])**   The COMPARE function compares *String1* with *String2*. If the strings are

identical, it returns 0. Otherwise, it returns the position of the first nonmatching character in *String1*. You can use the pad character to represent repeating characters at the end of a string if *String1* is longer than *String2*. REXX uses a blank as the default pad character.

✳ **CONDITION([*Option*])**   Using this function by itself (which is the same as using the Instruction option) returns the instruction that REXX executed prior to the currently trapped condition. There are two instructions that cause trap conditions: Call and Signal. If there is no trap condition, the function returns a null string. There are three other pieces of error trapping information that you can check using the function. Condition Name returns the name of the currently trapped condition. Description returns a string that describes the currently trapped condition. If the condition does not provide a descriptive string, then the function returns a null string. Status returns the status of the currently trapped conditions. There are three status conditions. On means that the trapped condition is enabled. Likewise, Off means that the trapped condition is disabled. Delayed means that the future occurrences of the condition are delayed. If there is no trapped condition, REXX returns a null string.

✳ **COPIES(*String, Number*)**   This function returns zero or more copies of the string that you specify in *String*. *Number* determines the number of copies.

✳ **DATATYPE(*Variable*)**   This function returns one of two values: CHAR or NUM depending on the data type of the variable that you supply. You can use this function to check user input for the right data type prior to processing it. This reduces the chance that your application will stop executing due to faulty user input.

✳ **DATE([*Option*])**   This function returns the current date. It normally displays the date in a *DD MMM YYYY* format. However, you can specify an option to change the format. Table 1-2 shows the formats available.

The REXX Date() function formats	Table 1-2

Format	Description
B	Base Date—Returns the number of days since 01/01/0001.
D	Days—Returns the number of days, including the current day, since the beginning of the year.
E	European Formatted Date—Returns the short form of the European formatted date.
L	Long Date—Returns the date in long format. This includes the full month name and four digit year.
M	Month—Returns the current month in long form.
N	Normal—Returns the date in normal format. You can accomplish the same thing by leaving the option blank.
O	Ordered Form—Returns the date in a format suitable for sorting. It uses the YY/MM/DD format.
S	Sorted Form—Returns the date in a format suitable for sorting. It uses the YYYYMMDD format.
U	USA Format—Returns the date in the format used by the United States: MM/DD/YY.
W	Weekday—Returns the day of the week in long form.

✳ **DELSTRING(*String, Characters* [, *Length*])**   This function returns a substring of *String*. It starts deleting characters from the end of the *String* starting at position *Characters*. If you specify a length, the function stops deleting characters when it deletes the number specified by *Length*. Otherwise, it deletes to the end of the string. If *Characters* is larger than the length of the string, REXX returns the string unchanged.

✳ **DELWORD(*String, Word* [, *Length*])**   This function returns a substring of *String*. It starts deleting words from the end of the *String* starting at position *Word*. If you specify a length, the function stops deleting words when it deletes the number specified by Length. Otherwise, it deletes to the end of the string. If *Word* is larger than the length of the string, REXX returns the string unchanged.

✳ **DIGITS()**   Returns the current numeric digits setting.

✳ **D2C(*Number* [, *Positions*])**   The D2C function converts a decimal number to its ASCII equivalent. For example, decimal number 67 converts to ASCII character *C*. *Positions* allows you to define the number of digits in the final result. *Number* must contain a positive number unless you supply a value for *Positions*. It must always contain a whole number.

✳ **D2X(*Number* [, *Positions*])**   The D2X function converts a decimal number to a string containing its hexadecimal equivalent. *Positions* allows you to define the number of digits in the final result. If you specify a longer result than the decimal number holds, then REXX pads the result with leading 0s for a positive result or Fs for a negative result. *Number* must contain a positive number unless you supply a value for *Positions*. It must always contain a whole number.

✳ **DIRECTORY([*NewDirectory*])**   When used by itself, this function returns the current directory. You can supply an optional value in *NewDirectory* that changes the current directory to the new directory, then returns the value of the original directory to the caller.

✳ **ERRORTEXT(*Number*)**   Returns the error text associated with the specified error number.

✳ **FILESPEC(*Option, FileSpecification*)**   This function returns the requested element of a file specification. *Option* contains the element that you want returned: drive, path, or name. *FileSpecification* contains a string with the file specification you want to parse.

✳ **FORM()**   Returns the current setting of numeric form.

✳ **FORMAT(*Number* [, [*Before*] [, [*After*] [, [*ExponentPlaces*] [, *ExponentTrigger*]]]])**   This function returns a formatted string. *Number* contains the number that you want to format. If you don't specify a *Before* and *After* value, REXX uses the default setup. It always rounds a number that contains too many digits for the set of formatting rules. *Before* contains the number of digits before the decimal point. *After* contains the number of digits after the decimal point. *ExponentPlaces* contains the number of digits in the exponent. This setting takes effect only when *Number* exceeds the value in *ExponentTrigger*.

* **FUZZ()**   Returns the current setting of numeric fuzz.

* **INSERT(*String, Target* [, [*Position*] [,[*Length*] [, *Pad*]]])**   The INSERT function places *String* within *Target*. This allows you to combine two strings. *Position* tells REXX where to place *String* within *Target*. *Length* tells REXX how long to make *String* before making the insertion. REXX normally uses spaces as a pad character, but you can specify any other character using *Pad*.

* **LASTPOS(*String1, String2* [, *Start*])**   This function returns the last position of *String1* within *String2*. For example, if *String1* contained a space and *String2* contained a variety of characters including two spaces, then LASTPOS would return the second occurrence of the space. You can override this default setting by supplying a value for *Start*. REXX uses this value as the last character it looks at, then searches backward to the beginning of *String2*.

* **LEFT(*String, Length* [, *Pad*])**   The LEFT function returns the left part of *String*. *Length* contains the length of the result. If *String* is shorter than *Length*, the REXX pads the right side of the string to make it long enough. Normally, it uses a space to pad the string as necessary. You can override this default by providing a value for *Pad*.

* **LENGTH(*String*)**   Returns the length of *String*.

* **LINEIN([*Name*] [, [*Line*] [, *Count*]])**   When used by itself, LINEIN returns one line of characters from the keyboard (STDIN). *Name* contains the name of another input stream if you don't want to use the keyboard. If this source is a persistent input like a file, then you can provide a value for *Line*. This value tells REXX what line of the file you want to start reading. *Count* contains the number of lines that you want to read from the input stream.

* **LINEOUT([*Name*] [, [*String*] [, *Line*]])**   When used by itself, LINEOUT sends a carriage return/line feed combination to the console (STDOUT). *Name* contains the name of an output device. If this is a persistent output device like a file, you can provide a value for *Line*. This tells REXX what line you want to start writing at. *String* contains the data that you want to output. If you do not provide a value for *String*, then REXX assumes a null value and

writes only the carriage return/line feed to the output stream. LINEOUT returns 0 if the write is successful or 1 if not.

* **LINES([*Name*])**   Returns 1 if there are any more lines of data to read from the input stream or *0* if none exists.

* **MAX(*Number* [, *Number*...])**   Returns the maximum number in a list of numbers.

* **MIN(*Number* [, *Number*...])**   Returns the minimum number in a list of numbers.

* **OVERLAY(*String, Target* [, [*Position*] [, [*Length*] [, *Pad*]]])**
The OVERLAY function places *String* over *Target*. This allows you to combine two strings by overwriting the data in one with the data in the other. *Position* tells REXX where to place *String* within *Target*. *Length* tells REXX how long to make *String* before overwriting *Target*. REXX normally uses spaces as a pad character, but you can specify any other character using *Pad*.

* **POS(*String1, String2* [, *Start*])**   This function returns the first position of *String1* within *String2*. For example, if *String1* contained a space and *String2* contained a variety of characters including two spaces, then POS would return the first occurrence of the space. You can override this default setting by supplying a value for *Start*. REXX uses this value as the first character it looks at, then searches forward to the end of *String2*.

* **QUEUED()**   Returns the number of lines remaining in the current queue.

* **RANDOM([*Number1*] [, [*Number2*] [, *Seed*]])**   Returns a pseudo-random number. When used by itself, RANDOM returns a number between 0 and 999 as a default. You can specify a maximum number in *Number1*. If you want to specify both a maximum and minimum number, place the maximum number in *Number1* and the minimum in *Number2*. *Number1* must contain a number larger than *Number2*. You can vary the output of RANDOM by providing a value for *Seed*. RANDOM always returns a whole number.

✳ **REVERSE**(*String*)   REVERSE reverses the order of the characters in *String*.

✳ **RIGHT(*String, Length* [, *Pad*])**   The RIGHT function returns the right part of *String*. *Length* contains the length of the result. If *String* is shorter than *Length*, the REXX pads the left side of the string to make it long enough. Normally, it uses a space to pad the string as necessary. You can override this default by providing a value for *Pad*.

✳ **RXFUNCADD(*Name, Module, Procedure*)**   Use this function to register a new function with REXX. *Name* contains the name that you want to assign to the new function. *Module* contains the name of the module that holds the function you want to register. *Procedure* contains the name of the function as it appears within the native module. The function returns 0 for successful completion.

✳ **RXFUNCDROP(*Name*)**   Use this function to deregister a function that you previously registered using the RXFUNCADD function. *Name* contains the name of the module that you want to deregister. The function returns 0 for successful completion.

✳ **RXFUNCQUERY(*Name*)**   The RXFUNCQUERY function checks the list of available functions for a specific function. *Name* contains the function that you want to check. It returns a 0 if the function is registered or 1 if it is not.

✳ **RXQUEUE(GET ¦ SET *NewQueueName* ¦ CREATE [, *QueueName*] ¦ DELETE *QueueName*)**   You can use this function to manage REXX queues. It provides four different management tools. GET returns the name of the queue that REXX is using. SET also returns the name of the queue that REXX is using. You set the name of the new queue by providing its name in *NewQueueValue*.

The DELETE option allows you to destroy an old queue. You supply the name of the queue you want to destroy in *QueueName*. The function returns 0 for a successful deletion. There are five error values that the function can return: 5 (not a valid queue name), 9 (queue does not exist), 10 (queue is busy), 12 (memory failure), and 1000 (initialization error, check the OS/2.INI file).

The CREATE option allows you to create a new queue. You can supply a name in *QueueName*. If you don't supply a name, then REXX creates a name for you. In either case, the function returns the name of the newly created queue.

✳ **SIGN(*Number*)**   Returns the sign of number.

✳ **SOURCELINE([*Number*])**   Returns the number of lines in the current source file when used by itself. If you supply a number for *Number*, then SOURCELINE returns that line from the source file.

✳ **SPACE(*String* [, [*Number*] [, *Pad*]])**   Use this function with strings to remove or add spaces. *String* contains the string you want to format. *Number* contains the number of spaces that you want between each word in *String*. If you specify a value of 0, then REXX removes all spaces from the string. It always removes leading and trailing spaces. You can specify another fill character by providing a value for *Pad*.

✳ **STREAM(*Name* [, [C, *StreamCommand*] ┊ [D] ┊ [S]])**   This function returns a string that describes the success or failure of an operation on a character stream. *Name* contains the name of the character stream. C (command) performs the command specified in *StreamCommand* on the character stream. D returns a description of the character stream status. The standard statement is followed by a colon and (if appropriate) an extended error number. S is the default setting for this function. It returns the state of the character stream. There are four values returns by Stream as follows.

➤ Error—The character stream experienced some type of error. This includes any input, output, or other character stream errors. You usually can get a more detailed description using the D option.

➤ Ready—The character stream is ready for use. You can perform any operation, including input and output. This does not guarantee that the operation will succeed.

➤ NotReady—The character stream is not ready for use. Any attempt at using it probably will result in failure.

➤ Unknown—The state of the stream is not known. This usually means that you failed to open a file before checking its state. It could mean that the file or other stream does not exist.

❋ **STRIP(*String* [, [*Option*] [, *Character*]])**   The STRIP function allows you to remove characters from string. The default character is a blank. *Option* contains a removal option: leading, trailing, or both. The default option is to remove both leading and trailing character. You can specify a different character for this function by adding a single character value to *Character*.

❋ **SUBSTR(*String, FirstCharacter, Length*)**   You can use this function to obtain a part of a string. The *String* variable contains the original string. *FirstCharacter* contains the number of the first character that you want in the resultant string. *Length* contains the length of the resultant string.

❋ **SUBWORD(*String, Position* [,*Length*])**   The SUBWORD function returns a substring of *String* starting at *Position*. The function uses a default of the remainder of the string. You can modify this behavior by specifying *Length*. In this case, SUBWORD returns only the number of words that you specify. This function always removes leading and training blanks. If you specify a starting position larger than the number of words in the sentence, SUBWORD returns a null string.

❋ **SYMBOL(*Symbol*)**   Returns the current state of *Symbol*. There are three different conditions. REXX returns Bad if the symbol does not exist. It returns Var if the symbol is a variable. Lit represents a literal symbol, which is a constant or variable with an unassigned value.

❋ **SYSCLS**   This function clears the display.

❋ **SYSCREATEOBJECT(*ClassName, Title, Location* [, *Setup*])**
The SYSCREATEOBJECT function allows you to create a new object. *ClassName* contains the name of the object class that you want to create *Title* contains the title for the object. *Location* is a description of where REXX can find the object class definition. You can use either a descriptive or file system path. The *Setup* parameter allows you to pass information to the object class in the form of a string. The function returns 1 if successful or 0 if unsuccessful.

✳ **SYSCURPOS ([*Row, Col*])**   There are two ways to use this function. If you call it without any parameters, then REXX returns the current cursor position without changing it. Adding parameters moves the cursor but still returns the previous cursor position. The cursor row and column start in the upper left corner at coordinates 0, 0.

✳ **SYSCURSTATE (ON ¦ OFF)**   Use this function to set the state of the cursor (either on or off).

✳ **SYSDEREGISTEROBJECTCLASS(*ClassName*)**   This function allows you to deregister a class registered with the SYSREGISTEROBJECTCLASS function. *ClassName* contains the name of the object class that you want to deregister. The function returns 1 if successful or 0 if unsuccessful.

✳ **SYSDRIVEINFO(*Drive*)**   The SYSDRIVEINFO function returns the drive letter, free space, total space, and volume label in a string. You must provide a drive letter as input. The function returns an empty string if the drive doesn't exist or isn't available.

✳ **SYSDRIVEMAP ([*Drive*], [*Options*])**   This function reports the drives available to the system. It uses a default of a beginning drive of C and all accessible drives, whether local or remote. The string returned by this function contains a list of drive letters followed by colons and separated by spaces. You can specify a different starting drive using the *Drive* parameter. There also are several search options that you can use as listed here:

> ➤ Used—This is the default option. It returns every drive that the system can access whether in use or not. It includes both local and remote drives.

> ➤ Free—This option reports both local and remote drives that are not in use. In other words, you can access these drives immediately.

> ➤ Local—Use this option if you want a listing of local drives whether they are in use or not.

> ➤ Remote—The Remote option provides a list of remote drives. It does not matter if the drives are currently in use by someone else.

> ➤ Detached—Use the Detached option when you need a list of detached network resources. In other words, the user could normally access the drive but current cannot for some reason.

✳ **SYSDROPFUNCS** Always use this function with care. It drops all the loaded REXXUtil functions from memory. This is a great way to free up memory for applications. Unfortunately, it also means that the REXXUtil functions are unavailable to any OS/2 session (essentially making REXX unavailable for use).

✳ **SYSFILEDELETE (*File*)** The SYSFILEDELETE function allows you to remove a file from disk. It does not support wildcard characters; you must supply a specific filename. The function returns the following codes:

0	File Deleted Successfully
2	File Not Found
3	Path Not Found
5	Access Denied
26	Not DOS Disk
32	Sharing Violation
36	Sharing Buffer Exceeded
87	Invalid Parameter
206	Filename Exceeds Range Error

✳ **SYSFILESEARCH (*String, Filename, Variable, [Options]*)**
The SYSFILESEARCH function allows you to find a string within a file. *String* contains the string that you want to search for. *Filename* contains the name of the file that you want to search. *Variable* contains the results of the search. This is an array containing one entry for each string, containing the search value. Element 0 of this array contains the total number of entries in the array.

There are two options that you can use with this function. The C option forces a case-sensitive search. The default setup uses a case-insensitive search. The N options tells REXX to provide you with line numbers when reporting hits. Normally, REXX reports only the string, not the line number within the search file.

✳ **SYSFILETREE (*Files, Variable, [Options], [TAttributes], [NAttributes]*)** Use this function to search for the files specified by the *Files* variable. You can use wildcard characters within the search criteria. *Variable* is an array that contains the results of the search upon return from the function. Element 0 of the array contains the total number of array entries.

The *Options* parameter allows you to search for specific file types. You can use the following options: B (default setting of files and directories), D (directories only), F (files only), O (report only fully qualified filenames), S (scan subdirectories recursively), and T (return time and date in the form *YY/MM/DD/HH/MM*). You can combine the options to achieve various effects.

The *TAttributes* and *NAttributes* options allow you to work with specific file attributes. The *TAttributes* variable allows you to specify a search attribute. The *NAttributes* variable allows you to specify a new attribute for the files that you find. Each attribute variable uses a positional mask in the following order: archive, directory, hidden, read-only, and system. You use the following symbols within the mask: * (attribute is either set or clear, it doesn't matter which), + (attribute set), and – (attribute clear). For example, if you wanted to search for files with the hidden and system attributes set you would use the following mask: **+*+. Likewise, if you wanted to reset the archive attribute of a file you would use the following mask –****. As you can see, it is quite simple to search for and change attributes using this method.

✳ **SYSGETEA(*Filename, ExtendedAttributeName, Variable*)**
Use the SYSGETEA function to retrieve an extended attribute from a file. It returns 0 if the function succeeds. *Filename* contains the name of the file that you want to examine. *ExtendedAttributeName* is the name of the extended attribute that you want to look for. Use *Variable* to hold the results of the search.

✳ **SYSGETKEY([*Option*])**   Use this function to retrieve a key from the keyboard buffer. If there is no keystroke in the buffer, the function waits until the user presses a key. Unlike the standard CHARIN() function, the user does not need to press Enter to return the keystroke.

There are two options you can use with this function. ECHO is the default setting. REXX automatically echoes any keystrokes to the display. NOECHO retrieves the keystroke without displaying it on screen. This is a useful setting for applications like password entry screens where you wouldn't want anyone to see the keystrokes typed by the user.

❋ **SYSGETMESSAGE(*Number, [File], [String1],...[String9]*)**
Instead of using the standard method to define messages for your
application, you can use the SYSGETMESSAGE function to retrieve
them from a file. The default file is 0S0001.MSG. Using a file allows
you to provide National Language Support (NLS) with your
application. Instead of creating a new version of your application for
each nationality, you can simply create different message files—one
for each language that you want to support. *Number* contains the
number of the message you want to use within the file. *File* contains
the name of a file that you want to use as a message source. You
must use the MKMSGF utility to build this file. *String1* through
String9 are variables used as replacement strings. They replace the
%1 through %9 parameters contained in the message string file.

❋ **SYSMKDIR(*Directory*)**   Use this function to create a new
directory. It returns one of the following codes to signal success or
failure:

0	Directory Created Successfully
2	File Not Found
3	Path Not Found
5	Access Denied
26	Not DOS Disk
87	Invalid Parameter
108	Drive Locked
206	Filename Exceeds Range Error

❋ **SYSOS2VER()**   The SYSOS2VER function returns a string
containing the current OS/2 version number in the form *x.xx*.

❋ **SYSPUTEA(*Filename, ExtendedAttributeName, Variable*)**
Use this function to write an extended attribute to a file specified by
Filename. *ExtendedAttributeName* contains the name of the extended
attribute to write to the file. *Variable* contains the value that you want
to write to the file. This function returns a 0 if it succeeds.

❋ **SYSQUERYCLASSLIST *List***   Use this function to obtain a list of
active object classes. *List* is an array that contains the information on
return from the call. Element 0 of the array contains the number of
items in the list.

✳ **SYSREGISTEROBJECTCLASS(*ClassName, ModuleName*)**
Use this function to register a new object class definition. *ClassName* contains the name of the class that you want to register. *ModuleName* contains the name of the file that contains the definition of the object class. All object class definitions appear in a SOM DLL. The function returns 1 if successful or 0 if unsuccessful.

✳ **SYSRMDIR(*Directory*)**   The SYSRMDIR function removes the specified directory from the drive. It returns one of the following error codes to indicate success or failure:

0	Directory Deleted Successfully
2	File Not Found
3	Path Not Found
5	Access Denied
16	Current Directory
26	Not DOS Disk
87	Invalid Parameter
108	Drive Locked
206	Filename Exceeds Range Error

✳ **SYSSEARCHPATH(*Path, Filename*)**   Use this function to search for a file within the specified path. The function returns the fully qualified filename if it finds the file. Otherwise, it returns a blank string. *Path* contains the path that you want to search. *Filename* contains the file that you want to search for. This function will not allow you to use wildcard characters.

✳ **SYSSETICON(*Filename, IconName*)**   This function allows you to assign a particular icon to a file. Filename contains the name of the file that you want to change. *IconName* is the name of an icon filename. You must use OS/2 specific icons; files from other operating systems/environments will not work. The function returns a value of 1 if it set the icon. It returns a value of 0 if the function fails.

✳ **SYSSLEEP(*Seconds*)**   Use this function to put the application to sleep for a specific amount of time.

✳ **SYSTEMPFILENAME(*Template,* [*Filter*])**   You can use the SYSTEMPFILENAME function to obtain the name of a file or

directory that does not currently exist. This allows you to quickly create a temporary file without overwriting an existing file by mistake. The *Template* variable contains a string that defines the temporary filename that you want returned. It contains filter and mandatory characters. REXX creates a filename containing all the mandatory characters in the specified positions. It fills the filter character positions with numbers. The standard filter character is the question mark (?). However, you can use any character that you want to for a filter by specifying a value in the *Filter* variable.

✳ **SYSTEXTSCREENREAD(*Row, Column,* [*Length*])**   This function retrieves the character information contained on a text screen. *Row* contains the starting row, and *Column* contains the starting column. You would use values of 0 for *Row* and 0 for *Column* if you wanted to start at the very beginning of the screen. The optional *Length* variable allows you to specify how many characters to return. The default setting reads until it reaches the end of the screen. This function does not store any color information. As a result, if you store a screen, then later restore it, the new screen will not contain any of the color information of the original. The SYSREADSCREEN function does retain any carriage returns and line feeds found in the original screen.

✳ **SYSTEXTSCREENSIZE()**   Use this function to determine the number of rows and columns in the current screen. It returns a string containing the number of rows as the first entry and the number of columns as the second entry.

✳ **SYSWAITNAMEDPIPE(*Name,* [*Timeout*])**   This function allows you to perform a timed wait on a particular named pipe. *Name* contains the name of the pipe in the form \PIPE*PipeName*. The optional *Timeout* value allows you to specify how long the function should wait for the named pipe before it returns. Using a value of 0 tells REXX to use the default timeout period. A value of –1 specifies an unlimited wait period. Any other positive value is the time to wait in microseconds. DOSWAITNAMEDPIPE always returns one of the following values:

   0   Named Pipe is no Longer Busy
   2   Named Pipe Not Found
 231   Function Timed Out Before Named Pipe Became Available

❋ **TIME([***Option***])**   Use this function to display the current time. The TIME function normally displays the time in military format *HH:MM:SS*. Like the DATE function, you can add an option to change the form of the TIME function output. Table 1-3 shows the available formats.

Table 1-3   **The REXX TIME( ) function formats**

Format	Description
L	Long Format—Shows the complete time in military format (24-hour clock) including hundredths of a second.
H	Hours—Shows the number of hours since midnight.
M	Minutes—Shows the number of minutes since midnight. It uses the equation (Hours × 60) + Minutes to determine the total number of minutes.
S	Seconds—Shows the number of seconds since midnight. It uses the equation (((Hours × 60) + Minutes) × 60) + Seconds to determine the total number of seconds.
N	Normal Time—Use this option to display the time in normal format. You can obtain the same results by not using any option at all.
C	Civilian Format—Shows the time in am/pm format (12-hour clock) instead of military format.

❋ **TRACE([Option])**   Returns the trace options currently in effect. You can check for a specific trace option by specifying the first character of the option in Option. See the TRACE command for further details.

❋ **TRANSLATE(*String* [, [*Output*] [, [*Input*] [, *Pad*]]])**   This function allows you to substitute one character in a string for another. *String* contains the string that you want to translate. *Output* contains the string that you want to use in the final result in place of the string specified by Input. If *Input* is larger than *Output*, REXX substitutes spaces for the missing characters. You can change this default by adding a value to *Pad*.

❋ **TRUNC(*Number*, [*Places*])**   Normally, the TRUNC function returns the integer part of *Number*. It does not perform any rounding. You can modify this behavior by supplying a value for

Places. This tells REXX how many decimal places to preserve in the result.

* **VALUE(*Name* [, [*NewValue*] [, *Selector*]])** Returns the current value of the variable specified by *Name.* You optionally can assign a new value to *Name* by providing it in *NewValue.* This function normally looks at internal variables only. You can specify external variables by providing a value for *Selector.* For example, if you use OS2ENVIRONMENT for *Selector,* then you can look at OS/2 environment variables.

* **VERIFY(*String, Reference* [, [*Option*] [, *Start*]])** This function returns a value that indicates whether all characters in *String* also appear in *Reference.* If not, it returns a number that indicates the first nonmatching character. Verify returns 0 if all the characters match. You can change this default behavior by adding a value to *Option.* N (nonmatch) is the standard behavior. M (match) finds the first character in *String* that matches *Reference* instead of finding the first nonmatching character. Normally, VERIFY starts at the first character of *String.* You can specify an alternate starting point with *Start.*

* **WORD(*String, Position*)** Returns the word at the position specified by *Position* in *String.* If you specify a position that is larger than the number of words in *String,* WORD returns a null string.

* **WORDINDEX(*String, Position*)** Returns the first character of the word at the position specified by *Position* in *String.* If you specify a position that is larger than the number of words in *String,* WORDINDEX returns a blank character.

* **WORDLENGTH(*String, Position*)** Returns the length of the word at the position specified by *Position* in *String.* If you specify a position that is larger than the number of words in *String,* WORDLENGTH returns 0.

* **WORDPOS(*Search, String* [, *Start*])** Searches for the string contained in *Search* within the string *String.* It returns the position of the first word in *String* that matches *Search.* Normally, WORDPOS starts at the first word of *String.* You can specify a different starting position using *Start.*

✳ **WORDS(*String*)**   Returns the number of blank delimited words in *String*.

✳ **XRANGE([*Start*] [, *End*])**   This function returns a string with all the codes between *Start* and *End*. For example, if you used XRANGE(a, d), the function would return a string containing "abcd." The default value for *Start* is 00h. The default value for *End* is FFh. You can specify hexadecimal sequences by following the code character with an X.

✳ **X2B(*HexString*)**   Converts a hexadecimal string to a binary string. The resulting string is four times longer than the original and does not contain any blanks.

✳ **X2C(*HexString*)**   Converts a hexadecimal string to ASCII characters. Each two character hexadecimal sequence becomes one character. You can place spaces at word boundaries in the string for ease of reading. REXX automatically pads the left side of the string with a 0 if there are an uneven number of hexadecimal digits.

✳ **X2D(*HexString* [, *Length*])**   Converts a hexadecimal string to a decimal string. *Length* contains the length of the resulting string. REXX pads the string with zeros as required to create a string of the desired length.

⇨ **PMREXX functions**

OS/2 provides a GUI environment for users. As a result, REXX also needs to provide constructs to handle that GUI environment. The following paragraphs describe functions that you can use under PMREXX in addition to those listed in the previous section. As you can see, this list of functions provides everything that you need to create a reasonably complex application using REXX as the base language. Even though you could build a complete application using these constructs, REXX really is suited for short utility projects. Remember, REXX is essentially a glorified batch language.

✳ **RxMessageBox(*Text*, [*Title*], [*Button*], [*Icon*])**   You use this function to create a message box. Text contains the information that

you want to appear in the message box. There is almost no limit to the messages that you can provide the user. The optional *Button* variable tells REXX the type and number of buttons that you want to display on screen.

⇨ Programming

Every REXX program starts with the same line: a comment field. Some people simply place a blank comment at the top of their REXX file, but you can use it for a lot more. If you create more than a few batch files to automate your everyday work, it becomes necessary to document them in some way. Using this initial comment to leave yourself a note about some of the particulars of this particular file can reduce confusion later and make your program easier for someone else who uses it. A standard REXX program should begin with the following entries as part of the comment:

```
/* Name: Your Name
   Date: Date of Initial Program Creation
   Purpose: The purpose of this program.
   Notes: Any notes about the program in general. Some people
   include psuedocode (a form of programmers notation) here.
*/
```

Of course, you can modify this initial entry any way you see fit. However, the more information you put here, the less frustration you'll have later when it's time to modify your program.

✳ **Expressions**   One of the more powerful features of REXX is its ability to interpret expressions. There are two forms of expression that you will use quite often in your REXX programs. The first form is string concatenation. For example, if you type the following statements:

```
Var1 = "Hello"
Var2 = "World"
Var3 = Var1 + Var2
SAY Var3
```

you will see Hello World displayed on your screen. Concatenation is useful when you want to combine program text with user input. Often, you'll use it as part of information or result screens.

The other form of expression is the result of an equation. REXX provides quite a few math operators as shown in Table 1-4.

Table 1-4 **The REXX math operators**

Operator	Description
+	Adds two numbers together. For example, 2 + 4 results in an output of 6.
−	Subtracts one number from another. For example, 4 − 2 results in an output of 2.
*	Multiplies one number by another. For example, 4 * 2 results in an output of 8.
/	Divides one number by another. For example, 5 / 2 results in an output of 2.5.
%	Returns only the integer portion of a division. For example, 5 % 2 results in an output of 2. REXX truncates the decimal portion of the answer.
//	Returns only the decimal portion of a division. For example, 5 // 2 returns an output of .5. REXX removes the integer portion of the result.
()	Changes the normal order of precedence. REXX normally evaluates the multiplication and division portion of an expression first, then the addition and subtraction. It also evaluates an expression from left to right, just like you normally would read it. For example, 2 + 3 / 2 results in an output of 3.5. Using the parenthesis will force REXX to evaluate the part of the expression you want evaluated first. For example, (2 + 3) / 2 results in an output of 2.5 instead of the 3.5 that you received before. You can nest the parenthesis as needed to achieve the desired result. For example, 2 + (3 + 4) / 2 results in an answer of 5.5, while (2 + (3 + 4)) / 2 results in 4.5.

✳ **Formatting**   There are a variety of formatting techniques that people use to increase the readability of their batch files. One system is not necessarily better than any other. However, you should use a system of some sort to help you read your batch files.

Indentation is one way that people use to format their programs. For example, if you want to make a control structure obvious, you can format it as follows:

```
IF SomeExp
   THEN
```

```
    Do Something
ELSE
    Do Something Else
```

As you can see, this is a lot more readable than placing all the statements in a straight line. There is no doubt that this is a control structure or where each of the elements end.

Another form of formatting is capitalization. For example, you could type all REXX commands in all uppercase, variables with initial capital letters only, and OS/2 commands in all lowercase. Using this formatting scheme reduces confusion when you edit your batch file. There is no doubt which words are variables, which are REXX commands, and which are OS/2 commands.

These are just a few ways that you can make your batch files easier to read and modify. As you become more proficient at creating REXX programs, you probably will find other ways to improve the appearance and readability of your code.

✳ **Getting down to business**   Now that you know what elements make a REXX program, it's time to start putting them together. Menuing systems are one of the projects that many people tackle using a batch programming language. While OS/2 reduces the need for using such a menuing system, you still can use one for commands that you must execute from the OS/2 prompt. The following program shows one simple way of using REXX to automate a process using a menuing system:

```
/* NAME: Your Name
   DATE: 8/23/92
   PURPOSE: This program shows you how to create a menuing system using REXX. */

Answer = 0                 /* Initialize our answer variable. */
DO WHILE \(Answer=3)       /* Do this procedure until the user enters Quit. */
   CLS                     /* Clear the display */
   SAY DATE()
   SAY TIME()
   SAY CENTER("This is my menu", 80)   /* Center the heading. */
   SAY
   SAY "1. Display the current directory"
   SAY "2. Change drive and/or directory"
```

```
      SAY "3. Quit"
      SAY "Enter your selection"
      PULL Answer
      SELECT
         WHEN Answer = 1
            THEN CALL DispDir
         WHEN Answer = 2
            THEN CALL ChngIt
         OTHERWISE
            SAY "Good-bye"
      END
END
EXIT

/* This function displays the directory on screen, then returns
   the user to the original menu.  Some OS/2 commands require
   that you enclose them in quotes.  Otherwise, REXX assumes that
   they are internal commands and processes them.
*/


DispDir:
cls
dir "|more"    /* Surround MORE with quotes it will execute. */
SAY "Press any key when ready..."
PULL
RETURN

/* This function allows the user to change the current drive and directory. */


ChngIt:
cls

/* Get the new drive from the user, then change it. */


SAY "Enter a new drive or press Enter to retain the current drive."
PULL Drive
IF \(Drive = "")        /* If user pressed Enter, ignore change.  */
   THEN Drive":"

/* Get the new directory from the user, then change it. */
SAY "Enter new directory or press Enter to retain current one."
PULL Directory
IF \(Directory = "")    /* If user pressed Enter, ignore change.  */
   THEN CD Directory


RETURN
```

As you can see, this menuing system is quite simple to create and it does automate the process of performing a task under OS/2. In many

cases, a menuing system can do more than just help you when you don't remember a specific command. It can prompt you for the correct information. For example, in this example program, the menuing system prompts you for the information that is needed to change drive and directory. You don't have to remember the command itself, simply what you wanted to do with it.

Automating your work environment through the Workplace Shell

The Workplace Shell (WPS) provides the means to automate your work environment in several ways. First, unlike DOS programming, you do not need to close, then reopen the environment before you switch between programming and debugging. Even though modern IDEs make this task automatic, you still waste time switching between environments under DOS. Under Windows, you had to worry about overloading the environment by opening too many windows at the same time. Under the WPS, both of these problems are solved. You can write, compile, test, and debug your application by simply switching windows without any loss of speed. Of course, this form of automation becomes very obvious once you think about it.

However, there are other automation features of the WPS that you might not think about using. For one thing, you can use REXX to duplicate the batch files that you use under DOS. REXX provides much greater flexibility as you can see from the previous section. Making optimal use of the features that REXX provides can greatly reduce the time that you need to perform tasks. Under OS/2, you can perform many of these tasks in the background. For example, how many times have you waited for a printout of your application before you could proceed to fix some critical bug? Under OS/2, you can perform this task in the background while you work on some other section of the program. Using REXX to automate some of these tasks could reduce your participation level to almost nothing.

Using the WPS to full advantage requires a change in thinking as well. You need to plan ahead if you want to use its full capability. For

example, you could use an automated test program to test your
application in the background while you print some of your program
modules and edit yet other modules. The keyword here is planning. If
you don't plan to use these capabilities, then you won't make the best
use of the programming environment. In coding, the bottom line is
not only to get your code written well, but fast.

Finally, you can arrange the desktop to meet a variety of needs and
work styles. Some people leave their desktop a mess, which is fine
if you work better in a disorganized environment; however, most
people do benefit from a little organization. For example, you
could place all your drives and other devices at the bottom of the
screen, as shown in Fig. 1-1. This makes them handy when you're
in the middle of an application and need to check something.
Instead of minimizing your application, you can simply open the
new one by double clicking one of the drive icons. Another good
practice is to place your applications and application folders at the
top of the screen. This allows you to grab them quickly without

Figure 1-1

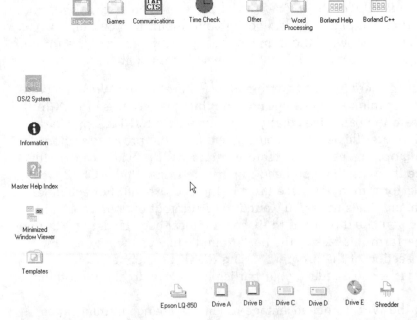

OS/2 Workplace Shell (WPS).

minimizing your current application. It usually helps to place all your OS/2 default folders at the side of the screen since you normally won't use them with other applications.

You can go even further in the optimization process by setting application settings to optimize that application's environment. Choosing to minimize an application to the desktop saves time when you use several applications together. Using the default setting keeps applications out of the way when you don't need them. Cluttering your display with excess icons is the last thing you want to do when programming.

No amount of planning for OS/2's multitasking environment removes the work that you need to do. That is a constant that remains unchanged no matter what environment you propose to use. However, the fact that you can use tools to automate part of the process is a real help in a world full of deadlines.

 # Optimizing the programming environment

Once you optimize the OS/2 environment as a whole, you need to optimize your programming environment. This usually involves several steps that you might or might not perform automatically. Like most optimizations, this one starts at product installation. Have you ever noticed how many software packages install more extraneous than useful files? Magazines and books both make money telling you how to rid yourself of this excess baggage. While you will always end up with a few extraneous files, there are a number of ways that you can reduce the clutter. The following paragraphs provide some suggestions you can use:

> ➤ Only create the libraries that you need for current projects when you install your compiler. Most (if not all) compiler installation programs provide the means for adding new libraries later. Extra libraries simply take space, and there is no guarantee that you will need them later.

> ➤ Some compiler packages allow you to choose which features to install. Take the time required to read the vendor manual before you start the installation. Install only those features that you actually will use; any additional features will waste space and slow down the environment without any substantial payback. Some programmers install these extra features thinking that they will take the time to learn them later. Always wait until you have the time to learn to use a new feature before you install it.

> ➤ You can save a substantial amount of hard disk space by not installing online help if you don't use it. Some programmer's force themselves to use online help, even though it makes them less productive. Other programmer's never touch the documentation, relying exclusively on the online help. Still other programmer's install the online help and never use it. If you fall into the first or third categories, think about how you plan to use the online help before you install it. Likewise, if you fall into the paper documentation category, you might want to print any README files, then erase them from your hard disk.

> ➤ Never select the default installation. This is the best way to ensure that the programming environment that you get won't meet your needs. If you want an environment that makes the most of the time you spend programming, always select the custom installation option.

Figure 1-2 shows a typical compiler installation screen. Notice the two buttons at the top of the dialog box. The first one allows you to change the default tools and library options, the other allows you to change the miscellaneous options.

Clicking the Tools and Library button displays the dialog box shown in Fig. 1-3. Notice that every box in the dialog box is checked. This means that, if you used the default installation, you would encumber your hard disk with every feature of this compiler. There is no way that the vendor can predict what pieces of the compiler that you will need, so this is a very predictable setup. You need to change this configuration to meet your needs or suffer the consequences of an overly full hard disk that might slow your work.

 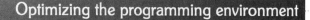

Figure 1-2

*Borland C++ Main
Installation dialog box.*

Figure 1-3

*Borland C++ Installation Options
dialog box.*

Once you get your compiler installed, take the time to check a few
things out. For example, changing the size of your disk cache can
make a significant difference in the speed of compilation. While you
could perform this task in the background, very few programmers do
so unless they want to perform a complete compilation of an entire
application. Because this is one of the foreground tasks that you'll
perform, it pays to optimize compilation speed as much as possible.
Check out the compilation speed of several average sized modules
using different cache sizes and other settings, then set the cache size
to the one that gives you best performance.

Check out the operation of your debugger on your largest
application. Make sure that you use settings that offer the best speed,
memory usage, and least risk of compiler-induced errors. Nothing is a
bigger time waster than thinking that you have a bug in your
application, only to find out later that you had set your debugger up
wrong. Take the time to perform the setups on your editor and other
utilities as well.

One size fits all usually doesn't work. You usually need to perform some setups for each application that you build. While most programming environments provide some method of saving your compiler environment from one session to the next for each application, they don't save the settings for your debugger and other utilities. You might want to keep a disk file or printed output with these settings. That way, you can quickly restore them when you need to take an application out of storage.

You can use these suggestions as a starting place for creating your own customized programming environment. However, it's only a start. Take a little time now to make things as easy as you can. The little time that you spend now can net big savings later. For example, a minute might not seem like much when it comes to compilation speed. However, over hundreds of compilation cycles, that minute starts to build into hours, then days. You effectively could save yourself days of programming effort in a year by reducing the time it takes to compile an application. Seconds taken from the time it takes to perform a repetitive task almost always pay big dividends later.

 # Creating a complete test environment

There is a whole world of ideas for testing applications. There isn't room in this book to explore them all, but we can take a look at several different test environments. Each of the following paragraphs looks at one test method that you can employ to test your application.

The most common test method is to get a number of beta testers to check your application for problems. The viability of this method is directly proportional to how your beta test group represents the people who normally use your application. If you use a sufficient number of beta testers who represent a wide enough variety of environments, you should deliver a fairly bug-free application. Of course, there are more variables than first meets the eye. For example, how do you know your beta testers actually are reporting every problem or even using the application? As you can see, even though this method is theoretically good, implementation details could prove difficult.

Some vendors turn to in-house testers using automated test suites to supplement their beta testers. This has several advantages and disadvantages. The advantages include the ability to test your application using the same sequence of steps every time that you test it. Using automated testing software means that you can perform the test in the background while you do something more productive in the foreground. Of course, there is no way that you can test every possible combination of keystrokes or even make sure that the keystrokes that you do test are reasonable in the real world. As a result, most vendors who use automated test suites create them from reproducible problems submitted by beta testers. Part of the input for a bug report includes the keystrokes that reproduce the error. You can tie these keystrokes directly into the test suite to make sure that the bug gets fixed and that no interaction bugs pop up to break the software again.

Some vendors employ directed testing. This method uses task scripts that new or experienced users follow. The vendor has observers stationed behind one-way glass to observe the reactions of the testers as they perform the tasks. Not only can this help the vendor improve the usability of a product, but it can alert the vendor to logic errors in the product as well. The biggest disadvantage to this test method is that it costs a lot. The vendor might make a big investment in labor-intensive testing that might not yield significant results.

You also can use keystroke recording to test the application. The vendor creates a special version of the program that records each user keystroke to a file on disk. The software also records the test environment, hardware conditions, and specific performance measures as part of the file. Each error that the user encounters also appears in the file. This method provides the vendor with superior test and usability analysis materials. The big disadvantage to this method is getting the beta testers to return the file to the vendor. There isn't much that you can do to evaluate the performance of your application unless you can get consistent returns from your users. Another problem with this approach is that you can't test everything. As a result, you cannot test everything that you need to check to ensure the application runs reliably.

As you can see, testing is part science, part art, part luck, and part magic. Coming up with the right test methods and techniques could

easily require an entire book by itself. Suffice it to say that these techniques will get you started on the right track. Honing these methods to a set of tests that always produce the desired results requires both time and patience.

Using the Developer Connection for OS/2

The Developer Connection provides you with many tools in addition to the ones that you'll find with the standard OS/2 package. One item that it usually contains is a set of the latest OS/2 operating system beta components. This means that you can buy the Developer Connection and not need to worry if you are developing for the latest version of OS/2. There also is a complete set of other IBM beta products (a beta version of a C++ compiler for example) provided with the package. The first version of this product includes a full copy of OS/2 version 2.1, but there is no guarantee that IBM will include it with future versions of the product. Some of the items provided with the first Developer Connection disk include:

> Multimedia Presentation Manager/2 Version 1.1

> Multimedia UltiMotion

> Motion Video AVI Files

> Communications Manager for OS/2 (single user)

> Networking Services/DOS (NSDOS)

> PL/I Workstation/2

> TCP/IP for OS/2

> HyperWrite

> PM Automated Test Environment (PMATE)

> Workstation Interactive Test Tool (WITT)

It's the additional items that really add value to the Developer Connection. There isn't room here to provide you with a detailed description of every product on the current disk; besides, the contents of

each disk are different. However, the following paragraphs do provide you with an overview of the features in some of the more interesting applications. I chose to concentrate on the most interesting applications that you should see with every version of Developer Connection. You'll need to use them to find out just how easy they are to use and which tools apply to your particular situation. Make sure you don't read the description and decide that these tools aren't for you. Take the time to actually test them; descriptions often leave out important applications that you will see immediately.

One of the big reasons to buy this package is the documentation. This is a constant for Developer Connection; you will always receive the latest OS/2 documentation. The first version of the product includes the following documentation:

➤ OS/2 Technical Library

➤ Communications Manager Technical Library

➤ REXX information

➤ TCP/IP information

➤ Using Workplace OS/2

➤ Pen for OS/2 Developer's Toolkit information

⇨ Presentation Manager Automated Test Environment (PMATE)

I talked about the importance of testing in a previous section of this chapter. One of the biggest obstacles to companies actually implementing these solutions is the cost involved. After all, test software doesn't come for free; it usually costs a great deal more than companies are willing to pay. In essence, automated test software is the UPS of the computer industry. Very few companies can justify the cost of using a UPS on each workstation even though it makes sense to do so. Some companies fall into the same trap with software testing, leaving it up to some specialized department that doesn't even interact with the department responsible for software development (or worse yet, not doing much in-house testing at all). PMATE resolves this problem when programming under OS/2. Figure 1-4 shows the main menu of this

Figure 1-4

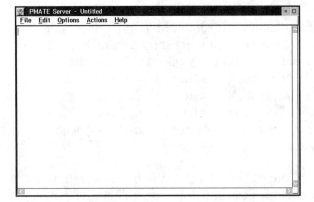

Presentation Manager Automated Test Environment (PMATE) main window.

utility. You get this automated test environment as part of the Developer Connection. It is located in the PMATE subdirectory of the TSTTOOLS directory on your CD-ROM. As a result, management is happy about the bottom line and the programmers are happy because they have the proper tools.

As you can see, the PMATE screen looks essentially like an editor. It allows you to record, load, and run script files that test your application. More importantly, PMATE provides a batch mode that you can call from within a REXX application. This means that you could compile and test your application in the background without ever leaving your foreground session. You still need to perform the setups required to make this work. While the payoff on large projects can more than pay for the time required to set up this level of automation, you might want to consider its feasibility on small projects.

 # Production tools

The PRODTOOL directory contains a number of production tools that you can use to enhance your program. More importantly, some of these tools could serve as inspiration for your own application; they show some of the things that you can do with a typical OS/2 application. Some of these tools provide a standalone environment that you enhance using macros; other tools simply provide the programmer with useful information. For example, PM Globe is a fun program that you can run from REXX using macros. This means that

you could put on a show using this application, shut it down, then go on to do some other work with your REXX application. Figure 1-5 shows the PM Globe display. As you can see, there is nothing earth shaking about this application, but it does serve to show how you can use some of the utilities provided with the Developer Connection. One interesting feature of this application is the distance calculator shown in the lower left corner of the screen.

Figure 1-5

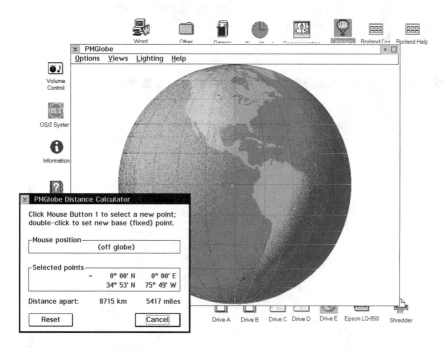

PMGlobe main window.

DInfo is one of those utilities that fall into the useful category even if it doesn't provide any command-line interface that you can use within a REXX application. Essentially, this application tells you about the swap file for your system. The default statistics include the SWAPPER.DAT size and the amount of free space. You can include several other statistics including two alarms.

PMTree is more than a simple tool that you can use to dress up an application, and it really falls outside the utility category as well. This application provides the programmer with essential information about

the PM environment. Figure 1-6 shows a typical PMTree display. Notice that this is a hierarchical display of all the active PM windows. The leftmost window provides a description of all the properties of that window. Double clicking on another window displays a description of its properties and children. As you can see from the figure, PMTree displays the process ID, thread ID, and other characteristics of the "head" window. You can use this information to see how other developers arrange their applications or as part of the debugging effort for your own applications. The number of uses is virtually unlimited.

Figure 1-6

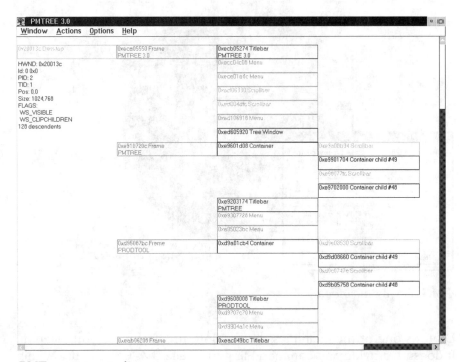

PMTree main window.

There are many other production tools provided as part of the Developer Connection. All of them fall into one of the three previously described areas. As you can see, each tool provides an added level of productivity that you can rely on to help you in your programming endeavors.

⇨ Editors

It might not seem like a programmer would need yet another editor for creating applications. Yet, the Developer Connection provides four rather unique editors that you can use to create your applications. Rather than simply assume that the editor provided with your compiler will do all the work that you need it to do, you might want to take a look at one or more of these useful utilities.

Tiny (T.EXE in the TINYED subdirectory of the EDITORS directory) is an editor that consumes a mere 9K of RAM. One of the unique features of this editor is that it is a DOS application; you can use it anywhere within OS/2 or when you boot DOS to check something out during the development cycle. For this reason, Tiny is more useful than many editors that you might want to use. In addition, its small memory footprint means that you can load all but the very largest source code files. The flexibility provided by this editor even allows you to write documentation or other longer texts. Tiny can't provide all the bells and whistles of a full-featured word processor, but it does the job in a pinch.

SlickEdit is a fully functional programmer's editor. It provides the hooks required to make it an integrated development environment (IDE) if you want. For example, there are built-in menu commands for compiling your application. The IDE even includes a limited number of debugging aids like finding the last error recorded by the compiler. Figure 1-7 shows the SlickEdit display. One of the unique features of this editor is that it comes in versions for a variety of operating systems including DOS and Windows NT. This means that you could learn one interface for all the environments that you use.

EPM is another one of the editors included with the Developer Connection. This one should look familiar to anyone who has used the enhanced editor provided with OS/2 (Fig. 1-8). Essentially, this is an exact copy of that editor. The only difference is that the Developer Connection provides the tools for you, the programmer, to modify the behavior of this power editor. The package includes one very important tool to assist you in this goal. The macro compiler allows you to create add-ons to the enhanced editor that you can distribute to users of your

Figure 1-7

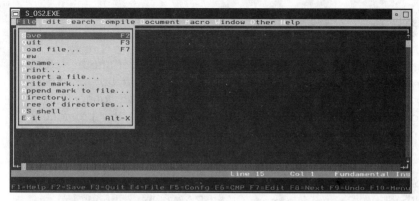

Slick Edit main window.

Figure 1-8

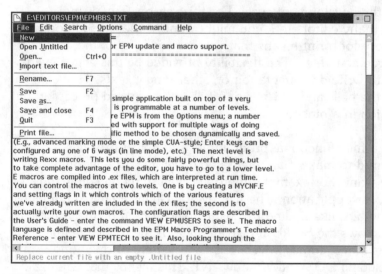

EPM main window.

product or use for a variety of other purposes. Besides the macro compiler, the Developer Connection provides some debugging aids and documentation for creating macros for EPM.

The fourth editor, Hyperwrite/E, really is not an editor in the conventional sense. What it provides is an advanced help and documentation creation utility. It provides an environment where you can create fully animated help and documentation files that really help

the user understand your application. This includes both graphics and sound, besides the usual toolbars and other aids associated with a hypertext environment. Of course, it takes time and patience to learn to use a tool of this nature. The Developer Connection also provides a number of training aids in the form of samples that you can use to learn this product. (You also will find a tutorial conspicuously located under the Help menu.) Figure 1-9 shows a typical screen from Hyperwrite/E.

Figure 1-9

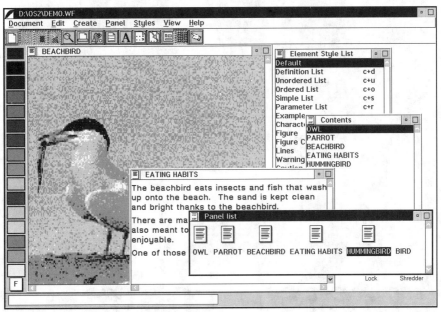

HyperWrite main window.

Hyperwrite/E includes several aids besides the editor. For example, it includes a compiler that allows you to create either a HLP file that you can call within an application or an INF file you execute from the OS/2 prompt. The output looks much like any other help screen that you might have used in the past. The big difference is the ease with which you create it and the ability to add both graphics and sound.

As you can see, the editors provided with the Developer Connection help you to automate a variety of tasks. Don't pass up the opportunity to use these rather unique tools; add them to your programmer's toolbox as soon as possible. Especially important is the Hyperwrite/E editor. This is one tool that can greatly reduce the time required to document your new application.

Processor commands
and interfaces

T he processor represents the central control for any application that you create. It's a combination traffic cop and "brain" for your computer system. Just about everything that goes on in your computer goes through the processor first. Using the maximum level of commands for the platform that you want to target with your application ensures that it will run as quickly as possible. For example, it is much faster to push all the registers on the stack at one time using the PUSHA command rather than pushing them one at a time. Using this command also ensures that you will not run into any bugs associated with popping the registers in a different order than you push them. So using the appropriate command set for the platform that you want to target not only makes the application run faster, but your debugging time less as well.

This chapter discusses processor-specific commands. It arranges them in mnemonic alphabetical order within functional areas. There are sections for the 8086/8088, 8087, 80286, 80287, 80386, 80387, and 80486 processors. Each general-purpose processor builds upon the commands available to its predecessor; therefore, each command appears once. The math coprocessor commands require a little different treatment. While each math coprocessor does build on the capabilities of its predecessor, some math coprocessor commands do not appear in all versions of the chip. As a result, the applicable processor appears in parentheses beside the command.

⇨ 8086/8088 and 8087 commands

The following paragraphs describe each 8086/8088 processor specific command. Table 2-1 lists the 8086/8088 processor instructions by functional area. The 80286, 80386, 80486, and Pentium processors use these commands as well. Table 2-2 lists the 8087 math coprocessor commands. The 80287, 80387, and 80487 math coprocessors use some of these commands as well. Each command identifies which processor uses it.

Table 2-1   **8088/8086 command summary**

Command	Description
Arithmetic instructions	
ASCII Adjust for Addition (AAA)	The ASCII Adjust for Addition instruction changes the AL register contents from packed to unpacked decimal format. Zero the auxiliary carry flag (AF) before using this command.
ASCII Adjust for Division (AAD)	The ASCII Adjust for Division instruction changes the AX register contents from unpacked to packed decimal format.
ASCII Adjust for Multiplication (AAM)	The ASCII Adjust for Multiplication instruction corrects the result of multiplying two unpacked decimal format numbers.
ASCII Adjust for Subtraction (AAS)	The ASCII Adjust for Subtraction instruction corrects the results of subtracting of two unpacked decimal format numbers. Zero the auxiliary carry flag (AF) before using this command.
Add with Carry (ADC)	Use the Add with Carry instruction to add two numbers and accounts for carries generated from previous additions.
Add Without Carry (ADD)	This instruction adds two operands without regard for CF status.
Convert Byte to Word (CBW)	This instruction converts a byte value stored in AL to a word value by extending the sign-bit in AL through AH.
Compare (CMP)	This instruction compares by subtracting the value of the destination from the value of the source. It updates the AF, CF, OF, PF, SF, and ZF registers to reflect the subtraction results but does not place the results in the destination.
Convert Word to Doubleword (CWD)	Use this instruction to convert a word value to a doubleword value. It extends the sign-bit in AX through DX.
Decimal Adjust for Addition (DAA)	The Decimal Adjust for Addition instruction corrects the result of adding two packed decimal operands.
Decimal Adjust for Subtraction (DAS)	The Decimal Adjust for Subtraction instruction corrects the result of subtracting two packed decimal operands.
Decrement (DEC)	This instruction reduces the contents of a register or memory variable by one.
Divide (DIV)	The divide instruction performs unsigned division. It divides the quantity in the accumulator by the divisor. When using byte values, the quotient appears in AL and the remainder appears in AH. The value divided appears in AX. When using word values, the quotient appears in AX and the remainder appears in DX. The value divided appears in the AX:DX register pair. Using doubleword values places the quotient in EAX and the remainder in EDX. The processor divides the numerator in the EAX:EDX register pair by the divisor.
Integer Divide (IDIV)	The Integer Divide instruction performs signed division on the value

Command	Description
	contained in the accumulator. When using byte values, the quotient appears in AL and the remainder appears in AH. The value divided appears in AX. When using word values, the quotient appears in AX and the remainder appears in DX. The value divided appears in the AX:DX register pair. Using doubleword values places the quotient in EAX and the remainder in EDX. The processor divides the numerator in the EAX:EDX register pair by the divisor.
Integer Multiply (IMUL)	This instruction performs signed multiplication on the value in the accumulator by the multiplicand. When using byte values, the AX register contains the double length result. Using word values returns the result in the AX:DX register pair. Doubleword values return a result in the EAX:EDX register pair.
Increment (INC)	This instruction increases the contents of a register or memory variable by one.
Multiply (MUL)	This instruction performs unsigned multiplication on the value in the accumulator by the multiplicand. When using byte values, the AX register contains the double length result. Using word values returns the result in the AX:DX register pair. Doubleword values return a result in the EAX:EDX register pair.
Negate (NEG)	This instruction calculates the two's complement of the destination operand. This is effectively the same as subtracting the destination operand from 0.
Subtract with Borrow (SBB)	This instruction subtracts the source value from the destination value and stores the result in the destination. It decrements the result by one if CF = 1. The subtract with borrow instruction affects AF, CF, OF, PF, SF, and ZF.
Subtract (SUB)	The subtract instruction subtracts the value in the source from the destination. It affects AF, CF, OF, PF, SF, and ZF.

Bit-manipulation instructions

Command	Description
Logical AND on Bits (AND)	Use this instruction to logically AND two values together at the bit level.
Logical NOT on Bits (NOT)	The NOT instruction produces the one's complement of the destination operand by inverting its bits. This instruction does not affect any flags.
Logical OR on Bits (OR)	This instruction performs an inclusive OR of the source and destination operands. It places the results in the destination operand. A bit equals 1 in the destination operand when either or both operands contain a 1 in that bit position.
Rotate Left through Carry (RCL)	This instruction rotates the bits in the destination to the left the number of places specified in the count operand. The carry flag receives the value dropped from the high-order bit. The low-order bit receives the value contained in the carry flag.

Table 2-1   **Continued**

Command	Description
Rotate Right through Carry (RCR)	This instruction rotates the bits in the destination to the right the number of places specified in the count operand. The carry flag receives the value dropped from the low-order bit. The high-order bit receives the value contained in the carry flag.
Rotate Left (ROL)	This instruction rotates the bits in the destination to the left the number of places specified in the count operand. It affects both OF and CF.
Rotate Right (ROR)	This instruction rotates the bits in the destination to the right the number of places specified in the count operand. It affects both OF and CF.
Arithmetic Shift Left (SAL)	The Arithmetic Shift Left instruction shifts all bits in the destination operand left the number of bits specified by the source operand. It affects CF, OF, PF, SF, ZF, and AF (undefined).
Arithmetic Shift Right (SAR)	The Arithmetic Shift Right instruction shifts all bits in the destination operand right the number of bits specified by the source operand. It affects CF, OF, PF, SF, ZF, and AF (undefined).
Shift Left (SHL)	The Shift Left instruction shifts all bits in the destination operand left the number of bits specified by the source operand. It affects CF, OF, PF, SF, ZF, and AF (undefined).
Shift Right (SHR)	The Shift Right instruction shifts all bits in the destination operand right the number of bits specified by the source operand. It affects CF, OF, PF, SF, ZF, and AF (undefined).
Test Bits (TEST)	This instruction performs a logical AND of two operands then updates the flags. The flags reflect how the two operands compared. Test does nothing with the results. The flags it affects include CF, OF, PF, SF, ZF, and AF (undefined).
Logical Exclusive-OR on Bits (XOR)	This instruction performs an exclusive OR on two operands. It returns a value in the destination operand. XOR sets a bit in the destination operand if the corresponding bits in the comparison opperands are different. The exclusive or instruction affects CF, OF, PF, SF, ZF, and AF (undefined).

Control-transfer instructions

Execute a Subprogram (CALL)	The call instruction executes a subprogram. Two types of call instruction exist. The first type is a near call to subprograms ±32 Kbytes or less distant from the current instruction. For this type, the processor updates IP to the next instruction position and pushes this value on the stack. It then places the new instruction value in IP and continues execution until a return instruction appears. The second type is a far call to subprograms greater than ±32Kbytes distant from the current instruction. The processor pushes CS and replaces it with the segment of the call instruction. Then, the processor

Command	Description
	updates IP to the next instruction position and pushes this value on the stack. It then places the new instruction value in IP and continues execution until a return instruction appears.
Software Interrupt (INT)	This instruction activates the following interrupt processing procedure: (1) Decrement SP by 2. Push the flags on the stack using the same format as PUSHF. (2) Clear TF and IF to prevent other single-step or maskable interrupts from occurring. (3) Decrement SP. Push CS. (4) Calculate the interrupt pointer address by multiplying the interrupt type by four. Place the second word of the interrupt pointer in CS. (5) Decrement SP, and push IP. Place the first word of the interrupt pointer in IP.

The assembler generates a 1-byte form of the instruction for interrupt 3 (known as the breakpoint interrupt). Only device drivers or operating systems normally create their own interrupt code. The only flags affected are IF and TF, which the interrupt processor sets to 1. |
Interrupt on Overflow (INTO)	Use this instruction to generate an interrupt 4 when the overflow flag (OF) equals 1. It operates in all respects like the interrupt instruction when executed. If OF equals 0, the processor ignores this instruction.
Return from Interrupt (IRET)	This instruction returns control to a procedure calling an interrupt after the interrupt completes. It pops CS, IP, and all flags.
Jump if Above (JA)	This instruction transfers control to the instruction pointed to by IP + Displacement when CF and ZF equal 0.
Jump if Above or Equal (JAE)	This instruction transfers control to the instruction pointed to by IP + Displacement when CF equals 0.
Jump if Below (JB)	This instruction transfers control to the instruction pointed to by IP + Displacement when CF equals 1.
Jump if Below or Equal (JBE)	This instruction transfers control to the instruction pointed to by IP + Displacement when CF or ZF equal 1.
Jump on Carry (JC)	This instruction transfers control to the instruction pointed to by IP + Displacement when CF equals 1.
Jump if CX Equals Zero (JCXZ)	This instruction transfers control to the instruction pointed to by IP + Displacement when CX equals 0.
Jump if Equal (JE)	This instruction transfers control to the instruction pointed to by IP + Displacement when ZF equals 1.
Jump if Greater Than (JG)	This instruction transfers control to the instruction pointed to by IP + Displacement when SF equals OF or ZF equals 0.
Jump if Greater Than or Equal (JGE)	This instruction transfers control to the instruction pointed to by IP + Displacement when SF equals OF.
Jump if Less Than	This instruction transfers control to the instruction pointed to by IP

Table 2-1   **Continued**

Command	Description
(JL)	+ Displacement when SF does not equal OF.
Jump if Less Than or Equal (JLE)	This instruction transfers control to the instruction pointed to by IP + Displacement when SF does not equal OF or ZF equals 1.
Jump Unconditionally (JMP)	This instruction unconditionally transfers control to the instruction referenced by an operand. There are three types of unconditional jump. The first type, short, allows jumps of only ±127 bytes but produces only 2 bytes of code. The second type, near, allows jumps of ±32 Kbytes. It produces 3 bytes of code. The third type uses both CS and IP for far jumps. It uses 5 bytes of code.
Jump if Not Above (JNA)	This instruction transfers control to the instruction pointed to by IP + Displacement when CF or ZF equal 1.
Jump if Not Above or Equal (JNAE)	This instruction transfers control to the instruction pointed to by IP + Displacement when CF equals 1.
Jump if Not Below (JNB)	This instruction transfers control to the instruction pointed to by IP + Displacement when CF equals 0.
Jump if Not Below or Equal (JNBE)	This instruction transfers control to the instruction pointed to by IP + Displacement when CF and ZF equal 0.
Jump on No Carry (JNC)	This instruction transfers control to the instruction pointed to by IP + Displacement when CF equals 0.
Jump if Not Equal (JNE)	This instruction transfers control to the instruction pointed to by IP + Displacement when ZF equals 0.
Jump if Not Greater Than (JNG)	This instruction transfers control to the instruction pointed to by IP + Displacement when SF does not equal OF or ZF equals 1.
Jump if Not Greater Than or Equal (JNGE)	This instruction transfers control to the instruction pointed to by IP + Displacement when SF does not equal OF.
Jump if Not Less Than (JNL)	This instruction transfers control to the instruction pointed to by IP + Displacement when SF equals OF.
Jump if Not Less Than or Equal (JNLE)	This instruction transfers control to the instruction pointed to by IP + Displacement when SF equals OF or ZF equals 0.
Jump on No Overflow (JNO)	This instruction transfers control to the instruction pointed to by IP + Displacement when OF equals 0.
Jump on No Parity) (JNP	This instruction transfers control to the instruction pointed to by IP + Displacement when PF equals 0.
Jump on Not Sign (JNS)	This instruction transfers control to the instruction pointed to by IP + Displacement when SF equals 0.
Jump on Not Zero	This instruction transfers control to the instruction pointed to by IP

Command	Description
(JNZ)	+ Displacement when ZF equals 0.
Jump on Overflow (JO)	This instruction transfers control to the instruction pointed to by IP + Displacement when OF equals 1.
Jump on Parity (JP)	This instruction transfers control to the instruction pointed to by IP + Displacement when PF equals 1.
Jump on Parity Even (JPE)	This instruction transfers control to the instruction pointed to by IP + Displacement when PF equals 1.
Jump on Parity Odd (JPO)	This instruction transfers control to the instruction pointed to by IP + Displacement when PF equals 0.
Jump on Sign (JS)	This instruction transfers control to the instruction pointed to by IP + Displacement when SF equals 1.
Jump on Zero (JZ)	This instruction transfers control to the instruction pointed to by IP + Displacement when ZF equals 1.
Loop (LOOP)	The Loop instruction decrements CX by 1, then tests to see if CX equals 0. If CX is greater than 0, Loop transfers control to the target instruction. Otherwise, it passes control to the next inline instruction.
Loop While Equal (LOOPE)	The loop instruction decrements CX by 1, then tests to see if CX equals 0. If CX is greater than 0 and ZF equals 1, Loop transfers control to the target instruction. Otherwise, it passes control to the next inline instruction.
Loop While Not Equal (LOOPNE)	The loop instruction decrements CX by 1, then tests to see if CX equals 0. If CX is greater than 0 and ZF equals 0, Loop transfers control to the target instruction. Otherwise, it passes control to the next inline instruction.
Loop While Not Zero (LOOPNZ)	The loop instruction decrements CX by 1, then tests to see if CX equals 0. If CX is greater than 0 and ZF equals 0, Loop transfers control to the target instruction. Otherwise, it passes control to the next inline instruction.
Loop While Zero (LOOPZ)	The loop instruction decrements CX by 1, then tests to see if CX equals 0. If CX is greater than 0 and ZF equals 1, Loop transfers control to the target instruction. Otherwise, it passes control to the next inline instruction.
Return from a Subprogram (RET)	Use this instruction at the end of a subprogram to return control to the calling program. The assembler generates two types of return: far and near. The near return pops only IP from the stack. A far return pops both IP and CS from the stack.

Data-transfer instructions

Input Data from Port (IN)	This instruction allows data input from a port to the AX register. Use either the DX register or a constant to specify port number less

Table 2-1   **Continued**

Command	Description
	than 256. For port number greater than 255, use the DX register only. This instruction does not affect the flags.
Load the AH Register with Flags (LAHF)	Use this instruction during assembly language conversions from 8080/8085 processor to 8086/8088 processor format. It transfers the low-order byte of the flags register to AH. The flags transferred include SF, ZF, AF, PF, and CF.
Load the DS Register (LDS)	This instruction transfers a 32-bit pointer from the source operand (memory only) to the destination operand (offset) and the DS register (segment). The destination operand is any 16-bit general purpose register.
Load the Effective Address (LEA)	The load effective address instruction transfers the offset of the source operand (rather than its value) to the destination operand. The source operand is always a memory variable. The destination is always a general purpose 16-bit register.
Load the ES Register (LES)	This instruction transfers a 32-bit pointer from the source operand (memory only) to the destination operand (offset) and the ES register (segment). The destination operand is any 16-bit general purpose register.
Move (MOV)	This instruction transfers data from the source operand to a destination operand of the same length.
Output Data to Port (OUT)	This instruction allows data output to a port from the AX register. Use either the DX register or a constant to specify port numbers less than 256. For port numbers greater than 255, use the DX register only. This instruction does not affect the flags.
Remove Data from the Stack (POP)	POP removes the word pointed to by the stack pointer (SP) and places it in a memory operand or register. It then increments SP by 2.
Remove Flags from the Stack (POPF)	POPF removes the word pointed to by the stack pointer (SP) and places it in the flag register. It then increments SP by 2.
Place Data on the Stack (PUSH)	PUSH decrements SP by 2. It then adds the word contained in a register or memory operand to the location pointed to by the stack pointer (SP).
Place Flags on the Stack (PUSHF)	PUSHF decrements SP by 2. It then adds the flag register contents to the location pointed to by the stack pointer (SP).
Store AH into the Flag Register (SAHF)	Use this instruction during assembly language conversions from 8080/8085 processor to 8086/8088 processor format. It transfers the contents of AH to low-order byte of the flags register. The flags transferred include SF, ZF, AF, PF, and CF.
Exchange (XCHG)	This instruction swaps the contents of the source and destination operands. It does not affect any flags.

Command · Description

Translate (XLAT) The translate instruction places the value in a table pointed to by BX in AL. The AL register initially contains an offset into the table. The translate instruction does not affect any flags.

Flag- and processor-control instructions

Clear the Carry Flag (CLC) The Clear the Carry Flag instruction sets CF to zero.

Clear the Direction Flag (CLD) The Clear the Direction Flag instruction sets DF to zero.

Clear the Interrupt Flag (CLI) The Clear the Interrupt Flag instruction sets IF to zero.

Complement the Carry Flag (CMC) This instruction toggles the value of CF.

Escape (ESC) The escape instruction provides a means for co-processing chips to access data using the 8086/8088/80286/80386 processing stream. It causes the processor to place the operand on the bus while internally performing a no operation (NOP) instruction.

Halt (HLT) This instruction stops the processor temporarily while waiting for an interrupt. It provides a means of creating a wait state without resorting to endless software loops. The halt instruction does not affect any flags.

Lock the Bus (LOCK) The lock instruction prevents interference by any coprocessors during the next instruction. Always use lock with other instructions.

No Operation (NOP) This instruction tells the CPU to do nothing.

Set the Carry Flag (STC) This instruction sets CF reguardless of its present condition.

Set the Direction Flag (STD) This instruction sets DF reguardless of its present condition.

Set the Interrupt Flag (STI) This instruction sets IF reguardless of its present condition.

Wait (WAIT) This instuction causes the CPU to enter its wait state until it receives an external interrupt on the test line. Wait does not affect any flags.

String-manipulation instructions

Compare Strings, Byte-by-Byte (CMPSB) This instruction changes the value of the AF, CF, OF, PF, SF, and ZF flags to show the relationship between two bytes in a string. The results of the comparison do not affect the contents of either operand. After comparing the two string bytes, the instruction updates both SI and DI to point to the next string element. DF controls the direction of comparison.

Compare Strings, This instruction changes the value of the AF, CF, OF, PF, SF, and ZF

Table 2-1   **Continued**

Command	Description
Word-by-Word (CMPSW)	flags to show the relationship between two words in a string. The results of the comparison do not affect the contents of either operand. After comparing the two string words, the instruction updates both SI and DI to point to the next string element. DF controls the direction of comparison.
Load a Byte from String into AL (LODSB)	Use this instruction to transfer a byte from the string pointed to by SI to AL. The SI register automatically advances to the next string element in the direction pointed to by the direction flag.
Load a Word from String into AX (LODSW)	Use this instruction to transfer a word from the string pointed to by SI to AX. The SI register automatically advances to the next string element in the direction pointed to by the direction flag.
Move String Byte-by-Byte (MOVSB)	This instruction moves the byte pointed to by SI to the destination pointed to by DI. Using the REP instruction with this instruction, repeats the move the number of times shown in CX. After each move, the instruction advances both SI and DI to the next position in the direction indicated by DF.
Move String Word-by-Word (MOVSW)	This instruction moves the word pointed to by SI to the destination pointed to by DI. Using the REP instruction with this instruction, repeats the move the number of times shown in CX. After each move, the instruction advances both SI and DI to the next position in the direction indicated by DF.
Repeat (REP)	Use this instruction with string manipulation instructions to repeat the instruction the number of times specified in CX.
Repeat if Equal (REPE)	Use this instruction with string manipulation instructions to repeat the instruction the number of times specified in CX. It repeats only while ZF = 1 when used with the CMPSB, CMPSW, SCASB, or SCASW instructions.
Repeat if Not Equal (REPNE)	Use this instruction with string manipulation instructions to repeat the instruction the number of times specified in CX. It repeats only while ZF = 0 when used with the CMPSB, CMPSW, SCASB, or SCASW instructions.
Repeat if Not Zero (REPNZ)	Use this instruction with string manipulation instructions to repeat the instruction the number of times specified in CX. It repeats only while ZF = 0 when used with the CMPSB, CMPSW, SCASB, or SCASW instructions.
Repeat if Zero (REPZ)	Use this instruction with string manipulation instructions to repeat the instruction the number of times specified in CX. It repeats only while ZF = 1 when used with the CMPSB, CMPSW, SCASB, or SCASW instructions.
Scan String for Byte	Use this instruction with any of the repeat instructions to scan

Command	Description
(SCASB)	strings for the value contained in AL. After each scan, DI advances to point to the next string element. This instruction affects AF, CF, OF, PF, SF, and ZF.
Scan String for Word (SCASW)	Use this instruction with any of the repeat instructions to scan strings for the value contained in AX. After each scan, DI advances to point to the next string element. This instruction affects AF, CF, OF, PF, SF, and ZF.
Store Byte in AL at String (STOSB)	Use this instruction alone or with any repeat instruction to send the value in AL to the string pointed at by DI. DI automatically advances to the next string location after each store operation. This instruction does not affect any flags.
Store Word in AX at String (STOSW)	Use this instruction alone or with any repeat instruction to send the value in AX to the string pointed at by DI. DI automatically advances to the next string location after each store operation. This instruction does not affect any flags.

8087 command summary

Table 2-2

Command	Description
Arithmetic instructions	
Absolute Value (FABS) (8087/80287/ 80387)	Use this instruction to replace the top stack element with its absolute value. It affects the IE status bit.
Add Real (FADD) (8087/80287/ 80387)	The Add Real instruction adds two numbers together and places the result in the destination operand. The instruction uses the stack as the default destination. This instruction affects the PE, UE, OE, DE, and IE status bits.
Add Real and Pop (FADDP) (8087/80287/ 80387)	This instruction adds two operands, places the result at the destination, and pops a value from the stack. The instruction uses the stack as the default destination. This instruction affects the PE, UE, OE, DE, and IE status bits.
Change Sign (FCHS) (8087/80287/ 80387)	Use this instruction to change the sign of the top stack element. It affects the IE status bit.
Divide Real (FDIV) (8087/80287/ 80387)	This instruction divides the destination by the source operand. It places the result in the destination. The instruction uses the stack as the default destination. The divide real instruction affects the PE, UE, OE, ZE, DE, and IE status bits.
Divide Real and Pop (FDIVP) (8087/80287/	This instruction divides the destination by the source operand. It places the result in the destination and pops the stack. The instruction uses the stack as the default destination. The divide real

Table 2-2   **Continued**

Command	Description
80387)	and pop instruction affects the PE, UE, OE, ZE, DE, and IE status bits.
Divide Real Reversed (FDIVR) (8087/80287/ 80387)	This instruction divides the source by the destination operand. It places the result in the destination. The instruction uses the stack as the default destination. The divide real reversed instruction affects the PE, UE, OE, ZE, DE, and IE status bits.
Divide Real Reversed and Pop (FDIVRP) (8087/80287/ 80387)	This instruction divides the source by the destination operand. It places the result in the destination and pops the stack. The instruction uses the stack as the default destination. The divide real reversed and pop instruction affects the PE, UE, OE, ZE, DE, and IE status bits.
Integer Add (FIADD) (8087/80287/ 80387)	This instruction adds two operands as integers and stores the result at the destination. It assumes a default stack destination. The integer add instruction affects the PE, OE, DE, and IE status bits.
Integer Divide (FIDIV) (8087/80287/ 80387)	The integer divide instruction divides the destination by the source operand as integers. It stores the result in the destination operand. The instruction uses the stack as the default destination. If affects the PE, UE, OE, ZE, DE, and IE status bits.
Integer Divide Reversed (FIDIVR) (8087/80287/ 80387)	The integer divide reversed instruction divides the source by the destination operand as integers. It stores the result in the destination operand. The instruction uses the stack as the default destination. It affects the PE, UE, OE, ZE, DE, and IE status bits.
Integer Multiply (FIMUL) (8087/80287/ 80387)	The integer multiply instruction multiplies the destination by the source operand as integers. It stores the result in the destination operand. The instruction uses the stack as the default destination. It affects the PE, OE, DE, and IE status bits.
Integer Subtract (FISUB) (8087/80287/ 80387)	This instruction subtracts the source from the destination operand and places the result in the destination. The instruction assumes a stack default destination. The arithmetic instruction affects the PE, OE, DE, and IE status bits.
Integer Subtract Reversed (FISUBR) (8087/80287/ 80387)	This instruction subtracts the destination from the source operand and places the result in the destination. The instruction assumes a stack default destination. The arithmetic instruction affects the PE, OE, DE, and IE status bits.
Multiply Real (FMUL) (8087/80287/ 80387)	This instruction multiplies the source by the destination operand. It stores the result in the destination operand. The instruction assumes a default stack destination. The multiply real instruction affects the PE, UE, OE, DE, and IE status bits.
Multiply Real and Pop (FMULP)	This instruction multiplies the source by the destination operand. It stores the result in the destination operand, then pops the stack.

Command	Description
(8087/80287/80387)	The instruction assumes a default stack destination. The multiply real instruction affects the PE, UE, OE, DE, and IE status bits.
Partial Remainder (FPREM) (8087/80287/80387)	The partial arctangent instruction calculates the modulo of the top two stack elements. It performs this by successively subtracting the second element from the first. The calculated remainder remains in the first element. The instruction affects the C0, C1, C3, UE, DE, and IE status bits.
Round to an Integer (FRNDINT) (8087/80287/80387)	This instruction rounds the number located on the top stack element to an integer. It affects the PE and IE status bits.
Square Root (FSQRT) (8087/80287/80387)	Use this instruction to calculate the square root of the top stack element. The square root value replaces the old stack value. This instruction affects the PE, DE, and IE status bits.
Subtract Real (FSUB) (8087/80287/80387)	This instruction subtracts the source from the destination operand and places the result in the destination. The instruction assumes a default destination of stack. It affects the PE, UE, OE, DE, and IE status bits.
Subtract Real and Pop (FSUBP) (8087/80287/80387)	This instruction subtracts the source from the destination operand and places the result in the destination. Upon instruction completion, it pops the stack. The instruction assumes a default destination of stack. It affects the PE, UE, OE, DE, and IE status bits.
Subtract Real Reversed (FSUBR) (8087/80287/80387)	This instruction subtracts the destination from the source operand and places the result in the destination. The instruction assumes a default destination of stack. It affects the PE, UE, OE, DE, and IE status bits.
Subtract Real Reversed and Pop (FSUBRP) (8087/80287/80387)	This instruction subtracts the destination from the source operand and places the result in the destination. It pops the stack upon instruction completion. The instruction assumes a default destination of stack. It affects the PE, UE, OE, DE, and IE status bits.
Extract Exponent and Significand (FXTRACT) (8087/80287/80387)	This instruction pops the top stack element, separates the exponent from the significand, and pushes both values on the stack. It affects only the IE status bit.

Comparison instructions

Command	Description
Compare Real (FCOM) (8087/80287/80387)	This instruction compares the top stack element with the second stack element or other specified operand. It affects the C0, C1, C3, DE, and IE status bits.

Table 2-2   **Continued**

Command	Description
Compare Real and Pop (FCOMP) (8087/80287/ 80387)	This instruction compares the top stack element with the second stack element or other specified operand. It then pops the stack. The compare real and pop instruction affects the C0, C1, C3, DE, and IE status bits.
Compare Real and Pop Twice (FCOMPP) (8087/80287/ 80387)	This instruction compares the top stack element with the second stack element or other specified operand. It then pops the stack twice. The compare real and pop instruction affects the C0, C1, C3, DE, and IE status bits.
Integer Compare (FICOM) (8087/80287/ 80387)	This instruction converts the operand to an integer (if required) and compares it to the top stack element. It then changes the condition of the status word bits to match the comparison result. The status word bits affected include C0, C2, C3, DE, and IE.
Integer Compare and Pop (FICOMP) (8087/80287/ 80387)	This instruction converts the operand to an integer (if required) and compares it to the top stack element. It then changes the condition of the status word bits to match the comparison result and pops the stack. The status word bits affected include C0, C2, C3, DE, and IE.
Test (FTST) (8087/80287/ 80387)	This instruction compares the top stack element with zero and sets the status bits accordingly. It affects the C0, C2, C3, DE, and IE status bits.
Examine (FXAM) (8087/80287/ 80387)	This instruction examines the top stack element and updates the status bits to reflect its condition. The examine instruction affects the C0, C1, C2, and C3 status bits.
Constant instructions	
Load Value of 1.0 (FLD1) (8087/80287/ 80387)	This instruction pushes the constant 1.0 on the stack. It affects the IE status bit.
Load Value of $\log_2 e$ (FLDL2E) (8087/80287/ 80387)	This instruction pushes the value of $\log_2 e$ onto the stack. It affects the IE status bit.
Load Value of $\log_2 10$ (FLDL2T) (8087/80287/ 80387)	This instruction pushes the value of $\log_2 10$ onto the stack. It affects the IE status bit.
Load Value of $\log_{10} 2$ (FLDLG2) (8087/80287/ 80387)	This instruction pushes the value of $\log_{10} 2$ onto the stack. It affects the IE status bit.
Load Value of $\log_e 2$	This instruction pushes the value of $\log_e 2$ onto the stack. It affects

Command	Description
(FLDLN2) (8087/80287/ 80387)	the IE status bit.
Load Value of Pi (FLDPI) (8087/80287/ 80387)	This instruction pushes the value of Pi onto the stack. It affects the IE status bit.
Load Value of 0.0 (FLDZ) (8087/80287/ 80387)	This instruction pushes 0 onto the stack. It affects the IE status bit.

Data-transfer instructions

Command	Description
BCD Load (FBLD) (8087/80287/ 80387)	Use this instruction to convert a BCD number (at the specified operand address) to a temporary real format and pushes it on the stack. This instruction affects the IE status bit.
BCD Store and POP (FBSTP) (8087/80287/ 80387)	This instruction pops a value from the stack, converts it to a BCD integer, and places it at the operand address. It affects the IE status bit.
Integer Load (FILD) (8087/80287/ 80387)	This instruction converts the binary integer pointed to by the operand address to a temporary real format and pushes it on the stack. It affects only the IE status bit.
Integer Store (FIST) (8087/80287/ 80387)	Use this instruction to round the top stack element to a binary integer and store it at the operand address. This instruction affects the PE and IE status bits.
Integer Store and Pop (FISTP) (8087/80287/ 80387)	Use this instruction to round the top stack element to a binary integer and store it at the operand address. It pops the stack after storing the integer. This instruction affects the PE and IE status bits.
Load Real (FLD) (8087/80287/ 80387)	Use this instruction to push the source operand on the stack. It affects the DE and IE status bits.
Store Real (FST) (8087/80287/ 80387)	The store real instruction copies the top stack element value to the position pointed to by the destination operand. This instruction affects the PE, UE, OE, and IE status bits.
Store Real and Pop (FSTP) (8087/80287/ 80387)	The store real instruction copies the top stack element value to the position pointed to by the destination operand. It pops the stack after transferring the value. This instruction affects the PE, UE, OE, and IE status bits.
Exchange Registers (FXCH) (8087/80287/ 80387)	This instruction switches the value contained in the top stack element with the destination operand. It only affects the IE status bit.

Table 2-2 **Continued**

Command	Description
Processor-control instructions	
Clear Exceptions with Wait (FCLEX) (8087/80287/80387)	Precede this instruction with a CPU wait prefix. It clears the B, PE, UE, OE, ZE, DE, IE, and IR status bits.
Decrement the Stack Pointer (FDECSTP) (8087/80287/80387)	This instruction decrements the 8087 status word stack pointer. It affects only the ST status bits.
Disable Interrupts with Wait (FDISI) (8087 Only)	Precede this instruction with a CPU wait prefix. It sets the IEM control word bit preventing the 8087 from generating interrupts. This instruction does not affect the status word.
Enable Interrupts with Wait (FENI) (8087 Only)	Precede this instruction with a CPU wait prefix. It clears the IEM control word bit allowing the 8087 to generate interrupts. This instruction does not affect the status word.
Free Register (FFREE) (8087/80287/80387)	This instruction changes the specified stack register tag to indicate an empty element. It does not affect the status word.
Increment the Stack Pointer (FINCSTP) (8087/80287/80387)	This instruction increments the stack status word bits.
Initialize the Processor with Wait (FINIT) (8087/80287/80387)	This instruction equals a hardware reset instruction for the math coprocessor chip. Precede this instruction with a CPU wait prefix.
Load a Control Word (FLDCW) (8087/80287/80387)	Use this instruction to load the control word with the value pointed to by the source operand. This instruction does not affect any status bits.
Load the Environment (FLDENV) (8087/80287/80387)	The load the environment instruction restores all the environment variables from the 14-word memory location pointed to by the source operand. It affects all the status bits.
Clear Exceptions (FNCLEX) (8087/80287/80387)	Use this instruction to clear the exception flags, interrupt request, and busy flags of the status word without using a CPU wait prefix. It affects the B, IR, PE, UE, OE, ZE, DE, and IE status bits.
Disable Interrupts (FNDISI)	This instruction sets the interrupt enable mask of the control word without using a CPU wait prefix. It prevents the coprocessor from

Command	Description
(8087 Only)	issuing interrupts. The disable interrupts instruction does not affect any status bits.
Enable Interrupts (FNENI) (8087 Only)	This instruction clears the interrupt enable mask of the control word without using a CPU wait prefix. It enables the coprocessor to issue interrupts. The disable interrupts instruction does not affect any status bits.
Initialize Processor (FNINIT) (8087/80287/ 80387)	This instruction initializes the math coprocessor without issuing a CPU wait prefix. It is functionally equivalent to a hardware reset.
No Operation (FNOP) (8087/80287/ 80387)	This instruction tells the CPU to do nothing. This instruction does not affect the status bits.
Save State (FNSAVE) (8087/80287/ 80387)	This instruction saves the contents of all math coprocessor registers and environment variables, without issuing a CPU wait, to the place pointed to by the destination operand. It requires 94 words of memory per save for an 8087 math coprocessor. The instruction then issues the equivalent of an FNINIT instruction.
Store Control Word (FNSTCW) (8087/80287/ 80387)	This instruction copies the control word to the place pointed to by the destination operand without using a CPU wait prefix. It does not affect any status bits.
Store Environment (FNSTENV) (8087/80287/ 80387)	This instruction copies the environment variable to the place pointed to by the destination operand without using a CPU wait prefix. The store requires 14 words when using an 8087 math coprocessor. It does not affect any status bits.
Store Status Word (FNSTSW) (8087/80287/ 80387)	This instruction copies the status word to the place pointed to by the destination operand without using a CPU wait prefix. It does not affect any status bits.
Restore State (FRSTOR) (8087/80287/ 80387)	This instruction restores the state of all registers and environment variables from the location pointed to by the destination operand. It affects all the status bits.
Save State with Wait (FSAVE) (8087/80287/ 80387)	This instruction saves the contents of all math coprocessor registers and environment variables to the place pointed to by the destination operand. It uses the CPU wait prefix and requires 94 words of memory per save for an 8087 math coprocessor. The instruction then issues the equivalent of an FINIT instruction.
Store Control Word with Wait (FSTCW) (8087/80287/ 80387)	This instruction copies the control word to the place pointed to by the destination operand using a CPU wait prefix. It does not affect any status bits.

Table 2-2   **Continued**

Command	Description
Store Environment with Wait (FSTENV) (8087/80287/ 80387)	This instruction copies the environment variable to the place pointed to by the destination operand using a CPU wait prefix. The store requires 14 words when using an 8087 math coprocessor. It does not affect any status bits.
Store Status Word with Wait (FSTSW) (8087/80287/ 80387)	This instruction copies the status word to the place pointed to by the destination operand using a CPU wait prefix. It does not affect any status bits.
CPU Wait (FWAIT) (8087/80287/ 80387)	The CPU wait instruction performs essentially the same function for the math coprocessor as it does for the main processor. This permits synchronization of both processors. The main processor suspends operations until the coprocessor completes its activities.

Trancendental instructions

Command	Description
Value of $2^X - 1$ (F2XM1) (8087/80287/ 80387)	This instruction calculates the value of $Y = 2^X - 1$. X is the top stack element. Y replaces X as the top stack element. This instruction affects the PE and UE status bits.
Partial Arctangent (FPATAN) (8087/80287/ 80387)	This instruction computes $\phi = \text{ARCTAN}(Y/X)$, where X is the top stack element and Y is the second stack element. It pops both stack elements and places the result on the stack. This instruction performs no input number validation. It affects the PE and UE status bits.
Partial Tangent (FPTAN) (8087/80287/ 80387)	This instruction computes $Y/X = \text{TAN}(\phi)$ where ϕ is the top stack element. The instruction replaces the top stack element with Y, then pushes the computed X. This instruction performs no input value checking. It affects the PE and IE status bits.
Scale (FSCALE) (8087/80287/ 80387)	Use this instruction to calculate the value of $X = X \times 2^Y$, where X is the value of the top stack element and Y is the second stack element. This instruction affects the UE, OE, and IE status bits.
Value of $Y \times \log_2 X$ (FYL2X) (8087/80287/ 80387)	This instruction calculates the value of $Z = Y \times \log_2 X$, where X is the top stack element and Y is the second stack element. The instruction pops both stack elements and pushes the new value, Z, onto the stack. This instruction does not validate the input values. It affects the PE status bit.
Value of $Y \times \log_2$ $(X + 1)$ (FYL2XP1) (8087/80287/ 80387)	This instruction calculates the value of $Z = Y \times \log_2 (X + 1)$, where X is the top stack element and Y is the second stack element. The instruction pops both stack elements and pushes the new value, Z, onto the stack. This instruction does not validate the input values. It affects the PE status bit.

All the 80x86 processors allow you to monitor conditions through the use of a flag register. Each flag provides feedback on a specific area. For example, the overflow flag tells you when a processor overflow occurs. The flags used for various 8086/8088 instructions include the following:

➤ Overflow (OF)

➤ Direction (DF)

➤ Interrupt (IF)

➤ Trap (TF)

➤ Sign (SF)

➤ Zero (ZF)

➤ Auxiliary Carry (AF)

➤ Parity (PF)

➤ Carry (CF)

The math coprocessor can greatly enhance the execution speed of math intensive applications. It makes use of several coprocessor specific commands to tell you what type of coprocessor (if any) you have installed in your machine. The program reports an 80486 machine as having an 80387 coprocessor installed because there is no difference in functionality. As with the 8086/8088 processor example, this example appears in assembly language for maximum clarity of the coprocessor specific commands. There are no listings for BASIC, C, and Pascal because it is impossible to see the coprocessor commands using these languages. In most cases, these languages invoke the math coprocessor automatically when detected. (Detection and use of the math coprocessor by high-level languages is determined by the library support you load within the application.)

The 8087/80287/80387 math coprocessors do not use flags to provide your application with status information. (Remember that the 80486 comes with built-in math coprocessor support. The 80486SX chip provides math coprocessor support through the 80487 math coprocessor—essentially the other half of a fully functional 80486DX chip.) They use a status and control word instead. The status word

indicates the current math coprocessor condition. The control word affects math coprocessor operation. The breakdown for both the control word and status word is shown here:

Status Word (bit)
0	Invalid Operation Exception (IE)
1	Denormalized Operation Exception (DE)
2	Zero Divide Exception (ZE)
3	Overflow Exception (OE)
4	Underflow Exception (UE)
5	Precision Exception (PE)
7	Interrupt Request (IR)
8	Condition Code 0 (C0)
9	Condition Code 1 (C1)
10	Condition Code 2 (C2)
11-13	Stack Top Pointer (ST)
14	Condition Code 3 (C3)
15	Busy Signal (B)

Control Word (bit)
0	Invalid Operation Exception Mask (IM)
1	Denormalized Operation Exception Mask (DM)
2	Zero Divide Exception Mask (ZM)
3	Overflow Exception Mask (OM)
4	Underflow Exception Mask (UM)
5	Precision Exception Mask (PM)
7	Interrupt Enable Mask (IEM); 0 = Enabled, 1 = Disabled
8-9	Precision Control (PC); 00 = 24 bits, 01 = (Reserved), 10 = 53 bits, 11 = 64 bits
10-11	Rounding Control (RC); 00 = Round to Nearest or Even, 01 = Round Down, 10 = Round Up, 11 = Truncate
12	Infinity Control (IC); 0 = Projective, 1 = Affine
13-15	Reserved

Each math coprocessor contains 8 stack elements that are 80 bits long. Bits 11 through 13 of the coprocessor status word tell you which element appears at the top of the stack. For example, if element 8 was at the top of the stack, then element 1 would appear second. Each element uses a floating point format consisting of 64 significant bits, 15 exponent bits, and 1 sign bit. The coprocessors

use these stack elements for most math operations. Figure 2-1 depicts the relationship between the stack elements. It also shows how the math coprocessor stores real numbers.

Figure 2-1

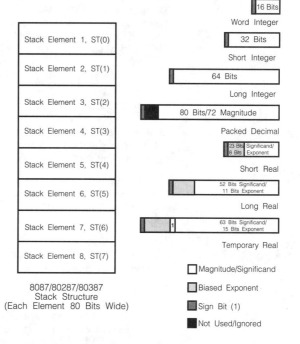

Math coprocessor internal logical structure.

8087/80287/80387
Stack Structure
(Each Element 80 Bits Wide)

80286 and 80287 command additions

The 80286 really added little functionality to the DOS programmer's toolbox; even the 80286's protected mode is of dubious value. The 80287 math coprocessor added even less. The 80286 did add a few interesting commands that can reduce your workload. For example, the 80286 instruction set adds the PUSHA and POPA instructions. Table 2-3 lists the 80286 processor additions to the 8086/8088 instruction set, while Table 2-4 lists the 80287 coprocessor additions to the 8087 instruction set. See Table 2-1 for a listing of 8086/8088 processor instruction by functional area and Table 2-2 for a listing of 8087 instructions.

Table 2-3   **80286 command summary**

Command	Description
Bit-manipulation instructions	
Adjust RPL Field of Selector (ARPL)	Use this instruction to compare the two RPL bits (bits 0 and 1) of the first operand with those in the second. If the RPL bits of the first operand are less than those of the second, the instruction sets the first operand's RPL bits equal to those of the second. The adjust RPL field of selector instruction affects ZF only. It then sets ZF. Otherwise, this instruction clears ZF.
Data-transfer instructions	
Input String from Port (INS)	This instruction allows string input from a port to the destination operand. Use the DX register to specify the port number and the DI register to specify destination. The instruction automatically switches between word or byte to accommodate the size of the destination operand. This instruction does not affect the flags.
Input String Byte from Port (INSB)	This instruction allows byte input from a port to the destination operand. Use the DX register to specify the port number and the DI register to specify destination. This instruction does not affect the flags.
Input String Word from Port (INSW)	This instruction allows word input from a port to the destination operand. Use the DX register to specify the port number and the DI register to specify destination. This instruction does not affect the flags.
Load Access-Rights Byte (LAR)	This instruction overwrites the high byte of the destination with the access-rights byte and zeros the low byte. The instruction operates only when the discriptor appears at the current privilege level and at the selector RPL. The instruction sets ZF when successful.
Load Global Descriptor Table Register (LGDT)	Use this instruction to load the global descriptor table from the memory address operand specified. The global descriptor table is six bytes long. Normally this instruction appears in protected mode operating system software only. It does not affect any registers.
Load Interrupt Descriptor Table Register (LIDT)	Use this instruction to load the interrupt descriptor table from the memory address operand specified. The interrupt descriptor table is six bytes long. Normally, this instruction appears in protected mode operating system software only. It does not affect any registers.
Load Local Descriptor Table Register (LLDT)	Use this instruction to transfer the global descriptor table to the local descriptor table based on the current selector. Normally, this instruction appears in protected mode operating system software only. It does not affect any registers.
Load Machine Status Word (LMSW)	The load machine status word instruction transfers the value of the operand to the machine status word. Normally, this instruction appears in operating system software only. It does not affect any registers.

Command	Description
Load Segment Limit (LSL)	This instruction loads the descriptor's limit field (if present) into the destination operand based on the selector specified in the source operand. When successful, the instruction sets ZF; otherwise, it clears ZF.
Load Task Register (LTR)	Use this instruction to load the task register with the value contained in the source operand. Normally, this instruction appears in operating system software only. It does not affect any registers.
Output String to Port (OUTS)	This instruction allows string output to a port from the source operand. Use the DX register to specify the port number and the SI register to specify source. The instruction automatically switches between word or byte to accommodate the size of the destination operand. This instruction does not affect the flags.
Output String Byte to Port (OUTSB)	This instruction allows byte output to a port from the source operand. Use the DX register to specify the port number and the SI register to specify source. This instruction does not affect the flags.
Output String Word to Port (OUTSW)	This instruction allows byte output to a port from the source operand. Use the DX register to specify the port number and the SI register to specify source. This instruction does not affect the flags.
Pop All General Registers (POPA)	POPA removes the general-purpose registers from the stack and discards the SP value. It then increments SP by 16.
Push All General Registers (PUSHA)	PUSHA decrements SP by 2 for each value pushed. It then adds the register contents to the location pointed to by the stack pointer (SP) The SP value pushed equals SP before instruction execution begins.
Store Global Descriptor Table Register (SGDT)	Use this instruction to transfer the six bytes of the global descriptor table to the memeory address operand. Normally, this instruction appears in protected mode operating system software only. It does not affect any registers.
Store Interrupt Descriptor Table Register (SIDT)	Use this instruction to transfer the six bytes of the interrupt descriptor table to the memeory address operand. Normally, this instruction appears in protected mode operating system software only. It does not affect any registers.
Store Local Descriptor Table Register (SLDT)	Use this instruction to transfer the two bytes of the local descriptor table to the memeory address operand. Normally, this instruction appears in protected mode operating system software only. It does not affect any registers.
Store Machine Status Word (SMSW)	Use this instuction to transfer the machine status word to the operand. Normally, this instruction appears in operating system software only.
Store Task Register (STR)	Use this instuction to transfer the task register contents to the operand. Normally, this instruction appears in operating system software only.

Table 2-3   **Continued**

Command	Description
Flag- and processor-control instructions	
Check Array Index Against Bounds (BOUND)	This instruction compares the signed value of the first operand against the values pointed to by the second operand. The word at the second word is the lower boundary. The word after the second word is the upper boundary. This instruction generates an interrupt 5 whenever the first operand falls outside of either boundary. The bound instruction affects none of the flags.
Clear the Task Switched Flag (CLTS)	This instruction (normally used in operating systems) clears the task switched flag of the machine register.
Make Stack Frame for Procedure Parameters (ENTER)	Use this instruction to modify the stack for entry into a high level language. The first operand specifies the number of stack storage bytes to allocate. The second operand indicates the routine nesting level. This instruction does not modify any of the flags.
High Level Procedure Exit (LEAVE)	Use this instruction when leaving a high-level language procedure to reverse the effects of the ENTER instruction. It deallocates all variables, then restores SP and BP to their original state. This instruction does not affect any flags.
Verify a Segment for Reading (VERR)	Use this instruction to determine if the selector specified by the operand appears at the current privilege level and is readable. The instruction sets ZF for accessible selectors.
Verify a Segment for Writing (VERW)	Use this instruction to determine if the selector specified by the operand appears at the current privilege level and is writeable. The instruction sets ZF for accessible selectors.

Table 2-4   **80287 command summary**

Command	Description
Processor-control instruction	
Set Protected Mode (FSETPM) (80287 Only)	This instruction sets the 80287 to protected mode operation.

The 80286 uses a variety of flags that the 8086/8088 processor does not provide. Most of these flags are related to the protected mode instructions provided by the 80286. In most cases, you will not need to use them unless you create an application that handles its own protected mode interface. These flags include the following.

➤ Nested Task (NT)

➤ Input/Output Privilege Level (IOPL)

➤ Overflow (OF)

➤ Direction (DF)

➤ Interrupt (IF)

➤ Trap (TF)

➤ Sign (SF)

➤ Zero (ZF)

➤ Auxiliary Carry (AF)

➤ Parity (PF)

➤ Carry (CF)

As you can see from Table 2-4, the 80287 provides only one command in addition to those provided by the 8087 processor. As with the 8087 math coprocessor, the 80287 math coprocessor does not use flags. It uses a status and control word. The status word indicates the current math coprocessor condition. The control word affects math coprocessor operation. There is a minor difference between the status and control word used by the 8087 and the 80287. The breakdown for both the 80287 control word and status word is shown here:

Status Word (bit)
0	Invalid Operation Exception (IE)
1	Denormalized Operation Exception (DE)
2	Zero Divide Exception (ZE)
3	Overflow Exception (OE)
4	Underflow Exception (UE)
5	Precision Exception (PE)
7	Error Summary Status (ES)
8	Condition Code 0 (C0)
9	Condition Code 1 (C1)
10	Condition Code 2 (C2)
11-13	Stack Top Pointer (ST)
14	Condition Code 3 (C3)
15	Busy Signal (B)

Control Word (bit)
0	Invalid Operation Exception Mask (IM)
1	Denormalized Operation Exception Mask (DM)
2	Zero Divide Exception Mask (ZM)

3	Overflow Exception Mask (OM)
4	Underflow Exception Mask (UM)
5	Precision Exception Mask (PM)
8-9	Precision Control (PC); 00 = 24 bits, 01 = (Reserved), 10 = 53 bits, 11 = 64 bits
10-11	Rounding Control (RC); 00 = Round to Nearest or Even, 01 = Round Down, 10 = Round Up, 11 = Truncate
12	Infinity Control (IC); 0 = Projective, 1 = Affine
13-15	Reserved

80386 and 80387 command additions

The 80386 and 80387 processors provide a lot of capability that the average DOS programmer will never use. Not only do they provide a much better protected mode interface than the 80286/80287 processor combination, but a Virtual 86 mode as well. In addition to this new mode, both the 80386 and 80387 processors provide a wide variety of time-saving commands that you can use to reduce your workload. For example, the 80386 chip provides a wide variety of new bit-testing instructions. The 80387 chip provides a fully functional tangent instruction. It even has a combination sine/cosine function. Tables 2-5 and 2-6 list the 80386 processor and 80387 coprocessor additions respectively.

Table 2-5

80386 command summary

Command	Description
Arithmetic instruction	
Convert Doubleword to Quadword (CDQ)	Use this instruction to convert a doubleword value to a quadword value. It extends the sign-bit in EAX through EDX.
Convert Word to Doubleword Extended (CWDE)	Use this instruction to convert a word value to a doubleword value. It extends the sign-bit in AX through EAX.
Bit-manipulation instructions	
Bit Scan Forward (BSF)	Use this instruction to scan the bits of the second operand (beginning at the low-order bit) for any set bits. If the instruction

Command	Description
	finds a set bit, it places the bit number in the first operand and clears ZF. If it does not find any set bits, it sets ZF and does nothing to the first operand.
Bit Scan Reverse (BSR)	Use this instruction to scan the bits of the second operand (beginning at the high order bit) for any set bits. If the instruction finds a set bit, it places the bit number in the first operand and clears ZF. If it does not find any set bits, it sets ZF and does nothing to the first operand.
Bit Test (BT)	This instruction uses the value of the second operand as a bit index to the first operand. It copies the bit at the indexed position to the carry flag.
Bit Test and Complement (BTC)	This instruction uses the value of the second operand as a bit index to the first operand. It copies the complement of the bit at the indexed position to the carry flag.
Bit Test and Reset (BTR)	This instruction uses the value of the second operand as a bit index to the first operand. It copies the bit at the indexed position to the carry flag and clears the original bit.
Bit Test and Set (BTS)	This instruction uses the value of the second operand as a bit index to the first operand. It copies the bit at the indexed position to the carry flag and sets the original bit.
Shift Left Double Precision (SHLD)	The Shift Left Double Precision instruction shifts all bits in the first operand left the number of bits specified by the third operand. It loses high-order bits and copies low-order bits from the second operand starting at the second operand's low-order bit. This instruction affects CF, OF, PF, SF, ZF, and AF (undefined).
Shift Right Double Precision (SHRD)	The Shift Right Double Precision instruction shifts all bits in the first operand right the number of bits specified by the third operand. It loses the low-order bits and copies the high-order bits from the second operand start and the second operand's high-order bit. This instruction affects CF, OF, PF, SF, ZF, and AF (undefined).

Control-transfer instructions

Jump if ECX Equals Zero (JECXZ)	This instruction transfers control to the instruction pointed to by IP + Displacement when ECX equals 0.

Data-transfer instructions

Input String Doubleword from Port (INSD)	This instruction allows doubleword input from a port to the destination operand. Use the DX register to specify the port number and the EDI register to specify destination. This instruction does not affect the flags.
Load the FS Register (LFS)	This instruction transfers a 32-bit pointer from the source operand (memory only) to the destination operand (offset) and the FS register (segment). The destination operand is any 16-bit general purpose register.

Table 2-5   **Continued**

Command	Description
Load the GS Register (LGS)	This instruction transfers a 32-bit pointer from the source operand (memory only) to the destination operand (offset) and the GS register (segment). The destination operand is any 16-bit general purpose register.
Load the SS Register (LSS)	This instruction transfers a 32-bit pointer from the source operand (memory only) to the destination operand (offset) and the SS register (segment). The destination operand is any 16-bit general purpose register.
Move with Sign Extended (MOVSX)	Use this instruction to move data from a smaller to larger operand. It extends the sign-bit of the second operand to fill the first operand.
Move with Zero Extended (MOVZX)	Use this instruction to move data from a smaller to larger operand. It clears the bits in the first operand not filled by the second operand.
Output String Doubleword to Port (OUTSD)	This instruction allows doubleword output to a port from the source operand. Use the EDX register to specify the port number and the ESI register to specify source. This instruction does not affect the flags.
Pop All General Doubleword Registers (POPAD)	POPAD removes the extended general-purpose registers from the stack and discards the ESP value. It then increments ESP by 32.
Remove Extended Flags from Stack (POPFD)	POPFD removes the two words pointed to by the stack pointer (ESP) and places it in the extended flag register. It then increments ESP by 4.
Push All General Doubleword Registers (PUSHAD)	PUSHAD decrements ESP by 4 for each value pushed. It then adds the register contents to the location pointed to by the stack pointer (ESP). The ESP value pushed equals ESP before instruction execution begins.
Place Extended Flags on Stack (PUSHFD)	PUSHF decrements ESP by 4. It then adds the extended flag register contents to the location pointed to by the stack pointer (ESP).
Set Byte if Above (SETA)	This instruction checks the status of both CF and ZF. If both flags equal 0, then the instruction stores a 1 in the operand; otherwise, it stores a 0 in the operand.
Set Byte if Above or Equal (SETAE)	This instruction checks the status of CF. If CF equals 0, then the instruction stores a 1 in the operand; otherwise, it stores a 0 in the operand.
Set Byte if Below (SETB)	This instruction checks the status of CF. If CF equals 1, then the instruction stores a 1 in the operand; otherwise, it stores a 0 in the operand.
Set Byte if Below or	This instruction checks the status of CF and ZF. If CF or ZF equals

Command	Description
Equal (SETBE)	1, then the instruction stores a 1 in the operand; otherwise, it stores a 0 in the operand.
Set Byte on Carry (SETC)	This instruction checks the status of CF. If CF equals 1, then the instruction stores a 1 in the operand; otherwise, it stores a 0 in the operand.
Set Byte if Equal (SETE)	This instruction checks the status of ZF. If ZF equals 1, then the instruction stores a 1 in the operand; otherwise, it stores a 0 in the operand.
Set Byte if Greater Than (SETG)	This instruction checks the status of ZF, SF and OF. If ZF equals 0 or SF equals OF, then the instruction stores a 1 in the operand; otherwise, it stores a 0 in the operand.
Set Byte if Greater Than or Equal (SETGE)	This instruction checks the status of SF and OF. If SF equals OF, then the instruction stores a 1 in the operand; otherwise, it stores a 0 in the operand.
Set Byte if Less Than (SETL)	This instruction checks the status of SF and OF. If SF does not equal OF, then the instruction stores a 1 in the operand; otherwise, it stores a 0 in the operand.
Set Byte if Less Than or Equal (SETLE)	This instruction checks the status of ZF, SF and OF. If SF does not equal OF or ZF equals 1, then the instruction stores a 1 in the operand; otherwise, it stores a 0 in the operand.
Set Byte if Not Above (SETNA)	This instruction checks the status of CF and ZF. If CF or ZF equals 1, then the instruction stores a 1 in the operand; otherwise, it stores a 0 in the operand.
Set Byte if Not Above or Equal (SETNAE)	This instruction checks the status of CF. If CF equals 1, then the instruction stores a 1 in the operand; otherwise, it stores a 0 in the operand.
Set Byte if Not Below (SETNB)	This instruction checks the status of CF. If CF equals 0, then the instruction stores a 1 in the operand; otherwise, it stores a 0 in the operand.
Set Byte if Not Below or Equal (SETNBE)	This instruction checks the status of both CF and ZF. If both flags equal 0, then the instruction stores a 1 in the operand; otherwise, it stores a 0 in the operand.
Set Byte on No Carry (SETNC)	This instruction checks the status of CF. If CF equals 0, then the instruction stores a 1 in the operand; otherwise, it stores a 0 in the operand.
Set Byte if Not Equal (SETNE)	This instruction checks the status of ZF. If ZF equals 0, then the instruction stores a 1 in the operand; otherwise, it stores a 0 in the operand.
Set Byte if Not Greater Than (SETNG)	This instruction checks the status of ZF, SF and OF. If SF does not equal OF or ZF equals 1, then the instruction stores a 1 in the operand; otherwise, it stores a 0 in the operand.

Table 2-5

Continued

Command	Description
Set Byte if Not Greater Than or Equal (SETNGE)	This instruction checks the status of SF and OF. If SF does not equal OF, then the instruction stores a 1 in the operand; otherwise, it stores a 0 in the operand.
Set Byte if Not Less Than (SETNL)	This instruction checks the status of SF and OF. If SF equals OF, then the instruction stores a 1 in the operand; otherwise, it stores a 0 in the operand.
Set Byte if Not Less Than or Equal (SETNLE)	This instruction checks the status of ZF, SF and OF. If ZF equals 0 or SF equals OF, then the instruction stores a 1 in the operand; otherwise, it stores a 0 in the operand.
Set Byte on No Overflow (SETNO)	This instruction checks the status of OF. If OF equals 0, then the instruction stores a 1 in the operand; otherwise, it stores a 0 in the operand.
Set Byte on No Parity (SETNP)	This instruction checks the status of PF. If PF equals 0, then the instruction stores a 1 in the operand; otherwise, it stores a 0 in the operand.
Set Byte on Not Sign (SETNS)	This instruction checks the status of SF. If SF equals 0, then the instruction stores a 1 in the operand; otherwise, it stores a 0 in the operand.
Set Byte on Not Zero (SETNZ)	This instruction checks the status of ZF. If ZF equals 0, then the instruction stores a 1 in the operand; otherwise, it stores a 0 in the operand.
Set Byte on Overflow (SETO)	This instruction checks the status of OF. If OF equals 1, then the instruction stores a 1 in the operand; otherwise, it stores a 0 in the operand.
Set Byte on Parity (SETP)	This instruction checks the status of PF. If PF equals 1, then the instruction stores a 1 in the operand; otherwise, it stores a 0 in the operand.
Set Byte on Parity Even (SETPE)	This instruction checks the status of PF. If PF equals 1, then the instruction stores a 1 in the operand; otherwise, it stores a 0 in the operand.
Set Byte on Parity Odd (SETPO)	This instruction checks the status of PF. If PF equals 0, then the instruction stores a 1 in the operand; otherwise, it stores a 0 in the operand.
Set Byte on Sign (SETS)	This instruction checks the status of SF. If SF equals 1, then the instruction stores a 1 in the operand; otherwise, it stores a 0 in the operand.
Set Byte on Zero (SETZ)	This instruction checks the status of ZF. If ZF equals 1, then the instruction stores a 1 in the operand; otherwise, it stores a 0 in the operand.

Command	Description
String-manipulation instructions	
Compare Strings Doubleword-by-Doubleword (CMPSD)	This instruction changes the value of the AF, CF, OF, PF, SF, and ZF flags to show the relationship between two doublewords in a string. The results of the comparison do not affect the contents of either operand. After comparing the two string words, the instruction updates both ESI and EDI to point to the next string element. DF controls the direction of comparison.
Load a Doubleword from String into EAX (LODSD)	Use this instruction to transfer a doubleword from the string pointed to by ESI to EAX. The ESI register automatically advances to the next string element in the direction pointed to by the direction flag.
Move String, Doubleword-by-Doubleword (MOVSD)	This instruction moves the doubleword pointed to by ESI to the destination pointed to by EDI. Using the REP instruction with this instruction, repeats the move the number of times shown in ECX. After each move, the instruction advances both ESI and EDI to the next position in the direction indicated by DF.
Scan String for Doubleword (SCASD)	Use this instruction with any of the repeat instructions to scan strings for the value contained in EAX. After each scan, EDI advances to point to the next string element. This instruction affects AF, CF, OF, PF, SF, and ZF.
Store Doubleword in EAX at String (STOSD)	Use this instruction alone or with any repeat instruction to send to value in EAX to the string pointed at by EDI. EDI automatically advances to the next string location after each store operation. This instruction does not affect any flags.

80387 command summary

Table 2-6

Command	Description
Arithmetic instruction	
IEEE Partial Remainder (FPREM1) (80387 Only)	The partial arctangent instruction calculates the modulo of the top two stack elements. It performs this by successively subtracting the second element from the first. The calculated remainder remains in the first element. The instruction affects the C0, C1, C3, UE, DE, and IE status bits.
Comparison instruction	
Unordered Compare (FUCOM) (80387 Only)	This instruction converts the operand to an integer (if required) and compares it to the top stack element. It then changes the condition of the status word bits to match the comparison result. The difference between this instruction and the standard compare is that noncomparable results do not raise the invalid operation exception. The status word bits affected include C0, C2, C3, DE, and IE.
Unordered Compare	This instruction converts the operand to an integer (if required) and

Table 2-6   **Continued**

Command	Description
and Pop (FUCOMP) (80387 Only)	compares it to the top stack element. It then changes the condition of the status word bits to match the comparison result and pops the stack. The difference between this instruction and the standard compare and pop is that noncomparable results do not raise the invalid operation exception. The status word bits affected include C0, C2, C3, DE, and IE.
Unordered Compare and Pop Twice (FUCOMPP) (80387 Only)	This instruction converts the operand to an integer (if required) and compares it to the top stack element. It then changes the condition of the status word bits to match the comparison result and pops the stack twice. The difference between this instruction and the standard compare and pop twice is that noncomparable results do not raise the invalid operation exception. The status word bits affected include C0, C2, C3, DE, and IE.

Trancendental instruction

Command	Description
Cosine (FCOS) (80387 Only)	This instruction computes $Y = COS(\phi)$, where ϕ is the top stack element. The instruction replaces the top stack element with Y. If ϕ exceeds 26^3, then the instruction sets C2; otherwise, it clears C2. It affects the C2, PE, and IE status bits.
Sine (FSIN) (80387 Only)	This instruction computes $Y = SIN(\phi)$, where ϕ is the top stack element. The instruction replaces the top stack element with Y. If ϕ exceeds 26^3, then the instruction sets C2; otherwise, it clears C2. It affects the C2, PE, and IE status bits.
Sine and Cosine (FSINCOS) (80387 Only)	This instruction computes $Y = SIN(\phi)$ and $X = COS(\phi)$, where ϕ is the top stack element. The instruction replaces the top stack element with Y, then pushes X. If ϕ exceeds 26^3, then the instruction sets C2; otherwise, it clears C2. It affects the C2, PE, and IE status bits.

The 80386 flag register is 32-bits wide. As a result, it provides you with a little more information than the 8088/8086 or 80286 processors. The 80386 chip does reserve the upper 14 bits of this register. The flags used for the various instructions include:

➤ Virtual Mode (VM)

➤ Resume (R)

➤ Nested Task (NT)

➤ Input/Output Privilege Level (IOPL)

➤ Overflow (OF)

> Direction (DF)

> Interrupt (IF)

> Trap (TF)

> Sign (SF)

> Zero (ZF)

> Auxiliary Carry (AF)

> Parity (PF)

> Carry (CF)

The 80387 math coprocessor uses many of the 8087 commands. It does not use any 80287 specific commands. Just like the 8087 and 80287 math coprocessors, the 80387 math coprocessor does not use flags to convey information to the programmer. It uses a status and control word. The status word indicates the current math coprocessor condition. The control word affects math coprocessor operation. The 80387 provides some added functionality in the status and control words that the other two math coprocessors do not provide. The breakdown for both the control word and status word is shown here:

Status Word (bit)
0	Invalid Operation Exception (IE)
1	Denormalized Operation Exception (DE)
2	Zero Divide Exception (ZE)
3	Overflow Exception (OE)
4	Underflow Exception (UE)
5	Precision Exception (PE)
6	Stack Flag (SF); When SF = 1 and C0 = 0 then stack underflow. When SF = 1 and C0 = 1 then stack overflow.
7	Error Summary Status (ES)
8	Condition Code 0 (C0)
9	Condition Code 1 (C1)
10	Condition Code 2 (C2)
11-13	Stack Top Pointer (ST)
14	Condition Code 3 (C3)
15	Busy Signal (B)

Control Word (bit)

0	Invalid Operation Exception Mask (IM)
1	Denormalized Operation Exception Mask (DM)
2	Zero Divide Exception Mask (ZM)
3	Overflow Exception Mask (OM)
4	Underflow Exception Mask (UM)
5	Precision Exception Mask (PM)
8-9	Precision Control (PC); 00 = 24 bits, 01 = (Reserved), 10 = 53 bits, 11 = 64 bits
10-11	Rounding Control (RC); 00 = Round to Nearest or Even, 01 = Round Down, 10 = Round Up, 11 = Truncate
12	Infinity Control (IC); 0 = Projective, 1 = Affine
13-15	Reserved

80486 command additions

The 80486 is a lot more than simply a fast 80386 processor with an attached 80387 math coprocessor. This chip provides the basis for future programming endeavors on the PC. Along with three commands unique to its caching capability, the 80486 provides a few additional instructions that you can use to make programming a little easier. Table 2-7 lists the 80486 processor additions.

Table 2-7   **80486 command summary**

Command	Description
Arithmetic instructions	
Compare and Exchange (CMPXCHG)	This instruction compares the contents in the destination register to the contents of the AL, AX, or EAX register depending on the size of the destination. If the size is equal, then the contents of the source is copied to the destination. If they are not equal, then the destination is copied to the AL, AX, or EAX register. This instruction affects the same flags as the CMP instruction: AF, CF, OF, PF, SF, and ZF.
Exchange and Add (XADD)	Adds the source and destination operands, then stores the result in the destination. The destination is copied to the source before the result is stored. This instruction affects the following flags: AF, CF, OF, PF, SF, and ZF.

Command	Description
Data-transfer instructions	
Byte Swap (BSWAP)	Use this instruction to convert 80486 register storage to the 8086/8088 scheme. It swaps the first and the fourth, and the second and the third bytes. Instruction does not affect the flags.
Flag- and processor-control instructions	
Invalidate Data Cache (INVD)	An OS level instruction that invalidates the data cache without writing the contents to memory. Instruction does not affect the flags.
Invalidate Translation Lookaside Buffer Entry (INVLPG)	An OS level instruction that invalidates the Translation Lookaside Buffer (TLB) used by the demand paging system of virtual memory operation systems. Instruction does not affect the flags.
Write Back and Invalidate Data Cache (WBINVD)	An OS level instruction that invalidates the data cache after writing the contents to memory. Instruction does not affect the flags.

The 80486 uses the same flags of the 80386 processor. It also provides the full functionality of the 80387 math coprocessor. While the 80486SX processor does provide all the 80486 instructions, it does not provide this math coprocessing capability. You must add an 80487SX math coprocessor to gain the full 80486 functionality. The easiest way to determine the difference between an 80486 and an 80486SX from a programming perspective is to test for the presence of a math coprocessor. If your application determines that the host machine contains an 80486 processor but no coprocessor, then it really contains an 80486SX. If the machine also contains an 80487SX processor, then programming is essentially identical to the 80486 chip.

 Pentium processor command additions

The Pentium processor offers many features like the dual execution units that this chapter doesn't discuss. It also offers a 128-bit and 256-bit internal bus, and a 64-bit external bus that speeds program execution but really doesn't matter from a programming perspective. These are the speed enhancements that receive a lot of media attention. The programmer is more interested in the unique programmable features that this processor offers. The following paragraphs provide you with the full details of these enhancements.

There actually are four programming modes for the Pentium processor. It supports real, virtual 86, and protected modes like any other member of the Intel family. However, the Pentium processor also supports a new mode called System Management Mode (SMM). This new mode actually started to appear with the 80386SL processor. It isn't a new operating mode; the other three modes fulfill this function. Essentially, this new mode allows either an application program or the operating system to perform power management. For example, you could power down the processor during user "think" time on a laptop. In most cases, the OS/2 programmer will not need to worry about this new mode (unless your company writes power-management software), but it is important to realize that the new mode does exist. You enter SMM by activating the external interrupt pin (SMI#). This switches the CPU to a separate address space and saves the entire CPU context. Once you enter SMM, your application can execute any required code. The CPU context automatically is restored when you exit from SMM using the Resume from System Management Mode (RSM) instruction described later.

Besides these new features, the Pentium processor sports several new commands. Table 2-8 provides a complete list of all these new commands. Some of these instructions are extensions to the 80486 command set. For example, the Pentium processor provides a new compare and exchange instruction called CMPXCHG8B. Other instructions are completely new to the Pentium processor. For example, the CPUID instruction allows you to identify the vendor, family, model, and stepping of the microprocessor installed in your machine. Still other instructions aid the programmer in working with the realities of protected mode. For example, the IRETD command supports 32-bit operands in place of the 16-bit operands used by the IRET command.

Table 2-8
Pentium processor command summary

Command	Description
Arithmetic instructions	
Compare and Exchange 8 Bytes (CMPXCHG8B)	This instruction compares the contents in the destination register to the contents of the EDX:EAX register pair. If the two values are equal, then the contents of the source is copied to the destination. If they are not equal, then the destination is copied to the EDX:EAX register pair. This instruction affects the same flags as the CMP

Command	Description
	instruction: AF, CF, OF, PF, SF, and ZF.

Control-transfer instructions

| Return from Interrupt Double (IRETD) | This instruction returns control to a procedure calling an interrupt after the interrupt completes. The main difference between this instruction and the IRET instruction is that IRETD uses a 32-bit operand. It pops CS, IP, and all flags. There are three types of IRETD instructions versus 4 for IRET. The IRETD instruction does not support an interrupt return from real or Virtual 86 mode. |

Flag- and processor-control instructions

CPU Identification (CPUID)	This instruction provides the vendor, family, model, and stepping of the microprocessor installed in the machine. The value in EAX determines what information CPUID returns. Placing a 0 in EAX returns the highest value understood by the CPUID instruction in EAX and a vendor identification string in EBX:EDX:ECX. Placing a 1 in EAX returns the stepping ID (bits 0 through 3), model (bits 4 through 7), and family (bits 8 through 11) in EAX. Bits 12 through 31 of EAX are reserved. EDX contains the feature flags as follows: FPU on chip (bit 0), Advanced Features (bits 1 through 6), Machine Check Exception (bit 7), and CMPXCHG8B Instruction (bit 8). The rest of the EDX register bits are reserved. Passing a value higher than the highest acceptable value returns an undefined value in the EAX, EBX, ECX, and EDX registers.
Read from Model Specific Register (RDMSR)	Use this instruction to retrieve the contents of a model specific register. These registers vary by processor type and vendor, so check your processor vendor manual for complete details on the types of registers available to you. ECX always contains the number of the register that you want to check. The EDX:EAX register pair contains the register value on return from the call. There are two common register values you can retrieve. A value of 00h in ECX returns the Machine Check Address (the address of the cycle causing an exception). A value of 01h in ECX returns the Machine Check Type (the cycle type of cycle type of cycle causing an exception). Most Intel versions of the Pentium processor also return values used to perform cache, TLB, and BTB testing and performance monitoring. You must execute this instruction from priveledge level 0 or from within real mode. Intel reserves ECX values of 03h, 0Fh, and all values above 13h.
Resume from System Management Mode (RSM)	The RSM instruction returns the processor to its state before entering SMM mode. All standard registers are returned to their previous state using the contents of the SMM dump. None of the model-specific registers are affected by this instruction. Execution always continues where it ceased prior to entering SMM. The processor does check for invalid state information before it turns control over to the application program. If it detects an invalid state, it enters a shutdown state. There are three conditions which place the processor in an invalid state.

Table 2-8 **Continued**

Command	Description
	• The value stored in the State Dump Base field is not a 32KB aligned address.
	• Any reserved bit of CR4 is set to 1.
	• CR0 contains any combination of illegal bits. This includes (PG=1 and PE=0) or (NW=1 and CD=0).
Write to Model Specific Register (WRMSR)	Use this instruction to write to a model specific register. There are two common register values that you can write. These registers vary by processor type and vendor, so check your processor vendor manual for complete details on the types of registers available to you. ECX always contains the number of the register that you want to write to. The EDX:EAX register pair contains the register value you want to write. A value of 00h in ECX writes to the Machine Check Address (the address of the cycle causing an exception). A value of 01h in ECX write to the Machine Check Type (the cycle type of cycle causing an exception). Most Intel versions of the Pentium processor also return values used to perform cache, TLB, and BTB testing and performance monitoring. You must execute this instruction from priveledge level 0 or from within real mode. Intel reserves ECX values of 03h, 0Fh, and all values above 13h.

Like the 80386 and 80486 chip, the Pentium process provides a 32-bit register for flags. The Pentium process supports all the flags of the 80386 process. It also supports a few additional flags. The following list shows all the flags supported by the Pentium processor:

➢ ID Flag (ID)

➢ Virtual Interrupt Pending (VIP)

➢ Virtual Interrupt Flag (VIF)

➢ Alignment Check (AC)

➢ Virtual Mode (VM)

➢ Resume (R)

➢ Nested Task (NT)

➢ Input/Output Privilege Level (IOPL)

➢ Overflow (OF)

➢ Direction (DF)

> Interrupt (IF)

> Trap (TF)

> Sign (SF)

> Zero (ZF)

> Auxiliary Carry (AF)

> Parity (PF)

> Carry (CF)

Like the 80486, the Pentium process includes the equivalent of an 80387 math coprocessor internally. This includes both the control and status word used by that coprocessor. There is no difference between programming the 80387 math coprocessor and the Pentium processor. The only differences are internal design features that speed math computation processing. These features are invisible to the programmer.

⇨ Conclusion

This chapter provided you with all that you need to know about the "brain" of your computer—the processor. Each section described one member of the Intel family in detail. As applications continue to grow in complexity, you might find that you need to use the increased capacity of the higher-level processor in lieu of compatibility with older processor versions. This chapter provides you with a stepped view of what each processor can provide in addition to the base instruction set provided by the 8086/8088 processor and 8087 math coprocessor.

3

Video API

It doesn't matter how much work your application can perform if it can't interact with the user. This usually means that you must provide some type of visual feedback as a minimum. Today's GUI environment provides a lot more in the way of programmer's tools to create displays that are both functional and visually appealing. This chapter describes the video application programming interface (API) provided by OS/2. This chapter views programming from the business application viewpoint. Because OS/2 does not allow direct hardware manipulation by "ring 3" applications, the programmer must use the tools supplied by the operating system. (You can always choose to create your own device drivers and DLLs to perform any required work.)

The example programs in this chapter also assume that you want to program for the Presentation Manager. While most of the VIO functions work only in a full-screen character-mode OS/2 session, you can even use some of them within the Presentation Manager. (The text will note whether you can use a particular call for character- and graphics-mode applications.) The main area addressed by this chapter is the drawing functions OS/2 provides. The programmer needs to know how to use this capability to program in OS/2.

⇨ Drawing

Whether or not you consider yourself an artist, almost *every* GUI program requires some type of drawing. Even graphs and charts are considered drawing by most people. Of course, *every* program includes an icon and other interesting graphics as well. The following paragraphs describe the commands that you can use for drawing within OS/2.

⇨ VIO functions

There are many video input/output (VIO) functions provided in the OS/2 API. Most of these functions affect the way that OS/2 sees your application screen space. For example, VioEndPopup ends a

pop-up screen displayed over your standard screen. Version 1.1 of OS/2 provided many VIO functions in addition to the ones that were documented for Version 1.3. These functions appear in Table 3-1. There is no guarantee that they will work in the OS/2 2.*x* environment or that IBM will support them in the future.

Table 3-1   **AVIO function listing**

Function	Description
UShort VioAssociate (hDC, hvPS)	The VioAssociate function associates an AVIO presentation space with a device context. hDC contains a device context handle. hvPS contains a presentation space handle.
	You need to make subsequent calls to VioShowPS or VioShowBuf functions to direct output to this device context. You can use only screen devices as the device contents for the presentation space. Any previous associations are disassociated when you use this function. In addition, using a Null device context disassociates the presentation space with the current device context. You must call VioCreatePS prior to using this function. Any return value other than 0 indicates an error condition.
UShort VioCreateLogFont (pFAttr, lCID, pStr8Name, hvPS)	The VioCreateLogFont function creates a logical font for the specified presentation space. pFAttr contains a point to a font attribute table. lCID contains the local font identifier. pStr8Name contains a pointer to a descriptive name for the logical font. hvPS contains a presentation space handle.
	A logical font contains a complete description of all the attributes required to create the font itself. When it comes time to use the font, OS/2 selects the one that most closely matches the font description. Setting the szFaceName field to Null and all other attributes (except code page) to 0 in the FAttr structure selects the system default font. Any return value other than 0 indicates an error condition. The FAttr structure contains the following elements:

Offset	Length	Description
00h	2	Length of structure
02h	2	Font characteristics: italic (bit 0), underline (bit 1), reverse (bit 2), outline (bit 3), and strikeout (bit 4). All other bits are reserved.
04h	4	Match number from VioQueryFonts call (use 0 to use the best match).
08h	32	ASCIIZ typeface name
28h	2	Font registry number
2Ah	2	Code page identifier

Function	Description

Description

Offset	Length	Description
2Eh	4	Maximum baseline extent
32h	4	Average character width
36h	2	Width class
38h	2	Weight class
3Ah	2	Kerning and proportional space flags: reserved (bit 0), nonproportional font (bit 1), kernable font (bit 2, always set to 0), reserved (bits 3 through 15).
3Ch	2	Font quality: default (bit 0, always set to 1), draft (bit 1, always set to 0), proof (bit 2, always set to 0), reserved (bits 3 through 15)
3Eh	2	Reserved, always set to 0.

Function	Description
UShort VioCreatePS (phvPS, cRows, cColumns, fFormat, cAttrBytes, hvPS)	The VioCreatePS functions creates an AVIO presentation space. phvPS contains a pointer to a variable used to hold the presentation space handle. cRows contains the height of the presentation space. cColumns contains the width of the presentation space. fFormat contains attribute byte format flags. The only value that you currently can use for this entry is 0. cAttrBytes contains the number of attribute bytes per character cell. Use a value of 1 for the FORMAT_CGA setting or 3 for the FORMAT_4BYTE setting. hvPS contains a presentation space handle (always set this entry to 0).

The size of the presentation space (cRows × cColumns × (cAttrBytes + 1)) must not exceed 32K. The FORMAT_CGA setting include the following information: character code (byte 0) and text mode attribute (byte 1). The FORMAT_4BYTE setting includes the following information: character code (byte 0), foreground/background colors (byte 1), underline/reverse/blink/font ID (byte 2), and user information (byte 3). Any return value other than 0 indicates an error condition. |
UShort VioDeleteSetId (lCID, hvPS)	The VioDeleteSetId function releases a logical font identifier assigned using the VioCreateFont function. lCID contains the local font identifier. hvPS contains a presentation space handle. You can release all font identifiers by using a lCID value of −1. Any return value other than 0 indicates an error condition.
UShort VioDestroyPS (hvPS)	The VioDestroyPS function releases the specified AVIO presentation space. hvPS contains a presentation space handle. You must obtain this handle using the VioCreatePS function. Any return value other than 0 indicates an error condition.
UShort VioGetDeviceCellSize (pcRows, pcColumns, hvPS)	The VioGetDeviceCellSize retrieves the size of the current device cell. pcRows contains a pointer to a variable containing the cell height. pcColumns contains a pointer to a variable containing the cell width. hvPS contains a presentation space handle. Any return value other than 0 indicates an error condition.

Table 3-1 **Continued**

Function	Description
UShort VioGetOrg (psRow, psColumn, hvPS)	The VioGetOrg function retrieves the origin of the AVIO presentation space. psRow contains a pointer to a variable containing the row number of the upper-left corner of the window. pcColumns contains a pointer to a variable containing the column number of the upper-left corner of the window. hvPS contains a presentation space handle. Any return value other than 0 indicates an error condition.
UShort VioQueryFonts (pcbMetrics, pFM, cbMetrics, pcFonts, pszFacename, flOptions, hvPS)	The VioQueryFonts function retrieves a font metric structure containing the characteristics of one or more fonts. pcbMetrics contains a pointer to a variable holding the structure length. pFM contains a pointer to the front metric structure. cb Metrics contains the structure length. pcFonts contains a pointer to a variable holding the number of fonts. pszFacename contains a pointer to an ASCIIZ string holding the face name string. flOptions contains the enumeration options. hvPS contains a presentation space handle.

The size of pFM determines the absolute number of font metric structures that OS/2 returns. OS/2 fills the structure until it either runs out of fonts that match the string in pszFacename or room in the structure. You can use the VioCreateLogFont function to select any of the fonts returned in the structure. Specifying a value of 0 in the pcFonts parameter returns the number of available fonts for the specified face name. Any return value other than 0 indicates an error condition or the number of fonts not retrieved. The font metrics structure uses the following format:

Offset	Length	Description
00h	32	Family name of the font. This is a null-terminated string up to 31 characters long. For the purposes of this table, I assume a 31-character length.
20h	32	Typeface name of the font. This is a null-terminated string up to 31 characters long. For the purposes of this table, I assume a 31-character length.
40h	2	Font registry number (always set to 0)
42h	2	Code page that application should use with the font (set to 850 in most cases).
44h	4	Average height of uppercase characters.
48h	4	Average height of lowercase characters.
4Ch	4	Maximum height of any character (ascender).

Function	Description		
	Offset	**Length**	**Description**
	50h	4	Maximum depth of any character (descender).
	54h	4	Maximum height of any lowercase character.
	58h	4	Maximum depth of any lowercase character.
	5Ch	4	Amount of space reserved at the top of each character cell for accent marks.
	60h	4	Amount of space that should appear between adjacent rows of text.
	64h	4	Average character width for each character in the font.
	68h	4	Maximum increment between characters in the font.
	6Ch	4	Width of an uppercase M.
	70h	4	Maximum ascender and descender values.
	74h	2	Stroke angle in degrees and minutes. Bits 0 through 8 contain the degrees, bits 9 through 14 contain the minutes, and bits 15 and 16 are reserved. Normal fonts are always zero; italic fonts are always nonzero.
	76h	2	Angle in degrees and minutes of the next character in a string (baseline). Bits 0 through 8 contain the degrees, bits 9 through 14 contain the minutes, and bits 15 and 16 are reserved. Swiss fonts are always 0, while Hebrew fonts are always 180.
	78h	2	Angle of the baseline rotation used for aligning characters in a string. The font designer determines this value. Bits 0 through 8 contain the degrees, bits 9 through 14 contain the minutes, and bits 15 and 16 are reserved.
	7Ah	2	Thickness of the strokes that form the character. The following values determine stroke width: ultra-light (1), extra-light (2), light (3), semi-light (4), medium (5), semi-bold (6), bold (7), extra bold (8), and ultra-bold (9).
	7Ch	2	Font aspect ratio when compared to a standard font in this family. The following nine values determine the font aspect ratio: ultra-condensed (1), extra-condensed (2), condensed (3), semi-condensed (4), normal (5), semi-expanded (6), expanded (7), extra-expanded (8), and ultra-expanded (9).

Table 3-1   **Continued**

Function	Description		
	Offset	**Length**	**Description**
	7Eh	2	Horizontal resolution of the device for which the font originally was designed in pels.
	80h	2	Vertical resolution of the device for which the font originally was designed in pels.
	82h	2	Code point for the first character in the font.
	84h	2	Code point for the last character in the font.
	86h	2	Code point for the default character in the font. This is the font that OS/2 uses when an application requests a font outside the normal range of font's code page.
	88h	2	Code point for the space character in the font.
	8Ah	2	Nominal font height in decipoints ($\frac{1}{20}$ of an inch).
	8Ch	2	Minimum font height in decipoints.
	8Eh	2	Maximum font height in decipoints.
	90h	2	Font type including zero or more of the following values: FM_TYPE_FIXED, FM_TYPE_LICENSED, FM_TIME_KERNING, FM_TYPE_DBCS, FM_TYPE_MBCS, and FM_TYPE_64K.
	92h	2	Font definition including zero or more of the following values: FN_DEFN_OUTLINE and FN_DEFN_GENERIC.
	94h	2	Character drawing specification including zero or more of the following values: FM_SEL_ITALIC, FM_SEL_UNDERSCORE, FM_SEL_NEGATIVE, FM_SEL_OUTLINE, FM_SEL_STRIKEOUT, and FM_SEL_BOLD.
	96h	2	If this field contains the value FM_CAP_NOMIX, you cannot mix it with graphics; otherwise, you can use the font with graphics.
	98h	4	Horizontal size of font subscripts.
	9Ch	4	Vertical size of font subscripts.
	9Eh	4	Horizontal offset of font subscripts from the left edge of the character cell.
	100h	4	Vertical offset of the font subscripts from the character cell baseline.

Function	Description		
	Offset	**Length**	**Description**
	104h	4	Horizontal size of font superscripts.
	108h	4	Vertical size of font superscripts.
	10Ch	4	Horizontal offset of font superscripts from the left edge of the character cell.
	110h	4	Vertical offset of the font superscripts from the character cell baseline.
	114h	4	Width of the font underscore.
	118h	4	Distance from font baseline to underscore.
	11Ch	4	Width of the font overstrike.
	120h	4	Distance from font baseline to overstrike.
	124h	2	Number of kerning pairs for the font in the kerning pair table.
	126h	2	Font family class and subclass.
	128h	4	Contains a long integer value that gets copied to the FAttrs structure when the GpiCreateLogFont function is called. The system selects a font that contains the metrics associated with the field.
UShort VioQuerySetIds (palCIDs, pachNames, palTypes, cSets, hvPS)	The VioQuerySetIds function retrieves information about all available logical fonts. palCIDs contains a pointer to an array of local identifiers for fonts. pachNames contains a pointer to an array of font names. palTypes contains a pointer to an array of object types. cSets contains the number of local identifiers currently in use. hvPS contains a presentation space handle. Any return value other than 0 indicates an error condition.		
UShort VioSetDeviceCellSize (cRows, cColumns, hvPS)	The VioSetDeviceCellSize sets the size of the current device cell. cRows contains the cell height in pels. cColumns contains the cell width in pels. hvPS contains a presentation space handle. Any return value other than 0 indicates an error condition.		
UShort VioSetOrg (sRow, sColumns, hvPS)	The VioSetOrg function sets the origin of the AVIO presentation space. sRow contains the row number of the upper-left corner of the window. cColumns contains the column number of the upper-left corner of the window. hvPS contains a presentation space handle. Any return value other than 0 indicates an error condition.		
UShort VioShowPS (cRows, cColumns, off, hvPS)	The VioShowPS updates the display by copying all the changes in the specified window to the display. cRows contains the window height in pels. cColumns contains the width in pels. off contains the upper left corner of the window. This position is relative to the first character in the AVIO presentation space. hvPS contains a presentation space handle. Any return value other than 0 indicates an error condition.		

The Borland compiler does provide access to these functions through the PMAVIO.H include file. You might need to check the include files for your compiler to find references to these functions because most vendors do not document them. In some cases, the vendor uses a new name for the function. Fortunately, most vendors include a file with #defines that allow you to use the original names.

The remaining VIO functions do appear in OS/2 version 1.3 and above in their original state. Many of these functions have limitations regarding the Presentation Manager. There is at least one of the following three classifications assigned to each function. You can use FAPI functions in a family API application; a family API application runs equally well in DOS or OS/2. Presentation Manager will not allow you to use a xPM function within an application designed for that environment. However, you can use these functions in a windowed OS/2 character-mode session. A final restriction is that xWPM functions cannot appear in windowed OS/2 character-mode sessions; you must restrict their use to full screen sessions only.

The Borland compiler provides access to these functions through the BSESUB.H include file. You might need to check the include files for your compiler to find references to these functions, because most vendors do not document them. In some cases, the vendor uses a new name for the function. Fortunately, most vendors include a file with #defines that allow you to use the original names.

Table 3-2 contains a complete list of these functions. Remember that these are the functions supported by OS/2 versions 1.3 and above in their original version 1.1 state. The table includes the parameters for calling the functions, any restrictions, a complete description of the function, and a full listing of error codes that the function returns. It does not include any compiler specific calls like the VioCheckCharType function supported by the Borland compiler.

VIO function listing

Table 3-2

Function	Description

xWPM
UShort
VioDeRegister
(Void)
	The VioDeRegister function deregisters a video subsystem previously registered within a session (all the processes in the current screen group). VioDeRegister must be issued by the same process that issued the previous VioRegister. After VioDeRegister is issued, subsequent video calls are processed by the Base Video Subsystem. VioDeRegister returns one of the following values:
	
	    0 NO_ERROR
	  404 ERROR_VIO_DEREGISTER
	  430 ERROR_VIO_ILLEGAL_DURING_POPUP
	  465 ERROR_VIO_DETACHED
	  494 ERROR_VIO_EXTENDED_SG

xPM
UShort VioEndPopUp
(hvio)
	The VioEndPopUp function closes a pop-up screen and restores the video buffer to its previous state. hvio contains a handle to the video buffer. Only the process that issued a VioPopUp can call this function to end it. Always use a handle value of 0 for Presentation Manager applications.
	
	There are some instances where this call will not restore the screen fully. For example, if your application modified the contents of any of the display adapter registers, it would have to restore the state of these registers before the VioEndPopUp function executes. Use the VioModeWait function to request that OS/2 notify you of the change in video conditions. VioEndPopUp returns one of the following values:
	
	    0 NO_ERROR
	  405 ERROR_VIO_NO_POPUP
	  436 ERROR_VIO_INVALID_HANDLE

xPM
UShort VioGetAnsi
(pfANSI, hvio)
	The VioGetAnsi function retrieves the state of the ANSI flag. This determines whether OS/2 can process ANSI escape sequences. pfANSI is a pointer to a variable which receives the ANSI flag. hvio contains a handle to the video buffer. Always use a handle value of 0 for Presentation Manager applications. Character mode applications must provide a handle obtained using the VioCreatePS function. VioGetAnsi returns one of the following values:
	
	    0 NO_ERROR
	  436 ERROR_VIO_INVALID_HANDLE
	  465 ERROR_VIO_DETACHED

FAPI UShort VioGetBuf (pulLVB, pcbLVB, hvio)	The VioGetBuf function retrieves the address of a logical video buffer (LVB). pulLVB contains a pointer to a variable that holds the address of the LVB. Never assume the offset portion of this variable is 0. pcbLVB contains a pointer to a variable which holds the length of the LVB. The buffer length equals Rows × Columns × Cell Size. hvio contains a handle to the video buffer. A process can modify the LVB at any time—even while it executes in the background. In most cases, the LVB and physical display

Table 3-2 **Continued**

Function	Description

Function   **Description**

buffer (PDB) are the same when the application is in the foreground. OS/2 automatically updates the PDB when the application switches to the foreground. This changes if you issue a VioGetPhysBuf call. OS/2 stops updating the PDB even if the application is in the foreground. The application can display the contents of the LVB using the VioShowBuf function. You can use the VioGetMode function to determine the size of the buffer. Issuing a VioSetMode call changes the size of the logical buffer to match the dimensions of the new mode. VioGetAnsi returns one of the following values:

```
  0  NO_ERROR
355  ERROR_VIO_MODE
430  ERROR_VIO_ILLEGAL_DURING_POPUP
436  ERROR_VIO_INVALID_HANDLE
465  ERROR_VIO_DETACHED
```

FAPI
UShort VioGetConfig
(usConfiguration,
pvioIn, hvio)

The VioGetConfig function returns the video display configuration including: display adapter type, display type, and amount of video memory. usConfiguration determines which display configuration the call retrieves. You can use any of the following values: 0 for current, 1 for primary, and 2 for secondary. pvioIn contains the address of the display configuration structure. hvio contains a handle to the video buffer. The display configuration structure consists of the following elements:

Offset	Length	Description
00h	2	Length of structure.
02h	2	Display adapter type including: 0 monochrome, 1 CGA, 2 EGA, 3 VGA, 4-6 reserved, 7 8514/A, 8 PS/2 Image Adapter/A, or 9 XGA.
04h	2	Display type including: 0 monochrome, 1 CGA, 2 EGA, 3 PS/2 monochrome (8503), 4 PS/2 color (8512 and 8513), 5-8 reserved, 9 PS/2 color (8514), 10 IBM plasma display panel, 11 monochrome (8507 and 8604), 12 PS/2 color, or 13 reserved.
06h	4	Amount of display adapter memory in bytes.
0Ah	2	The number of the display adapter used to used to derive this information. It comes from the video subsystem rather than the Base Video Handler (HVH).
0Ch	2	Reserved
0Eh	2	Flags
	0	Power up display configuration
		1–15 Reserved

Function	Description		
	Offset	**Length**	**Description**
	10h	4	The BVH buffer size in bytes. This is the number of bytes used to store the full hardware state excluding the physical display buffer.
	14h	4	The maximum BVH buffer size in bytes. This is the amount of memory required to store the full physical display buffer.
	18h	4	The pop-up BVH buffer size in bytes. This is the amount of memory required to store the area of the physical display buffer overlaid by a pop-up.
	1Ch	2	This entry provides an offset into the configuration data structure that contains a description of what other display adapters this adapter emulates. Each emulation entry contains the data shown in the following paragraphs.
	1Eh	2	Contains the a count of the number of words to follow.
	20h	2	Display adapters emulated by this display adapter. Each bit represents a different display adapter type.

0	Monochrome
1	CGA
2	EGA
3	VGA or PS/2 Display Adapter
4–6	Reserved
7	8514/A
8	PS/2 Image Adapter/A
9	XGA
10–15	Reserved

	22h	2	Reserved
	24h	2	Reserved
	26h	2	This entry provides an offset into the configuration data structure that contains a description of what other displays this display emulates. Each emulation entry contains the data shown in the following paragraphs.
	28h	2	Displays emulated by this display. Each bit represents a different display type.

0	5151 Monochrome
1	5153 CGA
2	5154 EGA
3	8503 Monochrome

Table 3-2			Continued

Function	Description

	Offset	Length	Description
		4	8512 or 8513 Color
		5–8	Reserved
		9	8514 Color
		10	IBM Plasma Display Panel
		11	8507 and 8604 Monochrome
		12	8515 Color
		13–15	Reserved
	2Ah	2	Reserved
	2Ch	2	Reserved

VioGetConfig returns one of the following values.

0	NO_ERROR
421	ERROR_VIO_INVALID_PARMS
436	ERROR_VIO_INVALID_HANDLE
438	ERROR_VIO_INVALID_LENGTH
465	ERROR_VIO_DETACHED

xPM
UShort VioGetCp
(usReserved,
pIDCodePage, hvio)

The VioGetCp function returns the current code page used to display text data. usReserved contains a value of zero. pIDCodePage contains a pointer to a word used to store the code page number. A return value of 0 indicates that the current code page is the ROM font provided by the display adapter. hvio contains a handle to the video buffer. VioGetCp returns one of the following values:

0	NO_ERROR
355	ERROR_VIO_MODE
436	ERROR_VIO_INVALID_HANDLE
465	ERROR_VIO_DETACHED
468	ERROR_VIO_USER_FONT

FAPI
UShort
VioGetCurPos
(pusRow,
pusColumn, hvio)

The VioGetCurPos function returns the current row and column coordinates of the cursor. pusRow contains a pointer to the row variable. pusColumn contains a pointer to the column variable. A return value of 0 in both variables indicates the cursor is in the upper left corner of the display. hvio contains a handle to the video buffer. VioGetCurPos returns one of the following values:

0	NO_ERROR
355	ERROR_VIO_MODE
436	ERROR_VIO_INVALID_HANDLE
465	ERROR_VIO_DETACHED

FAPI
UShort
VioGetCurType
(pvioCursorInfo,
hvio)

The VioGetCurType function returns the cursor type. pvioCursorInfo contains a pointer to a structure containing the cursor information. hvio contains a handle to the video buffer. The pvioCursorInfo data structure consists of the following elements:

Function	Description		

Description

Offset	Length	Description
00h	2	The top horizontal scan line of the cursor within a character cell.
02h	2	The bottom horizontal scan line of the cursor within a character cell.
04h	2	Cursor Width. In character mode, the cursor width equals the number of character columns on the display. In graphics mode, the cursor width is measured in pels.
06h	2	Cursor Attribute. A value of −1 indicates a hidden cursor. Any other value in text mode indicates that the user can see the cursor. In graphics mode, any other number indicates the color of the cursor.

VioGetCurType returns one of the following values:

```
  0  NO_ERROR
355  ERROR_VIO_MODE
436  ERROR_VIO_INVALID_HANDLE
465  ERROR_VIO_DETACHED
468  ERROR_VIO_USER_FONT
```

FAPI xWPM
UShort VioGetFont
(pviofi, hvio)

The VioGetFont function returns a font table for the font in use or the one you specify. pviofi contains a pointer to a table used to store the font data. hvio contains a handle to the video buffer. The pviofi data structure consists of the following elements:

Offset	Length	Description
00h	2	Length of structure.
02h	2	Request Type. A value of 0 gets the current RAM font for EGA, VGA, or SVGA display adapters. A value of 1 gets the ROM font for CGA, EGA, VGA, or SVGA display adapters.
04h	2	Pel columns in character cell.
06h	2	Pel rows in character cell.
08h	4	Pointer to a block of storage space in the application data area. This area contains the font table when this function returns.
0Ch	2	Length of the caller-supplied font table storage area in bytes.

VioGetFont returns one of the following values:

```
0    NO_ERROR
```

Table 3-2   **Continued**

Function	Description
	355 ERROR_VIO_MODE 421 ERROR_VIO_INVALID_PARMS 438 ERROR_VIO_INVALID_LENGTH 465 ERROR_VIO_DETACHED 467 ERROR_VIO_FONT 494 ERROR_VIO_EXTENDED_SG
FAPI xPM UShort VioGetMode (pvioModeInfo, hvio)	The VioGetMode function returns the current display mode information. pvioModeInfo contains a pointer to a table used to store the mode data. hvio contains a handle to the video buffer. The pvioModeInfo data structure consists of the following elements:

Offset	Length	Description
00h	2	Length of structure. The value that you supply controls the amount of display mode data returned. The minimum value is 2, and the maximum is 34. A length of 2 returns the maximum structure size required to return all mode data.
02h	1	Mode characteristics bit mask

0		0 = Monochrome compatible mode
		1 = Other
1		0 = Text mode
		1 = Graphics mode
2		0 = Enable color burst
		1 = Disable color burst
3		0 = VGA compatible modes 0-13h
		1 = Native mode
4–7		Reserved

Offset	Length	Description
03h	1	Number of colors defined as a power of two:

0 = monochrome
1 = 2 colors
2 = 4 colors
4 = 16 colors
8 = 256 colors

Offset	Length	Description
04h	2	Number of text columns.
06h	2	Number of text rows.
08h	2	Horizontal resolution in pels.
0Ah	2	Vertical resolution in pels.
0Ch	1	Format of the attributes.
0Dh	1	Number of attributes in a character cell.

Function	Description

Description

Offset	Length	Description
0Eh	4	32-bit address of the physical display buffer for this mode.
12h	4	Length of the physical display buffer for this mode.
16h	4	Size of the buffer required for a full save of the physical display buffer for this mode.
1Ah	4	Size of the buffer required for a partial (pop-up) save of the physical display buffer for this mode.
1Dh	4	Far address to the extended mode data structure. The format of this structure varies by display adapter and is unknown to OS/2.

VioGetMode returns one of the following values:

0	NO_ERROR
436	ERROR_VIO_INVALID_HANDLE
438	ERROR_VIO_INVALID_LENGTH
465	ERROR_VIO_DETACHED
494	ERROR_VIO_EXTENDED_SG

FAPI xWPM
UShort
VioGetPhysBuf
(pvioPhysBuf,
usReserved)

The VioGetPhysBuf function obtains an address to the physical display buffer. pvioModeInfo contains a pointer to a table used to store the physical display buffer data. usReserved contains a value of zero. The pvioModeInfo data structure consists of the following elements:

Offset	Length	Description
00h	4	Pointer to the 32-bit start address of the physical display buffer. This address range must fall between A0000h and BFFFFh, inclusive. If the display buffer length is 0, then VioGetPhysBuf returns one selector corresponding to the address of the current display mode.
04h	4	Display buffer length.
08h-XX	2 per selector	Physical display buffer selector list. Each selector points to one 64K block of the physical display buffer. The last selector points to either a whole or partial 64K block (depending on the size of the buffer).
XX+2	2	Length of the physical buffer in bytes.
XX+4-YY	2 per selector	Each selector points to one 64K block of the physical video buffer.

Issuing a VioGetPhysBuf after a VioGetBuf call sends all VioWrtXX calls to the physical display buffer instead of the LVB. An application can only issue this call while operating in the foreground. It must issue a VioScrLock call prior to using the physical display buffer.

Table 3-2 **Continued**

Function	Description
	VioGetPhysBuf returns one of the following values:

    0 NO_ERROR
350 ERROR_VIO_PTR
429 ERROR_VIO_IN_BG
430 ERROR_VIO_ILLEGAL_DURING_POPUP
436 ERROR_VIO_INVALID_HANDLE
465 ERROR_VIO_DETACHED
494 ERROR_VIO_EXTENDED_SG

FAPI xWPM
UShort VioGetState
(pState, hvio)

The VioGetState function returns one of several types of information about the video adapter. This includes the various types of register information. pState contains a pointer to a structure. There are six different structures; each one corresponds to a particular structure. The structure types include: get palette registers (0), get overscan color (1), get blink/background intensity switch (2), get color registers (3), get the scan line for underlining (5), and get target display configuration (6). Types 4 and 7 currently are reserved. hvio contains a handle to the video buffer. The pState data structure consists of the following elements (depending on the type of request you make):

Offset	Length	Description

Get palette registers (VioPalState)

00h	2	Length of structure. (Maximum length of 38 allowed.)
02h	2	Set to 0 for palette registers.
04h-XX	2 per entry	Input only. One entry for each palette register. The length of the structure determines the number of palette registers returned. The palette registers are numbered 0 through 15.
04h-XX	2 per entry	Output only. One entry for each palette register that you wish to set. You may specify a maximum of 16 register entries.

Get overscan color (VioOverscan)

00h	2	Length of structure. The only valid value is 6.
02h	2	Set to 1 for overscan (border) color.
04h	2	Color Value

Get blink/background intensity switch (VioIntensity)

00h	2	Length of structure. The only valid value is 6.
02h	2	Set to 2 for blink/background intensity switch.
04h	2	Use the following values to set the switch:

Function	Description		
	Offset	**Length**	**Description**

		0 = Blinking colors enabled
		1 = High Intensity colors enabled

Get color registers (VioColorReg)

Offset	Length	Description
00h	2	Length of structure. The only valid value is 12.
02h	2	Set to 3 for color registers.
04h	2	Value of the first color register value to retrieve (0–255). The color registers are returned in sequential order.
06h	2	Number of color registers that you want returned (1–256).
08h	4	Pointer to a data area to use to store the register values. Multiply the number of registers that you want to retrieve by 3 bytes to determine the size of the data area needed. Each register entry contains one byte each of color information in the following order: red, green, and blue.

Get the scan line for underlining (VioSetUlineLoc)

Offset	Length	Description
00h	2	Length of structure. The only valid value is 6.
02h	2	Set to 5 to get the scan line for underlining. You can only use this feature if the foreground color is 1 or 9. You cannot use this value in a family API application.
04h	2	Value of the scan line in the range 0 to 31. Setting this entry to 32 disables underlining.

Get target display configuration (VioSetTarget)

Offset	Length	Description
00h	2	Length of structure. The only valid value is 6.
02h	2	Set to 6 to get the display configuration that you want to select as the target for the next VioSetMode function call. You cannot use this value in a family API application.
04h	2	Configuration value: 0 for default selection, 1 for primary, or 2 for secondary.

VioGetState returns one of the following values:

0	NO_ERROR
355	ERROR_VIO_MODE
421	ERROR_VIO_INVALID_PARMS
436	ERROR_VIO_INVALID_HANDLE
438	ERROR_VIO_INVALID_LENGTH
465	ERROR_VIO_DETACHED
494	ERROR_VIO_EXTENDED_SG

Table 3-2   **Continued**

Function	Description
xWPM UShort VioGlobalReg (pszModName, pszEntryName, flFun1, flFun2, usReturn)	The VioGlobalReg function allows an application to receive notification of the completion of any VIO call by any full-screen session. pszModName contains the address of a one to eight character ASCIIZ string that identifies the subsystem. You must use a DLL for the subsystem name. Do not include the DLL extension as part of the name. pszEntryName contains an address to a one to thirty-two character ASCIIZ string that identifies the entry point within the DLL. This is the routine that receives control when another thread executes a registered VIO function in a full-screen session. flFun1 contains a bit mask that identifies the video functions that you want registered. Push the high-order 16 bits onto the stack first, then the low-order 16 bits. Each bit registers one or more of the following functions: VioGetCurPos (0), VioGetCurType (1), VioGetMode (2), VioGetBuf (3), VioGetPhysBuf (4), VioSetCurPos (5), VioSetCurType (6), VioSetMode (7), VioShowBuf (8), VioReacCharStr (9), VioReadCellStr (10), VioWrtNChar (11), VioWrtNAttr (12), VioWrtNCell (13), VioWrtTTY (14), VioWrtCharStr (15), VioWrtCharStrAtt (16), VioWrtCellStr (17), VioScrollUp (18), VioScrollDn (19), VioScrollLf (20), VioScrollRt (21), VioSetAnsi (22), VioGetAnsi (23), VioPrtSc (24), VioScrLock (25), VioScrUnlock (26), VioSavRedrawWait (27), VioSavRedrawUndo (28), VioPopUp (29), VioEndPopUp (30), and VioPrtScToggle (31). flFun2 contains a bit mask similar to flFun1. The only difference is the functions that it registers. Each bit registers one or more of the following functions: VioModeWait (0), VioModeUndo (1), VioGetFont (2), VioGetConfig (3), VioSetCP (4), VioGetCP (5), VioSetFont (6), VioGetState (7), VioSetState (8), VioRegister (9), and VioDeRegister (10). You must always set bits 11 through 31 to zero. usReturn is reserved; always set it to zero. VioGlobalReg returns one of the following values: 0 NO_ERROR 349 ERROR_VIO_INVALID_MASK 403 ERROR_VIO_INVALID_ASCIIZ 426 ERROR_VIO_REGISTER 494 ERROR_VIO_EXTENDED_SG When OS/2 routes control to the entry point of your DLL, it passes four additional values: index number (WORD), a near pointer (WORD), the caller's DS register (WORD), and the return address to the VIO router (DWORD). Each registered function has its own index number as shown here:

0 VioGetPhysBuf	4 VioGetCurType	8 VioSetMode
1 VioGetBuf	5 VioGetMode	9 VioReadCharStr
2 VioShowBuf	6 VioSetCurPos	10 VioReadCellStr
3 VioGetCurPos	7 VioSetCurType	11 VioWrtNChar

Function	Description

Function

Description

12 VioWrtNAttr	23 VioGetAnsi	34 VioGetFont
13 VioWrtNCell	24 VioPrtSc	35 VioGetConfig
14 VioWrtCharStr	25 VioScrLock	36 VioSetCp
15 VioWrtCharStrAtt	26 VioScrUnlock	37 VioGetCp
16 VioWrtCellStr	27 VioSavRedrawWait	38 VioSetFont
17 VioWrtTTY	28 VioSavRedrawUndo	39 VioGetState
18 VioScrollUp	29 VioPopUp	40 VioSetState
19 VioScrollDn	30 VioEndPopUp	41 VioRegister
20 VioScrollLf	31 VioPrtScToggle	42 VioDeRegister
21 VioScrollRt	32 VioModeWait	
22 VioSetAnsi	33 VioModeUndo	

xWPM
UShort
VioModeUndo
(usOwnerInd,
usKillInd,
usReserved)

The VioModeUndo function allows a thread to cancel a VioModeWait issued by another thread in the same process. usOwnerInd tells OS/2 whether the thread wants to reserve ownership of VioModeWait for its process. It can contain two values: reserve ownership (0) or give up ownership (1). usKillInd tells OS/2 to return an error code or terminate the thread with the outstanding VioModeWait. It can contain two values: return error code (0) or terminate thread (1). usReserved is a reserved word; always set it to 0. VioModeUndo returns one of the following values:

```
  0  NO_ERROR
421  ERROR_VIO_INVALID_PARMS
422  ERROR_VIO_FUNCTION_OWNED
427  ERROR_VIO_NO_MODE_THREAD
430  ERROR_VIO_ILLEGAL_DURING_POPUP
465  ERROR_VIO_DETACHED
486  ERROR_VIO_BAD_RESERVE
494  ERROR_VIO_EXTENDED_SG
```

xWPM
UShort VioModeWait
(usReqType,
pNotifyType,
usReserved)

The VioModeWait function provides a graphics mode application with the means for automatically restoring its video mode, state, and modified display adapter registers. The application must perform this task each time this function returns. usReqType determines the event that VioModeWait monitors. The only acceptable value is 0, which notifies the application after a pop-up to restore its display. pNotifyType contains the address of the restoration routine. Restore mode (0) is the only type of notification returned. usReserved is a reserved word; always set it to 0. VioModeWait returns one of the following values:

```
  0  NO_ERROR
421  ERROR_VIO_INVALID_PARMS
422  ERROR_VIO_FUNCTION_OWNED
423  ERROR_VIO_RETURN
```

Table 3-2   **Continued**

Command	Description
	424 ERROR_SCS_INVALID_FUNCTION 428 ERROR_VIO_NO_SAVE_RESTORE_THD 430 ERROR_VIO_ILLEGAL_DURING_POPUP 465 ERROR_VIO_DETACHED 494 ERROR_VIO_EXTENDED_SG
xPM UShort VioPopUp (pflags, hvio)	The VioPopUp function provides a temporary screen that an application can use to display messages to the user. OS/2 allows only one pop-up at any time. You normally use a pop-up to inform the user of an error condition or other emergency information. The current foreground application cannot continue until the thread that issued the VioPopUp issues a VioEndPopUp. pflags contains the address of the flags used to set up the pop-up. Bit 0 returns a unique error code if a pop-up is not available when set to 0. It waits for a pop-up if one is not available when set to 1. Bit 1 selects nontransparent operation when set to 0 or transparent operation when set to 1. OS/2 automatically selects text mode (3, 3*, 3+, 7, or 7+) when you select nontransparent mode. It also clears the display and places the cursor in the upper-left corner. No mode changes occur if the display adapter already is in modes 2, 3, or 7 when using transparent mode. OS/2 does not clear the display or change the cursor position. If the display is not in a text mode or the foreground process has a VioSavRedrawWait thread, then OS/2 returns an error code. Bits 2 through 15 are reserved; always set them to 0. hvio contains a handle to the video buffer. VioPopUp returns one of the following values: 0 NO_ERROR 405 ERROR_VIO_NO_POPUP 406 ERROR_VIO_EXISTING_POPUP 483 ERROR_VIO_TRANSPARENT_POPUP
xWPM UShort VioPrtSc (hvio)	The VioPrtSc function sends the contents of the screen buffer to the printer. It supports text video modes 0 through 3 and 7. This is the call issued by the session manager when the user presses PrtSc. Application programs cannot issue this call. hvio contains a handle to the video buffer. VioPrtSc returns one of the following values: 0 NO_ERROR 355 ERROR_VIO_MODE 402 ERROR_VIO_SMG_ONLY 436 ERROR_VIO_INVALID_HANDLE 465 ERROR_VIO_DETACHED
xWPM UShort VioPrtScToggle (hvio)	The VioPrtScToggle function changes the Ctrl–PrtSc state of the foreground session. Setting this state on sends all output to the printer. This is the call issued by the session manager when the user presses Ctrl–PrtSc. Application programs cannot issue this call. hvio contains a handle to the video buffer. VioPrtScToggle returns one of the following values:

Function	Description
	0 NO_ERROR 355 ERROR_VIO_MODE 402 ERROR_VIO_SMG_ONLY 430 ERROR_VIO_ILLEGAL_DURING_POPUP 436 ERROR_VIO_INVALID_HANDLE 465 ERROR_VIO_DETACHED
FAPI UShort VioReadCellStr (pchCellStr, pcb, usRow, usColumn, hvio)	The VioReadCellStr function reads a string of character-attribute pairs from the screen starting at the specified location. pchCellStr contains the address of the buffer used to store the character-attribute pairs. pcb contains the address of the variable that stores the buffer length. Each character-attribute entry consumes two or four bytes (depending on mode). usRow contains the starting row to read (0 is at the top of the display). usColumn contains the starting column to read (0 is at the left side of the display). hvio contains a handle to the video buffer. VioReadCellStr returns one of the following values:
	0 NO_ERROR 355 ERROR_VIO_MODE 358 ERROR_VIO_ROW 359 ERROR_VIO_COL 436 ERROR_VIO_INVALID_HANDLE 465 ERROR_VIO_DETACHED
FAPI UShort VioReadCharStr (pchCellStr, pcb, usRow, usColumn, hvio)	The VioReadCharacterStr function reads a string of characters from the screen starting at the specified location. pchCellStr contains the address of the buffer used to store the characters. pcb contains the address of the variable that stores the buffer length. usRow contains the starting row to read (0 is at the top of the display). usColumn contains the starting column to read (0 is at the left side of the display). hvio contains a handle to the video buffer. VioReadCharacterStr returns one of the following values:
	0 NO_ERROR 355 ERROR_VIO_MODE 358 ERROR_VIO_ROW 359 ERROR_VIO_COL 436 ERROR_VIO_INVALID_HANDLE 465 ERROR_VIO_DETACHED
xWPM UShort VioRegister (pszModName, pszEntryName, flFun1, flFun2)	The VioRegister function registers an alternate video subsystem within the session. pszModName contains the address of a one to eight character ASCIIZ string that identifies the subsystem. You must use a DLL for the subsystem name. Do not include the DLL extension as part of the name. pszEntryName contains an address to a 1- to 32-character ASCIIZ string that identifies the entry point within the DLL. This is the routine that receives control when another thread executes a registered VIO function in a full screen session. flFun1 contains a bit mask that identifies the video functions that you want registered. Push the

Table 3-2   **Continued**

Function	**Description**

high-order 16 bits onto the stack first, then the low-order 16 bits. Each bit registers one or more of the following functions: VioGetCurPos (0), VioGetCurType (1), VioGetMode (2), VioGetBuf (3), VioGetPhysBuf (4), VioSetCurPos (5), VioSetCurType (6), VioSetMode (7), VioShowBuf (8), VioReacCharStr (9), VioReadCellStr (10), VioWrtNChar (11), VioWrtNAttr (12), VioWrtNCell (13), VioWrtTTY (14), VioWrtCharStr (15), VioWrtCharStrAtt (16), VioWrtCellStr (17), VioScrollUp (18), VioScrollDn (19), VioScrollLf (20), VioScrollRt (21), VioSetAnsi (22), VioGetAnsi (23), VioPrtSc (24), VioScrLock (25), VioScrUnlock (26), VioSavRedrawWait (27), VioSavRedrawUndo (28), VioPopUp (29), VioEndPopUp (30), and VioPrtScToggle (31). flFun2 contains a bit mask similar to flFun1. The only difference is the functions that it registers. Each bit registers one or more of the following functions: VioModeWait (0), VioModeUndo (1), VioGetFont (2), VioGetConfig (3), VioSetCP (4), VioGetCP (5), VioSetFont (6), VioGetState (7), VioSetState (8), VioRegister (9), and VioDeRegister (10). You must always set bits 11 through 31 to zero. VioRegister returns one of the following values:

```
  0   NO_ERROR
349   ERROR_VIO_INVALID_MASK
403   ERROR_VIO_INVALID_ASCIIZ
426   ERROR_VIO_REGISTER
430   ERROR_VIO_ILLEGAL_DURING_POPUP
465   ERROR_VIO_DETACHED
494   ERROR_VIO_EXTENDED_SG
```

When OS/2 routes control to the entry point of your DLL, it passes four additional values: index number (WORD), a near pointer (WORD), the caller's DS register (WORD), and the return address to the VIO router (DWORD). Each registered function has its own index number as shown here:

0 VioGetPhysBuf	9 VioReadCharStr	18 VioScrollUp
1 VioGetBuf	10 VioReadCellStr	19 VioScrollDn
2 VioShowBuf	11 VioWrtNChar	20 VioScrollLf
3 VioGetCurPos	12 VioWrtNAttr	21 VioScrollRt
4 VioGetCurType	13 VioWrtNCell	22 VioSetAnsi
5 VioGetMode	14 VioWrtCharStr	23 VioGetAnsi
6 VioSetCurPos	15 VioWrtCharStrAtt	24 VioPrtSc
7 VioSetCurType	16 VioWrtCellStr	25 VioScrLock
8 VioSetMode	17 VioWrtTTY	26 VioScrUnlock

Function

Description

27	VioSavRedrawWait	33	VioModeUndo	39	VioGetState
28	VioSavRedrawUndo	34	VioGetFont	40	VioSetState
29	VioPopUp	35	VioGetConfig	41	VioRegister
30	VioEndPopUp	36	VioSetCp	42	VioDeRegister
31	VioPrtScToggle	37	VioGetCp		
32	VioModeWait	38	VioSetFont		

The router interprets the return code from a registered function as follows:

0 = No Error. Do not invoke the corresponding Base Video Subsystem routine. Return to the caller with a return code of 0.

−1 = No Error. Invoke the corresponding Base Video Subsystem routine. Return to the caller with a return value from the Base Video Subsystem.

Other Number = Error. Do not invoke the corresponding Base Video Subsystem routine. Return the error number to the caller.

xWPM
UShort
VioSavRedraw-
Undo
(usOwnerInd,
usKillInd
usReserved)

The VioSavRedrawUndo function allows a thread to cancel a VioSavRedrawWait issued by another thread in the same process. usOwnerInd tells OS/2 whether the thread wants to reserve ownership of VioSavRedrawWait for its process. It can contain two values: reserve ownership (0) or give up ownership (1). usKillInd tells OS/2 to return an error code or terminate the thread with the outstanding VioSavRedrawWait. It can contain two values: return error code (0) or terminate thread (1). usReserved is a reserved word; always set it to 0. VioSavRedrawUndo returns one of the following values:

```
  0  NO_ERROR
421  ERROR_VIO_INVALID_PARMS
422  ERROR_VIO_FUNCTION_OWNED
428  ERROR_VIO_NO_SAVE_RESTORE_THD
430  ERROR_VIO_ILLEGAL_DURING_POPUP
465  ERROR_VIO_DETACHED
494  ERROR_VIO_EXTENDED_SG
```

xWPM
UShort
VioSavRedrawWait
(usRedrawInd,
pNotifyType,
usReserved)

The VioSavRedrawWait function notifies a graphics-mode application when it should save or redraw the screen. Only one process per session can issue this call. The application must perform this task each time this function returns. usRedrawInd determines the event that VioSavRedrawWait monitors. There are two different values for the parameter. A value of 0 notifies the application of both save and redraw operations. A value of 1 notifies the application of redraw operations only. pNotifyType contains the address of the operation routine. A value of 0 saves the screen image. A value of 1 restores the screen image. usReserved is a

Table 3-2 **Continued**

Function	Description
	reserved word; always set it to 0. VioSavRedrawWait returns one of the following values: 0 NO_ERROR 421 ERROR_VIO_INVALID_PARMS 422 ERROR_VIO_FUNCTION_OWNED 423 ERROR_VIO_RETURN 430 ERROR_VIO_ILLEGAL_DURING_POPUP 436 ERROR_VIO_INVALID_HANDLE 465 ERROR_VIO_DETACHED 494 ERROR_VIO_EXTENDED_SG
FAPI xWPM UShort VioScrLock (fwait, pfNot Locked, hvio)	The VioScrLock function requests ownership of the physical display buffer. This locks out any other application that might want to use it. OS/2 disables screen switching while the lock is in place. Only one thread can own the screen locks. fwait contains a flag that tells OS/2 whether the process wants to wait until the screen I/O can take place. A value of 0 returns immediately if the screen I/O is not available. A value of 1 waits until the screen I/O is available. pfNotLocked contains a pointer to a variable which contains a flag showing whether the lock is successful. On return from the call a value of 0 indicates success, while a value 1 indicates failure. hvio contains a handle to the video buffer (a reserved word of zeros in this case). VioScrLock returns one of the following values: 0 NO_ERROR 366 ERROR_VIO_WAIT_FLAG 430 ERROR_VIO_ILLEGAL_DURING_POPUP 434 ERROR_VIO_LOCK 436 ERROR_VIO_INVALID_HANDLE 465 ERROR_VIO_DETACHED 494 ERROR_VIO_EXTENDED_SG
FAPI UShort VioScrollDn (usTopRow, usBotRow, usLeftCol, usRightCol, hvio) pCell, hvio)	The VioScrollDn function scrolls the entire or defined area of the screen down. A value of 0 for both usTopRow and usLeftCol equates to the upper-left corner of the display. Using a value of 0 for usTopRow and usLeftCol, and a value of 65,535 (–1 for assembler) for usBotRow, usRightCol, and cbLines fills the entire area with the contents of pCell. usTopRow contains the top row to scroll. usLeftCol contains the leftmost column to scroll. usBotRow contains the bottom row to scroll. usRightCol contains the rightmost column to scroll. cbLines tells how many lines to scroll. pCell contains the address of a variable that contains a fill character to use for the scrolled lines. hvio contains a handle to the video buffer. VioScrollDn returns one of the following values: 0 NO_ERROR 355 ERROR_VIO_MODE 358 ERROR_VIO_ROW

Function	Description
	359 ERROR_VIO_COL 436 ERROR_VIO_INVALID_HANDLE 465 ERROR_VIO_DETACHED
FAPI UShort VioScrollLf (usTopRow, usLeftCol, usBotRow, usRightCol, cbCol, pCell, hvio)	The VioScrollLf function scrolls the entire or defined area of the screen to the left. A value of 0 for both usTopRow and usLeftCol equates to the upper-left corner of the display. Using a value of 0 for usTopRow and usLeftCol, and a value of 65,535 (–1 for assembler) for usBotRow, usRightCol, and cbCol fills the entire area with the contents of pCell. usTopRow contains the top row to scroll. usLeftCol contains the leftmost column to scroll. usBotRow contains the bottom row to scroll. usRightCol contains the rightmost column to scroll. cbCol tells how many columns to scroll. pCell contains the address of a variable that contains a fill character to use for the scrolled lines. hvio contains a handle to the video buffer. VioScrollLf returns one of the following values:
	0 NO_ERROR 355 ERROR_VIO_MODE 358 ERROR_VIO_ROW 359 ERROR_VIO_COL 436 ERROR_VIO_INVALID_HANDLE 465 ERROR_VIO_DETACHED
FAPI UShort VioScrollRt (usTopRow, usLeftCol, usBotRow, usRightCol, cbCol,pCell, hvio)	The VioScrollRt function scrolls the entire or defined area of the screen to the right. A value of 0 for both usTopRow and usLeftCol equates to the upper-left corner of the display. Using a value of 0 for usTopRow and usLeftCol, and a value of 65,535 (–1 for assembler) for usRightCol, and cbCol fills the entire area with the contents of pCell. usTopRow contains the top row to scroll. usLeftCol contains the leftmost column to scroll. usBotRow contains the bottom row to scroll. usRightCol contains the rightmost column to scroll. cbCol tells how many lines to scroll. pCell contains the address of a variable that contains a fill character to use for the scrolled lines. hvio contains a handle to the video buffer. VioScrollRt returns one of the following values:
	0 NO_ERROR 355 ERROR_VIO_MODE 358 ERROR_VIO_ROW 359 ERROR_VIO_COL 436 ERROR_VIO_INVALID_HANDLE 465 ERROR_VIO_DETACHED
FAPI UShort VioScrollUp (usTopRow, usLeftCol, usBotRow, usRightCol, cbLines,pCell, hvio)	The VioScrollUp function scrolls the entire or defined area of the screen up. A value of 0 for both usTopRow and usLeftCol equates to the upper-left corner of the display. Using a value of 0 for usTopRow and usLeftCol, and a value of 65,535 (–1 for assembler) for usBotRow, usRightCol, and cbLines fills the entire area with the contents of pCell. usTopRow contains the top row to scroll. usLeftCol contains the leftmost column to scroll. usBotRow contains

Table 3-2	**Continued**
Command	**Description**

	the bottom row to scroll. usRightCol contains the rightmost column to scroll. cbLines tells how many lines to scroll. pCell contains the address of a variable that contains a fill character to use for the scrolled lines. hvio contains a handle to the video buffer. VioScrollUp returns one of the following values:
	
	    0 NO_ERROR
	  355 ERROR_VIO_MODE
	  358 ERROR_VIO_ROW
	  359 ERROR_VIO_COL
	  436 ERROR_VIO_INVALID_HANDLE
	  465 ERROR_VIO_DETACHED

FAPI xWPM
UShort
VioScrUnLock (hvio)
	The VioScrUnLock function releases ownership of the physical display buffer. This unlocks the physical display buffer so that all applications can use it. Only the thread that issued the VioScrLock call can call this function. hvio contains a handle to the video buffer (a reserved word of zeros in this case). VioScrUnLock returns one of the following values:
	
	    0 NO_ERROR
	  367 ERROR_VIO_UNLOCK
	  430 ERROR_VIO_ILLEGAL_DURING_POPUP
	  436 ERROR_VIO_INVALID_HANDLE
	  465 ERROR_VIO_DETACHED
	  494 ERROR_VIO_EXTENDED_SG

xPM
UShort VioSetAnsi
(fAnsi, hvio)
	The VioSetAnsi function sets the state of the ANSI flag. This determines whether OS/2 can process ANSI escape sequences. fAnsi is a pointer to a variable that contains the ANSI flag. Setting this flag to 1 activates ANSI support. hvio contains a handle to the video buffer. VioSetAnsi returns one of the following values:
	
	    0 NO_ERROR
	  355 ERROR_VIO_MODE
	  421 ERROR_VIO_ILLEGAL_PARMS
	  430 ERROR_VIO_ILLEGAL_DURING_POPUP
	  436 ERROR_VIO_INVALID_HANDLE
	  465 ERROR_VIO_DETACHED

xPM UShort VioSetCp (usReserved, idCodePage, hvio)	The VioSetCp function sets the current code page used to display text data. usReserved contains a value of zero. idCodePage contains a word used to store the code page number. There are four code page values that you can use: 0 (default ROM), −1 (user front code page), −2 (disables user font code page and returns system to either a prepared or ROM code page), or a value specified with the CODEPAGE= statement in CONFIG.SYS. You cannot use values of −1 or −2 for Presentation Manager sessions. hvio contains a handle to the video buffer. VioSetCp returns one of the following values:

Function	Description
	0 NO_ERROR 355 ERROR_VIO_MODE 436 ERROR_VIO_INVALID_HANDLE 465 ERROR_VIO_DETACHED 469 ERROR_VIO_BAD_CP 470 ERROR_VIO_NO_CP 471 ERROR_VIO_NA_CP
FAPI UShort VioSetCurPos (usRow, usColumn, hvio)	The VioSetCurPos function returns the current row and column coordinates of the cursor. usRow contains the row setting. pusColumn contains the column setting. A value of 0 in both variables indicates the cursor is in the upper left corner of the display. hvio contains a handle to the video buffer. VioSetCurPos returns one of the following values: 0 NO_ERROR 355 ERROR_VIO_MODE 358 ERROR_VIO_ROW 359 ERROR_VIO_COL 436 ERROR_VIO_INVALID_HANDLE 465 ERROR_VIO_DETACHED
FAPI UShort VioSetCurType (pvioCursorInfo, hvio)	The VioSetCurType function changes the cursor type. pvioCursorInfo contains a pointer to a structure containing the cursor information. hvio contains a handle to the video buffer. The pvioCursorInfo data structure consists of the following elements:

Offset	Length	Description
00h	2	The top horizontal scan line of the cursor within a character cell. You also can specify this number as a percentage of the total scan lines by supplying a negative number in the range 0 to –100.
02h	2	The bottom horizontal scan line of the cursor within a character cell. You also can specify this number as a percentage of the total scan lines by supplying a negative number in the range 0 to –100.
04h	2	Cursor Width. In character mode, the cursor width equals the number of character columns on the display. In graphics mode, the cursor width is measured in pels.
06h	2	Cursor Attribute. A value of –1 indicates a hidden cursor. Any other value in text mode indicates that the user can see the cursor. In graphics mode, any other number indicates the color of the cursor.

VioSetCurType returns one of the following values:

0 NO_ERROR

Table 3-2   **Continued**

Function	Description
	355 ERROR_VIO_MODE 356 ERROR_VIO_WIDTH 421 ERROR_VIO_INVALID_PARMS 436 ERROR_VIO_INVALID_HANDLE 465 ERROR_VIO_DETACHED
FAPI xWPM UShort VioSetFont (pviofi, hvio)	The VioSetFont function changes the display font to a font that is specified. You must use a font that is compatible with the current video mode. pviofi contains a pointer to a table used to store the font data. hvio contains a handle to the video buffer. The pviofi data structure consists of the following elements:

Offset	Length	Description
00h	2	Length of structure. 14 is the only correct value.
02h	2	Request Type. A value of 0 uses the current RAM font for EGA, VGA, or SVGA display adapters.
04h	2	Pel columns in character cell.
06h	2	Pel rows in character cell.
08h	4	Pointer to a block of storage space in the application data area that contains the font table.
0Ch	2	Length of the caller-supplied font table storage area in bytes.

VioSetFont returns one of the following values:

```
  0  NO_ERROR
355  ERROR_VIO_MODE
421  ERROR_VIO_INVALID_PARMS
436  ERROR_VIO_INVALID_HANDLE
438  ERROR_VIO_INVALID_LENGTH
465  ERROR_VIO_DETACHED
467  ERROR_VIO_FONT
468  ERROR_VIO_USER_FONT
494  ERROR_VIO_EXTENDED_SG
```

FAPI xPM
UShort VioSetMode
(pvioModeInfo,
hvio)

The VioSetMode function changes the current display mode information. It also initializes the cursor position and type. It does not clear the screen. pvioModeInfo contains a pointer to a table used to store the mode data. hvio contains a handle to the video buffer. The pvioModeInfo data structure consists of the following elements:

Offset	Length	Description
00h	2	Length of structure. The value that you supply controls the amount of display mode data

Function	Description		
	Offset	**Length**	**Description**
			changed. The minimum value is 3 and the maximum is 34.
	02h	1	Mode characteristics bit mask. The disable color burst setting works only with CGA and VGA displays.

0	0 = Monochrome compatible mode
	1 = Other
1	0 = Text mode
	1 = Graphics mode
2	0 = Enable color burst
	1 = Disable color burst
3	0 = VGA compatible modes 0-13h
	1 = Native mode
4–7	Reserved

Offset	Length	Description
03h	1	Number of colors defined as a power of two:

0 = monochrome
1 = 2 colors
2 = 4 colors
4 = 16 colors
8 = 256 colors

Offset	Length	Description
04h	2	Number of text columns
06h	2	Number of text rows
08h	2	Horizontal resolution in pels
0Ah	2	Vertical resolution in pels
0Ch	1	Format of the attributes
0Dh	1	Number of attributes in a character cell.
0Eh	4	32-bit address of the physical display buffer for this mode.
12h	4	Length of the physical display buffer for this mode.
16h	4	Size of the buffer required for a full save of the physical display buffer for this mode.
1Ah	4	Size of the buffer required for a partial (pop-up) save of the physical display buffer for this mode.
1Dh	4	Far address to the extended mode data structure. The format of this structure varies by display adapter and is unknown to OS/2. Set this value to 0 if there is no extended mode data.

VioSetMode returns one of the following values:

    0 NO_ERROR
355 ERROR_VIO_MODE
430 ERROR_VIO_ILLEGAL_DURING_POPUP

Table 3-2 | **Continued**

Function	Description

Function

Description

436 ERROR_VIO_INVALID_HANDLE
438 ERROR_VIO_INVALID_LENGTH
465 ERROR_VIO_DETACHED
467 ERROR_VIO_FONT
468 ERROR_VIO_USER_FONT
494 ERROR_VIO_EXTENDED_SG

FAPI xWPM
UShort
VioSetState
(pState, hvio)

The VioSetState function changes one of several types of information about the video adapter. This includes the various types of register information. pState contains a pointer to a structure. There are six different structures; each one corresponds to a particular structure. The structure types include: set palette registers (0), set overscan color (1), set blink/background intensity switch (2), set color registers (3), set the scan line for underlining (5), and set target display configuration (6). Types 4 and 7 currently are reserved. hvio contains a handle to the video buffer. The pState data structure consists of the following elements (depending on the type of request you make):

Offset	Length	Description

Set palette registers (VioPalState)

Offset	Length	Description
00h	2	Length of structure. (Maximum length of 38 allowed.)
02h	2	Set to 0 for palette registers.
04h	2	First palette register in the register sequence. You must supply a value between 0 and 15.
06h-XX	2 per entry	One entry for each palette register that you want to set. You can specify a maximum of 16 register entries.

Set overscan color (VioOverscan)

Offset	Length	Description
00h	2	Length of structure. The only valid value is 6.
02h	2	Set to 1 for overscan (border) color.
04h	2	Color Value

Set blink/background intensity switch (VioIntensity)

Offset	Length	Description
00h	2	Length of structure. The only valid value is 6.
02h	2	Set to 2 for blink/background intensity switch.
04h	2	Use the following values to set the switch:

0 = Blinking colors enabled
1 = High-intensity colors enabled

Function	Description		
	Offset	**Length**	**Description**

Set color registers (VioColorReg)

	Offset	Length	Description
	00h	2	Length of structure. The only valid value is 12.
	02h	2	Set to 3 for color registers.
	04h	2	Value of the first color register value to set (0–255). The color registers are changed in sequential order.
	06h	2	Number of color registers that you want to set (1–256).
	08h	4	Pointer to a data area to use to store the register values. Multiply the number of registers that you want to retrieve by 3 bytes to determine the size of the data area that is needed. Each register entry contains one byte of color information in the following order: red, green, and blue.

Set the scan line for underlining (VioSetUlineLoc)

	Offset	Length	Description
	00h	2	Length of structure. The only valid value is 6.
	02h	2	Set to 5 to set the scan line for underlining. You can use this feature only if the foreground color is 1 or 9. You cannot use this value in a family API application.
	04h	2	Value of the scan line in the range 0 to 31. Setting this entry to 32 disables underlining.

Set target display configuration (VioSetTarget)

	Offset	Length	Description
	00h	2	Length of structure. The only valid value is 6.
	02h	2	Set to 6 to set the display configuration that you want to select as the target for the next VioSetMode function call. You cannot use this value in a family API application.
	04h	2	Configuration value: 0 for default selection, 1 for primary, or 2 for secondary.

VioSetState returns one of the following values:

0	NO_ERROR
355	ERROR_VIO_MODE
421	ERROR_VIO_INVALID_PARMS
436	ERROR_VIO_INVALID_HANDLE
438	ERROR_VIO_INVALID_LENGTH
465	ERROR_VIO_DETACHED
494	ERROR_VIO_EXTENDED_SG

Table 3-2 **Continued**

Function	Description
xPM UShort VioShowBuf (offLVB, cb, hvio)	The VioShowBuf function updates the physical display buffer (PDB) with the contents of the logical video buffer (LVB). offLVB contains the starting position within the LVB to use to update the PDB. cb contains the length of the update. hvio contains a handle to the video buffer. VioShowBuf returns one of the following values: 0 NO_ERROR 355 ERROR_VIO_MODE 430 ERROR_VIO_ILLEGAL_DURING_POPUP 436 ERROR_VIO_INVALID_HANDLE 465 ERROR_VIO_DETACHED
FAPI UShort VioWrtCellStr (pchCellStr, cb, usRow, usColumn, hvio)	The VioWrtCellStr function writes a string of character-attribute pairs to the screen starting at the specified location. The write always terminates at the end of the physical display even if the buffer is not exhausted. pchCellStr contains the address of the buffer used to store the character-attribute pairs. cb contains the length of the string. Each character-attribute entry consumes two or four bytes (depending on the mode). usRow contains the starting row to write (0 is at the top of the display). usColumn contains the starting column to write (0 is at the left side of the display). hvio contains a handle to the video buffer. VioWrtCellStr returns one of the following values: 0 NO_ERROR 355 ERROR_VIO_MODE 358 ERROR_VIO_ROW 359 ERROR_VIO_COL 436 ERROR_VIO_INVALID_HANDLE 465 ERROR_VIO_DETACHED
FAPI UShort VioWrtCharStr (pch, cb, usRow, usColumn, hvio)	The VioWrtCharStr function writes a string of characters to the screen starting at the specified location. The write always terminates at the end of the physical display even if the buffer is not exhausted. pch contains the address of the buffer used to store the string. cb contains length of the string. usRow contains the starting row to write (0 is at the top of the display). usColumn contains the starting column to write (0 is at the left side of the display). hvio contains a handle to the video buffer. VioWrtCharStr returns one of the following values: 0 NO_ERROR 355 ERROR_VIO_MODE 358 ERROR_VIO_ROW 359 ERROR_VIO_COL 436 ERROR_VIO_INVALID_HANDLE 465 ERROR_VIO_DETACHED
FAPI UShort VioWrtCharStrAtt (pch, cb, usRow,	The VioWrtCharStrAtt function writes a string of character string with a repeated attribute to the screen starting at the specified location. The write always terminates at the end of the physical cb, display even if the buffer is not exhausted. pch contains the address

Function	Description
usColumn, pAttr, hvio)	of the buffer used to store the string. cb contains the length of the string. usRow contains the starting row to write (0 is at the top of the display). usColumn contains the starting column to write (0 is at the left side of the display). pAttr contains the address of the buffer used to store the attribute for the string (either one or three bytes). hvio contains a handle to the video buffer. VioWrtCharStrAtt returns one of the following values:

0	NO_ERROR
355	ERROR_VIO_MODE
358	ERROR_VIO_ROW
359	ERROR_VIO_COL
436	ERROR_VIO_INVALID_HANDLE
465	ERROR_VIO_DETACHED

Function	Description
FAPI UShort VioWrtNAttr (pAttr, cb, usRow, usColumn, hvio)	The VioWrtNAttr function writes an attribute to the screen a specified number of times. The write always terminates at the end of the physical display even if the attribute does not appear the requested number of times. pAttr contains the address of the buffer used to store the attribute (either one or three bytes). cb contains the number of times to write the attribute. usRow contains the starting row to write (0 is at the top of the display). usColumn contains the starting column to write (0 is at the left side of the display). hvio contains a handle to the video buffer. VioWrtNAttr returns one of the following values:

0	NO_ERROR
355	ERROR_VIO_MODE
358	ERROR_VIO_ROW
359	ERROR_VIO_COL
436	ERROR_VIO_INVALID_HANDLE
465	ERROR_VIO_DETACHED

Function	Description
FAPI UShort VioWrtNCell (pCell, cb, usRow, usColumn, hvio)	The VioWrtNCell function writes a character-attribute pair to the screen a specified number of times. The write always terminates at the end of the physical display even if the character-attribute pair does not appear the requested number of times. pCell contains the address of the buffer used to store the character-attribute pair (either two or four bytes). cb contains the number of times to write the character-attribute pair. usRow contains the starting row to write (0 is at the top of the display). usColumn contains the starting column to write (0 is at the left side of the display). hvio contains a handle to the video buffer. VioWrtNCell returns one of the following values:

0	NO_ERROR
355	ERROR_VIO_MODE
358	ERROR_VIO_ROW
359	ERROR_VIO_COL
436	ERROR_VIO_INVALID_HANDLE
465	ERROR_VIO_DETACHED

Function	Description
FAPI UShort VioWrtNChar	The VioWrtNChar function writes a character to the screen a specified number of times. The write always terminates at the end of

Table 3-2   **Continued**

Function	Description
(pchChar, cb, usRow, usColumn, hvio)	the physical display even if the character does not appear the requested number of times. pchChar contains the address of the buffer used to store the character (either one or three bytes). cb contains the number of times to write the character. usRow contains the starting row to write (0 is at the top of the display). usColumn contains the starting column to write (0 is at the left side of the display). hvio contains a handle to the video buffer. VioWrtNChar returns one of the following values: 0 NO_ERROR 355 ERROR_VIO_MODE 358 ERROR_VIO_ROW 359 ERROR_VIO_COL 436 ERROR_VIO_INVALID_HANDLE 465 ERROR_VIO_DETACHED
FAPI UShort VioWrtTTY (pch, cb, hvio)	The VioWrtTTY function writes a string of characters to the screen starting at the current location. The write always continues, even if it is at the end of the physical display. OS/2 simply scrolls the display to accommodate the extra text. pch contains the address of the buffer used to store the string. cb contains length of the string. hvio contains a handle to the video buffer. VioWrtCharStr returns one of the following values: 0 NO_ERROR 355 ERROR_VIO_MODE 436 ERROR_VIO_INVALID_HANDLE 465 ERROR_VIO_DETACHED

NOTE IBM did not choose to document these functions after version 1.3 of OS/2 because they are machine specific and IBM plans to port OS/2 to other platforms. The current OS/2 implementation encourages the developer to write to the less machine-specific

You still can use all these functions within your current applications, but there is no guarantee that IBM will support them in future versions of OS/2. Use Presentation Manager specific functions whenever possible in your applications.

Some functions, like VioSetMode, require a mode number to work. The mode numbers for MDA, Hercules, CGA, and EGA adapters are standardized. VGA and SVGA adapters present a little more of a problem. Early VGA vendors had no standard to follow when they designed extensions to their display adapters. (IBM, the leader at the time, chose to make the 8514/A display its upgrade to the VGA.)

SVGA vendors faced the same problem. As a result, every display adapter used its own set of codes for extended modes and every programmer had to take these modes into account. The Video Electronics Standards Association (VESA) worked with vendors to correct this situation. While every display adapter still uses its own set of modes, some display adapters also come with support for the VESA supported modes. You usually need to load this support through one of the display drivers.

Table 3-3 provides a list of the modes commonly used with everything from CGA to SVGA displays. Notice that the table shows you the VESA specific display modes for the VGA and SVGA adapter types. Some vendors implement these same modes as 7-bit mode numbers accessed through standard BIOS calls.

Standard display adapter display modes   Table 3-3

Mode	Type	Colors	Resolution	Glyph Cell***
0h	Text	16	400 by 360 (25 by 40 characters)	9 by 16
1h	Text	16	400 by 360 (25 by 40 characters)	9 by 16
2h	Text	16	400 by 720	9 by 16
3h	Text	16	400 by 720	9 by 16
4h	Graphics	4	200 by 320 (25 by 40 characters)	8 by 8
5h	Graphics	4	200 by 320 (25 by 40 characters)	8 by 8
6h	Graphics	2	200 by 640	8 by 8
7h	Text	Mono	400 by 720	9 by 16
Dh	Graphics	16	200 by 320 (25 by 40 characters)	8 by 8
Eh	Graphics	16	200 by 640	8 by 8
Fh	Graphics	Mono	350 by 640	8 by 14
10h	Graphics	16	350 by 640	8 by 14
11h	Graphics	2	480 by 640	8 by 16
12h	Graphics	16	480 by 640	8 by 16
13h	Graphics	256	200 by 320	8 by 8

Table 3-3   **Continued**

Mode	Type	Colors	Resolution	Glyph Cell***
6AH*	Graphics	16	600 by 600	10 by 24
(100h*	Graphics	256	400 by 640	8 by 16
101h*	Graphics	256	480 by 640	8 by 16
102h*	Graphics	16	600 by 800	10 by 24
103h*	Graphics	256	600 by 800	10 by 24
104h*	Graphics	16	768 by 1024	12 by 30
105h*	Graphics	256	768 by 1024	12 by 30
106h*	Graphics	16	1024 by 1280	16 by 40
107h*	Graphics	256	1024 by 1280	16 by 40
108h**	Text	16	600 by 800 (80 by 60 characters)	10 by 10
109h**	Text	16	600 by 800 (132 by 25 characters)	6 by 24
10Ah**	Text	16	600 by 800 (132 by 43 characters)	6 by 14
10Bh**	Text	16	600 by 800 (132 by 50 characters)	6 by 12
10Ch**	Text	16	600 by 800 (132 by 60 characters)	6 by 10
10Dh**	Graphics	32K	200 by 320 (25 by 40 characters)	8 by 8
10Eh**	Graphics	64K	200 by 320 (25 by 40 characters)	8 by 8
10Fh**	Graphics	16.8M	200 by 320 (25 by 40 characters)	8 by 8
110h**	Graphics	32K	480 by 640	8 by 16
111h	Graphics	64K	480 by 640	8 by 16
112h	Graphics	16.8M	480 by 640	8 by 16
113h	Graphics	32K	600 by 800	10 by 24
114h	Graphics	64K	600 by 800	10 by 24
115h	Graphics	16.8M	600 by 800	10 by 24
116h	Graphics	32K	768 by 1024	12 by 30
117h	Graphics	64K	768 by 1024	12 by 30

Mode	Type	Colors	Resolution	Glyph Cell***
118h	Graphics	16.8M	768 by 1024	12 by 30
119h	Graphics	32K	1024 by 1280	16 by 40
11Ah	Graphics	64K	1024 by 1280	16 by 40
11Bh	Graphics	16.8M	1024 by 1280	16 by 40

* 15-bit mode numbers are based on VESA (Video Electronics Standards Association) standard VS891001 for Super VGA resolution. Not all manufacturers use the 15-bit sequence. Some Super VGA display adapters use a 7-bit mode from 14h-7Fh. Mode 6Ah is the only 7-bit Super VGA mode currently supported by the VESA standard. (See standard 800401 for more information on using the mode 6Ah extension.)

** 15-bit mode numbers are based on VESA (Video Electronics Standards Association) standard VS911022 for Super VGA resolution. There are no 7-bit extensions for the modes added by this standard. All extensions are 15-bit numbers. This standard does recognize the mode 6Ah extension of previous standards.

*** Glyph cell size is determined by an 80×25 character display unless otherwise stated. The resolution is always stated.

Some of the VIO functions will not work with advanced display adapters at all. The reason is simple, these adapters provide a host interface that makes their registers inaccessible to the standard OS/2 routines. For example, the standard OS/2 routines will not support mode changes (VioSetMode) with advanced adapters like the 8514/A and XGA. Nor can you use VioGetMode to determine the current adapter mode. Notice that, even though VioGetConfig does provide limited support for advanced display adapters, it does not provide everything you need. As a result, you must program and read the registers of these adapters directly.

Compare the VGA block diagram in Fig. 3-1 to those found in the TIGA, and XGA sections. A quick check makes it apparent that OS/2 cannot access these adapters without a lot more information that a device driver could provide. The VGA allows full access to the CRTC, the registers, and all BIOS extensions; the advanced adapters usually accomplish their tasks through a processor or coprocessor. This is the reason that you must access these adapters directly to obtain the full range of flexibility and programming options they provide. The following paragraphs provide everything you need to perform this task.

✳ **8514/A display adapter**   The 8415/A display adapter provides a host interface that you use to access the registers. This display adapter does not usually operate by itself. It requires the addition of a VGA to access lower-resolution compatibility modes.

Figure 3-1

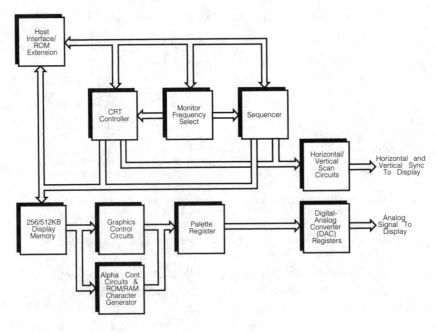

VGA block diagram.

Table 3-4 shows the display modes accessible with a system equipped with an 8514/A display adapter. You can use these modes in addition to the ones shown in Table 3-3.

Table 3-4

8514/A display modes

Mode[1]	Type	Colors	Resolution	Glyph Cell
14h	Graphics	16/256[1]	480 by 640	8 by 16
15h	Graphics	16/256[1]	768 by 1024	12 by 20
16h	Graphics	16/256[1]	768 by 1024	8 by 14
17h	Graphics	16/256[1]	768 by 1024	7 by 15

[1] Application Interface (AI) specific modes. Some 8514/A adapters support additional modes through the use of direct register programming.

As stated previously, the standard 8514/A AI consists of an OS/2 device driver. To access this program, use interrupt 7Fh after loading AX with the value 0105h. If successful, the CX:DX pair returns a segment and offset to the program entry table and the carry flag

equals 0. The table contains 59 segment offset pairs for the calls
listed in Table 3-5 in the order listed.

8514/A Application Interface (AI) commands

Table 3-5

Command	Number	Function
ABLOCKCGA	53	Writes a CGA-formatted alphanumeric character block.
ABLOCKMF1	52	Writes an alphanumeric character block.
ACURSOR	56	Sets the alphanumeric cursor position.
AERASE	54	Erases a character cell rectangle.
ASCROLL	55	Scrolls the character cell rectangle.
ASCUR	57	Sets the alphanumeric cursor shape.
ASFONT	58	Selects the alphanumeric character font.
AXLATE	59	Selects the alphanumeric attribute color index table.
HBAR	5	Begins a filled area.
HBBC	14	Performs Bit-BLT exclusively in display memory.
HBBCHN	13	Performs Bit-BLT to or from system memory.
HBBR	12	Defines the Bit-BLT source at an absolute address.
HBBW	10	Defines the Bit-BLT destination at an absolute address.
HCBBW	11	Defines the Bit-BLT destination at the current cursor position.
HCCHST	50	Places a text string at the current cursor position.
HCHST	49	Places a text string at an absolute position.
HCLINE	2	Draws an absolute polyline starting at the current cursor position.
HCLOSE	16	Closes the display adapter interface.
HCMRK	9	Draws a marker symbol at the current cursor position.
HEAR	6	Ends a filled area.
HEGS	26	Clears the screen.
HESC	37	Terminate adapter processing.
HINIT	20	Initializes the task-dependent state buffer.
HINT	22	Waits for the vertical retrace signal.
HLDPAL	29	Load a palette.
HLINE	1	Draws an absolute polyline starting at an absolute cursor position.
HMRK	8	Draws a marker symbol at an absolute position.

Table 3-5   **Continued**

Command	Number	Function
HOPEN	15	Opens the display adapter interface.
HQCOORD	35	Gets the coordinate types.
HQCP	18	Gets the current cursor position.
HQDFPAL	19	Get default palette information.
HQDPS	38	Gets drawing process buffer size.
HQMODE	24	Gets the display adapter mode.
HQMODES	25	Sees if a display adapter mode is available.
HRCLINE	4	Draws a relative polyline starting at the current cursor position.
HRECT	7	Draws a filled rectangle.
HRLINE	3	Draws a relative polyline starting at an absolute position.
HRLPC	33	Restores a saved line pattern position.
HRPAL	31	Restores a saved palette.
HSBCOL	45	Sets the background color.
HSBP	34	Sets the display and masking bitplane controls.
HSCMP	47	Sets the color comparison register.
HSCOL	44	Sets the foreground color.
HSCOORD	36	Sets the coordinate types.
HSCP	17	Moves the cursor to an absolute position.
HSCS	48	Selects a character set.
HSGQ	27	Sets the graphics quality/drawing styles.
HSHS	28	Clips a rectangle (scissors).
HSLPC	32	Saves the current line pattern position.
HSLT	42	Sets the current line type.
HSLW	43	Sets the current line width.
HSMARK	39	Sets the current marker shape.
HSMODE	23	Sets the display adapter mode.
HSMX	46	Sets the drawing raster operation (mix).
HSPAL	30	Save the current palette.
HSPATT	40	Sets the current pattern shape.
HSPATTO	41	Sets the current pattern origin.
HSYNC	21	Sets the adapter to a task-dependent state.
HXLATE	51	Assigns a color index table for text.

However, you can directly access the ports on an 8514/A adapter. VESA has adopted a standard set of register names, mnemonics, and addresses (standards VS890804 and VS900601) as listed in Table 3-6. (*Note*: The VS900601 standard also includes C header and assembler files that you can use while programming the 8514/A adapter.) As indicated in the table, some registers use the read-only attribute, while others use the read-write attribute. Because each vendor could provide different functionality for each register, you should refer to the vendor manual for a detailed description of the register functions. A generalized listing of register functions as listed in Chips and Technologies 82C480 Programmer's Spec (Rev 2.1) follows.

Standard 8514/A registers   Table 3-6

Port	Register name	Mnemonic	Type
0100*	Setup Mode Identification	SETUP_ID1	Read-Only
0101*	Setup Mode Identification	SETUP_ID2	Read-Only
0102*	Setup Mode Option	SETUP_OPT	Read-Write
02E8	Display Status	DISP_STAT	Read-Only
02E8	Horizontal Total	H_TOTAL	Write-Only
02EA	DAC Mask	DAC_MASK	Read-Write
02EB	DAC Read Index	DAC_R_INDEX	Read-Write
02EC	DAC Write Index	DAC_W_INDEX	Read-Write
02ED	DAC Data	DAC_DATA	Read-Write
06E8	Horizontal Displayed	H_DISP	Read-Write
0AE8	Horizontal Sync Start	H_SYNC_STRT	Read-Write
0EE8	Horizontal Sync Width	H_SYNC_WID	Read-Write
12E8	Vertical Total	V_TOTAL	Read-Write
16E8	Vertical Displayed	V_DISP	Read-Write
1AE8	Vertical Sync Start	V_SYNC_STRT	Read-Write
1EE8	Vertical Sync Width	V_SYNC_WID	Read-Write
22E8	Display Control	DISP_CNTL	Read-Write
42E8	Subsystem Status	SUBSYS_STAT	Read-Only
42E8	Subsystem Control	SUBSYS_CNTL	Write-Only

Table 3-6   **Continued**

Port	Register name	Mnemonic	Type
46E8	ROM Page Select	ROM_PAGE_SEL	Read-Write
4AE8	Advanced Function Control	ADVFUNC_CNTL	Read-Write
82E8	Current Y Position	CUR_Y	Read-Write
86E8	Current X Position	CUR_X	Read-Write
8AE8	Destination Y Position/ Axial Step Constant	DESTY_AXSTP	Read-Write
8EE8	Destination X Position/ Axial Step Constant	DESTX_AXSTP	Read-Write
92E8	Error Term	ERR_TERM	Read-Write
96E8	Major Axis Pixel Count	MAJ_AXIS_PCNT	Read-Write
9AE8	Graphics Processor Status	GP_STAT	Read-Only
9AE8	Command	CMD	Write-Only
9EE8	Short Stroke Vector Transfer	SHORT_STROKE	Read-Write
A2E8	Background Color	BKGD_COLOR	Read-Write
A6E8	Foreground Color	FRGD_COLOR	Read-Write
AAE8	Write Mask	WRT_MASK	Read-Write
AEE8	Read Mask	RD_MASK	Read-Write
B2E8	Color Compare	COLOR_CMP	Read-Write
B6E8	Background Mix	BKGD_MIX	Read-Write
BAE8	Foreground Mix	FRGD_MIX	Read-Write
BEE8	Multi-Function Control	MULTIFUNC_CNTL	N/A
BEE8 Index 0	Minor Axis Pixel Count	MIN_AXIS_PCNT	Read-Write
BEE8 Index 1	Top Scissors	SCISSORS_T	Read-Write
BEE8 Index 2	Left Scissors	SCISSORS_L	Read-Write
BEE8 Index 3	Bottom Scissors	SCISSORS_B	Read-Write
BEE8 Index 4	Right Scissors	SCISSORS_R	Read-Write
BEE8 Index 5	Memory Control	MEM_CNTL	Read-Write

Port	Register name	Mnemonic	Type
BEE8 Index 8	Fixed Pattern Low	PATTERN_L	Read-Write
BEE8 Index 9	Fixed Pattern High	PATTERN_H	Read-Write
BEE8 Index A	Pixel Control	PIX_CNTL	Read-Write
E2E8	Pixel Data Transfer	PIX_TRANS	Read-Write

* These register addresses do not appear in the VS900601 standard. They do appear in the VS890804 standard.

Ports 100h, 101h, and 102h are Micro Channel Architecture (MCA) specific. You can read, but not write, to ports 100h and 101h. They provide the POS ID for the installed card. The IBM 8514/A adapter returns a value of EF7Fh. Use this port to determine if the machine contains an 8514/A adapter. Port 102h enables or disables the 8514/A adapter. Placing a 1 in bit zero enables the card. You must set all other bits to zero.

Ports 2E8h, 6E8h, AE8h, EE8h, 12E8h, 16E8h, 1AE8h, and 1EE8h provide information about the vertical and horizontal sync parameters. Port 2E8h provides sync status when read. It sets the horizontal total register when written. The horizontal total equals the total length of the scan line including blanking. Horizontal total always begins with the first pixel of the scan line. Table 3-7 contains a complete bit listing for port 2E8h. Ports 6E8h, AE8h, and EE8h provide the means to read and write the remaining horizontal registers. These parameters include horizontal blank, horizontal sync, and horizontal sync pulse. Tables 3-8 through 3-10 provide bit information about these ports. Ports 12E8h, 16E8h, 1AE8h, and 1EE8h provide read and write capability for all vertical registers. These registers include vertical total, vertical displayed, vertical sync start, and vertical sync width. Tables 3-11 through 3-14 provide bit information about these ports.

Sync status and horizontal total (Port 02E8h)   Table 3-7

Bit Function

Read - Sync Status

0   Video Sense
       0 - No Monitor Attached

Table 3-7   **Continued**

Bit	Function
1	Monitor Attached
1	Horizontal Sync - End of Scan Line
2	Vertical Sync - Start of Vertical Retrace
3–15	Not Used

Write - Horizontal Total

Bit	Function
0–7	Horizontal Total - Total Scan Line Width
8–15	Not Used

Table 3-8   **Horizontal displayed (Port 6E+8h)**

Bit	Function
0–7	Horizontal Blank - Start of Blank Pulse
8–15	Not Used

Table 3-9   **Horizontal sync start (Port AE8h)**

Bit	Function
0–7	Horizontal Sync Start
8–15	Not Used

Table 3-10   **Horizontal sync width (Port EE8h)**

Bit	Function
0–4	Horizontal Sync Width
5	Horizontal Sync Polarity 1 - Negative 0 - Positive
6–15	Not Used

Vertical total (Port 12E8h)

Table 3-11

Bit	Function
1–11	Vertical Total - The total number of half scan lines in the frame.
12–15	Not Used

Vertical displayed (Port 16E8h)

Table 3-12

Bit	Function
1–11	Vertical Blank - The starting position of the vertical blank pulse in half scan lines.
12–15	Not Used

Vertical sync start (Port 1AE8h)

Table 3-13

Bit	Function
1–11	Vertical Sync Pulse
12–15	Not Used

Vertical sync width (Port 1EE8h)

Table 3-14

Bit	Function
1–4	Vertical Sync Width
5	Vertical Sync Polarity 1 - Negative 0 - Positive
6–15	Not Used

The DAC register set includes ports 2EAh, 2EBh, 2ECh, and 2EDh. These registers include: DAC Mask, DAC Read Index, DAC Write Index, and DAC Data. All four registers contain eight bits of information. The 8514/A ANDs the bit stream with the contents DAC Mask register before sending them to the palette. This allows you to remove one or more bit planes from the data stream prior to display. The DAC Read Index addresses data at a specific address for the host.

Use this register in combination with the DAC Data register (port 2EDh) to read a palette location. The DAC Write Index addresses a specific palette location for writing. The host uses the DAC Data register to place information at the specified palette location.

The control register set consists of ports 22E8h, 42E8h, 46E8h, 4AE8h, and 9AE8h. This includes the Display Control, Subsystem Status, Subsystem Control, ROM Page Select, Advanced Function Control, Graphics Processor Status, and Command registers. Each register controls a different area of 8514/A operation. Tables 3-15 through 3-19 describe the display elements controlled by each register. Note that you can read the Subsystem Status and Graphics Processor Status registers. The Subsystem Control and Command registers are write-only.

Table 3-15 | **Display control register (Port 22E8h)**

Bit	Function
0	Nugget Phase Enable (Not used on some 8514/A implementations.)
1–2	Pre-Scaler Bits 00 - Divide NCLK by 2 (Pseudo 8-Plane Mode) 01 - Divide NCLK by 4 (Standard 8514/A) 10 - Divide NCLK by 6 (Not Used) 11 - Divide NCLK by 8 (Not Used)
3	Double Scan Select 1 - Display each scan line once (normal). 0 - Display each scan line twice.
4	Interlaced Sync Select 1 - Interlaced Sync 0 - Non-Interlaced Sync
5–6	Display Enable 11 - Disable HSYNC, VSYNC, and BLANK* 10 - Disable HSYNC, VSYNC, and BLANK* 01 - Enable HSYNC, VSYNC, and BLANK* 00 - Not Used
7–15	Not Used

* Not Function (Setting bit disables input or output.)

Subsystem status/control register (Port 42E8h)   Table 3-16

Bit	Function

Read - Subsystem Status

0–3   IRQ - Interrupt Request (Determines state of interrupt request lines.)
1XXX - Idle. The 8514/A is idle and waiting for input. This bit provides the same information as the BSY bit of the Queue Status Register.
X1XX - Queue Overflow/Underflow. The host attempted to write to a full write queue or read from an empty read queue.
XX1X - Inside Scissor Rectangle. The 8514/A drew current object within an area bounded by a scissor rectangle. You can use this bit to determine when two objects coincide.
XXX1 - Vertical Blanking Active. Shows when it is safe to send data to the 8514/A for display.

4–6   Monitor Sense - Determines type monitor attached to 8514/A.
000 - Reserved
001 - 8507 (1024 X 768 Interlaced Monochrome)
010 - 8514 (1024 X 768 Interlaced Color)
011 - Reserved
100 - Reserved
101 - 8503 (640 X 480 Non-Interlaced Monochrome)
110 - 8512/8513 (640 X 480 Non-Interlaced Color)
111 - Reserved

7   8-Bit Plane Select (8BP)
0 - 4 Bit Planes
1 - 8 Bit Planes

8–15   Not Used

Write - Subsystem Control

0–3   IRQ Clear - Interrupt Request (Write 1 to clear flag.)
1XXX - Idle.
X1XX - Queue Overflow/Underflow.
XX1X - Inside Scissor Rectangle.
XXX1 - Vertical Blanking Active.

8–11   IRQ Enable - Interrupt Request (Write 1 to enable flag.)
1XXX - Idle.
X1XX - Queue Overflow/Underflow.
XX1X - Inside Scissor Rectangle.
XXX1 - Vertical Blanking Active.

12–13   Memory Controller Disable
00 - No Effect
01 - Enable synchronization with memory controller chip.
10 - Disable synchronization from memory controller chip. (8514/A does not operate correctly.)

Table 3-16   **Continued**

Bit	Function
	11 - Disable synchronization from memory controller chip. (8514/A does not operate correctly.)
14–15	Graphics Processor Reset 00 - No Effect 01 - Enable Chip 10 - Reset Chip$$ 11 - Reset Chip

Table 3-17   **ROM Page select register (Port 46#8h)**

Bit	Function
0–2	ROM Page Number - Remaps one of eight 4 KByte ROM pages into the address area from C0000h - C5FFFh.
3–15	Not Used

Table 3-18   **Advanced function control register (Port 4AE8h)**

Bit	Function
0	Advanced Function Mode Select 0 - VGA drives video connector. 1 - 8514/A drives video connector.
1	Not Used
2–4	Clock Select - Not Used, Set To 0
5–7	Not Used

Table 3-19   **Graphics processor status/command**
registers (Port 9EE8h)

Bit	Function
	Read - Graphics Processor Status Register
0–7	Queue Full Status 00000000 - 8 Words Available (Queue Empty) 00000001 - 7 Words Available 00000011 - 6 Words Available 00000111 - 5 Words Available 00001111 - 4 Words Available

Bit	Function

00011111 - 3 Words Available
00111111 - 2 Words Available
01111111 - 1 Words Available
11111111 - 0 Words Available (Queue Full)

8   Variable Data Ready
0 - Data Not Ready
1 - Data Ready to Read from Data Register

9   Busy
0 - 8514/A Not Busy
1 - 8514/A Executing a Drawing Command

10–15   Not Used

Write - Command Register

0   Pixel Write Operation
0 - Write disabled. Rectangle commands copy rectangular blocks from bitmap to system memory.
1 - Write enabled. Rectangle commands copy rectangular blocks from system memory to bitmap.

1   Across Planes
0 - Through Plane Mode
1 - Across Plane Mode

2   Last Pixel Null
0 - 8514/A draws last pixel for line and SVV commands.
1 - 8514/A moves current position pointer without drawing pixel. Use this with commands that produce the wrong pixel color on the last pixel of a row. For example, XOR.

3   Short Stroke Enable
0 - Short stroke vectors not enabled.
1 - Short stroke vectors enabled. 8514/A draws contents of SSV register after each data write.

4   Marking Enable
0 - Marking disabled for line and BITBLTS (bit block transfers). 8514/A moves current position without changing pixels.
1 - Marking enabled.

5   Increment X Positive
0 - 8514/A draws lines in X negative direction (right).
1 - 8514/A draws lines in X positive direction (left).

6   Y Major Axis
0 - X is major (independent) axis for Bresenham algorithm.
1 - Y is major (independent) axis for Bresenham algorithm.

7   Increment Y Positive
0 - 8514/A draws lines in Y negative direction (up).
1 - 8514/A draws lines in Y positive direction (down).

Table 3-19   **Continued**

Bit	Function
8	Variable Data Enable 0 - 8514/A draws normally. 1 - 8514/A waits for read/write of variable data from host.
9	16-bit Operation (16B) 0 - SSV and VAR are accessed as 8-bit registers. 1 - SSV and VAR are accessed as 16-bit registers.
10	Read Byte Swap (RBS) - 8514/A reads bytes in opposite order written. RBS & 16B = 0 - No Swap RBS & 16B = 1 - Swap
11	Always set to zero.
12	Byte Order (Does not affect 16-bit registers.) 0 - Read high byte first. 1 - Read low byte first.
13–15	Draw Command 000 - No Operation 001 - Line 010 - Fill rectangle in X direction. 011 - Fill rectangle in Y direction. 100 - Fast filled rectangle. 101 - Outline 110 - Copy Rectangle 111 - Illegal (Generates error IRQ.)

The graphics register set includes position, status, and control registers. The position registers consist of Current X Position (port 82E8h), Current Y Position (port 86E8h), Destination X Position (port 8AE8h), and Destination Y Position (port 8EE8h). Each of these ports contain a number representing the start and finish of a graphics operation. The Y Position register contains a 10-bit number; all other registers contain 11-bit numbers.

The status registers consist of Error Term (port 92E8h) and Major Axis Pixel Count (port 96E8h). The Error Term register contains a 12-bit number used as a constant for the Bresenham algorithm. The host must place a number equal to $2 \times dy - dx$ in the register before starting the algorithm. The 8514/A automatically updates the register as it draws. The Major Axis Pixel Count register contains a 10-bit number. The 8514/A uses this number for CopyRect commands and as the constant dx term for the Bresenham algorithm. You must use a positive number for dx. The 8514/A automatically updates this register.

Finally, the control registers consist of Short Stroke Vector Transfer, Background Color, Foreground Color, Write Mask, Read Mask, Color Compare, Background Mix, Foreground Mix, Multi-Function Control, and Pixel Data Transfer. Table 3-20 contains a bit description of the Short Stroke Vector Transfer Register (port 9EE8h). Notice that you can write two SSVs at once in 16-bit mode. The Background Color (port A2E8h) and Foreground Color (port A6E8h) registers contain 8-bit numbers. The 8514/A uses the contents of the Background Color register for writing pixels if you select Foreground Color Mix and FSS=00 or select the Background Color Mix and BSS=00. Likewise, it uses the contents of the Foreground Color register for writing pixels if you select the Foreground Color Mix and FSS=01 or select the Background Color Mix and BSS=01. The Write Mask register (port AAE8h) contains 8 bits—one for each plane. Placing a 1 in a bit allows writing to that plane's bit. Bit 0 corresponds to plane 0.

Short stroke vector (SSV) transfer register (Port 9EE8h)　　　　Table 3-20

Bit	Function
0–3	Length - The number of pixels that the 8514/A moves the Current Position pointer. If length contains 0, the 8514/A does not change Current Position.
4	Mark Pixels 0 - Move Current Position, but do not mark vector. 1 - Mark Pixels
5–7	Direction 000 -　　0° 001 -　　45° 010 -　　90° 011 -　135° 100 -　180° 101 -　225° 110 -　270° 111 -　315°
8–11	Length - The number of pixels that the 8514/A moves the Current Position pointer. If length contains 0, the 8514/A does not change Current Position.
12	Mark Pixels 0 - Move Current Position, but do not mark vector. 1 - Mark Pixels
13–15	Direction 000 -　　0° 001 -　　45° 010 -　　90°

Table 3-20   **Continued**

Bit   Function
011 - 135°
100 - 180°
101 - 225°
110 - 270°
111 - 315°

The Read Mask register (port AEE8h) contains 8 bits, one for each
plane. Placing a 0 in a bit allows reading of the selected plane's bit. Bit
0 corresponds to plane 0. The Color Compare register (port B2E8h)
contains an 8-bit color number. The 8514/A compares the value of
this color to the value of the destination during BITBLT operations. If
the comparison is true, the CPU changes the destination. The
comparison can use any type of equality including greater-than and
less-than. The 8514/A uses the contents of bits 3, 4, and 5 of the
Pixel Control register (port BEE8 index A) to control the comparison
type. The 8514/A uses the contents of the Background Mix (port
B6E8h) and Foreground Mix (port BAE8h) registers to control display
color during drawing operations. This includes selection of both the
mix color source and mix method. The Pixel Control register controls
the selection of either the Foreground Mix or Background Mix register.
Tables 3-21 and 3-22 describe these two registers.

Table 3-21   **Background mix register (Port B6E8h)**

Bit   Function
0–5   Mix Method
00000 - ~DST
00001 - 0 (Destination always false.)
00010 - 1 (Destination always true.)
00011 - DST
00100 - ~SRC
00101 - SRC ^ DST
00110 - ~ (SRC ^ DST)
00111 - SRC
01000 - ~ (SRC * DST)
01001 - ~ (SRC * ~DST)
01010 - ~ (~SRC * DST)
01011 - ~ (~SRC * ~DST)
01100 - SRC * DST
01101 - SRC * ~DST
01110 - ~SRC * DST

Bit   Function

01111 - ~SRC * ~DST
10000 - min(SRC,DST)
10001 - DST – SRC (With Underflow)
10010 - SRC – DST (With Underflow)
10011 - SRC + DST (With Overflow)
10100 - max(SRC,DST)
10101 - (DST – SRC)/2 (With Underflow)
10110 - (SRC – DST)/2 (With Underflow)
10111 - (SRC + DST)/2 (With Overflow)
11000 - DST – SRC (With Saturate)
11001 - DST – SRC (With Saturate)
11010 - SRC – DST (With Saturate)
11011 - SRC + DST (With Saturate)
11100 - (DST – SRC)/2 (With Saturate)
11101 - (DST – SRC)/2 (With Saturate)
11110 - (SRC – DST)/2 (With Saturate)
11111 - (SRC + DST)/2 (With Saturate)

5–7   Background Source Select
00 - Background Color Register Contents
01 - Foreground Color Register Contents
10 - Variable Data
11 - Bitmap Data

Legend:

DST	Destination
SRC	Source
~	Not
^	XOR
*	And
+	Numeric Addition
–	Numeric Subtraction
/	Integer Division

Foreground mix register (Port BAE8h)   Table 3-22

Bit   Function

0–5   Mix Method
00000 - ~DST
00001 - 0 (Destination always false.)
00010 - 1 (Destination always true.)
00011 - DST
00100 - ~SRC
00101 - SRC ^ DST
00110 - ~ (SRC ^ DST)

155

Table 3-22   **Continued**

Bit	Function
	00111 - SRC
	01000 - ~ (SRC * DST)
	01001 - ~ (SRC * ~DST)
	01010 - ~ (~SRC * DST)
	01011 - ~ (~SRC * ~DST)
	01100 - SRC * DST
	01101 - SRC * ~DST
	01110 - ~SRC * DST
	01111 - ~SRC * ~DST
	10000 - min(SRC,DST)
	10001 - DST – SRC (With Underflow)
	10010 - SRC – DST (With Underflow)
	10011 - SRC + DST (With Overflow)
	10100 - max(SRC,DST)
	10101 - (DST – SRC)/2 (With Underflow)
	10110 - (SRC – DST)/2 (With Underflow)
	10111 - (SRC + DST)/2 (With Overflow)
	11000 - DST – SRC (With Saturate)
	11001 - DST – SRC (With Saturate)
	11010 - SRC – DST (With Saturate)
	11011 - SRC + DST (With Saturate)
	11100 - (DST – SRC)/2 (With Saturate)
	11101 - (DST – SRC)/2 (With Saturate)
	11110 - (SRC – DST)/2 (With Saturate)
	11111 - (SRC + DST)/2 (With Saturate)
5–7	Foreground Source Select
	00 - Background Color Register Contents
	01 - Foreground Color Register Contents
	10 - Variable Data
	11 - Bitmap Data

Legend:

DST	Destination
SRC	Source
~	Not
^	XOR
*	And
+	Numeric Addition
–	Numeric Subtraction
/	Integer Division

The Multi-Function Control register (port BEE8h) provides multiple services. You access each service by using an index number as part of the input. In all cases, bits 12 through 15 contain the index number.

Index 0 accesses the Minor Axis Pixel Count register. This register contains an 11-bit number that determines the rectangular height for BITBLTs. The next four indexes (1 through 4) control the scissors registers. The Top Scissors register (index 1) determines the upper limit of the boundary. The Left Scissors register (index 2) determines the minimum X limit of the boundary. The Bottom Scissors register (index 3) determines the lower limit of the boundary. Finally, the Right Scissors register (index 4) determines the maximum (right) X limit of the boundary. Each register contains a 12-bit number. Each time the 8514/A draws an object within the boundary described by these four registers, it outputs an interrupt (when enabled). The Memory Control register (index 5) determines the physical configuration of memory on the adapter. Table 3-23 describes the bit contents of this register. The Pattern X and Pattern Y registers (index 8 and 9) mix colors on a pixel-by-pixel basis. The Pattern X register contains the mix for even-numbered nuggets (four bits per plane) and the Pattern Y register contains the mix for odd numbered nuggets. Each register uses bits 1 through 4 to provide the mix pattern. Bit 4 controls pixel 0. The Pixel Control register (index A) determines the color mix modes and methods logic. Table 3-24 describes each bit in this register.

Memory control register (Port BEE8h Index 5) Table 3-23

Bit	Function
0	Not Used
1	X Coordinate Divisor - Determines the memory bank interleave factor in a horizontal direction. 0 - 1 Bank, No Interleave 1 - 2 Horizontally Interleaved Banks (Normal)
2–3	Y Coordinate Divisor - Determines the memory bank interleave factor in a vertical direction. 00 - 2 banks of 256 Kbyte VRAM. Extended modes, no pseudo 8-plane mode. 01 - 4 banks of 256 Kbyte or 1 bank of 1 Mbyte VRAM. 8514/A compatible modes. 10 - 2 banks of 1 Mbyte VRAM. Extended modes. 11 - 4 banks of 1 Mbyte VRAM. Extended modes.
4	SWP - Active in Pseudo 8 Plane Mode (Always Set to 0 When Not in Use.) 0 - Select buffer number zero, lower four planes. 1 - Select buffer number one, upper four planes.
5–11	Not Used
12–15	Index - Always Equals 5

Table 3-24   **Pixel control register (Port BEE8h Indesx Ah)**

Bit	Function
0	Not Used
1	MOD1 0 - Normal Operation 1 - Disables mixes. Opposite polarity of MOD2.
2	MOD2 0 - Normal Operation 1 - Disables mixes and prevents VRAM RMW cycles if bits 3 through 5 equal zero.
3–5	Color Comparison 000 - Always False 001 - Always True 010 - DST >= CCMP 011 - DST < CCMP 100 - DST = CCMP 101 - DST = CCMP 110 - DST <= CCMP 111 - DST > CCMP
6–7	Foreground Select 00 - Foreground Mix register is always used. 01 - PATX and PATY select mix (1 equals Foreground Mix register). 10 - Variable data selects mix (1 equals Foreground Mix register). 11 - SRC selects mix (used to implement transparency).
8–11	Not Used
12–15	Index - Always Equals 10

Legend:

DST	Destination
SRC	Source
CCMP	Color Comparison

✳ TMS340*x*0 Graphics System Processor (GSP)

TMS340*x*0 Graphics System Processor (GSP) programming requires three pieces of information. First, the programmer must know the memory mapping used by the interface software/ROM to provide access to the GSP. Second, the programmer must know how to use the registers provided by the GSP to manipulate data in program and display memory. Some vendor boards do not allow direct access to either memory area. To read or write host data, you first must program the register set, then use processor commands to initiate the transfer. Third, the programmer must know the GSP instruction set.

Refer to the vendor manual for your GSP to obtain the addresses of
various GSP components. You can eliminate this requirement by
using the TIGA interface. The following paragraphs describe both the
GSP registers and instruction set. Figure 3-2 shows a typical
TMS34010 implementation. Notice that the block diagram looks
similar to the other display implementations. The big difference is the
graphics processor provided with this setup. The programmability of
the GSP adds to the functionality provided by this system. The
block diagram shows a generalized version of a typical GSP
implementation. Most manufacturers deviate from this basic design.

Figure 3-2

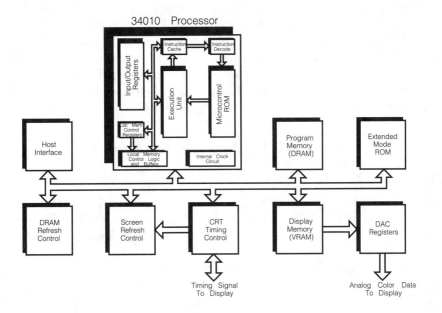

Typical 30410 block diagram.

The TMS340x0 GSP contains four sets of registers: general-purpose,
special-purpose, input/output, and memory-control. Each register set
performs a specific task and contains more than one register. The
general-purpose registers work with the execution unit to manipulate
data. The special-purpose registers contain CPU execution flags and
settings. The input/output registers provide an interface between the
GSP, host, and external display related devices. The memory-control

registers affect the internal memory operations of the GSP. The following paragraphs describe the registers in detail.

The general-purpose registers consist of two banks of 15 registers (30 total registers). You refer to the first bank as Register File A and the second bank as Register File B. The GSP does not use Register File A for any special purpose. Therefore, you can use Register File A to store any semi-permanent variables. The GSP does use Register File B for special purposes. This includes PIXBLT and line drawing operations. Table 3-25 describes the special uses for Register File B. Always load Register File B with the required information before executing a line drawing or PIXBLT operation. When not in use, Register File B reacts exactly like Register File A. In addition to standard registers, each register file contains a stack pointer (SP). The 340x0 locks the two stack pointers together, meaning that the GSP provides one physical SP. The reason that each register file contains a reference to SP is to reduce the number of clock cycles required to perform a task. You can use SP like any other general register.

Table 3-25   **TMS34010 register file B functions**

Register	Function
B0	Source Address (SADDR) - Contains a linear or XY address describing the upper left corner (lower address in array) of the source pixel array.
B1	Source Pitch (SPTCH) - The distance between adjacent rows of the source pixel array.
B2	Destination Address (DADDR) - Contains a linear or XY address describing the upper left corner (lower address in array) of the destination pixel array.
B3	Destination Pitch (DPTCH) - The distance between adjacent rows of the destination pixel array.
B4	Offset (OFFSET) - Linear address of the XY coordinate origin (X = 0, Y = 0). The GSP uses this address during XY to linear address conversions.
B5	Window Start Address (WSTART) - An address describing the upper left corner (lowest address) of the window area.
B6	Window End Address (WEND) - An address describing the lower right corner (highest address) of the window area.
B7	Delta X/Delta Y (DYDX) - Two 16-bit numbers describing the width (DX) and height (DY) of the destination array. The MSB holds DY, while the LSB holds DX.
B8	Color 0 (COLOR0) - The 16 MSB bits contain the background color used for

Register   Function

fill, color expand, or draw and advance operations. The 16 LSB bits contain all ones or a pattern of ones and zeros for dithered output. The 34010 ignores the 16 MSB bits during color expand operations.

B9 | Color 1 (COLOR1) - The 16 MSB bits contain the foreground color used for fill, color expand, or draw and advance operations. The 16 LSB bits contain all ones or a pattern of ones and zeros for dithered output. The 34010 ignores the 16 MSB bits during color expand operations.

B10–B14 (PIXBLT) | Temporary Storage (TEMP) - Contain temporary information during PIXBLT operations.

B10 (Line Draw) | Count (COUNT) - Contains the number of pixels drawing during a line draw operation.

B11 (Line Draw) | Increment 1 (INC1) - Contains the X and Y values for a diagonal step.

B12 (Line Draw) | Increment 2 (INC2) - Contains the X and Y values for a non-diagonal step.

B13 (Line Draw) | Pattern (PATTRN) - Future Expansion. Always set this register to 0FFFFFFFFh (all ones) before performing a line draw operation. Failure to do so will result in software compatibility problems.

SP | Stack Pointer - Points to the top (lowest address) of the stack.

There are three special-purpose registers: status, program counter, and instruction cache. Each special-purpose register is 32 bits long. The status register (ST) contains information about CPU status. Table 3-26 describes the status information contained in this register. The program counter (PC) points to the next instruction in the execution sequence. The GSP aligns all instructions on 16-bit boundaries. Therefore, the four LSB bits of this register always contain 0. An instruction can consist of more than one instruction word. As the GSP retrieves each instruction word, it automatically updates PC. There are occasions when the GSP replaces the contents of PC with another value. Table 3-27 describes each occurrence.

34010 status register

Table 3-26

Bit   Function

0–4 | Field Size 0 (FS0) - Length of the first data field in bits. A field size of 00001b corresponds to a 1-bit field length. A field size of 11111b corresponds to a 31-bit field length. A field size of 00000b corresponds to the maximum field length of 32 bits.

Table 3-26   **Continued**

Bit	Function
5	Field Extend 0 (FE0) - Determines method of extending field 0 when loaded into a 32-bit register. 0 - Zero extend field. 1 - Sign extend field.
6–10	Field Size 1 (FS1) - Length of the second data field in bits. A field size of 00001b corresponds to a 1-bit field length. A field size of 11111b corresponds to a 31-bit field length. A field size of 00000b corresponds to the maximum field length of 32 bits.
11	Field Extend 1 (FE1) - Determines method of extending field 1 when loaded into a 32-bit register. 0 - Zero extend field. 1 - Sign extend field.
12–20	Not Used
21	Interrupt Enable (IE) 0 - Disables all maskable interrupts. 1 - Enables all maskable interrupts.
22–24	Not Used
25	PIXBLT Executing (PBX) - Indicates if an interrupt occurred in the middle of a PIXBLT or FILL instruction. 0 - Interrupt occurred at PIXBLT or FILL instruction boundary. 1 - Interrupt occurred in the middle of a PIXBLT or FILL instruction.
26–27	Not Used
28	Overflow Flag (V) - Set according to instruction execution parameters.
29	Zero Flag (Z) - Set according to instruction execution parameters.
30	Carry Flag (C) - Set according to instruction execution parameters.
31	Negative Flag (N) - Set according to instruction execution parameters.

Table 3-27   **34010 program counter replace values**

Type	GSP Replace Value
Standard Instructions (Non-Branch)	GSP increments PC by 16 (10h) after each instruction word retrieval. Execution proceeds with the next instruction in sequence.
Absolute Branch To Instruction Address (TRAP, CALL, JAxx)	GSP loads specified address (instruction word contents after instruction). It automatically zeros four LSB bits. Execution proceeds with instruction pointed to by PC.

Type	GSP Replace Value
Relative Branch To Instruction Address (JRxx, DSJxx)	GSP shifts instruction offset by four bits to zero four LSB bits. It adds the offset to PC. Execution proceeds with instruction pointed to by PC.
Indirect Branch To Register Address (JUMP, EXGPC)	GSP loads PC with register contents. It automatically zeros four LSB bits. Execution proceeds with instruction pointed to by PC.

The instruction cache is 256 bytes long. It contains four segments. Each segment provides access to 64 bytes of cache memory. The segments are further broken down into 8 subsegments (also called data registers). Each subsegment contains 8 bytes (four 16-bit words) of code or data. The GSP aligns each segment on an even 32-bit word boundary. It addresses each word within the segment, as shown in Table 3-28. The GSP provides access to the cache register pointed to by PC. A program cannot read the contents of any of the other cache registers.

34010 instruction cache segment start address (SSA) format

Table 3-28

Bit	Contents/Value
0–3	Always set to zero.
4–5	Instruction word address within subsegment. 00 - First Word 01 - Second Word 10 - Third Word 11 - Fourth Word
6–8	Subsegment address within segment. 000 - Subsegment 1 001 - Subsegment 2 010 - Subsegment 3 011 - Subsegment 4 100 - Subsegment 5 101 - Subsegment 6 110 - Subsegment 7 111 - Subsegment 8
9–31	Segment Start Address (SSA). Corresponds to segment address in main memory.

The instruction cache uses a least-recently used algorithm to replace the contents of the cache. Each time the GSP requests a segment not currently in memory, the cache controller fetches a new 64-byte

segment from main memory. It replaces the least-recently used segment with the new segment contents.

The input/output register affects most display parameters used by the 340x0. Both the host and 340x0 can access the input/output register. There are 28 different input/output registers. As shown in Table 3-29, a program can access a register by name or address. The host accesses the registers through the host interface registers. It does this by loading the input/output register address in HSTADRL and HSTADRH registers. It then reads or writes the contents of the HSTDATA register. These registers occupy the address range from C0000000h to C00001FFh.

Table 3-29   **34010 input/output registers**

Address	Register	Function
C0000170h–C00001A0h	RESERVED	These register addresses reserved for future expansion.
Host Interface Registers		
C00000C0h	HSTDATA	Host Interface Data - A buffer used to transfer data between the host and the 34010 local memory.
C00000D0h	HSTADRL	Host Interface Address Low Word - This register contains the 16 LSB bits of the local memory address accessed by the host computer. Local memory addresses include register addresses.
C00000E0h	HSTADRH	Host Interface Address High Word - This register contains the 16 MSB bits of the local memory address accessed by the host computer. Local memory addresses include register addresses.
C00000F0h	HSTCTLL	Host Interface Control Low Byte - Controls host interface functions as shown below.

Bit	Function
0–2	Input Message Buffer (MSGIN)
3	Input Interrupt Bit (INTIN)
4–6	Output Message Buffer (MSGOUT)
7	Output Interrupt Bit (INTOUT)
8–15	Reserved

Address	Register	Function
C0000100h	HSTCTLH	Host Interface Control High Byte - Controls host interface functions as shown below.

Address	Register	Function

Bit Function

0–7 Reserved
8 Nonmaskable Interrupt (NMI)
9 NMI Mode Bit
10 Reserved
11 Increment Pointer Address on Write (INCW)
12 Increment Pointer Address on Read (INCR)
13 Lower Byte Last (LBL)
14 Cache Flust (CF)
15 Halt 34010 Execution (HLT)

Local Memory Interface Registers

C00000B0h CONTROL Memory Control - Controls local memory interface operations as shown below.

Bit Function

0–1 Reserved
2 DRAM Refresh Mode (RM)
3–4 DRAM Refresh Rate (RR)
5 Transparency Enable (T)
6–7 Window Violation Detection Mode (W)
8 PIXBLT Horizontal Direction (PBH)
9 PIXBLT Vertical Direction (PBV)
10–14 Pixel Processing Operation Select (PPOP)
15 Cache Disable (CD)

C0000130h CONVSP Source Pitch Conversion Factor - Used by 34010 during XY to linear conversion of a source memory address.

C0000140h CONVDP Destination Pitch Conversion Factor - Used by 34010 during XY/linear conversion of a memory address.

C0000150h PSIZE Pixel Size Register - Specifies the pixel size in bits. Possible sizes include 1, 2, 4, 8, and 16 bits (2, 4, 16, 256, and 65,536 colors).

C0000160h PMASK Plane Mask Register - Enables/disables bits in the bit map plane. For example, setting bit 0 to 1 enables bit plane 0.

C00001F0h REFCNT Refresh Count Register - Generates the addresses output during DRAM refresh cycles and counts delay between next refresh cycles.

Bit Function

0–1 Reserved
2–7 Refresh Interval Counter (RINTVL)
8–15 Row Address (ROWADR)

Table 3-29 | **Continued**

Address	Register	Function
Interrupt Control Registers		
C0000110h	INTENB	Interrupt Enable - Selectively enables or disables three internal and two external interrupts as shown below.

Bit	Function
0	Reserved
1	External Interrupt 1 Enable (X1E)
2	External Interrupt 2 Enable (X2E)
3–8	Reserved
9	Host Interrupt Pending (HIP)
10	Display Interrupt Pending (DIP)
11	Window Violation Interrupt Pending (WVP)
12–15	Reserved

Address	Register	Function
C0000120h	INTPEND	Interrupt Pending - Shows which interrupts are pending using the same bit mask as INTENB.
Video Timing and Refresh Registers		
C0000000h	HESYNC	Horizontal End Sync - Contains the ending value of the horizontal sync interval.
C0000010h	HEBLNK	Horizontal End Blank - Contains the ending value of the horizontal blank interval.
C0000020h	HSBLNK	Horizontal Start Blank - Contains the starting value of the horizontal blank interval.
C0000030h	HTOTAL	Horizontal Total - Contains the total value of the horizontal scan line in VCLK periods.
C0000040h	VESYNC	Vertical End Sync - Contains the ending value of the vertical sync interval.
C0000050h	VEBLNK	Vertical End Blank - Contains the ending value of the vertical blank interval.
C0000060h	VSBLNK	Vertical Start Blank - Contains the starting value of the vertical blank interval.
C0000070h	VTOTAL	Vertical Total - Contains the total value of the vertical scan line in VCLK periods.
C0000080h	DPYCTL	Display Control - Controls several video timing signal values as shown below.

Bit	Function
0	Horizontal Sync Direction (HSD)
1	Reserved
2–9	Display Address Update (DUDATE)
10	Screen Origin Select (ORG)

Address	Register	Function

		Bit	**Function**
		11	VRAM Serial Register Transfer Enable (SRT)
		12	Screen Refresh Enable (SRE)
		13	Disable External Video (DXV)
		14	Noninterlaced Video Enable (NIL)
		15	Enable Video (ENV)

Address	Register	Function
C0000090h	DPYSTRT	Display Start Address - Controls the automatic memory-to-register cycles required to refresh a screen as shown below.

		Bit	**Function**
		0–1	Specifies the number of scan lines displayed between refresh cycles. (LCSTRT)
		2–15	Starting Screen-Refresh Address. (SRSTRT)

Address	Register	Function
C00000A0h	DPYINT	Display Interrupt - Contains the number of the next scan line which causes a display interrupt request.
C00001B0h	DPYTAP	Display Tap Point Address - Used during shift register transfer cycles. Contains a VRAM tap point address.
C00001C0h	HCOUNT	Horizontal Count - Contains the number of VCLK cycles per horizontal scan line.
C00001D0h	VCOUNT	Vertical Count - Contains the number of horizontal scan lines in a display.
C00001E0h	DPYADR	Display Address - Counts the number of scan lines output between screen refresh cycles. Also contains the source of the row and column addresses output during a screen refresh cycle as shown below.

		Bit	**Function**
		0-1	Scan Line Counter (LNCNT)
		2–15	Screen Refresh Address (SRFADR)

Each of the registers shown in Table 3-29 fall into one of four groups. Each group performs a specific task. The host interface registers provide host to 340x0 communications. The host computer performs most communication with the display adapter through this interface. The local memory-control register controls how the 340x0 manipulates data in VRAM. This includes the size of various display adapter constructs like pixel depth and window size. The interrupt-control register provides status information to the 340x0 and host computer. The host computer can perform display-related tasks more efficiently by monitoring these two registers. The physical characteristics of the display adapter and display mode affect the video timing and screen refresh registers.

In addition to registers, the 340x0 uses the instruction set summarized in Table 3-30. Notice that this instruction set contains instructions specifically designed for display data manipulation. Also, note that, although Texas Instruments optimized the 340x0 for graphic operations, it also uses generalized instructions like jump. This differentiates the 340x0 from both a standard display adapter BIOS or coprocessor and a general-purpose processor like the 8088. The 340x0 can perform any task performed by a general-purpose processor. This gives it display data manipulation capabilities not found in standard display adapter BIOS or coprocessor chips.

Table 3-30   **34010 instruction set**

Instruction	Type	Function
ABS	Arithmetic	Stores the absolute value of a number in a destination register.
ADD	Arithmetic	Adds the source register to the destination register.
ADDC	Arithmetic	Adds the source register to the destination register and sets the carry flag if necessary.
ADDI	Arithmetic	Adds an immediate value to the destination register. The immediate value may be 16 or 32-bits long.
ADDK	Arithmetic	Adds a 5-bit constant to the destination register.
ADDXY	Arithmetic	Adds the source register to the destination register in XY mode.
AND	Logical	Performs a logical AND of the value in the destination register with the source register.
ANDI	Logical	Performs a logical AND of the value in the destination register with a 32-bit immediate value.
ANDN	Logical	Performs a logical AND of the value in the destination register with the source register, then complements the result.
ANDNI	Logical	Complements a 32-bit immediate value, then performs a logical AND of the value in the destination register with the 32-bit immediate value.
BTST	Compare	Tests the bit specified by a constant or source register in the destination register.
CALL	Program Control and Context Switching	Calls the subroutine address placed in the source register.
CALLA	Program Control and	Calls the absolute subroutine address specified by an immediate value.

Instruction	Type	Function
	Context Switching	
CALLR	Program Control and Context Switching	Calls the relative subroutine address specified by an immediate value.
CLR	Compare	Clears the specified register.
CLRC	Compare	Clears the carry flag.
CMP	Compare	Nondestructively compares the value in the source register to the destination register. Sets or clears the appropriate status bits.
CMPI	Compare	Nondestructively compares an immediate value to the destination register. Sets or clears the appropriate status bits. The immediate value may be 16 or 32-bits long.
CMPXY	Compare	Nondestructively compares the X and Y half of a register. Sets or clears the appropriate status bits.
CPW	Graphics	Compares a point specified by an X and Y coordinate in the source register to the window limits in the WEND or WSTART registers. X and Y are 16-bit signed values. WEND and WSTART must contain positive values. Used to reject objects drawn outside the confines of a window.
CVXYL	Graphics	Convert an XY address to a linear address.
DEC	Arithmetic	Reduces the contents of the specified register by one.
DINT	Program Control and Context Switching	Disable maskable interrupts.
DIVS	Arithmetic	Perform a signed division of the destination register by the source register. The 34010 performs the division on a 64-bit number if the destination register number is even (for example A14). Otherwise, it performs the division on a 32-bit number. The source and destination registers must appear in the same register file.
DIVU	Arithmetic	Perform an unsigned division of the destination register by the source register. The 34010 performs the division on a 64-bit number if the destination register number is even (for example A14). Otherwise, it performs the division on a 32-bit number. The source and destination registers must appear in the same register file.
DRAV	Graphics	Draws a pixel at the address pointed to by the destination register using the color in COLOR1. The 34010 then adds the value in the source register to the destination register.

Table 3-30   **Continued**

Instruction	Type	Function
DSJ	Jump	If the destination register is greater than 0, the 34010 decrements it by one and advances to the specified address. Otherwise, it skips the jump and proceeds with the next sequential instruction.
DSJEQ	Jump	This instruction first checks to see if the zero flag (Z) is set. If Z = 1, then the 34010 skips the jump. Otherwise, if the destination register is greater than 0, the 34010 decrements it by one and advances to the specified address. Otherwise, it skips the jump and proceeds with the next sequential instruction.
DSJNE	Jump	This instruction first checks to see if the zero flag (Z) is clear. If Z = 0, then the 34010 skips the jump. Otherwise, if the destination register is greater than 0, the 34010 decrements it by one and advances to the specified address. Otherwise, it skips the jump and proceeds with the next sequential instruction.
DSJS	Jump	If the destination register is greater than 0, the 34010 decrements it by one. If the direction bit (D) equals 0, the 34010 adds the specified value to the program counter. Otherwise, the 34010 subtracts the specified value from the program counter. If the destination register equals 0, the 34010 skips the jump and proceeds with the next sequential instruction.
EINT	Program Control and Context Switching	Enable maskable interrupts.
EMU	Program Control and Context Switching	The 34010 enters emulation mode. This instruction is intended for systems level programming only.
EXGF	Program Control and Context Switching	Exchanges the six LSB bits of the destination register with the specified field bits. The 34010 clears the upper 26-bits of the destination register.
EXGPC	Program Control and Context Switching	Exchanges the value contained in the destination register with the program counter. Program execution continues with the new program counter address.
FILL L	Graphics	Fills a two dimensional array with the value contained in COLOR1. DADDR contains the pixel array starting address

Instruction	Type	Function
		(linear value). DPTCH contains the pixel array pitch (linear value). DYDX contains the pixel array dimensions.
FILL XY	Graphics	Fills a two dimensional array with the value contained in COLOR1. DADDR contains the pixel array starting address (XY value). DPTCH contains the pixel array pitch (linear value). OFFSET contains the address of the screen origin (linear value). WSTART contains the window starting address (XY value). WEND contains the window ending address (XY value). DYDX contains the pixel array dimensions.
GETPC	Program Control and Context Switching	Increments the program counter value by 16 (to point past the current instruction) and places the value in the destination register.
GETST	Program Control and Context Switching	Copies the contents in the status register to the destination register.
INC	Arithmetic	Increases the contents of the specified register by one.
JAcc	Jump	Jump to the specified address (absolute) if the status flag(s) listed below contain the correct values.

cc	NCZV	NCZV	NCZV
B	X1XX		
C	X1XX		
EQ	XX1X		
GE	0XX0	1XX1	
GT	0X00	1X01	
HI	X00X		
HS	X00X	XX1X	
LE	0XX1	1XX0	XX1X
LO	X1XX		
LS	XX1X	X1XX	
LT	0XX1	1XX0	
N	1XXX		
NB	X0XX		
NC	X0XX		
NE	XX0X		
NN	0XXX		

Table 3-30   **Continued**

Instruction	Type	Function

		cc	NCZV	NCZV	NCZV
		NV	XXX0		
		NZ	XX0X		
		P	0X0X		
		UC	XXXX		
		V	XXX1		
		Z	XX1X		

JRcc	Jump	Add the specified value to the program counter (relative jump) if the status flag(s) listed below contain the correct values.

cc	NCZV	NCZV	NCZV
C	X1XX		
GE	0XX0	1XX1	
GT	0X00	1X01	
HI	X00X		
LE	0XX1	1XX0	XX1X
LS	XX1X	X1XX	
LT	0XX1	1XX0	
N	1XXX		
NC	X0XX		
NN	0XXX		
NV	XXX0		
NZ	XX0X		
P	0X0X		
UC	XXXX		
V	XXX1		
Z	XX1X		

Instruction	Type	Function
JUMP	Jump	Perform an absolute jump to the specified address.
LINE [0,1]	Graphics	Selects one of two available line drawing algorithms.
LMO	Compare	Locates the leftmost 1 in the source register and places the 1's complement of its location in the destination register (5

Instruction	Type	Function
		LSB bits). If the source register does not contain a 1, the 34010 loads the destination register with zeros and sets the zero flag.
MMFM	Move	Moves the contents of memory to the specified register list. All registers in the list must appear in the same register file.
MMTM	Move	Moves the contents of a specified register list to memory. All registers in the list must appear in the same register file.
MODS	Arithmetic	Returns the signed remainder of the division of the destination register by the source register. Both registers always contain a 32-bit number. Both registers must appear in the same register file.
MODU	Arithmetic	Returns the unsigned remainder of the division of the destination register by the source register. Both registers always contain a 32-bit number. Both registers must appear in the same register file.
MOVB	Move	Moves a byte from the source register to the memory address pointed to by the destination register. Both registers must appear in the same register file.
MOVE	Move	Moves the contents of the source register, source register address, or explicitly specified memory address to the destination register, the memory address pointed to by the destination register, or an explicitly specified memory address.
MOVI	Move	Stores a 16-bit, sign extended or 32-bit immediate value in the destination register.
MOVK	Move	Stores a 5-bit constant in the destination register.
MOVX	Move	Moves the X half of the source register to the X half of the destination register. Does not affect the Y half of either register. Both registers must appear in the same register file.
MOVY	Move	Moves the Y half of the source register to the Y half of the destination register. Does not affect the X half of either register. Both registers must appear in the same register file.
MPYS	Arithmetic	Performs a signed multiplication of the source register by the destination register. The 34010 stores a 32-bit result if the destination register is odd. Otherwise, it stores a 64-bit result. Both registers must appear in the same register file.
MPYU	Arithmetic	Performs an unsigned multiplication of the source register by the destination register. The 34010 stores a 32-bit result if the destination register is odd. Otherwise, it stores a 64-bit result. Both registers must appear in the same register file.
NEG	Arithmetic	Stores the 2s complement of the number in the destination register back into the destination register.

Table 3-30   **Continued**

Instruction	Type	Function
NEGB	Arithmetic	Stores the 2s complement of the number in the destination register back into the destination register. The 34010 decrements the result by one if the borrow bit is set.
NOP	Program Control and Context Switching	The processor does not perform any instruction. The program counter is set to the next instruction.
NOT	Logical	Stores the 1s complement of the number in the destination register back into the destination register.
OR	Logical	Performs a logical OR of the source register with the destination register. Both registers must appear in the same register file.
ORI	Logical	Performs a logical OR of an immediate value with the destination register.
PIXBLT B, L	Graphics	Pixel Block Transfers the contents of a binary pixel array to a linear array.
PIXBLT B, XY	Graphics	Pixel Block Transfers the contents of a binary pixel array to an XY array.
PIXBLT L, L	Graphics	Pixel Block Transfers the contents of a linear pixel array to a linear array.
PIXBLT L, XY	Graphics	Pixel Block Transfers the contents of a linear pixel array to an XY array.
PIXBLT XY, L	Graphics	Pixel Block Transfers the contents of an XY pixel array to a linear array.
PIXBLT XY, XY	Graphics	Pixel Block Transfers the contents of an XY pixel array to an XY array.
PIXT	Graphics	Transfers the contents of the source register to the address pointed to by the destination register. It can also transfer the contents of the address pointed to by the source register to the destination register. PSIZE determines the size of the pixel. The address contained in the source or destination register is either XY or linear.
POPST	Program Control and Context Switching	Pops the status register from the stack and increments SP by 32.
PUSHST	Program Control and	Pushes the status register onto the stack and decrements SP by 32.

Instruction	Type	Function
	Context Switching	
PUTST	Program Control and Context Switching	Places the contents of the specified register into the status register.
RETI	Program Control and Context Switching	Returns to an interrupted routine from an interrupt service routine. ST and PC are popped from the stack and SP is incremented by 64.
RETS N	Program Control and Context Switching	Returns to an interrupted routine from a subroutine. This return may contain an optional stack increment value (32 + 16N). If N is not specified, SP is incremented by 32.
REV	Program Control and Context Switching	Returns the revision number of the TMS34010 installed on the display adapter.
RL	Shift	Rotate the value in the destination register left by the amount specified in a constant or the source register.
SETC	Compare	Sets the carry bit of the status register to 1.
SETF	Program Control and Context Switching	Loads the field size and field extension values into the status register. This does not affect the value of the flags.
SEXT	Arithmetic	Sign extends the right justified field of the destination register using the MSB of the field.
SLA	Shift	Shifts the destination register field left by the value contained in a constant or the five LSB bits of the source register. The MSB of the destination register is always shifted to the carry bit of the status register. This instruction provides overflow detection and sets the overflow bit of the status register as required.
SLL	Shift	Shifts the destination register field left by the value contained in a constant. The MSB of the destination register is always shifted to the carry bit of the status register. This instruction does not provide overflow detection.
SRA	Shift	Shifts the destination register field right by the value contained in a constant or the five LSB bits of the source register. The LSB of the destination register is always shifted to the carry bit of the status register. This instruction provides overflow detection and sets the overflow bit of the status register as required.

Table 3-30   **Continued**

Instruction	Type	Function
SRL	Shift	Shifts the destination register field left by the value contained in a constant. The LSB of the destination register is always shifted to the carry bit of the status register. This instruction does not provide overflow detection.
SUB	Arithmetic	Subtracts the value in the source register from the destination register and stores the result in the destination register.
SUBB	Arithmetic	Subtracts the value in the source register and carry bit of the status register from the destination register and stores the result in the destination register.
SUBI	Arithmetic	Subtracts a 16 or 32-bit immediate value from the destination register and stores the result in the destination register.
SUBK	Arithmetic	Subtracts a 5-bit constant value from the destination register and stores the result in the destination register.
SUBXY	Arithmetic	Individually subtract the X and Y halves of the source register from the X and Y halves of the destination register and stores the result in the destination register.
TRAP N	Program Control and Context Switching	Executes the software interrupt specified by N. Trap pushes PC and ST on the stack, then places the address pointed to by the track number. N is a number from 0 to 31 as shown below.

N	Trap Function
0	Reset
1	External Interrupt 1
2	External Interrupt 2
3–7	Traps 3 through 7
8	Nonmaskable Interrupt
9	Host Interrupt
10	Display Interrupt
11	Window Violation
12–29	Traps 12 through 29
30	Illegal Opcode
31	Trap 31

Instruction	Type	Function
XOR	Logical	Performs a logical XOR of the contents of the destination register with the source register and stores the results in the destination register.
XORI	Logical	Performs a logical XOR of the contents of the destination register with an immediate value and stores the results in the destination register.
ZEXT	Arithmetic	Zero extends the right justified field in the destination register. If the field size is not specified, the 34010 uses the default field size as a reference.

As you can see from Tables 3-29 and 3-30, the 340x0 provides a complex, but flexible, programming interface. This book cannot provide the detailed information required by the novice programmer to create programs for the 340x0. Refer to the Texas Instruments TMS340x0 Software Development Kit for detailed programming information. However, you can use the tables in this book as a quick reference to the 340x0. In addition to the information provided by the tables, you need to know the addresses used by the display adapter for the host interface. Obtain this information from the manufacturer's technical manuals.

✳ **Texas Instruments Graphics Architecture (TIGA)**   The Texas Instruments Graphics Architecture (TIGA) application interface allows you to program the TMS340x0 using the simplified procedures provided in multiple assembly and C libraries. Table 3-31 provides a summary of the TIGA instructions and their use. As with the processor instructions, this book does not provide the detailed instruction required by the novice programmer. Unlike the processor instructions, you must own a copy of the software development kit to use the TIGA interface. However, this book does provide a quick reference to the TIGA instruction set. In addition to the information provided by Table 3-31, you need to know the addresses used by the display adapter for the host interface. Obtain this information from the manufacturer's technical manuals.

TIGA instruction set   Table 3-31

Instruction	Type	Function
Void BITBLT (Width, Height, SRCX, SRCY, DSTX, DSTY)	Pixel Array (Extended)	Copies data from the source bitmap to the destination bitmap. Width and height describe the size of both bitmaps. SRCX and SRCY describe the starting coordinates of the source. DSTX and DSTY describe the starting coordinates of the destination.
Int CD_IS_ALIVE ( )	Graphics System Initialization (Core)	Returns 0 if the communication driver is not installed. Otherwise, returns a nonzero result.
Void CLEAR_FRAME_BUFFER (Color)	Clear (Core)	Clears the entire display memory by setting it to the specified color. Use the CLEAR_SCREEN function to preserve offscreen data.

Table 3-31   **Continued**

Instruction	Type	Function
Void CLEAR_PAGE (Color)	Clear (Core)	Clears the current drawing page by setting it to the specified color. Use the CLEAR_SCREEN function to preserve offscreen data.
Void CLEAR_SCREEN (Color)	Clear (Core)	Clears only the visible portion of display memory by setting it to the specified color.
Void COP2GSP (COPID, COPADDR, GSPADDR, Length)	Communication (Core)	Copies data from the coprocessor address space to the TMS340 address space. Transfers occur in 32-bit length words.
Short CPW (X, Y)	Graphics Attribute Control (Core)	Outputs a 4-bit outcode based on a pixel's position within a window as shown here:

Code **Function**

0000	Point lies within window.
01XX	Point lies above window.
10XX	Point lies below window.
XX01	Point lies left of window.
XX10	Point lies right of window.

Instruction	Type	Function
Int CREATE_ALM (RLM_Name, ALM_Name)	Extensibility (Core)	Converts a relocatable load module to an absolute load module. Exits with a value of 0 if successful.
Int CREATE_ESYM (GM_Name)	Extensibility (Core)	Creates an external symbol table of global symbols. The linking loader uses this table to resolve references in a relocatable load module. Exits with a value of 0 if successful.
Int DELETE_FONT (ID)	Text (Extended)	Removes the font specified by ID (number) from the font table. Returns 0 if the font was not installed. Returns nonzero value if font removed successfully.
Void DRAW_LINE (X1, Y1, X2, Y2)	Graphics Output (Extended)	Draws a line onscreen. X1 and Y1 contain the starting coordinate. X2 and Y2 contain the ending coordinate.
Void DRAW_OVAL (W, H, XLeft, YTop)	Graphics Output (Extended)	Draws an oval onscreen. W contains the width. H contains the height. XLeft and YTop contain the coordinates of the upper-left corner of the oval.

Instruction	Type	Function
Void DRAW_OVALARC (W, H, XLeft, YTop, Theta, Arc)	Graphics Output (Extended)	Draws an elliptical arc onscreen. W contains the width. H contains the height. XLeft and YTop contain the coordinates of the upper-left corner of the oval. Theta contains the start angle. Arc contains the number of degrees of arc.
Void DRAW_PIEARC (W, H, XLeft, YTop, Theta, Arc)	Graphics Output (Extended)	Draws an elliptical arc onscreen. Two lines emanate from the center of the arc to each end. W contains the width. H contains the height. XLeft and YTop contain the coordinates of the upper-left corner of the oval. Theta contains the start angle. Arc contains the number of degrees of arc.
Void DRAW_POINT (X, Y)	Graphics Output (Extended)	Draws a single pixel onscreen. X and Y contain the coordinate of the pixel.
Void DRAW_POLYLINE (N, Points)	Graphics Output (Extended)	Draws a group of lines whose end points are supplied as a set of points. N indicates the number of lines to draw. Each point consists of an X and Y coordinate. To draw a closed polygon, use the same coordinates for the first and last set of points.
Void DRAW_POLYLINE (N, Points)	Poly Drawing (Extended)	See previous description.
Void DRAW_RECT (W, H, XLeft, YTop)	Graphics Output (Extended)	Draws a rectangle onscreen. W contains the width. H contains the height. XLeft and YTop contain the coordinates of the upper-left corner.
Unsigned Long FIELD_EXTRACT (GPTR, FS)	Communication (Core)	Returns the 32-bit data in the TMS340 memory space pointed to by GPTR. FS contains the field size (number of significant bits).
Void FIELD_INSERT (GPTR, FS, Data)	Communication (Core)	Writes Data to the address in TMS340 memory pointed to by GPTR. FS contains the field size.
Void FILL_CONVEX (N, Points)	Graphics Output (Extended)	Draws a filled convex polygon. N indicates the number of vertices in the polygon. Each point consists of an X and Y coordinate. To draw a closed polygon, use the same coordinates for the first and last set of points.

Table 3-31   **Continued**

Instruction	Type	Function
Void FILL_CONVEX (N, Points)	Poly Drawing (Extended)	See previous description.
Void FILL_OVAL (W, H, XLeft, YTop)	Graphics Output (Extended)	Draws a filled oval onscreen. W contains the width. H contains the height. XLeft and YTop contain the coordinates of the upper-left corner of the oval.
Void FILL_PIEARC (W, H, XLeft, YTop, Theta, Arc)	Graphics Output (Extended)	Draws a filled pie-shaped wedge onscreen. W contains the width. H contains the height. XLeft and YTop contain the coordinates of the upper-left corner of the oval. Theta contains the start angle. Arc contains the number of degrees of arc.
Void FILL_POLYGON (N, Points)	Graphics Output (Extended)	Draws a filled polygon. N indicates the number of vertices in the polygon. Each point consists of an X and Y coordinate. To draw a closed polygon, use the same coordinates for the first and last set of points.
Void FILL_POLYGON (N, Points)	Poly Drawing (Extended)	See previous description.
Void FILL_POLYGON (N, Points)	Workspace (Extended)	See previous description.
Void FILL_RECT (W, H, XLeft, YTop)	Graphics Output (Extended)	Draws a filled rectangle onscreen. W contains the width. H contains the height. XLeft and YTop contain the coordinates of the upper-left corner.
Int FLUSH_ESYM ( )	Extensibility (Core)	Flushes an external symbol table of external symbols. The linking loader uses this table to resolve references in a relocatable load module. Exits with a value of 0 if successful.
Void FLUSH_EXTENDED ( )	Extensibility (Core)	Flushes the TIGA extended functions and installed user functions. Then, removes the symbol table stored on the host.
Void FRAME_OVAL (W, H, XLeft, Ytop, DX, DY)	Graphics Output (Extended)	Fills the area between two concentric ovals with the current foreground color. W contains the width. H contains the height. XLeft and YTop contain the

Instruction	Type	Function
		coordinates of the upper-left corner of the oval. DX specifies the horizontal distance between the outer and inner ovals. DY specifies the vertical distance between the two ovals.
Void FRAME_RECT (W, H, XLeft, Ytop, DX, DY)	Graphics Output (Extended)	Fills the area between two concentric rectangles with the current foreground color. W contains the width. H contains the height. XLeft and YTop contain the coordinates of the upper-left corner. DX specifies the horizontal distance between the outer and inner rectangles. DY specifies the vertical distance between the two rectangles.
Int FUNCTION_IMPLEMENTED (Function Code)	Graphics System Initialization (Core)	Queries if a board supports a specific function. Some TIGA implementations do not support the following functions:
		COP2GSP GET_PALET GET_PALET_ENTRY GSP2COP INIT_PALET SET_PALET SET_PALET_ENTRY SET_TRANSP
Void GET_COLORS (FColor, BColor)	Graphics Attribute Control (Core)	Obtains the foreground and background color values.
Void GET_CONFIG (Config)	Graphics System Initialization (Core)	Obtains the current display adapter configuration and returns it in a structure.
Int GET_CURS_STATE ( )	Cursor (Core)	Returns 0 if the cursor is not enabled.
Void GET_CURS_XY (PX, PY)	Cursor (Core)	Returns the coordinates of the cursor. Coordinates are relative to the upper-left corner of the visible screen.
Void GET_ENV (Env)	Graphics Attribute Control (Core)	Returns the current graphics environment variable status in the structure pointed to by ENV.
Int GET_FONTINFO (ID, PFontInfo)	Text (Core)	Returns information about the current font in a structure pointed to by PFontInfo. ID determines which font the function polls. 0 returns system font information. −1 returns current font information.

Table 3-31   **Continued**

Instruction	Type	Function
Void GET_ISR_PRIORITIES (NumISRs, PTR)	Extensibility (Core)	Returns the priorities of interrupt service routines installed using the INSTALL_RLM and INSTALL_ALM functions. NumISRs contains the number of ISRs installed. PTR points to an array of short containing the priority data.
Int GET_MODEINFO (Index, ModeInfo)	Graphics System Initialization (Core)	Returns a structure containing the board configuration supported by the current board and monitor. Index contains the mode number.
Long GET_NEAREST_COLOR (R, G, B, I)	Palette (Core)	Obtains the color number that most closely matches the specified parameters. R is red, G is green, B is blue, and I is intensity.
Void GET_OFFSCREEN_MEM-ORY (Num_Blocks, Offscreen)	Pointer-Based Memory Management (Core)	Returns a description of the offscreen memory areas that are not in use. These blocks normally consist of display memory that is not used for the frame buffer or alternate frame buffer. You obtain the Num_Blocks parameter using the GET_CONFIG function. Offscreen is a pointer to memory allocated for offscreen entry storage.
Void GET_PALET (Palet Size, Palet)	Palette (Core)	Reads an entire palette register into the palette array. You obtain the Palet Size parameter using the GET_CONFIG function.
Int GET_PALET_ENTRY (Index, R, G, B, I)	Palette (Core)	Reads the color values contained in a single palette. Index specifies which palette to read. R is red, G is green, B is blue, and I is intensity. This function returns 0 if you specify an invalid index.
Long GET_PIXEL (X, Y)	Graphics Utility (Extended)	Returns the value of the pixel at the address specified by X and Y. The coordinate is relative to the drawing origin.
Long GET_PMASK ( )	Graphics Attribute Control (Core)	Returns the value of the plane mask (planes enabled/disabled for writing).

Instruction	Type	Function
Int GET_PPOP ( )	Graphics Attribute Control (Core)	Returns a 5-bit code for the current pixel processing operation.

Code	Function
0	Source
1	Source AND Destination
2	Source AND NOT Destination
3	All 0s
4	Source OR NOT Destination
5	Source EQU Destination
6	NOT Destination
7	Source NOR Destination
8	Source OR Destination
9	Destination
10	Source XOR Destination
11	NOT Source AND Destination
12	All 1s
13	NOT Source OR Destination
14	Source NAND Destination
15	NOT Source
16	Source + Destination
17	ADDS (Source, Destination)
18	Destination – Source
19	SUBS (Destination, Source)
20	MAX (Source, Destination)
21	MIN (Source, Destination)

Instruction	Type	Function
Int GET_TEXTATTR (PControl, Count, Arg)	Text (Extended)	Obtains the text rendering attributes. PControl is a pointer to a list of desired attributes. Current attribute values include %a (top left alignment = 0, baseline = 1) and %e (additional intercharacter spacing). Count contains the number of attributes in the control string.
Int GET_TRANSP ( )	Graphics Attribute Control (Core)	Gets the state of the transparency (T) bit of the control register. Returns 0 if transparency is disabled.
Unsigned Long GET_VECTOR (TrapNum)	Communication (Core)	Obtains the address of the trap vector specified by TrapNum.
Int GET_VIDEOMODE ( )	Graphics System Initialization (Core)	Returns the current video mode emulation number.
Int GET_WINDOWING ( )	Graphics Attribute Control (Core)	Gets the 2-bit windowing code in the control I/O register as shown here:

Table 3-31 **Continued**

Instruction	Type	Function

		Code	**Function**
		00	No Windowing
		01	Interrupt Request on Write In Window
		10	Interrupt Request on Write Outside Window
		11	Clip to Window

Instruction	Type	Function
Short GET_WKSP (Addr, Pitch)	Workspace (Core)	Returns parameters defining the current offscreen workspace. If the function returns a nonzero value, then Addr and Pitch contain the address and pitch of the workspace area.
Long GSP_CALLOC (NMemB, Size)	Pointer-Based Memory Management (Core)	Allocates enough TMS340 memory to contain NMemB objects of Size. Returns 0 if not enough memory remains. Otherwise, returns a pointer to the memory area.
Void GSP_EXECUTE (Entry Point)	Graphics System Initialization (Core)	Loads and executes a non-application function. In other words, this function provides a portable COFF loader.
Int GSP_FREE (PTR)	Pointer-Based Memory Management (Core)	Deallocates the memory allocated by the GSP_MALLOC, GSP_CALLOC, or GSP_REALLOC functions. PTR points to the beginning of the memory area. Returns 0 if not successful.
Long GSP_MALLOC (Size)	Pointer-Based Memory Management (Core)	Allocates the amount of TMS340 memory specified by Size. Returns 0 if not enough memory remains. Otherwise, returns a pointer to the memory area.
Long GSP_MAXHEAP ( )	Pointer-Based Memory Management (Core)	Returns the largest amount of heap available for allocation.
Void GSP_MINIT (Stack Size)	Pointer-Based Memory Management (Core)	Deallocates all dynamically allocated memory in the TMS340 heap. Also changes the size of the stack. Providing a value of −1 allocates the default stack size.
Long GSP_REALLOC (PTR,	Pointer-Based	Changes the size of the previously

184

Instruction	Type	Function
Size)	Memory Management (Core)	allocated memory block pointed to by PTR. Size determines the new size of memory allocation. Returns 0 if not successful.
Void GSP2COP (COPID, GSPAddr, COPAddr, Length)	Communication (Core)	A TMS34020 and above specific function that copies data from the TMS340 address space to the coprocessor address space.
Void GSP2GSP (Addr1, Addr2, Length)	Pointer-Based Memory Management (Core)	Copies data within the TMS340 address area. Addr1 contains the source address, Addr2 contains the destination address, and Length contains the length of the data.
Void GSP2HOST (GPTR, HPTR, Length, Swizzle)	Communication (Core)	Transfers data from TMS340 memory (GPTR) to host memory (HPTR). Length contains the length of data to transfer. If Swizzle is nonzero, the 34010 reverses the order of the bits in each byte before transfer.
Void GSP2HOSTXY (SAddr, SPTCH, DAddr, DPTCH, SX, SY, DX, DY, XExt, YExt, PSize, Swizzle)	Communication (Core)	Transfers a rectangular area of the TMS340 bitmap to the host. SAddr contains the source address; DAddr contains the destination address. The source area starts at SX, SY and is transferred to DX, DY. XExt and YExt define the size of the area to transfer. PSize contains the size of the pixels transferred. SPTCH and DPTCH contain the source and destination pitch. If Swizzle is nonzero, the 34010 reverses the order of the bits in each byte before transfer.
Void HOST2GSP (GPTR, HPTR, Length, Swizzle)	Communication (Core)	Transfers data from host memory (HPTR) to TMS340 memory (GPTR). Length contains the length of data to transfer. If Swizzle is nonzero, the 34010 reverses the order of the bits in each byte before transfer.
Void HOST2GSPXY (SAddr, SPTCH, DAddr, DPTCH, SX, SY, DX, DY, XExt, YExt, PSize, Swizzle)	Communication (Core)	Transfers a rectangular area of host memory to the TMS340. SAddr contains the source address; DAddr contains the destination address. The source area starts at SX, SY and transfers to DX, DY. XExt and YExt

185

Table 3-31   **Continued**

Instruction	Type	Function
		define the area to transfer. PSize contains the size of the pixels. SPTCH and DPTCH contain source and destination pitch. If Swizzle is nonzero, the 34010 reverses the order of the bits in each byte before transfer.
Void INIT_PALET ( )	Palette (Core)	Initializes the first 16 palette entries to the EGA default palette.
Void INIT_TEXT ( )	Text (Core)	Removes any installed fonts from memory and selects the standard font. Resets all text drawing attributes.
Int INSTALL_ALM (ALM Name)	Extensibility (Core)	Installs the absolute load module into the TIGA graphics manager and returns a module identifier. Use the module identifier to invoke the ALM extended functions. Returns a negative number if not successful.
Short INSTALL_FONT (PFont)	Text (Extended)	Use this function to install a font into the font table after loading it into TMS340 memory. PFont points to the location of the font file in memory. The function returns an ID number when successful. Otherwise, it returns 0.
Int INSTALL_PRIMITIVES ( )	Graphics System Initialization (Core)	Loads extended graphics primitives in memory. Returns a positive number identifier when successful. Returns a negative number error otherwise.
Int INSTALL_PRIMITIVES ( )	Extensibility (Core)	See previous description.
Int INSTALL_RLM (RLM Name)	Extensibility (Core)	Installs a relocatable load module into the TIGA graphics manager and returns a module identifier. Use the module identifier to invoke the RLM extended functions. Returns a negative number if not successful.
Void INSTALL_USERERROR (Function Name)	Graphics System Initialization (Core)	Substitutes the default host communication error messages with a user supplied error handling routine.
Int LMO (N)	Graphics Utility (Core)	Calculates the position of the leftmost 1 in N. This function treats N as a 32-bit number. Returns −1 if no one

Instruction	Type	Function
		found. Otherwise, returns the bit position of the one.
Unsigned Long LOADCOFF (Filename)	Graphics System Initialization (Core)	Provides the capability to load portable COFF code into the graphics manager. Not generally used by application programs.
Short PAGE_BUSY ( )	Graphics Utility (Core)	Used with the PAGE_FLIP function. Returns a nonzero number while page flipping in progress. Otherwise, it returns 0.
Int PAGE_FLIP (Display, Drawing)	Graphics Utility (Core)	Used with multiple frame buffers to set the display page to a particular frame buffer and the drawing page for subsequent drawing operations.
Void PATNFILL_CONVEX (N, Points)	Graphics Output (Extended)	Fills a convex polygon with a pattern. N defines the number of vertices in the polygon. Points is an array containing the coordinates of each of the vertices in the polygon. The first and last X,Y coordinate in Points should be the same to make sure the polygon is closed. Uses the currently defined pattern for fill.
Void PATNFILL_CONVEX(N, Points)	Poly Drawing (Extended)	See previous description.
Void PATNFILL_OVAL (W, H, XLeft, YTop)	Graphics Output (Extended)	Draws a pattern-filled oval onscreen. W contains the width. H contains the height. XLeft and YTop contain the coordinates of the upper-left corner of the oval. Uses the currently defined pattern for fill.
Void PATNFILL_PIEARC (W, H, XLeft, YTop, Theta, Arc)	Graphics Output (Extended)	Draws a pattern-filled pie-shaped wedge onscreen. W contains the width. H contains the height. XLeft and YTop contain the coordinates of the upper-left corner of the oval. Theta contains the start angle. Arc contains the number of degrees of arc. Uses the currently defined pattern for fill.
Void PATNFILL_POLYGON (N, Points)	Graphics Output (Extended)	Draws a pattern-filled polygon. N indicates the number of vertices in the polygon. Each point consists of an X and Y coordinate. To draw a closed

Table 3-31   **Continued**

Instruction	Type	Function
		polygon, use the same coordinates for the first and last set of points. Uses the currently defined pattern for fill.
Void PATNFILL_POLYGON (N, Points)	Poly Drawing (Extended)	See previous description.
Void PATNFILL_POLYGON (N, Points)	Workspace (Extended)	See previous description.
Void PATNFILL_RECT (W, H, XLeft, YTop)	Graphics Output (Extended)	Draws a pattern-filled rectangle onscreen. W contains the width. H contains the height. XLeft and YTop contain the coordinates of the upper-left corner. Uses the currently defined pattern for fill.
Void PATNFRAME_OVAL (W, H, XLeft, Ytop, DX, DY)	Graphics Output (Extended)	Pattern fills the area between two concentric ovals. W contains the width. H contains the height. XLeft and YTop contain the coordinates of the upper left corner of the oval. DX specifies the horizontal distance between the outer and inner ovals. DY specifies the vertical distance between the two ovals. Uses the currently defined pattern for fill.
Void PATNFRAME_RECT (W, H, XLeft, YTop, DX, DY)	Graphics Output (Extended)	Pattern fills the area between two concentric rectangles. W contains the width. H contains the height. XLeft and YTop contain the coordinates of the upper-left corner. DX specifies the horizontal distance between the outer and inner rectangles. DY specifies the vertical distance between the two rectangles. Uses the currently defined pattern for fill.
Void PATNPEN_LINE (X1, Y1, X2, Y2)	Graphics Output (Extended)	Draws a patterned line onscreen. X1 and Y1 contain the starting coordinate. X2 and Y2 contain the ending coordinate. Uses the currently defined pattern for drawing. Use the SET_PENSIZE function to change pen width and height.
Void PATNPEN_OVALARC (W, H, XLeft, YTop, Theta, Arc)	Graphics Output (Extended)	Draws a patterned elliptical arc onscreen. W contains the width. H contains the height. XLeft and YTop

Instruction	Type	Function
		contain the coordinates of the upper-left corner. Theta contains the start angle. Arc contains the degrees of arc. Uses the currently defined pattern for drawing. Use the SET_PENSIZE function to change pen width and height.
Void PATNPEN_PIEARC (W, H, XLeft, YTop, Theta, Arc)	Graphics Output (Extended)	Draws a patterned elliptical arc onscreen. Two lines emanate from the center of the arc to each end. W contains the width. H contains the height. XLeft and YTop contain the coordinates of the upper-left corner. Theta contains the start angle. Arc contains the degrees of arc. Uses the currently defined pattern for drawing. Use the SET_PENSIZE function to change pen width and height.
Void PATNPEN_POINT (X, Y)	Graphics Output (Extended)	Draws rectangular set of pixels onscreen (corresponds to pen height and width). The pixel color depends on its position within the currently defined pattern. X and Y contain the coordinate of the pixel. Use the SET_PENSIZE function to change pen width and height.
Void PATNPEN_POLYLINE (N, Points)	Graphics Output (Extended)	Draws a group of patterned lines whose end points are supplied as a set of points. N indicates the number of lines to draw. Each point consists of an X and Y coordinate. To draw a closed polygon, use the same coordinates for the first and last set of points. Uses the currently defined pattern for drawing. Use the SET_PENSIZE function to change pen width and height.
Void PATNPEN_POLYLINE (N, Points)	Poly Drawing (Extended)	See previous description.
Long PEEK_BREG (BREG)	Graphics Utility (Core)	Returns a 32-bit number containing the value of a B-file register. BREG contains a number from 0 to 15 corresponding to a file register number.
Void PEN_LINE (X1, Y1, X2,	Graphics Output	Draws a line the width and height of

189

Table 3-31   **Continued**

Instruction	Type	Function
Y2)	(Extended)	of the current pen onscreen. X1 and Y1 contain the starting coordinate. X2 and Y2 contain the ending coordinate. Use the SET_PENSIZE function to change pen width and height.
Void PEN_OVALARC (W, H, XLeft, YTop, Theta, Arc)	Graphics Output (Extended)	Draws an arc the width and height of the current pen onscreen. W contains the width. H contains the height. XLeft and YTop contain the coordinates of the upper-left corner. Theta contains the start angle. Arc contains the degrees of arc. Use the SET_PENSIZE function to change pen width and height.
Void PEN_PIEARC (W, H, XLeft, YTop, Theta, Arc)	Graphics Output (Extended)	Draws an arc the width and height of the current pen onscreen. Two lines emanate from the center of the arc to each end. W contains the width. H contains the height. XLeft and YTop contain the coordinates of the upper-left corner. Theta contains the start angle. Arc contains the degrees of arc. Use the SET_PENSIZE function to change pen width and height.
Void PEN_POINT (X, Y)	Graphics Output (Extended)	Draws a rectangular set of pixels onscreen (corresponds to pen height and width). X and Y contain the coordinate of the pixel. Use the SET_PENSIZE function to change pen width and height.
PEN_POLYLINE (N, Points)	Graphics Output (Extended)	Draws a group of lines the width and height of the current pen whose end points are supplied as a set of points. N indicates the number of lines to draw. Each point consists of an X and Y coordinate. To draw a closed polygon, use the same coordinates for the first and last set of points. Use the SET_PENSIZE function to change pen width and height.
PEN_POLYLINE (N, Points)	Poly Drawing (Extended)	See previous description.
Void POKE_BREG (BREG, Value)	Graphics Utility (Core)	Writes Value to the B-file register specified by BREG. Value is a 32-bit number.

Instruction	Type	Function
Int RMO (N)	Graphics Utility (Core)	Calculates the position of the rightmost 1 in N. This function treats N as a 32-bit number. Returns −1 if no one found. Otherwise, returns the bit position of the one.
Int SEED_FILL (XSeed, YSeed, Buffer, Maxbytes)	Graphics Output (Extended)	Fills a region of connected pixels starting a specified seed pixel. XSeed and YSeed contain the coordinates of the seed pixel. Buffer is an area of memory set aside for working storage. Maxbytes is the number of 8-bit bytes in the storage area.
Int SEED_PATNFILL (XSeed, YSeed, Buffer, Maxbytes)	Graphics Output (Extended)	Pattern fills a region of connected pixels starting a specified seed pixel. XSeed and YSeed contain the coordinates of the seed pixel. Buffer is an area of memory set aside for working storage. Maxbytes is the number of 8-bit bytes in the storage area. Uses the currently defined pattern for fill.
Int SELECT_FONT (ID)	Text (Extended)	Selects a previously installed font for use. ID is the number returned after font installation.
Void SET_BCOLOR (Color)	Graphics Attribute Control (Core)	Changes the background color specified in the COLOR0 B-file register to Color.
Void SET_CLIP_RECT (W, H, XLeft, YTop)	Graphics Attribute Control (Core)	Sets the current clipping rectangle by updating the B-file registers WSTART and WEND to match the W and H parameters. XLeft and YTop are relative to the drawing origin.
Void SET_COLORS (FColor, BColor)	Graphics Attribute Control (Core)	Changes the foreground color specified in the COLOR1 B-file register to FColor. Also changes the background color specified in the COLOR0 B-file register to BColor.
Int SET_CONFIG (Graphics Mode, Init Draw)	Graphics System Initialization (Core)	The SET_CONFIG function changes the mode to match Graphics Mode. If the mode is invalid, returns 0. Otherwise, returns a nonzero result. Init Draw causes the function to reset the following parameters when set true (nonzero).

Table 3-31   **Continued**

Instruction	Type	Function
		Transparency is disabled (CONTROL I/O Register).
		Window Clipping is set (CONTROL I/O Register).
		Pixel Processing is set to replace (CONTROL I/O Register).
		PMASK I/O Register is set to 0.
		Foreground color is set to light gray and background color to black.
		Source and destination bitmaps are set to the screen.
		Drawing origin is set to 0, 0.
		Pen width and height are set to 1.
		Current pattern address is set to 0.
		All installed fonts are removed and the current selected font set to the system font.
		Graphics cursor placed in the center of the screen, turned off, and set to the default shape.
		Temporary workspace is initialized.
Void SET_CURS_SHAPE (Shape)	Cursor (Core)	Defines the size and shape of the cursor. Shape is a structure containing size, color, and shape bitmaps.
Void SET_CURS_STATE (Enable)	Cursor (Core)	Displays the cursor if Enable is nonzero. Removes cursor if Enable is zero.
Void SET_CURS_XY (X, Y)	Cursor (Core)	Sets the pixel coordinates of the cursor hotspot. The cursor coordinates are relative to the upper-left corner of the screen.
Void SET_DRAW_ORIGIN (X, Y)	Graphics Attribute Control (Extended)	Sets the drawing origin for future drawing operations.
Void SET_DSTBM (Addr, Pitch, XExt, YExt, PSize)	Pixel Array (Extended)	Sets the destination bitmap for future BITBLT operations. An address value of 0 sets the destination to screen.

Instruction	Type	Function
Void SET_FCOLOR (Color)	Graphics Attribute Control (Core)	Changes the foreground color specified in the COLOR1 B-file register to Color.
Void SET_INTERRUPT (Level, Priority, Enable, Scan Line)	Extensibility (Core)	Enables or disables a previously installed interrupt service routine. The Scan Line parameter is used for display interrupts only. It sets the scan line at which the interrupt becomes enabled.
Void SET_PALET (Count, Index, Palet)	Palette (Core)	Loads an entire palette into memory. Count contains the number of palette entries. Index contains the palette loading start point. Palet contains groups of four values (R, G, B, and I). Each group defines one palette value.
Void SET_PALET_ENTRY (Index, R, G, B, I)	Palette (Core)	Loads a single palette into memory. Index contains the palette entry to replace. R, G, B, and I contain the color values for the palette entry.
Void SET_PATN (P)	Graphics Attribute Control (Extended)	Defines the pattern used for drawing operations. P is a pointer to a structure containing the height, width, depth, and bit pattern.
Void SET_PENSIZE (W, H)	Graphics Attribute Control (Extended)	Sets the width (W) and height (H) of the drawing pen.
Void SET_PMASK (Mask)	Graphics Attribute Control (Core)	Defines which plane mask bits are writable. A zero in a bit position enables writing. A one in a bit position disables writing.
Void SET_PPOP (PPOP Code)	Graphics Attribute Control (Core)	Defines the pixel processing for future drawing operations.

Code	Function
0	Source
1	Source AND Destination
2	Source AND NOT Destination
3	All 0s
4	Source OR NOT Destination
5	Source EQU Destination
6	NOT Destination
7	Source NOR Destination
8	Source OR Destination
9	Destination
10	Source XOR Destination
11	NOT Source AND Destination

193

Table 3-31   **Continued**

Instruction	Type	Function
		Code **Function**
		12 All 1s
		13 NOT Source OR Destination
		14 Source NAND Destination
		15 NOT Source
		16 Source + Destination
		17 ADDS (Source, Destination)
		18 Destination – Source
		19 SUBS (Destination, Source)
		20 MAX (Source, Destination)
		21 MIN (Source, Destination)
Void SET_SRCBM (Addr, Pitch, XExt, YExt, PSize)	Pixel Array (Extended)	Sets the source bitmap for future BITBLT operations. An address value of 0 sets the source to screen.
Int SET_TEXTATTR (PControl, Count, Arg)	Text (Extended)	Sets the text rendering attributes. PControl is a pointer to a list of desired attributes. Current attribute values include %a (top left alignment = 0, baseline = 1) and %e (additional intercharacter spacing). Count contains the number of attributes in the control string.
Void SET_TIMEOUT (Value)	Graphics System Initialization (Core)	Sets the time in milliseconds that the host waits for a TMS340 function to complete before calling the error function.
Void SET_TRANSP (Mode)	Graphics Attribute Control (Core)	Changes the transparency mode (TMS34020 and above only) as shown here (TMS34010 uses mode 2 only):
		Mode **Function**
		0 Source transparency = 0
		1 Source transparency = COLOR0
		2 Result transparency = 0
		3 Result transparency = COLOR0
Unsigned SET_VECTOR (TrapNum, NewAddr)	Communication (Core)	Sets the specified trap number to NewAddr. Returns the address of the old interrupt.
Int SET_VIDEOMODE (Mode, Style)	Graphics System Initialization (Core)	The SET_VIDEOMODE function changes the current video mode and determines how to initialize the new mode. Mode can contain one of the following values: TIGA, MDA,

Instruction	Type	Function
		HERCULES, CGA, EGA, VGA, AI_8514, or PREVIOUS. Style determines the initialization method. It can contain one of the following values: NO_INIT, INIT_GLOBALS, INIT, or CLR_SCREEN.
Void SET_WINDOWING (Enable)	Graphics Attribute Control (Core)	Sets the 2-bit windowing code in the control I/O register as shown here:

Code	Function
00	No Windowing
01	Interrupt Request on Write In Window
10	Interrupt Request on Write Outside Window
11	Clip to Window

Instruction	Type	Function
Void SET_WKSP (Addr, Pitch)	Workspace (Core)	Sets parameters defining the current offscreen workspace. Addr and Pitch contain the address and pitch of the workspace area.
Void STYLED_LINE (X1, Y1, X2, Y2, Style, Mode)	Graphics Output (Extended)	Uses Bresenham's algorithm to draw a styled line from X1, Y1 to X2, Y2. Style is a 32-bit value containing a repeating pattern. Mode changes the method used for drawing:

Mode	Function
0	Do not draw background pixels, leave gaps. Load new line-style from style argument.
1	Draw background pixels using COLOR0. Load new line-style from style argument.
2	Do not draw background pixels, leave gaps. Do not load new line-style from style argument.
3	Draw background pixels using COLOR0. Do not load new line-style from style argument.

Instruction	Type	Function
Void SWAP_BM ( )	Pixel Array (Extended)	Exchanges pointers to the structures containing the source and destination bitmaps.

Table 3-31   **Continued**

Instruction	Type	Function
Void SYNCHRONIZE ( )	Graphics System Initialization (Core)	Synchronizes operations between two processors. Ensures the TMS340 completes an operation before the host CPU tries to manipulate the resulting data.
Int TEXT_OUT (X, Y, PString)	Text (Core)	Sends an ASCII string pointed to by PString to the display using the current font. X and Y specify the starting coordinates for the string.
Int TEXT_WIDTH (PString)	Text (Extended)	Returns the length of the specified string in pixels (using the current font for reference).
Void TRANSP_OFF ( )	Graphics Attribute Control (Core)	Disables transparency for future drawing operations.
Void TRANSP_ON ( )	Graphics Attribute Control (Core)	Enables transparency for future drawing operations.
Void WAIT_SCAN (Line)	Graphics Utility (Core)	Causes a wait state until the processor scans the specified scan line. Control returns to the calling procedure. Synchronizes drawing operations with the display.
Void ZOOM_RECT (WS, HS, XS, YS, WD, HD, XD, YD, LineBuf)	Pixel Array (Extended)	Expands or shrinks the specified rectangle to fit on the display. WS contains the source width. HS contains the source height. XS and YS contain the coordinates of the upper-left corner of the source screen. WD contains the destination width. HD contains the destination height. XD and YD contain the coordinates of the upper-left corner of the destination screen. LineBuf is a buffer large enough to contain one line of the display.

As shown by Table 3-31, the TIGA instruction set falls into 14 main categories. In addition, each instruction also falls into one of two types. TIGA instruction types include core and extended. Core instructions are always available. They remain constant over the entire range of TIGA compatible boards. You must load an extended function into the TIGA environment before using it. This allows you to substitute one instruction for another. Always consult the manufacturer documentation before using an extended function.

There are 14 TIGA instruction categories. The graphics system initialization functions allow you to determine the presence of a TIGA compatible board and place the 340xx in a predefined state. There are different methods of performing this task. Each instruction performs the task of initialization in a different way. The clear functions allow you to clear all or part of display memory. The graphics attribute control functions allow you to change how the graphics processor executes various instructions. These attributes include foreground color, background color, plane mask, pixel processing, transparency, windowing, drawing origin, fill pattern, and drawing pen. The palette function allows you to change the final color used to paint the display on screen. These functions vary in scope from manufacturer to manufacturer. The graphics output function performs the actual drawing of objects in display memory. The poly drawing function provides extended graphics drawing functions. The workspace functions provide a method of temporarily allocating memory to manipulate a graphics object. The pixel array functions allow you to define pixel blocks and move them within display memory. The text functions provide the means to send text to the display. These functions depend on the availability of TIGA font files. You must install a font before using these functions. The cursor functions change the appearance and position of the cursor on-screen. The graphics utility functions consist of miscellaneous housekeeping instructions. The pointer-based memory-management functions allow you to allocate and deallocate dynamic memory. In addition, these functions provide statistics on memory status. The communication functions determine how and when the display adapter communicates with the host. Finally, the extensibility functions allow you to add or delete functions from the TIGA environment.

As you can see, each category of TIGA instruction performs a specific task in relation to the graphics environment. Using this interface not only allows you to create portable code, but also to develop programs quickly and easily.

✳ **Extended Graphics Array (XGA)**   The XGA is one of the newest display adapters on the market. It provides higher resolution and more colors than the 8514/A display adapter. The XGA also outperforms most SVGA display adapters. The best part is that the

XGA delivers this performance at a lower cost than buying a processor-driven display adapter like those designed around the TMS340x0 chip. IBM originally designed this adapter for the PS/2, but several vendors have made a commitment to produce it for other platforms as well.

Figure 3-3 shows a typical XGA implementation. Most vendors deviate from this design, but the one here tells you a lot about this design of this adapter. Notice that it does not follow the VGA or TMS34010 designs at all. It provides many new function blocks including the sprite and attribute controls. In addition, the coprocessor controls all advanced functions on this display adapter. There are some similarities. For example, all three adapters use a DAC to convert their digital signals to analog output.

Figure 3-3

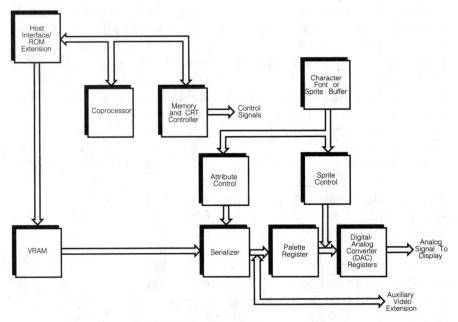

XGA Block diagram.

The XGA does provide full VGA register level compatibility, so you can use the registers described in the previous section with this adapter. It also provides many other display features that are not documented as part of the VGA register set. VESA hopes to avoid

the proliferation of interface techniques that plagued the VGA and the SVGA adapter by producing an XGA standard for these additional capabilities early. This standard is VXE 1.0. The following paragraphs outline the register level aspect of this standard. This book pursues the VESA standard rather than looking at the IBM XGA directly to ensure that applications you create will run on the widest range of available hardware.

Note: The VESA standard does refer to the IBM documentation contained in the "Update for the Personal System/2 Hardware Interface Technical Reference Common Interfaces" part number 04G3281 (form number S04G-3281-00).

The XGA uses a different mechanism than other display adapters for positioning itself in system memory and I/O address space. Rather than use fixed addresses like the VGA or device driver addresses like the TMS34010, the XGA uses a POS setup to determine its location in memory. Each vendor receives a POS identification for their card from either IBM or VESA. The list of POS IDs include: 8FD8h, 8FD9h, 8FDAh, and 8FDBh. The way that the vendor implements the POS identification code varies by system as follows:

➢ MCA machines—You must place each board to setup mode and query it. Use the IBM-prescribed interrupt 15h service C4h BIOS call to check all the expansion boards. Write 0Dh to port 94h to set the onboard system video to setup mode, then write 0FFh to port 94h to enable it.

➢ ISA machines—Directly access the POS registers using the I/O address range from 108h to 10Fh. Make sure you follow any vendor specific addressing schemes for this method.

➢ EISA Machines—Read the POS data directly from slot addresses zC88h through zC8Fh. You also can use the EISA setup to enable the POS registers.

Once you locate an XGA in the system, you must determine several addresses from the remainder of the POS bytes including: ROM address, XGA instance, and video memory address. Simply add the required offset to the base address and read the port. Never write to these ports.

The first two offsets (base address + 0 and base address + 1) contain the low and high bytes of the subsystem identification register, respectively. You use this identification number to see if the board installed in the current slot is an XGA.

The POS register (base address + 2) contains four pieces of information. Bit 0 is the subsystem enable. Bits 1 through 3 are the XGA instance number. Cross reference this instance number to an I/O base address using the following equation: I/O Address = 2100h + (10 × Instance Number). For example, if you wanted to look at XGA instance 1, the base I/O address is 2110h. Bits 4 through 7 contain the ROM address. The ROM address space is 8K. The first 7K of this range is occupied by the ROM; the remaining 1K is occupied by the coprocessor memory mapped registers. To convert the ROM address number to an address use the following equation: C0000h + (2000h × ROM Address Number). For example, if you were looking for the second instance of ROM address 3, then the ROM address would equal C6000. Once you calculate the ROM address, you can use this information to find the coprocessor register base address using the following equation: ROM Address + 1C00h + (80h × XGA Instance Number).

Offset base address + 4 contains two pieces of information. Bit 0 contains the video memory enable flag. Bits 1 through 7 contain the seven most significant bits of the video memory base address. This is a 32-bit number where bits 0 through 21 are the location in video memory that you want to look at (set to zero to get the base address), bits 22 through 24 are the instance number (from bits 1 through 3 of the register at base address + 2), and bits 25 through 31 are the most significant bits from the current register (bits 1 through 7 of base address + 4).

The sixth offset (base address + 5) contains the 1MB aperture base address. If this register contains 0, then the aperture is disabled. Otherwise, you can find the base address by multiplying the base address number by 100000h.

The XGA also provides direct access to a number of internal registers. (Remember, these registers are in addition to the VGA registers described in the previous section.) Table 3-32 contains a

complete list of the registers you can access directly. The *x* in the address represents the instance number of the adapter. For example, if you wanted to access the Memory Access Mode register for the second XGA instance, you would use I/O address 2129h.

XGA registerset   Table 3-32

I/O Address	Description
21x0	Operating Mode
21x1	Aperture Control
21x2–21x3	Reserved
21x4	Interrupt Enable
21x5	Interrupt Status
21x6	Virtual Memory Control
21x7	Virtual Memory Interrupt Status
21x8	Aperture Index
21x9	Memory Access Mode
21xA	Index
21xB–21xF	Data

Each of the direct access registers allows you to perform specific tasks with the extended modes of the XGA. Tables 3-33 through 3-40 contain detailed information about these registers. The registers allow you full read and write capability. In addition, you can assume all the registers provide 8-bit access unless otherwise specified.

Operating mode register (Port 21x0)   Table 3-33

Bit	Description
0–2	Display Mode Field 000—VGA Mode (Address Decode Disabled) 001—VGA Mode (Address Decode Enabled) 010—132-Column Text Mode (Address Decode Disabled) 011—132-Column Text Mode (Address Decode Enabled) 100—Extended Graphics Mode 101 through 111—Reserved
3	Coprocessor Register Interface Format Field—Determines whether the coprocessor uses the Intel or Motorola register format. Setting this bit to 0 selects the Intel format. When you select the Intel format, the byte positions of the registers are reversed. The only exceptions to this rule are the Direction Steps and the PEL Operations registers.
4–7	Reserved

Table 3-34 **Aperature control register (Port 21x1h)**

Bit	Description
0–1	Aperture Size and Location Field 00—No 64K Aperture 01—64K Aperture at A0000h 10—64K Aperture at B0000h 11—Reserved
2–7	Reserved

Table 3-35 **Interrupt enable register (Port 21x4h)**

Bit	Description
0	Start of Blanking Enable—Setting this field to 1 enables the start of blanking interrupt.
1	Start of Picture Enable—Setting this field to 1 enables the start of picture interrupt.
2	Sprite Display Complete Enable—Setting this field to 1 enables the sprite display complete interrupt.
3–5	Reserved
6	Coprocessor Access Rejected Enable—Setting this field to 1 enables the coprocessor access rejected interrupt.
7	Coprocessor Operation Complete Enable—Setting this field to 1 enables the coprocessor operation complete interrupt.

Table 3-36 **Interrupt status register (Port 21x5h)**

Bit	Description
0	Start of Blanking—A 1 indicates that start of blanking occurred.
1	Start of Picture—A 1 indicates that start of picture occurred.
2	Sprite Display Complete—A 1 indicates that sprite display generation is complete.
3–5	Reserved
6	Coprocessor Access Rejected—A 1 indicates that a process tried to access the coprocessor and failed.
7	Coprocessor Operation Complete—A 1 indicates that a process tried to access the coprocessor and succeeded. It also indicates that the coprocessor carried out the operation successfully.

Virtual memory control register (Port 21x6h)   Table 3-37

Bit   Description

0   Enable Virtual Address Lookup—This field controls the virtual memory address translation function. If you don't set this bit, there are a number of conditions that must exist including: all bit maps must be resident, the PEL map addresses represent physical locations, the coprocessor must generate physical addresses, and nonpaged operating systems are supported.

1   Reserved

2   User/Supervisor Selection—When set to 1, the current process is operating a privilege level 3 (user).

3–5   Reserved

6   Virtual Memory Protection Violation Interrupt Enable—Setting this bit to 1 allows the adapter to send an interrupt to the system processor when it detects a protection violation.

7   Virtual Memory Page Not Present Interrupt—Setting this bit to 1 allows the adapter to send an interrupt to the system processor when it needs a memory page read from disk.

Virtual memory interrupt status register (Port 21x7h)   Table 3-38

Bit   Description

0–5   Reserved

6   Virtual Memory Protection Violation—This bit is set when a protection error occurs. You reset this bit to 0 by writing a 1 to it. Once you reset the bit, the adapter retries the page translation that caused the error. If the process does not repair the fault condition prior to resetting the bit, then the adapter generates another interrupt.

7   Virtual Memory Page Not Present—This bit is set when the adapter detects that it needs a page of memory read from disk. You reset this bit to 0 by writing a 1 to it. Once you reset the bit, the adapter looks for the page in memory again. If the process does not read the page of memory from disk prior to resetting the bit, then the adapter generates another interrupt.

Aperature index register (Port 21x8h)   Table 3-39

Bit   Description

0–5   Aperture Index—Defines the position of the 64K or 1MB window within the range of memory installed on the adapter. All six bits are used for a 64K windows. The 1MB windows only uses bits 4 and 5. (You must write 0 to bits 0 through 3 when using the 1MB aperture size.)

6–7   Reserved

Table 3-40   **Memory accessmode register (Port 21x9h)**

Bit	Description
0–2	PEL Size—Determines the size of the PEL. 000—1 bit 001—2 bits 010—4 bits 011—8 bits 100—16 bits 101 through 111—Reserved
3	PEL Order—Controls the ordering method used for the PELs. 1 selects Intel ordering, while 0 selects Motorola ordering.
4–7	Reserved

The index register (Port 21xAh) allows you to indirectly access a number of registers as well. Data registers (Port 21xB through 21xFh) allow you to read and write the indexed registers. You can access the data using byte, word, or double word values. Table 3-41 provides a list of these registers.

Table 3-41   **Index register (Port 21xAh)**

Index Value	Description
00h–03h	Reserved
04h	Auto-Configuration
05h–0Bh	Reserved
0Ch	Coprocessor Save/Restore Data A
0Dh	Coprocessor Save/Restore Data B
0Eh–0Fh	Reserved
10h	Horizontal Total Low
11h	Horizontal Total High
12h	Horizontal Display End Low
13h	Horizontal Display End High
14h	Horizontal Blanking Start Low
15h	Horizontal Blanking Start High
16h	Horizontal Blanking End Low
17h	Horizontal Blanking End High
18h	Horizontal Sync Pulse Start Low
19h	Horizontal Sync Pulse Start High
1Ah	Horizontal Sync Pulse End Low
1Bh	Horizontal Sync Pulse End High
1Ch	Horizontal Sync Position
1Dh	Reserved
1Eh	Horizontal Sync Position
1Fh	Reserved

Index Value   Description

Index Value	Description
20h	Vertical Total Low
21h	Vertical Total High
22h	Vertical Display End Low
23h	Vertical Display End High
24h	Vertical Blanking Start Low
25h	Vertical Blanking Start High
26h	Vertical Blanking End Low
27h	Vertical Blanking End High
28h	Vertical Sync Pulse Start Low
29h	Vertical Sync Pulse Start High
2Ah	Vertical Sync Pulse End
2Bh	Reserved
2Ch	Vertical Line Compare Low
2Dh	Vertical Line Compare High
2Eh–2Fh	Reserved
30h	Sprite Horizontal Start Low
31h	Sprite Horizontal Start High
32h	Sprite Horizontal Preset
33h	Sprite Vertical Start Low
34h	Sprite Vertical Start High
35h	Sprite Vertical Preset
36h	Sprite Control
37h	Reserved
38h	Sprite Color 0 Red
39h	Sprite Color 0 Green
3Ah	Sprite Color 0 Blue
3Bh	Sprite Color 1 Red
3Ch	Sprite Color 1 Green
3Dh	Sprite Color 1 Blue
3Eh-3Fh	Reserved
40h	Display PEL Map Offset Low
41h	Display PEL Map Offset Middle
42h	Display PEL Map Offset High
43h	Display PEL Map Width Low
44h	Display PEL Map Width High
45h–4Fh	Reserved
50h	Display Control 1
51h	Display Control 2
52h	Display ID and Comparator
53h	Reserved
54h	Clock Frequency Select 1
55h	Boarder Color
56h–5Fh	Reserved
60h	Sprite/Palette Index Low
61h	Sprite Index High
62h	Sprite/Palette Prefetch Index Low
63h	Sprite Prefetch Index High
64h	Palette Mask
65h	Palette Data

Table 3-41   **Continued**

Index Value	Description
66h	Palette Sequence
67h	Palette Red Prefetch
68h	Palette Green Prefetch
69h	Palette Blue Prefetch
6Ah	Sprite Data
6Bh	Sprite Prefetch
6Ch–6Fh	Reserved
70h	Clock Frequency Select 2

⇨ GPI functions

The Graphics Programming Interface (GPI) functions provide the
programmer with everything needed to work with the display and
other devices like printers and plotters. Think of the GPI functions as
the detailed tools that work outside the purview of windows. They
work with windows, but not within the confines of windows. These
functions are very device and as a result presentation space oriented.
In most cases, they also provide a higher level of accuracy than their
WIN counterparts (where counterparts exist).

There are three essential function areas: drawing, graphics
management, and translation. The drawing functions further divide
into five areas: lines, patterned areas, text, marker symbols, and
images. The drawing functions allow you to create and shade the
images that you want to display and save. The graphics
management functions allow you to control devices, save your data
to disk, and perform other necessary functions. The translation
functions allow you to transform one set of image characteristics
for another. For example, you might want to change the unit of
measurement from twipps to inches. When combined, all three
areas allow you total control over the drawing device. This device
could be anything: memory, the display, a printer, or any other
physical medium. The combination of device independent function
calls and translation utilities allow you to work in the graphics
environment without worrying about the ultimate destination of
your graphic images.

The GPI functions are only the start of your programmer's tool kit. You require other functions to get any real work done; the GPI functions merely embody the part of your program the user sees. Table 3-42 contains a complete list of the GPI functions. It includes the calling syntax, a brief description of what task the function performs, and descriptions of each variable that the function requires.

GPI function listing   Table 3-42

Function	Description
lChanged = GpiAnimatePalette (hpal, ulFormat, ulStart, ulCount, aulTable)	The GpiAnimatePalette function changes the color values of animating indexes in a palette. An animating index is one that has the PC_RESERVED flag set. lChanged contains the number of remapped colors or an error code on return from the function call. hpal contains a palette handle. ulFormat contains the format of entries in the table. ulStart contains the starting index. ulCount contains the number of elements in aulTable. aulTable contains the start of the application data area. GpiAnimatePalette returns one of the following values:

−1   PAL_ERROR
Other   Number of remapped colors

You can retrieve the last error using WinGetLastError. These errors include:

0x203E PMERR_INSUFFICIENT_MEMORY
0x2054 PMERR_INV_COLOR_DATA
0x2055 PMERR_INV_COLOR_FORMAT
0x2058 PMERR_INV_COLOR_START_INDEX
0x2085 PMERR_INV_IN_AREA
0x2092 PMERR_INV_LENGTH_OR_COUNT
0x2111 PMERR_INV_HPAL
0x2112 PMERR_PALETTE_BUSY

Function	Description
fSuccess = GpiAssociate (hps, hdc)	The GpiAssociate function associates a graphics presentation space with a device context. You also can use this function to disassociate the presentation space by using a null handle. fSuccess contains true if this function is successful. hps contains a presentation space handle. hdc contains a device context handle. You can retrieve the last error using WinGetLastError. These errors include:

0x2005 PMERR_AREA_INCOMPLETE
0x2017 PMERR_DC_IS_ASSOCIATED
0x207C PMERR_INV_HDC
0x207F PMERR_INV_HPS
0x20A1 PMERR_INV_MICROPS_FUNCTION
0x20EC PMERR_PATH_INCOMPLETE
0x20F4 PMERR_PS_BUSY

Table 3-42   **Continued**

Function	Description
	0x20F5 PMERR_PS_IS_ASSOCIATED 0x20F7 PMERR_REALIZE_NOT_SUPPORT
fSuccess = GpiBeginArea (hps, flOptions)	The GpiBeginArea function begins the construction of an area. fSuccess contains true if this function is successful. hps contains a presentation space handle. flOptions contains the area options. These flags include: BA_NOBOUNDARY, BA_BOUNDARY, BA_ALTERNATE, and BA_WINDING. You can retrieve the last error using WinGetLastError. These errors include: 0x2001 PMERR_ALREADY_IN_AREA 0x2041 PMERR_INV_AREA_CONTROL 0x207F PMERR_INV_HPS 0x208B PMERR_INV_IN_PATH 0x20F4 PMERR_PS_BUSY
fSuccess = GpiBeginElement (hps, lType, pszDesc)	The GpiBeginElement function defines the start of an element within a segment. fSuccess contains true if this function is successful. hps contains a presentation space handle. lType contains the type to associate with the element. Use the values between 81000000h and FFFFFFFFh to avoid conflicts with system generated elements when starting application-defined elements. pszDesc contains a variable-length string that describes the element. You can retrieve the last error using WinGetLastError. These errors include: 0x2002 PMERR_ALREADY_IN_ELEMENT 0x2018 PMERR_DESC_STRING_TRUNCATED 0x207F PMERR_INV_HPS 0x20F4 PMERR_PS_BUSY
fSuccess = GpiBeginPath (hps, lPath)	The GpiBeginPath function defines the start of a path. fSuccess contains true if this function is successful. hps contains a presentation space handle. lPath contains the path identifier (always set to a value of 1). You can retrieve the last error using WinGetLastError. These errors include: 0x2003 PMERR_ALREADY_IN_PATH 0x207F PMERR_INV_HPS 0x2085 PMERR_INV_IN_AREA 0x20AE PMERR_INV_PATH_ID 0x20F4 PMERR_PS_BUSY
lHits = GpiBitBlt (hpsTarget, hpsSource, lCount, aptlPoints, lRop, flOptions)	The GpiBitBlt function copies a rectangle of bit-map image data. lHits contains the correlation and error indicators. hpsTarget contains the target presentation space handle. hpsSource contains the source presentation space handle. lCount contains the number of points (array element pairs) in aptlPoints. Providing three points forces GpiBitBlt to use a source rectangle that matches the target

| Function | Description |

Function

Description

rectangle in size. When you supply four points, GpiBitBlt performs any required stretching or compression. aptlPoints contains an array of coordinate pairs. The pairs appear in the following order: Tx1, Ty1, Tx2, Ty2, Sx1, Sy1, Sx2, and Sy2. The first set of coordinates refers to the lower-left corner, while the second set refers to the upper-right corner. lRop contains the mixing function required. There are fifteen different mixing actions including: ROP_SRCCOPY, ROP_SRCPAINT, ROP_SRCAND, ROP_SRCINVERT, ROP_SRCERASE, ROP_NOTSRCCOPY, ROP_NOTSRCERASE, ROP_MERGECOPY, ROP_MERGEPAINT, ROP_PATCOPY, ROP_PATPAINT, ROP_PATINVERT, ROP_DSTINVERT, ROP_ZERO, and ROP_ONE. flOptions contains a list of applicable options. You can use bits 15 through 31 for unique modes supported by particular devices. Other values for this parameter include: BBO_OR, BOO_AND, and BBO_IGNORE. GpiBitBlt returns one of the following values:

```
0000   GPI_ERROR
0001   GPI_OK
0002   GPI_HITS
```

You can retrieve the last error using WinGetLastError. These errors include:

```
0x200A   PMERR_BITMAP_NOT_FOUND
0x203A   PMERR_INCOMPATIBLE_BITMAP
0x203C   PMERR_INCORRECT_DC_TYPE
0x2046   PMERR_INV_BITBLT_MIX
0x2047   PMERR_INV_BITBLT_STYLE
0x205B   PMERR_INV_COORDINATE
0x207F   PMERR_INV_HPS
0x2092   PMERR_INV_LENGTH_OR_COUNT
0x20BD   PMERR_INV_RECT
0x20E4   PMERR_NO_BITMAP_SELECTED
0x20F4   PMERR_PS_BUSY
```

lHits = GpiBox (hps, lControl, pptlPoint, lHRound, lVRound)

The GpiBox function draws a rectangular box using the current cursor position for one corner and a designated coordinate for the opposing corner. lHits contains the correlation and error indicators. hps contains a presentation space handle. lControl contains the outline and fill control. These values include: DRO_FILL, DRO_OUTLINE, and DRO_OUTLINEFILL. pptlPoint contains the coordinates of the second corner. lHRound is the horizontal length of the ellipse used for rounding at each corner. lVRound is the vertical length of the ellipse used for rounding at each corner. GpiBox returns one of the following values:

```
0000   GPI_ERROR
0001   GPI_OK
0002   GPI_HITS
```

Table 3-42   **Continued**

Function	Description
	You can retrieve the last error using WinGetLastError. These errors include:
	0x2049 PMERR_INV_BOX_CONTROL
	0x204A PMERR_INV_BOX_ROUNDING_PARM
	0x205B PMERR_INV_COORDINATE
	0x207F PMERR_INV_HPS
	0x20F4 PMERR_PS_BUSY
lHits = GpiCallSegment-Matrix (hps, lSegment, lCount, pmatlfArray, lOptions)	The GpiCallSegmentMatrix function calls a segment and applies an instance transform to it. lHits contains the correlation and error indicators. hps contains a presentation space handle. lSegment contains the identifier of the segment that you want to call. lCount contains the number of elements in pmatlfArray. If lCount contains a value less than 9, the remaining elements in pmatlfArray default to the corresponding elements in the identity matrix. (The function defaults to the identity matrix if lCount contains a value of zero.) pmatlfArray contains an instance of the transform matrix. Elements three, six, and nine must contain 0, 0, and 1 respectively. lOptions contains the transform options. These options include: TRANSFORM_REPLACE, TRANSFORM_ADD, and TRANSFORM_PREEMPT. GpiCallSegmentMatrix returns one of the following values:
	0000 GPI_ERROR
	0001 GPI_OK
	0002 GPI_HITS
	You can retrieve the last error using WinGetLastError. These errors include:
	0x200D PMERR_CALLED_SEG_IS_CHAINED
	0x200E PMERR_CALLED_SEG_IS_CURRENT
	0x200F PMERR_CALLED_SEG_NOT_FOUND
	0x207F PMERR_INV_HPS
	0x2092 PMERR_INV_LENGTH_OR_COUNT
	0x209B PMERR_INV_MATRIX_ELEMENT
	0x20A1 PMERR_INV_MICROPS_FUNCTION
	0x20C7 PMERR_INV_SEG_NAME
	0x20D0 PMERR_INV_TRANSFORM_TYPE
	0x20F4 PMERR_PS_BUSY
	0x20FC PMERR_SEG_CALL_STACK_EMPTY
lHits = GpiCharString (hps, lCount, pchString)	The GpiCharString function draws a character string starting at the current cursor position. lHits contains the correlation and error indicators. hps contains a presentation space handle. lCount contains the number of characters in pchString. pchString contains the string you want to draw. GpiCharString returns one of the following values:

Function	Description

0000   GPI_ERROR
0001   GPI_OK
0002   GPI_HITS

You can retrieve the last error using WinGetLastError. These errors include:

0x202D   PMERR_FONT_AND_MODE_MISMATCH
0x207F   PMERR_INV_HPS
0x2092   PMERR_INV_LENGTH_OR_COUNT
0x20F4   PMERR_PS_BUSY

**lHits =
GpiCharStringAt
(hps, pptlPoint,
lCount, pchString)**

The GpiCharStringAt function draws a character string starting at the specified cursor position. lHits contains the correlation and error indicators. hps contains a presentation space handle. pptlPoint contains the coordinates of the starting position. lCount contains the number of characters in pchString. pchString contains the string you want to draw. GpiCharStringAt returns one of the following values:

0000   GPI_ERROR
0001   GPI_OK
0002   GPI_HITS

You can retrieve the last error using WinGetLastError. These errors include:

0x202D   PMERR_FONT_AND_MODE_MISMATCH
0x205B   PMERR_INV_COORDINATE
0x207F   PMERR_INV_HPS
0x2092   PMERR_INV_LENGTH_OR_COUNT
0x20F4   PMERR_PS_BUSY

**lHits =
GpiCharStringPos
(hps, prclRect,
flOptions, lCount,
pchString, alAdx)**

The GpiCharStringPos function draws a character string starting at the current cursor position. It includes formatting. lHits contains the correlation and error indicators. hps contains a presentation space handle. prclRect defines the rectangle that bounds the characters you draw. It is used to provide a background color for the text. OS/2 ignores this parameter unless you use the CHS_OPAQUE or CHS_CLIP options. flOptions contains the formatting flag. These flags include: CHS_OPAQUE, CHS_VECTOR, CHS_LEAVEPOS, CHS_CLIP, CHS_UNDERSCORE, and CHS_STRIKEOUT. lCount contains the number of characters in pchString. pchString contains the string that you want to draw. alAdx contains the increment values in world coordinates. This controls the spacing between characters. OS/2 treats any negative values as zeros. GpiCharStringPos returns one of the following values:

0000   GPI_ERROR
0001   GPI_OK
0002   GPI_HITS

Table 3-42   **Continued**

Function	Description
	You can retrieve the last error using WinGetLastError. These errors include:

0x202D   PMERR_FONT_AND_MODE_MISMATCH
0x204E   PMERR_INV_CHAR_POS_OPTIONS
0x207F   PMERR_INV_HPS
0x2092   PMERR_INV_LENGTH_OR_COUNT
0x20BD   PMERR_INV_RECT
0x20F4   PMERR_PS_BUSY

lHits =
GpiCharStringPosAt
(hps, pptlStart,
prclRect, flOptions,
lCount, pchString,
alAdx)

The GpiCharStringPosAt function draws a character string starting at the specified cursor position. It includes formatting. lHits contains the correlation and error indicators. hps contains a presentation space handle. pptlStart contains the coordinates of the starting position. prclRect defines the rectangle that bounds the characters that you draw. It is used to provide a background color for the text. OS/2 ignores this parameter unless you use the CHS_OPAQUE or CHS_CLIP options. flOptions contains the formatting flag. These flags include: CHS_OPAQUE, CHS_VECTOR, CHS_LEAVEPOS, CHS_CLIP, CHS_UNDERSCORE, and CHS_STRIKEOUT. lCount contains the number of characters in pchString. pchString contains the string that you want to draw. alAdx contains the increment value in world coordinates. This controls the spacing between characters. OS/2 treats any negative values as zeros. GpiCharStringPosAt returns one of the following values:

0000   GPI_ERROR
0001   GPI_OK
0002   GPI_HITS

You can retrieve the last error using WinGetLastError. These errors include:

0x202D   PMERR_FONT_AND_MODE_MISMATCH
0x204E   PMERR_INV_CHAR_POS_OPTIONS
0x205B   PMERR_INV_COORDINATE
0x207F   PMERR_INV_HPS
0x2092   PMERR_INV_LENGTH_OR_COUNT
0x20BD   PMERR_INV_RECT
0x20F4   PMERR_PS_BUSY

fSuccess =
GpiCloseFigure (hps)

The GpiCloseFigure function closes a figure within a path specification. fSuccess contains true if this function is successful. hps contains a presentation space handle. You can retrieve the last error using WinGetLastError. These errors include:

0x207F   PMERR_INV_HPS
0x20F4   PMERR_PS_BUSY

Function	Description
fSuccess = GpiCloseSegment (hps)	The GpiCloseSegment function closes the current segment. fSuccess contains true if this function is successful. hps contains a presentation space handle. You can retrieve the last error using WinGetLastError. These errors include:

0x2004   PMERR_AREA_INCOMPLETE
0x207F   PMERR_INV_HPS
0x20A1   PMERR_INV_MICROPS_FUNCTION
0x20E3   PMERR_NOT_IN_SEG
0x20EC   PMERR_PATH_INCOMPLETE
0x20F4   PMERR_PS_BUSY

| lComplexity = GpiCombineRegion (hps, hrgnDest, hrgnSrc1, hrgnSrc2, lmode) | The GpiCombineRegion function combines two regions. The source and destination regions must be the same device class. lComplexity contains the complexity of the resulting region or an error indicator on return from the function call. hps contains a presentation space handle. hrgnDest contains the destination handle. You can use one of the source destinations for this handle. hrgnSrc1 and hrgnSrc2 contain the source destination handles. lMode determines the method of combination. These values include: CRGN_OR, CRGN_COPY, CRGN_XOR, CRGN_AND, and CRGN_DIFF. GpiCombineRegion returns one of the following values: |

0000   RGN_ERROR
0001   RGN_NULL
0002   RGN_RECT
0003   RGN_COMPLEX

You can retrieve the last error using WinGetLastError. These errors include:

0x2034   PMERR_HRGN_BUSY
0x207F   PMERR_INV_HPS
0x2080   PMERR_INV_HRGN
0x20BF   PMERR_INV_REGION_MIX_MODE
0x20F4   PMERR_PS_BUSY
0x20F8   PMERR_REGION_IS_CLIP_REGION

| fSuccess = GpiComment (hps, lLength, pbData) | The GpiComment function adds a comment to the current segment. You can use this area to maintain application specific data. fSuccess contains true if this function is successful. hps contains a presentation space handle. lLength contains the length of the comment string. pbData contains the comment string. You can retrieve the last error using WinGetLastError. These errors include: |

0x207F   PMERR_INV_HPS
0x2092   PMERR_INV_LENGTH_OR_COUNT
0x20F4   PMERR_PS_BUSY

| fSuccess = GpiConvert (hps, lSrc, lTarg, lCount, | The GpiConvert function converts an array of coordinate pairs from one coordinate space to another. fSuccess contains true if this function is successful. hps contains a presentation space handle. |

Table 3-42   **Continued**

Function	Description
aptlPoints)	lSrc contains the source coordinate space. lTarg contains the target coordinate space. Valid values for these two parameters include: CVTC_WORLD, CVTC_MODEL, CVTC_DEFAULTPAGE, CVTC_PAGE, and CVTC_DEVICE. lCount contains the number of coordinate pairs. aptlPoints is an array of coordinate pairs. You can retrieve the last error using WinGetLastError. These errors include: 0x2014 PMERR_COORDINATE_OVERFLOW 0x207F PMERR_INV_HPS 0x205A PMERR_INV_COORD_SPACE 0x205B PMERR_INV_COORDINATE 0x2092 PMERR_INV_LENGTH_OR_COUNT 0x20F4 PMERR_PS_BUSY
fSuccess = GpiConvertWith-Matrix (hps, lCount, aptlPoints, lCount, pmatlfArray)	The GpiConvertWithMatrix function converts an array of coordinate pairs from one coordinate space to another, using the supplied transform matrix. fSuccess contains true if this function is successful. hps contains a presentation space handle. lCount contains the number of coordinate pairs and the number of elements in pmatlfArray. If the number of transform matrix elements is less than nine, OS/2 defaults to the identity matrix for the remaining elements. In addition, it uses the identity matrix if the number of elements is zero. aptlPoints is an array of coordinate pairs. pmatlfArray contains the transform matrix. Elements 3, 6, and 9 must be 0, 0, and 1 respectively. You can retrieve the last error using WinGetLastError. These errors include: 0x2014 PMERR_COORDINATE_OVERFLOW 0x205B PMERR_INV_COORDINATE 0x207F PMERR_INV_HPS 0x2092 PMERR_INV_LENGTH_OR_COUNT 0x20F4 PMERR_PS_BUSY
hmfNew = GpiCopyMetaFile (hmf)	The GpiCopyMetaFile function creates a new metafile and copies the contents of a metafile that you loaded into memory into it. Only the process that creates the metafile can use it. OS/2 automatically deletes the metafile when the process terminates. hmfNew contains the handle of the new metafile or an error indicator. hmf contains the handle of the source metafile. GpiCopyMetaFile returns one of the following values: 0000 GPI_ERROR <>0 New metafile handle You can retrieve the last error using WinGetLastError. These errors include: 0x207E PMERR_INV_HMF 0x20D9 PMERR_METAFILE_IN_USE

Function	Description

0x2106   PMERR_TOO_MANY_METAFILES_IN_USE

lNumHits =
GpiCorrelateChain
(hps, lType, pptlPick,
lMaxHits, lMaxDepth,
alSegTag)

The GpiCorrelateChain function compares a segment chain with an aperture. It returns a set of segment and tag pairs whenever the segment chain appears within the aperture. lNumHits contains the number of hits or an error indicator (a value of 0). hps contains a presentation space handle. lType contains the segment type. There are two values for this parameter: PICKSEL_VISIBLE and PICKSEL_ALL. pptlPick contains the center of the aperture. lMaxHits contains the maximum number of hits that alSegTag can hold. lMaxDepth contains the number of segment identifier and tag pairs that the function returns each hit. alSegTag is an array of segment identifier and tag pairs. You can retrieve the last error using WinGetLastError. These errors include:

0x205B   PMERR_INV_COORDINATE
0x205C   PMERR_INV_CORRELATE_DEPTH
0x205D   PMERR_INV_CORRELATE_TYPE
0x207F   PMERR_INV_HPS
0x209C   PMERR_INV_MAX_HITS
0x20A1   PMERR_INV_MICROPS_FUNCTION
0x20F4   PMERR_PS_BUSY

lNumHits =
GpiCorrelateFrom
(hps, lFirstSegment,
lSecondSegment,
lType, pptlPick,
lMaxHits, lMaxDepth,
alSegTag)

The GpiCorrelateFrom function compares a segment chain with an aperture. It returns a set of segment and tag pairs whenever the segment chain appears within the aperture. lNumHits contains the number of hits or an error indicator (a value of 0). hps contains a presentation space handle. lFirstSegment contains the first segment that you want to compare. lLastSegment contains the last segment you want to compare. lType contains the segment type. There are two values for this parameter: PICKSEL_VISIBLE and PICKSEL_ALL. pptlPick contains the center of the aperture. lMaxHits contains the maximum number of hits that alSegTag can hold. lMaxDepth contains the number of segment identifier and tag pairs that the function returns each hit. alSegTag is an array of segment identifier and tag pairs. You can retrieve the last error using WinGetLastError. These errors include:

0x205B   PMERR_INV_COORDINATE
0x205C   PMERR_INV_CORRELATE_DEPTH
0x205D   PMERR_INV_CORRELATE_TYPE
0x207F   PMERR_INV_HPS
0x209C   PMERR_INV_MAX_HITS
0x20A1   PMERR_INV_MICROPS_FUNCTION
0x20C8   PMERR_INV_SEG_NAME
0x20F4   PMERR_PS_BUSY
0x20FF   PMERR_SEG_NOT_CHAINED
0x2100   PMERR_SEG_NOT_FOUND

lNumHits =
GpiCorrelate

The GpiCorrelateSegment function compares a segment with an aperture. It returns a set of segment and tag pairs whenever the

Table 3-42   **Continued**

Function	Description
Segment (hps, lSegment, lType, pptlPick, lMaxHits, lMaxDepth, alSegTag)	segment chain appears within the aperture. lNumHits contains the number of hits or an error indicator (a value of 0). hps contains a presentation space handle. lSegment contains the identifier of the segment that you want to compare. lType contains the segment type. There are two values for this parameter: PICKSEL_VISIBLE and PICKSEL_ALL. pptlPick contains the center of the aperture. lMaxHits contains the maximum number of hits that alSegTag can hold. lMaxDepth contains the number of segment identifier and tag pairs that the function returns each hit. alSegTag is an array of segment identifier and tag pairs. You can retrieve the last error using WinGetLastError. These errors include: 0x205B PMERR_INV_COORDINATE 0x205C PMERR_INV_CORRELATE_DEPTH 0x205D PMERR_INV_CORRELATE_TYPE 0x207F PMERR_INV_HPS 0x209C PMERR_INV_MAX_HITS 0x20A1 PMERR_INV_MICROPS_FUNCTION 0x20C8 PMERR_INV_SEG_NAME 0x20F4 PMERR_PS_BUSY 0x2100 PMERR_SEG_NOT_FOUND
hbm = GpiCreateBitmap (hps, pbmp2New, flOptions, pbInitData, pbmi2InfoTable)	The GpiCreateBitmap function creates a bit map and returns a handle to it. hbm contains bitmap handle (0 for an error condition). hps contains a presentation space handle. pbmp2New contains the bitmap information header that defines the bitmap format. flOptions contains the CBM_INIT bitmap option. You can initialize bits 16 through 31 with any options supported by a specific device driver. pbInitData contains the initialization data when you set CBM_INIT in flOptions. pbmi2InfoTable contains the bitmap information table that defines the format of pbInitData. You can retrieve the last error using WinGetLastError. These errors include: 0x207F PMERR_INV_HPS 0x208F PMERR_INV_INFO_TABLE 0x20F4 PMERR_PS_BUSY
fSuccess = GpiCreateLogColor-Table (hps, flOptions, lFormat, lStart, lCount, alTable)	The GpiCreateLogColorTable function defines the entries of a logical color table. fSuccess contains true if this function is successful. hps contains a presentation space handle. flOptions contains one of the following options: LCOL_RESET and LCOL_PURECOLOR. lFormat determines the format of the table entries including: LCOLF_INDRGB, LCOLF_CONSECRGB, and LCOLF_RGB. lStart contains the starting index when using the LCOLF_CONSECRGB format. lCount contains the number of entries in alTable. alTable contains the color table definition data. You can retrieve the last error using WinGetLastError. These errors include:

216

Function	Description
	0x2054 PMERR_INV_COLOR_DATA
	0x2055 PMERR_INV_COLOR_FORMAT
	0x2057 PMERR_INV_COLOR_OPTIONS
	0x2058 PMERR_INV_COLOR_START_INDEX
	0x207F PMERR_INV_HPS
	0x2092 PMERR_INV_LENGTH_OR_COUNT
	0x20F4 PMERR_PS_BUSY
	0x20F6 PMERR_REALIZE_NOT_SUPPORTED
	0x210F PMERR_PALETTE_SELECTED

lMatch =
GpiCreateLogFont
(hps, pName, lLcid,
pAttrs)

The GpiCreateLogFont function provides a logical font definition. hps contains a presentation space handle. pName contains an 8-character logical font name. lLcid contains the local identifier in the range from 0 (default) to 254. pAttrs is a pointer to the font attributes. GpiCreateLogFont returns one of the following values:

0000   GPI_ERROR
0001   FONT_DEFAULT
0002   FONT_MATCH

You can retrieve the last error using WinGetLastError. These errors include:

0x202F   PMERR_FONT_NOT_LOADED
0x2072   PMERR_INV_FONT_ATTRS
0x207F   PMERR_INV_HPS
0x20CA   PMERR_INV_SETID
0x20D5   PMERR_KERNING_NOT_SUPPORTED
0x20F4   PMERR_PS_BUSY
0x2102   PMERR_SETID_IN_USE

hpal =
GpiCreatePalette
(hab, flOptions,
lFormat, lCount,
alTable)

The GpiCreatePalette function creates and initializes a color palette. hpal contains the palette handle (0 for an error condition). hab contains the anchor block handle. flOptions determines the color entry table options including: LCOL_PURECOLOR and LCOL_OVERRIDE_DEFAULT_COLORS. lFormat specifies the color entry table format including: LCOLF_CONSECRGB. lCount is the number entries in alTable. alTable is an array of color entries. Each entry is a 4-byte integer with the following value: $(F \times 16777216) + (R \times 65536) + (G \times 256) + B$. F is one of the following flags: PC_RESERVED or PC_EXPLICIT. R, G, and B are the color values. You can retrieve the last error using WinGetLastError. These errors include:

0x203F   PMERR_INSUFFICIENT_MEMORY
0x2054   PMERR_INV_COLOR_DATA
0x2055   PMERR_INV_COLOR_FORMAT
0x2057   PMERR_INV_COLOR_OPTIONS
0x2058   PMERR_INV_COLOR_START_INDEX
0x2092   PMERR_INV_LENGTH_OR_COUNT

hps = GpiCreatePS

The GpiCreatePS function creates a presentation space. hps

217

Table 3-42   **Continued**

Function	Description
(hab, hdc, psizlSize, flOptions)	contains the presentation space handle (0 for an error condition). hab contains the anchor block handle. hdc contains the device context handle. This is mandatory for a micro presentation space. psizlSize contains the presentation space page size. flOptions contains the presentation space options. There are five fields: PS_UNITS, PS_FORMAT, PS_TYPE, PS_MODE, and PS_ASSOCIATE. Simply OR the correct values for each field together to create the parameter. PS_UNITS includes: PU_ARBITRARY, PU_PELS, PU_LOMETRIC, PU_HIMETRIC, PU_LOENGLISH, PU_HIENGLISH, and PU_TWIPS. PS_FORMAT includes: GPIF_DEFAULT, GPIF_SHORT, and GPIF_LONG. PS_TYPE includes: GPIT_NORMAL and GPIT_MICRO. Always assume that the PS_MODE entry is 0. PS_ASSOCIATE includes: GPIA_NOASSOC and GPIA_ASSOC. You can retrieve the last error using WinGetLastError. These errors include: 0x2017 PMERR_DC_IS_ASSOCIATED 0x207C PMERR_INV_HDC 0x20A9 PMERR_INV_OR_INCOMPAT_OPTIONS 0x20BA PMERR_INV_PS_SIZE
hrgn = GpiCreateRegion (hps, lCount, arclRectangles)	The GpiCreateRegion function creates a region for a particular class of device using a series of rectangles. hrgn contains the region handle (0 for an error condition). hps contains the presentation space handle. lCount determines the number of rectangles. arclRectangles is an array of rectangles. You can retrieve the last error using WinGetLastError. These errors include: 0x205B PMERR_INV_COORDINATE 0x207F PMERR_INV_HPS 0x2092 PMERR_INV_LENGTH_OR_COUNT 0x20BD PMERR_INV_RECT 0x20F4 PMERR_PS_BUSY
fSuccess = GpiDeleteBitmap (hbm)	The GpiDeleteBitmap function deletes a bitmap. fSuccess contains true if this function is successful. hbm contains the handle of the bitmap you want to delete. You can retrieve the last error using WinGetLastError. These errors include: 0x2008 PMERR_BITMAP_IS_SELETED 0x2032 PMERR_HBITMAP_BUSY 0x207B PMERR_INV_HBITMAP
fSuccess = GpiDeleteElement (hps)	The GpiDeleteElement function deletes the specified element. fSuccess contains true if this function is successful. hps contains the presentation space handle. You can retrieve the last error using WinGetLastError. These errors include: 0x207F PMERR_INV_HPS

Function	Description
	0x2089 PMERR_INV_IN_ELEMENT 0x20A1 PMERR_INV_MICROPS_FUNCTION 0x20E2 PMERR_NOT_IN_RETAIN_MODE 0x20E6 PMERR_NO_CURRENT_SEG 0x20F4 PMERR_PS_BUSY
fSuccess = GpiDeleteElement- Range (hps, lFirstElement, lLastElement)	The GpiDeleteElementRange function deletes the specified element range. fSuccess contains true if this function is successful. hps contains the presentation space handle. lFirstElement and lLastElement contain the number of the first and last elements to delete. You can retrieve the last error using WinGetLastError. These errors include:
	0x207F PMERR_INV_HPS 0x2089 PMERR_INV_IN_ELEMENT 0x20A1 PMERR_INV_MICROPS_FUNCTION 0x20E2 PMERR_NOT_IN_RETAIN_MODE 0x20E6 PMERR_NO_CURRENT_SEG 0x20F4 PMERR_PS_BUSY
fSuccess = GpiDeleteElements- BetweenLabels (hps, lFirstLabel, lLastLabel)	The GpiDeleteElementBetweenLabels function deletes the elements between the specified labels. fSuccess contains true if this function is successful. hps contains the presentation space handle. lFirstLabel and lLastLabel contains the labels marking the start and end of the range of elements to delete. You can retrieve the last error using WinGetLastError. These errors include:
	0x207F PMERR_INV_HPS 0x2089 PMERR_INV_IN_ELEMENT 0x20A1 PMERR_INV_MICROPS_FUNCTION 0x20D6 PMERR_LABEL_NOT_FOUND 0x20E2 PMERR_NOT_IN_RETAIN_MODE 0x20E6 PMERR_NO_CURRENT_SEG 0x20F4 PMERR_PS_BUSY
fSuccess = GpiDeleteMetaFile (hmf)	The GpiDeleteMetaFile function deletes a metafile. fSuccess contains true if this function is successful. hmf contains the metafile handle that you want to delete. You can retrieve the last error using WinGetLastError. These errors include:
	0x207E PMERR_INV_HMF 0x20D9 PMERR_METAFILE_IN_USE 0x2106 PMERR_TOO_MANY_METAFILES_IN_USE
fSuccess = GpiDeletePalette (hpal)	The GpiDeletePalette function deletes a color palette. fSuccess contains true if this function is successful. hpal contains the color palette handle that you want to delete. You can retrieve the last error using WinGetLastError. These errors include:
	0x201F PMERR_PALETTE_SELECTED 0x2111 PMERR_INV_HPAL 0x2112 PMERR_PALETTE_BUSY

Table 3-42   **Continued**

Function	Description
fSuccess = GpiDeleteSegment (hps, lSegid)	The GpiDeleteSegment function deletes a retained segment. fSuccess contains true if this function is successful. hps contains the presentation space handle. lSegid contains the segment identification. You can retrieve the last error using WinGetLastError. These errors include: 0x207F PMERR_INV_HPS 0x20A1 PMERR_INV_MICROPS_FUNCTION 0x20C8 PMERR_INV_SEG_NAME 0x20F4 PMERR_PS_BUSY
fSuccess = GpiDeleteSegments (hps, lFirstSegment, lLastSegment)	The GpiDeleteSegments function deletes a range of retained segments. fSuccess contains true if this function is successful. hps contains the presentation space handle. lFirstSegment and lLastSegment contain the first and last segment identifiers in the range that you want to delete. You can retrieve the last error using WinGetLastError. These errors include: 0x207F PMERR_INV_HPS 0x20A1 PMERR_INV_MICROPS_FUNCTION 0x20C8 PMERR_INV_SEG_NAME 0x20F4 PMERR_PS_BUSY
fSuccess = GpiDeleteSetId (hps, lLcid)	The GpiDeleteSetId function deletes a logical font or bitmap tag. Bitmaps are simply untagged; the handle to them still is valid. OS/2 deletes fonts from memory. fSuccess contains true if this function is successful. hps contains the presentation space handle. lLcid contains the identifier of the object that you want to delete. Specifying a value of LCID_ALL deletes all fonts and untags all bitmaps. It also restores the original default font. You can retrieve the last error using WinGetLastError. These errors include: 0x207F PMERR_INV_HPS 0x20CA PMERR_INV_SETID 0x20F4 PMERR_PS_BUSY 0x2102 PMERR_SETID_IN_USE 0x2103 PMERR_SETID_NOT_FOUND
fSuccess = GpiDestroyPS (hps)	The GpiDestroyPS function destroys the presentation space. It also destroys any objects owned by the presentation space. fSuccess contains true if this function is successful. hps contains the presentation space handle. You can retrieve the last error using WinGetLastError. These errors include: 0x207F PMERR_INV_HPS 0x20F4 PMERR_PS_BUSY 0x20F5 PMERR_PS_IS_ASSOCIATED
fSuccess = GpiDestroyRegion	The GpiDestroyRegion function destroys a region. fSuccess contains true if this function is successful. hps contains the

Function	Description
(hps, hrgn)	presentation space handle. hrgn contains the region handle that you want to destroy. You can retrieve the last error using WinGetLastError. These errors include:

0x2034   PMERR_HRGN_BUSY
0x207F   PMERR_INV_HPS
0x2080   PMERR_INV_HRGN
0x20F4   PMERR_PS_BUSY
0x20F8   PMERR_REGION_IS_CLIP_REGION

Function	Description
lHits = GpiDrawBits (hpsTarget, pBits, pbmi2InfoTable, lCount, aptlPoints, lRop, flOptions)	The GpiDrawBits function draws (copies) a rectangle of bits from a storage area to the specified device context. lHits contains the correlation and error indicators. hpsTarget contains the presentation space handle of the target. pBits contains a pointer to the source bits (must use a standard bitmap format). pbmi2InfoTable contains a bitmap information table that describes the format of the source bits. lCount is always equal to 4. aptlPoints contains an array of lCount points. These points are: Tx1, Ty1, Tx2, Ty2, Sx1, Sy1, Sx2, and Sy2. The first set of points is the bottom-left corner. The second set of points is the upper-right corner. lRop contains the mixing function required. There are 15 different mixing actions including: ROP_SRCCOPY, ROP_SRCPAINT, ROP_SRCAND, ROP_SRCINVERT, ROP_SRCERASE, ROP_NOTSRCCOPY, ROP_NOTSRCERASE, ROP_MERGECOPY, ROP_MERGEPAINT, ROP_PATCOPY, ROPPATPAINT, ROP_PATINVERT, ROP_DSTINVERT, ROP_ZERO, and ROP_ONE. flOptions contains a list of applicable options. You can use bits 15 through 31 for unique modes supported by particular devices. Other values for this parameter include: BBO_OR, BOO_AND, and BBO_IGNORE. GpiBitBlt returns one of the following values:

0000   GPI_ERROR
0001   GPI_OK
0002   GPI_HITS

You can retrieve the last error using WinGetLastError. These errors include:

0x203C   PMERR_INCORRECT_DC_TYPE
0x2046   PMERR_INV_BITBLT_MIX
0x2047   PMERR_INV_BITBLT_STYLE
0x205B   PMERR_INV_COORDINATE
0x207F   PMERR_INV_HPS
0x2092   PMERR_INV_LENGTH_OR_COUNT
0x20BD   PMERR_INV_RECT
0x20F4   PMERR_PS_BUSY

Function	Description
fSuccess = GpiDrawChain (hps)	The GpiDrawChain function draws the segments that are in a segment chain. fSuccess contains true if this function is successful. hps contains the presentation space handle. You can retrieve the last error using WinGetLastError. These errors include:

Table 3-42   **Continued**

Function	Description
	0x207F PMERR_INV_HPS 0x20A1 PMERR_INV_MICROPS_FUNCTION 0x20F4 PMERR_PS_BUSY
fSuccess = GpiDrawDynamics (hps)	The GpiDrawDynamics function redraws the dynamic segments (segments with the ATTR_DYNAMIC segment attribute) in or called from the segment chain. fSuccess contains true if this function is successful. hps contains the presentation space handle. You can retrieve the last error using WinGetLastError. These errors include: 0x2074 PMERR_INV_FOR_THIS_DC_TYPE 0x207F PMERR_INV_HPS 0x20A1 PMERR_INV_MICROPS_FUNCTION 0x20F4 PMERR_PS_BUSY
fSuccess = GpiDrawFrom (hps, lFirstSegment, lLastSegment)	The GpiDrawFrom function draws a section of the segment chain. fSuccess contains true if this function is successful. hps contains the presentation space handle. lFirstSegment and lLastSegment contain the identifiers of the first and last segments that you want to draw. You can retrieve the last error using WinGetLastError. These errors include: 0x207F PMERR_INV_HPS 0x20A1 PMERR_INV_MICROPS_FUNCTION 0x20C8 PMERR_INV_SEG_NAME 0x20F4 PMERR_PS_BUSY 0x20FF PMERR_SEG_NOT_CHAINED 0x2100 PMERR_SEG_NOT_FOUND
fSuccess = GpiDrawSegment (hps, lSegment)	The GpiDrawSegment function draws the specified segment. fSuccess contains true if this function is successful. hps contains the presentation space handle. lSegment contains the identifier of the segment that you want to draw. You can retrieve the last error using WinGetLastError. These errors include: 0x207F PMERR_INV_HPS 0x20A1 PMERR_INV_MICROPS_FUNCTION 0x20C8 PMERR_INV_SEG_NAME 0x20F4 PMERR_PS_BUSY 0x2100 PMERR_SEG_NOT_FOUND
lHits = GpiElement (hps, lType, pszDesc, lLength, pbData)	The GpiElement function adds a single element to the current segment. lHits contains the correlation and error indicators. hps contains the presentation space handle. lType contains the type you want to associate with the element. Application-defined types should use the range 81000000h to FFFFFFFFh to avoid conflict with system-generated elements. pszDesc contains a string that describes the element. lLength contains the length of the data for the element. pbData is a pointer to the buffer containing the data.

Function	Description
	GpiElement returns one of the following values:
	0000 GPI_ERROR 0001 GPI_OK 0002 GPI_HITS
	You can retrieve the last error using WinGetLastError. These errors include:
	0x2002 PMERR_ALREADY_IN_ELEMENT 0x207F PMERR_INV_HPS 0x2092 PMERR_INV_LENGTH_OR_COUNT 0x20A0 PMERR_INV_MICROPS_FUNCTION 0x20D4 PMERR_DATA_TOO_LONG 0x20F4 PMERR_PS_BUSY
lHits = GpiEndArea (hps)	The GpiEndArea function ends the construction of a shaded area. OS/2 automatically adds a closing line (if required) before ending the construction. lHits contains the correlation and error indicators. hps contains the presentation space handle. GpiEndArea returns one of the following values:
	0000 GPI_ERROR 0001 GPI_OK 0002 GPI_HITS
	You can retrieve the last error using WinGetLastError. These errors include:
	0x2014 PMERR_COORDINATE_OVERFLOW 0x207F PMERR_INV_HPS 0x20DD PMERR_NOT_IN_AREA 0x20F4 PMERR_PS_BUSY
fSuccess = GpiEndElement (hps)	The GpiEndElement function terminates an element started by GpiBeginElement. fSuccess contains true if this function is successful. hps contains the presentation space handle. You can retrieve the last error using WinGetLastError. These errors include:
	0x207F PMERR_INV_HPS 0x20DF PMERR_NOT_IN_ELEMENT 0x20F4 PMERR_PS_BUSY
fSuccess = GpiEndPath (hps)	The GpiEndPath function ends the specification of a path started by GpiBeginPath. fSuccess contains true if this function is successful. hps contains the presentation space handle. You can retrieve the last error using WinGetLastError. These errors include:
	0x207F PMERR_INV_HPS 0x20E1 PMERR_NOT_IN_PATH 0x20F4 PMERR_PS_BUSY
lEquality = GpiEqualRegion	The GpiEqualRegion function compares to regions of equal device class for equality. lEquality contains the equality and error

Table 3-42   **Continued**

Function	Description
(hps, hrgnSrc1, hrgnSrc2)	indicators. hps contains the presentation space handle. hrgnSrc1 contains the handle of the first region. hrgnSrc2 contains the handle of the second region. GpiEqualRegion returns one of the following values: 0000 EQRGN_ERROR 0001 EQRGN_NOTEQUAL 0002 EQRGN_EQUAL You can retrieve the last error using WinGetLastError. These errors include: 0x2034 PMERR_HRGN_BUSY 0x207F PMERR_INV_HPS 0x2080 PMERR_INV_HRGN 0x20F4 PMERR_PS_BUSY 0x20F8 PMERR_REGION_IS_CLIP_REGION
fSuccess = GpiErase (hps)	The GpiErase function clears the output area of the device context associated with a particular presentation space. It uses the current background color and observes all clipping limitations. fSuccess contains true if this function is successful. hps contains the presentation space handle. You can retrieve the last error using WinGetLastError. These errors include: 0x207F PMERR_INV_HPS 0x20F4 PMERR_PS_BUSY
lOff = GpiErrorSegment-Data (hps, plSegment, plContext)	The GpiErrorSegmentData function returns data about the last segment drawing error. This includes the segment name, context, and byte offset or element number. lOff contains the position of the error or an error indicator (a return value of 0). hps contains the presentation space handle. plSegment contains the segment in which the error occurred. plContext contains the context of the error including: GPIE_SEGMENT, GPIE_ELEMENT, and GPIE_DATA. You can retrieve the last error using WinGetLastError. These errors include: 0x207F PMERR_INV_HPS 0x20A0 PMERR_INV_MICROPS_FUNCTION 0x20F4 PMERR_PS_BUSY
lComplexity = GpiExcludeClip-Rectangle (hps, prclRectangle)	The GpiExcludeClipRectangle function excludes the interior of a rectangular area from the clipping region. It creates a clipping region if one does not exist already. lComplexity contains the complexity of clipping or an error indicator. hps contains the presentation space handle. prclRectangle contains the coordinates of the rectangle that you want to exclude in world coordinates. GpiExcludeClipRectangle returns one of the following values:

Function	Description
	0000 RGN_ERROR 0001 RGN_NULL 0002 RGN_RECT 0003 RGN_COMPLEX

You can retrieve the last error using WinGetLastError. These errors include:

0x205B   PMERR_INV_COORDINATE
0x207F   PMERR_INV_HPS
0x20BD   PMERR_INV_RECT
0x20F4   PMERR_PS_BUSY

lHits = GpiFillPath (hps, lPath, lOptions)

The GpiFillPath function fills the interior of a path using the area attributes. It automatically closes any open figures within the path, then deletes the path once it completes the task. lHits contains the correlation and error indicators. hps contains the presentation space handle. lPath is the identifier of the path that you want to draw (always a value of 1). lOptions contains the fill option including: FPATH_ALTERNATE and FPATH_WINDING. GpiFillPath returns one of the following values:

0000   GPI_ERROR
0001   GPI_OK
0002   GPI_HITS

You can retrieve the last error using WinGetLastError. These errors include:

0x2070   PMERR_INV_FILL_PATH_OPTIONS
0x207F   PMERR_INV_HPS
0x20AE   PMERR_INV_PATH_ID
0x20F4   PMERR_PS_BUSY
0x20FF   PMERR_PATH_UNKNOWN

lHits = GpiFloodFill (hps, lOptions, lColor)

The GpiFloodFill function fills an area bounded by a specific color or while on a specific color. The area attributes define the fill. The results of this function are very device dependent. lHits contains the correlation and error indicators. hps contains the presentation space handle. lOptions defines the flood fill options that include: FF_BOUNDARY and FF_SURFACE. lColor contains the boundary or surface color. GpiFloodFill returns one of the following values:

0000   GPI_ERROR
0001   GPI_OK
0002   GPI_HITS

You can retrieve the last error using WinGetLastError. These errors include:

0x1641   PMERR_FUNCTION_NOT_SUPPORTED
0x203E   PMERR_INSUFFICIENT_MEMORY
0x2053   PMERR_INV_COLOR_ATTR
0x207F   PMERR_INV_HPS
0x2085   PMERR_INV_IN_AREA

Table 3-42 **Continued**

Function	Description

0x208B PMERR_INV_IN_PATH
0x20F4 PMERR_PS_BUSY
0x210D PMERR_INV_FLOOD_FILL_OPTIONS
0x2113 PMERR_START_POINT_CLIPPED
0x2114 PMERR_NO_FILL

lHits = GpiFrameRegion (hps, hrgn, psizlThickness)

The GpiFrameRegion function draws a frame within a region using the current pattern attributes. lHits contains the correlation and error indicators. hps contains the presentation space handle. hrgn contains the region handle. psizlThickness contains the thickness of the frame. There are two coordinates, one for the X-axis and another for the Y-axis. GpiFrameRegion returns one of the following values:

0000 GPI_ERROR
0001 GPI_OK
0002 GPI_HITS

You can retrieve the last error using WinGetLastError. These errors include:

0x2034 PMERR_HRGN_BUSY
0x207F PMERR_INV_HPS
0x2080 PMERR_INV_HRGN
0x20F4 PMERR_PS_BUSY
0x20F8 PMERR_REGION_IS_CLIP_REGION

lHits = GpiFullArc (hps, lControl, fxMultiplier)

The GpiFullArc function draws an arc with the current cursor position as its center. lHits contains the correlation and error indicators. hps contains the presentation space handle. lControl contains the interior and outline control values including: DRO_FILL, DRO_OUTLINE, and DRO_OUTLINEFILL. fxMultiplier determines the size of the arc in relation to an arc with the current arc parameters. GpiFullArc returns one of the following values:

0000 GPI_ERROR
0001 GPI_OK
0002 GPI_HITS

You can retrieve the last error using WinGetLastError. These errors include:

0x2040 PMERR_INV_ARC_CONTROL
0x207F PMERR_INV_HPS
0x20A7 PMERR_INV_MULTIPLIER
0x20F4 PMERR_PS_BUSY

lCount = GpiGetData (hps, lSegid, plOffset, lFormat,

The GpiGetData function retrieves a set of drawing orders from the specified segment and places them in the supplied buffer. lCount contains the number of bytes of drawing data returned in pbData or

Function	Description
lLength, pbData)	an error indicator (a return value of 0). The drawing information in pbData probably is incomplete if lCount equals the value of lLength on return from this call. hps contains a handle to the presentation space. lSegid contains the segment identifier. plOffset contains the segment offset. Always set this value to 0 the first time that you call GpiGetData and to the position of the last segment data retrieved on subsequent calls. lFormat contains the coordinate type required (currently a value of DFORM_NOCONV). lLength is the length of the data buffer. pbData contains the drawing data. You can retrieve the last error using WinGetLastError. These errors include:

0x200F   PMERR_SEG_IS_CURRENT
0x2016   PMERR_DATA_TOO_LONG
0x2079   PMERR_INV_GETDATA_CONTROL
0x207F   PMERR_INV_HPS
0x2092   PMERR_INV_LENGTH_OR_COUNT
0x20A1   PMERR_INV_MICROPS_FUNCTION
0x20C8   PMERR_INV_SEG_NAME
0x20C9   PMERR_INV_SEG_OFFSET
0x20F4   PMERR_PS_BUSY
0x2100   PMERR_SEG_NOT_FOUND

Function	Description
lHits = GpiImage (hps, lFormat, psizlImageSize, lLength, pbData)	The GpiImage function draws a rectangular image with the top-left corner at the current cursor position. lHits contains the correlation and error indicators. hps contains the presentation space handle. lFormat contains the format of the image data (always set to 0). psizlImageSize contains the width and height of the image area in pels. lLength contains the length of pbData in bytes. pbData contains the image data. Each row must contain a multiple of 8 bits. For example, if the pel data contains 12-bits, you must pad it to 16. The value in lLength must reflect the length of the padded data. GpiImage returns one of the following values:

0000   GPI_ERROR
0001   GPI_OK
0002   GPI_HITS

You can retrieve the last error using WinGetLastError. These errors include:

0x207F   PMERR_INV_HPS
0x2082   PMERR_INV_IMAGE_DATA_LENGTH
0x2083   PMERR_INV_IMAGE_DIMENSION
0x2084   PMERR_INV_IMAGE_FORMAT
0x20F4   PMERR_PS_BUSY

Function	Description
lComplexity = GpiIntersectClip-	The GpiIntersectClipRectangle function sets the new clip region to the intersection of the current clip region and the specified

Table 3-42   **Continued**

Function	Description
Rectangle (hps, prclRectangle)	rectangle. lComplexity contains the complexity of the resulting region or an error indicator on return from the function call. hps contains a presentation space handle. prclRectangle contains the rectangle coordinates in world coordinates. GpiIntersectClip Rectangle returns one of the following values: 0000 RGN_ERROR 0001 RGN_NULL 0002 RGN_RECT 0003 RGN_COMPLEX You can retrieve the last error using WinGetLastError. These errors include: 0x205B PMERR_INV_COORDINATE 0x207F PMERR_INV_HPS 0x20BD PMERR_INV_RECT 0x20F4 PMERR_PS_BUSY
fSuccess = GpiLabel (hps, lLabel)	The GpiLabel function generates an element containing a label. fSuccess contains true if this function is successful. hps contains the presentation space handle. lLabel contains the label that you want to assign to the element. You can retrieve the last error using WinGetLastError. These errors include: 0x207F PMERR_INV_HPS 0x2089 PMERR_INV_IN_ELEMENT 0x20A1 PMERR_INV_MICROPS_FUNCTION 0x20F4 PMERR_PS_BUSY
lHits = GpiLine (hps, pptlEndPoint)	The GpiLine function draws a line from the current cursor position to the specified end point. OS/2 uses the current line color, mix, width, and type values. lHits contains the correlation and error indicators. hps contains the presentation space handle. pptlEndPoint contains the coordinates of the end point of the line. GpiEndArea returns one of the following values: 0000 GPI_ERROR 0001 GPI_OK 0002 GPI_HITS You can retrieve the last error using WinGetLastError. These errors include: 0x205B PMERR_INV_COORDINATE 0x207F PMERR_INV_HPS 0x20A8 PMERR_INV_NESTED_FIGURES 0x20F4 PMERR_PS_BUSY
hbm =	The GpiLoadBitmap function loads a bitmap from a resource and

Function	Description
GpiLoadBitmap (hps, Resource, idBitmap, lWidth, lHeight)	returns a handle to it. hbm contains the bitmap handle (or 0 for an error condition). hps contains the presentation space handle. Resource contains the bitmap identity. It contains NULLHANDLE when you want to use the EXE file of the application. idBitmap is the identification of the bitmap within the resource file. lWidth is the width of the bitmap in pels. lHeight is the height in pels. OS/2 stretches the bitmap to fit within lWidth and lHeight; use a value of zero to load the bitmap without stretching it. You can retrieve the last error using WinGetLastError. These errors include: 0x200A PMERR_BITMAP_NOT_FOUND 0x2047 PMERR_INV_BITMAP_DIMENSION 0x207F PMERR_INV_HPS 0x20F4 PMERR_PS_BUSY
fSuccess = GpiLoadFonts (hab, pszFilename)	The GpiLoadFonts function loads one or more fonts from the specified resource file. fSuccess contains true if this function is successful. hab contains the anchor block handle. pszFilename contains the font filename (OS/2 assumes a FON extension). You can retrieve the last error using WinGetLastError. These errors include: 0x2073 PMERR_INV_FONT_FILE_DATA
hmf = GpiLoadMetaFile (hab, pszFilename)	The GpiLoadMetaFile function loads data from a file into a metafile. hmf contains the metafile handle (a value of 0 signifies an error). hab contains the anchor block handle. pszFilename contains the filename. You can retrieve the last error using WinGetLastError. These errors include: 0x2024 PMERR_DOSOPEN_FAILURE 0x2025 PMERR_DOSREAD_FAILURE
fSuccess = GpiLoadPublicFonts (hab, pszFilename)	The GpiLoadPublicFonts function loads one or more fonts from the specified resource file. Any application can use these fonts. fSuccess contains true if this function is successful. hab contains the anchor block handle. pszFilename contains the font filename (OS/2 assumes a FON extension). You can retrieve the last error using WinGetLastError. These errors include: 0x203F PMERR_INSUFFICIENT_MEMORY 0x2073 PMERR_INV_FONT_FILE_DATA
lHits = GpiMarker (hps, pptlPoint)	The GpiMarker function draws a marker centered at the specified location. lHits contains the correlation and error indicators. hps contains the presentation space handle. pptlPoint contains the center point coordinates. GpiMarker returns one of the following values: 0000 GPI_ERROR 0001 GPI_OK 0002 GPI_HITS

Table 3-42   **Continued**

Function	Description
	You can retrieve the last error using WinGetLastError. These errors include:

0x205B   PMERR_INV_COORDINATE
0x207F   PMERR_INV_HPS
0x20F4   PMERR_PS_BUSY

| fSuccess = GpiModifyPath (hps, lPath, lMode) | The GpiModifyPath function modifies the specified path. fSuccess contains true if this function is successful. hps contains the presentation space handle. lPath contains the path identifier (always set to 1). lMode contains the type of modification required (MPATH_STROKE is the only valid value). You can retrieve the last error using WinGetLastError. These errors include: |

0x2014   PMERR_COORDINATE_OVERFLOW
0x207F   PMERR_INV_HPS
0x20A6   PMERR_INV_MODIFY_PATH_MODE
0x20AE   PMERR_INV_PATH_ID
0x20F4   PMERR_PS_BUSY
0x20FF   PMERR_PATH_UNKNOWN

| fSuccess = GpiMove (hps, pptlPoint) | The GpiMove function moves the cursor from the current position to the specified position. fSuccess contains true if this function is successful. hps contains the presentation space handle. pptlPoint contains the new cursor position in world coordinates. You can retrieve the last error using WinGetLastError. These errors include: |

0x205B   PMERR_INV_COORDINATE
0x207F   PMERR_INV_HPS
0x20F4   PMERR_PS_BUSY

| lComplexity = GpiOffsetClipRegion (hps, pptlPoint) | The GpiOffsetClipRegion function moves the clipping region to a new position. lComplexity contains the complexity of the resulting region or an error indicator on return from the function call. hps contains a presentation space handle. pptlPoint contains the clipping region position offset in world coordinates. GpiOffsetClipRegion returns one of the following values: |

0000   RGN_ERROR
0001   RGN_NULL
0002   RGN_RECT
0003   RGN_COMPLEX

You can retrieve the last error using WinGetLastError. These errors include:

0x2014   PMERR_COORDINATE_OVERFLOW
0x207F   PMERR_INV_HPS
0x20F4   PMERR_PS_BUSY

fSuccess =
GpiOffsetElement-
Pointer (hps, lOffset)

The GpiOffsetElementPointer function moves the element pointer within the current segment by the specified offset. fSuccess contains true if this function is successful. hps contains the presentation space handle. lOffset contains the element position offset in world coordinates. You can retrieve the last error using WinGetLastError. These errors include:

0x207F PMERR_INV_HPS
0x2089 PMERR_INV_IN_ELEMENT
0x20A1 PMERR_INV_MICROPS_FUNCTION
0x20E2 PMERR_NOT_IN_RETAIN_MODE
0x20E6 PMERR_NO_CURRENT_SEG
0x20F4 PMERR_PS_BUSY

fSuccess =
GpiOffsetRegion
(hps, hrgn,
pptlOffset)

The GpiOffsetRegion moves a range by the specified offset. fSuccess contains true if this function is successful. hps contains the presentation space handle. hrgn contains the region handle. pptlOffset contains the region position offset in world coordinates. You can retrieve the last error using WinGetLastError. These errors include:

0x2034 PMERR_HRGN_BUSY
0x205B PMERR_INV_COORDINATE
0x207F PMERR_INV_HPS
0x2080 PMERR_INV_HRGN
0x20F4 PMERR_PS_BUSY
0x20F8 PMERR_REGION_IS_CLIP_REGION

fSuccess =
GpiOpenSegment
(hps, lSegment)

The GpiOpenSegment function opens a segment using the specified identification number. fSuccess contains true if this function is successful. hps contains the presentation space handle. lSegment contains the segment identification number. A value of zero always results in a new segment, even if there is one using that identifier. However, OS/2 chains zero segments together; you cannot refer to a single segment. A positive (nonzero) number creates a new retained segment if one that uses that identifier does not exist already. If one does exist, OS/2 reopens it in retain mode. You can retrieve the last error using WinGetLastError. These errors include:

0x2004 PMERR_ALREADY_IN_SEG
0x2005 PMERR_AREA_INCOMPLETE
0x2029 PMERR_DYNAMIC_SEG_ZERO_INV
0x207F PMERR_INV_HPS
0x20A1 PMERR_INV_MICROPS_FUNCTION
0x20A4 PMERR_INV_MODE_FOR_OPEN_DYN
0x20A5 PMERR_INV_MODE_FOR_REOPEN_SEG
0x20C8 PMERR_INV_SEG_NAME
0x20F4 PMERR_PS_BUSY
0x20FC PMERR_PATH_INCOMPLETE
0x2108 PMERR_UNCHAINED_SEG_ZERO_INV

lHits =
GpiOutlinePath (hps,

The GpiOutlinePath function draws the outline of a path. lHits contains the correlation and error indicators. hps contains the

Table 3-42   **Continued**

Function	Description
lPath, lOptions)	presentation space handle. lPath is the path identifier (always set to 1). lOptions is reserved (always set to 0). GpiOutlinePath returns one of the following values:

0000   GPI_ERROR
0001   GPI_OK
0002   GPI_HITS

You can retrieve the last error using WinGetLastError. These errors include:

0x207F   PMERR_INV_HPS
0x20AE   PMERR_INV_PATH_ID
0x20C1   PMERR_INV_RESERVED_FIELD
0x20F4   PMERR_PS_BUSY
0x20FF   PMERR_PATH_UNKNOWN

| lHits =
GpiPaintRegion
(hps, hrgn) | The GpiPaintRegion function pains a region into a presentation space using the current pattern attributes. lHits contains the correlation and error indicators. hps contains the presentation space handle. hrgn contains the region handle. GpiPaintRegion returns one of the following values: |

0000   GPI_ERROR
0001   GPI_OK
0002   GPI_HITS

You can retrieve the last error using WinGetLastError. These errors include:

0x2034   PMERR_HRGN_BUSY
0x207F   PMERR_INV_HPS
0x2080   PMERR_INV_HRGN
0x20F4   PMERR_PS_BUSY
0x20F8   PMERR_REGION_IS_CLIP_REGION

| lHits = GpiPartialArc
(hps, pptlCenter,
fxMultiplier,
fxStartAngle,
fxSweepAngle) | The GpiPartialArc function draws a straight line followed by an arc. lHits contains the correlation and error indicators. hps contains the presentation space handle. pptlCenter contains the center point coordinates. fxMultiplier determines the size of the arc in relation to an arc with the current arc parameters. fxStartAngle contains the start angle in degrees (always positive). fsSweepAngle contains the sweep angle in degrees (always positive). GpiPartialArc returns one of the following values: |

0000   GPI_ERROR
0001   GPI_OK
0002   GPI_HITS

You can retrieve the last error using WinGetLastError. These errors include:

Function	Description
	0x203F PMERR_INV_ANGLE_PARM 0x205B PMERR_INV_COORDINATE 0x207F PMERR_INV_HPS 0x20A7 PMERR_INV_MULTIPLIER 0x20A8 PMERR_INV_NESTED_FIGURES 0x20F4 PMERR_PS_BUSY
hrgn = GpiPathToRegion (hps, lPath, flOptions)	The GpiPathToRegion function converts a path to a region. It automatically closes any open figures within the path. You cannot reuse the path for other purposes once you convert it. hrgn contains the region handle (0 for an error condition). hps contains the presentation space handle. lPath contains the path identifier (always set to 1). flOptions contains the fill options, which include: FPATH_ALTERNATE and FPATH_WINDING. You can retrieve the last error using WinGetLastError. These errors include: 0x207F PMERR_INV_HPS 0x20AE PMERR_INV_PATH_ID 0x20F4 PMERR_PS_BUSY 0x20FF PMERR_PATH_UNKNOWN
lHits = GpiPlayMetaFile (hps, hmf, lCount1, alOptarray, plSegCount, lCount2, pszDesc)	The GpiPlayMetaFile function plays (executes) a metafile into a presentation space. lHits contains the correlation and error indicators. hps contains the presentation space handle. hmf contains the metafile handle. lCount1 contains the number of elements in alOptarray. alOptarray contains the options for playing the metafile. There are nine fields within alOptarray. The PMF_SEGBASE and PMF_RESOLVE fields are reserved, set them to zero. The PMF_LOADTYPE field can contain any of the following values: LT_DEFAULT, LT_NOMODIFY and LT_ORIGINALVIEW. The PMF_LCIDS field can contain any of the following values: LC_DEFAULT, LC_NOLOAD, and LC_LOADDISC. The PMF_RESET field can contain any of the following values: RES_DEFAULT, RES_NORESET, and RES_RESET. The PMF_SUPRESS field can contain any of the following values: SUP_DEFAULT, SUP_NOSUPPRESS, and SUP_SUPPRESS. The PMF_COLORTABLES field can contain any of the following values: CTAB_DEFAULT, CTAB_NOMODIFY, CTAB_REPLACE, and CTAB_REPLACEPALETTE. The PMF_COLORREALIZE field can contain any of the following values: CREA_DEFAULT, CREA_DOREALIZE, and CREA_NOREALIZE. The PMF_DEFAULTS field can contain any of the following values: DDEF_DEFAULT, DDEF_IGNORE, and DDEF_LOADDISC. plSegCount is a reserved parameter, OS/2 always sets it to zero. lCount2 contains the number of bytes in pszDesc. pszDesc contains a descriptive record for the metafile on return from the function call. It is always null terminated. GpiPlayMetaFile returns one of the following values: 0000 GPI_ERROR 0001 GPI_OK

Table 3-42   **Continued**

Function	Description
	0002 GPI_HITS

You can retrieve the last error using WinGetLastError. These errors include:

0x203B	PMERR_INCOMPATIBLE_METAFILE
0x206B	PMERR_INV_ELEMENT_POINTER
0x207E	PMERR_INV_HMF
0x207F	PMERR_INV_HPS
0x2087	PMERR_INV_IN_CURRENT_EDIT_MODE
0x2092	PMERR_INV_LENGTH_OR_COUNT
0x209D	PMERR_INV_METAFILE
0x20A2	PMERR_INV_MICROPS_ORDER
0x20AC	PMERR_INV_OUTSIDE_DRAW_MODE
0x20B8	PMERR_INV_PLAY_METAFILE_OPTION
0x20F2	PMERR_PROLOG_ERROR
0x20F4	PMERR_PS_BUSY
0x2105	PMERR_STOP_DRAW_OCCURRED
0x5004	PMERR_DUP_SEG

lHits = GpiPointArc (hps, aptlPoints)

The GpiPointArc function creates an arc using the current arc parameters (through three points) starting at the current cursor position. lHits contains the correlation and error indicators. hps contains the presentation space handle. aptlPoints contains the intermediate and end points. GpiPointArc returns one of the following values:

0000   GPI_ERROR
0001   GPI_OK
0002   GPI_HITS

You can retrieve the last error using WinGetLastError. These errors include:

0x205B	PMERR_INV_COORDINATE
0x207F	PMERR_INV_HPS
0x20A8	PMERR_INV_NESTED_FIGURES
0x20F4	PMERR_PS_BUSY

lHits = GpiPolyFillet (hps, lCount, aptlPoints)

The GpiPolyFillet function draws a curve starting at the current position. The curve is defined by the points that you supply. lHits contains the correlation and error indicators. hps contains the presentation space handle. lCount contains the number of points in aptlPoints. aptlPoints contains an array of points. GpiPolyFillet returns one of the following values:

0000   GPI_ERROR
0001   GPI_OK
0002   GPI_HITS

Function	Description
	You can retrieve the last error using WinGetLastError. These errors include:

0x205B   PMERR_INV_COORDINATE
0x207F   PMERR_INV_HPS
0x2092   PMERR_INV_LENGTH_OR_COUNT
0x20A8   PMERR_INV_NESTED_FIGURES
0x20F4   PMERR_PS_BUSY

lHits = GpiPolyFilletSharp (hps, lCount, aptlPoints, afxSharpness)

The GpiPolyFilletSharp function draws a series of connected lines starting at the current position. The line endpoints are defined by the points you supply. lHits contains the correlation and error indicators. hps contains the presentation space handle. lCount contains the number of points in aptlPoints. aptlPoints contains an array of points. afxSharpness contains an array of sharpness values which affect the sharpness of successive fillets. GpiPolyFilletSharp returns one of the following values:

0000   GPI_ERROR
0001   GPI_OK
0002   GPI_HITS

You can retrieve the last error using WinGetLastError. These errors include:

0x205B   PMERR_INV_COORDINATE
0x207F   PMERR_INV_HPS
0x2092   PMERR_INV_LENGTH_OR_COUNT
0x20A8   PMERR_INV_NESTED_FIGURES
0x20CD   PMERR_INV_SHARPNESS_PARM
0x20F4   PMERR_PS_BUSY

lHits = GpiPolygons (hps, lCount, alPolygons, lOptions, lModel)

The GpiPolygons function draws a closed set of polygons. lHits contains the correlation and error indicators. hps contains the presentation space handle. lCount contains the number of polygons listed in alPolygons. alPolygons contains an array of polygons. lOptions contains a list of drawing options, which include: POLYGON_NOBOUNDARY, POLYGON_BOUNDARY, POLYGON_ALTERNATE, and POLYGON_WINDING. lModel contains the drawing model, which includes: POLYGON_INCL and POLYGON_EXCL. GpiPolygons returns one of the following values:

0000   GPI_ERROR
0001   GPI_OK
0002   GPI_HITS

You can retrieve the last error using WinGetLastError. These errors include:

0x2001   PMERR_ALREADY_IN_AREA
0x2041   PMERR_INV_AREA_CONTROL
0x207F   PMERR_INV_HPS
0x208B   PMERR_INV_IN_PATH
0x20F4   PMERR_PS_BUSY

Table 3-42   **Continued**

Function	Description
lHits = GpiPolyLine (hps, lCount, aptlPoints)	The GpiPolyLine function draws a series of straight lines starting at the current cursor location and connecting the specified points. lHits contains the correlation and error indicators. hps contains the presentation space handle. lCount contains the number of points in aptlPoints. aptlPoints contains an array of points. GpiPolyLine returns one of the following values: 0000 GPI_ERROR 0001 GPI_OK 0002 GPI_HITS You can retrieve the last error using WinGetLastError. These errors include: 0x205B PMERR_INV_COORDINATE 0x207F PMERR_INV_HPS 0x2092 PMERR_INV_LENGTH_OR_COUNT 0x20A8 PMERR_INV_NESTED_FIGURES 0x20F4 PMERR_PS_BUSY
lHits = GpiPolyLineDisjoint (hps, lCount, aptlPoints)	The GpiPolyLineDisjoint function draws a series of disjoint straight lines using the endpoint pairs that you supply. lHits contains the correlation and error indicators. hps contains the presentation space handle. lCount contains the number of points in aptlPoints. aptlPoints contains an array of points. GpiPolyLineDisjoint returns one of the following values: 0000 GPI_ERROR 0001 GPI_OK 0002 GPI_HITS You can retrieve the last error using WinGetLastError. These errors include: 0x205B PMERR_INV_COORDINATE 0x207F PMERR_INV_HPS 0x2092 PMERR_INV_LENGTH_OR_COUNT 0x20A8 PMERR_INV_NESTED_FIGURES 0x20F4 PMERR_PS_BUSY
lHits = GpiPolyMarker (hps, lCount, aptlPoints)	The GpiPolyMarker function draws markers with their centers at the points specified. lHits contains the correlation and error indicators. hps contains the presentation space handle. lCount contains the number of points in aptlPoints. aptlPoints contains an array of points. GpiPolyMarker returns one of the following values: 0000 GPI_ERROR 0001 GPI_OK 0002 GPI_HITS You can retrieve the last error using WinGetLastError. These errors include:

Function	Description
	0x205B PMERR_INV_COORDINATE 0x207F PMERR_INV_HPS 0x2092 PMERR_INV_LENGTH_OR_COUNT 0x20F4 PMERR_PS_BUSY
lHits = GpiPolySpline (hps, lCount, aptlPoints)	The GpiPolySpline function creates a succession of Bezier splines. lHits contains the correlation and error indicators. hps contains the presentation space handle. lCount contains the number of points in aptlPoints. aptlPoints contains an array of points. GpiPolySpline returns one of the following values: 0000 GPI_ERROR 0001 GPI_OK 0002 GPI_HITS You can retrieve the last error using WinGetLastError. These errors include: 0x205B PMERR_INV_COORDINATE 0x207F PMERR_INV_HPS 0x2092 PMERR_INV_LENGTH_OR_COUNT 0x20A8 PMERR_INV_NESTED_FIGURES 0x20F4 PMERR_PS_BUSY
fSuccess = GpiPop (hps, lCount)	The GpiPop function allows you to restore the primitives that you saved on the stack. This allows you to reset the previous conditions one or more steps at a time. fSuccess contains true if this function is successful. hps contains a presentation space handle. lCount contains the number of attributes that you want to restore. You can retrieve the last error using WinGetLastError. These errors include: 0x207F PMERR_INV_HPS 0x2092 PMERR_INV_LENGTH_OR_COUNT 0x20A1 PMERR_INV_MICROPS_FUNCTION 0x20F4 PMERR_PS_BUSY 0x20FC PMERR_SEG_CALL_STACK_EMPTY
lInside = GpiPtInRegion (hps, hrgn, pptlPoint)	The GpiPtInRegion function checks to see if the specified point is within a region. lInside contains the inside and error indicators. hps contains the presentation space handle. hrgn contains the region handle. pptlPoint contains points that you want to check in device coordinates. GpiPtInRegion returns one of the following values: 0000 PRGN_ERROR 0001 PRGN_OUTSIDE 0002 PRGN_INSIDE You can retrieve the last error using WinGetLastError. These errors include: 0x2034 PMERR_HRGN_BUSY 0x205B PMERR_INV_COORDINATE 0x207F PMERR_INV_HPS

Table 3-42   **Continued**

Function	Description
	0x2080 PMERR_INV_HRGN 0x20F4 PMERR_PS_BUSY 0x20F8 PMERR_REGION_IS_CLIP_REGION
lVisibility = GpiPtVisible (hps, pptlPoint)	The GpiPtVisible function checks whether a point is visible within the clipping region of the device associated with the specified presentation space. lVisibility contains the visibility and error indicators. hps contains the presentation space handle. pptlPoint contains the point that you want to check in world coordinates. GpiPtVisible returns one of the following values: 0000 PVIS_ERROR 0001 PVIS_INVISIBLE 0002 PVIS_VISIBLE You can retrieve the last error using WinGetLastError. These errors include: 0x205B PMERR_INV_COORDINATE 0x207F PMERR_INV_HPS 0x20F4 PMERR_PS_BUSY
lHits = GpiPutData (hps, lFormat, plLength, pbData)	The GpiPutData function passes a buffer of graphics orders to the current segment. You also can use it to draw the orders. lHits contains the correlation and error indicators. hps contains the presentation space handle. lFormat contains the coordinate type used including: DFORM_NOCONV, DFORM_S370SHORT, DFORM_PCSHORT, and DFORM_PCLONG. plLength contains the length of the graphic data in pbData. pbData is a buffer containing the orders that you want copied. GpiPutData returns one of the following values: 0000 GPI_ERROR 0001 GPI_OK 0002 GPI_HITS You can retrieve the last error using WinGetLastError. These errors include: 0x206B PMERR_INV_ELEMENT_POINTER 0x207F PMERR_INV_HPS 0x2092 PMERR_INV_LENGTH_OR_COUNT 0x20A1 PMERR_INV_MICROPS_FUNCTION 0x20BB PMERR_INV_PUTDATA_FORMAT 0x20C0 PMERR_INV_REPLACE_MODE_FUNC 0x20D4 PMERR_DATA_TOO_LONG 0x20E8 PMERR_ORDER_TOO_BIG 0x20F4 PMERR_PS_BUSY
fSuccess =	The GpiQueryArcParams function returns the current arc

Function	Description
GpiQueryArcParams (hps, parcpArcParams)	parameters. This includes full, partial, and 3-point arcs. fSuccess contains true if this function is successful. hps contains a presentation space handle. parcpArcParams contains the arc parameters on function return. You can retrieve the last error using WinGetLastError. These errors include:

0x2060   PMERR_INV_DC_TYPE
0x207F   PMERR_INV_HPS
0x208C   PMERR_INV_IN_RETAIN_MODE
0x20F4   PMERR_PS_BUSY

Function	Description
lMode GpiQueryAttrMode (hps)	The GpiQueryAttrMode function returns the current attribute mode value (as set by GpiSetAttrMode). lMode contains the current attribute mode (or 0 to indicate an error). hps contains the presentation space handle. You can retrieve the last error using WinGetLastError. These errors include:

0x207F   PMERR_INV_HPS
0x20F4   PMERR_PS_BUSY

Function	Description
lDefMask = GpiQueryAttrs (hps, lPrimType, flAttrMask, ppbunAttrs)	The GpiQueryAttrs function retrieves the current attributes for the specified primitive type. lDefMask returns the defaults mask (values can be equal to or greater than 0). A return value of −1 signifies an error. hps contains the presentation space handle. lPrimType contains the primitive type, which includes: PRIM_LINE, PRIM_CHAR, PRIM_MARKER PRIM_AREA, and PRIM_IMAGE. flAttrMask contains the attributes mask. Each flag that you set returns the corresponding flag in lDefMask. If the attribute is not at its default value, OS/2 returns it in ppbunAttrs. ppbunAttrs contains the attributes that are not at their default value. You can retrieve the last error using WinGetLastError. These errors include:

0x2060   PMERR_INV_DC_TYPE
0x207F   PMERR_INV_HPS
0x208C   PMERR_INV_IN_RETAIN_MODE
0x20B9   PMERR_INV_PRIMITIVE_TYPE
0x20F4   PMERR_PS_BUSY
0x2109   PMERR_UNSUPPORTED_ATTR

Function	Description
lColor = GpiQueryBackColor (hps)	The GpiQueryBackColor function returns the current background color attribute. lColor contains the background color and error indicators. hps contains the presentation space handle. GpiQueryBackColor returns one of the following values:

0000   CLR_ERROR
−0003   CLR_DEFAULT
Other   Background color index.

You can retrieve the last error using WinGetLastError. These errors include:

0x2060   PMERR_INV_DC_TYPE

Table 3-42   **Continued**

Function	Description
	0x207F PMERR_INV_HPS 0x208C PMERR_INV_IN_RETAIN_MODE 0x20F4 PMERR_PS_BUSY
lColor = GpiQueryBackMix (hps)	The GpiQueryBackMix function returns the current background color-mixing mode. lColor contains the background color and error indicators. hps contains the presentation space handle. GpiQueryBackMix returns one of the following values: 0000 BM_DEFAULT –0001 BM_ERROR >0 Background mix mode. You can retrieve the last error using WinGetLastError. These errors include: 0x2060 PMERR_INV_DC_TYPE 0x207F PMERR_INV_HPS 0x208C PMERR_INV_IN_RETAIN_MODE 0x20F4 PMERR_PS_BUSY
lScansReturned = GpiQueryBitmapBits (hps, lScanStart, lScans, pbBuffer, pbmi2InfoTable)	The GpiQueryBitmapBits function returns data from a bitmap and places it in application storage. lScansReturned contains the number of scan lines actually returned (values can be equal to or greater than 0). A return value of –1 signifies an error. hps contains the presentation space handle. lScanStart contains the starting scan line number (0 is the bottom line). lScans contains the number of scan lines that you want returned. pbBuffer contains the returned scan data. pbmi2InfoTable contains the bitmap information table (including the associated color table). You can retrieve the last error using WinGetLastError. These errors include: 0x2060 PMERR_INV_DC_TYPE 0x207F PMERR_INV_HPS 0x208F PMERR_INV_INFO_TABLE 0x2092 PMERR_INV_LENGTH_OR_COUNT 0x20C4 PMERR_INV_SCAN_START 0x20E4 PMERR_NO_BITMAP_SELECTED 0x20F4 PMERR_PS_BUSY
fSuccess = GpiQueryBitmap- Dimension (hbm, psizlBitmap Dimension)	The GpiQueryBitmapDimension function returns the height and width of the specified bitmap. fSuccess contains true if this function is successful. hbm contains the bitmap handle. psizlBitmap Dimension contains the size of the bitmap in 0.1 millimeter units. You can retrieve the last error using WinGetLastError. These errors include: 0x2032 PMERR_HBITMAP_BUSY 0x207B PMERR_INV_HBITMAP

Function	Description
hbm = GpiQueryBitmap-Handle (hps, ILcid)	The GpiQueryBitmapHandle function returns the handle of the bitmap currently tagged with the specified identifier. hbm contains the bitmap handle (0 indicated an error condition). hps contains the presentation space handle. ILcid contains the local identifier. You can retrieve the last error using WinGetLastError. These errors include:

0x2036   PMERR_ID_HAS_NO_BITMAP
0x207F   PMERR_INV_HPS
0x20CA PMERR_INV_SETID
0x20F4   PMERR_PS_BUSY

Function	Description
fSuccess = GpiQueryBitmapInfo-Header (hbm, pbmp2Data)	The GpiQueryBitmapInfoHeader function returns information about the bitmap identified by the specified bitmap handle. fSuccess contains true if this function is successful. hbm contains the bitmap handle. pbmp2Data contains the bitmap information header. You can retrieve the last error using WinGetLastError. These errors include:

0x2032   PMERR_HBITMAP_BUSY
0x207B   PMERR_INV_HBITMAP

Function	Description
fSuccess = GpiQueryBitmap-Parameters (hbm, pbmpData)	The GpiQueryBitmapParameters function returns information about the bitmap identified by the bitmap handle. fSuccess contains true if this function is successful. hbm contains the bitmap handle. pbmpData contains the bitmap information header. You can retrieve the last error using WinGetLastError. These errors include:

0x2032   PMERR_HBITMAP_BUSY
0x207B   PMERR_INV_HBITMAP

Function	Description
fSuccess = GpiQueryBoundary-Data (hps, prclBoundary)	The GpiQueryBoundaryData function returns the boundary data. fSuccess contains true if this function is successful. hps contains the presentation space handle. prclBoundary data including the following fields: xmin, ymin, xmax, and ymax. You can retrieve the last error using WinGetLastError. These errors include:

0x2014   PMERR_COORDINATE_OVERFLOW
0x2060   PMERR_INV_DC_TYPE
0x207F   PMERR_INV_HPS
0x20F4   PMERR_PS_BUSY

Function	Description
fSuccess = GpiQueryCharAngle (hps, pgradlAngle)	The GpiQueryCharAngle function returns the current value of the character baseline angle. fSuccess contains true if this function is successful. hps contains the presentation space handle. pgradlAngle contains the character baseline angle vector (the default is 0, 0). You can retrieve the last error using WinGetLastError. These errors include:

0x2060   PMERR_INV_DC_TYPE
0x207F   PMERR_INV_HPS
0x208C   PMERR_INV_IN_RETAIN_MODE
0x20F4   PMERR_PS_BUSY

241

Table 3-42   **Continued**

Function	Description
fSuccess = GpiQueryCharBox (hps, psizlfxSize)	The GpiQueryCharBox function returns the current value of the character box attribute. fSuccess contains true if this function is successful. hps contains the presentation space handle. psizlfxSize contains the character height and width. You can retrieve the last error using WinGetLastError. These errors include: 0x2060 PMERR_INV_DC_TYPE 0x207F PMERR_INV_HPS 0x208C PMERR_INV_IN_RETAIN_MODE 0x20F4 PMERR_PS_BUSY
fSuccess = GpiQueryCharBreak-Extra (hps, pfxBreakExtra)	The GpiQueryCharBreakExtra function returns the current value of the character-break-extra attribute. fSuccess contains true if this function is successful. hps contains the presentation space handle. pfxBreakExtra contains the character-break-extra attribute. You can retrieve the last error using WinGetLastError. These errors include: 0x207F PMERR_INV_HPS 0x208C PMERR_INV_IN_RETAIN_MODE 0x20F4 PMERR_PS_BUSY
lDirection = GpiQueryChar-Direction (hps)	The GpiQueryCharDirection function returns the character direction attribute. lDirection contains the character direction and error indicators. hps contains the presentation space handle. GpiQuery CharDirection returns one of the following values: 0000 CHDIRN_DEFAULT –0001 CHDIRN_ERROR >0 Character direction You can retrieve the last error using WinGetLastError. These errors include: 0x2060 PMERR_INV_DC_TYPE 0x207F PMERR_INV_HPS 0x208C PMERR_INV_IN_RETAIN_MODE 0x20F4 PMERR_PS_BUSY
fSuccess = GpiQueryCharExtra (hps, pfxExtra)	The GpiQueryCharExtra function returns the current value of the character-extra attribute. fSuccess contains true if this function is successful. hps contains the presentation space handle. pfxExtra contains the character-extra attribute. You can retrieve the last error using WinGetLastError. These errors include: 0x207F PMERR_INV_HPS 0x208C PMERR_INV_IN_RETAIN_MODE 0x20F4 PMERR_PS_BUSY
lMode = GpiQueryCharMode	The GpiQueryCharMode function returns the current value of the character-mode attribute. lMode contains the character-mode

Function	Description
(hps)	attribute and error indicators. hps contains the presentation space handle. GpiQueryCharMode returns one of the following values:

0000   CM_DEFAULT
–0001 CM_ERROR
>0   Character mode

You can retrieve the last error using WinGetLastError. These errors include:

0x2060   PMERR_INV_DC_TYPE
0x207F   PMERR_INV_HPS
0x208C   PMERR_INV_IN_RETAIN_MODE
0x20F4   PMERR_PS_BUSY

Function	Description
lLcid = GpiQueryCharSet (hps)	The GpiQueryCharSet function returns the character-set local identifier (lLcid). lLcid contains the character-set local identifier and error indicators. hps contains the presentation space handle. GpiQueryCharDirection returns one of the following values:

0000   LCID_DEFAULT
–0001 LCID_ERROR
>0   Character-set local identifier

You can retrieve the last error using WinGetLastError. These errors include:

0x2060   PMERR_INV_DC_TYPE
0x207F   PMERR_INV_HPS
0x208C   PMERR_INV_IN_RETAIN_MODE
0x20F4   PMERR_PS_BUSY

Function	Description
fSuccess = GpiQueryCharShear (hps, pptlShear)	The GpiQueryCharShear function returns the current character-shear angle. fSuccess contains true if this function is successful. hps contains the presentation space handle. pptlShear contains the character shear angle vector (the default value is 0, 1). You can retrieve the last error using WinGetLastError. These errors include:

0x2060   PMERR_INV_DC_TYPE
0x207F   PMERR_INV_HPS
0x208C   PMERR_INV_IN_RETAIN_MODE
0x20F4   PMERR_PS_BUSY

Function	Description
fSuccess = GpiQueryCharString- Pos (hps, flOptions, lCount, pchString, alXincrements, aptlPositions)	The GpiQueryCharStringPos function processes a string as if you drew it using the current character attributes. It returns the drawing positions for each character in the string in world coordinates. fSuccess contains true if this function is successful. hps contains the presentation space handle. flOptions contains the option flags, which include: CHS_VECTOR. lCount contains the number of characters in pchString. pchString contains the string that you want to draw. alXincrements contains the increment values in world coordinates. aptlPositions contains an array of points

Table 3-42   **Continued**

Function	Description
	corresponding to each character position. You can retrieve the last error using WinGetLastError. These errors include:

0x2014   PMERR_COORDINATE_OVERFLOW
0x204F   PMERR_INV_CHAR_POS_OPTIONS
0x205B   PMERR_INV_COORDINATE
0x2060   PMERR_INV_DC_TYPE
0x207F   PMERR_INV_HPS
0x208C   PMERR_INV_IN_RETAIN_MODE
0x2092   PMERR_INV_LENGTH_OR_COUNT
0x20F4   PMERR_PS_BUSY

Function	Description
fSuccess = GpiQueryCharString-PosAt (hps, pptlStart, flOptions, lCount, pchString, alXincrements, aptlPositions)	The GpiQueryCharStingPosAt function processes a string as if you drew it using the current character attributes. It returns the drawing positions for each character in the string in world coordinates. fSuccess contains true if this function is successful. hps contains the presentation space handle. pptlStart contains the string starting position. flOptions contains the option flags which include: CHS_VECTOR. lCount contains the number of characters in pchString. pchString contains the string that you want to draw. alXincrements contains the increment values in world coordinates. aptlPositions contains an array of points corresponding to each character position. You can retrieve the last error using WinGetLastError. These errors include:

0x2014   PMERR_COORDINATE_OVERFLOW
0x204F   PMERR_INV_CHAR_POS_OPTIONS
0x205B   PMERR_INV_COORDINATE
0x2060   PMERR_INV_DC_TYPE
0x207F   PMERR_INV_HPS
0x208C   PMERR_INV_IN_RETAIN_MODE
0x2092   PMERR_INV_LENGTH_OR_COUNT
0x20F4   PMERR_PS_BUSY

Function	Description
lComplexity = GpiQueryClipBox (hps, prclBound)	The GpiQueryClipBox function returns the dimensions of the smallest box that could fit around all the current clipping definitions. lComplexity contains the complexity of the resulting region or an error indicator. hps contains a presentation space handle. ppclBound contains the bounding rectangle dimensions in world coordinates. GpiQueryClipBox returns one of the following values:

0000   RGN_ERROR
0001   RGN_NULL
0002   RGN_RECT
0003   RGN_COMPLEX

You can retrieve the last error using WinGetLastError. These errors include:

Function	Description
	0x2014 PMERR_COORDINATE_OVERFLOW 0x207F PMERR_INV_HPS 0x20F4 PMERR_PS_BUSY
hrgn = GpiQueryClipRegion (hps)	The GpiQueryClipRegion function returns the handle of the currently selected clip region. hrgn contains the region handle (0 indicates an error). It returns a NULLHANDLE if there is no region selected. hps contains the presentation space handle. You can retrieve the last error using WinGetLastError. These errors include: 0x207F PMERR_INV_HPS 0x20F4 PMERR_PS_BUSY
lColor = GpiQueryColor (hps)	The GpiQueryColor function returns the current character color attribute. lColor contains the background color and error indicators. hps contains the presentation space handle. GpiQueryColor returns one of the following values: 0000 CLR_ERROR –0003 CLR_DEFAULT Other Character color index You can retrieve the last error using WinGetLastError. These errors include: 0x2060 PMERR_INV_DC_TYPE 0x207F PMERR_INV_HPS 0x208C PMERR_INV_IN_RETAIN_MODE 0x20F4 PMERR_PS_BUSY
fSuccess = GpiQueryColorData (hps, lCount, alArray)	The GpiQueryColorData function returns the current logical color table or the selected palette. fSuccess contains true if this function is successful. hps contains the presentation space handle. lCount contains the number of elements in alArray. alArray contains the the color information in a set of fields. QCD_LCT_FORMAT contains one of the following values: LCOLF_DEFAULT, LCOLF_INDRGB, LCOLF_RGB, or LCOLF_PALETTE. QCD_LCT_LOINDEX contains the smallest color index in the color table or palette. QCD_LCT_HIINDEX contains the largest color in the color table or palette. QCD_LCT_OPTIONS contains one or more of the following values: LCOL_PURECOLOR and LCOL_OVERRIDE_DEFAULT_COLORS. You can retrieve the last error using WinGetLastError. These errors include: 0x207F PMERR_INV_HPS 0x2092 PMERR_INV_LENGTH_OR_COUNT 0x20F4 PMERR_PS_BUSY
lIndex = GpiQueryColorIndex (hps, ulOptions, lRgbColor)	The GpiQueryColorIndex function returns the device color index closest to the specified RGB value for the device connected to the specified presentation space. lIndex contains the index of the color that most closely matches the RGB value (–1 indicates an error). hps contains the presentation space handle. ulOptions is a reserved

Table 3-42   **Continued**

Function	Description
	variable (set to 0). lRgbColor contains a color in RGB terms. You can retrieve the last error using WinGetLastError. These errors include: 0x2057 PMERR_INV_COLOR_OPTIONS 0x207F PMERR_INV_HPS 0x20C3 PMERR_INV_RGBCOLOR 0x20F4 PMERR_PS_BUSY
ulCodePage = GpiQueryCp (hps)	The GpiQueryCp function returns the currently selected graphics code page (set by GpiSetCp or default for presentation space). ulCodePage contains the current code page (0 indicates an error). hps contains the presentation space handle. You can retrieve the last error using WinGetLastError. These errors include: 0x207F PMERR_INV_HPS 0x20F4 PMERR_PS_BUSY
fSuccess = GpiQueryCurrent-Position (hps, pptlPoint)	The GpiQueryCurrentPosition function returns the current position. fSuccess contains true if this function is successful. hps contains the presentation space handle. pptlPoint contains the current position. You can retrieve the last error using WinGetLastError. These errors include: 0x2060 PMERR_INV_DC_TYPE 0x207F PMERR_INV_HPS 0x208C PMERR_INV_IN_RETAIN_MODE 0x20F4 PMERR_PS_BUSY
fSuccess = GpiQueryDefArc-Params (hps, parcpArcParams)	The GpiQueryDefArcParams function returns the default arc parameters set by GpiSetDefArcParams. fSuccess contains true if this function is successful. hps contains the presentation space handle. parcpArcParams contains the default arc parameters. You can retrieve the last error using WinGetLastError. These errors include: 0x207F PMERR_INV_HPS 0x20F4 PMERR_PS_BUSY
fSuccess = GpiQueryDefAttrs (hps, lPrimType, flAttrMask, ppbunAttrs)	The GpiQueryDefAttrs function returns the default attribute values for the specified primitive type. fSuccess contains true if this function is successful. hps contains the presentation space handle. lPrimType contains the following primitive types: PRIM_LINE, PRIM_CHAR, PRIM_MARKER, PRIM_AREA, or PRIM_IMAGE. flAttrMask contains the attribute mask. Each flag that you set returns the corresponding attribute in ppbunAttrs. ppbunAttrs is a pointer to the attribute buffer. You can retrieve the last error using WinGetLastError. These errors include: 0x207F PMERR_INV_HPS

Function	Description
	0x20B9 PMERR_INV_PRIMITIVE_TYPE 0x20F4 PMERR_PS_BUSY 0x2109 PMERR_UNSUPPORTED_ATTR
fSuccess = GpiQueryDefault- ViewMatrix (hps, lCount, pmatlfArray)	The GpiQueryDefaultViewMatrix returns the current default viewing transform. fSuccess contains true if this function is successful. hps contains the presentation space handle. lCount contains the number of elements in pmatlfArray. pmatlfArray contains the transform matrix. You can retrieve the last error using WinGetLastError. These errors include: 0x207F PMERR_INV_HPS 0x2092 PMERR_INV_LENGTH_OR_COUNT 0x20F4 PMERR_PS_BUSY
hps = GpiQueryDefChar- Box (hps, psizlSize)	The GpiQueryDefCharBox function returns the current size of the default character box in world coordinates. fSuccess contains true if this function is successful. hps contains the presentation space handle. psizlSize contains the default character box size. You can retrieve the last error using WinGetLastError. These errors include: 0x207F PMERR_INV_HPS 0x208C PMERR_INV_IN_RETAIN_MODE 0x20F4 PMERR_PS_BUSY
fSuccess = GpiQueryDefTag (hps, plTag)	The GpiQueryDefTag function returns the default value of the tag identifier. fSuccess contains true if this function is successful. hps contains the presentation space handle. plTag contains the default tag identifier. You can retrieve the last error using WinGetLastError. These errors include: 0x207F PMERR_INV_HPS 0x20A1 PMERR_INV_MICROPS_FUNCTION 0x20F4 PMERR_PS_BUSY
fSuccess = GpiQueryDefViewing- Limits (hps, prclLimits)	The GpiQueryDefViewingLimits function returns the default value of the viewing limits. fSuccess contains true if this function is successful. hps contains the presentation space handle. prclLimits contains the default viewing limits. You can retrieve the last error using WinGetLastError. These errors include: 0x207F PMERR_INV_HPS 0x20F4 PMERR_PS_BUSY
hdc = GpiQueryDevice (hps)	The GpiQueryDevice function returns the handle of a currently associated device. hdc contains the device context handle, 0 to signify an error condition, or NULLHANDLE if no device context is associated. hps contains the presentation space handle. You can retrieve the last error using WinGetLastError. These errors include: 0x207F PMERR_INV_HPS 0x20F4 PMERR_PS_BUSY

Table 3-42   **Continued**

Function	Description
fSuccess = GpiQueryDevice-BitmapFormats (hps, lCount, alArray)	The GpiQueryDeviceBitmapFormats function returns the formats of the bitmaps supported internally by a device driver. fSuccess contains true if this function is successful. hps contains the presentation space handle. lCount contains the number of elements in alArray. alArray contains the format data in pairs of cPlanes, cBitCount elements. You can retrieve the last error using WinGetLastError. These errors include: 0x207F PMERR_INV_HPS 0x2092 PMERR_INV_LENGTH_OR_COUNT 0x20F4 PMERR_PS_BUSY
lValue = GpiQueryDraw-Control (hps, lControl)	The GpiQueryDrawControl function returns the draw control set by GpiSetDrawControl. lValue contains the value of the control and error indicators. hps contains the presentation space handle. lControl contains one of the following control types: DCTL_ERASE, DCTL_DISPLAY, DCTL_BOUNDARY, DCTL_DYNAMIC, or DCTL_CORRELATE. GpiQueryColor returns one of the following values: –0001 DCTL_ERROR 0000 DCTL_OFF 0001 DCTL_ON You can retrieve the last error using WinGetLastError. These errors include: 0x2063 PMERR_INV_DRAW_CONTROL 0x207F PMERR_INV_HPS 0x20A0 PMERR_INV_MICROPS_DRAW_CONTROL 0x20F4 PMERR_PS_BUSY
lMode = GpiQueryDrawing-Mode (hps)	The GpiQueryDrawingMode function returns the current drawing mode. lMode contains the current drawing mode or 0 to signify an error condition. hps contains the presentation space handle. You can retrieve the last error using WinGetLastError. These errors include: 0x207F PMERR_INV_HPS 0x20A1 PMERR_INV_MICROPS_FUNCTION 0x20F4 PMERR_PS_BUSY
GpiQueryEditMode	The GpiQueryEditMode function returns the current editing mode. lMode contains the current drawing mode or 0 to signify an error condition. hps contains the presentation space handle. GpiQueryEditMode returns one of the following values: 0000 SEGEM_ERROR 0001 SEGEM_INSERT 0002 SEGEM_REPLACE

Function	Description
	You can retrieve the last error using WinGetLastError. These errors include:
	0x207F PMERR_INV_HPS 0x20A1 PMERR_INV_MICROPS_FUNCTION 0x20F4 PMERR_PS_BUSY
lRetLength = GpiQueryElement (hps, lOff, lMaxLength, pbData)	The GpiQueryElement function returns element content data. This is for the element currently pointed at by the element pointer. lRetLength contains the number of bytes returns (–1 indicates an error). hps contains the presentation space handle. lOff contains the starting byte offset within the element. lMaxLength contains the size of pbData. pbData contains the element content data. You can retrieve the last error using WinGetLastError. These errors include:
	0x206A PMERR_INV_ELEMENT_OFFSET 0x207F PMERR_INV_HPS 0x2089 PMERR_INV_IN_ELEMENT 0x2092 PMERR_INV_LENGTH_OR_COUNT 0x20A1 PMERR_INV_MICROPS_FUNCTION 0x20E2 PMERR_NOT_IN_RETAIN_MODE 0x20E5 PMERR_NO_CURRENT_ELEMENT 0x20E6 PMERR_NO_CURRENT_SEG 0x20F4 PMERR_PS_BUSY
lElement = GpiQueryElement-Pointer (hps)	The GpiQueryElementPointer function returns the current element pointer. lElement contains the current element pointer (–1 indicates an error). hps contains the presentation space handle. You can retrieve the last error using WinGetLastError. These errors include:
	0x207F PMERR_INV_HPS 0x20A1 PMERR_INV_MICROPS_FUNCTION 0x20E2 PMERR_NOT_IN_RETAIN_MODE 0x20E6 PMERR_NO_CURRENT_SEG 0x20F4 PMERR_PS_BUSY
lReqLength = GpiQueryElement-Type (hps, plType, lLength, pszData)	The GpiQueryElementType function returns information about the element pointed to by the element pointer. lReqLength contains the size of the buffer required to hold the element content (–1 indicates an error). hps contains the presentation space handle. plType contains the element type. lLength contains the size of pszData. pszData contains a description of the data buffer. You can retrieve the last error using WinGetLastError. These errors include:
	0x207F PMERR_INV_HPS 0x2089 PMERR_INV_IN_ELEMENT 0x2092 PMERR_INV_LENGTH_OR_COUNT 0x20A1 PMERR_INV_MICROPS_FUNCTION 0x20E2 PMERR_NOT_IN_RETAIN_MODE 0x20E5 PMERR_NO_CURRENT_ELEMENT 0x20E6 PMERR_NO_CURRENT_SEG 0x20F4 PMERR_PS_BUSY

249

Table 3-42   **Continued**

Function	Description
cbRetLength = GpiQueryFaceString (hps, pszFamily Name, pfndFace Attrs, lLength, pszCompoundFace Name)	The GpiQueryFaceString returns a compound face name for a font. cbRetLength contains the length of the compound face name (0 indicates an error). hps contains the presentation space handle. pszFamilyName contains the family. pfndFaceAttrs contains the face name description (a set of font characteristics). lLength contains the size of pszCompoundFaceName. pszCompoundFaceName contains the generated compound face name for the font. You can retrieve the last error using WinGetLastError. These errors include: 0x201D PMERR_INV_FACENAME 0x202F PMERR_FONT_NOT_LOADED 0x207F PMERR_INV_HPS 0x20F4 PMERR_PS_BUSY 0x2115 PMERR_INV_FACENAMEDESC
flActions = GpiQueryFontAction (hab, flOptions)	The GpiQueryFontAction function determines if the available fonts have changed since the last time you called the function. flActions contains the actions and error indicators. hab contains the anchor block handle. flOptions contains one or more of the following options: QFA_PUBLIC and QFA_PRIVATE. GpiQueryFontAction returns one of the following values: –0001 QFA_ERROR 0001 QFA_PUBLIC 0002 QFA_PRIVATE You can retrieve the last error using WinGetLastError. These errors include: 0x20A9 PMERR_INV_OR_INCOMPAT_OPTIONS
lRemFonts = GpiQueryFontFile-Descriptions (hab, pszFilename, plCount, affdescsNames)	The GpiQueryFontFileDescriptions function determines whether a file is a font resource file. If so, it returns the family and face names for the fonts that it contains. lRemFonts contains the number of fonts that affdescsNames could not hold (–1 indicates an error). hab contains the anchor block handle. pszFilename contains the font file name. plCount contains the number of family and face names that you want returned. affdescsNames is an array of file descriptors. Each field is 32-bytes long. You can retrieve the last error using WinGetLastError. These errors include: 0x2073 PMERR_INV_FONT_FILE_DATA 0x2092 PMERR_INV_LENGTH_OR_COUNT
fSuccess = GpiQueryFontMetrics (hps, lMetricsLength, pfmMetrics)	The GpiQueryFontMetrics function returns a record containing the font metrics (in world coordinates) for the currently selected logical font. fSuccess contains true if this function is successful. hps contains the presentation space handle. lMetricsLength contains the size of pfmMetrics. pfmMetrics contains the font metrics for the

Function	Description
	currently selected logical font. You can retrieve the last error using WinGetLastError. These errors include: 0x2014 PMERR_COORDINATE_OVERFLOW 0x207F PMERR_INV_HPS 0x2092 PMERR_INV_LENGTH_OR_COUNT 0x20F4 PMERR_PS_BUSY
lRemFonts = GpiQueryFonts (hps, flOptions, pszFacename, plReqFonts, lMetricsLength, afmMetrics)	The GpiQueryFonts function returns a record that provides details for the fonts that match pszFacename. lRemFonts contains the number of fonts that affdescsNames could not hold (–1 indicates an error). hps contains the presentation space handle. flOptions contains the flags that control which fonts get listed. This includes: QF_PUBLIC, QF_PRIVATE, QF_NO_DEVICE, and QF_NOGENERIC. pszFacename contains the font face name. A null handle forces OS/2 for query all fonts. plReqFonts contains the number of fonts that you want queried; it returns the actual number of fonts queried. lMetricsLength contains the size of pfmMetrics. afmMetrics is an array that contains the font metrics for the queried fonts. You can retrieve the last error using WinGetLastError. These errors include: 0x2014 PMERR_COORDINATE_OVERFLOW 0x207F PMERR_INV_HPS 0x2092 PMERR_INV_LENGTH_OR_COUNT 0x20F4 PMERR_PS_BUSY
lRemFonts = GpiQueryFullFontFileDescs (hab, pszFilename, plCount, pNames, plNamesBuffLength)	The GpiQueryFullFontFileDescs function determines whether a file is a font resource file. If so, it returns the family and face names for the fonts that it contains. lRemFonts contains the number of fonts that affdescsNames could not hold (–1 indicates an error). hab contains the anchor block handle. pszFilename contains the font file name. plCount contains the number of family and face names that you want returned. pNames is a buffer containing the font file descriptors. Each entry contains one font file family and face name pair. plNamesBuffLength contains the size of pNames. You can retrieve the last error using WinGetLastError. These errors include: 0x2073 PMERR_INV_FONT_FILE_DATA 0x2092 PMERR_INV_LENGTH_OR_COUNT
fSuccess = GpiQueryGraphicsField (hps, prclField)	The GpiQueryGraphicsField function returns the bottom-left and top-right corners of the graphics field (in presentation page units). fSuccess contains true if this function is successful. hps contains the presentation space handle. prclField contains the graphics field coordinates. You can retrieve the last error using WinGetLastError. These errors include: 0x207F PMERR_INV_HPS 0x20F4 PMERR_PS_BUSY
lValue =	The GpiQueryInitialSegmentAttrs function returns the current value

Table 3-42 **Continued**

Function	Description
GpiQueryInitial-SegmentAttrs (hps, lAttribute)	of a particular initial segment attribute. lValue contains the segment attribute value or error indicator. hps contains the presentation space handle. lAttribute contains the attribute you want to query. These attributes include: ATTR_DETECTABLE, ATTR_VISIBLE, ATTR_CHAINED, ATTR_DYNAMIC, ATTR_FASTCHAIN, ATTR_PROP_DETECTABLE, and ATTR_PROP_VISIBLE. GpiQueryInitialSegmentAttrs returns one of the following values:

–0001 ATTR_ERROR
0000 ATTR_OFF
0001 ATTR_ON

You can retrieve the last error using WinGetLastError. These errors include:

0x207F PMERR_INV_HPS
0x20A1 PMERR_INV_MICROPS_FUNCTION
0x20C5 PMERR_INV_SEG_ATTR
0x20F4 PMERR_PS_BUSY

| lReturned = GpiQueryKerning-Pairs (hps, lCount, akrnprData) | The GpiQueryKerningPairs function returns the kerning pair information for the logical font identified by the current value of the character set attribute. lReturned contains the number of kerning pairs returned or an error indicator (a value of –1). hps contains the presentation space handle. lCount contains the number of elements in akrnprData. akrnprData is an array that contains the kerning pairs. You can retrieve the last error using WinGetLastError. These errors include: |

0x2014 PMERR_COORDINATE_OVERFLOW
0x207F PMERR_INV_HPS
0x2092 PMERR_INV_LENGTH_OR_COUNT
0x20F4 PMERR_PS_BUSY

| lLineEnd = GpiQueryLineEnd (hps) | The GpiQueryLineEnd function returns the current line-end attribute. lLineEnd contains the line end attribute, LINEEND_DEFAULT, or an error indicator (a value of –1). hps contains the presentation space handle. You can retrieve the last error using WinGetLastError. These errors include: |

0x2060 PMERR_INV_DC_TYPE
0x207F PMERR_INV_HPS
0x208C PMERR_INV_IN_RETAIN_MODE
0x20F4 PMERR_PS_BUSY

| lLineJoin = GpiQueryLineJoin (hps) | The GpiQueryLineJoin function returns the current line-join attribute. lLineJoin contains the line join attribute, LINEJOIN_DEFAULT, or an error indicator (a value of –1). hps contains the presentation space handle. You can retrieve the last error using WinGetLastError. These errors include: |

Function	Description
	0x2060 PMERR_INV_DC_TYPE 0x207F PMERR_INV_HPS 0x208C PMERR_INV_IN_RETAIN_MODE 0x20F4 PMERR_PS_BUSY
lLineType = GpiQueryLineType (hps)	The GpiQueryLineType function returns the current line-type attribute. lLineType contains the line type attribute, LINETYPE_DEFAULT, or an error indicator (a value of −1). hps contains the presentation space handle. You can retrieve the last error using WinGetLastError. These errors include: 0x2060 PMERR_INV_DC_TYPE 0x207F PMERR_INV_HPS 0x208C PMERR_INV_IN_RETAIN_MODE 0x20F4 PMERR_PS_BUSY
lLineWidth = GpiQueryLineWidth (hps)	The GpiQueryLineWidth function returns the current cosmetic line-width attribute. lLineWidth contains the line width attribute, LINEWIDTH_DEFAULT, or an error indicator (a value of −1). hps contains the presentation space handle. You can retrieve the last error using WinGetLastError. These errors include: 0x2060 PMERR_INV_DC_TYPE 0x207F PMERR_INV_HPS 0x208C PMERR_INV_IN_RETAIN_MODE 0x20F4 PMERR_PS_BUSY
lLineWidth = GpiQueryLineWidth- Geom (hps)	The GpiQueryLineWidthGeom function returns the current geometric line-width attribute. lLineWidth contains the line width attribute or an error indicator (a value of −1). hps contains the presentation space handle. You can retrieve the last error using WinGetLastError. These errors include: 0x2060 PMERR_INV_DC_TYPE 0x207F PMERR_INV_HPS 0x208C PMERR_INV_IN_RETAIN_MODE 0x20F4 PMERR_PS_BUSY
lRetCount = GpiQueryLogColor- Table (hps, flOptions, lStart, lCount, alArray)	The GpiQueryLogColorTable function returns the logical color table. lRetCount contains the number of returned elements and error indicators. hps contains the presentation space handle. flOptions contains the option values including: LCOLOPT_INDEX. lStart contains the starting index. lCount contains the number of elements in alArray. alArray contains the returned color table. If the LCOLOPT_INDEX flag is not set, then alArray contains an array of RGB values. It is set, then alArray contains alternating color indexes and RGB values. GpiQueryLogColorTable returns one of the following values: −0002 QLCT_RGB −0001 QLCT_ERROR >0 Number of returned elements

Table 3-42   **Continued**

Function	Description
	You can retrieve the last error using WinGetLastError. These errors include:

0x2057 PMERR_INV_COLOR_OPTIONS
0x2058 PMERR_INV_COLOR_START_INDEX
0x207F PMERR_INV_HPS
0x2092 PMERR_INV_LENGTH_OR_COUNT
0x20F4 PMERR_PS_BUSY
0x210F PMERR_PALETTE_SELECTED

fSuccess = GpiQueryLogicalFont (hps, lLcid, pName, pfatAttrs, lAttrsLength)

The GpiQueryLogicalFontFunction returns a description of a logical font. fSuccess contains true if this function is successful. hps contains the presentation space handle. lLcid contains the local font identifier in the range from 0 (default) to 254. pName contains an 8-character logical font name. pfatAttrs contains the font attributes. lAttrsLength contains the length of the pfatAttrs buffer. You can retrieve the last error using WinGetLastError. These errors include:

0x207F PMERR_INV_HPS
0x2092 PMERR_INV_LENGTH_OR_COUNT
0x20CA PMERR_INV_SETID
0x20F4 PMERR_PS_BUSY
0x2102 PMERR_SETID_IN_USE

lSymbol = GpiQueryMarker (hps)

The GpiQueryMarker function returns the current value of the marker symbol attribute (set by the GpiSetMarker function). lSymbol contains the marker symbol value and error indicators. hps contains the presentation space handle. GpiQueryMarker returns one of the following values:

−0001 MARKSYM_ERROR
0000 MARKSYM_DEFAULT
>0 Marker symbol

You can retrieve the last error using WinGetLastError. These errors include:

0x2060 PMERR_INV_DC_TYPE
0x207F PMERR_INV_HPS
0x208C PMERR_INV_IN_RETAIN_MODE
0x20F4 PMERR_PS_BUSY

fSuccess = GpiQueryMarkerBox (hps, psizfxSize)

The GpiQueryMarkerBox function returns the current value of the marker-box attribute (set by the GpiSetMarkerBox function). fSuccess contains true if this function is successful. hps contains the presentation space handle. psizlfxSize contains the size of the marker box in world coordinates. You can retrieve the last error using WinGetLastError. These errors include:

0x2060 PMERR_INV_DC_TYPE

Function	Description
	0x207F PMERR_INV_HPS 0x208C PMERR_INV_IN_RETAIN_MODE 0x20F4 PMERR_PS_BUSY
lSet = GpiQueryMarkerSet (hps)	The GpiQueryMarkerSet function returns the current value of the marker-set attribute (set by the GpiSetMarkerSet function). lSet contains the marker set value and error indicators. hps contains the presentation space handle. GpiQueryMarker returns one of the following values:

–0001   LCID_ERROR
0000   LCID_DEFAULT
>0   Marker set local identifier

You can retrieve the last error using WinGetLastError. These errors include:

0x2060   PMERR_INV_DC_TYPE
0x207F   PMERR_INV_HPS
0x208C   PMERR_INV_IN_RETAIN_MODE
0x20F4   PMERR_PS_BUSY

Function	Description
fSuccess = GpiQueryMetaFile- Bits (hmf, lOffset, lLength, pbData)	The GpiQueryMetaFileBits function stores a metafile to application storage. fSuccess contains true if this function is successful. hmf contains the metafile handle. lOffset contains the offset within the metafile where you want to start the data transfer. lLength contains the amount of metafile data to copy in bytes. pbData is a pointer to the metafile data storage area. You can retrieve the last error using WinGetLastError. These errors include:

0x207E   PMERR_INV_HMF
0x209E   PMERR_INV_METAFILE_LENGTH
0x209F   PMERR_INV_METAFILE_OFFSET
0x20D9   PMERR_METAFILE_IN_USE
0x2106   PMERR_TOO_MANY_METAFILES_IN_USE

Function	Description
lLength = GpiQueryMetaFile- Length (hmf)	The GpiQueryMetaFileLength function returns the length of a memory metafile in bytes. lLength contains the total length of the metafile in bytes (–1 indicates an error). hmf contains the metafile handle. You can retrieve the last error using WinGetLastError. These errors include:

0x207E   PMERR_INV_HMF
0x2106   PMERR_TOO_MANY_METAFILES_IN_USE

Function	Description
lMixMode = GpiQueryMix (hps)	The GpiQueryMix function returns the current value of the character foreground color mixing mode (set by the GpiSetMix function). lMixMode contains the foreground color mixing mode and error indicators. hps contains the presentation space handle. GpiQueryMix returns one of the following values:

–0001   FM_ERROR
0000   FM_DEFAULT
>0   Mix mode

Table 3-42   **Continued**

Function	Description
	You can retrieve the last error using WinGetLastError. These errors include: 0x2060 PMERR_INV_DC_TYPE 0x207F PMERR_INV_HPS 0x208C PMERR_INV_IN_RETAIN_MODE 0x20F4 PMERR_PS_BUSY
fSuccess = GpiQueryModel-TransformMatrix (hps, lCount, pmatlfArray)	The GpiQueryModelTransformMatrix function returns the current model transform. fSuccess contains true if this function is successful. hps contains the presentation space handle. lCount contains the number of elements in pmatlfArray. pmatlfArray contains the transform matrix. You can retrieve the last error using WinGetLastError. These errors include: 0x2060 PMERR_INV_DC_TYPE 0x207F PMERR_INV_HPS 0x208C PMERR_INV_IN_RETAIN_MODE 0x2092 PMERR_INV_LENGTH_OR_COUNT 0x20F4 PMERR_PS_BUSY
lRbgOut = GpiQueryNearest-Color (hps, ulOptions, lRgbln)	The GpiQueryNearestColor function returns the color on the current devices that most closely matches the specified color (both colors use RGB terms). This function returns a pure color, it does not take dithered colors into account. lRgbOut contains the color that most closely matches the specified color (–1 indicates an error). hps contains the presentation space handle. ulOptions is a reserved parameter, set it to zero. lRgbln contains the required color. You can retrieve the last error using WinGetLastError. These errors include: 0x2057 PMERR_INV_COLOR_OPTIONS 0x207F PMERR_INV_HPS 0x20C3 PMERR_INV_RGBCOLOR 0x20F4 PMERR_PS_BUSY
lCount = GpiQueryNumber-SetIds (hps)	The GpiQueryNumberSetIds function returns the number of local identifiers (lcids) that refer to fonts or bitmaps currently in use. lCount contains the number of lcids (–1 indicates an error). hps contains the presentation space handle. You can retrieve the last error using WinGetLastError. These errors include: 0x207F PMERR_INV_HPS 0x20F4 PMERR_PS_BUSY
fSuccess = GpiQueryPage-Viewport (hps, prclViewport)	The GpiQueryViewport function returns the current viewport. fSuccess contains true if this function is successful. hps contains the presentation space handle. prclViewport contains the size and position of the page viewport in device units. You can retrieve the last error using WinGetLastError. These errors include:

Function	Description
	0x2060 PMERR_INV_DC_TYPE 0x207F PMERR_INV_HPS 0x208C PMERR_INV_IN_RETAIN_MODE 0x20F4 PMERR_PS_BUSY
hpal = GpiQueryPalette (hps)	The GpiQueryPalette function returns the handle of the palette currently selected into a presentation space. hpal contains the palette handle, a NULLHANDLE if no palette is selected, or −1 to indicate an error. hps contains the presentation space handle. You can retrieve the last error using WinGetLastError. These errors include: 0x207F PMERR_INV_HPS 0x20F4 PMERR_PS_BUSY
lRetCount = GpiQueryPaletteInfo (hpal, hps, flOptions, lStart, lCount, alArray)	The GpiQueryPaletteInfo function returns the specified palette's information. It uses the same information required to create a palette using GpiCreatePalette. lRetCount contains the number of returned elements (−1 to indicate an error). hpal contains the palette handle. Passing a null handle in this parameter returns the information for the currently selected presentation space palette. hps contains the presentation space handle. flOptions contains the option values including: LCOLOPT_INDEX. lStart contains the starting index. lCount contains the number of elements in alArray. alArray contains the returned color table. If the LCOLOPT_INDEX flag is not set, then alArray contains an array of RGB values. If it is set, then alArray contains alternating color indexes and RGB values. You can retrieve the last error using WinGetLastError. These errors include: 0x2057 PMERR_INV_COLOR_OPTIONS 0x2058 PMERR_INV_COLOR_START_INDEX 0x207F PMERR_INV_HPS 0x2092 PMERR_INV_LENGTH_OR_COUNT 0x20F4 PMERR_PS_BUSY 0x2111 PMERR_INV_HPAL 0x2112 PMERR_PALETTE_BUSY
lPatternSymbol = GpiQueryPattern (hps)	The GpiQueryPattern function returns the current value of the shading-pattern symbol (set by the GpiSetPattern function). lPatternSymbol contains the pattern symbol and error indicators. hps contains the presentation space handle. GpiQueryPattern returns one of the following values: −0001 PATSYM_ERROR 0000 PATSYM_DEFAULT >0 Pattern Symbol You can retrieve the last error using WinGetLastError. These errors include: 0x2060 PMERR_INV_DC_TYPE

Table 3-42   **Continued**

Function	Description
	0x207F PMERR_INV_HPS 0x208C PMERR_INV_IN_RETAIN_MODE 0x20F4 PMERR_PS_BUSY
fSuccess = GpiQueryPatternRef-Point (hps, pptlRefPoint)	The GpiQueryPatternRefPoint function returns the current pattern reference point (set by the GpiSetPatternRefPoint function). fSuccess contains true if this function is successful. hps contains the presentation space handle. pptlRefPoint contains the pattern reference point (default is 0, 0). You can retrieve the last error using WinGetLastError. These errors include: 0x2060 PMERR_INV_DC_TYPE 0x207F PMERR_INV_HPS 0x208C PMERR_INV_IN_RETAIN_MODE 0x20F4 PMERR_PS_BUSY
lSet = GpiQueryPatternSet (hps)	The GpiQueryPatternSet function returns the current value of the pattern-set identifier (set by the GpiSetPatternSet function). lSet contains the pattern set local identifier and error indicators. hps contains the presentation space handle. GpiQueryPatternSet returns one of the following values: –0001 LCID_ERROR 0000 LCID_DEFAULT >0 Pattern Symbol You can retrieve the last error using WinGetLastError. These errors include: 0x2060 PMERR_INV_DC_TYPE 0x207F PMERR_INV_HPS 0x208C PMERR_INV_IN_RETAIN_MODE 0x20F4 PMERR_PS_BUSY
lColor = GpiQueryPel (hps, pptlPoint)	The GpiQueryPal function returns the color of a pel (as an RGB value) at a position specified in world coordinates. lColor returns the color index of the pel, CLR_NOINDEX, or –1 to indicate an error. hps contains the presentation space handle. pptlPoint contains the pel position in world coordinates. You cannot specify a point outside any of the current clipping objects. You can retrieve the last error using WinGetLastError. These errors include: 0x205B PMERR_INV_COORDINATE 0x2060 PMERR_INV_DC_TYPE 0x207F PMERR_INV_HPS 0x20E4 PMERR_NO_BITMAP_SELECTED 0x20EF PMERR_PEL_IS_CLIPPED 0x20F0 PMERR_PEL_NOT_AVAILABLE 0x20F4 PMERR_PS_BUSY

Function	Description

fSuccess = GpiQueryPick-AperturePosition (hps, pptlPoint)

The GpiQueryPickAperturePosition function returns the center of the pick aperture. fSuccess contains true if this function is successful. hps contains the presentation space handle. pptlPoint contains the pick aperture center point. You can retrieve the last error using WinGetLastError. These errors include:

0x2060   PMERR_INV_DC_TYPE
0x207F   PMERR_INV_HPS
0x20F4   PMERR_PS_BUSY

fSuccess = GpiQueryPick-ApertureSize (hps, psizlSize)

The GpiQueryPickApertureSize function returns the current size of the pick aperture (set by the GpiSetPickAperture function). fSuccess contains true if this function is successful. hps contains the presentation space handle. psizlSize contains the pick aperture size in presentation page coordinates. You can retrieve the last error using WinGetLastError. These errors include:

0x2060   PMERR_INV_DC_TYPE
0x207F   PMERR_INV_HPS
0x20F4   PMERR_PS_BUSY

lOptions = GpiQueryPS (hps, psizlSize)

The GpiQueryPS function returns the page parameters for the presentation space. lOptions contains the presentation space options. This includes the following fields: PS_UNITS, PS_FORMAT, PS_TYPE, and PS_MODE. hps contains the presentation space handle. psizlSize contains the presentation-page size. You can retrieve the last error using WinGetLastError. These errors include:

0x207F   PMERR_INV_HPS
0x20F4   PMERR_PS_BUSY

lRetCount = GpiQueryRealColors (hps, ulOptions, lStart, lCount, alColors)

The GpiQueryRealColors function returns the RGP values of the distinct colors available on the currently associated device. lRetCount contains the number of returned elements (–1 to indicate an error). hps contains the presentation space handle. ulOptions contains the option values including: LCOLOPT_INDEX. lStart contains the starting color number. lCount contains the number of elements in alColors. alColors contains the returned color table. If the LCOLOPT_INDEX flag is not set, then alArray contains an array of RGB values. If it is set, then alArray contains alternating color indexes and RGB values. You can retrieve the last error using WinGetLastError. These errors include:

0x2057   PMERR_INV_COLOR_OPTIONS
0x2058   PMERR_INV_COLOR_START_INDEX
0x207F   PMERR_INV_HPS
0x2092   PMERR_INV_LENGTH_OR_COUNT
0x20F4   PMERR_PS_BUSY

lComplexity = GpiQueryRegionBox

The GpiQueryRegionBox returns the dimensions of the smallest rectangle able to bound the region. lComplexity contains the

Table 3-42   **Continued**

Function	Description
(hps, hrgn, prclBound)	complexity of the resulting region or an error indicator. hps contains a presentation space handle. hrgn contains the region handle. ppclBound contains the bounding rectangle dimensions in world coordinates. GpiQueryRegionBox returns one of the following values:

0000   RGN_ERROR
0001   RGN_NULL
0002   RGN_RECT
0003   RGN_COMPLEX

You can retrieve the last error using WinGetLastError. These errors include:

0x2034   PMERR_HRGN_BUSY
0x207F   PMERR_INV_HPS
0x2080   PMERR_INV_HRGN
0x20F4   PMERR_PS_BUSY
0x20F8   PMERR_REGION_IS_CLIP_REGION

Function	Description
fSuccess = GpiQueryRegion-Rects (hps, hrgn, prclBound, prgnrcControl, arclRects)	The GpiQueryRegionRects returns the rectangles used to define the specified region. fSuccess contains true if this function is successful. hps contains the presentation space handle. hrgn contains the region handle. ppclBound contains the bounding rectangle dimensions in world coordinates. A value of NULL returns all the rectangles in the region. prgnrcControl contains the processing control structure. arclRects contains an array of rectangle structures. You can retrieve the last error using WinGetLastError. These errors include:

0x2034   PMERR_HRGN_BUSY
0x205B   PMERR_INV_COORDINATE
0x207F   PMERR_INV_HPS
0x2080   PMERR_INV_HRGN
0x20BD   PMERR_INV_RECT
0x20BE   PMERR_INV_HRGN_CONTROL
0x20F4   PMERR_PS_BUSY
0x20F8   PMERR_REGION_IS_CLIP_REGION

Function	Description
lRgbColor= GpiQueryRGBColor (hps, FlOptions, lColorIndex)	The GpiQueryRGBColor function returns the actual RGB color residing at a particular index on the currently-associated device. (If you load an RGB logical color table, then this function returns the same value as the GpiQueryNearestColor function.) lRgbColor contains the RGB color providing the closest match to the specified color index (−1 indicates an error). hps contains the presentation, space handle. flOptions contains the option values including: LCOLOPT_INDEX. lStart contains the starting color number. lColorIndex contains any normally valid color index value except CLR_DEFAULT. You can retrieve the last error using WinGetLastError. These errors include:

0x2056   PMERR_INV_COLOR_INDEX

Function	Description

Function   **Description**

0x2057   PMERR_INV_COLOR_OPTIONS
0x207F   PMERR_INV_HPS
0x20F4   PMERR_PS_BUSY

lValue =
GpiQuerySegment-
Attrs (hps, lSegid,
lAttribute)

The GpiQuerySegmentAttrs function returns the current value of the specified attribute (set by the GpiSetSegmentAttrs function). lValue contains the segment attribute value or error indicator. hps contains the presentation space handle. lSegid contains the segment identifier. lAttribute contains the attribute you want to query. These attributes include: ATTR_DETECTABLE, ATTR_VISIBLE, ATTR_CHAINED, ATTR_DYNAMIC, ATTR_FASTCHAIN, ATTR_PROP_DETECTABLE, and ATTR_PROP_VISIBLE. GpiQuerySegmentAttrs returns one of the following values:

–0001   ATTR_ERROR
0000   ATTR_OFF
0001   ATTR_ON

You can retrieve the last error using WinGetLastError. These errors include:

0x207F   PMERR_INV_HPS
0x20A1   PMERR_INV_MICROPS_FUNCTION
0x20C5   PMERR_INV_SEG_ATTR
0x20C8   PMERR_INV_SEG_NAME
0x20F4   PMERR_PS_BUSY
0x2100   PMERR_SEG_NOT_FOUND

lRetCount =
GpiQuerySegment-
Names (hps,
lFirstSegid,
lLastSegid, lMax,
alSegids)

The GpiQuerySegmentNames function returns the identifiers of all segments that exist with identifiers in a specified range. (This function does not return nonretained segments.) lRetCount contains the number of returned elements (–1 to indicate an error). hps contains the presentation space handle. lFirstSeg and lLastSeg contain the identifiers of the first and last segments that you want to query. lMax contains the number of segment identifiers that you want returned in alSegids. alSegids is an array containing the required segment identifiers. You can retrieve the last error using WinGetLastError. These errors include:

0x207F   PMERR_INV_HPS
0x2092   PMERR_INV_LENGTH_OR_COUNT
0x20A1   PMERR_INV_MICROPS_FUNCTION
0x20C8   PMERR_INV_SEG_NAME
0x20F4   PMERR_PS_BUSY

lSegid =
GpiQuerySegment-
Priority (hps,
lRefSegid, lOrder)

The GpiQuerySegmentPriority function returns the identifier of the segment chained immediately before (lower priority) or after (higher priority) a specified reference segment. lSegid contains the segment identifier: 0 when the segment is either the highest (lOrder = HIGHER_PRI) or lowest (lOrder = LOWER_PRI) priority segment, or –1 to indicate an error. hps contains the presentation space handle. lRefSegid contains the reference segment identifier. lOrder contains a flag that shows whether you want a lower (LOWER_PRI)

Table 3-42   **Continued**

Function   **Description**

or higher (HIGHER_PRI) priority segment. You can retrieve the last
error using WinGetLastError. These errors include:

0x207F   PMERR_INV_HPS
0x20A1   PMERR_INV_MICROPS_FUNCTION
0x20AB   PMERR_INV_ORDERING_PARM
0x20C8   PMERR_INV_SEG_NAME
0x20F4   PMERR_PS_BUSY
0x20FF   PMERR_SEG_NOT_CHAINED
0x2100   PMERR_SEG_NOT_FOUND

fSuccess =   The GpiQuerySegmentTransformMatrix function returns the
GpiQuerySegment-   elements of the transform of the specified segment. fSuccess
TransformMatrix   contains true if this function is successful. hps contains the
(hps, lSegid, lCount,   presentation space handle. lSegid contains the segment identifier.
pmatlfArray)   lCount contains the number of elements in pmatlfArray.
                                pmatlfArray contains the transform matrix. You can retrieve the last
                                error using WinGetLastError. These errors include:

0x207F   PMERR_INV_HPS
0x2092   PMERR_INV_LENGTH_OR_COUNT
0x20A1   PMERR_INV_MICROPS_FUNCTION
0x20C8   PMERR_INV_SEG_NAME
0x20F4   PMERR_PS_BUSY
0x2100   PMERR_SEG_NOT_FOUND

fSuccess =   The GpiQuerySetIds function returns information about all fonts
GpiQuerySetIds   created by the GpiCreateLogFont function and tagged bitmaps.
(hps, lCount,   fSuccess contains true if this function is successful. hps contains
alTypes, aNames,   the presentation space handle. lCount contains the number of items
allcids)   you want to query. alTypes contains a list of the object types that
                                you want to retrieve. They include: LCIDT_FONT and
                                LCIDT_BITMAP. aNames contains an array of 8-character font
                                names. (Bitmaps set the array entry to zero.) allcids is an array of
                                local identifiers. You can retrieve the last error using
                                WinGetLastError. These errors include:

0x207F   PMERR_INV_HPS
0x2092   PMERR_INV_LENGTH_OR_COUNT
0x20F4   PMERR_PS_BUSY

lValue =   The GpiQueryStopDraw function returns the status of the "stop
GpiQueryStopDraw   draw" condition. lValue contains the stop draw condition or error
(hps)   indicator. hps contains the presentation space handle.
                                GpiQueryStopDraw returns one of the following values:

–0001   SDW_ERROR
0000   SDW_OFF
0001   SDW_ON

You can retrieve the last error using WinGetLastError. These errors
include:

Function	Description
	0x207F PMERR_INV_HPS 0x20A1 PMERR_INV_MICROPS_FUNCTION
fSuccess = GpiQueryTag (hps, plTag)	The GpiQueryTag function returns the current value of the tag identifier (set by the GpiSegTag function). fSuccess contains true if this function is successful. hps contains the presentation space handle. plTag contains the tag identifier. You can retrieve the last error using WinGetLastError. These errors include: 0x207F PMERR_INV_HPS 0x20A1 PMERR_INV_MICROPS_FUNCTION 0x20F4 PMERR_PS_BUSY
fSuccess = GpiQueryText- Alignment (hps, plHorizontal, plVertical)	The GpiQueryTextAlignment function returns the current value of the text alignment attribute (set by the GpiSetTextAlignment function). fSuccess contains true if this function is successful. hps contains the presentation space handle. plHorizontal contains the horizontal alignment value. plVertical contains the vertical alignment value. You can retrieve the last error using WinGetLastError. These errors include: 0x2060 PMERR_INV_DC_TYPE 0x207F PMERR_INV_HPS 0x208C PMERR_INV_IN_RETAIN_MODE 0x20F4 PMERR_PS_BUSY
fSuccess = GpiQueryTextBox (hps, lCount1, pchString, lCount2, aptlPoints)	The GpiQueryBox function returns the relative coordinates of the four corners of a text box. fSuccess contains true if this function is successful. hps contains the presentation space handle. lCount1 contains the number of characters in pchString. pchString contains the character string. lCount2 contains the number of points that you want returned in aptlPoints. Using TXTBOX_COUNT returns the maximum amount of information. aptlPoints contains a list of points in world coordinates. You can retrieve the last error using WinGetLastError. These errors include: 0x2014 PMERR_COORDINATE_OVERFLOW 0x2060 PMERR_INV_DC_TYPE 0x207F PMERR_INV_HPS 0x208C PMERR_INV_IN_RETAIN_MODE 0x2092 PMERR_INV_LENGTH_OR_COUNT 0x20F4 PMERR_PS_BUSY
fSuccess = GpiQueryViewing- Limits (hps, prclLimits)	The GpiQueryViewingLimits function returns the current value of the viewing limits (set by the GpiSetViewingLimits function). fSuccess contains true if this function is successful. hps contains the presentation space handle. prclLimits contains the viewing limits. You can retrieve the last error using WinGetLastError. These errors include: 0x2060 PMERR_INV_DC_TYPE 0x207F PMERR_INV_HPS

Table 3-42   **Continued**

Function	Description
	0x208C PMERR_INV_IN_RETAIN_MODE 0x20F4 PMERR_PS_BUSY
fSuccess = GpiQueryViewing-TransformMatrix (hps, lCount, pmatlfArray)	The GpiQueryViewingTransformMatrix function returns the current viewing transform. fSuccess contains true if this function is successful. hps contains the presentation space handle. lCount contains the number of elements in pmatlfArray. pmatlfArray contains the transform matrix. You can retrieve the last error using WinGetLastError. These errors include:
	0x207F PMERR_INV_HPS 0x2092 PMERR_INV_LENGTH_OR_COUNT 0x20A1 PMERR_INV_MICROPS_FUNCTION 0x20F4 PMERR_PS_BUSY
fSuccess = GpiQueryWidthTable (hps, lFirstChar, lCount, alData)	The GpiQueryWidthTable returns the width table information for the logical font identified by the value of the character-set attribute. fSuccess contains true if this function is successful. hps contains the presentation space handle. lFirstChar contains the codepoint of the first character that you want width table information for. lCount contains the number of elements in alData. alData contains the width table information. You can retrieve the last error using WinGetLastError. These errors include:
	0x2014 PMERR_COORDINATE_OVERFLOW 0x2071 PMERR_INV_FIRST_CHAR 0x207F PMERR_INV_HPS 0x2092 PMERR_INV_LENGTH_OR_COUNT 0x20F4 PMERR_PS_BUSY
lInside = GpiRectInRegion (hps, hrgn, prclRect)	The GpiRectInRegion function checks whether any part of a rectangle lies within the specified region. lInside contains the inside and error indicators. hps contains the presentation space handle. hrgn contains the region handle. prclRect contains the rectangle that you want to check in device coordinates. GpiRectInRegion returns one of the following values:
	0000 RRGN_ERROR 0001 RRGN_OUTSIDE 0002 RRGN_PARTIAL 0003 RRGN_INSIDE
	You can retrieve the last error using WinGetLastError. These errors include:
	0x2034 PMERR_HRGN_BUSY 0x205B PMERR_INV_COORDINATE 0x207F PMERR_INV_HPS 0x2080 PMERR_INV_HRGN

Function	Description
	0x20BD PMERR_INV_RECT 0x20F4 PMERR_PS_BUSY 0x20F8 PMERR_REGION_IS_CLIP_REGION
lVisibility = GpiRectVisible (hps, prclRectangle)	The GpiRectVisible function checks whether any part of a rectangle lies within the clipping region of the device associated with the specified presentation space. lVisibility contains the visibility and error indicators. hps contains the presentation space handle. prclRectangle contains the rectangle that you want to check in world coordinates. GpiRectVisible returns one of the following values: 0000 RVIS_ERROR 0001 RVIS_INVISIBLE 0002 RVIS_PARTIAL 0003 RVIS_VISIBLE You can retrieve the last error using WinGetLastError. These errors include: 0x205B PMERR_INV_COORDINATE 0x207F PMERR_INV_HPS 0x20BD PMERR_INV_RECT 0x20F4 PMERR_PS_BUSY
fSuccess = GpiRemove- Dynamics (hps, lFirstSegid, lLastSegid)	The GpiRemoveDynamics function removes the parts of a displayed image drawn from the dynamic segments section of the segment chain. (This includes any parts drawn by calls from these dynamic segments.) fSuccess contains true if this function is successful. hps contains the presentation space handle. lFirstSegid contains the first segment in the section. lLastSegid contains the last segment in the section. You can retrieve the last error using WinGetLastError. These errors include: 0x2074 PMERR_INV_FOR_THIS_DC_TYPE 0x207F PMERR_INV_HPS 0x20A1 PMERR_INV_MICROPS_FUNCTION 0x20C8 PMERR_INV_SEG_NAME 0x20F4 PMERR_PS_BUSY
fSuccess = GpiResetBoundary- Data (hps)	The GpiResetBoundaryData function resets the boundary data to null. fSuccess contains true if this function is successful. hps contains the presentation space handle. You can retrieve the last error using WinGetLastError. These errors include: 0x207F PMERR_INV_HPS 0x20F4 PMERR_PS_BUSY
fSuccess = GpiResetPS (hps, flOptions)	The GpiResetPS function resets the presentation space. fSuccess contains true if this function is successful. hps contains the presentation space handle. flOptions contains one of three reset options including: GRES_ATTRS, GRES_SEGMENTS, or

Table 3-42   **Continued**

Function	Description
	GRES_ALL. You can retrieve the last error using WinGetLastError. These errors include:
	0x207F PMERR_INV_HPS 0x20C2 PMERR_INV_RESET_OPTIONS 0x20F4 PMERR_PS_BUSY
fSuccess = GpiRestorePS (hps, IPSid)	The GpiRestorePS function restores the state of the presentation space to the one that existed when you issued the corresponding GpiSavePS call. (You do not need to restore the most recent save; any interim saves are discarded.) fSuccess contains true if this function is successful. hps contains the presentation space handle. IPSid contains the identifier of the presentation space that you want to restore. You can retrieve the last error using WinGetLastError. These errors include:
	0x207F PMERR_INV_HPS 0x2081 PMERR_INV_ID 0x20DE PMERR_NOT_IN_DRAW_MODE 0x20F4 PMERR_PS_BUSY
fSuccess = GpiRotate (hps, pmatlfArray, IOptions, fxAngle, pptlCenter)	The GpiRotate function applies a rotation to a transform matrix. fSuccess contains true if this function is successful. hps contains the presentation space handle. pmatlfArray contains the transform matrix. The first, second, fourth, and fifth elements are of type FIXED. They have an assumed binary point between the second and third bytes (1.0 is represented as 65,536). You must provide values of 0, 0, 1 for the third, sixth, and ninth elements respectively. IOptions contains the transform options, which include: TRANSFORM_REPLACE and TRANSFORM_ADD. fxAngle contains the rotation angle. pptlCenter contains the center of rotation. You can retrieve the last error using WinGetLastError. These errors include:
	0x20D0 PMERR_INV_TRANSFORM_TYPE
fSuccess = GpiSaveMetaFile (hmf, pszFilename)	The GpiSaveMetaFile function saves a metafile to a disk file. (This action removes the metafile from memory and invalidates the handle). fSuccess contains true if this function is successful. hmf contains the metafile handle. pszFilename contains the name of the file that you want to use for storage. OS/2 does not allow you to use an existing filename. You can retrieve the last error using WinGetLastError. These errors include:
	0x2024 PMERR_DOSOPEN_FAILURE 0x203D PMERR_INSUFFICIENT_DISK_SPACE 0x207E PMERR_INV_HMF 0x20D9 PMERR_METAFILE_IN_USE 0x2106 PMERR_TOO_MANY_METAFILES_IN_USE

Function	Description
lPSid = GpiSavePS (hps)	The GpiSavePS function saves information about the presentation space on a LIFO stack. lPSid contains the presentation space identifier (0 indicates an error). hps contains the presentation space handle. You can retrieve the last error using WinGetLastError. These errors include: 0x207F PMERR_INV_HPS 0x20DF PMERR_NOT_IN_DRAW_MODE 0x20F4 PMERR_PS_BUSY
fSuccess = GpiScale (hps, pmatlfArray, lOptions, afxScale, pptlCenter)	The GpiScale function applies a scaling component to a transform matrix. fSuccess contains true if this function is successful. hps contains the presentation space handle. pmatlfArray contains the transform matrix. The first, second, fourth, and fifth elements are of type FIXED. They have an assumed binary point between the second and third bytes (1.0 is represented as 65,536). You must provide values of 0, 0, 1 for the third, sixth, and ninth elements respectively lOptions contains the transform options, which include: TRANSFORM_REPLACE and TRANSFORM_ADD. afxScale is an array of scaling factors; the first element is the X-scale factor and the second is the Y-scale factor. pptlCenter contains the center of scale. You can retrieve the last error using WinGetLastError. These errors include: 0x20D0 PMERR_INV_TRANSFORM_TYPE
hpalOld = GpiSelectPalette (hps, hpal)	The GpiSelectPalette function selects a palette into a presentation space. hpalOld contains the old palette handle (NULLHANDLE if the application was using the default palette) or a −1 to indicate an error. hps contains the presentation space handle. hpal contains the palette handle. Providing a value of NULLHANDLE resets the presentation space to the default palette. You can retrieve the last error using WinGetLastError. These errors include: 0x203F PMERR_INSUFFICIENT_MEMORY 0x207F PMERR_INV_HPS 0x2085 PMERR_INV_IN_AREA 0x20F4 PMERR_PS_BUSY 0x2111 PMERR_INV_HPAL 0x2112 PMERR_PALETTE_BUSY
fSuccess = GpiSetArcParams (hps, parcpArcParams)	The GpiSetArcParams function sets the current arc parameters. fSuccess contains true if this function is successful. hps contains the presentation space handle. parcpArcParams contains the arc parameters that consist of four elements: p, q, r, and s. You can retrieve the last error using WinGetLastError. These errors include: 0x205B PMERR_INV_COORDINATE 0x207F PMERR_INV_HPS 0x20F4 PMERR_PS_BUSY
fSuccess =	The GpiSetAttrMode function sets the current attribute mode. The

Table 3-42   **Continued**

Function	Description
GpiSetAttrMode (hps, lMode)	setting of this mode affects whether a primitive attribute is saved on the stack when another attribute replaces it. You can restore the original attribute using the GpiPop function. fSuccess contains true if this function is successful. hps contains the presentation space handle. lMode contains the attribute mode, which includes: AM_PRESERVE and AM_NOPRESERVE. You can retrieve the last error using WinGetLastError. These errors include: 0x2043 PMERR_INV_ATTR_MODE 0x2060 PMERR_INV_DC_TYPE 0x207F PMERR_INV_HPS 0x20A1 PMERR_INV_MICROPS_FUNCTION 0x20F4 PMERR_PS_BUSY
fSuccess = GpiSetAttrs (hps, lPrimType, flAttrMask, flDefMask, ppbunAttrs)	The GpiSetAttrs function sets the attributes of the specified primitive type. fSuccess contains true if this function is successful. hps contains the presentation space handle. lPrimType contains the primitive type that you want to change. This includes: PRIM_LINE, PRIM_CHAR, PRIM_MARKER, PRIM_AREA, and PRIM_IMAGE. flAttrMask contains the attributes mask. Each flag that you set indicates that there is a corresponding setting value in either flDefMask or ppbunAttrs. The line attributes include: LBB_COLOR, LBB_MIX_MODE, LBB_WIDTH, LBB_GEOM_WIDTH, LBB_TYPE, LBB_END, and LBB_JOIN. The character attribute types include: CBB_COLOR, CBB_BACK_COLOR, CBB_MIX_MODE, CBB_BACK_MIX_MODE, CBB_SET, CBB_MODE, CBB_BOX, CBB_ANGLE, CBB_SHEAR, and CBB_DIRECTION. The marker attribute types include: MBB_COLOR, MBB_BACK_COLOR, MBB_MIX_MODE, MBB_BACK_MIX_MODE, MBB_SET, MBB_SYMBOL, and MBB_BOX. The pattern attribute types include: ABB_COLOR, ABB_BACK_COLOR, ABB_MIX_MODE, ABB_BACK_MIX_MODE, ABB_SET, ABB_SYMBOL, and ABB_REF_POINT. The image attribute types include: IBB_COLOR, IBB_BACK_COLOR, IBB_MIX_MODE, and IBB_BACK_MIX_MODE. flDefMask contains the defaults mask. ppbunAttrs contains the attributes. Each primitive type uses its own structure as follows: LINEBUNDLE, CHARBUNDLE, MARKERBUNDLE, AREABUNDLE, and IMAGEBUNDLE. You can retrieve the last error using WinGetLastError. These errors include: 0x2035 PMERR_HUGE_FONTS_NOT_SUPPORTED 0x2044 PMERR_INV_BACKGROUND_COL_ATTR 0x204B PMERR_INV_CHAR_ANGLE_ATTR 0x204C PMERR_INV_CHAR_DIRECTION_ATTR 0x204D PMERR_INV_CHAR_MODE_ATTR 0x204F PMERR_INV_CHAR_SET_ATTR

Function	Description
	0x2050 PMERR_INV_CHAR_SHEAR_ATTR 0x2053 PMERR_INV_COLOR_ATTR 0x205B PMERR_INV_COORDINATE 0x2078 PMERR_INV_GEOM_LINE_WIDTH_ATTR 0x207F PMERR_INV_HPS 0x2093 PMERR_INV_LINE_END_ATTR 0x2094 PMERR_INV_LINE_JOIN_ATTR 0x2095 PMERR_INV_LINE_TYPE_ATTR 0x2096 PMERR_INV_LINE_WIDTH_ATTR 0x2099 PMERR_INV_MARKER_SET_ATTR 0x209A PMERR_INV_MARKER_SYMBOL_ATTR 0x20A3 PMERR_INV_MIX_ATTR 0x20AF PMERR_INV_PATTERN_ATTR 0x20B2 PMERR_INV_PATTERN_SET_ATTR 0x20B9 PMERR_INV_PRIMITIVE_TYPE 0x20F4 PMERR_PS_BUSY 0x2109 PMERR_UNSUPPORTED_ATTR 0x210A PMERR_UNSUPPORTED_ATTR_VALUE
fSuccess = GpiSetBackColor (hps, lColor)	The GpiSetBackColor function sets the current background color index attribute to the specified value. Each primitive type gets set individually. fSuccess contains true if this function is successful. hps contains the presentation space handle. lColor contains the background color. You can use a color index number or one of the following values: CLR_FALSE, CLR_TRUE, CLR_DEFAULT, CLR_WHITE, CLR_BLACK, CLR_BACKGROUND, CLR_BLUE, CLR_RED, CLR_PINK, CLR_GREEN, CLR_CYAN, CLR_YELLOW, CLR_NEUTRAL, CLR_DARKGRAY, CLR_DARKBLUE, CLR_DARKRED, CLR_DARKPINK, CLR_DARKGREEN, CLR_DARKCYAN, CLR_BROWN, or CLR_PALEGRAY. You can retrieve the last error using WinGetLastError. These errors include: 0x2044 PMERR_INV_BACKGROUND_COL_ATTR 0x207F PMERR_INV_HPS 0x20F4 PMERR_PS_BUSY
fSuccess = GpiSetBackMix (hps, lMixMode)	The GpiSetBackMix function individually sets the background mix attribute for each primitive type. fSuccess contains true if this function is successful. hps contains the presentation space handle. lMixMode controls the background color mix mode. You can use any of the following mix modes: BM_DEFAULT, BM_OR, BM_OVERPAINT, BM_XOR, or BM_LEAVEALONE. You can retrieve the last error using WinGetLastError. These errors include: 0x2044 PMERR_INV_BACKGROUND_COL_ATTR 0x207F PMERR_INV_HPS 0x20F4 PMERR_PS_BUSY
hbmOld = GpiSetBitmap (hps, hbm)	The GpiSetBitmap function selects a bitmap in a memory device context. hbmOld contains the old bitmap handle, a NULLHANDLE (if there is no old bitmap handle), or a value of −1 to indicate an

Table 3-42 | **Continued**

Function	Description

Function | **Description**

error. hps contains the presentation space handle. hbm contains the bitmap handle. You can retrieve the last error using WinGetLastError. These errors include:

0x2008 PMERR_BITMAP_IN_USE
0x2032 PMERR_HBITMAP_BUSY
0x203A PMERR_INCOMPATIBLE_BITMAP
0x207B PMERR_INV_HBITMAP
0x207F PMERR_INV_HPS
0x20F4 PMERR_PS_BUSY

lScanSet = GpiSetBitmapBits (hps, lScanStart, lScans, pbBuffer, pbmi2InfoTable)

The GpiSetBitmapBits functions transfers bitmap data from application storage to a bitmap. lScanSet contains the number of scan lines actually sent (values can be equal to or greater than 0). A return value of −1 signifies an error. hps contains the presentation space handle. lScanStart contains the starting scan line number (0 is the bottom line). lScans contains the number of scan lines that you want to send. pbBuffer contains the bitmap data. pbmi2InfoTable contains the bitmap information table (including the associated color table). You can retrieve the last error using WinGetLastError. These errors include:

0x2060 PMERR_INV_DC_TYPE
0x207F PMERR_INV_HPS
0x208F PMERR_INV_INFO_TABLE
0x2092 PMERR_INV_LENGTH_OR_COUNT
0x20C4 PMERR_INV_SCAN_START
0x20E4 PMERR_NO_BITMAP_SELECTED
0x20F4 PMERR_PS_BUSY

fSuccess = GpiSetBitmap-Dimension (hps, psizlBitmap Dimension)

The GpiSetBitmapDimension function associates a width and height with a bitmap. The system does not use these settings. An application can retrieve them using the GpiQueryBitmapDimension function. fSuccess contains true if this function is successful. hps contains the presentation space handle. psizBitmapDimension contains the width and height of the bitmap (using units of 0.1 millimeter). You can retrieve the last error using WinGetLastError. These errors include:

0x2032 PMERR_HBITMAP_BUSY
0x207B PMERR_INV_HBITMAP

fSuccess = GpiSetBitmapId (hps, hbm, lLcid)

The GpiSetBitmapId function tags a bitmap with a local identifier. This allows you to use it as a pattern set containing a single member. fSuccess contains true if this function is successful. hps contains the presentation space handle. hbm contains the bitmap handle. lLcid contains the local identifier. You can retrieve the last error using WinGetLastError. These errors include:

Function	Description
	0x2008 PMERR_BITMAP_IN_USE
	0x2032 PMERR_HBITMAP_BUSY
	0x207F PMERR_INV_HPS
	0x207B PMERR_INV_HBITMAP
	0x20CA PMERR_INV_SETID
	0x20F4 PMERR_PS_BUSY
	0x2102 PMERR_SETID_IN_USE

fSuccess = GpiSetCharAngle (hps, pgradlAngle)

The GpiSetCharAngle function sets the baseline angle used to draw characters as a relative vector. fSuccess contains true if this function is successful. hps contains the presentation space handle. pgradlAngle contains the baseline angle as a coordinate (a gradient to the origin of 0, 0). Providing a value of 0, 0 resets the angle to default. The standard default is 1, 0. You can retrieve the last error using WinGetLastError. These errors include:

0x207F   PMERR_INV_HPS
0x20F4   PMERR_PS_BUSY

fSuccess = GpiSetCharBox (hps, psizfxBox)

The GpiSetCharBox function sets the current character-box attribute to the specified value. fSuccess contains true if this function is successful. hps contains the presentation space handle. psizfxBox contains the size of the box in world coordinates. You can retrieve the last error using WinGetLastError. These errors include:

0x207F   PMERR_INV_HPS
0x20F4   PMERR_PS_BUSY

fSuccess = GpiSetCharBreak-Extra (hps, fxBreakExtra)

The GpiSetCharBreakExtra function specifies an extra increment used for spacing break characters in a string. fSuccess contains true if this function is successful. hps contains the presentation space handle. fxBreakExtra contains the character-break-extra value. Using a 0 value results in normal spacing, a negative value reduces the spacing, and a positive value increases spacing. You can retrieve the last error using WinGetLastError. These errors include:

0x207F   PMERR_INV_HPS
0x20F4   PMERR_PS_BUSY

fSuccess = GpiSetCharDirection (hps, lDirection)

The GpiSetCharDirection function determines the direction OS/2 draws characters along the baseline. fSuccess contains true if this function is successful. hps contains the presentation space handle. lDirection determines the character draw direction, which includes: CHDIRN_DEFAULT, CHDIRN_LEFTRIGHT, CHDIRN_TOPBOTTOM, CHDIRN_RIGHTLEFT, or CHDIRN_BOTTOMTOP. You can retrieve the last error using WinGetLastError. These errors include:

0x204C   PMERR_INV_CHAR_DIRECTION_ATTR
0x207F   PMERR_INV_HPS
0x20F4   PMERR_PS_BUSY

271

Table 3-42   **Continued**

Function	Description
fSuccess = GpiSetCharExtra (hps, fxExtra)	The GpiSetCharExtra function specified an extra increment used to space characters in a string. fSuccess contains true if this function is successful. hps contains the presentation space handle. fxExtra contains the character-extra value. Using a 0 value results in normal spacing, a negative value reduces the spacing, and a positive value increases spacing. You can retrieve the last error using WinGetLastError. These errors include: 0x207F PMERR_INV_HPS 0x20F4 PMERR_PS_BUSY
fSuccess = GpiSetCharMode (hps, lMode)	The GpiSetCharMode function sets the character mode used to draw a character string. fSuccess contains true if this function is successful. hps contains the presentation space handle. lMode contains the character mode, which includes: CM_DEFAULT, CM_MODE1, CM_MODE2, or CM_MODE3. You can retrieve the last error using WinGetLastError. These errors include: 0x204D PMERR_INV_CHARACTER_MODE_ATTR 0x207F PMERR_INV_HPS 0x20F4 PMERR_PS_BUSY
fSuccess = GpiSetCharSet (hps, lLcid)	The GpiSetCharSet function sets the current value of the character-set attribute. fSuccess contains true if this function is successful. hps contains the presentation space handle. lLcid contains the character set local identifier, which includes: LCID_DEFAULT, or 1 through 254 for a logical font. You can retrieve the last error using WinGetLastError. These errors include: 0x2035 PMERR_HUGE_FONTS_NOT_SUPPORTED 0x204F PMERR_INV_CHAR_SET_ATTR 0x207F PMERR_INV_HPS 0x20F4 PMERR_PS_BUSY
fSuccess = GpiSetCharShear (hps, pptlAngle)	The GpiSetCharShear function sets the character-shear attribute. fSuccess contains true if this function is successful. hps contains the presentation space handle. pptlAngle contains the shear angle as a coordinate (a gradient to the origin of 0, 0). You can retrieve the last error using WinGetLastError. These errors include: 0x2050 PMERR_INV_CHAR_SHEAR_ATTR 0x205B PMERR_INV_COORDINATE 0x207F PMERR_INV_HPS 0x20F4 PMERR_PS_BUSY
fSuccess = GpiSetClipPath (hps, lPath, lOptions)	The GpiSetClipPath function selects a path as the current clip path. fSuccess contains true if this function is successful. hps contains the presentation space handle. lPath contains the path control flag. A value of 0 resets the current clip path to no clipping, while a value

Function	Description

of 1 intersects the current path with the defined path. IOptions contains the option bits, which include: SCP_ALTERNATE and SCP_WINDING. You can retrieve the last error using WinGetLastError. These errors include:

0x2051	PMERR_INV_CLIP_PATH_OPTIONS
0x207F	PMERR_INV_HPS
0x20AE	PMERR_INV_PATH_ID
0x20F4	PMERR_PS_BUSY
0x20FF	PMERR_PATH_UNKNOWN

IComplexity = GpiSetClipRegion (hps, hrgn, phrgnOld)

The GpiSetClipRegion function sets the current clip region for any drawing that takes place through the specified presentation space. IComplexity contains the complexity of the resulting region or an error indicator on return from the function call. hps contains a presentation space handle. hrgn contains the region handle (NULLHANDLE resets clipping to no clipping). phrgnOld contains a pointer to the old region handle. GpiSetClipRegion returns one of the following values:

0000	RGN_ERROR
0001	RGN_NULL
0002	RGN_RECT
0003	RGN_COMPLEX

You can retrieve the last error using WinGetLastError. These errors include:

0x2034	PMERR_HRGN_BUSY
0x207F	PMERR_INV_HPS
0x2080	PMERR_INV_HRGN
0x20F4	PMERR_PS_BUSY

fSuccess = GpiSetColor (hps, IColor)

The GpiSetColor function sets the current color attribute for each primitive type. Each primitive type gets set individually. fSuccess contains true if this function is successful. hps contains the presentation space handle. IColor contains the foreground color. You can use a color index number or one of the following values: CLR_FALSE, CLR_TRUE, CLR_DEFAULT, CLR_WHITE, CLR_BLACK, CLR_BACKGROUND, CLR_BLUE, CLR_RED, CLR_PINK, CLR_GREEN, CLR_CYAN, CLR_YELLOW, CLR_NEUTRAL, CLR_DARKGRAY, CLR_DARKBLUE, CLR_DARKRED, CLR_DARKPINK, CLR_DARKGREEN, CLR_DARKCYAN, CLR_BROWN, or CLR_PALEGRAY. You can retrieve the last error using WinGetLastError. These errors include:

0x2053	PMERR_INV_COLOR_ATTR
0x207F	PMERR_INV_HPS
0x20F4	PMERR_PS_BUSY

fSuccess = GpiSetCp (hps,

The GpiSetCp function sets the current graphics code page. fSuccess contains true if this function is successful. hps contains

Table 3-42   **Continued**

Function	Description
ulCodePage)	the presentation space handle. ulCodePage contains the code page identifier. You can retrieve the last error using WinGetLastError. These errors include: 0x2052 PMERR_INV_CODEPAGE 0x207F PMERR_INV_HPS 0x20F4 PMERR_PS_BUSY
fSuccess = GpiSetCurrent-Position (hps, pptlPoint)	The GpiSetCurrentPosition function sets the current position to the specified point. This function is equivalent to the GpiMove function. It does save the current position on the stack if the AM_PRESERVE attribute is in effect. This allows you to restore the previous position using GpiPop. Each primitive type gets set individually. fSuccess contains true if this function is successful. hps contains the presentation space handle. pptlPoint contains the new position coordinates. You can retrieve the last error using WinGetLastError. These errors include: 0x205B PMERR_INV_COORDINATE 0x207F PMERR_INV_HPS 0x20F4 PMERR_PS_BUSY
fSuccess = GpiSetDefArcParams (hps, parcpArcParams)	The GpiSetDefArcParams function sets the default arc parameters. The initial default values are: p=1, q=1, r=0, and s=0. Each primitive type gets set individually. fSuccess contains true if this function is successful. hps contains the presentation space handle. parcpArcParams contains the new default arc parameters in a four element structure (p, q, r, and s). You can retrieve the last error using WinGetLastError. These errors include: 0x205B PMERR_INV_COORDINATE 0x207F PMERR_INV_HPS 0x20F4 PMERR_PS_BUSY
fSuccess = GpiSetDefAttrs (hps, lPrimType, flAttrMask, ppbunAttrs)	The GpiSetDefAttrs sets the default attributes for the specified primitive. fSuccess contains true if this function is successful. hps contains the presentation space handle. lPrimType contains the primitive type that you want to change. This includes: PRIM_LINE, PRIM_CHAR, PRIM_MARKER, PRIM_AREA, and PRIM_IMAGE. flAttrMask contains the attributes mask. Each flag that you set indicates that there is a corresponding setting value in ppbunAttrs. The line attributes include: LBB_COLOR, LBB_MIX_MODE, LBB_WIDTH, LBB_GEOM_WIDTH, LBB_TYPE, LBB_END, and LBB_JOIN. The character attribute types include: CBB_COLOR, CBB_BACK_COLOR, CBB_MIX_MODE, CBB_BACK_MIX_MODE, CBB_SET, CBB_MODE, CBB_BOX, CBB_ANGLE, CBB_SHEAR, and CBB_DIRECTION. The marker attribute types include: MBB_COLOR, MBB_BACK_COLOR,

Function	Description

Function

Description

MBB_MIX_MODE, MBB_BACK_MIX_MODE, MBB_SET, MBB_SYMBOL, and MBB_BOX. The pattern attribute types include: ABB_COLOR, ABB_BACK_COLOR, ABB_MIX_MODE, ABB_BACK_MIX_MODE, ABB_SET, ABB_SYMBOL, and ABB_REF_POINT. The image attribute types include: IBB_COLOR, IBB_BACK_COLOR, IBB_MIX_MODE, and IBB_BACK_MIX_MODE. ppbunAttrs contains the attributes. Each primitive type uses its own structure as follows: LINEBUNDLE, CHARBUNDLE, MARKERBUNDLE, AREABUNDLE, and IMAGEBUNDLE. You can retrieve the last error using WinGetLastError. These errors include:

0x2035	PMERR_HUGE_FONTS_NOT_SUPPORTED
0x2044	PMERR_INV_BACKGROUND_COL_ATTR
0x204B	PMERR_INV_CHAR_ANGLE_ATTR
0x204C	PMERR_INV_CHAR_DIRECTION_ATTR
0x204D	PMERR_INV_CHAR_MODE_ATTR
0x204F	PMERR_INV_CHAR_SET_ATTR
0x2050	PMERR_INV_CHAR_SHEAR_ATTR
0x2053	PMERR_INV_COLOR_ATTR
0x205B	PMERR_INV_COORDINATE
0x2078	PMERR_INV_GEOM_LINE_WIDTH_ATTR
0x207F	PMERR_INV_HPS
0x2093	PMERR_INV_LINE_END_ATTR
0x2094	PMERR_INV_LINE_JOIN_ATTR
0x2095	PMERR_INV_LINE_TYPE_ATTR
0x2096	PMERR_INV_LINE_WIDTH_ATTR
0x2099	PMERR_INV_MARKER_SET_ATTR
0x209A	PMERR_INV_MARKER_SYMBOL_ATTR
0x20A3	PMERR_INV_MIX_ATTR
0x20AF	PMERR_INV_PATTERN_ATTR
0x20B2	PMERR_INV_PATTERN_SET_ATTR
0x20B3	PMERR_INV_PATTERN_SET_FONT
0x20B9	PMERR_INV_PRIMITIVE_TYPE
0x20F4	PMERR_PS_BUSY
0x2109	PMERR_UNSUPPORTED_ATTR
0x210A	PMERR_UNSUPPORTED_ATTR_VALUE

fSuccess = GpiSetDefaultView-Matrix (hps, lCount, pmatlfArray, lOptions)

The GpiSetDefViewMatrix function sets the default viewing transform that OS/2 applies to the entire picture. fSuccess contains true if this function is successful. hps contains the presentation space handle. lCount contains the number of elements in pmatlfArray. pmatlfArray contains the transform matrix. The first, second, fourth, and fifth elements are of type FIXED. They have an assumed binary point between the second and third bytes (1.0 is represented as 65,536). You must provide values of 0, 0, 1 for the third, sixth, and ninth elements respectively. lOptions contains the transform options, which include: TRANSFORM_REPLACE, TRANSFORM_ADD, and TRANSFORM_PREEMPT. You can retrieve the last error using WinGetLastError. These errors include:

Table 3-42   **Continued**

Function	Description
	0x207F PMERR_INV_HPS 0x2092 PMERR_INV_LENGTH_OR_COUNT 0x209B PMERR_INV_MATRIX_ELEMENT 0x20D0 PMERR_INV_TRANSFORM_TYPE 0x20F4 PMERR_PS_BUSY
fSuccess = GpiSetDefTag (hps, lTag)	The GpiSetDefTag function specifies the default primitive tag value. fSuccess contains true if this function is successful. hps contains the presentation space handle. lTag contains the default tag identifier. You can retrieve the last error using WinGetLastError. These errors include: 0x207F PMERR_INV_HPS 0x20A1 PMERR_INV_MICROPS_FUNCTION 0x20F4 PMERR_PS_BUSY
fSuccess = GpiSetDefViewing-Limits (hps, prclLimits)	The GpiSetDefViewingLimits function sets the default viewing limits value. fSuccess contains true if this function is successful. hps contains the presentation space handle. prclLimits contains the default viewing limits. You can retrieve the last error using WinGetLastError. These errors include: 0x205B PMERR_INV_COORDINATE 0x207F PMERR_INV_HPS 0x20F4 PMERR_PS_BUSY
fSuccess = GpiSetDrawControl (hps, lControl, lValue)	The GpiSetDrawControl function sets options for the subsequent drawing operations. fSuccess contains true if this function is successful. hps contains the presentation space handle. lControl contains a drawing control which include the following: DCTL_ERASE, DCTL_DISPLAY, DCTL_BOUNDARY, DCTL_DYNAMIC, and DCTL_CORRELATE. lValue contains the requests value for the control, which includes: DCTL_OFF and DCTL_ON. You can retrieve the last error using WinGetLastError. These errors include: 0x2063 PMERR_INV_DRAW_CONTROL 0x2064 PMERR_INV_DRAW_VALUE 0x207F PMERR_INV_HPS 0x2085 PMERR_INV_IN_AREA 0x2089 PMERR_INV_IN_ELEMENT 0x208B PMERR_INV_IN_PATH 0x208D PMERR_INV_IN_SEG 0x20A0 PMERR_INV_MICROPS_DRAW_CONTROL 0x20F4 PMERR_PS_BUSY
fSuccess = GpiSetDrawingMode (hps, lMode)	The GpiSetDrawingMode function sets the drawing mode to control handle subsequent individual drawing primitive and attribute calls. fSuccess contains true if this function is successful. hps contains the presentation space handle.

Function	Description
	lMode contains the mode to use for subsequent drawing calls. This includes: DM_DRAW, DM_RETAIN, and DM_DRAWANDRETAIN. You can retrieve the last error using WinGetLastError. These errors include:

0x2065   PMERR_INV_DRAWING_MODE
0x207F   PMERR_INV_HPS
0x2085   PMERR_INV_IN_AREA
0x2089   PMERR_INV_IN_ELEMENT
0x208B   PMERR_INV_IN_PATH
0x208D   PMERR_INV_IN_SEG
0x20A1   PMERR_INV_MICROPS_FUNCTION
0x20F4   PMERR_PS_BUSY

Function	Description
fSuccess = GpiSetEditMode (hps, lMode)	The GpiSetEditMode function sets the current editing mode (insert or replace an element within the segment). fSuccess contains true if this function is successful. hps contains the presentation space handle. lMode contains the editing mode, which includes: SEGEM_INSERT and SEGEM_REPLACE. You can retrieve the last error using WinGetLastError. These errors include:

0x2069   PMERR_INV_EDIT_MODE
0x207F   PMERR_INV_HPS
0x2089   PMERR_INV_IN_ELEMENT
0x20A1   PMERR_INV_MICROPS_FUNCTION
0x20F4   PMERR_PS_BUSY

Function	Description
fSuccess = GpiSetElement-Pointer (hps, lElement)	The GpiSetElementPointer function sets the element pointer to the specified position within the current segment. The element pointer normally points to the end of the segment. fSuccess contains true if this function is successful. hps contains the presentation space handle. lElement contains the number of the element that you want to point at. You can retrieve the last error using WinGetLastError. These errors include:

0x207F   PMERR_INV_HPS
0x2089   PMERR_INV_IN_ELEMENT
0x20A1   PMERR_INV_MICROPS_FUNCTION
0x20E2   PMERR_NOT_IN_RETAIN_MODE
0x20E6   PMERR_NO_CURRENT_SEG
0x20F4   PMERR_PS_BUSY

Function	Description
fSuccess = GpiSetElement-PointerAtLabel (hps, lLabel)	The GpiSetElementPointerAtLabel functions sets the element pointer to point at the specified label within the current segment. The element pointer normally points to the end of the segment. fSuccess contains true if this function is successful. hps contains the presentation space handle. lLabel contains the label that you want to point at. You can retrieve the last error using WinGetLastError. These errors include:

0x207F   PMERR_INV_HPS
0x2089   PMERR_INV_IN_ELEMENT

Table 3-42   **Continued**

Function	Description
	0x20A1 PMERR_INV_MICROPS_FUNCTION 0x20D6 PMERR_LABEL_NOT_FOUND 0x20E2 PMERR_NOT_IN_RETAIN_MODE 0x20E6 PMERR_NO_CURRENT_SEG 0x20F4 PMERR_PS_BUSY
fSuccess = GpiSetGraphicsField (hps, prclField)	The GpiSetGraphicsField function sets the size and position of the graphics fields (measured in presentation page units). fSuccess contains true if this function is successful. hps contains the presentation space handle. prclField contains the coordinates of the graphics field. You can retrieve the last error using WinGetLastError. These errors include: 0x205B PMERR_INV_COORDINATE 0x207A PMERR_INV_GRAPHICS_FIELD 0x207F PMERR_INV_HPS 0x20F4 PMERR_PS_BUSY
fSuccess = GpiSetInitialSegment-Attrs (hps, lAttribute, lValue)	The GpiSetInitialSegmentAttrs function sets the segment attribute used when your application creates a segment. fSuccess contains true if this function is successful. hps contains the presentation space handle. lAttribute contains the segment attribute you want to set including: ATTR_DETECTABLE, ATTR_VISIBLE, ATTR_CHAINED, ATTR_DYNAMIC, ATTR_FASTCHAIN, ATTR_PROP_DETECTABLE, and ATTR_PROP_VISIBLE. lValue contains the attribute value, which includes: ATTR_ON and ATTR_OFF. You can retrieve the last error using WinGetLastError. These errors include: 0x207F PMERR_INV_HPS 0x20A1 PMERR_INV_MICROPS_FUNCTION 0x20C5 PMERR_INV_SEG_ATTR 0x20C6 PMERR_INV_SEG_ATTR_VALUE 0x20F4 PMERR_PS_BUSY
fSuccess = GpiSetLineEnd (hps, lLineEnd)	The GpiSetLineEnd function sets the current line-end attribute. fSuccess contains true if this function is successful. hps contains the presentation space handle. lLineEnd contains the line end style, which includes: LINEEND_DEFAULT, LINEEND_FLAT, LINEEND_SQUARE, and LINEEND_ROUND. You can retrieve the last error using WinGetLastError. These errors include: 0x207F PMERR_INV_HPS 0x2093 PMERR_INV_LINE_END_ATTR 0x20F4 PMERR_PS_BUSY
fSuccess = GpiSetLineJoin (hps, lLineJoin)	The GpiSetLineJoin function sets the current line-join attribute. fSuccess contains true if this function is successful. hps contains the presentation space handle. lLineJoin contains the line join style,

Function	Description
	which includes: LINEJOIN_DEFAULT, LINEJOIN_BEVEL, LINEJOIN_ROUND, and LINEJOIN_MITRE. You can retrieve the last error using WinGetLastError. These errors include: 0x207F PMERR_INV_HPS 0x2094 PMERR_INV_LINE_JOIN_ATTR 0x20F4 PMERR_PS_BUSY
fSuccess = GpiSetLineType (hps, fxLineWidth)	The GpiSetLineType function sets the current cosmetic line-type attribute. fSuccess contains true if this function is successful. hps contains the presentation space handle. lLineType contains the line end style, which includes: LINETYPE_DEFAULT, LINETYPE_DOT, LINETYPE_SHORTDASH, LINETYPE_DASHDOT, LINETYPE_DOUBLEDOT, LINETYPE_LONGDASH, LINETYPE_DASHDOUBLEDOT, LINETYPE_SOLID, LINETYPE_ALTERNATE, and LINETYPE_INVISBLE. You can retrieve the last error using WinGetLastError. These errors include: 0x207F PMERR_INV_HPS 0x2094 PMERR_INV_LINE_TYPE_ATTR 0x20F4 PMERR_PS_BUSY
GpiSetLineWidth	The GpiSetLineWidth function sets the current cosmetic line-width attribute. fSuccess contains true if this function is successful. hps contains the presentation space handle. fxLineWidth contains the line width multiplier, which includes: LINEWIDTH_DEFAULT, LINEWIDTH_NORMAL, and LINEWIDTH_THICK. You can retrieve the last error using WinGetLastError. These errors include: 0x207F PMERR_INV_HPS 0x2096 PMERR_INV_LINE_WIDTH_ATTR 0x20F4 PMERR_PS_BUSY
fSuccess = GpiSetLineWidth-Geom (hps, lLineWidth)	The GpiSetLineWidthGeom function sets the current geometric line-width attribute. fSuccess contains true if this function is successful. hps contains the presentation space handle. lLineWidth contains the line width in world coordinates. You can retrieve the last error using WinGetLastError. These errors include: 0x207F PMERR_INV_HPS 0x2078 PMERR_INV_GEOM_LINE_WIDTH_ATTR 0x20F4 PMERR_PS_BUSY
fSuccess = GpiSetMarker (hps, lSymbol)	The GpiSetMarker function sets the value of the marker-symbol attribute. fSuccess contains true if this function is successful. hps contains the presentation space handle. lSymbol contains the marker symbol. 0 selects the default symbol. You can retrieve the last error using WinGetLastError. These errors include: 0x207F PMERR_INV_HPS 0x209A PMERR_INV_MARKER_SYMBOL_ATTR 0x20F4 PMERR_PS_BUSY

Table 3-42   **Continued**

Function	Description
fSuccess = GpiSetMarkerBox (hps, psizfxSize)	The GpiSetMarkerBox function sets the current marker-box attribute. fSuccess contains true if this function is successful. hps contains the presentation space handle. psizlfxSize contains the size of the marker box in world coordinates. You can retrieve the last error using WinGetLastError. These errors include:
	0x207F PMERR_INV_HPS
	0x20F4 PMERR_PS_BUSY
GpiSetMarkerSet	The GpiSetMarkerSet function sets the current marker-set attribute. fSuccess contains true if this function is successful. hps contains the presentation space handle. lSet contains the marker set local identifier. You can use a value of LCID_DEFAULT or an identifier in the range 1 to 254. You can retrieve the last error using WinGetLastError. These errors include:
	0x207F PMERR_INV_HPS
	0x2099 PMERR_INV_MARKER_SET_ATTR
	0x20F4 PMERR_PS_BUSY
fSuccess = GpiSetMetaFileBits (hmf, lOffset, lLength, pbBuffer)	The GpiSetMetaFileBits functions transfers metafile data from application storage to a memory metafile. fSuccess contains true if this function is successful. hmf contains the metafile handle. lOffset contains the offset within the metafile where you want the transfer to start. lLength contains the length of the metafile data. pbBuffer contains the metafile data. You can retrieve the last error using WinGetLastError. These errors include:
	0x207E PMERR_INV_HMF
	0x209E PMERR_INV_METAFILE_LENGTH
	0x209F PMERR_INV_METAFILE_OFFSET
	0x20D9 PMERR_METAFILE_IN_USE
fSuccess = GpiSetMix (hps, lMixMode)	The GpiSetMix function individually sets the foreground mix attribute for each primitive type. fSuccess contains true if this function is successful. hps contains the presentation space handle. lMixMode controls the background color mix mode. You can use any of the following mix modes: FM_DEFAULT, FM_OR, FM_OVERPAINT, FM_XOR, FM_LEAVEALONE, FM_AND, FM_SUBTRACT, FM_MARKSRCNOT, FM_ZERO, FM_NOTMERGESRC, FM_NOTXORSRC, FM_INVERT, FM_MERGESRCNOT, FM_NOTCOPYSRC, FM_MERGENOTSRC, FM_NOTMASKSRC, or FM_ONE. You can retrieve the last error using WinGetLastError. These errors include:
	0x207F PMERR_INV_HPS
	0x20A3 PMERR_INV_MIX_ATTR
	0x20F4 PMERR_PS_BUSY

Function	Description
fSuccess = GpiSetModel-TransformMatrix (hps, lCount, pmatlfArray, lOptions)	The GpiSetModelTransformMatrix function sets the model transform matrix for subsequent primitives. fSuccess contains true if this function is successful. hps contains the presentation space handle. lCount contains the number of elements in pmatlfArray. pmatlfArray contains the transform matrix. The first, second, fourth, and fifth elements are of type FIXED. They have an assumed binary point between the second and third bytes (1.0 is represented as 65,536). You must provide values of 0, 0, 1 for the third, sixth, and ninth elements, respectively. lOptions contains the transform options, which include: TRANSFORM_REPLACE, TRANSFORM_ADD, and TRANSFORM_PREEMPT. You can retrieve the last error using WinGetLastError. These errors include:

0x207F   PMERR_INV_HPS
0x2092   PMERR_INV_LENGTH_OR_COUNT
0x209B   PMERR_INV_MATRIX_ELEMENT
0x20D0   PMERR_INV_TRANSFORM_TYPE
0x20F4   PMERR_PS_BUSY

Function	Description
fSuccess = GpiSetPageViewport (hps, prclViewport)	The GpiSetPageViewport function sets the page viewport within the device space. fSuccess contains true if this function is successful. hps contains the presentation space handle. prclViewport contains the size and position of the page viewport in device units. You can retrieve the last error using WinGetLastError. These errors include:

0x205B   PMERR_INV_COORDINATE
0x207F   PMERR_INV_HPS
0x20AD   PMERR_INV_PAGE_VIEWPORT
0x20F4   PMERR_PS_BUSY

Function	Description
fSuccess = GpiSetPaletteEntries (hpal, ulFormat, ulStart, ulCount, aTable)	The GpiSetPaletteEntries function changes the entries in a palette. (You will not see the results until you call WinRealizePalette.) fSuccess contains true if this function is successful. hpal contains the color palette handle. ulFormat contains the format of the table entries, which includes: LCOLF_CONSECRGB. ulStart contains the starting index. ulCount contains the number of entries in aTable. aTable is an array of color values. Each color value is a 4-byte integer with a value of $(F \times 16777216) + (R \times 65536) + (G \times 256) + B$. F is one of the following flags: PC_RESERVED or PC_EXPLICIT. R, G, and B are the color values. You can retrieve the last error using WinGetLastError. These errors include:

0x2111   PMERR_INV_HPAL
0x2112   PMERR_PALETTE_BUSY
0x203F   PMERR_INSUFFICIENT_MEMORY
0x2054   PMERR_INV_COLOR_DATA
0x2055   PMERR_INV_COLOR_FORMAT
0x2058   PMERR_INV_COLOR_START_INDEX
0x2085   PMERR_INV_IN_AREA
0x2092   PMERR_INV_LENGTH_OR_COUNT

Table 3-42 **Continued**

Function	Description
fSuccess = GpiSetPattern (hps, lPatternSymbol)	The GpiSetPattern function sets the current value of the pattern-symbol attribute. fSuccess contains true if this function is successful. hps contains the presentation space handle. lPatternSymbol contains the identifier of the shading symbol that you want to use in the range from 0 to 255 (0 selects the default pattern). Possible patterns include: PATSYM_DEFAULT, PATSYM_DENSE1 through PATSYM_DENSE8, PATSYM_VERT, PATSYM_HORIZ, PATSYM_DIAG1 through PATSYM_DIAG4, PATSYM_NOSHADE, PATSYM_SOLID, PATSYM_HALFTONE, and PATSYM_BLANK. You can retrieve the last error using WinGetLastError. These errors include: 0x207F　PMERR_INV_HPS 0x20B0　PMERR_INV_PATTERN_ATTR 0x20F4　PMERR_PS_BUSY
fSuccess = GpiSetPatternRef-Point (hps, pptlRefPoint)	The GpiSetPatternRefPoint function sets the current pattern reference point to the specified value. fSuccess contains true if this function is successful. hps contains the presentation space handle. pptlRefPoint contains the pattern reference point in world coordinates (the default setting is 0, 0). You can retrieve the last error using WinGetLastError. These errors include: 0x205B　PMERR_INV_COORDINATE 0x207F　PMERR_INV_HPS 0x20F4　PMERR_PS_BUSY
fSuccess = GpiSetPatternSet (hps, lSet)	The GpiSetPatternSet function sets the current pattern-set attribute to the specified value. fSuccess contains true if this function is successful. hps contains the presentation space handle. lSet contains the pattern set local identifier that can contain numbers in the range 1 to 254 or LCID_DEFAULT. You can retrieve the last error using WinGetLastError. These errors include: 0x2035　PMERR_HUGE_FONTS_NOT_SUPPORTED 0x207F　PMERR_INV_HPS 0x20B2　PMERR_INV_PATTERN_SET_ATTR 0x20B3　PMERR_INV_PATTERN_SET_FONT 0x20F4　PMERR_PS_BUSY
lHits = GpiSetPel (hps, pptlPoint)	The GpiSetPel function sets a pel color using the current color and mix. You must specify the pel position in world coordinates. lHits contains the correlation and error indicators. hps contains the presentation space handle. pptlPoint contains the pel position in world coordinates. GpiSetPel returns one of the following values: 0000　GPI_ERROR 0001　GPI_OK 0002　GPI_HITS

Function	Description
	You can retrieve the last error using WinGetLastError. These errors include: 0x205B PMERR_INV_COORDINATE 0x207F PMERR_INV_HPS 0x20F4 PMERR_PS_BUSY
fSuccess = GpiSetPickAperture- Position (hps, pptlPick)	The GpiSetPickAperturePosition function sets the center of the pick aperture in the presentation page space. This affects subsequent nonretained correlation operations. fSuccess contains true if this function is successful. hps contains the presentation space handle. pptlPick contains the center of the pick aperture in presentation page coordinates. You can retrieve the last error using WinGetLastError. These errors include: 0x205B PMERR_INV_COORDINATE 0x207F PMERR_INV_HPS 0x20F4 PMERR_PS_BUSY
fSuccess = GpiSetPickAperture- Size (hps, lOptions, psizlSize)	The GpiSetPickApertureSize function sets the pick aperture size. fSuccess contains true if this function is successful. hps contains the presentation space handle. lOptions contains the setting options, which include: PICKAP_DEFAULT and PICKAP_REC. psizlSize contains the pick aperture size. You can retrieve the last error using WinGetLastError. These errors include: 0x207F PMERR_INV_HPS 0x20B4 PMERR_INV_PICK_APERTURE_OPTION 0x20B6 PMERR_INV_PICK_APERTURE_SIZE 0x20F4 PMERR_PS_BUSY
fSuccess = GpiSetPS (hps, psizlSize, flOptions)	The GpiSetPS sets the presentation space size, units, and format. fSuccess contains true if this function is successful. hps contains the presentation space handle. psizlSize contains the presentation space size. flOptions contains the presentation options. Each field provides one or more values as follow. The PS_UNITS field can contain: PU_ARBITRARY, PU_PELS, PU_LOMETRIC, PU_HIMETRIC, PU_LOENGLISH, PU_HIENGLISH, or PU_TWIPS. The PS_FORMAT field can contain: GPIF_DEFAULT, GPIF_SHORT, or GPIF_LONG. The PS_TYPE field contains the presentation space type (this value is ignored). The PS_MODE field contains the presentation space mode information (this value is ignored). The PS_ASSOCIATE field contains the association indicator (this value is ignored). The PS_NORESET field contains the inhibit full reset field. You can retrieve the last error using WinGetLastError. These errors include: 0x2074 PMERR_INV_FOR_THIS_DC_TYPE 0x207C PMERR_INV_HDC 0x207F PMERR_INV_HPS 0x20A9 PMERR_INV_OR_INCOMPAT_OPTIONS 0x20BA PMERR_INV_PS_SIZE 0x20F4 PMERR_PS_BUSY

Table 3-42   **Continued**

Function	Description
fSuccess = GpiSetRegion (hps, hrgn, lCount, arclRectangles)	The GpiSetRegion function changes a region to the logical-OR of the rectangles that define it. fSuccess contains true if this function is successful. hps contains the presentation space handle. hrgn contains the region handle. lCount contains the number of elements in arclRectangles. arclRectangles contains an array of rectangles specified in device coordinates. You can retrieve the last error using WinGetLastError. These errors include:

0x2034	PMERR_HRGN_BUSY
0x205B	PMERR_INV_COORDINATE
0x207F	PMERR_INV_HPS
0x2080	PMERR_INV_HRGN
0x2092	PMERR_INV_LENGTH_OR_COUNT
0x20BD	PMERR_INV_RECT
0x20F4	PMERR_PS_BUSY
0x20F8	PMERR_REGION_IS_CLIP_REGION

Function	Description
fSuccess = GpiSetSegmentAttrs (hps, lSegid, lAttribute, lValue)	The GpiSetSegmentAttrs function sets a segment attribute. fSuccess contains true if this function is successful. hps contains the presentation space handle. lSegid contains the segment identifier. lAttribute contains the segment attributes. This includes: ATTR_DETECTABLE, ATTR_VISIBLE, ATTR_CHAINED, ATTR_DYNAMIC, ATTR_FASTCHAIN, ATTR_PROP_DETECTABLE, and ATTR_PROP_VISIBLE. lValue contains the attribute value, which includes: ATTR_ON and ATTR_OFF. You can retrieve the last error using WinGetLastError. These errors include:

0x207F	PMERR_INV_HPS
0x20A1	PMERR_INV_MICROPS_FUNCTION
0x20C5	PMERR_INV_SEG_ATTR
0x20C6	PMERR_INV_SEG_ATTR_VALUE
0x20C8	PMERR_INV_SEG_NAME
0x20F4	PMERR_PS_BUSY
0x2100	PMERR_SEG_NOT_FOUND

Function	Description
fSuccess = GpiSetSegment-Priority (hps, lSegid, lRefSegid, lOrder)	The GpiSetSegmentPriority function changes the position of a segment within the segment chain. It also can add a segment to the chain. fSuccess contains true if this function is successful. hps contains the presentation space handle. lSegid contains the segment identifier of the segment that you want to change. lRefSegid contains the identifier of the reference segment. OS/2 places the segment that you want to change before or after the reference segment. lOrder determines the position of the segment when you change it. This parameter can have two values: LOWER_PRI or HIGHER_PRI. You can retrieve the last error using WinGetLastError. These errors include:

Function	Description
	0x207F PMERR_INV_HPS 0x20A1 PMERR_INV_MICROPS_FUNCTION 0x20AB PMERR_INV_ORDERING_PARM 0x20C8 PMERR_INV_SEG_NAME 0x20F4 PMERR_PS_BUSY 0x20FA PMERR_SEG_AND_REFSEG_ARE_SAME 0x2100 PMERR_SEG_NOT_FOUND
fSuccess = GpiSetSegment-TransformMatrix (hps, lSegid, lCount, pmatlfArray, lOptions)	The GpiSetSegmentTransformMatrix function sets the segment transform that normally applies to all primitives in the specified segment. fSuccess contains true if this function is successful. hps contains the presentation space handle. lSegid contains the segment identifier. lCount contains the number of elements in pmatlfArray. pmatlfArray contains the transform matrix. The first, second, fourth, and fifth elements are of type FIXED. They have an assumed binary point between the second and third bytes (1.0 is represented as 65,536). You must provide values of 0, 0, 1 for the third, sixth, and ninth elements respectively. lOptions contains the transform options, which include: TRANSFORM_REPLACE, TRANSFORM_ADD, and TRANSFORM_PREEMPT. You can retrieve the last error using WinGetLastError. These errors include: 0x207F PMERR_INV_HPS 0x2092 PMERR_INV_LENGTH_OR_COUNT 0x209B PMERR_INV_MATRIX_ELEMENT 0x20A1 PMERR_INV_MICROPS_FUNCTION 0x20C8 PMERR_INV_SEG_NAME 0x20D0 PMERR_INV_TRANSFORM_TYPE 0x20F4 PMERR_PS_BUSY 0x2100 PMERR_SEG_NOT_FOUND
fSuccess = GpiSetStopDraw (hps, lValue)	The GpiStopDraw function sets or clears the "stop draw" condition. fSuccess contains true if this function is successful. hps contains the presentation space handle. lValue contains the stop draw condition: SDW_OFF or SDW_ON. You can retrieve the last error using WinGetLastError. These errors include: 0x207F PMERR_INV_HPS 0x20A1 PMERR_INV_MICROPS_FUNCTION 0x20CF PMERR_INV_STOP_DRAW_VALUE
fSuccess = GpiSetTag (hps, lTag)	The GpiSetTag function sets the tag used to reference the following primitives. fSuccess contains true if this function is successful. hps contains the presentation space handle. lTag contains the tag identifier. You can retrieve the last error using WinGetLastError. These errors include: 0x207F PMERR_INV_HPS 0x20A1 PMERR_INV_MICROPS_FUNCTION 0x20F4 PMERR_PS_BUSY
fSuccess =	The GpiSetTextAlignment function determines the alignment of the

Table 3-42   **Continued**

Function	Description
GpiSetTextAlignment (hps, lHorizontal, lVertical)	characters in a string. fSuccess contains true if this function is successful. hps contains the presentation space handle. lHorizontal contains the horizontal alignment. lVertical contains the vertical alignment. You can retrieve the last error using WinGetLastError. These errors include: 0x207F PMERR_INV_HPS 0x20F4 PMERR_PS_BUSY 0x2117 PMERR_INV_CHAR_ALIGN_ATTR
fSuccess = GpiSetViewingLimits (hps, prclLimits)	The GpiSetViewingLimits function sets a clipping rectangle in model space. fSuccess contains true if this function is successful. hps contains the presentation space handle. prclLimits contains the viewing limits in model space. You can retrieve the last error using WinGetLastError. These errors include: 0x205B PMERR_INV_COORDINATE 0x207F PMERR_INV_HPS 0x20F4 PMERR_PS_BUSY
fSuccess = GpiSetViewing-TransformMatrix (hps, lCount, pmatlfArray, lOptions)	The GpiSetViewingTransformMatrix function sets the viewing transform that OS/2 applies to any subsequently opened segments. fSuccess contains true if this function is successful. hps contains the presentation space handle. lCount contains the number of elements in pmatlfArray. pmatlfArray contains the transform matrix. The first, second, fourth, and fifth elements are of type FIXED. They have an assumed binary point between the second and third bytes (1.0 is represented as 65,536). You must provide values of 0, 0, 1 for the third, sixth, and ninth elements respectively. lOptions contains the transform options, which include: TRANSFORM_REPLACE, TRANSFORM_ADD, and TRANSFORM_PREEMPT. You can retrieve the last error using WinGetLastError. These errors include: 0x207F PMERR_INV_HPS 0x208D PMERR_INV_IN_SEG 0x2092 PMERR_INV_LENGTH_OR_COUNT 0x209B PMERR_INV_MATRIX_ELEMENT 0x20A1 PMERR_INV_MICROPS_FUNCTION 0x20D0 PMERR_INV_TRANSFORM_TYPE 0x20E2 PMERR_NOT_IN_RETAIN_MODE 0x20F4 PMERR_PS_BUSY
lHits = GpiStroke-Path (hps, lPath, flOptions)	The GpiStrokePath function strokes a path, then draws it. lHits contains the correlation and error indicators. hps contains the presentation space handle. lPath contains the identifier to stroke (must contain 1). flOptions contains the stroke option (reserved, set it to zero). GpiSetPel returns one of the following values:

Function	Description
	0000 GPI_ERROR 0001 GPI_OK 0002 GPI_HITS
	You can retrieve the last error using WinGetLastError. These errors include:
	0x207F PMERR_INV_HPS 0x20AE PMERR_INV_PATH_ID 0x20C1 PMERR_INV_RESERVED_FIELD 0x20F4 PMERR_PS_BUSY 0x20FF PMERR_PATH_UNKNOWN
fSuccess = GpiTranslate (hps, pmatlfArray, lOptions, pptlTranslation)	The GpiTranslate function applies a translation to a translation matrix. fSuccess contains true if this function is successful. hps contains the presentation space handle. pmatlfArray contains the transform matrix. The first, second, fourth, and fifth elements are of type FIXED. They have an assumed binary point between the second and third bytes (1.0 is represented as 65,536). You must provide values of 0, 0, 1 for the third, sixth, and ninth elements respectively. lOptions contains the transform options, which include: TRANSFORM_REPLACE, and TRANSFORM_ADD. pptlTranslation contains the coordinates of a point, relative to the origin, that defines the required translation. You can retrieve the last error using WinGetLastError. These errors include:
	0x20D0 PMERR_INV_TRANSFORM_TYPE
fSuccess = GpiUnloadFonts (hps, pszFilename)	The GpiUnloadFonts function unloads any fonts previously loaded by GpiLoadFonts. fSuccess contains true if this function is successful. hps contains the presentation space handle. pszFilename contains the fully qualified font name. (OS/2 assumes an extension of FON.) You can retrieve the last error using WinGetLastError. These errors include:
	0x202E PMERR_FONT_FILE_NOT_LOADED 0x20EB PMERR_OWN_SET_ID_REFS
GpiUnloadPublic-Fonts	The GpiUnloadFonts function unloads one or more generally available fonts previously loaded by GpiLoadPublicFonts. fSuccess contains true if this function is successful. hps contains the presentation space handle. pszFilename contains the fully qualified font name. (OS/2 assumes an extension of FON.) You can retrieve the last error using WinGetLastError. These errors include:
	0x202E PMERR_FONT_FILE_NOT_LOADED 0x20EB PMERR_OWN_SET_ID_REFS
lHits = GpiWCBitBlt (hpsTarget, hbmSource, lCount, aptlPoints, lRop, flOptions)	The GpiWCBitBlt function copies a rectangle of bitmap image data. lHits contains the correlation and error indicators. hpsTarget contains the presentation space handle of the target. hbmSource contains the source bitmap handle. lCount contains the point count (must contain a value of 4). aptlPoints contains an array of lCount

Table 3-42   **Continued**

Function	Description
	points. These points are: Tx1, Ty1, Tx2, Ty2, Sx1, Sy1, Sx2, and Sy2. The first set of points is the bottom-left corner. The second set of points is the upper-right corner. lRop contains the mixing function required. There are 15 different mixing actions including: ROP_SRCCOPY, ROP_SRCPAINT, ROP_SRCAND, ROP_SRCINVERT, ROP_SRCERASE, ROP_NOTSRCCOPY, ROP_NOTSRCERASE, ROP_MERGECOPY, ROP_MERGEPAINT, ROP_PATCOPY, ROPPATPAINT, ROP_PATINVERT, ROP_DSTINVERT, ROP_ZERO, and ROP_ONE. flOptions contains a list of applicable options. You can use bits 15 through 31 for unique modes supported by particular devices. Other values for this parameter include: BBO_OR, BOO_AND, and BBO_IGNORE. GpiWCBitBlt returns one of the following values:

0000   GPI_ERROR
0001   GPI_OK
0002   GPI_HITS

You can retrieve the last error using WinGetLastError. These errors include:

0x200A   PMERR_BITMAP_NOT_FOUND
0x2032   PMERR_HBITMAP_BUSY
0x203A   PMERR_INCOMPATIBLE_BITMAP
0x203C   PMERR_INCORRECT_DC_TYPE
0x2046   PMERR_INV_BITBLT_MIX
0x2047   PMERR_INV_BITBLT_STYLE
0x205B   PMERR_INV_COORDINATE
0x207B   PMERR_INV_HBITMAP
0x207F   PMERR_INV_HPS
0x2092   PMERR_INV_LENGTH_OR_COUNT
0x20BD   PMERR_INV_RECT
0x20E4   PMERR_NO_BITMAP_SELECTED
0x20F4   PMERR_PS_BUSY

 # WIN functions

Everything that you do with the Presentation Manager (PM) is based on a window. One of the very first things that you do when you write a PM application is create one or more windows. Every activity seems to involve some interaction with windows. The WIN functions work within windows; the device aspect of using these functions is hidden from the programmer in many cases. Very few WIN functions even

mention the device context or the presentation space; their sole concern is the window. The WIN functions allow you to create, delete, and manipulate the windows required to create a PM application.

Many of the WIN functions appear to overlap the GPI functions. In most cases, the GPI function is more accurate than its faster WIN counterpart. This is an important programming consideration. If you need speed, then use the WIN version of the function. If you need accuracy, use the GPI version. A perfect example of this relationship is the WinSubtractRect and GpiCombineRegion functions. Both of them perform about the same task. The main difference between these two functions is their speed and accuracy. The WinSubtractRect function is much faster than its GpiCombineRegion counterpart. Keep these differences in mind as you select functions for your applications.

Table 3-43 contains a complete listing of the WIN function. It includes the calling syntax, a brief description of what task the function performs, and descriptions of each variable that the function requires. The table also includes references to other functions that act like the current function or that you need to call before calling this function. The descriptions contain any pertinent notes and warnings but might not tell you about every facet of the function.

WIN function listing   Table 3-43

Function	Description
atom = WinAddAtom (hatomtblAtomTbl, pszAtomName)	The WinAddAtom function adds an atom to an atom table. An integer atom always adds a new element to the table. A name atom updates the atom count by one if the atom already exists, or it adds a new atom if it does not exist. atom contains the atom associated with the passed string (0 indicates an error). hatomtblAtomTbl contains the atom table handle. pszAtomName contains the atom name. You can retrieve the last error using WinGetLastError. These errors include: 0x1013 PMERR_INVALID_HATOMTBL 0x1015 PMERR_INVALID_ATOM_NAME 0x1016 PMERR_INVALID_INTEGER_ATOM 0x1017 PMERR_ATOM_NAME_NOT_FOUND
hswitchSwitch = WinAddSwitchEntry	The WinAddSwitchEntry function adds an entry to the Window List. (This is the list of applications displayed to the

Table 3-43 **Continued**

Function	Description
(pswctlSwitchData)	user by the operating system.) hswitchSwitch contains the Window List handle (NULLHANDLE indicates an error). pswctlSwitchData contains information about the Window List entry. You can retrieve the last error using WinGetLastError. These errors include: 0x1201 PMERR_NO_SPACE 0x1206 PMERR_INVALID_WINDOW 0x120B PMERR_INVALID_SESSION_ID
fResult = WinAlarm (hwndDesktop, flStyle)	The WinAlarm function generates an audible alarm. fResult contains true if this function is successful. hwndDesktop can contain HWND_DESKTOP or a handle to another desktop window. flStyle determines the type of alarm, which includes: WA_WARNING, WA_NOTE, and WA_ERROR. You can retrieve the last error using WinGetLastError. These errors include: 0x1001 PMERR_INVALID_HWND 0x1019 PMERR_INVALID_FLAG
fSuccess = WinAssociateHelpInstance (hwndHelpInstance, hwndApp)	The WinAssociateHelpInstance function associates the specified instance of the Help Manager with the window chain of the specified application window. fSuccess contains true if this function is successful. hwndHelpInstance contains a handle of an instance of the Help Manager. A value of NULLHANDLE disassociates the Help Manager instance from the window chain. hwndApp contains the handle of an application window.
Henum = WinBeginEnumWindows (hwndParent)	The WinBeginEnumWindows function starts the enumeration process for all immediate child windows of a specified window. Enumeration does not extend to the children of the child windows. Henum contains the enumeration handle. Use it with the WinGetNextWindow function to return the immediate child-window handles in succession. hwndParent contains the handle of the parent window. You can use the following values: HWND_DESKTOP, HWND_OBJECT, or any other window handle. You can retrieve the last error using WinGetLastError. These errors include: 0x1001 PMERR_INVALID_HWND
hpsPaintPS = WinBeginPaint (hwnd, hps, prclRect)	The WinBeginPaint function obtains a presentation space. It readies the associated update region for drawing in a specified window. hpsPaintPS contains a presentation space handle (NULLHANDLE indicates an error). hwnd contains the window handle (HWND_DESKTOP or other window handle). hps contains the presentation space handle. NULLHANDLE

Function	Description
	obtains a cache presentation space. prclRect contains the bounding rectangle coordinates. A value of NULL indicates that the window does not require repainting. You can retrieve the last error using WinGetLastError. These errors include: 0x1001 PMERR_INVALID_HWND 0x207F PMERR_INV_HPS
fSuccess = WinBroadcastMsg (hwndParent, ulMsgId, mpParam1, mpParam2, flCmd)	The WinBroadcastMsg function broadcasts a message to multiple windows. This function posts messages to all the immediate child windows of hwndParent unless flCmd is BMSG_DESCENDANTS. fSuccess contains true if this function is successful. hwndParent contains the parent window handle. ulMsgId contains the message identifier. mpParam1 contains the first parameter. mpParam2 contains the second parameter. flCmd contains the broadcast message command, which includes: BMSG_POST, BMSG_SEND, BMSG_POSTQUEUE, BMSG_DESCENDANTS, and BMSG_FRAMEONLY.
fSuccess = WinCalcFrameRect (hwnd, prclRect, fFrame)	The WinCalcFrameRect function calculates a client rectangle from a frame rectangle or a frame rectangle from a client rectangle. fSuccess contains true if this function is successful. hwnd contains the frame window handle. prclRect contains the coordinates of the window rectangle. fFrame contains the frame indicator: TRUE (frame rectangle provided) or FALSE (child-area rectangle provided). You can retrieve the last error using WinGetLastError. These errors include: 0x1001 PMERR_INVALID_HWND
fHookRet = WinCallMsgFilter (hab, pqmsgpqmsg, ulFilter)	The WinCallMsgFilter function calls a message-filter hook. fHookRet contains true if this function is successful. hab contains the anchor block handle. pqmsgpqmsg contains the message that you want to send to the message-filter hook. ulFilter contains the message-filter code that you want to pass to the message-filter hook.
fSuccess = WinCancelShutdown (hmq, fCancelAlways)	The WinCancelShutdown function cancels a request to shut an application down. fSuccess contains true if this function is successful. hmq contains the message queue handle for the current thread. fCancelAlways contains TRUE if you do not want to place a WM_QUIT message on the queue during system shutdown, or FALSE if the application will ignore any outstanding WM_QUIT messages, but you want it to receive the message during any other system shutdowns.
ulRetCode = WinChangeSwitchEntry (hswitchSwitch, pswctlSwitchData)	The WinChangeSwitchEntry function changes the information in a Window List entry. usRetCode contains a 0 for successful completion, any other value is an error indication. hswitchSwitch contains the Window List handle.

Table 3-43   **Continued**

Function	Description
	pswctlSwitchData contains information about the Window List entry. You can retrieve the last error using WinGetLastError. These errors include: 0x1202 PMERR_INVALID_SWITCH_HANDLE 0x1206 PMERR_INVALID_WINDOW
usRetChkst = WinCheckButton (hwndDlg, usId, usChkstate)	The WinCheckButton function sets the checked state of the specified control button. It returns the previous state of the button. usRetChkst contains the previous button value. hwndDlg contains the dialog window handle. usId contains the button control identity. usChkstate contains the current checked state of the button.
fSuccess = WinCheckMenuItem (hwndMenu, usId, fCheck)	The WinCheckMenuItem function sets the check state of the specified menu item. fSuccess contains true if this function is successful. hwndMenu contains the menu window handle. usId contains the item identity. fCheck contains the current checked state of the item.
fSuccess = WinCloseClipbrd (hab)	The WinCloseClipbrd function closes the clipboard. This allows other applications to open it using the WinOpenClipbrd function. fSuccess contains true if this function is successful. hab contains the anchor block handle.
ulResult = WinCompareStrings (hab, idCodepage, idCountryCode, pszString1, pszString2, flOptions)	The WinCompareStrings function compares two null-terminated strings. They must use the same code page. ulResult contains the comparison result or an error indicator. hab contains the anchor block handle. idCodepage contains the codepage identity for both strings. idCountryCode contains the country code. pszString1 and pszString2 contain the strings that you want to compare. flOptions is a reserved parameter (set it to 0). WinCompareStrings returns one of the following values: 0000 WIN_ERROR 0001 WIN_EQ 0002 WIN_LT 0003 WIN_GT You can retrieve the last error using WinGetLastError. These errors include: 0x100B PMERR_INVALID_STRING_PARM
ulCopied = WinCopyAccelTable (hAccel, pacctAccelTable, ulCopyMax)	The WinCopyAccelTable function retrieves accelerator table data corresponding to an accelerator table handle. You also can use it to determine the size of the accelerator table data. ulCopied contains the amount of data copied into the data area or the size of the data area required for the complete accelerator table (0 indicates an error). hAccel contains the

Function	Description
	accelerator table handle. pacctAccelTable contains a pointer to the accelerator table data area (NULL if you want OS/2 to return the size of the accelerator table in bytes). ulCopyMax contains the size of the data area. You can retrieve the last error using EinGetLastError. These errors include:
	0x101A PMERR_INVALID_HACCEL
fSuccess = WinCopyRect (hab, prclDest, prclSrc)	The WinCopyRect function copies a rectangle from prclSrc to prclDest. fSuccess contains true if this function is successful. hab contains the anchor block handle. prclDest is a pointer to the destination rectangle. prclSrc is a pointer to the source rectangle.
ucDest = WinCpTranslateChar (hab, idCpSource, ucSource, idCpDest)	The WinCpTranslateChar function translates a character from one codepage to another. (If a character does not directly map to the new codepage, OS/2 uses a substitution character.) ucDest contains the converted character (0 indicates an error). hab contains the anchor block handle. idCpSource contains the source character codepage. ucSource contains the character that you want to translate. idCpDest contains the destination character codepage. You can retrieve the last error using WinGetLastError. These errors include:
	0x100B PMERR_INVALID_STRING_PARM 0x101D PMERR_INVALID_SRC_CODEPAGE 0x101E PMERR_INVALID_DST_CODEPAGE
fSuccess = WinCpTranslateString (hab, idCpSource, pszSource, idCpDest, cbLenDest, pszDest)	The WinCpTranslateString function translates a string from one codepage to another. (If a character does not directly map to the new codepage, OS/2 uses a substitution character.) fSuccess contains true if this function is successful. hab contains the anchor block handle. idCpSource contains the source character codepage. pszSource contains the string that you want to translate. idCpDest contains the destination character codepage. cbLenDest contains the length of the output string. pszDest contains the converted string. You can retrieve the last error using WinGetLastError. These errors include:
	0x1003 PMERR_PARAMETER_OUT_OF_RANGE 0x100B PMERR_INVALID_STRING_PARM 0x101D PMERR_INVALID_SRC_CODEPAGE 0x101E PMERR_INVALID_DST_CODEPAGE
hAccel = WinCreateAccelTable (hab, pacctAccelTable)	The WinCreateAccelTable function creates an accelerator table from the accelerator definitions in memory. hAccel contains the accelerator table handle. hab contains the anchor block handle. pacctAccelTable contains a pointer to the accelerator table.
hatomtblAtomTbl = WinCreateAtomTable (ulInitial, ulBuckets)	The WinCreateAtomTable creates an atom table of the specified size. The minimum atom table size is 16+(2 × ulBuckets). hatomtblAtomTbl contains the atom table handle

Table 3-43   **Continued**

Function	Description

Function **Description**

(NULLHANDLE indicates the call failed). ulInitial contains the initial size of the table in bytes. ulBuckets contains the size of the atom table hash table. Providing a value of 0 creates a hash table that uses the default size of 37. Always provide a prime number.

fSuccess = WinCreateCursor (hwnd, lx, ly, lcx, lcy, ulrgf, prclClip)

The WinCreateCursor function creates or changes a text input cursor for a specified window. It automatically destroys any existing cursors. fSuccess contains true if this function is successful. hwnd contains the window handle. lx contains the cursor X position. ly contains the cursor Y position. lcx contains the cursor X size (0 specifies a nominal cursor size). lcy contains the cursor Y size (0 specifies a nominal cursor size). ulrgf controls the cursor appearance. This includes: CURSOR_SOLID, CURSOR_HALFTONE, CURSOR_FRAME, CURSOR_FLASH, or CURSOR_SETPOS. prclClip contains the cursor rectangle coordinates. This is the area where the cursor is visible to the user. A NULL value uses the entire window area as the cursor clipping area. You can retrieve the last error using WinGetLastError. These errors include:

0x1001   PMERR_INVALID_HWND
0x1019   PMERR_INVALID_FLAG

hwndDlg = WinCreateDlg (hwndParent, hwndOwner, pDlgProc, pdlgtDlgTmp, pCreateParams)

The WinCreateDlg function creates a dialog window. hwndDlg contains the dialog window handle (NULLHANDLE indicates an error). hwndParent contains the parent window handle: HWND_DESKTOP, HWND_OBJECT, or any other window handle. hwndOwner contains the owner window handle. pDlgProc contains the dialog procedure for the dialog window. pdlgtDlgTmp contains a pointer to the dialog template. pCreateParams contains a pointer to the application data area. You can retrieve the last error using WinGetLastError. These errors include:

0x1001   PMERR_INVALID_HWND
0x1015   PMERR_INVALID_ATOM_NAME
0x1016   PMERR_INVALID_INTEGER_ATOM
0x1017   PMERR_ATOM_NAME_NOT_FOUND

fSuccess = WinCreateFrameControls (hwndFrame, pFcdata, pszTitle)

The WinCreateFrameControls function creates the standard frame controls for the specified window. fSuccess contains true if this function is successful. hwndFrame contains the frame window handle: HWND_DESKTOP, HWND_OBJECT, or any other window handle. pFcdata contains the frame control data (any combination of frame creation flags). pszTitle contains the title bar string. You can retrieve the last error using WinGetLastError. These errors include:

Function	Description
	0x1001 PMERR_INVALID_HWND 0x1019 PMERR_INVALID_FLAG
hwndHelp = WinCreateHelpInstance (hab, phinitHMInitStructure)	The WinCreateHelpInstance function creates an instance of the Help Manager. This allows you to request Help Manager functions. hwndHelp contains the Help Manager handle (NULLHANDLE indicates an error, the Help Manager returns the error code in the ulReturnCode parameter of the HELPINIT structure). hab contains the anchor block handle. phinitHMInitStructure contains the Help Manager initialization structure.
fSuccess = WinCreateHelpTable (hwndHelpInstance, pthHelpTable)	The WinCreateHelpTable function identifies or changes a help table. fSuccess contains true if this function is successful. hwndHelpInstance contains the Help Manager instance handle created using the WinCreateHelpInstance function. pthHelpTable contains the help table allocated by the application.
hwndMenu = WinCreateMenu (hwndOwner, pmtMenutmp)	The WinCreateMenu function creates a menu from the menu template. hwndMenu contains the menu window handle. hwndOwner contains the owner and parent window handle: HWND_DESKTOP, HWND_OBJECT, or any other window handle. pmtMenutmp contains the menu template in binary format. You can retrieve the last error using WinGetLastError. These errors include: 0x1001 PMERR_INVALID_HWND
hmq = WinCreateMsgQueue (hab, lQueuesize)	The WinCreateMsgQueue function creates a message queue. You must issue this call immediately after WinInitialize, but before any Presentation Manager calls. Only issue this call once per thread. hmq contains the message queue handle (NULLHANDLE indicates an error). hab contains the anchor block handle. lQueuesize contains the maximum number of messages that you can queue. Providing a value of 0 uses the system default queue size. You can retrieve the last error using WinGetLastError. These errors include: 0x100A PMERR_RESOURCE_NOT_FOUND 0x1011 PMERR_HEAP_OUT_OF_MEMORY 0x1012 PMERR_HEAP_MAX_SIZE_REACHED 0x1051 PMERR_NOT_IN_A_PM_SESSION 0x1052 PMERR_MSG_QUEUE_ALREADY_EXISTS
hSuccess = WinCreateObject (pszClassName, pszTitle, pszSetupString, pszLocation, ulFlags)	The WinCreateObject function creates an instance of object class pszClassName. It uses a title pszTitle and places the icon and title in the location referred to by pszLocation. hSuccess contains the handle for the object (NULLHANDLE indicates an error). pszClassName contains the name of the object class. pszTitle contains the title that appears on the title when OS/2 displays the object. pszSetupString contains a pointer to a

Table 3-43   **Continued**

Function	Description
	setup string. pszLocation contains the location of the object as follows: "<WP_NOWHERE>", "<WP_DESKTOP>", "<WP_OS2SYS>", "<WP_TEMPS>", "<WP_CONFIG>", "<WP_START>", "<WP_INFO>", "<WP_DRIVES>", or a fully qualified path name. ulFlags contains the creation flags: CO_FAILIFEXISTS or COREPLACEIFEXISTS. The pszSetupString parameter contains the following *keyname = value* pairs. Each pair is separated by a comma.
	These values affect the behavior of the class. All parameters in this structure have safe defaults, you never need to pass unnecessary parameters.

Keyname	Value	Description
TITLE	Title	Contains the object's title.
ICON	filename	Contains the filename of the object's icon.
HELPPANEL	id	Sets the object's default help panel.
TEMPLATE	YES	Sets the object's template property.
	NO	Resets the object's template property.
NODELETE	YES	Sets the object's no delete property.
	NO	Resets the object's no delete property.
NOCOPY	YES	Sets the object's no copy property.
	NO	Resets the object's no copy property.
NOMOVE	YES	Sets the object's no move property.
	NO	Resets the object's no move property.
NOLINK	YES	Sets the object's no link property.
	NO	Resets the object's no link property.

Function	Description
hptr = WinCreatePointer (hwndDesktop, hbmBitMap, fPointerSize, lxHotspot, lyHotspot)	The WinCreatePointer function creates a pointer (either pointer or icon size) from a bitmap. hptr contains the pointer handle (NULLHANDLE indicates an error). hwndDesktop contains the desktop window handle (HWND_DESKTOP). hbmBitMap contains the bitmap handle. fPointerSize contains the pointer size indicator: TRUE (stretch bitmap to conform to system

Function	Description
	pointer dimensions) or FALSE (stretch bitmap to conform to system icon dimensions). lxHotspot contains the X offset of the hotspot from the lower left corner in pels. lyHotspot contains the Y offset of the hotspot from the lower left corner in pels. You can retrieve the last error using WinGetLastError. These errors include: 0x1001 PMERR_INVALID_HWND 0x2032 PMERR_HBITMAP_BUSY
hptr = WinCreatePointerIndirect (hwndDesktop, pptriPointerInfo)	The WinCreatePointer function creates a colored pointer (either pointer or icon size) from a bitmap. hptr contains the pointer handle (NULLHANDLE indicates an error). hwndDesktop contains the desktop window handle (HWND_DESKTOP). pptriPointerInfo contains the pointer information structure. This includes the following fields: ulPointer, xHotspot, yHotspot, hbmPointer, and hbmColor. You can retrieve the last error using WinGetLastError. These errors include: 0x1001 PMERR_INVALID_HWND 0x2032 PMERR_HBITMAP_BUSY
hwndFrame = WinCreateStdWindow (hwndParent, flStyle, pflCreateFlags, pszClassClient, pszTitle, flStyleClient, Resource, ulId, phwndClient)	The WinCreateStdWindow function creates a standard window. hwndFrame contains the frame window handle (NULLHANDLE indicates an error). hwndParent contains the parent window handle. Use HWND_DESKTOP to create a main window. flStyle contains the frame window style. This includes any combination of Window Styles (WSs) and Frame Styles (FSs). pflCreateFlags contains the frame create flags. This includes any combination of Frame Creation Flags (FCFs). pszClassClient contains the client window class name. OS/2 does not create a client area if pszClassClient is NULL. pszTitle contains the title bar text. flStyleClient contains the client window style. Resource contains a resource identifier (ignored unless you specify the FCF_MENU, FCF_STANDARD, FCF_ACCELTABLE, or FCF_ICON flags). NULLHANDLE indicates that the resources are contained in the application EXE file. ulId contains the frame window identifier. phwndClient contains the client window handle. You can retrieve the last error using WinGetLastError. These errors include: 0x1001 PMERR_INVALID_HWND 0x1015 PMERR_INVALID_ATOM_NAME 0x1016 PMERR_INVALID_INTEGER_ATOM 0x1017 PMERR_ATOM_NAME_NOT_FOUND 0x1019 PMERR_INVALID_FLAG
hswitchSwitch = WinCreateSwitchEntry (hab, pswctlSwitchData)	The WinCreateSwitchEntry function adds an entry to the Window List. (This is the list of applications displayed to the user by the operating system.) hswitchSwitch contains the

Table 3-43	Continued
Function	**Description**
	Window List handle (NULLHANDLE indicates an error). pswctlSwitchData contains information about the Window List entry. You can retrieve the last error using WinGetLastError. These errors include: 0x1201 PMERR_NO_SPACE 0x1206 PMERR_INVALID_WINDOW 0x120B PMERR_INVALID_SESSION_ID
hwnd = WinCreateWindow (hwndParent, pszClassName, pszName, flStyle, lxCoord, lyCoord, lWidth, lHeight, hwndOwner, hwndBehind, id, pCtlData, pPressParams)	The WinCreateWindow function creates a new window of class pszClassName and returns hwnd. hwnd contains the window handle (NULLHANDLE indicates an error). hwndParent contains the parent window handle. Use HWND_DESKTOP to create a main window. Use HWND_OBJECT or an object window handle to create an object window. pszClassName contains the registered class name. (You can use a WC constant to define this parameter.) pszName contains the window text. It is class specific. flStyle contains the frame window style. This includes any combination of Window Styles (WSs) and Frame Styles (FSs). lxCoord contains the window X-coordinate position relative to the origin of the parent window. lyCoord contains the window Y-coordinate position relative to the origin of the parent window. lWidth contains the width of the window in window coordinates. lHeight contains the height of the window in window coordinates. hwndOwner contains the owner window handle. hwndBehind contains the sibling window handle, which includes: HWND_BOTTOM and HWND_TOP. You can retrieve the last error using WinGetLastError. These errors include: 0x1001 PMERR_INVALID_HWND 0x1015 PMERR_INVALID_ATOM_NAME 0x1016 PMERR_INVALID_INTEGER_ATOM 0x1017 PMERR_ATOM_NAME_NOT_FOUND 0x1019 PMERR_INVALID_FLAG
fSuccess = WinDdeInitiate (hwndClient, pszAppName, pszTopicName, pContext)	The WinDdeInitiate function initiates a dynamic data exchange (DDE) conversation between a client and one or more other applications. It uses a national language conversation context. fSuccess contains true if this function is successful. hwndClient contains the client window handle. pszAppName contains the application name (the server name). A zero length string allows any application to respond. pszTopic contains the topic name. A zero length string allows the application to respond once for each topic it can support. pContext contains the conversation context.
fSuccess =	The WinDdeRespond function allows an application to post a

Function

**WinDdePostMsg
(hwndTo, hwndFrom,
usMsgId, pData,
ulOptions)**

Description

message to another application that it is carrying out a dynamic
data exchange (DDE) conversation with using a national
language conversation context. fSuccess contains true if this
function is successful. hwndTo contains the target handle.
hwndFrom contains the originator handle. usMsgId contains
the message identifier, which includes: WM_DDE_ACK,
WM_DDE_ADVISE, WM_DDE_DATA, WM_DDE_EXECUTE,
WM_DDE_POKE, WM_DDE_REQUEST,
WM_DDE_TERMINATE, and WM_DDE_UNADVISE. pData
points to a DDE structure. You must always use a 16-bit address
for this parameter. usOptions contains the DDE options, which
include: DDEPM_RETRY and DDEPM_NOFREE.

**mresReply =
WinDdeRespond
(hwndClient, hwndServer,
pszAppName,
pszTopicName,
pContext)**

The WinDdeRespond function allows a dynamic data exchange
(DDE) server to indicate that it can support a DDE conversation
on a particular topic with a national language conversation
context. mresReply contains the message return information.
hwndClient contains the client handle. hwndServer contains
the server handle. pszAppName contains the application name
(the server name). pszTopic contains the topic name. pContext
contains the conversation context.

**mresReply =
WinDefDlgProc
(hwndDlg, ulMsgId,
mpParam1, mpParam2)**

The WinDefDlgProc invokes the default dialog procedure. This
provides a method of processing messages that the application
does not wish to handle. mresReply contains the message
return data. hwndDlg contains the dialog window handle.
ulMsgId contains the message identity. mpParam1 contains
the first parameter. mpParam2 contains the second parameter.
You can retrieve the last error using WinGetLastError. These
errors include:

0x1001   PMERR_INVALID_HWND

**mresReply =
WinDefFileDlgProc
(hwndDlg, ulMsgId,
mpParam1, mpParam2)**

The WinDefFileDlgProc function is the default dialog procedure
for the file dialog. mresReply contains the message return data
hwndDlg contains the dialog window handle. ulMsgId contains
the message identity. mpParam1 contains the first parameter.
mpParam2 contains the second parameter.

**mresReply =
WinDefFintDlgProc
(hwndDlg, ulMsgId,
mpParam1, mpParam2)**

The WinDefFontDlgProc function is the default dialog
procedure for the font dialog. mresReply contains the message
return data. hwndDlg contains the dialog window handle.
ulMsgId contains the message identity. mpParam1 contains
the first parameter. mpParam2 contains the second parameter.

**mresReply =
WinDefWindowProc
(hwnd, ulMsgId,
mpParam1, mpParam2)**

The WinDefWindowProc invokes the default window procedure.
This provides a method of processing messages that the
application does not wish to handle. mresReply contains the
message return data. hwnd contains the window handle.
ulMsgId contains the message identity. mpParam1 contains
the first parameter. mpParam2 contains the second parameter.

Table 3-43   **Continued**

Function	Description
	You can retrieve the last error using WinGetLastError. These errors include: 0x1001 PMERR_INVALID_HWND
hatomtblReturnCode = WinDeleteAtom (hatomtblAtomTbl, atom)	The WinDeleteAtom function removes an atom from an atom table. If the atom has an atom name, its use count is decremented by one. The atom is removed from the table if its use count is zero. hatomtblReturnCode contains a zero for a successful completion. Any other value indicates an error. hatomtblAtomTbl contains the atom table handle. atom contains an identifier for the atom that you want to delete. You can retrieve the last error using WinGetLastError. These errors include: 0x1013 PMERR_INVALID_HATOMTBL 0x1014 PMERR_INVALID_ATOM
sItems = WinDeleteLboxItem (hwndLbox, sIndex)	The WinDeleteLboxItem function removes an indexed item from a list box. sItems contains the number of items left. hwndLbox contains the listbox handle. sIndex contains the index of the listbox item you want to remove.
fDeleted = WinDeleteLibrary (hab, hlibLibhandle)	The WinDeleteLibrary function deletes a library that you previously loaded using the WinLoadLibrary function. fDeleted contains the library deletion indicator; TRUE indicates that OS/2 deleted the library. hab contains the anchor block handle. hlibLibhandle contains the library handle.
fSuccess = WinDeleteProcedure (hab, pwndProc)	The WinDeleteProcedure function deletes the window or dialog procedure that you previously loaded using the WinLoadProcedure function. fSuccess contains true if this function is successful. hab contains the anchor block handle. pwndProc contains the identifier of the window or dialog procedure that you want to delete.
fSuccess = WinDeregisterObjectClass (pszClassName)	The WinDeregisterObjectClass function deregisters a workplace object class. fSuccess contains true if this function is successful. pszClassName contains the name of the class you want to deregister.
fSuccess = WinDestroyAccelTable (haccelAccel)	The WinDestroyAccelTable function destroys an accelerator table. fSuccess contains true if this function is successful. haccelAccel contains the accelerator table handle. You can retrieve the last error using WinGetLastError. These errors include: 0x101A PMERR_INVALID_HACCEL
hatomtblReturnCode =	The WinDestroyAtomTable function destroys an atom table that

Function	Description
WinDestroyAtomTable (hatomtblAtomTbl)	you created using the WinCreateAtomTable function. OS/2 will not allow you to destroy the system atom table. hatomtblReturnCode contains a zero for a successful completion. Any other value indicates an error. hatomtblAtomTbl contains the atom table handle. You can retrieve the last error using WinGetLastError. These errors include: 0x1013 PMERR_INVALID_HATOMTBL
fSuccess = WinDestroyCursor (hwnd)	The WinDestroyCursor function destroys the current cursor if it belongs to the specified window. fSuccess contains true if this function is successful. hwnd contains the window handle. You can retrieve the last error using WinGetLastError. These errors include: 0x1001 PMERR_INVALID_HWND
fSuccess = WinDestroyHelpInstance (hwndHelpInstance)	The WinDestroyHelpInstance function destroys the specified help instance of the Help Manager. fSuccess contains true if this function is successful. hwndHelpInstance contains the handle of the instance of the Help Manager that you want to destroy.
fDestroyed = WinDestroyMsgQueue (hmq)	The WinDestroyMsgQueue function destroys a message queue. Always call this function before you terminate a thread or application that uses a message queue. fDestroyed contains true if this function is successful. hmq contains the message queue handle. You can retrieve the last error using WinGetLastError. These errors include: 0x1002 PMERR_INVALID_HMQ
fSuccess = WinDestoryObject (hobject)	The WinDestroyObject function destroys a workplace object. fSuccess contains true if this function is successful. hobject contains the object handle.
fSuccess = WinDestroyPointer (hptrPointer)	The WinDestroyPointer function destroys a pointer or icon. Never attempt to destroy the system icons or pointers. fSuccess contains true if this function is successful. hptrPointer contains the handle of the pointer or icon that you want to destroy. You can retrieve the last error using WinGetLastError. These errors include: 0x101B PMERR_INVALID_HPTR
fSuccess = WinDestroyWindow (hwnd)	The WinDestroyWindow function destroys a window and its children. fSuccess contains true if this function is successful. hwnd contains the window handle. You can retrieve the last error using WinGetLastError. These errors include: 0x1001 PMERR_INVALID_HWND
fSuccess =	The WinDismissDlg function hides a modal dialog window or

Table 3-43   **Continued**

Function	Description
WinDismissDlg (hwndDlg, ulResult)	destroys a modal dialog window. This causes the WinProcessDlg and WinDlgBox functions to return. fSuccess contains true if this function is successful. hwndDlg contains the dialog window handle. ulResult contains the reply value returned to the caller of the WinProcessDlg or WinDlgBox functions. You can retrieve the last error using WinGetLastError. These errors include: 0x1001 PMERR_INVALID_HWND
mresReply = WinDispatchMsg (hab, pqmsgMsg)	The WinDispatchMsg function invokes a window procedure. mresReply contains the message reply data. hab contains the anchor block handle. pqmsgMsg contains the message structure.
ulResult = WinDlgBox (hwndParent, hwndOwner, pDlgProc, Resource, ulDlgId, pCreateParams)	The WinDlgBox function loads and processes a modal dialog box window. It returns the result value established by the WinDismissDlg call. ulResult contains the reply value (DID_ERROR indicates an error). hwndParent contains the parent window handle: HWND_DESKTOP, HWND_OBJECT, or other specified window. hwndOwner contains the handle of the actual window owner. pDlgProc contains a pointer to the procedure for the created dialog window. Resource contains the resource identity containing the dialog template (NULLHANDLE uses the application's EXE file). ulDlgid contains the dialog template identity within the resource file. pCreateParams contains the application defined data area. You can retrieve the last error using WinGetLastError. These errors include: 0x1001 PMERR_INVALID_HWND 0x100A PMERR_RESOURCE_NOT_FOUND 0x1015 PMERR_INVALID_ATOM_NAME 0x1016 PMERR_INVALID_INTEGER_ATOM 0x1017 PMERR_ATOM_NAME_NOT_FOUND
fSuccess = WinDrawBitmap (hps, hbm, prclSrc, pptlDest, lForeColor, lBackColor, flRgf)	The WinDrawBitmap function draws a bitmap using the current image colors and mixes. fSuccess contains true if this function is successful. hps contains the presentation space handle. hbm contains the bitmap handle. prclSrc contains the subrectangle of the bitmap to draw. Use a value of NULL to draw the entire bitmap. pptlDest contains the bitmap destination in device coordinates. lForeColor contains the foreground color of a monochrome bitmap (color bitmap colors are not changed). lBackColor contains the bitmap background color. flRgf contains the flags that determine how OS/2 draws the bitmap. These flags include: DBM_NORMAL, DBM_INVERT, DBM_STRETCH, DBM_HALFTONE, and DBM_IMAGEATTRS. You can retrieve the last error using WinGetLastError. These errors include:

Function	Description
	0x1019 PMERR_INVALID_FLAG 0x2032 PMERR_HBITMAP_BUSY
fSuccess = WinDrawBorder (hps, prclRectangle, lVertSideWidth, lHorizSideWidth, lBorderColor, lInteriorColor, flCmd)	The WinDrawBorder function draws the borders and interior of a rectangle. fSuccess contains true if this function is successful. hps contains the presentation space handle. prclRectangle contains the bounding rectangle for the border in device coordinates. lVertSideWidth contains the width of the border's vertical sides in device coordinates. lHorizSideWidth contains the width of the border's horizontal sides in device coordinates. lBorderColor contains the color of the edge border. lInteriorColor contains the color of the interior border. flCmd contains a list of flags that control how OS/2 draws the border. These flags include: DB_PATCOPY, DB_PATINVERT, DB_DESTINVERT, or DB_AREAMIXMODE. Only one of these flags is significant. Other flags include: DB_ROP, DB_INTERIOR, DB_AREAATTRS, DB_STANDARD, and DB_DLGBORDER. You can retrieve the last error using WinGetLastError. These errors include: 0x1019 PMERR_INVALID_FLAG 0x2068 PMERR_INVALID_DRAW_BORDER_OPTION
fSuccess = WinDrawPointer (hps, lX, lY, hptrPointer, ulHalftone)	The WinDrawPointer function draws a pointer. fSuccess contains true if this function is successful. hps contains the presentation space handle. lX contains the pointer X coordinate. lY contains the pointer Y coordinate. hptrPointer contains the pointer handle. ulHalftone controls the pointer shading. This includes: DP_NORMAL, DP_HALFTONED, and DP_INVERTED. You can retrieve the last error using WinGetLastError. These errors include: 0x1019 PMERR_INVALID_FLAG 0x101B PMERR_INVALID_HPTR
lChars = WinDrawText (hps, lCount, pchText, prclRectangle, lForeColor, lBackColor, flCmd)	The WinDrawText function draws a single line of formatted (using the current font and colors) text within the specified rectangle. lChars contains the number of characters drawn within the rectangle (0 indicates an error). hps contains the presentation space handle. lCount contains the number of characters in the string (use −1 for a null-terminated string). pchText is a pointer to the string. prclRectangle contains the text bounding rectangle in world coordinates. lForeColor contains the foreground color. lBackColor contains the background color. flCmd is an array of flags that determine how OS/2 draws the text. There are three groups of mutually exclusive flags. The first group includes: DT_LEFT, DT_CENTER, and DT_RIGHT. The second group includes:

Table 3-43   **Continued**

Function	Description
	DT_TOP, DT_VCENTER, and DT_BOTTOM. The third group includes: DT_HALFTONE, DT_ERASERECT, and DT_MNEMONIC. You can retrieve the last error using WinGetLastError. These errors include: 0x1019 PMERR_INVALID_FLAG
fSuccess = WinEmptyClipbrd (hab)	The WinEmptyClipboard function empties the clipboard of all handles to data. fSuccess contains true if this function is successful. hab contains the anchor block handle.
fSuccess = WinEnableControl (hwndDlg, usId, fEnable)	The WinEnableControl function sets the enable flag of the specified item in the dialog template. fSuccess contains true if this function is successful. hwndDlg contains the dialog window handle. usId contains the identity of the item. fEnable contains the enable flag.
fSuccess = WinEnableMenuItem (hwndMenu, usId, fEnable)	The WinEnableMenuItem function sets the enable flag of the specified item in the menu. fSuccess contains true if this function is successful. hwndMenu contains the menu window handle. usId contains the identity of the item. fEnable contains the enable flag.
fOldInputState = WinEnablePhysInput (hwndDesktop, fNewInputState)	The WinEnablePhysInput function enables or disables queuing of physical input (mouse or keyboard). fOldInputState contains the previous state. TRUE indicates that the device and keyboard input are queued. hwndDesktop contains the desktop window handle (HWND_DESKTOP in most cases). fNewInputState contains the new state for queuing physical input. You can retrieve the last error using WinGetLastError. These errors include: 0x1001 PMERR_INVALID_HWND
fSuccess = WinEnableWindow (hwnd, fNewEnabled)	The WinEnableWindow function sets the window enabled state. fSuccess contains true if this function is successful. hwnd contains the window handle. fNewEnabled contains the enable flag. You can retrieve the last error using WinGetLastError. These errors include: 0x1001 PMERR_INVALID_HWND
fSuccess = WinEnableWindowUpdate (hwnd, fNewVisibility)	The WinEnableWindowUpdate function sets the window visibility state for subsequent drawing. It does not cause any change to the window on the device. fSuccess contains true if this function is successful. hwnd contains the window handle. fNewVisibility contains the enable flag. You can retrieve the last error using WinGetLastError. These errors include: 0x1001 PMERR_INVALID_HWND

Function	Description
	0x1019 PMERR_INVALID_FLAG
fSuccess = WinEndEnumWindows (henum)	The WinEndEnumWindows function ends the enumeration process for a specified enumeration. fSuccess contains true if this function is successful. henum contains the enumeration handle. You can retrieve the last error using WinGetLastError. These errors include:
	0x101C PMERR_INVALID_HENUM
fSuccess = WinEndPaint (hps)	The WinEndPaint function completes the redrawing of a window. (It normally appears as a part of WM_PAINT message processing.) fSuccess contains true if this function is successful. hps contains the presentation space handle.
ulNext = WinEnumClipbrdFmts (hab, ulPrev)	The WinEnumClipbrdFmts function enumerates the list of available clipboard data formats. ulNext contains the next clipboard data index (0 indicates that enumeration is complete). hab contains the anchor block handle. ulPrev contains the previous clipboard data format index (always start at 0).
hwndItem = WinEnumDlgItem (hwndDlg, hwnd, ulCode, fLock)	The WinEnumDlgItem returns the window handle of a dialog item within a dialog window. hwndItem contains the item handle. hwndDlg contains the dialog window handle. hwnd contains the child window handle. You can use a value of NULLHANDLE if ulCode is EDI_FIRSTTABITEM or EDI_LASTTABITEM. ulCode contains the item type code, which includes: EDI_PREVTABITEM, EDI_NEXTABITEM, EDI_FIRSTTABITEM, EDI_LASTTABITEM, EDI_PREVGROUPITEM, EDI_NEXTGROUPITEM, EDI_FIRSTGROUPITEM, or EDI_FIRSTGROUPITEM. fLock contains the lock indicator. OS/2 versions 1.2 and above ignore this parameter. You can retrieve the last error using WinGetLastError. These errors include:
	0x1001 PMERR_INVALID_HWND
fSuccess = WinEnumObjectClasses (pObjClass, pSize)	The WinEnumObjectClasses function returns a list of all the registered workplace object classes. fSuccess contains true if this function is successful. pObjClass contains a pointer to the buffer used to store the object class list. pSize contains the length of pObjClass in bytes.
fEqual = WinEqualRect (hab, prclRect1, prclRect2)	The WinEqualRect function compares two rectangles for equality. (OS/2 considers two empty rectangles equal even though their coordinate values are different.) fEqual contains true if the two rectangles are equal. hab contains the anchor block handle. prclRect1 contains the coordinates of the first rectangle. prclRect2 contains the coordinates of the second rectangle.
lComplexity =	The WinExcludeUpdateRegion function subtracts the update

Table 3-43   **Continued**

Function	Description
WinExcludeUpdate-Region (hps, hwnd)	region of a window from the clipping region of a presentation space. lComplexity contains the complexity of the resulting region or an error indicator. hps contains a presentation space handle. hwnd contains the window handle. WinExcludeUpdateRegion returns one of the following values: 0000 EXRGN_ERROR 0001 EXRGN_NULL 0002 EXRGN_RECT 0003 EXRGN_COMPLEX You can retrieve the last error using WinGetLastError. These errors include: 0x1001 PMERR_INVALID_HWND
hwndDlg = WinFileDlg (hwndParent, hwndOwner, pfFiledlg)	The WinFileDlg function creates and displays the file dialog box and returns the user's selections. hwndDlg contains the file dialog window handle. If the FDS_MODELESS flag is set, then the return value is the handle of the file dialog NULLHANDLE indicates that OS/2 cannot create the dialog. If the FDS_MODELESS flag is not set, then the return value is TRUE for successful creation (NULLHANDLE indicates an unsuccessful attempt). hwndParent contains the parent window handle (HWND_DESKTOP or other specified window). hwndOwner contains the owner window handle. pfFiledlg contains a pointer to FILEDLG structure.
fSuccess = WinFillRect (hps, prclRect, lColor)	The WinFillRect function draws a filled rectangular area. fSuccess contains true if this function is successful. hps contains the presentation space handle. prclRect contains the coordinates in world coordinates of the rectangle that you want to fill. lColor contains the color that you want to use to fill the rectangle. You can use either a color index or an RGB color value.
atom = WinFindAtom (hatomtblAtomTbl, pszAtomName)	The WinFindAtom function finds an atom in the atom table. atom contains the atom value (0 indicates an invalid atom table handle or name specified). hatomtblAtomTbl contains the atom table handle. pszAtomName contains the atom name. You can retrieve the last error using WinGetLastError. These errors include: 0x1013 PMERR_INVALID_HATOMTBL 0x1015 PMERR_INVALID_ATOM_NAME 0x1016 PMERR_INVALID_INTEGER_ATOM 0x1017 PMERR_ATOM_NAME_NOT_FOUND
fSuccess =	The WinFlashWindow function starts or stops window flashing.

Function	Description
WinFlashWindow (hwnd, fFlash)	fSuccess contains true if this function is successful. hwnd contains the window handle. fFlash contains the flashing indicator; a value of TRUE starts window flashing. You can retrieve the last error using WinGetLastError. These errors include: 0x1001 PMERR_INVALID_HWND
fSuccess = WinFocusChange (hwndDesktop, hwndNewFocus, flFocusChange)	The WinFocusChange function changes the focus window. fSuccess contains true if this function is successful. hwndDesktop contains the desktop window handle (HWND_DESKTOP or other desktop window handle). hwndNewFocus contains the handle of the window that will receive focus. flFocusChange contains the focus change indicator. This includes: FC_NOSETFOCUS, FC_NOLOSEFOCUS, FC_NOSETACTIVE, FC_NOLOSEACTIVE, FC_NOSETSELECTION, FC_NOBRINGTOTOP, FC_NOBRINGTOTOPFIRSTWINDOW, and FC_SETACTIVEFOCUS. You can retrieve the last error using WinGetLastError. These errors include: 0x1001 PMERR_INVALID_HWND
hwndDlg = WinFontDlg (hwndParent, hwndOwner, pfntdFontdlg)	The WinFontDlg function creates and displays the font dialog box and returns the user's selections. hwndDlg contains the font dialog window handle. If the FNTS_MODELESS flag is set, then the return value is the handle of the file dialog (NULLHANDLE indicates that OS/2 cannot create the dialog). If the FNTS_MODELESS flag is not set, then the return value is TRUE for successful creation (NULLHANDLE indicates an unsuccessful attempt). hwndParent contains the parent window handle (HWND_DESKTOP or other specified window). hwndOwner contains the owner window handle. pfntdFiledlg contains a pointer to FILEDLG structure.
fSuccess = WinFreeErrorInfo (perriErrorInfo)	The WinFreeErrorInfo function releases memory allocated for an error information block. fSuccess contains true if this function is successful. perriErrorInfo contains a pointer to the error information block.
fSuccess = WinFreeFileDlgList (papszFQFilename)	The WinFreeFileDlgList function frees the storage allocated by the file dialog when the FDS_MULTPLESEL flag is set. fSuccess contains true if this function is successful. papszFQFilename contains a pointer to a table of pointers to fully qualified filename returned by the dialog.
fSuccess = WinFreeFileIcon (hptr)	The WinFreeFileIcon function frees the pointer to an icon allocated by the WinLoadFileIcon function. fSuccess contains true if this function is successful. hptr contains the pointer handle.
hps = WinGetClipPS	The WinGetClipPS function obtains a clipped cache

307

Table 3-43   **Continued**

Function	Description
(hwnd, hwndClipWindow, ulClipflags)	presentation space. hps contains the presentation space handle. hwnd contains the window handle. hwndClipWindow contains the handle of the window used for clipping. You can specify one of the following values: HWND_BOTTOM, HWND_TOP, or NULLHANDLE. ulClipflags contains the clipping control flags, which include: PSF_CLIPSIBLINGS, PSF_CLIPCHILDREN, PSF_CLIPUPWARDS, PSF_CLIPDOWNWARDS, PSF_LOCKWINDOWUPDATE, and PSF_PARENTCLIP. You can retrieve the last error using WinGetLastError. These errors include: 0x1001 PMERR_INVALID_HWND
ulTime = WinGetCurrentTime (hab)	The WinGetCurrentTime function returns the current time. ulTime contains the system time count in milliseconds from the system Initial Program Load (IPL). hab contains the anchor block handle.
fResult = WinGetDlgMsg (hwndDlg, pqmsgMsg)	The WinGetDlgMsg function gets a message from the application queue associated with the specified dialog. fResult contains TRUE if the message returned is not a WM_QUIT message and the dialog was not dismissed. hwndDlg contains the dialog window handle. pqmsgMsg contains a pointer to the message structure. You can retrieve the last error using WinGetLastError. These errors include: 0x1001 PMERR_INVALID_HWND
perriErrorInfo = WinGetErrorInfo (hab)	The WinGetErrorInfo function returns detailed error information. (The memory allocated by this function is not released until you call the WinFreeErrorInfo function.) perriErrorInfo contains a pointer to the error information structure (NULL if no error information is available). hab contains the anchor block handle.
lKeyState = WinGetKeyState (hwndDesktop, lVk)	The WinGetKeyState function returns the state of the key at the time that the last message from the queue was posted. lKeyState contains the key state. It is an OR combination of the following values: 0x0001 (the key was pressed an odd number of times since the system started) and 0x8000 (the key is down). hwndDesktop contains the desktop window handle (HWND_DESKTOP or other desktop window handle). lVk contains the virtual key value in the low-order byte and zero in the high-order byte. You can retrieve the last error using WinGetLastError. These errors include: 0x1001 PMERR_INVALID_HWND
erridErrorCode =	The WinGetLastError function returns the error state set by the

Function	Description
WinGetLastError (hab)	failure of a PM function. It automatically sets the error code to zero. erridErrorCode contains the last error state. hab contains the anchor block handle.
fSuccess = WinGetMaxPosition (hwnd, pSwp)	The WinGetMaxPosition function fills an SWP structure with the maximized window size and position. fSuccess contains true if this function is successful. hwnd contains the frame window handle. pSwp contains a pointer to the SWP structure.
fSuccess = WinGetMinPosition (hwnd, pSwp, pptlPoint)	The WinGetMinPosition function fills an SWP structure with the minimized window size and position. fSuccess contains true if this function is successful. hwnd contains the frame window handle. pSwp contains a pointer to the SWP structure. pptlPoint contains the preferred position. Use NULL if you want the system to choose the position.
fResult = WinGetMsg (hab, pqmsgMsg, hwndFilter, ulFirst, ulLast)	The WinGetMsg function gets a message from the thread's message queue. It waits until a message that conforms to the filtering criteria is available. fResult returns TRUE if the message returned is not a WM_QUIT message. hab contains the anchor block handle. pqmsgMsg contains a pointer to the message structure. hwndFilter contains the filter window handle. ulFirst contains the first message identity. ulLast contains the last message identity. You can retrieve the last error using WinGetLastError. These errors include: 0x1001 PMERR_INVALID_HWND
hwndNext = WinGetNextWindow (henum)	The WinGetNextWindow function gets the handle of the next window in an enumeration list. hwndNext contains the handle of the next window in the enumeration list (NULLHANDLE indicates an error). henum contains the enumeration handle. You can retrieve the last error using WinGetLastError. These errors include: 0x101C PMERR_INVALID_HENUM
lKeyState = WinGetPhysKeyState (hwndDesktop, lScancode)	The WinGetPhysKeyState function returns the physical key state. lKeyState contains the key state. It is an OR combination of the following values: 0x0001 (the key was pressed an odd number of times since the system started), 0x0002 (the key was pressed since the last time the application called this function), and 0x8000 (the key is down). hwndDesktop contains the desktop window handle (HWND_DESKTOP or other desktop window handle). lScancode contains the hardware key value in the low-order byte and zero in the high-order byte. You can retrieve the last error using WinGetLastError. These errors include: 0x1001 PMERR_INVALID_HWND
hps = WinGetPS (hwnd)	The WinGetPS function returns the handle to a cache

Table 3-43   **Continued**

Function	Description
	presentation space. hps contains the presentation space handle. hwnd contains the window handle (HWND_DESKTOP or other window handle). You can retrieve the last error using WinGetLastError. These errors include:
	0x1001 PMERR_INVALID_HWND
hpsScreenPS = WinGetScreenPS (hwndDesktop)	The WinGetScreenPS function returns a handle to a presentation space that you can use for drawing anywhere on the display. As a result, you must exercise extreme caution not to draw on the windows of other applications when using this function. hpsScreenPS contains the presentation space handle (NULLHANDLE indicates an error). hwndDesktop contains the desktop window handle (HWND_DESKTOP or other desktop window handle). You can retrieve the last error using WinGetLastError. These errors include:
	0x1001 PMERR_INVALID_HWND
hbm = WinGetSysBitmap (hwndDesktop, ulIndex)	The WinGetSysBitmap function returns a handle to one of the standard bitmaps provided by the system. You can use this bitmap for any normal bitmap operation; it is a copy of the original system bitmap. hbm contains the bitmap handle (NULLHANDLE indicates an error). hwndDesktop contains the desktop window handle (HWND_DESKTOP or other desktop window handle). ulIndex contains the system bitmap index value, which includes: SBMP_SYSMENU, SBMP_SYSMENUDEP, SBMP_SBUPARROW, SBMP_SBUPARROWDEP, SBMP_SBUPARROWDIS, SBMP_SBDNARROW, SBMP_SBDNARROWDEP, SBMP_SBDNARROWDIS, SBMP_SBRGARROW, SBMP_SBRGARROWDEP, SBMP_SBRGARROWDIS, SBMP_SBLFARROW, SBMP_SBLFARROWDEP, SBMP_SBLFARROWDIS, SBMP_MENUCHECK, SBMP_MENUATTACHED, SBMP_CHECKBOXES, SBMP_COMBODOWN, SBMP_BTNCORNERS, SBMP_MINBUTTON, SBMP_MINBUTTONDEP, SBMP_MAXBUTTON, SBMP_MAXBUTTONDEP, SBMP_RESTOREBUTTON, SBMP_RESTOREBUTTONDEP, SBMP_CHILDSYSMENU, SBMP_CHILDSYSMENUDEP, SBMP_DRIVE, SBMP_FILE, SBMP_FOLDER, SBMP_TREEPLUS, SBMP_TREEMINUS, SBMP_CLOSEBUTTON, SBMP_CLOSEBUTTONDEP, SBMP_PROGRAM, and SBMP_SIZEBOX. You can retrieve the last error using WinGetLastError. These errors include:
	0x1001 PMERR_INVALID_HWND 0x1003 PMERR_PARAMETER_OUT_OF_RANGE 0x100A PMERR_RESOURCE_NOT_FOUND

Function

Description

fSuccess =
WinInflateRect (hab,
prclRect, lcX, lcY)

The WinInflateRect expands or contracts a rectangle. fSuccess
contains true if this function is successful. hab contains the
anchor block handle. prclRect contains the coordinates of the
rectangle that you want to expand. lcX contains the horizontal
expansion factor. lcY contains the vertical expansion factor.

hab = WinInitialize
(flOptions)

The WinInitialize function initializes the PM facilities. You must
issue this call prior to any other PM call. hab contains the
anchor block handle (NULLHANDLE indicates an error).
flOptions contains the initialization options (0 is the only
available option).

fProcessing =
WinInSendMsg (hab)

The WinInSendMsg function determines whether the current
thread is processing a message sent by another thread.
fProcessing contains the message processing indicator. TRUE
indicates that the current thread is processing a message sent by
another thread. hab contains the anchor block handle.

sRetIndex =
WinInsertLboxItem
(hwndLbox, sIndex,
pszText)

The WinInsertLboxItem inserts text into a list box at the
specified index. sRetIndex contains the actual index where the
text got inserted. hwndLbox contains the list box handle.
sIndex contains the index of the list box item. pszText contains
the text that you want to insert.

fSuccess =
WinIntersectRect
(hab, prclDest,
prclRect1, prclRect2)

The WinIntersectRect function calculates the intersection of two
rectangles and places the result in the destination rectangle. If
there is no intersection, OS/2 returns an empty rectangle.
fSuccess contains true if this function is successful. hab
contains the anchor block handle. prclDest contains the
intersection of prclRect1 and prclRect2. prclRect1 and
prclRect2 contain the two rectangles that you want to intersect.

fSuccess =
WinInvalidateRect
(hwnd, prclPrc,
fIncludeClippedChildren)

The WinInvalidateRect function adds a rectangle to a window's
update region. This makes the region within the rectangle
invalid; that area of the window requires redrawing. fSuccess
contains true if this function is successful. hwnd contains the
window handle (HWND_DESKTOP or other window handle).
prclPrc contains the update rectangle coordinates. A value of
NULL updates the entire window. fIncludeClippedChildren
contains the invalidation scope indicator. A value of TRUE
includes the children of hwnd in the update. You can retrieve
the last error using WinGetLastError. These errors include:

0x1001   PMERR_INVALID_HWND
0x1019   PMERR_INVALID_FLAG

WinInvalidateRegion

The WinInvalidateRegion function adds a region to the
window's update region. This makes the region invalid; that
area of the window requires redrawing. fSuccess contains true
if this function is successful. hwnd contains the window handle
(HWND_DESKTOP or other window handle). hrgn contains the
handle of the region that you want to add to the window. A value

Table 3-43   **Continued**

Function	Description
	of NULLHANDLE updates the entire window. fIncludeClippedChildren contains the invalidation scope indicator. A value of TRUE includes the children of hwnd in the update. You can retrieve the last error using WinGetLastError. These errors include:
	0x1001 PMERR_INVALID_HWND 0x1019 PMERR_INVALID_FLAG 0x2034 PMERR_HRGN_BUSY
fSuccess = WinInvertRect (hps, prclRect)	The WinInvertRect function inverts a rectangular area. This essentially flips the bits of each pel (logical NOT operation). fSuccess contains true if this function is successful. hps contains the presentation space handle. prclRect contains the coordinates of the rectangle that you want to invert.
fRelated = WinIsChild (hwndChild, hwndParent)	The WinIsChild function tests whether one window is a child of another window. fRelated contains TRUE if the child window is a descendent of the parent window. hwndChild contains the handle of the child window. hwndParent contains the handle of the parent window. You can retrieve the last error using WinGetLastError. These errors include:
	0x1001 PMERR_INVALID_HWND
fSuccess = WinIsControlEnabled (hwndDlg, usId)	The WinIsControlEnabled function returns the state of the specified item in the dialog template within a dialog box. fSuccess contains true if this function is successful. hwndDlg contains the dialog window handle. usId contains the item identifier.
fSuccess = WinIsMenuItemChecked (hwndMenu, usId)	The WinIsMenuChecked function returns the state of the specified item in the menu. fSuccess contains true if this function is successful. hwndMenu contains the menu window handle. usId contains the item identifier.
fSuccess = WinIsMenuItemEnabled (hwndMenu, usId)	The WinIsMenuEnabled function returns the state of the specified item in the menu. fSuccess contains true if this function is successful. hwndMenu contains the menu window handle. usId contains the item identifier.
fSuccess = WinIsMenuItemValid (hwndMenu, usId)	The WinIsMenuItemValid function returns true if the specified menu item is valid. fSuccess contains true if this function is successful. hwndMenu contains the menu window handle. usId contains the item identifier.
fSuccess = WinIsPhysInputEnabled (hwndDesktop)	The WinIsPhysInputEnabled function returns the hardware input status. fSuccess contains true if this function is successful. hwndDesktop contains the desktop window handle (HWND_DESKTOP).

Function	Description
fEmpty = WinIsRectEmpty (hab, prclPrc)	The WinIsRectEmpty function checks whether a rectangle is empty. fEmpty contains TRUE if the rectangle is empty. hab contains the anchor block handle. prclPrc contains the coordinates of the rectangle to check.
fActive = WinIsThreadActive (hab)	The WinIsThreadActive function determines if the active window belongs to the calling execution thread. fActive contains TRUE if the active window belongs to the calling thread. hab contains the anchor block handle.
fValid = WinIsWindow (hab, hwnd)	The WinIsWindow function determines if a window handle is valid. fValid returns true if the window handle is valid. hab contains the anchor block handle. hwnd contains the window handle. You can retrieve the last error using WinGetLastError. These errors include: 0x1001 PMERR_INVALID_HWND
fEnabled = WinIsWindowEnabled (hwnd)	The WinIsWindowEnabled function determines the enabled/disabled state of a window. fEnabled contains TRUE if the window is enabled. hwnd contains the window handle. You can retrieve the last error using WinGetLastError. These errors include: 0x1001 PMERR_INVALID_HWND
fShowing = WinIsWindowShowing (hwnd)	The WinIsWindowShowing function determines if any part of the window is visible. fShowing contains TRUE if some part of the window is visible. hwnd contains the window handle. You can retrieve the last error using WinGetLastError. These errors include: 0x1001 PMERR_INVALID_HWND
fVisible = WinIsWindowVisible (hwnd)	The WinIsWindowVisible function returns the visibility state of a window. (This function only returns the status of the WS_VISIBLE style bits; it does not determine if a window is obscured by other windows.) fVisible contains TRUE if the window and all its parents have the WS_VISIBLE style bit set on. hwnd contains the window handle. You can retrieve the last error using WinGetLastError. These errors include: 0x1001 PMERR_INVALID_HWND
haccelAccel = WinLoadAccelTable (hab, Resource, idAccelTable)	The WinLoadAccelTable loads an accelerator table. haccelAccel contains the accelerator table handle. hab contains the anchor block handle. Resource contains the resource identity containing the accelerator table. NULLHANDLE indicates the application module contains the accelerator table. idAccelTable contains the accelerator table identifier within the resource file. You can retrieve the last error using WinGetLastError. These errors include: 0x100A PMERR_RESOURCE_NOT_FOUND

313

Table 3-43   **Continued**

Function	Description
hwndDlg = WinLoadDlg (hwndParent, hwndOwner, pDlgProc, Resource, idDlgid, pCreateParams)	The WinLoadDlg function creates a dialog window from a dialog template. hwndDlg contains the dialog window handle (NULL indicates the the dialog was not created). hwndParent contains the parent window handle: HWND_DESKTOP, HWND_OBJECT, or any other window handle. hwndOwner contains the owner window handle. pDlgProc contains the dialog procedure for the dialog window. pDlgProc contains a pointer to the dialog template. Resource contains the identity of the resource containing the dialog template. A value of NULLHANDLE indicates the template is in the application's EXE file. idDlgid contains the dialog template identity. pCreateParams contains a pointer to the application data area. You can retrieve the last error using WinGetLastError. These errors include: 0x1001 PMERR_INVALID_HWND 0x100A PMERR_RESOURCE_NOT_FOUND 0x1015 PMERR_INVALID_ATOM_NAME 0x1016 PMERR_INVALID_INTEGER_ATOM 0x1017 PMERR_ATOM_NAME_NOT_FOUND
hptrSuccess = WinLoadFileIcon (pszFilename, fPrivate)	The WinLoadFileIcon function loads a file icon and returns a pointer to it. hptrSuccess contains the icon pointer (NULL indicates an error). pszFilename contains the icon filename. fPrivate contains TRUE if the application wants a private copy of the icon.
fSuccess = WinLoadHelpTable (hwndHelpInstance, idHelpTable, hModule)	The WinLoadHelpTable function provides the module handle and help table identity to an instance of the Help Manager. fSuccess contains true if this function is successful. hwndHelpInstance contains the help manager instance handle. idHelpTable contains the identity of the help table. hModule contains the handle of the module that contains the help table and help subtable resources.
hlibLibrary = WinLoadLibrary (hab, pszLibname)	The WinLoadLibrary function loads a library and makes it available to an application. hlibLibhandle contains the library handle (NULLHANDLE indicates that the library was not loaded). hab contains the anchor block handle. pszLibname contains the library name.
hwndMenu = WinLoadMenu (hwndOwner, Resource, idMenuid)	The WinLoadMenu function creates a menu window from a menu template. hwndMenu contains the menu window handle. hwndOwner contains the owner window handle (HWND_DESKTOP, HWND_OBJECT, or any other window handle). Resource contains the resource identifier (NULLHANDLE indicates that the resource is in the application EXE file). idMenuid contains the menu identifier within the resource.

Function	Description
lLength = WinLoadMessage (hab, hmodMod, ulId, lcchMax, pszBuffer)	The WinLoadMessage function loads a message from a resource, copies the message to the specified buffer, and adds a terminating null character. lLength contains the length of the returned string (0 indicates an error). hab contains the anchor block handle. hmodMod contains the module handle. ulId contains the message identifier. The resource ID is calculated from the id parameter value passed to this function as follows: resource ID = (id / 16) + 1. lcchMax specifies the size of the buffer. pszBuffer is a pointer to the message buffer.
hptr = WinLoadPointer (hwndDesktop, Resource, idPointer)	The WinLoadPointer function loads a pointer from a resource file into the system. OS/2 creates a new copy of the pointer each time that you call this function. hptr contains the pointer handle (NULLHANDLE indicates an error). hwndDesktop contains the desktop window handle (HWND_DESKTOP or other desktop window handle). Resource contains the identity of the pointer definition file (NULLHANDLE indicates the application's EXE file). idPointer contains the identity of the pointer that you want to load. You can retrieve the last error using WinGetLastError. These errors include: 0x1001 PMERR_INVALID_HWND 0x100A PMERR_RESOURCE_NOT_FOUND
pWndProc = WinLoadProcedure (hab, hlibLibhandle, pszProcname)	The WinLoadProcedure function loads a window or dialog procedure from a dynamic link library (DLL). pWndProc contains the window procedure identifier (NULL indicates that OS/2 could not load the procedure). hab contains the anchor block handle. hlibLibhandle contains the library handle. pszProcname contains the procedure name.
lLength = WinLoadString (hab, Resource, idString, lBufferMax, pszBuffer)	The WinLoadString function loads a string from a resource. It automatically adds a terminating null character. lLength contains the length of the returned string (0 indicates an error). hab contains the anchor block handle. Resource contains the resource identifier (NULLHANDLE indicates the application's EXE file). idString contains the string identifier. The resource ID is calculated from the id parameter value passed to this function as follows: resource ID = (id / 16) + 1. lMaxBuffer specifies the size of the buffer. pszBuffer is a pointer to the message buffer. You can retrieve the last error using WinGetLastError. These errors include: 0x100A PMERR_RESOURCE_NOT_FOUND
fLocked = WinLockVisRegions (hwndDesktop, fLock)	The WinLockVisRegions function locks or unlocks the visible regions of all the windows onscreen. This prevents any visible region from changing. fLocked contains TRUE if the screen is successfully locked. hwndDesktop contains the desktop window handle (HWND_DESKTOP or other desktop window handle). fLock contains TRUE if you want to lock the visible regions.

Table 3-43   **Continued**

Function	Description
	You can retrieve the last error using WinGetLastError. These errors include:
	0x1001 PMERR_INVALID_HWND
fSuccess = WinLockWindowUpdate (hwndDesktop, hwndLockUpdate)	The WinLockWindowUpdate function disables or enables output to a window and its descendants. fSuccess contains true if this function is successful. hwndDesktop contains the desktop window handle (HWND_DESKTOP or other desktop window handle). hwndLockUpdate contains the handle of the window where you want to prevent output (NULLHANDLE enables output in the locked window and its descendants).
fSuccess = WinMakePoints (hab, pwptppt, ccount)	The WinMakePoints function converts points to graphics points (from a WPOINT structure to a POINTL structure). fSuccess contains true if this function is successful. hab contains the anchor block handle. pwptppt contains the points that you want to convert. ccount contains the number of points to convert.
fSuccess = WinMakeRect (hab, pwrcprc)	The WinMakeRect function converts a rectangle to a graphics rectangle (from a WRECT structure to a RECTL structure). fSuccess contains true if this function is successful. hab contains the anchor block handle. pwrcprc contains the points that you want to convert.
fSuccess = WinMapDlgPoints (hwndDlg, aptlPoints, ulCount, fOptions)	The WinMapDlgPoints function maps points from dialog coordinates to window coordinates. It also can perform the reverse function. fSuccess contains true if this function is successful. hwndDlg contains the dialog window handle. aptlPoints contains the points that you want to map. ulCount contains the number of coordinate points. fOptions contains the calculation control. A value of TRUE maps the dialog coordinates into window coordinates relative to the window specified by the hwndDlg parameter. You can retrieve the last error using WinGetLastError. These errors include:
	0x1001 PMERR_INVALID_HWND
fSuccess = WinMapWindowPoints (hwndFrom, hwndTo, aptlPoints, lCount)	The WinMapWindowPoints function maps a set of points from the coordinate space of one window into the coordinate space of another window. fSuccess contains true if this function is successful. hwndFrom contains the first window handle (HWND_DESKTOP maps the points from screen coordinates). hwndTo contains the second window handle (HWND_DESKTOP maps the points to screen coordinates). aptlPoints contains the points that you want to map. lCount contains the number of coordinate points (should contain a value of 2). You can retrieve the last error using WinGetLastError. These errors include:
	0x1001 PMERR_INVALID_HWND

Function	Description
usResponse = WinMessageBox (hwndParent, hwndOwner, pszText, pszTitle, usWindow, flStyle)	The WinMessageBox function creates, displays, and operates a message box window. usResponse contains the user response value or an error indicator. hwndDesktop contains the desktop window handle (HWND_DESKTOP or other desktop window handle). hwndOwner contains the owner window handle. pszText contains the message box window text. pszTitle contains the message box window title (NULL displays the text Error as the title of the message box window). usWindow contains the message box window identity. flStyle contains the message box window style, which includes: MB_OK, MB_OKCANCEL, MB_CANCEL, MB_ENTERCANCEL, MB_RETRYCANCEL, MB_ABORTRETRYIGNORE, MB_YESNO, and MB_YESNOCANCEL. You can specify a help button using the MB_HELP style. You also can specify a color or icon using the following: MB_NOICON, MB_ICONHAND, MB_ICONQUESTION, MB_ICONEXCLAMATION, MB_ICONASTERISK, MB_INFORMATION, MB_QUERY, MB_WARNING, and MB_ERROR. Finally, you can specify a default action using: MB_DEFBUTTON1, MB_DEFBUTTON2, or MB_DEFBUTTON3. The modality indicators include: MB_APPLMODAL and MB_SYSTEMMODAL. OS/2 allows you to determine mobility using MB_MOVEABLE. WinMessageBox returns one of the following values:

```
0000   MBID_ERROR
0001   MBID_OK
0002   MBID_CANCEL
0003   MBID_ABORT
0004   MBID_RETRY
0005   MBID_IGNORE
0006   MBID_YES
0007   MBID_NO
```

You can retrieve the last error using WinGetLastError. These errors include:

```
0x1001   PMERR_INVALID_HWND
0x1019   PMERR_INVALID_FLAG
```

Function	Description
lWindows = WinMultWindowFromIDs (hwndParent, ahwnd, ulFirst, ulLast)	The WinMultWindowFromIDs function finds the handles of the child windows that belong to a window. You also can specify a range of window identities. (This function is much faster than using multiple calls to WinWindowFromID.) lWindows contains the number of window handles returned. hwndParent contains the parent window handle. ahwnd contains an array of window handles. ulFirst contains the identity of the first window value in the range. ulLast contains the identity of the last window value in the range. You can retrieve the last error using WinGetLastError. These errors include:

```
0x1001   PMERR_INVALID_HWND
```

Table 3-43   **Continued**

Function	Description
pszNextChar = WinNextChar (hab, ulCodePage, ulCountry, pszCurrentChar)	The WinNextChar function moves to the next character in a DBCS string. pszNextChar contains the next character in the string (NULL indicates that you reached the end of the string). hab contains the anchor block handle. ulCodePage contains the codepage. ulCountry contains the country code. pszCurrentChar contains the current character in a null terminated string. You can retrieve the last error using WinGetLastError. These errors include: 0x100B PMERR_INVALID_STRING_PARM
fSuccess = WinOffsetRect (hab, prclRect, lcX, lcY)	The WinOffsetRect function offsets a rectangle by adding the value of lcX to both the left and right coordinates and the value of lcY to both the top and bottom coordinates. fSuccess contains true if this function is successful. hab contains the anchor block handle. prclRect contains the rectangle coordinates. lcX contains the X offset. lcY contains the Y offset.
fSuccess = WinOpenClipbrd (hab)	The WinOpenClipbrd function opens the clipboard. Opening the clipboard allows you to read the objects in it; do not delete or modify them. fSuccess contains true if this function is successful. hab contains the anchor block handle.
hdc = WinOpenWindowDC (hwnd)	The WinOpenWindowDC function opens a device context for a window. (Do not attempt to close this device context using DevCloseDC; OS/2 automatically closes it when it closes the associated window.) hdc contains a device context handle. hwnd contains a window handle. You can retrieve the last error using WinGetLastError. These errors include: 0x1001 PMERR_INVALID_HWND
fResult = WinPeekMsg (hab, pqmsgMsg, hwndFilter, ulFirst, ulLast, flOptions)	The WinPeekMsg function inspects the thread's message queue and returns to the application with or without a message. fResult returns TRUE if the function returned a message. hab contains the anchor block handle. pqmsgMsg contains a pointer to the message structure. hwndFilter contains the filter window handle. ulFirst contains the first message identity. ulLast contains the last message identity. flOptions controls whether or not OS/2 removes the message (PM_REMOVE or PM_NOREMOVE). You can retrieve the last error using WinGetLastError. These errors include: 0x1001 PMERR_INVALID_HWND 0x1019 PMERR_INVALID_FLAG
fSuccess = WinPopupMenu (hwndParent,	The WinPopupMenu function presents a pop-up menu to the user. (This is the unanchored equivalent of a pull-down menu.) fSuccess contains true if this function is successful.

Function	Description
hwndOwner, hwndMenu, IX, IY, idItem, fsOptions)	hwndParent contains the parent window handle. hwndOwner contains the owner window handle. hwndMenu contains the menu handle. IX contains the menu position X coordinate. IY contains the menu position Y coordinate. idItem contains the item identity. Use this parameter if you specified either the PU_POSITIONITEM or PU_SELECTITEM parameters in fsOptions. fsOptions contains the menu options. There are several feature sets you can choose from. The position options include PU_POSITIONITEM. The restrain options include: PU_HCONSTRAIN and PU_VCONSTRAIN. The initial state options include: PU_MOUSEBUTTON1DOWN, PU_MOUSEBUTTON2DOWN, PU_MOUSEBUTTON3DOWN, and PU_NONE. The select options include PU_SELECTITEM. The usage items include: PU_KEYBOARD, PU_MOUSEBUTTON1, PU_MOUSEBUTTON2, and PU_MOUSEBUTTON3.
fResult = WinPostMsg (hwnd, ulMsgId, mpParam1, mpParam2)	The WinPostMsg function posts a message to the message queue associated with the specified window. (This function returns immediately while WinPostMsg waits for the receiver to return.) fResult contains TRUE if the message posted successfully. hwnd contains the window handle (NULL posts the message to the queue associated with the current thread). ulMsgId contains the message identity. mpParam1 contains the first parameter. mpParam2 contains the second parameter. You can retrieve the last error using WinGetLastError. These errors include: 0x1001 PMERR_INVALID_HWND
fSuccess = WinPostQueueMsg (hmq, ulMsgId, mpParam1, mpParam2)	The WinPostQueueMsg function posts a message to a message queue. fSuccess contains true if this function is successful. hmq contains the message queue handle. ulMsgId contains the message identity. mpParam1 contains the first parameter. mpParam2 contains the second parameter. You can retrieve the last error using WinGetLastError. These errors include: 0x1002 PMERR_INVALID_HMQ
pszPrevChar = WinPrevChar (hab, ulCodePage, ulCountry, pszStart, pszCurrentChar)	The WinPrevChar function moves to the previous character in a DBCS string. pszPrevChar contains the previous character in the string. hab contains the anchor block handle. ulCodePage contains the codepage. ulCountry contains the country code. pszStart contains the character string that contains pszCurrentChar. pszCurrentChar contains the current character. You can retrieve the last error using WinGetLastError. These errors include: 0x100B PMERR_INVALID_STRING_PARM
ulResult = WinProcessDlg	The WinProcessDlg function dispatches messages while it displays a modal dialog box. If this window has an owner, that

Table 3-43   **Continued**

Function	Description
(hwndDlg)	window is disabled. Of course, this disables all the child windows as well. ulResult contains the reply value (established by the WinDismissDlg function). hwndDlg contains the dialog window handle. You can retrieve the last error using WinGetLastError. These errors include: 0x1001 PMERR_INVALID_HWND
fSuccess = WinPtInRect (hab, prclRect, pptlPoint)	The WinPtInRect function determines whether a point lies within a rectangle. fSuccess contains true if this function is successful. hab contains the anchor block handle. prclRect contains the rectangle coordinates. pptlPoint contains the point coordinates.
haccelAccel = WinQueryAccelTable (hab, hwndFrame)	The WinQueryAccelTable function queries the window or queue accelerator table. haccelAccel contains the accelerator table handle (NULLHANDLE indicates an error). hab contains the anchor block handle. hwndFrame contains the frame window handle (NULLHANDLE returns the queue accelerator). You can retrieve the last error using WinGetLastError. These errors include: 0x1001 PMERR_INVALID_HWND
hwndActive = WinQueryActiveWindow (hwndParent)	The WinQueryActiveWindow function returns the active window for HWND_DESKTOP or other parent window. hwndActive contains the active window handle (NULLHANDLE if no window is active). hwndParent contains the parent window handle (HWND_DESKTOP or other parent window handle). You can retrieve the last error using WinGetLastError. These errors include: 0x1001 PMERR_INVALID_HWND
hab = WinQueryAnchorBlock (hwnd)	The WinQueryAnchorBlock function returns the anchor block handle for the calling window. hab contains the anchor block handle. hwnd contains the window handle. You can retrieve the last error using WinGetLastError. These errors include: 0x1001 PMERR_INVALID_HWND
ulRetLen = WinQueryAtomLength (hatomtblAtomTbl, atom)	The WinQueryAtomLength function returns the length of the specified atom. (This allows the application to determine the buffer size required for a WinQueryAtomName call.) ulRetLen contains the length of the atom (0 if the atom or atom table is invalid). hatomtblAtomTbl contains the atom table handle. atom contains the atom whose character-string length you desire. You can retrieve the last error using WinGetLastError. These errors include:

Function	Description
	0x1013 PMERR_INVALID_HATOMTBL 0x1014 PMERR_INVALID_ATOM
ulRetLen = WinQueryAtomName (hatomtblAtomTbl, atom, pszBuffer, ulBufferMax)	The WinQueryAtomName function returns the atom name associated with an atom. ulRetLen contains the length of the atom (0 if the atom or atom table is invalid). hatomtblAtomTbl contains the atom table handle. atom contains the atom you want to retrieve. pszBuffer contains a pointer to the buffer used to hold the atom character string. ulBufferMax contains length of the buffer in bytes. You can retrieve the last error using WinGetLastError. These errors include:
	0x100B PMERR_INVALID_STRING_PARM 0x1013 PMERR_INVALID_HATOMTBL 0x1014 PMERR_INVALID_ATOM
ulCount = WinQueryAtomUsage (hatomtblAtomTbl, atom)	The WinQueryAtomUsage function returns the number of times an atom was used. ulCount contains the use count of the atom. It returns 65,535 for an integer atom. A return value of 0 indicates an invalid atom or atom table. hatomtblAtomTbl contains the atom table handle. atom contains the atom whose use count that you want to retrieve. You can retrieve the last error using WinGetLastError. These errors include:
	0x1013 PMERR_INVALID_HATOMTBL 0x1014 PMERR_INVALID_ATOM
usRetChkst = WinQueryButton-Checkstate (hwndDlg, usId)	The WinQueryButtonCheckstate function returns the checked state of the specified button control. usRetChkst contains the checkstate of the specified button control. hwndDlg contains the dialog window handle. usId contains the button control identity.
hwnd = WinQueryCapture (hwndDesktop)	The WinQueryCapture function returns the handle of the window that has the pointer captured. hwnd contains the handle of the window with the pointer captured (NULLHANDLE indicates that either there is no window with the pointer captured or an error). hwndDesktop contains the desktop window handle (HWND_DESKTOP or other desktop window handle). You can retrieve the last error using WinGetLastError. These errors include:
	0x1001 PMERR_INVALID_HWND
fExists = WinQueryClassInfo (hab, pszClassName, pclsiClassInfo)	The WinQueryClassInfo function returns window class information. fExists contains TRUE if the class exists. hab contains the anchor block handle. pszClassName contains the class name. pclsiClassInfo contains a pointer to the class information structure. You can retrieve the last error using WinGetLastError. These errors include:
	0x1015 PMERR_INVALID_ATOM_NAME

321

Table 3-43   **Continued**

Function	Description
	0x1016 PMERR_INVALID_INTEGER_ATOM 0x1017 PMERR_ATOM_NAME_NOT_FOUND
lRetLen = WinQueryClassName (hwnd, lLength, pchBuffer)	The WinQueryClassName function copies the window class name into a buffer as a null-terminated string. lRetLen contains the returned class name length. hwnd contains the window handle. lLength contains the length of pchBuffer. pchBuffer contains the class name. You can retrieve the last error using WinGetLastError. These errors include: 0x1001 PMERR_INVALID_HWND 0x100B PMERR_INVALID_STRING_PARM
pthunkpr = WinQueryClassThunkProc (pszClassName)	The WinQueryClassThunkProc function queries the pointer conversion procedure associated with a class. pthunkpr contains the pointer conversion procedure identifier (NULL indicates that no pointer conversion procedure is associated with this class). pszClassName contains the window class name.
ulData = WinQueryClipbrdData (hab, ulfmt)	The WinQueryClipbrdData function returns a handle to the current clipboard data using a specified format. ulData contains a handle to the clipboard data (0 indicates that the format does not exist or an error occurred). hab contains the anchor block handle. ulfmt contains the data format.
fExists = WinQueryClipbrdFmtInfo (hab, ulfmt, pulFmtInfo)	The WinQueryClipbrdFmtInfo function determines whether the clipboard contains a particular data format. If the format exists, then the function returns information about it. fExists contains true if the ulfmt exists in the clipboard. hab contains the anchor block handle. ulfmt contains the format of the data you want to query. pulFmtInfo contains the memory model and usage flags. You can retrieve the last error using WinGetLastError. These errors include: 0x1019 PMERR_INVALID_FLAG
hwndClipbrdOwner = WinQueryClipbrdOwner (hab)	The WinQueryClipbrdOwner function returns the handle of the current clipboard owner. hwndClipbrdOwner contains the handle of the current clipboard owner (NULLHANDLE indicates there is no current clipboard owner or an error occurred). hab contains the anchor block handle.
hwndClipbrdViewer = WinQueryClipbrdViewer (hab)	The WinQueryClipbrdViewer function returns the handle of any current viewer Window. hwndClipbrdViewer contains the clipboard viewer window handle (NULLHANDLE indicates there is no current viewer or an error occurred). hab contains the anchor block handle.
ulCodePage = WinQueryCp (hmq)	The WinQueryCp function returns the queue codepage for the specified message queue. ulCodePage contains the codepage

Function	Description
	(0 indicates an error). hmq contains the message queue handle. You can retrieve the last error using WinGetLastError. These errors include:
	0x1002 PMERR_INVALID_HMQ
ulTotCount = WinQueryCpList (hab, ulCount, aulCodePage)	The WinQueryCpList function returns a list of available codepages. ulTotCount contains the total number of available codepages (0 indicates an error). hab contains the anchor block handle. ulCount contains the number of elements in aulCodePage. aulCodePage is an array of codepages. You can retrieve the last error using WinGetLastError. These errors include:
	0x1003 PMERR_PARAMETER_OUT_OF_RANGE
fCursor = WinQueryCursorInfo (hwndDesktop, pcsriCursorInfo)	The WinQueryCursorInfo function returns information about the current cursor. fCursor contains TRUE if the cursor exists. hwndDesktop contains the desktop window handle (HWND_DESKTOP or other desktop window handle). pcsriCursorInfo contains a pointer to a cursor information structure. You can retrieve the last error using WinGetLastError. These errors include:
	0x1001 PMERR_INVALID_HWND
fSuccess = WinQueryDesktopBkgnd (hwndDesktop, pDeskTopState)	The WinQueryDesktopBkgnd returns the desktop structure. This contains information about the current state of the desktop background. The application making this call must act as the OS/2 PM shell in place of the standard IBM shell. fSuccess contains true if this function is successful. hwndDesktop contains the desktop window handle (HWND_DESKTOP or other desktop window handle). pDeskTopState contains a pointer to the desktop state structure. You can retrieve the last error using WinGetLastError. These errors include:
	0x1001 PMERR_INVALID_HWND
hwndDesktop = WinQueryDesktopWindow (hab, hdc)	The WinQueryDesktopWindow function returns the desktop window handle. (In most cases, you can use the HWND_DESKTOP constant in place of this handle for functions that require a desktop window handle.) hwndDesktop contains the desktop window handle (NULLHANDLE indicates an error). hab contains the anchor block handle. hdc contains the device context handle (NULLHANDLE uses the default screen device). You can retrieve the last error using WinGetLastError. These errors include:
	0x207C PMERR_INVALID_HDC
fSuccess = WinQueryDlgItemShort (hwndDlg, idItem,	The WinQueryDlgItemShort function converts the text of a dialog item into an integer value. This function is useful for converting numeric text input to a binary number. fSuccess

Table 3-43   **Continued**

Function	Description
psResult, fSigned)	contains true if this function is successful. hwndDlg contains the dialog window handle. idItem contains the identity of the text entry to convert. psResult contains the integer value of the conversion. fSigned contains the sign indicator. A value of TRUE is signed text that is inspected for a minus sign. You can retrieve the last error using WinGetLastError. These errors include: 0x1001 PMERR_INVALID_HWND
ulRetLen = WinQueryDlgItemText (hwndDlg, idItem, lMaxText, pszText)	The WinQueryDlgItemText function returns a text string from a dialog item. You can use this function for any window with children. ulRetLen contains the actual number of characters returned (0 indicates an error). hwndDlg contains the dialog window handle. idItem contains the identity of the item to query. lMaxText contains the length of pszText. pszText contains the dialog item text string. You can retrieve the last error using WinGetLastError. These errors include: 0x1001 PMERR_INVALID_HWND
lRetLen = WinQueryDlgTextLength (hwndDlg, idItem)	The WinQueryDlgTextLength returns the length of the txt string in a dialog item. This does not include the null termination character. You can use this function for any window with children. lRetLen contains the text string length (0 indicates an error). hwndDlg contains the dialog window handle. idItem contains the identity of the item to query.
hwndFocus = WinQueryFocus (hwndDesktop)	The WinQueryFocus function returns the handle of the focus window. hwndFocus contains the handle of the focus window (NULL indicates there is no focus window). hwndDesktop contains the desktop window handle (HWND_DESKTOP or other desktop window handle). You can retrieve the last error using WinGetLastError. These errors include: 0x1001 PMERR_INVALID_HWND
hwndHelp = WinQueryHelpInstance (hwndApp)	The WinQueryHelpInstance function returns the handle of the instance of the Help Manager associated with the specified window handle. hwndHelp contains the Help Manager instance handle (NULLHANDLE indicates that no Help Manager instance is associated with the application window). hwndApp contains application window handle.
sResNumIt = WinQueryLboxCount (hwndLbox)	The WinQueryLboxCount function returns the number of items in the list box. sResNumIt contains the number of items in the list box. hwndLbox contains the list box handle.
sRetTxtL = WinQueryLboxItemText	The WinQueryLboxItemText function fills a buffer with the text of the indexed item. It also returns the length of the text.

Function	Description
(hwndLbox, sIndex, pszText, scchMax)	sRetTxtL contains the actual length of the copied text. hwndLbox contains the list box handle. sIndex contains the index of the list box item. pszText contains the null terminate string. scchMax contains the length of pszText.
sRetLen = WinQueryLboxItem-TextLength (hwndLbox, sIndex)	The WinQueryLboxItemTextLength function returns the length of the text in the list box item. sRetLen contains the text string length. hwndLbox contains the list box handle. sIndex contains the index of the list box item.
sRetIndex = WinQueryLbox-SelectedItem (hwndLbox)	The WinQueryLboxSelectedItem function returns the index of the selected list box item. sRetIndex contains the index of the selected item. hwndLbox contains the list box handle.
fSuccess = WinQueryMsgPos (hab, pptlPtrPos)	The WinQueryMsgPos function returns the pointer position when the last message obtained from the current message queue gets posted in screen coordinates. fSuccess contains true if this function is successful. hab contains the anchor block handle. pptlPtrPos contains the pointer position in screen coordinates.
ulTime = WinQueryMsgTime (hab)	The WinQueryMsgTime returns the message time for the last message retrieve using WinGetMsg or WinPeekMsg from the current message queue. This is the time, in milliseconds, since the system was started. ulTime contains the time in milliseconds. hab contains the anchor block handle.
hObject = WinQueryObject (pszObjectId)	The WinQueryObject function returns a handle to the specified object. hObject contains the object handle (NULLHANDLE indicates the object does not exist or that OS/2 could not awaken it). pszObjectId contains the object identification (WP_DESKTOP for example). You also can specify a fully qualified filename.
hwndObject = WinQueryObjectWindow (hwndDesktop)	The WinQueryObjectWindow function returns the desktop object window handle. hwndObject contains the object window handle. hwndDesktop contains the desktop window handle (HWND_DESKTOP or other desktop window handle). You can retrieve the last error using WinGetLastError. These errors include: 0x1001 PMERR_INVALID_HWND
hptrPointer = WinQueryPointer (hwndDesktop)	The WinQueryPointer function returns the pointer handle for hwndDesktop. hptrPointer contains the pointer handle (NULLHANDLE indicates an error). hwndDesktop contains the desktop window handle (HWND_DESKTOP or other desktop window handle). You can retrieve the last error using WinGetLastError. These errors include: 0x1001 PMERR_INVALID_HWND
fSuccess =	The WinQueryPointerInfo function returns pointer information.

Table 3-43   **Continued**

Function	Description
WinQueryPointerInfo (hptr, pptriPointerInfo)	fSuccess contains true if this function is successful. hptr contains the pointer handle. pptriPointerInfo contains a pointer to the pointer information structure. You can retrieve the last error using WinGetLastError. These errors include: 0x101B PMERR_INVALID_HPTR
fSuccess = WinQueryPointerPos (hwndDesktop, pptlPoint)	The WinQueryPointerPos function returns the pointer position of the last message obtained using the WinGetMsg or WinPeekMsg functions. fSuccess contains true if this function is successful. hwndDesktop contains the desktop window handle (HWND_DESKTOP or other desktop window handle). pptlPoint contains the pointer position in screen coordinates. You can retrieve the last error using WinGetLastError. These errors include: 0x1001 PMERR_INVALID_HWND
cbRetLen = WinQueryPresParam (hwnd, idAttrType1, idAttrType2, pidAttrTypeFound, cbAttrValueLen, pAttrValue, flOptions)	The WinQueryPresParam function returns the values of the presentation parameters for a window. cbRetLen contains the length of the parameter value passed back. hwnd contains the window handle. idAttrType1 and idAttrType2 contain the first and second attribute type identities. pidAttrTypeFound contains the attribute type identity found. cbAttrValueLen contains the size of pAttrValue in bytes. pAttrValue contains the attribute value. flOptions contains the options that control the query. These controls include: QPF_NOINHERIT, QPF_ID1COLORINDEX, QPF_ID2COLORINDEX, and QPF_PURERGBCOLOR. You can retrieve the last error using WinGetLastError. These errors include: 0x1001 PMERR_INVALID_HWND
fSuccess = WinQueryQueueInfo (hmq, pmqiMqinfo, cbCopied)	The WinQueryQueueInfo function returns information about the specified queue. fSuccess contains true if this function is successful. hmq contains the message queue handle. pmqiMqinfo contains a pointer to the message queue information structure. cbCopied contains the size of the message queue structure in bytes.
flStatus = WinQueryQueueStatus (hwndDesktop)	The WinQueryQueueStatus function returns a code indicating the status of the message queue associated with the caller. You can use this function to determine if the queue contains messages ready for processing. flStatus contains the queue status information including the following fields. The summary field contains one or more of the following values: QS_KEY, QS_MOUSE, QS_MOUSEBUTTON, QS_MOUSEMOVE, QS_TIMER, QS_PAINT, QS_SEM1, QS_SEM2, QS_SEM3, QS_SEM4, QS_POSTMSG, and QS_SENDMSG. The added

Function	Description
	field contains the message type additions. hwndDesktop contains the desktop window handle (HWND_DESKTOP or other desktop window handle).
ulRetCode = WinQuerySessionTitle (hab, ulSession, pszTitle, ulTitleLen)	The WinQuerySessionTitle function returns the title under which OS/2 started the specified application (or added it to the Window List). ulRetCode contains 0 to indicate successful completion; any other value signifies an error. hab contains the anchor block handle. ulSession contains the OS/2 session identity of the application (0 uses the session identity of the caller). pszTitle contains the Window List title. ulTitleLen contains the length of pszTitle in bytes. If pszTitle is not large enough to hold the full title, OS/2 truncates it.
ulRetCode = WinQuerySwitchEntry (hswitchSwitch, pswctlSwitchData)	The WinQuerySwitchEntry function returns a copy of the Window List data for a specific application. ulRetCode contains 0 to indicate successful completion; any other value signifies an error. hswitchSwitch contains the Window List entry handle. pswctlSwitchData contains a pointer to the switch control data.
hswitchSwitch = WinQuerySwitchHandle (hwnd, idProcess)	The WinQuerySwitchHandle function obtains the Window List handle belonging to a window. hswitchSwitch contains the switch list handle for the specified application (NULLHANDLE indicates that the application does not appear in the switch list). hwnd contains the window handle (NULLHANDLE indicates that application is not an OS/2 application). idProcess contains the process identity of the application.
ulCount = WinQuerySwitchList (hab, pswblkBlock, ulLength)	The WinQuerySwitchList function returns information about the entries in the Window List. ulCount contains the number of switch list entries (0 indicates an error). hab contains the anchor block handle. pswblkBlock contains a pointer to the switch entries block. Supplying a value of NULL for this parameter returns the number of entries in ulCount, but no actual data. ulLength contains the length of pswblkBlock in bytes. Use a 0 for this parameter if you use NULL in pswblkBlock.
lRgbColor = WinQuerySysColor (hwndDesktop, lColor, lReserved)	The WinQuerySysColor function returns the system color. lRgbColor contains the RGB value of the system color. hwndDesktop contains the desktop window handle (HWND_DESKTOP or other desktop window handle). lColor contains the system color index value. You must use one of the SYSCLR index values defined under the WinSetSysColors function. lReserved is always set to 0. You can retrieve the last error using WinGetLastError. These errors include:
	0x1001 PMERR_INVALID_HWND 0x1003 PMERR_PARAMETER_OUT_OF_RANGE
hwndSysModal = WinQuerySysModal-Window (hwndDesktop)	The WinQuerySysModalWindow function returns the handle of the current system modal window. hwndSysModal contains the system modal window handle (NULLHANDLE indicates there is

Table 3-43   **Continued**

Function	Description
	no system modal window). hwndDesktop contains the desktop window handle (HWND_DESKTOP or other desktop window handle). You can retrieve the last error using WinGetLastError. These errors include:
	0x1001 PMERR_INVALID_HWND
hptrPointer = WinQuerySysPointer (hwndDesktop, lIdentifier, fCopy)	The WinQuerySysPointer function returns the system pointer handle. hptrPointer contains the pointer handle. hwndDesktop contains the desktop window handle. lIdentifier contains the system pointer identifier, which includes: SPTR_ARROW, SPTR_TEXT, SPTR_WAIT, SPTR_SIZE, SPTR_MOVE, SPTR_SIZENWSE, SPTR_SIZENESW, SPTR_SIZEWE, SPTR_APPICON, SPTR_ICONINFORMATION, SPTR_ICONQUESTION, SPTR_ICONERROR, SPTR_ICONWARNING, SPTR_ILLEGAL, SPTR_FILE, SPTR_MULTFILE, SPTR_FOLDER, and SPTR_PROGRAM. fCopy contains TRUE if you want to create a copy of the system pointer and return its handle. Always use this option if you plan to modify the system pointer. You can retrieve the last error using WinGetLastError. These errors include:
	0x1001 PMERR_INVALID_HWND 0x1003 PMERR_PARAMETER_OUT_OF_RANGE
hatomtblAtomTbl = WinQuerySystem-AtomTable (VOID)	The WinQuerySystemAtomTable function returns the handle of the system atom table. hatomtblAtomTbl contains the system atom table handle.
lValue = WinQuerySysValue (hwndDesktop, lValueId)	The WinQuerySysValue function returns the specified system value. lValue contains the system value (0 indicates an error). hwndDesktop contains the desktop window handle (HWND_DESKTOP or other desktop window handle). lValueid contains the system value identifier, which includes: SV_CXSCREEN, SV_CYSCREEN, SV_CXVSCROLL, SV_CYHSCROLL, SV_CYVSCROLLARROW, SV_CXHSCROLLARROW, SV_CYTITLEBAR, SV_CXBORDER, SV_CYBORDER, SV_CXSIZEBORDER, SV_CYSIZEBORDER, SV_CXDLGFRAME, SV_CYDLFRAME, SV_CYVSLIDER, SV_CXHSLIDER, SV_CXMINMAXBUTTON, SV_CYMINMAXBUTTON, SV_CYMENU, SV_CXFULLSCREEN, SV_CYFULLSCREEN, SV_CXICON, SV_CYICON, SV_CXPOINTER, SV_CYPOINTER, SV_DEBUG, SV_CMOUSEBUTTONS, SV_POINTERLEVEL, SV_CTIMERS, SV_SWAPBUTTON, SV_CURSORRATE, SV_DBLCLKTIME, SV_CXDBLCLK, SV_CYDBLCLK, SV_ALARM, SV_WARNINGFREQ, SV_WARNINGDURATION, SV_NOTEFREQ,

Function	Description
	SV_NOTEDURATION, SV_ERRORFREQ, SV_ERRORDURATION, SV_FIRSTSCROLLRATE, SV_SCROLLRATE, SV_CURSORLEVEL, SV_TRACKRECTLEVEL, SV_CXBYTEALIGN, SV_CYBYTEALIGN, SV_SETLIGHTS, SV_INSERTMODE, SV_MENUROLLDOWNDELAY, SV_MENUROLLUPDELAY, SV_MOUSEPRESENT, SV_MONOICONS. SV_KBDALTERED, SV_PRINTSCREEN, SV_BEGINDRAG, SV_ENDDRAG, SV_BEGINSELECT, SV_ENDSELECT, SV_OPEN, SV_CONTEXTMENU, SV_TEXTEDIT, SV_CONTEXTMENUKB, or SV_TEXTEDITKB. You can retrieve the last error using WinGetLastError. These errors include: 0x1001 PMERR_INVALID_HWND 0x1003 PMERR_PARAMETER_OUT_OF_RANGE
ulRetCode = WinQueryTaskSizePos (hab, ulId, pswp)	The WinQueryTaskSizePos function returns the recommended size, position, and status for the first window of a newly started application (typically the main window). These values normally come from the initialization file. The system automatically generates values if the application does not have an initialization file. ulRetCode contains a 0 to indicate successful completion (any other value indicates an error). hab contains the anchor block handle. ulId contains the session identifier. A value of 0 uses the caller's session identifier. pswp contains the window position and size. It also contains flags showing window activation, minimized, or maximized.
ulRetCode = WinQueryTaskTitle (ulSession, pszTitle, ulTitleLen)	The WinQueryTaskTitle function returns the application's title in the Window List. Use the WinQuerySessionTitle function in place of this one whenever possible. ulRetCode contains a return code of 0 for successful completion (any other value indicates an error). ulSession contains the session identity of the application. A value of 0 uses the caller's identification. pszTitle contains the Window List title. ulTitleLen contains the length of pszTitle.
fSuccess = WinQueryUpdateRect (hwnd, prclPrc)	The WinQueryUpdateRect returns the rectangle that bounds the update region of a specified window. You can use this function to implement an incremental update scheme in place of the WinBeginPaint and WinEndPaint functions. fSuccess contains true if this function is successful. hwnd contains the window handle. prclPrc contains the rectangle boundaries in world coordinates. You can retrieve the last error using WinGetLastError. These errors include: 0x1001 PMERR_INVALID_HWND
lComplexity = WinQueryUpdateRegion	The WinQueryUpdateRegion function returns the update region of a window. You can use this function to implement an

Table 3-43 | **Continued**

Function	Description
(hwnd, hrgn)	incremental update scheme in place of the WinBeginPaint and WinEndPaint functions. lComplexity contains the complexity and error indicators. hwnd contains the window handle. hrgn contains the region handle. WinQueryUpdateRegion returns one of the following values: 0000 RGN_ERROR 0001 RGN_NULL 0002 RGN_RECT 0003 RGN_COMPLEX You can retrieve the last error using WinGetLastError. These errors include: 0x1001 PMERR_INVALID_HWND 0x2034 PMERR_HRGN_BUSY
flSysInf = WinQueryVersion (hab)	The WinQueryVersion function returns the version, revision level, and environment of the PM. flSysInf contains the system information in the following fields: SYSINF_ENV (QV_OS2 equals OS/2), SYSINF_MAJOR (the major version number), and SYSINF_MINOR (the minor version and revision level number). hab contains the anchor block handle.
hwndRelated = WinQueryWindow (hwnd, lCode)	The WinQueryWindow function returns the handle of a window that has a specified relationship to the specified window. hwndRelated contains the handle of the window related to hwnd. hwnd contains the window handle. lCode contains the type of information requested. This includes: QW_NEXT, QW_PREV, QW_TOP, QW_BOTTOM, QW_OWNER, QW_PARENT, QW_NEXTTOP, QW_PREVTOP, and QW_FRAMEOWNER. You can retrieve the last error using WinGetLastError. These errors include: 0x1001 PMERR_INVALID_HWND 0x1003 PMERR_PARAMETER_OUT_OF_RANGE
hdc = WinQueryWindowDC (hwnd)	The WinQueryWindowDC function returns the device context for the specified window. hdc contains the device context handle (NULLHANDLE indicates no device context or an error condition). hwnd contains the window handle. You can retrieve the last error using WinGetLastError. These errors include: 0x1001 PMERR_INVALID_HWND
ulModel = WinQueryWindow-Model (hwnd)	The WinQueryWindowModel function returns the memory associated with the specified window. Use this function to determine the memory model used by another application (for example, in a DDE transfer). OS/2 version 1.1 and 1.2 applications do not perform automatic pointer conversion; this

Function	Description
	function makes it possible for a 32-bit application to detect this condition and perform the appropriate actions. ulModel contains the memory model associated with the window: PM_MODEL_1X (16-bit) or PM_MODEL_2X (32-bit). hwnd contains the window handle.
fSuccess = WinQueryWindowPos (hwnd, pswp)	The WinQueryWindowPos function returns the window size and position of a visible window. fSuccess contains true if this function is successful. hwnd contains the window handle. pswp contains a pointer to the SWP structure. You can retrieve the last error using WinGetLastError. These errors include:

0x1001   PMERR_INVALID_HWND
0x1019   PMERR_INVALID_FLAG

Function	Description
fSuccess = WinQueryWindowProcess (hwnd, pidPid, pidTid)	The WinQueryWindowProcess function returns the process and thread identity of the thread that created the window. fSuccess contains true if this function is successful. hwnd contains the window handle. pidPid contains the process identity (PID) of the thread that created the window. pidTid contains the thread identity (TID) of the thread that created the window. You can retrieve the last error using WinGetLastError. These errors include:

0x1001   PMERR_INVALID_HWND

Function	Description
pp = WinQueryWindowPtr (hwnd, lb)	The WinQueryWindowPtr function retrieves a pointer value from the memory of the reserved window word. pp contains the pointer value (NULL indicates an error). hwnd contains the window handle. lb contains a zero-based index of the pointer value that you want to retrieve. The valid range is zero through (usExtra − 4). (usExtra is the WinRegisterClass parameter that defines the number of bytes available for application storage.) The lb parameter is valid only if all the bytes referenced reside within reserved memory. You can retrieve the last error using WinGetLastError. These errors include:

0x1001   PMERR_INVALID_HWND
0x1003   PMERR_PARAMETER_OUT_OF_RANGE

Function	Description
fSuccess = WinQueryWindowRect (hwnd, prclRect)	The WinQueryWindowRect function returns a window rectangle referenced to itself. The bottom-left corner is always at position (0, 0). fSuccess contains true if this function is successful. hwnd contains the window handle. prclRect contains the rectangle boundaries in world coordinates. You can retrieve the last error using WinGetLastError. These errors include:

0x1001   PMERR_INVALID_HWND

Function	Description
lRetLen = WinQueryWindowText	The WinQueryWindowText function copies window text into a buffer. lRetLen contains the length of the returned text. hwnd

Table 3-43   **Continued**

Function	Description
(hwnd, lLength, pchBuffer)	contains the window handle. lLength contains the length of pchBuffer. pchBuffer contains the window text. You can retrieve the last error using WinGetLastError. These errors include: 0x1001 PMERR_INVALID_HWND
lRetLen = WinQueryWindow-TextLength (hwnd)	The WinQueryWindowTextLength function returns the length of the window text. This does not include the null-termination character. lRetLen contains the length of the window text. hwnd contains the window handle. You can retrieve the last error using WinGetLastError. These errors include: 0x1001 PMERR_INVALID_HWND
pthunkpr = WinQueryWindowThunk-Proc (hwnd)	The WinQueryWindowThunkProc returns a pointer to the pointer-conversion procedure associated with a window. pThunkpr contains the pointer-conversion procedure pointer (NULL indicates there is no pointer-conversion procedure associated with this window). hwnd contains the window handle.
ulValue = WinQueryWindowULong (hwnd, lb)	The WinQueryWindowULong function returns the unsigned long integer value from a specified offset of the memory of the specified reserved window. ulValue contains the value at the specified offset. hwnd contains the window handle. lb contains a zero-based index of the pointer value that you want to retrieve. The valid range is zero through (usExtra – 4). (usExtra is the WinRegisterClass parameter that defines the number of bytes available for application storage.) You also can use the following QWL values: QWL_HMQ, QWL_STYLE, QWL_HHEAP, QWL_FOCUSSAVE, QWL_USER, and QWL_DEFBUTTON. You can retrieve the last error using WinGetLastError. These errors include: 0x1001 PMERR_INVALID_HWND 0x1003 PMERR_PARAMETER_OUT_OF_RANGE
ulValue = WinQueryWindowUShort (hwnd, lb)	The WinQueryWindowUShort function returns the unsigned short integer value from a specified offset of the memory of the specified reserved window. ulValue contains the value at the specified offset. hwnd contains the window handle. lb contains a zero-based index of the pointer value that you want to retrieve. The valid range is zero through (usExtra – 4). (usExtra is the WinRegisterClass parameter that defines the number of bytes available for application storage.) You also can use the following QWS values: QWS_ID, QWS_FLAGS, QWS_RESULT, QWS_XRESTORE, QWS_YRESTORE, QWS_CXRESTORE, QWS_CYRESTORE, QWS_XMINIMIZE, and QWS_YMINIMIZE. You can retrieve the last error using WinGetLastError. These errors include:

Function	Description
	0x1001 PMERR_INVALID_HWND 0x1003 PMERR_PARAMETER_OUT_OF_RANGE
lChanged = WinRealizePalette (hwnd, hps, pcclr)	The WinRealize function initiates the drawing process after palette selection. You normally use this function after GpiSelectPalette. lChanged contains the number of remapped colors (PAL_ERROR indicates an error). hwnd contains the window handle. hps contains the presentation space handle. pcclr contains the number of physical palette entries changed. You can retrieve the last error using WinGetLastError. These errors include:
	0x1001 PMERR_INVALID_HWND 0x2033 PMERR_HDC_BUSY 0x207C PMERR_INV_HDC 0x2085 PMERR_INV_IN_AREA 0x2110 PMERR_NO_PALETTE_SELECTED
fRegistered = WinRegisterClass (hab, pszClassName, pWndProc, flClassStyle, usExtra)	The WinRegisterClass function registers a window class. fRegistered contains TRUE if OS/2 successfully registered the class. hab contains the anchor block handle. pszClassName contains the window class name. pWndProc contains the window procedure identifier. Use NULL if the application does not provide its own window procedure. flClassStyle contains the default window style. usExtra contains the amount of reserved storage required for each window created of this class. You can retrieve the last error using WinGetLastError. These errors include:
	0x1013 PMERR_INVALID_HATOMTBL 0x1015 PMERR_INVALID_ATOM_NAME 0x1016 PMERR_INVALID_INTEGER_ATOM 0x1017 PMERR_ATOM_NAME_NOT_FOUND 0x1019 PMERR_INVALID_FLAG
fSuccess = WinRegisterObjectClass (pszClassName, pszModName) fSuccess = WinRegisterUserDatatype (hab, lDatatype, lCount, asTypes)	The WinRegisterObjectClass function registers a workplace object class. fSuccess contains true if this function is successful. pszClassName contains the window class name. pszModName contains the name of the DLL that holds the object definition. The WinRegisterUserDatatype function registers a data type and defines its structure. fSuccess contains true if this function is successful. hab contains the anchor block handle. lDatatype contains the code of the data type that you want to define. lCount contains the number of elements in asTypes. asTypes contains the data type codes. This includes system-defined data types and their pointer equivalents, application-defined data types and their pointer equivalents, and control data types. Simple data types include: DTYP_ATOM, DTYPE_BIT16,

Table 3-43   **Continued**

Function	Description
	DTYP_BIT32, DTYP_BIT8, DTYP_BOOL, DTYP_COUNT2, DTYP_COUNT2B, DTYP_COUNT2CH, DTYP_COUNT4B, DTYP_CPID, DTYP_ERRORID, DTYP_IDENTITY, DTYP_IDENTITY4, DTYP_INDEX2, DTYP_IPT, DTYP_LENGTH2, DTYP_LENGTH4, DTYP_LONG, DTYP_OFFSET2B, DTYP_PID, DTYP_PIX, DTYP_PROGCATEGORY, DTYP_PROPERTY2, DTYP_PROPERTY4, DTYP_RESID, DTYP_SEGOFF, DTYP_SHORT, DTYP_TID, DTYP_TIME, DTYP_UCHAR, DTYP_ULONG, DTYP_USHORT, DTYP_WIDTH4, and DTYP_WNDPROC. Handle data types include: DTYP_HAB, DTYP_HACCEL, DTYP_HAPP, DTYP_HATOMTBL, DTYP_HBITMAP, DTYP_HDC, DTYP_HENUM, DTYP_HINI, DTYP_HLIB, DTYP_HMF, DTYP_HMQ, DTYP_HPOINTER, DTYP_HPROGRAM, DTYP_HPS, DTYP_HRGN, DTYP_HSEM, DTYP_HSPL, DTYP_HSWITCH, and DTYP_HWND. Character, string, and buffer data types include: DTYP_BYTE, DTYP_CHAR, DTYP_STRL, DTYP_STR16, DTYP_STR32, DTYP_STR64, and DTYP_STR8. Structure data types include: DTYP_ACCEL, DTYP_ACCELTABLE, DTYP_ARCPARAMS, DTYP_AREABUNDLE, DTYP_BITMAPINFO, DTYP_BITMAPINFOHEADER, DTYP_BTNCDATA, DTYP_CATCHBUF, DTYP_CHARBUNDLE, DTYP_CLASSINFO, DTYP_CREATESTRUCT, DTYP_CURSORINFO, DTYP_DEVOPENSTRUC, DTYP_DLGTEMPLATE, DTYP_DLGITEM, DTYP_ENTRYFDATA, DTYP_FATTRS, DTYP_FFDESCS, DTYP_FIXED, DTYP_FONTMETRICS, DTYP_FRAMECDATA, DTYP_GRADIENTL, DTYP_HCINFO, DTYP_IMAGEBUNDLE, DTYP_KERNINGPAIRS, DTYP_LINEBUNDLE, DTYP_MARGSTRUCT, DTYP_MARKERBUNDLE, DTYP_MATRIXLF, DTYP_MLECTLDATA, DTYP_OVERFLOW, DTYP_OWNERITEM, DTYP_POINTERINFO, DTYP_POINTL, DTYP_PROGRAMENTRY, DTYP_PROGTYPE, DTYP_QMSG, DTYP_RECTL, DTYP_RGB, DTYP_RGNRECT, DTYP_SBCDATA, DTYP_SIZEF, DTYP_SIZEL, DTYP_SWBLOCK, DTYP_SWCNTRL, DTYP_SWENTRY, DTYP_SWP, DTYP_TRACKINFO, DTYP_USERBUTTON, DTYP_WNDPARAMS, DTYP_WPOINT, DTYP_WRECT, and DTYP_XYWINSIZE. Pointer data types include: DTYP_Pxxx. Minimum application data types include: DTYP_USER. Control data types include: DTYP_CTL_ARRAY, DTYP_CTL_LENGTH, DTYP_CTL_OFFSET, and DTYP_CTL_PARRAY.

Function	Description
	You can retrieve the last error using WinGetLastError. These errors include:
	0x103E PMERR_ARRAY_TOO_SMALL 0x103F PMERR_DATATYPE_ENTRY_BAD_INDEX 0x1040 PMERR_DATATYPE_ENTRY_CTL_BAD 0x1041 PMERR_DATATYPE_ENTRY_CTL_MISS 0x1043 PMERR_DATATYPE_ENTRY_NOT_NUM 0x1044 PMERR_DATATYPE_ENTRY_NOT_OFF 0x1046 PMERR_DATATYPE_NOT_UNIQUE 0x1048 PMERR_DATATYPE_TOO_SMALL
fSuccess = WinRegisterUserMsg (hab, ulMsgId, lType1, lDir1, lType2, lDir2, lTyper)	The WinRegisterUserMsg function registers a user message and defines its parameters. fSuccess contains true if this function is successful. hab contains the anchor block handle. ulMsgId contains the message identifier. You must use a value greater than WM_USER. OS/2 allows only one definition per message. lType1 contains the data type of message parameter 1. Valid data types include: DTYPE_BIT16, DTYPE_BIT32, DTYP_BIT8, DTYP_BOOL, DTYP_LONG, DTYP_SHORT, DTYP_UCHAR, DTYP_ULONG, DTYP_USHORT, DTYP_P*, and <-DTYP_USER. lDir1 contains the direction of message parameter 1. If the message parameter is a pointer, then the following direction values apply to the contents of the storage location: RUM_IN, RUM_OUT, and RUM_INOUT. lType2 contains the data type of message parameter 2. See the lType1 entry. lDir2 contains the direction of message parameter 2. See the lDir1 entry. lTyper contains the type of message reply. See the lType1 entry. The message reply is always an output parameter. You can retrieve the last error using WinGetLastError. These errors include:
	0x1045 PMERR_DATATYPE_INVALID 0x1047 PMERR_DATATYPE_TOO_LONG 0x104F PMERR_MSGID_TOO_SMALL
fSuccess = WinReleaseHook (hab, hmq, lHook, pAddress, hModule)	The WinReleaseHook function releases an application hook from the hook chain. fSuccess contains true if this function is successful. hab contains the anchor block handle. hmq contains the message queue handle (HMQ_CURRENT or NULLHANDLE). lHook contains the type of hook chain. pAddress contains the address of the hook routine. hModule contains the module handle (NULLHANDLE if the hook procedure is in the application's EXE file). You can retrieve the last error using WinGetLastError. These errors include:
	0x1002 PMERR_INVALID_HMQ 0x1003 PMERR_PARAMETER_OUT_OF_RANGE
fSuccess = WinReleasePS (hps)	The WinReleasePS function releases a cache presentation space obtained using the WinGetPS or WinGetScreen PS call. This

Table 3-43   **Continued**

Function	**Description**
	function works only with cache presentation spaces. fSuccess contains true if this function is successful. hps contains the presentation space handle.
fSuccess = WinRemovePresParam (hwnd, idAttrType)	The WinRemovePresParam function removes a presentation parameter associated with a specific window. fSuccess contains true if this function is successful. hwnd contains the window handle. idAttrType contains the attribute type identity; the type of presentation attribute that you want to remove. You can retrieve the last error using WinGetLastError. These errors include: 0x1001 PMERR_INVALID_HWND
usRetCode = WinRemoveSwitchEntry (hswitchSwitch)	The WinRemoveSwitchEntry function removes the specified entry from the Window List. usRetCode contains 0 to indicate a successful completion (any other value indicates an error). hswitchSwitch contains the switch list entry handle. You can retrieve the last error using WinGetLastError. These errors include: 0x1202 PMERR_INVALID_SWITCH_HANDLE 0x1206 PMERR_INVALID_WINDOW
fSuccess = WinReplaceObjectClass (pszOldClassName, pszNewClassName, fReplace)	The WinReplaceObjectClass function replaces a registered call with another registered class. The new class must be a descendant of the old class. fSuccess contains true if this function is successful. pszOldClassName contains a pointer to the zero-terminated name of the class that you want to replace. pszNewClassName contains the name of the new class. fReplace replaces the function of the old class with the new class when set to TRUE. A value of FALSE undoes the replacement by restoring the old class back to its original functionality.
ulRc = WinRequestMutexSem (hmtx, ulTimeout)	The WinRequestMutexSem function requests ownership of a mutex semaphore or waits for a PM message. This function is similar to the DosRequestMutexSem function. ulRc contains one of the following return codes: NO_ERROR (0), ERROR_INVALID_HANDLE (6), ERROR_INTERRUPT (95), ERROR_TOO_MANY_SEM_REQUESTS (103), ERROR_SEM_OWNER_DIED (105), or ERROR_TIMEOUT (640). hmtx contains the mutex semaphore handle. ulTimeout contains the time-out in milliseconds. This is the maximum time that the call will wait for a semaphore. You also can use a value of 0 to indicate an immediate return or −1 to indicate an indefinite wait.
fSuccess =	The WinRestoreWindowPos function restores the size and

Function	Description
WinRestoreWindowPos (pszAppName, pszKeyName, hwnd)	position of the window to its condition the last time you called WinStoreWindowPos with the same pszAppName and pszKeyName values. This function also restores the presentation parameters. fSuccess contains true if this function is successful. pszAppName contains the application name. pszKeyName contains the key name. hwnd contains the window handle.
fSuccess = WinSaveWindowPos (hsvwp, aswpAswp, ccSwp)	The WinSaveWindowPos function uses an array of SWP structures to save the position of a frame window. fSuccess contains true if this function is successful. hsvwp contains the frame window repositioning process identifier. aswpAswp contains an array of SWP structures. ccSwp contains the number of elements in aswpAswp.
lComplexity = WinScrollWindow (hwnd, lDx, lDy, prclScroll, prclClip, hrgnUpdateRgn, prclUpdate, flOptions)	The WinScrollWindow function scrolls the contents of a window rectangle. lComplexity contains the complexity and error indicators. hwnd contains the window handle. lDx contains the amount of horizontal scroll to the right in device units. lDy contains the amount of vertical scroll upward in device units. prclScroll contains the coordinates of the scroll rectangle. prclClip contains the coordinates of the clip rectangle. You can use a value of NULL to indicate there is no clip rectangle. hrgnUpdateRgn contains the update region. Use a value of NULLHANDLE to indicate there is no update region. prclUpdate contains the coordinates of the update rectangle. A value of NULL indicates there is no update rectangle. flOptions contains the scroll options including: SW_SCROLLCHILDREN and SW_INVALIDATERGN. WinScrollWindow returns one of the following values:

0000   RGN_ERROR
0001   RGN_NULL
0002   RGN_RECT
0003   RGN_COMPLEX

You can retrieve the last error using WinGetLastError. These errors include:

0x1001   PMERR_INVALID_HWND
0x1019   PMERR_INVALID_FLAG
0x2034   PMERR_HRGN_BUSY

Function	Description
mresReply = WinSendDlgItemMsg (hwndDlg, idItem, ulMsgId, mpParam1, mpParam2)	The WinSendDlgItemMsg function sends a message to the specified dialog item in a specific dialog window. This function is equivalent to the WinSendMsg function. It does not return until the dialog item processes the message. mresReply contains the message return information. hwndDlg contains the dialog window handle. idItem contains the child window identity. ulMsgId contains the message identity. mpParam1 and mpParam2 contain the first and second message

Table 3-43   **Continued**

Function	Description
	parameters. You can retrieve the last error using WinGetLastError. These errors include: 0x1001 PMERR_INVALID_HWND
mresReply = WinSendMsg (hwnd, ulMsgId, mpParam1, mpParam2)	The WinSendMsg function sends a message to the specified window. It also passes two parameters to the window. The function does not return until the window processes the message and provides a return message. mresReply contains the message return information. hwnd contains the window handle. ulMsgId contains the message identity. mpParam1 and mpParam2 contain the first and second message parameters. You can retrieve the last error using WinGetLastError. These errors include: 0x1001 PMERR_INVALID_HWND 0x1007 PMERR_WINDOW_NOT_LOCKED
fSuccess = WinSetAccelTable (hab, haccelAccel, hwndFrame)	The WinSetAccelTable function sets the window accelerator or queue accelerator table. fSuccess contains true if this function is successful. hab contains the anchor block handle. haccelAccel contains the accelerator table handle. A value of NULLHANDLE removes any accelerator table in effect for the window or queue. hwndFrame contains the frame window handle. A value of NULLHANDLE sets the queue accelerator table. You can retrieve the last error using WinGetLastError. These errors include: 0x1001 PMERR_INVALID_HWND 0x101A PMERR_INVALID_HACCEL
fSuccess = WinSetActiveWindow (hwndDesktop, hwnd)	The WinSetActiveWindow function makes the frame window the active window. fSuccess contains true if this function is successful. hwndDesktop contains the desktop window handle (HWND_DESKTOP or other desktop window handle). hwnd contains the window handle. You can retrieve the last error using WinGetLastError. These errors include: 0x1001 PMERR_INVALID_HWND
fSuccess = WinSetCapture (hwndDesktop, hwnd)	The WinSetCapture function captures all pointing device messages to hwnd. This sends all pointing device input to the window even if the pointing device is not near it at the time. fSuccess contains true if this function is successful. hwndDesktop contains the desktop window handle (HWND_DESKTOP or other desktop window handle). hwnd contains the window handle. You can retrieve the last error using WinGetLastError. These errors include: 0x1001 PMERR_INVALID_HWND

Function	Description
fSuccess = WinSetClassMsgInterest (hab, pszClassName, ulMsgClass, lControl)	The WinSetClassMsgInterest function sets the message interest of a window class. fSuccess contains true if this function is successful. hab contains the anchor block handle. pszClassName contains the window class name. ulMsgClass contains the message class for which you want to set an interest level (SHIM_ALL selects all messages). lControl contains the level of interest for the message class including: SMI_INTEREST, SMI_NOINTEREST, and SMI_AUTODISPATCH. You can retrieve the last error using WinGetLastError. These errors include: 0x1001 PMERR_INVALID_HWND
fSuccess = WinSetClassThunkProc (pszClassName, pthunkpr)	The WinSetClassThunkProc function associates a pointer conversion procedure with a window class. fSuccess contains true if this function is successful. pszClassName contains the window class name. pthunkpr contains the pointer conversion procedure identifier (NULL disassociates the procedure from this class).
fDataPlaced = WinSetClipbrdData (hab, ulh, ulFmt, flFmtInfo)	The WinSetClipbrdData function puts data into the clipboard. It also frees any data of the specified format already in the clipboard. fDataPlaced contains true if this function is successful. hab contains the anchor block handle. ulh contains a generic handle to the data object that you want to place in the clipboard. A value of NULLHANDLE sends a WM_RENDERFMT message to the clipboard owner window. ulFmt contains the format of the data object in ulh. The valid format types include: CF_TEXT, CF_DSPTEXT, CF_BITMAP, CF_DSPBITMAP, CF_METAFILE, CF_DSPMETAFILE, and CF_PALETTE. flFmtInfo contains information about the type of data referenced by ulh. The memory model field includes: CFI_POINTER and CFI_HANDLE. The usage flags include: CFI_OWNERFREE and CFI_OWNERDISPLAY. You can retrieve the last error using WinGetLastError. These errors include: 0x1016 PMERR_INVALID_INTEGER_ATOM 0x1019 PMERR_INVALID_FLAG
fSuccess = WinSetClipbrdOwner (hab, hwnd)	The WinSetClipbrdOwner function sets the current clipboard owner window. The owner window receives the following clipboard related messages: WM_DESTROYCLIPBOARD, WM_HSCROLLCLIPBOARD, WM_PAINTCLIPBOARD, WM_RENDERFMT, WM_RENDERALLFMTS, WM_SIZECLIPBOARD, and WM_VSCROLLCLIPBOARD. fSuccess contains true if this function is successful. hab contains the anchor block handle. hwnd contains the window handle. A value of NULLHANDLE releases the clipboard owner window without establishing a new one. You can retrieve the last error using WinGetLastError. These errors include: 0x1001 PMERR_INVALID_HWND

Table 3-43   **Continued**

Function	Description
fSuccess = WinSetClipbrdViewer (hab, hwndNewClipViewer)	The WinSetClipbrdViewer function sets the current clipboard viewer window to the specified window. The viewer window receives the WM_DRAWCLIPBOARD message when the clipboard contents change. fSuccess contains true if this function is successful. hab contains the anchor block handle. hwndNewClipViewer contains the handle of the viewer window. A value of NULLHANDLE releases the current owner without establishing a new one. You can retrieve the last error using WinGetLastError. These errors include: 0x1001 PMERR_INVALID_HWND
fSuccess = WinSetCp (hmq, ulCodePage)	The WinSetCp function sets the code page for a queue. fSuccess contains true if this function is successful. hmq contains the message queue handle. ulCodePage contains the code page (either of the two pages specified in CONFIG.SYS). You can retrieve the last error using WinGetLastError. These errors include: 0x1002 PMERR_INVALID_HMQ 0x100A PMERR_RESOURCE_NOT_FOUND
hbm = WinSetDesktopBkgnd (hwndDesktop, pDeskTopState)	The WinSetDesktopBkgnd function sets the desktop window state. This function allows an application to present an image in the background of the desktop window. The application must act as the OS/2 PM shell because the IBM supplied shell prevents this action. hbm contains the desktop background bitmap handle (NULLHANDLE indicates an error). hwndDesktop contains the desktop window handle. pDeskTopState contains a pointer to the desktop state structure. You can retrieve the last error using WinGetLastError. These errors include: 0x1001 PMERR_INVALID_HWND 0x101B PMERR_INVALID_HPTR
fSuccess = WinSetDlgItemShort (hwndDlg, idItem, usValue, fSigned)	The WinSetDlgItemShort function converts an integer value into the text of a dialog item. This function is valid for any window with children. fSuccess contains true if this function is successful. hwndDlg contains the dialog window handle. idItem contains the child window identity. usValue contains the integer value used to generate the dialog item text. fSigned contains TRUE if usValue contains a signed integer value. You can retrieve the last error using WinGetLastError. These errors include: 0x1001 PMERR_INVALID_HWND
fSuccess =	The WinSetDlgItemText function sets a text string in a dialog

Function	Description
WinSetDlgItemText (hwndDlg, idItem, pszText)	item. This function is valid for any window with children. fSuccess contains true if this function is successful. hwndDlg contains the dialog window handle. idItem contains the child window identifier. pszText contains the string that you want to set into the dialog item. You can retrieve the last error using WinGetLastError. These errors include: 0x1001 PMERR_INVALID_HWND
fSuccess = WinSetFileIcon (pszFilename, pIcon)	The WinSetFileIcon function sets a file's icon. fSuccess contains true if this function is successful. pszFilename contains the name of the file whose icon that you want to change. pIcon contains a pointer to an ICONINFO structure.
fSuccess = WinSetFocus (hwndDesktop, hwndNewFocus)	The WinSetFocus function sets the focus window. This is equivalent to the WinFocusChange function with the flFocusChange parameter set to 0. fSuccess contains true if this function is successful. hwndDesktop contains the desktop window handle (HWND_DESKTOP or other desktop window handle). hwndNewFocus contains the handle of the window to receive the focus. You can retrieve the last error using WinGetLastError. These errors include: 0x1001 PMERR_INVALID_HWND
fSuccess = WinSetHook (hab, hmq, lHookType, pHookProc, hModule)	The WinSetHook function installs an application procedure into a specified hook chain. fSuccess contains true if this function is successful. hab contains the anchor block handle. hmq contains the message queue handle. Setting hmq to NULLHANDLE places the hook in the system hook chain. A value of HMQ_CURRENT installs the hook in the message queue associated with the current thread. lHookType specifies the hook chain type, which includes: HK_CHECKFILTER, HK_CODEPAGECHANGE, HK_DESTROYWINDOW, HK_HELP, HK_INPUT, HK_JOURNALPLAYBACK, HK_JOURNALRECORD, HK_LOADER, HK_MSGCONTROL, HK_MSGFILTER, HK_REGISTERUSERMSG, and HK_SENDMSG. pHookProc contains the address of the application hook procedure. hModule contains the handle of the module that contains the application hook procedure. Use a value of NULLHANDLE when installing the queue hook into an application's own message queue. You can retrieve the last error using WinGetLastError. These errors include: 0x1002 PMERR_INVALID_HMQ 0x1003 PMERR_PARAMETER_OUT_OF_RANGE
fSuccess = WinSetKeyboardState Table (hwndDesktop, abKeyStateTable, fSet)	The WinSetKeyboardStateTable function gets or sets the keyboard state. This function changes the value returned by the WinGetKeyState function but not the WinGetPhysKeyState function, because it does not affect the physical state of the

Table 3-43   **Continued**

Function	Description
	keyboard. fSuccess contains true if this function is successful. hwndDesktop contains the desktop window handle (HWND_DESKTOP or other desktop window handle). abKeyStateTable is an array that contains a 256-byte table indexed by virtual key value. fSet sets the keyboard state from abKeyStateTable when set to TRUE. A value of FALSE copies the keyboard state into abKeyStateTable. You can retrieve the last error using WinGetLastError. These errors include:
	0x1001 PMERR_INVALID_HWND
fSuccess = WinSetLboxItemText (hwndLbox, sLboxIndx, pszText)	The WinSetLboxItemText function sets the text of the list box indexed item to a buffer. fSuccess contains true if this function is successful. hwndLbox contains the list box handle. sLboxIndx contains the index of the list box item. pszText contains a pointer to a null terminated string.
fSuccess = WinSetMenuItemText (hwndMenu, usId, pszText)	The WinSetMenuItemText function sets the text for menu indexed item to a buffer. fSuccess contains true if this function is successful. hwndMenu contains the menu handle. usId contains the menu item identifier. pszText contains a pointer to a null-terminated string.
fSuccess = WinSetMsgInterest (hwnd, ulMsgClass, lControl)	The WinSetMsgInterest function sets a window's message interest. fSuccess contains true if this function is successful. hwnd contains the window handle. ulMsgClass contains the message class. A value of SMIM_ALL sets all messages except for WM_QUIT if lControl is SMI_AUTODISPATCH or SMI_NOINTEREST. lControl contains the interest identifier for the message class. This includes: SMI_RESET, SMI_INTEREST, SMI_NOINTEREST, and SMI_AUTODISPATCH. You can retrieve the last error using WinGetLastError. These errors include:
	0x1001 PMERR_INVALID_HWND
fSuccess = WinSetMsgMode (hab, pszClassName, lControl)	The WinSetMsgMode function sets the mode for generating and processing messages for the private window class of an application. fSuccess contains true if this function is successful. hab contains the anchor block handle. pszClassName contains the window class name. lControl contains the message mode identifier, which includes: SMD_DELAYED and SMD_IMMEDIATE. You can retrieve the last error using WinGetLastError. These errors include:
	0x1001 PMERR_INVALID_HWND
fSuccess = WinSetMultWindowPos	The WinSetMultWindowPos function performs the WinSetWindowPos function for the specified number of

Function	Description
(hab, aSwp, cCount)	windows. It also uses an array of SWP structures; one for each window. All the windows must have the same parent. This function is more efficient than issuing multiple WinSetWindowPos calls. fSuccess contains true if this function is successful. hab contains the anchor block handle. aSwp contains an array of set window position (SWP) structures. cCount contains the number of windows you want to position (which corresponds to the number of elements in aSwp). You can retrieve the last error using WinGetLastError. These errors include: 0x1001　PMERR_INVALID_HWND 0x1019　PMERR_INVALID_FLAG
fSuccess = WinSetObjectData (hObject, pszSetupString)	The WinSetObjectData function sets data on a workplace object. fSuccess contains true if this function is successful. hObject contains a handle to the workplace object. pszSetupString contains a pointer to a null terminated string containing object specific parameters.
fSuccess = WinSetOwner (hwnd, hwndNewOwner)	The WinSetOwner function changes the owner window of the specified window. fSuccess contains true if this function is successful. hwnd contains the window handle. hwndNewOwner contains the handle of the new owner window (NULLHANDLE disowns the window). You can retrieve the last error using WinGetLastError. These errors include: 0x1001　PMERR_INVALID_HWND
fSuccess = WinSetParent (hwnd, hwndNewParent, fRedraw)	The WinSetParent function sets the parent for the specified window. fSuccess contains true if this function is successful. hwnd contains the window handle. hwndNewParent contains the handle of the new parent window. A value of HWND_DESKTOP turns the window into a main window. fRedraw forces a redraw of the window (if required) when set to TRUE. You can retrieve the last error using WinGetLastError. These errors include: 0x1001　PMERR_INVALID_HWND 0x1019　PMERR_INVALID_FLAG
fSuccess = WinSetPointer (hwndDesktop, hwndNewPointer)	The WinSetPointer function sets the desktop pointer handle. fSuccess contains true if this function is successful. hwndDesktop contains the desktop window handle (HWND_DESKTOP or other desktop window handle). hwndNewPointer contains the new pointer handle. A value of NULL removes the pointer from the screen. You can retrieve the last error using WinGetLastError. These errors include: 0x1001　PMERR_INVALID_HWND 0x101B　PMERR_INVALID_HPTR 0x205F　PMERR_INV_CURSOR_BITMAP

Table 3-43   **Continued**

Function	Description
fSuccess = WinSetPointerPos (hwndDesktop, IX, IY)	The WinSetPointerPos function sets the pointer position. fSuccess contains true if this function is successful. hwndDesktop contains the desktop window handle (HWND_DESKTOP or other desktop window handle). IX contains the X position of the pointer in screen coordinates. IY contains the Y position of the pointer in screen coordinates. You can retrieve the last error using WinGetLastError. These errors include: 0x1001 PMERR_INVALID_HWND
fSuccess = WinSetPresParam (hwnd, idAttrType, cbAttrValueLen, pAttrValue)	The WinSetPresParam function sets a presentation parameter for a window. fSuccess contains true if this function is successful. hwnd contains the window handle. idAttrType contains one of the system-defined presentation parameter attribute types or an application-defined attribute type. cbAttrValueLen contains the length of pAttrValue in bytes. pAttrValue contains the attribute value. You can retrieve the last error using WinGetLastError. These errors include: 0x1001 PMERR_INVALID_HWND
fSuccess = WinSetRect (hab, prclRect, ILeft, IBottom, IRight, ITop)	The WinSetRect function sets rectangle coordinates. fSuccess contains true if this function is successful. hab contains the anchor block handle. prclRect contains the coordinates of the rectangle you want to update. ILeft, IBottom, IRight, and ITop contain the new rectangle coordinates.
fSuccess = WinSetRectEmpty (hab, prclRect)	The WinSetRectEmpty function sets the coordinates of a rectangle to an empty rectangle. It is equivalent to a WinSetRect (hab, prclRect, 0, 0, 0, 0) call. fSuccess contains true if this function is successful. hab contains the anchor block handle. prclRect contains the rectangle coordinates.
fSuccess = WinSetSynchroMode (hab, IMode)	The WinSetSynchroMode function synchronizes the processing of messages in an application that uses a distributed message queue. fSuccess contains true if this function is successful. hab contains the anchor block handle. IMode contains the synchronization mode, which includes: SSM_SYNCHRONOUS, SSM_ASYNCHRONOUS, and SSM_MIXED.
fSuccess = WinSetSysColors (hwndDesktop, flOptions, ulFormat, IStart, ulTablen, alTable)	The WinSetSysColors function sets the system color values. It sends all main windows in the system a WM_SYSCOLORCHANGE message to indicate the change in color. After every main window receives this message, the system invalidates all windows. This allows the application to redraw them with the new colors. fSuccess contains true if this function is successful. hwndDesktop contains the desktop window handle (HWND_DESKTOP or other desktop window

Function	**Description**
	handle). flOptions contains the color options, which include: LCOL_RESET and LCOL_PURECOLOR. ulFormat contains the format of the table entries. This includes: LCOLF_INDRGB and LCOLF_CONSECRGB. lStart contains the starting color index. The color indexes in order include: SYSCLR_ENTRYFIELD, SYSCLR_MENUDISABLEDTEXT, SYSCLR_MENUHILITE, SYSCLR_MENUHILITBGND, SYSCLR_PAGEBACKGROUND, SYSCLR_FIELDBACKGROUND, SYSCLR_BUTTONLIGHT, SYSCLR_BUTTONMIDDLE, SYSCLR_BUTTONDARK, SYSCLR_BUTTONDEFAULT, SYSCLR_SHADOW, SYSCLR_ICONTEXT, SYSCLR_DIALOGBACKGROUND, SYSCLR_HILITEFOREGROUND, SYSCLR_HILITEBACKGROUND, SYSCLR_INACTIVETITLETEXTBKGD, SYSCLR_INACTIVETITLETEXT, SYSCLR_ACTIVETITLETEXT, SYSCLR_OUTPUTTEXT, SYSCLR_WINDOWSTATICTEXT, SYSCLR_SCROLLBAR, SYSCLR_BACKGROUND, SYSCLR_ACTIVETITLE, SYSCLR_INACTIVETITLE, SYSCLR_MENU, SYSCLR_WINDOW, SYSCLR_WINDOWFRAME, SYSCLR_MENUTEXT, SYSCLR_WINDOWTEXT, SYSCLR_TITLETEXT, SYSCLR_ACTIVEBORDER, SYSCLR_INACTIVEBORDER, SYSCLR_APPWORKSPACE, SYSCLR_HELPBACKGROUND, SYSCLR_HELPTEXT, SYSCLR_HELPHILITE, SYSCLR_SHADOWHILITEBGND, SYSCLR_SHADOWHILITEFGND, and SYSCLR_SHADOWTEXT. ulTablen contains the number of elements in alTable. alTable contains the start address of the application data area containing the color-table definition data. Each color value is a 4-byte entry that uses the following equation: (Red_Value × 65536) + (Green_Value × 256) + Blue_Value. The maximum intensity for each primary color is 255. You can retrieve the last error using WinGetLastError. These errors include:

0x1001 PMERR_INVALID_HWND
0x1003 PMERR_PARAMETER_OUT_OF_RANGE
0x1019 PMERR_INVALID_FLAG

fSuccess = WinSetSysModalWindow (hwndDesktop, hwnd)	The WinSetModalWindow function sets the system-modal window or ends the system-modal state. When input processing enters the system-modal state, all input gets directed to the system-modal window or one of its children. Input processing resumes its normal state when you destroy the system-modal window. fSuccess contains true if this function is successful. hwndDesktop contains the desktop window handle or HWND_DESKTOP. hwnd contains the window handle. A handle of NULLHANDLE ends the system-modal state and returns input processing to its normal state. You can retrieve the

Table 3-43   **Continued**

Function	**Description**
	last error using WinGetLastError. These errors include:
	0x1001 PMERR_INVALID_HWND
fSuccess = WinSetSysValue (hwndDesktop, lValueId, lValue)	The WinSetSysValue function sets a system value. fSuccess contains true if this function is successful. hwndDesktop contains the desktop window handle or HWND_DESKTOP. lValueid contains the system value identity, which includes: SV_CXSIZEBORDER, SV_CYSIZEBORDER, SV_SWAPBUTTON, SV_CURSORRATE, SV_DBLCLKTIME, SV_CXDBLCLK, SV_CYDBLCLK, SV_ALARM, SV_WARNINGFREQ, SV_WARNINGDURATION, SV_NOTEFREQ, SV_NOTEDURATION, SV_ERRORFREQ, SV_ERRORDURATION, SV_FIRSTSCROLLRATE, SV_SCROLLRATE, SV_SETLIGHTS, SV_INSERTMODE, SV_MENUROLLDOWNDELAY, SV_MENUROLLUPDELAY, and SV_PRINTSCREEN. lValue contains the system value. Use milliseconds for time and pels for dimensions. You can retrieve the last error using WinGetLastError. These errors include:
	0x1001 PMERR_INVALID_HWND 0x1003 PMERR_PARAMETER_OUT_OF_RANGE
fSuccess = WinSetWindowBits (hwnd, lb, flData, flMask)	The WindowSetWindowBits function sets a number of bits into the memory of the reserved window words. fSuccess contains true if this function is successful. hwnd contains the window handle. lb contains the zero-based index of the value you want to set. You can use any value from zero through (usExtra – 4). (usExtra is the WinRegisterClass parameter that defines the number of bytes available for application storage.) flData contains the bit data to store in the window words. flMask contains the bits to write indicator. A value of 1 indicates a bit that you want to write.
fSuccess = WinSetWindowPos (hwnd, hwndBehind, lX, lY, lCx, lCy, flOptions)	The WinSetWindowPos function sets the general positioning of a window. The window can receive messages from other processes or threads during the processing of this function. fSuccess contains true if this function is successful. hwnd contains the window handle. hwndBehind contains the relative window placement order, which includes: HWND_TOP, HWND_BOTTOM, or the handle of the sibling window. lX contains the X coordinate of the window position. lY contains the Y coordinate of the window position. lCx contains the window width in device units. lCy contains the window height in device units. flOptions contains the window positioning options. These options include: SWP_SIZE, SWP_MOVE, SWP_ZORDER, SWP_SHOW, SWP_HIDE, SWP_NOREDRAW, SWP_NOADJUST, SWP_ACTIVATE,

346

Function	Description
	SWP_DEACTIVATE, SWP_MINIMIZE, SWP_MAXIMIZE, and SWP_RESTORE. You can retrieve the last error using WinGetLastError. These errors include: 0x1001 PMERR_INVALID_HWND 0x1019 PMERR_INVALID_FLAG
fSuccess = WinSetWindowPtr (hwnd, lb, pp)	The WinSetWindowPtr function sets a pointer value into the memory of the reserved window words. fSuccess contains true if this function is successful. hwnd contains the window handle. lb contains the zero-based index of the value you want to set. You can use any value from zero through (usExtra – 4). (usExtra is the WinRegisterClass parameter that defines the number of bytes available for application storage.) pp contains the pointer value that you want to store in the window words. You can retrieve the last error using WinGetLastError. These errors include: 0x1001 PMERR_INVALID_HWND 0x1003 PMERR_PARAMETER_OUT_OF_RANGE
fResult = WinSetWindowText (hwnd, pszString)	The WinSetWindowText function sets the window text for the specified window. This function sends a WM_SETWINDOWPARAMS message to the window identified by hwnd. fResult contains true if this function is successful. hwnd contains the window handle. pszString contains the window text. You can retrieve the last error using WinGetLastError. These errors include: 0x1001 PMERR_INVALID_HWND
fSuccess = WinSetWindowThunkProc (hwnd, pthunkpr)	The WinSetWindowThunkProc function associates a pointer-conversion procedure with a window. fSuccess contains true if this function is successful. hwnd contains the window handle. pthunkpr contains a pointer to the pointer-conversion procedure identifier. A value of NULL disassociates any existing pointer-conversion procedure from this window.
fSuccess = WinSetWindowULong (hwnd, lb, ulValue)	The WinSetWindowULong function sets an unsigned long integer value into the memory of the reserved window words. hwnd contains the window handle. fSuccess contains true if this function is successful. lb contains a zero-based index of the pointer value that you want to set. The valid range is zero through (usExtra – 4). (usExtra is the WinRegisterClass parameter that defines the number of bytes available for application storage.) You also can use the following QWL values: QWL_HMQ, QWL_STYLE, QWL_HHEAP, QWL_FOCUSSAVE, QWL_USER, and QWL_DEFBUTTON. ulValue contains the value you want to place at the specified offset. You can retrieve the last error using WinGetLastError. These errors include:

Table 3-43   **Continued**

Function	Description
	0x1001 PMERR_INVALID_HWND 0x1003 PMERR_PARAMETER_OUT_OF_RANGE
fSuccess = WinSetWindowUShort (hwnd, lb, usValue)	The WinSetWindowUShort function sets an unsigned short integer value into the memory of the reserved window words. hwnd contains the window handle. fSuccess contains true if this function is successful. lb contains a zero-based index of the pointer value that you want to set. The valid range is zero through (usExtra − 4). (usExtra is the WinRegisterClass parameter that defines the number of bytes available for application storage.) You also can use the following QWS values: QWS_ID, QWS_FLAGS, QWS_RESULT, QWS_XRESTORE, QWS_YRESTORE, QWS_CXRESTORE, QWS_CYRESTORE, QWS_XMINIMIZE. ulValue contains the value that you want to place at the specified offset. You can retrieve the last error using WinGetLastError. These errors include: 0x1001 PMERR_INVALID_HWND 0x1003 PMERR_PARAMETER_OUT_OF_RANGE
fSuccess = WinShowCursor (hwnd, fShow)	The WinShowCursor function shows or hides the cursor associated with the specified window. fSuccess contains true if this function is successful. hwnd contains the window handle. fShow contains TRUE if you want to show the cursor. You can retrieve the last error using WinGetLastError. These errors include: 0x1001 PMERR_INVALID_HWND
fSuccess = WinShowPointer (hwndDesktop, fShow)	The WinShowPointer function shows or hides a pointer. fSuccess contains true if this function is successful. hwndDesktop contains the desktop window handle or HWND_DESKTOP. fShow contains TRUE if you want to show the pointer. You can retrieve the last error using WinGetLastError. These errors include: 0x1001 PMERR_INVALID_HWND
fSuccess = WinShowTrackRect (hwnd, fShow)	The WinShowTrackRect hides or shows the tracking rectangle. fSuccess contains true if this function is successful. hwnd contains the window handle. fShow contains TRUE if you want to show the tracking rectangle. You can retrieve the last error using WinGetLastError. These errors include: 0x1001 PMERR_INVALID_HWND
fSuccess = WinShowWindows (hwnd, fNewVisibility)	The WinShowWindows function sets the visibility state of a window. fSuccess contains true if this function is successful. hwnd contains the window handle. fNewVisibility contains TRUE if you want to make the window visible. You can retrieve

Function	Description
	the last error using WinGetLastError. These errors include:
	0x1001 PMERR_INVALID_HWND
fSuccess = WinShutdownSystem (hab, hmq)	The WinShutdownSystem function shuts the system down. fSuccess contains true if this function is successful. hab contains anchor block handle. hmq contains the message queue handle.
hApp = WinStartApp (hwndNotify, pDetails, pszParams, pReserved, ulOptions)	The WinStartApp function starts an application. hApp contains the application handle (NULL indicates that OS/2 did not start the application). hwndNotify contains the notification window handle. Use NULLHANDLE if you do not want OS/2 to post a notification message. pDetails contains a pointer to the program list structure. pszParams contains any parameters that you want to pass to the application. Use a value of NULL if you don't want to pass any parameters. pReserved is a reserved parameter, set it to 0. ulOptions contains the option indicators, which include: 0 (no options selected), SAF_INSTALLEDCMDLINE, and SAF_STARTCHILDAPP. You can retrieve the last error using WinGetLastError. These errors include:
	0x1200 PMERR_DOS_ERROR 0x1206 PMERR_INVALID_WINDOW 0x1208 PMERR_INVALID_PARAMETERS 0x1530 PMERR_INVALID_APPL 0x1532 PMERR_STARTED_IN_BACKGROUND
ulRet = WinStartTimer (hab, hwnd, idTimer, ulTimeout)	The WinStartTimer function starts a timer. The window created by this function sends out a WM_TIMER message each time the timer expires. hab contains the anchor block handle. hwnd contains the window handle. When you use a value of NULLHANDLE, OS/2 ignores the idTimer parameter and this function returns a unique non-zero identity that represents the timer. idTimer contains the timer identifier. ulTimeout contains the delay time in milliseconds. Using a value of 0 causes the timer to time-out as quickly as possible. This is usually an interval of $\frac{1}{18}$ second. You can retrieve the last error using WinGetLastError. These errors include:
	0x1001 PMERR_INVALID_HWND
fSuccess = WinStopTimer (hab, hwnd, ulTimer)	The WinStopTimer function stops a timer. fSuccess contains true if this function is successful. hab contains the anchor block handle. hwnd contains the window handle. ulTimer contains the timer identifier. You can retrieve the last error using WinGetLastError. These errors include:
	0x1001 PMERR_INVALID_HWND
fSuccess =	The WinStoreWindowPos function saves the current size and

Table 3-43

Continued

Function	Description
WinStoreWindowPos (pszAppName, pszKeyName, hwnd)	position of the specified window. It also saves the presentation parameters. fSuccess contains true if this function is successful. pszAppName contains the application name. pszKeyName contains the key name. hwnd contains the window handle.
pOldWindowProc = WinSubclassWindow (hwnd, pNewWindowProc)	The WinSubclassWindow function subclasses the specified window by replacing its window procedure with another window procedure. pOldWindowProc contains a pointer to the previous window procedure (0 indicates an error). hwnd contains the window handle. pNewWindowProc contains a pointer to the window procedure used to subclass the window. You can retrieve the last error using WinGetLastError. These errors include: 0x1001 PMERR_INVALID_HWND
lDestRet = WinSubstituteStrings (hwnd, pszSrc, lDestMax, pszDest)	The WinSubstituteStrings function replaces specific marker characters (%n, where n is a number) in a string with text supplied by the application. A value of %% places a "%" in the destination string without substitution. lDestRet contains the actual number of characters returned (0 indicates an error). hwnd contains the window handle. pszSrc contains the source string. lDestMax contains the size of pszDest. pszDest contains the destination string. You can retrieve the last error using WinGetLastError. These errors include: 0x1001 PMERR_INVALID_HWND
fNonempty = WinSubtractRect (hab, prclDest, prclSrc1, prclSrc2)	The WinSubtractRect function subtracts one rectangle from another. Because the subtraction does not always result in a rectangular area, this function provides only an approximation of the subtraction. When this occurs, it always returns a resultant rectangle that is larger than the true subtraction result. While this function is much faster than GpiCombineRegion, the GpiCombineRegion function always returns the true result of the subtraction. fNonempty contains true if the rectangle is not empty. hab contains the anchor block handle. prclDest contains the resultant rectangle. prclSrc1 and prclSrc2 contain the source rectangles.
ulRetCode = WinSwitchToProgram (hswitchSwitch)	The WinSwitchToProgram function makes a specific program the active program. Only the current foreground application can use this call. ulRetCode contains the return code. This includes the following values: 0 (successful completion), INV_SWITCH_LIST_ENTRY_HANDLE, and NOT_PERMITTED_TO_CAUSE_SWITCH. hswitchSwitch contains the Window List entry handle of the program you want to activate. You can retrieve the last error using

Function	Description
	WinGetLastError. These errors include: 0x1202 PMERR_INVALID_SWITCH_HANDLE
fTerminated = WinTerminate (hab)	The WinTerminate function terminates an application thread's use of the PM and releases all of its resources. Always destroy all windows and message queues and return any cached presentation spaces to the cache before issuing this call. fTerminated contains TRUE if the application successfully terminated. hab contains the anchor block handle.
fTerminated = WinTerminateApp (happ)	The WinTerminateApp function terminates an application started using the WinStartApp function using the SAF_STARTCHILDAPP option. fTerminated contains TRUE if the application successfully terminated. happ contains the application handle. You can retrieve the last error using WinGetLastError. These errors include: 0x1533 PMERR_INVALID_HAPP 0x1534 PMERR_CANNOT_STOP
fSuccess = WinTrackRect (hwnd, hps, ptiTrackinfo)	The WinTrackRect function draws a tracking rectangle. fSuccess contains true if this function is successful. hwnd contains the window handle or HWND_DESKTOP. hps contains the presentation space handle. A value of NULLHANDLE assumes that tracking takes place within hwnd and that you did not use the WS_CLIPCHILDREN window style. ptiTrackinfo contains the track information. You can retrieve the last error using WinGetLastError. These errors include: 0x1001 PMERR_INVALID_HWND
fSuccess = WinTranslateAccel (hab, hwnd, haccelAccel, pQmsg)	The WinTranslateAccel function translates a WM_CHAR message in the accelerator table. If haccelAccel contains NULL, then OS/2 assumes that you want to use the current table. fSuccess contains true if this function is successful. hab contains the anchor block handle. hwnd contains the window handle. haccelAccel contains the accelerator table handle. pQmsg contains the message that you want to translate. You can retrieve the last error using WinGetLastError. These errors include: 0x1001 PMERR_INVALID_HWND 0x101A PMERR_INVALID_HACCEL
fNonempty = WinUnionRect (hab, prclDesk, prclSrc1, prclSrc2)	The WinUnionRect function calculates a rectangle that bounds the two source rectangles. fNonempty contains true if the rectangle is not empty. hab contains the anchor block handle. prclDest contains the resultant rectangle. prclSrc1 and prclSrc2 contain the source rectangles.
fSuccess =	The WinUpdateWindow function forces an update of a window

Table 3-43   **Continued**

Function	Description
WinUpdateWindow (hwnd)	and its associated child windows. fSuccess contains true if this function is successful. hwnd contains the window handle. You can retrieve the last error using WinGetLastError. These errors include: 0x1001 PMERR_INVALID_HWND
ulRetLen = WinUpper (hab, ulCodePage, ulCountry, pszString)	The WinUpper function converts a string to uppercase. ulRetLen contains the length of the converted string. hab contains the anchor block handle. ulCodePage contains the codepage identifier. Use 0 if you want to use the current process code page. ulCountry contains the country code. Use 0 if you want to use the default country code in CONFIG.SYS. pszString contains the string that you want to convert. You can retrieve the last error using WinGetLastError. These errors include: 0x100B PMERR_INVALID_STRING_PARM
ulOutChar = WinUpperChar (hab, ulCodePage, ulCountry, ulInChar)	The WinUpperChar function translates a character to uppercase. ulOutChar contains the converted character (0 indicates an error). hab contains the anchor block handle. ulCodePage contains the codepage identifier. Use 0 if you want to use the current process code page. ulCountry contains the country code. Use 0 if you want to use the default country code in CONFIG.SYS. ulInChar contains the character you want to convert. You can retrieve the last error using WinGetLastError. These errors include: 0x100B PMERR_INVALID_STRING_PARM
fSuccess = WinValidateRect (hwnd, prclRect, fIncludeClippedChildren)	The WinValidateRect function subtracts a rectangle from the update region of an asynchronous paint window. It marks the part of the window that is visually valid. Do not use this function for CS_SYNCPAINT windows. fSuccess contains true if this function is successful. hwnd contains the window handle. prclRect contains the coordinates of the rectangle that you want to subtract from the window's update region. fIncludeClippedChildren contains TRUE if you want to include the descendants of hwnd in the valid rectangle. You can retrieve the last error using WinGetLastError. These errors include: 0x1001 PMERR_INVALID_HWND 0x1019 PMERR_INVALID_FLAG
fSuccess = WinValidateRegion (hwnd, hrgn, fIncludeClippedChildren)	The WinValidateRect function subtracts a region from the update region of an asynchronous paint window. It marks the part of the window that is visually valid. Do not use this function for CS_SYNCPAINT windows. fSuccess contains true if this

Function	Description
	function is successful. hwnd contains the window handle. hrgn contains the handle of the region that you want to subtract from the window's update region. fIncludeClippedChildren contains TRUE if you want to include the descendants of hwnd in the valid rectangle. You can retrieve the last error using WinGetLastError. These errors include: 0x1001 PMERR_INVALID_HWND 0x1019 PMERR_INVALID_FLAG 0x2034 PMERR_HRGN_BUSY
ulRc = WinWaitEventSem (hev, ulTimeout)	The WinWaitEventSem function waits for OS/2 to post an event semaphore or for a PM message. ulRc contains one of the following return codes: NO_ERROR (0), ERROR_INVALID_HANDLE (6), ERROR_NOT_ENOUGH_MEMORY (8), ERROR_INTERRUPT (95), or ERROR_TIMEOUT (640). hev contains the event semaphore handle. ulTimeout contains the timeout in milliseconds. You also can use a value of 0 to indicate an immediate return or −1 to indicate an indefinite wait.
ulRc = WinWaitMuxWaitSem (hmux, ulTimeout, pUser)	The WinWaitMuxWaitSem function waits for a muxwait semaphore to clear or for a PM message. ulRc contains one of the following return codes: NO_ERROR (0), ERROR_INVALID_HANDLE (6), ERROR_NOT_ENOUGH_MEMORY (8), ERROR_INVALID_PARAMETER (87), ERROR_INTERRUPT (95), or ERROR_TOO_MANY_SEM_REQUESTS (103), ERROR_SEM_OWNER_DIED (105), ERROR_EMPTY_MUXWAIT (286), ERROR_MUTEX_DIED (287), ERROR_WRONG_TYPE (292), ERROR_TIMEOUT (640). hmux contains the muxwait semaphore handle. ulTimeout contains the timeout in milliseconds. You also can use a value of 0 to indicate an immediate return or −1 to indicate an indefinite wait. pUser contains a pointer to receive the user field from the muxwait semaphore data structure of the semaphore that you posted or released.
fSuccess = WinWaitMsg (hab, ulFirst, ulLast)	The WinWaitMsg function waits for a filtered message. fSuccess contains true if this function is successful. hab contains the anchor block handle. ulFirst contains the first message identity. ulLast contains the last message identity.
hwnd = WinWindowFromDC (hdc)	The WinWindowFromDC contains the handle of the window corresponding to a particular device context. hwnd contains the window handle (NULLHANDLE indicates an error). hdc contains the device context handle.
hwnd = WinWindowFromID (hwndParent, ulIdentifier)	The WinWindowFromID function returns the handle of the child window with the specified identity. hwnd contains the window handle (NULLHANDLE indicates an error). hwndParent

Table 3-43   **Continued**

Function	**Description**
	contains the parent window handle. ulIdentifier contains the child window identifier. You can retrieve the last error using WinGetLastError. These errors include: 0x1001 PMERR_INVALID_HWND
hwndFound = WinWindowFromPoint (hwndParent, pptlPoint, fEnumChildren)	The WinWindowFromPoint function finds the window below a specified point. This is the descendent of the specified window. hwndFound contains the handle of the window beneath pptlPoint (NULLHANDLE indicates that pptlPoint is outside hwndParent). If this function returns the parent's handle, then the point lies outside any of the children associated with hwndParent. hwndParent contains the parent window handle or HWND_DESKTOP. pptlPoint contains the point that you want to test. fEnumChildren contains TRUE if you want to test all the descendent windows including child windows of child windows. You can retrieve the last error using WinGetLastError. These errors include: 0x1001 PMERR_INVALID_HWND

Keyboard and mouse API

CHAPTER 4

INTERACTING with the user is one of the main parts of any application in any environment. If you can't receive user input and react to it, there is no reason to run the application (unless this is a device driver or a background application). This fact doesn't change if you program in DOS or OS/2. Of course, there are differences. The principles of receiving input between the two environments are completely different. An OS/2 application must cope with many variables that a DOS application does not even need to recognize. How do you know that the current input is meant for your application? What do you need to do to interact with both the mouse and the keyboard? These are the questions that the OS/2 programmer must ask. This chapter provides many of the answers the programmer needs. It doesn't matter if you want to write a device driver, a character-mode application, or an application that works with the Workplace Shell (WPS).

This chapter describes the mouse and keyboard application programming interface (API) provided by OS/2. This does include user input; it does not include output of this information. Chapter 3 dealt with fonts and the methods that you use to display them. Think of this chapter as the input side of the issues dealt with in chapter 3. There are three main sections in this chapter: device driver programming, keyboard interface, and mouse interface.

The device driver section assumes that you want to write a "ring 2" device driver application. This section looks at the DOSDevIOCtl functions. You might need to write a special adapter for a unique keyboard or your application might need to address the needs of input in more than one language. Whatever your needs, this section looks at the tools OS/2 provides to help interpret user input.

The other two sections view programming from the business application viewpoint. This includes both the KBD and MOU functions. Because OS/2 does not allow direct hardware manipulation by "ring 3" applications, the programmer must use the tools supplied by the operating system. This chapter also assumes that you want to program for the WPS. (The text will note whether the reader can use a particular call for character and graphics mode applications.) A unique aspect of this section is that many of the calls that you see will work with "Family API" (FAPI) applications as well as standard OS/2 applications. This is a special class of application that allows you to run under DOS or OS/2. See the VIO functions in chapter 3 for a list of functions that allow you to provide output in a FAPI as well as input.

 DOSDevIOCtl functions

The DOSDevIOCtl "functions" all relate to the same OS/2 function call. This function provides an expandable IOCtl facility that allows you to support anything that OS/2 did not build in as part of the operating system kernel. It is very generic in nature, much like the DOS software interrupt system. In many respects, this is the closest that you ever come to programming in the DOS environment under OS/2. This "one call" approach contains the following function elements:

```
rc = DOSDevIOCtl (hDevHandle, ulCategory, ulFunction, pParmList,
ulParmLengthMax, pParmLengthInOut, pDataArea, ulDataLengthMax,
pDataLengthInOut)
```

The function provides only one return value. rc contains a return code that tells you if the function completed without error. It also contains an error code if it didn't. Table 4-1 provides a list of these error codes.

DOSDevIOCtl function return codes   Table 4-1

Error Number	Description
0	NO_ERROR
1	ERROR_INVALID_FUNCTION
6	ERROR_INVALID_HANDLE
15	ERROR_INVALID_DRIVE
31	ERROR_GEN_FAILURE
87	ERROR_INVALID_PARAMETER
111	ERROR_BUFFER_OVERFLOW
115	ERROR_PROTECTION_VIOLATION
117	ERROR_INVALID_CATEGORY
119	ERROR_BAD_DRIVER_LEVEL
163	ERROR_UNCERTAIN_MEDIA
165	ERROR_MONITORS_NOT_SUPPORTED

As you can see, there are more than a few parameters that you need to consider as well. There are three groups of parameters: call definition, parameter area parameters, and data area parameters. Each parameter group performs a different function as detailed in the paragraphs that follow.

NOTE OS/2 Version 1.0 and 1.1 device drivers do not understand generic IOCtl packets. As a result, the kernel does not pass the ulDataLengthMax, pDataLengthInOut, ulParmLengthMax, and pParmLengthInOut parameters to the device driver. You must mark device drivers level 2 or higher to support receipt of these fields.

The first group of parameters define the DOSDevIOCtl function call itself. hDevHandle contains a device handle returned by a DosOpen call or a standard (open) device handle. ulCategory contains the device category in the range from 0 to 255. Table 4-2 provides a list of typical device categories. Your computer setup might or might not provide other categories. A search of vendor documentation, the INI files on your hard drive, and some debugging of the device driver itself usually yields the category information for these devices. You also can look at the OS/2 2.x Physical Device Reference published by IBM. ulFunction contains a device specific function code in the range from 0 to 255. As with the category entry, you can find additional functions by looking through the vendor documentation, the INI files on your system, or the device driver itself. Table 4-3 provides a list of common function areas. You OR the required areas together to obtain the tens part of a function number. As you can see, all three of these parameters require an intimate knowledge of the device driver that you want to access and the device that you want to use.

Table 4-2   **DOSDevIOCtl typical categories**

Category	Device
0x0001	Serial device
0x0003	Video/screen/pointer draw control
0x0004	Keyboard
0x0005	Printer
0x0006	Light-pen (Reserved)

Category	Device
0x0007	Pointing-device (mouse)
0x0008	Disk/diskette
0x0009	Physical-disk control
0x000A	Character-monitor control
0x000B	General device control

DOSDevIOCtl typical function areas   Table 4-3

Function Area	Description
0x0020	Set this bit to retrieve data or information from the device. If you do not use this code (the bit is set to zero), then OS/2 sends information or data to the device.
0x0040	Set this bit to pass the command to the device driver. If you do not set this bit, the operating system kernel intercepts the command. (You must set this bit for most generic I/O operations.)
0x0080	Set this bit if you want the device driver to ignore any commands that it does not support. If you do not set this bit, the device driver always returns an error code if it does not support the command. (You do not set this bit for most generic I/O operations.)

There are three parameter area parameters. Each one defines a different part of the input process. pParmList contains the address of the command-specific argument list. ulParmLengthMax contains the maximum output length of pParmList in bytes. This is not the actual length of pParmList for both input and output. pParmLengthInOut contains a pointer to the actual length of pParmList. This value can exceed ulParmLengthMax on input, but not on output. If this function returns ERROR_BUFFER_OVERFLOW, then pParmLengthInOut contains the size of the buffer needed to hold the return parameters. A NULL value for pParmList tells OS/2 that there is no data area defined for this call. OS/2 automatically ignores the DataLengthMax and DataLengthInOut parameters.

There are three data area parameters. pDataArea contains the data area address. ulDataLengthMax contains the maximum output length of pDataArea in bytes. This is not the actual length of pDataArea for input and output. pDataLengthInOut contains the actual length of

pDataArea in bytes. The value of this parameter can exceed ulDataLengthMax on input, but not output. If this function returns ERROR_BUFFER_OVERFLOW, then pDataLengthInOut contains the size of the buffer needed to hold the return data. A NULL value for pDataArea tells OS/2 that there is no parameter list defined for this call. OS/2 automatically ignores the ParmLengthMax and ParmListInOut parameters.

OS/2 provides a number of default device driver functions that you can access using this function. Of course, your specific computer configuration provides even more opportunities to use it. It always pays to search the vendor documentation and the INI files on your system. You might want to check the device drivers themselves for additional information (provided the software licensing agreement does not prevent this action).

The Borland compiler provides access to these functions through the BSEDEV.H and BSEDOS.H include files. The BSEDEV.H file contains the entries that you need to actually use the DOSDevIOCtl function. The BSEDOS.H file contains the DOSDevIOCtl function declaration. Both files provide interesting bits of information. You might need to check the include files for your compiler to find references to these functions because most vendors do not document them. In some cases, the vendor uses a new name for the function. Fortunately, most vendors include a file with #defines that allow you to use the original names. Table 4-4 provides a complete list of the keyboard, mouse, and generic DOSDevIOCtl functions.

Table 4-4   **DOSDevIOCtl generic functions**

Function	Name	Description
Video, screen, and pointer draw control (Category 3)		
0x0070	Allocate an LDT Selector	This function allocates an LDT selector. The Screen device driver grants read/write access to any data area completely within the 0xA0000 to 0xBFFFF data range. It also grants read-only access to the areas between 0x00000 and 0xFFFFF. You cannot request access to any areas outside these ranges. The input parameter information includes: 32-bit physical address (DWORD) and data area length (WORD). The output data information includes an LDT selector (WORD).

Function	Name	Description
0x0071	Deallocate an LDT Selector	This function deallocates an LDT selector that you allocated using function 0x0070. The input parameter information includes an LDT selector (WORD). There is no data information.
0x0072	Query Pointer Draw Address	This function returns the pointer draw address. The mouse routine uses this address to update the pointer image on screen. There is no parameter information. The output data information includes: return code (WORD), pointer draw routine entry point (DWORD, selector:offset), and pointer draw routine data segment (WORD).
0x0073	Initialize Call Vector Table	This function initializes the Call Vector Table. There is no parameter information. The output data information includes the far address of the call vector table (DWORD).
0x0074	ABIOS Pass-Through	This function passes an ABIOS request block to Unit 0 of the video device opened by SCREEN$. It returns the request block to the caller when the function completes. OS/2 copies the parameter packet to the 64-byte work area used as an ABIOS request block. It overwrites the LID and UNIT fields with the logical ID of the ABIOS video device opened by SCREEN$ and Unit 0. The input and output parameter information includes an ABIOS request block. There is no data packet information.
0x0075	Allocate an LDT Selector with Offset	This function allocates an LDT selector with offset. The Screen device driver grants read/write access to any data area completely within the 0xA0000 to 0xBFFFF data range. It also grants read-only access to the areas between 0x00000 and 0xFFFFF. You cannot request access to any areas outside these ranges. The input parameter information includes: 32-bit physical address (DWORD) and data area length (WORD). The output data information includes: offset with new LDT selector (WORD) and LDT selector (WORD).
0x0076	Allocate an LDT Selector with Back Ground Validation Options	This function allocates an LDT selector with background validation options. The Screen device driver grants access plus a 16-bit option value to customize the allocated memory to any data area completely within the 0xA0000 to 0xBFFFF data range. It also grants read-only access to the areas between 0x00000 and 0xFFFFF. You cannot request access to any areas outside these ranges. The input parameter information includes: 32-bit physical address (DWORD), data area length (WORD), and an option (WORD). The output data information includes an LDT selector (WORD). The options include the following values:

Value   **Description**

0   Make the segment readable code without background validation.

Table 4-4   **Continued**

Function	Name	Description

Value **Description**

1   Make the segment writable data without background validation.

2   Free the selector.

3   Make the segment readable IOPL code.

4   Make the segment read/write IOPL data.

Keyboard (Category 4)

0x0050   Set Code   The function changes the device driver resident code page
         Page   for the system and updates the zero entry of the Code Page
                    Control Block. The input parameter information includes the
                    Code Page Translation Table. There is no data information.
                    The Code Page Translation Table contains the following
                    elements:

         Code Page | Offset | Length | Description |
         Translation |--------|--------|-------------|
         Table

         XHeader | 00h | 2 | usXTableId contains the code page number. |

         | 02h | 2 | fXTableFlags1 contains bits that represent the following information: use Shift–Alt instead of Ctrl–Alt (0), use the left Alt key as Alt-Graphics (1), use the right Alt key as Alt-Graphics (2), treat the Caps Lock key as the Shift–Lock key (3), default table for the language (4), toggle the Shift–Lock key when set to 1 (5), pass on accent keys and beep when set to 1 (6), Caps–Shift uses CHAR5 entry (7), machine dependent table (8), reserved (9-15). |

         | 04h | 2 | fXTableFlags2 is a reserved word; set it to 0. |

         | 06h | 2 | usKbdType contains the type of keyboard installed on the host machine. |

         | 08h | 2 | usKbdSubType is a reserved word; set it to 0. |

         | 0Ah | 2 | usXTableLen contains the length of the table. |

         | 0Ch | 2 | usEntryCount contains the number of KeyDef entries. |

Function	Name	Description		
		Offset	**Length**	**Description**
		0Eh	2	usEntryWidth contains the width of the KeyDef entries.
		10h	2	usCountry contains the language identifier.
		12h	2	usTableTypeID contains the type identifier The first byte contains the type identifier. The second byte contains the subtype identifier. OS/2 uses a default of 0x0100.
		14h	4	ulSubCountryID contains the sub-language identifier.
		18h	16	Reserved, set these words to 0.
	KeyDef[1]	3Ah	2	usXlatOp is a record that contains the accent flags (AccentFlags) in the first 7 bits and the key type (KeyType) in the next 9 bits. The AccentFlags field determines how OS/2 translates a standard key into its accented version. The KeyType field determines how OS/2 treats the key when used with various shift keys. There are different key types and each type receives different treatment. The following list includes the various key types: alpha key (01h), non-alpha special key (02h), non-alpha special key with Caps Lock (03h), non-alpha special key with Alt (04h), non-alpha special key with Caps Lock and Alt, function key (06h), pad key (07h), special Ctrl key (08h), PrtSc (09h), SysReq (0Ah), accent key (also known as a dead key) (0Bh), Shift key (0Ch), toggle key (like Caps Lock) (0Dh), Alt key (0Eh), Num Lock (0Fh), Caps Lock (10h), Scroll Lock (11h), extended Shift key (12h), extended toggle key (13h), special key with Ctrl and Shift (14h), special key with Alt and Shift (15h), extended key (1Ah), and reserved for the extended key except 1Ah (16h to 1FFh).
		3Ch	1	The value of charCHAR1 depends on the usKbdType entry.

[1]The Code Page Translation Table normally contains 127 KeyDef entries. This table assumes that you provided the entire 127 entries. The offset of the AccentTbl entry depends on this assumption.

Table 4-4 **Continued**

Function	Name	Description		
		Offset	**Length**	**Description**
		3Dh	1	The value of charCHAR2 depends on the usKbdType entry.
		3Eh	1	The value of charCHAR3 depends on the usKbdType entry.
		3Fh	1	The value of charCHAR4 depends on the usKbdType entry.
		40h	1	The value of charCHAR5 depends on the usKbdType entry.
	AccentTable[2]	3B3h	322	Seven 46-byte accent entries (AccentEntry). Each field represents one flag in the AccentFlag field of the usXlatOp entry. Each AccentEntry element contains the following fields: NonAccent (2 bytes), CtlAccent (2 bytes), AltAccent (2 bytes), Map 1 through 20 (2 bytes each)
0x0051	Set Input Mode	This function passes the current input mode to the Keyboard device driver. This driver maintains a separate entry for each session. You can retrieve this information using function 0x0071, 0x0074, or 0x0075. The default input mode is ASCII. The input parameter information contains Mode (BYTE). There are 3 modes as follow: 1xxxxxx1b (1 shift report), 0xxxxxx0b (ASCII mode), and 1xxxxxxxb (BINARY mode). There is no data information. This function returns the following error codes: 0x810C GENERAL_FAILURE 0x8113 INVALID_PARAMETER		
0x0052	Set Interim Character Flags	This function passes the current interim character flags to the Keyboard device driver. This driver maintains a separate entry for each session. The parameter information includes Flag (BYTE). The Flag field contains the following flags: reserved (bits 0 through 4), program requested on-the-spot conversion (bit 5), reserved (bit 6), and interim console flag on (bit 7). Set all reserved bits to 0. There is no data information. This function returns the following error code: 0x8113 INVALID_PARAMETER		
0x0053	Set Shift State	This function sets the current shift state of the keyboard. The Keyboard device driver maintains a separate shift state for each logical keyboard. The function overrides the shift state set by previous shift keystrokes; it does not affect subsequent		

[2] There are seven AccentTable entries; one for each accent table bit.

Function	Name	Description
		shift keystrokes. The parameter information includes: shift state (WORD) and NLS (BYTE). The shift state bits contain the following information: right Shift key down (0), left Shift key down (1), either Ctrl key down (2), either Alt key down (3), Scroll Lock on (4), Num Lock on (5), Caps Lock on (6), insert on (7), left Ctrl key down (8), left Alt key down (9), right Ctrl key down (10), right Alt key down (11), Scroll Lock key down (12), Num Lock key down (13), Caps Lock key down (14), and SysReq key down (15). The NLS field contains the NLS shift status. There is no data information.
0x0054	Set Typematic Rate And Display	This function sets the keyboard typematic rate and delay. The input parameter information includes: typematic delay in milliseconds (WORD) and typematic rate in characters per second (WORD). There is no data information.
0x0056	Set Session Manager Hot Key	The Session Manager uses this call to set a list of up to 16 keyboard hot keys. The physical Keyboard device driver searches this list and acts on each one the user types. The hot keys set by this function affect every OS/2 session. You can specify a variety of hot key combinations using shift flags and scan codes. This allows for key combinations like Ctrl–Esc. The input parameter information includes: state (WORD), make scan code (BYTE), break scan code (BYTE), and hot key identifier (WORD). The state bits contain the following information: right Shift key down (0), left Shift key down (1), reserved (2 through 7), left Ctrl key down (8), left Alt key down (9), right Ctrl key down (10), right Alt key down (11), and reserved (12 through 15). You cannot use the reserved value of 0xFFFF for the hot key identifier. There is no data information. This function returns the following error codes: 0x8103 BAD_COMMAND 0x8113 INVALID_PARAMETER
0x0057	Set KCB	This function binds the specified logical keyboard (KCB) to the physical keyboard for this session. You must not issue this call within the PM session. The input parameter information includes the KCB handle (WORD). The default handle is 0. There is no data information. This function returns the following error codes: 0x8103 BAD_COMMAND 0x810C GENERAL_FAILURE
0x0058	Set Code Page Number	This function sets the code page translation table used by the current KCB. You can call this function within a DOS session. The input parameter information includes: code page number (WORD) and code page layer (WORD). There are two code page layers: primary (0) and secondary (1). There is no data information. This function returns the following error codes:

Table 4-4   **Continued**

Function	Name	Description
		0x810C GENERAL_FAILURE 0x8113 INVALID_PARAMETER
0x0059	Set Read/ Peak Notification	This function sets the read/peak notification. It sets the DDFlags of a key packet. This instructs the keyboard device driver to send a special monitor packet down the monitor chain. The packet appears as part of every Read request seen by the physical Keyboard device driver. It continues until you terminate the screen group or disable it by calling this function again. The Keyboard device driver saves the PID of the first caller of this function. Use of this function by another PID results in an error. The parameter information includes: session number that you want to enable or disable (WORD) and read/peak notification flags (WORD). The read/peak flag bits include: enable read/peak notification when set to 1 (0) and reserved (1 through 15). There is no data information. This function returns the following error codes: 0x8103 BAD_COMMAND 0x8113 INVALID_PARAMETER
0x005A	Alter Keyboard LEDs	This function alters the keyboard LEDs without changing the keyboard's mode of scan generation. Only PM can call this function. In addition, this function will not change the LED status on 88/89 key enhanced keyboards. The parameter information includes the state of each LED (WORD). These status bits include: Scroll Lock (0), Num Lock (1), Caps Lock (2), and reserved (3 through 15). Setting the bit to 1 turns the LED on. There is no data information. This function returns the following error codes: 0x8103 BAD_COMMAND 0x8113 INVALID_PARAMETER
0x005C	Set NLS and Custom Code Page	This function sets the National Language Support (NLS) and custom code page. It installs one of two possible Code Page Translation tables into the device driver and updates the number 1 or 2 entry of the Code Page Control Block. A DOS session can call this function. The parameter information includes: Code Page Translation Table pointer (DWORD), code page number (WORD), and index to load (WORD). There are two standard code page indexes (1 or 2). Using a value of −1 indicates that you want to load a custom code page (not valid from a DOS session). There is no data information. This function returns the following error codes: 0x810C GENERAL_FAILURE 0x8113 INVALID_PARAMETER

Function	Name	Description
0x005D	Create a New Logical Keyboard	This function creates a new logical keyboard. Use either the default code page or one of the two optional code pages listed in CONFIG.SYS as the desired initial code page. You cannot use this function within a PM application. The input parameter information includes: the new logical keyboard KCB handle obtained with DosOpenHandle (WORD) and the initial code page to use with the new logical keyboard (WORD). There is no data information. This function returns the following error codes:

0x8103 BAD_COMMAND
0x810C GENERAL_FAILURE
0x8113 INVALID_PARAMETER

Function	Name	Description
0x005E	Destroy a Logical Keyboard	This function destroys an existing logical keyboard. You cannot call this function from a PM application. The input parameter information includes the logical keyboard handle (WORD). Use a value of zero for the default keyboard. There is no data information. This function returns the following error code:

0x810C GENERAL_FAILURE

Function	Name	Description
0x0071	Query Input Mode	This function returns the input mode of the session of the currently active process. There is no parameter information. The output data information includes the mode (BYTE). The default input mode is ASCII. The input parameter information contains Mode (BYTE). There are three modes as follow: 1xxxxxx1b (1 shift report), 0xxxxxx0b (ASCII mode), and 1xxxxxxxb (BINARY mode).
0x0072	Query Interim Character Flags	This function returns the interim character flags maintained by the physical Keyboard device driver. There is no parameter information. The data information includes Flag (BYTE). The Flag field contains the following flags: reserved (bits 0 through 4), program requested on-the-spot conversion (bit 5), reserved (bit 6), and interim console flag on (bit 7).
0x0073	Query Shift State	This function returns the shift state of the session of the currently active process. There is no parameter information. The data information includes: shift state (WORD) and NLS (BYTE). The shift state bits contain the following information: right Shift key down (0), left Shift key down (1), either Ctrl key down (2), either Alt key down (3), Scroll Lock on (4), Num Lock on (5), Caps Lock on (6), insert on (7), left Ctrl key down (8), left Alt key down (9), right Ctrl key down (10), right Alt key down (11), Scroll Lock key down (12), Num Lock key down (13), Caps Lock key down (14), and SysReq key down (15). The NLS field contains the NLS shift status.
0x0074	Read Character Data Records	This function returns one or more character data records from the keyboard input buffer (KIB) for the session

Table 4-4   **Continued**

Function	Name	Description
		of the currently active process. If you set shift report on, then the CharData record might contain a shift state change in place of a character. You cannot use this function within a PM session. The input parameter information includes the record transfer count (WORD). If you set this value to 0, then the function waits for the number of keystrokes that you request. A value of 1 causes the function to return immediately. The input/output data information includes the CharData record (10 bytes). The CharData fields include: ASCII character code (UCHAR), ASCII scan code (the numeric value of the character) (UCHAR), state of the keystroke event (Status) (UCHAR), reserved (UCHAR), the shift key status (WORD), and the time the user pressed the key in milliseconds since the system was started (ULONG). The Status field contains the shift status in bit 0 (if set to 1 the shift status returned without a character). Bit 1 contains a 0 if the scan code is a character. Bits 2 through 4 are reserved. Bit 5 requests immediate conversion when set to 1. Bits 6 and 7 contain the following information: 00—undefined, 01—final character with interim character turned off, 10—interim character, and 11—final character with interim character flag turned on. The shift status bits contain the following information: right Shift key down (0), left Shift key down (1), either Ctrl key down (2), either Alt key down (3), Scroll Lock on (4), Num Lock on (5), Caps Lock on (6), insert on (7), left Ctrl key down (8), left Alt key down (9), right Ctrl key down (10), right Alt key down (11), Scroll Lock key down (12), Num Lock key down (13), Caps Lock key down (14), and SysReq key down (15). This function returns the following error codes:
		0x8103 BAD_COMMAND 0x8111 CHAR_CALL_INTERRUPTED 0x8113 INVALID_PARAMETER
0x0075	Peek Character Data Record	This function returns one CharData record from the head of the keyboard input buffer (KIB) for the session of the currently active process. It does not remove the record from the KIB. If you set shift report on, then the CharData record might contain a shift state change in place of a character. You cannot use this function within a PM session. The parameter information includes the KIB status (WORD). Bit 0 contains 1 if the KIB contained a record. Bit 7 contains 1 if the current input mode is binary. The data information contains the CharData record (see function 0x0074 for further details). This function returns the following error codes:

Function	Name	Description
		0x8103 BAD_COMMAND 0x8111 CHAR_CALL_INTERRUPTED 0x8113 INVALID_PARAMETER
0x0076	Query Session Manager Hot Key	This function returns the scan code the physical Keyboard device driver uses for the Session Manager hot key. The parameter information includes the type of information to return (WORD). A value of 0 returns the maximum number of hot keys supported by the physical Keyboard device driver. A value of 1 returns the hot keys. The data information includes: state (WORD), make scan code (BYTE), break scan code (BYTE), and hot key identifier (WORD). The state bits contain the following information: right Shift key down (0), left Shift key down (1), reserved (2 through 7), left Ctrl key down (8), left Alt key down (9), right Ctrl key down (10), right Alt key down (11), and reserved (12 through 15). This function returns the following error code: 0x8113 INVALID_PARAMETER
0x0077	Query KeyboardType	This function returns the keyboard type. The 101- and 102-key enhanced, 88- and 89-key enhanced, 122-key enhanced, and MF1 keyboards returns a value of 01h to indicate their enhanced status. There is no parameter information. The output data information includes: keyboard type (WORD) and reserved (DWORD). The keyboard types include: 0000h—personal computer AT keyboard, 0001h—enhanced keyboard, and 0002h through 00FFh—reserved.
0x0078	Query Code Page Number	This function returns the code page in use by the current logical keyboard (KCB). You can call this function from a DOS session. The parameter information includes: code page number (WORD) and reserved (WORD). The code page number contains 0 for PC US 437 or –1 for a custom code page. Any other value indicates the true code page number. There is no data information.
0x0079	Translate Scan Code to ASCII	This function returns an ASCII character translated from a scan code. You can specify the code page that you want the function to use (default is the current code page). The parameter information includes: code page number (WORD) and reserved (WORD). The data information includes: CharData record (10 bytes, see function 0x0074 for details), keyboard device monitor packets (WORD), translation flags (WORD), translate state 1 (WORD), and translate state 2 (WORD). The translation flag bits include: translation complete (0) and reserved (1 through 15). Translation state 1 and 2 contain a 0 when you start the function call and the same value when the translation completes. You can reset them to zero if you want to stop the current translation and start a new one. This function returns the following error code:

Table 4-4   **Continued**

Function	Name	Description
		0x8113 INVALID_PARAMETER
0x007A	Query Keyboard Hardware Identification	This function returns the identifier for the currently attached keyboard. There is no parameter information. The input/ output data information includes: data length (WORD) and hardware identifier (WORD). On input the data length field contains the number of data bytes requested by the caller. On output, this field contains the maximum length of the data available (4 bytes). This function returns the following error code:

0x8113 INVALID_PARAMETER

The hardware identifiers include:

Hardware Identifier	Keyboard Type
0001h	PC AT standard keyboard
AB41h	101-key enhanced keyboard
AB41h	102-key enhanced keyboard
AB54h	88-key enhanced keyboard
AB54h	89-key enhanced keyboard
AB86h	122 key mainframe interactive (MFI) keyboard

Function	Name	Description
0x007B	Query Keyboard Code Page Support Information	This function returns the keyboard's current code page support information. This includes the active code page, country, and subcountry. There is no parameter information. The data information includes: data length (WORD), code page number (WORD), country code in ASCIIZ format (ASCIIZ), and subcountry code in ASCIIZ format (ASCIIZ). On input, the data length field contains the number of data bytes requested by the caller. On output, this field contains the maximum length of the data available. This function returns the following error code:

0x8113 INVALID_PARAMETER

Pointing-device (mouse) (Category 7)

Function	Name	Description
0x0051	Notification of Display Mode Change	This function notifies the physical Mouse device driver of a display mode change. The input parameter information includes: length of the data structure in bytes (34 bytes maximum) (WORD), mode type (BYTE), number of colors as a power of 2 (BYTE), number of text columns (WORD), number of text rows (WORD), horizontal resolution (WORD), vertical resolution (WORD), attribute format (BYTE), number of attributes per character cell (BYTE), 32-bit physical address buffer address (DWORD), buffer size required for a full save (DWORD), buffer size required for a partial save (DWORD),

Function	Name	Description
		and address of the extended mode data structure (DWORD). The mode type bits include: monochrome compatible mode (0), text mode when clear or graphics mode when set (1), enable color burst when clear (2), VGA compatible modes when clear (3), and reserved (4 through 7). The data information includes: length of the data structure in bytes (WORD), adapter type (WORD). display type (WORD), display memory in bytes (DWORD), display configuration number (WORD), device driver version number (WORD), flag bits (WORD), hardware state buffer size (DWORD), full save maximum buffer size (DWORD), partial save maximum buffer size (DWORD), and offset to mode data (WORD). The adapter types include: monochrome (0), CGA (1), EGA (2), VGA (3), reserved (4 through 6), and 8514/A (7). The display types include: monochrome (0), CGA (1), enhanced color (2), 8503 monochrome (3), 8512 or 8512 color (4), reserved (5 through 8), and 8514 (9). The flag bits include the following values: 0001h—power up display configuration, and 0002h—VGA pass through.
0x0053	Reassign Current Mouse Scaling Factors	This function reassigns the current mouse scaling factors. The default values are: 16 mickeys per 8 pixels for the vertical row ratio and 8 mickeys per 8 pixels for the horizontal column ratio. The parameter information includes: row coordinate scaling factor (WORD) and column coordinate scaling factor (WORD). There is no data information.
0x0054	Assign New Mouse Event Mask	This function assigns a new mouse event mask. The mask determines which event the Mouse driver queues. The parameter information includes the event mask (WORD). The event mask bits contain: all mouse motion (0), motion with button 1 down (1), button 1 is down (2), motion with button 2 down (3), button 2 is down (4), motion with button 3 down (5), button 3 is down (6), and reserved (7 through 15). There is no data information.
0x0056	Set Pointer Shape	This function sets the shape of the mouse pointer. The current video mode determines the mouse pointer size. The parameter information includes: length of the pointer image buffer (WORD), pointer image width in columns (WORD), pointer image height in rows (WORD), hot spot column offset (WORD), and hot spot row offset (WORD). The data information is a pointer to the AND pointer image followed by the XOR pointer image.
0x0057	Unmark Collision Area	This function frees the mouse to draw the pointer anywhere on the display. There is no parameter or data information.
0x0058	Mark Collision Area	This function creates a collision area that restricts the Mouse driver from drawing the mouse pointer in that area. The

Table 4-4   **Continued**

Function	Name	Description
		parameter information includes: starting row (WORD), starting column (WORD), ending row (WORD), and ending column (WORD). There is no data information.
0x0059	Specify/ ReplacePointer Screen Position	This function moves the mouse pointer from one area to another. It does not draw the pointer if it appears within a collision area. The parameter information includes: new row position (WORD) and new column position (WORD). There is no data information.
0x005A	Set OS/2 Mode Pointer Draw Device Driver Address	This function specifies the address of the physical Pointer Draw device driver. This is the routine that receives any mouse interrupt requests that affect the pointer image. You can use this function only in an OS/2 full-screen session. The parameter information includes: pointer draw device driver entry point (DWORD) and pointer draw data segment selector (DWORD). The second word of the pointer draw data segment selector entry is reserved; set it to 0. The data information includes: length of the data structure (WORD) and caller identification (WORD). Caller identities include: application (0) and base video subsystem (BVS) (1).
0x005C	Set Current Physical Mouse Device Driver Status Flags	This function sets a subset of the current physical Mouse device driver status flag. The parameter information includes a status flag (WORD). The status flag bits contain the following information: reserved (0 through 7), interrupt level pointer draw routine not called when set (8), mouse data returned in mickeys, not display units, when set (9), and reserved (10 through 15). There is no data information.
0x005D	Notification of Mode Switch Completion	This function informs the mouse that a display mode change occurred and that it can resume drawing operations. The parameter and data information contains a dummy FAR-16 pointer (DWORD).
0x0060	Query Number of Mouse Buttons Supported	This function returns the number of mouse buttons supported by the physical Mouse device driver. There is no parameter information. The data information includes the number of buttons supported (WORD).
0x0061	Query Mouse Device Motion Sensitivity	This function returns the mouse device motion sensitivity. There is no parameter information. The data information contains the mickeys/centimeter supported by the mouse device in the range of 1 to (32K − 1) (WORD).
0x0062	Query Current Physical Mouse Device Driver Status Flag	This function returns the current physical Mouse device driver status flags. There is no parameter information. The data information includes the status flags (WORD). The status flag bits contain the following information: event queue

Function	Name	Description
		busy with I/O when set (0), block read in progress when set (1), flush in progress when set (2), pointer draw routine disabled by unsupported mode when set (3), reserved (4 through 7), interrupt level pointer draw routine not called when set (8), mouse data returned in mickeys when set (9), and reserved (10 through 15).
0x0063	Read Mouse Event Queue	This function reads the FIFO mouse event queue and returns its contents. The parameter information includes the type of read you want to perform (WORD). There are two read types: wait until data is available (0) and return immediately (1). The data information includes: mouse event query mask (see function 0x0065) (WORD), event time stamp in milliseconds (DWORD), pointer row coordinate (WORD), and pointer column coordinate (WORD).
0x0064	Query Current Event Queue Status	This function returns the number of queued elements in the mouse queue. It also returns the maximum number of elements allowed in the mouse queue. There is no parameter information. The data information includes: the current number of queued elements (WORD) and the maximum queue size (WORD).
0x0065	Query Current Mouse Event Mask	This function returns the current mouse event mask that can include any combination of the event flags set with function 0x0054. There is no parameter information. The data information includes the event mask (WORD). The event mask bits contain: all mouse motion (0), motion with button 1 down (1), button 1 is down (2), motion with button 2 down (3), button 2 is down (4), motion with button 3 down (5), button 3 is down (6), and reserved (7 through 15).
0x0066	Query Current Mouse Scaling Factors	This function returns the current mouse scaling factors. The default values are: 16 mickeys per 8 pixels for the vertical row ratio and 8 mickeys per 8 pixels for the horizontal column ratio. There is no parameter information. The data information includes: row coordinate scaling factor (WORD) and column coordinate scaling factor (WORD).
0x0067	Query Current Pointer Screen Position	This function returns the current pointer screen position. The value that you receive depends on the video mode. Graphic modes return pixel values while text modes return character position values. There is no parameter information. The data information includes: current row position (WORD) and current column position (WORD).
0x0068	Query Pointer Shape	This function returns a pointer to the current pointer shape buffer. The buffer includes both AND XOR masks. The parameter information includes: length of the pointer image buffer (WORD), pointer image width in columns (WORD), pointer image height in rows (WORD), hot spot column

Table 4-4   **Continued**

Function	Name	Description
		offset (WORD), and hot spot row offset (WORD). The data information is a pointer to the AND pointer image followed by the XOR pointer image.
0x006A	Query Physical Mouse Device Driver Level and Version	This function returns the physical Mouse device driver level and version number. There is no parameter information. The data information includes the version number (WORD). There are two return values: 1 for OS/2 1.3 level support and 2 for OS/2 2.0 level support.
0x006B	Query Pointing Device Identification	This function returns the pointing device identifier. There is no parameter information. The data information includes: device identification (WORD) and the number of the COM port that it's attached to (WORD). OS/2 supports the following types of pointers:

Identifier	Pointer type
0	Unknown
1	Bus mouse
2	Serial mouse
3	Import mouse
4	PS/2 style mouse
5	IBM 8516 touch display
6-65535	Reserved

Character-monitor control (Category Ah)

Function	Name	Description
0x0040	Register a Monitor	This function registers a monitor. Character devices that support a monitor receive this request during application calls to the DosMonReg function. The parameter information includes command information (BYTE). This is a reserved field; set it to 0. The data information contains: placement flag (refer to the DosMonReg function for more information) (WORD), index (refer to the OS/2 Version 2.0 Physical Device Driver Reference for more information) (WORD), address of the monitor input buffer (DWORD), and offset of the monitor output buffer (WORD). This function returns the following error codes:

0x8103   BAD_COMMAND
0x810C   GENERAL_FAILURE
0x8112   NO_MONITOR_SUPPORT

Function	Name	Description
General device control (Category Bh)		
0x0001	Flush Input Buffer	This function flushes an input buffer. The parameter information includes command information (BYTE). This is a reserved field, set it to 0. The data information includes a reserved field, set it to 0 (BYTE).
0x0002	Flush Output Buffer	This function flushes an output buffer. The parameter information includes command information (BYTE). This is a reserved field, set it to 0. The data information includes a reserved field, set it to 0 (BYTE).
0x0041	System Notifications for Physical Device Drivers	This function notifies the physical device driver of any activities or modifications that occur during session switching. This includes any changes to the alternate-input-methods interfaces. The parameter information includes: length of the data structure in bytes (8, 12, and 24 are the only valid values) (BYTE) and notification calling condition (Action) made to the physical device driver (WORD). The Action field contains the following bit values: pre-session save (0), post-session save (1), post-session restore (2), session termination (3), session creation (4), start of session switch (5), end of session switch (6), AIM pre-save verification (7), AIM post-save verification (8), and reserved (9 through 15). The data information includes a reserved field, set it to 0 (BYTE). This function returns the following error codes: 0x810C GENERAL_FAILURE 0x8113 INVALID_PARAMETER
0x0060	Query Monitor Support	This function returns the monitor support status of a physical device driver. It returns a value of MONITORS_NOT_SUPPORTED or NO_ERROR. The parameter information includes command information (BYTE). This is a reserved field, set it to 0. The data information includes a reserved field, set it to 0 (BYTE).

Using Table 4-4 is quite simple. The previous paragraphs describe the calling syntax for this function. You obtain hDevHandle using an open call. The ulCategory entry appears in the heading for each group of function calls. The ulFunction entry appears in the first column of the table. The rest of the entries (pParmList, ulParmLengthMax, pParmLengthInOut, pDataArea, ulDataLengthMax, and pDataLengthInOut) appear in the function description. Of course, you need to provide the specifics required to make this function work.

⇨ KBD functions

The keyboard (KBD) functions provide an easier and more intuitive method of programming the keyboard than resorting to the DOSDevIOCtl function. Of course, you also give up a little flexibility to get this ease of use. The functions include the capability not only to process keystrokes, but also to perform all the functions required in a multitasking environment as well. For example, the KbdGetFocus function binds a logical keyboard to the physical keyboard.

If you could use every KBD function in every programming environment, you would seldom need the services of DOSDevIOCtl. Unfortunately, many of these functions have limitations regarding the Presentation Manager. There is at least one of the following three classifications assigned to each function. You can use FAPI functions in a family API application; a family API application runs equally well in DOS or OS/2. Presentation Manager will not allow you to use a xPM function within an application designed for that environment. However, you can use these functions in a windowed OS/2 character-mode session. A final restriction is that xWPM functions cannot appear in windowed OS/2 character mode sessions; you must restrict their use to full-screen sessions only.

The Borland compiler provides access to these functions through the BSESUB.H, BSEERR.H, and BSEDEV.H include files. The BSESUB.H file contains the function declarations. The BSEERR.H file contains all the error declarations. Finally, the BSEDEV.H file contains the constant declarations that you need to actually use the KBD functions. You might need to check the include files for your compiler to find references to these functions because most vendors do not document them. In some cases, the vendor uses a new name for the function. Fortunately, most vendors include a file with #defines that allow you to use the original names.

NOTE IBM did not choose to document these functions after version 1.3 of OS/2 because they are machine specific and IBM plans to port OS/2 to other platforms. The current OS/2 implementation encourages the developer to write to the less machine-specific Presentation Manager interface. You still can use all these functions within your current

applications, but there is no guarantee that IBM will support them in future versions of OS/2. Use Presentation Manager specific functions whenever possible in your applications.

Table 4-5 contains a complete listing of the KBD functions. Remember, these are the calls supported by OS/2 versions 1.3 and above. Versions before 1.3 might or might not support all the listed calls. Each entry contains the function classification, calling syntax, complete description, and any appropriate errors. It does not include any compiler specific calls supported by the Borland (or any other) compiler.

KBD function listing   Table 4-5

Function	Description
FAPI, xPM UShort KbdCharIn (pkbci, fWait, hkbd)	The KbdCharIn function returns a character data (CharData) structure from the keyboard. You must make two calls to this function to return DBCS (double-byte character codes). If you set the shift report with KbdSetStatus, then this function returns only the changed shift status information. The CharData structure does not include the time stamp when you use this function within a FAPI application. pkcbi contains a pointer to the character data structure. fWait contains 1 if you want to return immediately or 0 if you want to wait for a keystroke. hkbd contains the keyboard handle. The CharData structure consists of the following elements:

Offset	Length	Description
00h	1	Keyboard scan code translated into an ASCII character code.
01h	1	Code received from the keyboard.
02h	1	State of the keyboard event. This entry contains the following bits: shift status returned without character (0), scan code is a character when clear or scan code is an extended key code when set (1), reserved (2 through 4), immediate conversion requested (5), and character type (6 and 7). There are four character types: undefined (00), final character with interim flag off (01), interim character (10), and final character with interim flag on (11).
03h	1	NLS shift status. This is a reserved field; set it to 0.

Table 4-5   **Continued**

Function	Description

Function	**Description**
	Offset **Length** **Description**

	Offset	Length	Description
	04h	2	The shift key status bits contain the following information: right Shift key down (0), left Shift key down (1), either Ctrl key down (2), either Alt key down (3), Scroll Lock on (4), Num Lock on (5), Caps Lock on (6), insert on (7), left Ctrl key down (8), left Alt key down (9), right Ctrl key down (10), right Alt key down (11), Scroll Lock key down (12), Num Lock key down (13), Caps Lock key down (14), and SysReq key down (15).
	06h	4	Time of key press in milliseconds since the user started the system.

KbdCharIn returns one of the following values:

0	NO_ERROR
375	ERROR_KBD_INVALID_IOWAIT
439	ERROR_KBD_INVALID_HANDLE
445	ERROR_KBD_FOCUS_REQUIRED
447	ERROR_KBD_KEYBOARD_BUSY
464	ERROR_KBD_DETACHED
504	ERROR_KBD_EXTENDED_SG

xPM
UShort KbdClose
(hkdb)

The KbdClose function closes a logical keyboard. You normally use this function when the keyboard has the focus. Using it at other times could block other applications. hkbd contains the keyboard handle. KbdClose returns one of the following values:

0	NO_ERROR
439	ERROR_KBD_INVALID_HANDLE
464	ERROR_KBD_DETACHED
504	ERROR_KBD_EXTENDED_SG

xWPM
UShort
KbdDeRegister
(VOID)

The KbdDeRegister function deregisters a session's keyboard subsystem. KbdDeRegister returns one of the following values:

0	NO_ERROR
411	ERROR_KBD_DEREGISTER
464	ERROR_KBD_DETACHED
504	ERROR_KBD_EXTENDED_SG

FAPI, xPM
UShort
KbdFlushBuffer
(hkbd)

The KbdFlushBuffer function clears the keystroke buffer. hkbd contains the keyboard handle. You do not require a handle when using this function in a FAPI application. KbdFlushBuffer returns one of the following values:

0	NO_ERROR
439	ERROR_KBD_INVALID_HANDLE

Function	Description
	445 ERROR_KBD_FOCUS_REQUIRED
	447 ERROR_KBD_KEYBOARD_BUSY
	464 ERROR_KBD_DETACHED
	504 ERROR_KBD_EXTENDED_SG

xPM
UShort
KbdFreeFocus (hkbd)

The KbdFreeFocus function severs the bond created by KbdGetFocus between a logical and physical keyboard. KbdFreeFocus returns one of the following values:

0	NO_ERROR
439	ERROR_KBD_INVALID_HANDLE
445	ERROR_KBD_FOCUS_REQUIRED
464	ERROR_KBD_DETACHED
504	ERROR_KBD_EXTENDED_SG

xPM
UShort KbdGetCp
(ulReserved,
pidCP, hkbd)

The KbdGetCp function returns the code page used to translate scan codes to ASCII characters. ulReserved is a reserved parameter, set it to 0. pidCP contains the code page identifier. hkbd contains the keyboard handle. KbdGetCP returns one of the following values:

0	NO_ERROR
373	ERROR_KBD_PARAMETER
439	ERROR_KBD_INVALID_HANDLE
445	ERROR_KBD_FOCUS_REQUIRED
447	ERROR_KBD_KEYBOARD_BUSY
464	ERROR_KBD_DETACHED
504	ERROR_KBD_EXTENDED_SG

xPM
UShort KbdGetFocus
(fWait, hkbd)

The KbdGetFocus function binds the logical keyboard to the physical keyboard. fWait contains 0 if you want to wait until the physical keyboard is free to make the bond or 1 if you want the function to return immediately. hkbd contains the keyboard handle. KbdGetFocus returns one of the following values:

0	NO_ERROR
439	ERROR_KBD_INVALID_HANDLE
446	ERROR_KBD_FOCUS_ALREADY_ACTIVE
447	ERROR_KBD_KEYBOARD_BUSY
464	ERROR_KBD_DETACHED
504	ERROR_KBD_EXTENDED_SG

xPM
UShort KbdGetHWID
(pkbdHwID, hkbd)

The KbdGetStatus function returns the attached keyboard's hardware generated identification value. pkbdHwID contains the hardware identification structure. hkbd contains the keyboard handle. The hardware identification structure contains the following entries:

Offset	Length	Description
00h	2	Length of the structure.

Table 4-5   **Continued**

Function	Description

Description

Offset	Length	Description
02h	2	Keyboard identification number. This includes the following values: undefined (0000h), PC AT standard keyboard (0001h), 101- or 102-key enhanced (AB41h), 88- or 89-key enhanced (AB54h), or 122-key enhanced (AB85h).
04h	2	Reserved, set this field to 0.
06h	2	Reserved, set this field to 0.

KbdGetHWID returns one of the following values:

0	NO_ERROR
373	ERROR_KBD_PARAMETER
447	ERROR_KBD_KEYBOARD_BUSY
464	ERROR_KBD_DETACHED
504	ERROR_KBD_EXTENDED_SG

FAPI, xPM
UShort
KbdGetStatus
(pkbdInfo, hkbd)

The KbdGetStatus function returns the current keyboard status. FAPI applications ignore the keyboard handle value and always return a NULL value for NLS shift state. pkbdInfo contains the keyboard information structure. hkbd contains the keyboard handle. The pkbdInfo structure contains the following elements:

Offset	Length	Description
00h	2	Length of the structure (10 is the only valid value).
02h	2	The mask information bits include: echo on (0), echo off (1), binary mode on (2), ASCII mode on (3), shift state modified (4), interim character flags modified (5), turnaround character modified (6), turnaround character length (7), shift return on (8), and reserved (9 through 15).
04h	2	Definition of the turnaround character in ASCII and extended ASCII format. The turnaround character is the carriage return.
06h	2	The interim character flag bits include: reserved (0 through 4), application requested immediate conversion (5), reserved (6), interim character flag on (7), and NLS shift state (8 through 15).
08h	2	Shift state (see KbdCharIn).

KbdGetStatus returns one of the following values:

0	NO_ERROR
376	ERROR_KBD_INVALID_LENGTH

Function	Description

	439 ERROR_KBD_INVALID_HANDLE
	445 ERROR_KBD_FOCUS_REQUIRED
	447 ERROR_KBD_KEYBOARD_BUSY
	464 ERROR_KBD_DETACHED
	504 ERROR_KBD_EXTENDED_SG

xPM
UShort KbdOpen
(phkbd)

The KbdOpen function creates a new logical keyboard. phkbd contains a pointer to the keyboard handle. KbdOpen returns one of the following values:

0	NO_ERROR
440	ERROR_KBD_NO_MORE_HANDLE
441	ERROR_KBD_CANNOT_CREATE_KCB
464	ERROR_KBD_DETACHED
504	ERROR_KBD_EXTENDED_SG

FAPI, xPM
UShort KbdPeek
(pkbci, hkbd)

The KbdPeek function returns any available character record data from the keyboard without removing it from the buffer. You must make two calls to this function to return DBCS (double-byte character codes). If you set the shift report with KbdSetStatus, then this function returns only the changed shift status information. The CharData structure does not include the time stamp when you use this function within a FAPI application. pkbci contains the character data information structure (see KbdCharIn for details). hkbd contains the keyboard handle. KbdPeek returns one of the following values:

0	NO_ERROR
439	ERROR_KBD_INVALID_HANDLE
445	ERROR_KBD_FOCUS_REQUIRED
447	ERROR_KBD_KEYBOARD_BUSY
464	ERROR_KBD_DETACHED
504	ERROR_KBD_EXTENDED_SG

xWPM
UShort KbdRegister
(pszModName,
pszEntryPt,
fFunMask)

The KbdRegister function registers a keyboard subsystem within a session. You can have one pending KbdRegister function pending at a time. pszModName contains the dynamic link module name. name. pszEntryPt contains the entry point routine name that receives control when you call any of the registered functions. fFunMax contains the following registration bits: KbdCharIn (0), KbdPeek (1), KbdFlushRegister (2), KbdGetStatus (3), KbdSetStatus (4), KbdStringIn (5), KbdOpen (6), KbdClose (7), KbdGetFocus (8), KbdFreeFocus (9), KdbGetCp (10), KbdSetCp (11), KbdXlate (12), KbdSetCustXt (13), KbdGetHWID (14), and reserved (15 through 31). KbdRegister returns one of the following values:

0	NO_ERROR
408	ERROR_KBD_INVALID_ASCIIZ
409	ERROR_KBD_INVALID_MASK
410	ERROR_KBD_REGISTER
464	ERROR_KBD_DETACHED
504	ERROR_KBD_EXTENDED_SG

Table 4-5   **Continued**

Function	Description
xPM UShort KbdSetCp (usReserved, pidCP, hkbd)	The KbdSetCp function sets the code page used to translate scan codes into ASCII characters. usReserved is a reserved parameter, set it to 0. pidCP contains the code page identifier. Common code page values include: 0 (resident code page), 437 (IBM PC US), 850 (multilingual), 860 (Portuguese), 863 (Canadian-French), and 865 (Nordic). hkbd contains the keyboard handle. KbdSetCp returns one of the following values:

                                 0   NO_ERROR
                             375   ERROR_KBD_INVALID_IOWAIT
     439   ERROR_KBD_INVALID_HANDLE
     445   ERROR_KBD_FOCUS_REQUIRED
     447   ERROR_KBD_KEYBOARD_BUSY
     464   ERROR_KBD_DETACHED
     504   ERROR_KBD_EXTENDED_SG

Function	Description
xPM UShort KbdSetCustXt (usCodePage, hkbd)	The KbdSetCustXt function sets the translate table for the specified keyboard handle. usCodePage contains a pointer to the translation table used to translate a scan code to an ASCII character (see Category 4 Function 0x0050 of Table 4-4 for further details). hkbd contains the keyboard handle. KbdSetCustXt returns one of the following values:

        0   NO_ERROR
     377   ERROR_KBD_INVALID_ECHO_MASK
     378   ERROR_KBD_INVALID_INPUT_MASK
     439   ERROR_KBD_INVALID_HANDLE
     445   ERROR_KBD_FOCUS_REQUIRED
     447   ERROR_KBD_KEYBOARD_BUSY
     464   ERROR_KBD_DETACHED
     504   ERROR_KBD_EXTENDED_SG

Function	Description
xPM UShort KbdSetFgnd (VOID)	The KbdSetFgnd increases the priority of the foreground keyboard's thread. KbdSetFgnd returns one of the following values:

        0   NO_ERROR
     447   ERROR_KBD_KEYBOARD_BUSY
     504   ERROR_KBD_EXTENDED_SG

Function	Description
FAPI, xPM UShort KbdSetStatus (pkbdInfo, hkbd)	The KbdSetStatus function sets the keyboard characteristics. FAPI applications ignore the keyboard handle value. They do not support the interim or turnaround character. pkbdInfo contains the keyboard information structure (see KbdSetStatus for further details). hkbd contains the keyboard handle. KbdSetStatus returns one of the following values:

        0   NO_ERROR
     376   ERROR_KBD_INVALID_LENGTH

Function	Description
	377 ERROR_KBD_INVALID_ECHO_MASK
	378 ERROR_KBD_INVALID_INPUT_MASK
	439 ERROR_KBD_INVALID_HANDLE
	445 ERROR_KBD_FOCUS_REQUIRED
	447 ERROR_KBD_KEYBOARD_BUSY
	464 ERROR_KBD_DETACHED
	504 ERROR_KBD_EXTENDED_SG

FAPI, xPM
UShort
KbdStringIn (pch,
pchIn, fsWait, hkbd)

The KbdStringIn function returns a character string from the keyboard. You can echo the character string to the display by setting echo mode. OS/2 does not allow you to use echo mode with binary mode. The default input mode is ASCII. FAPI applications do not need to supply a keyboard handle. pch contains a pointer to the character string buffer. pchIn contains a pointer to the character string length (maximum length of 255). Template processing (meaningful in ASCII mode) returns two fields: cb (the length of the input buffer) and cchIn (the number of bytes read into the buffer). fsWait contains 0 if you want the function to wait for a character; otherwise, it contains 1 (no wait). hkbd contains the keyboard handle. KbdStringIn returns one of the following values:

    0   NO_ERROR
375   ERROR_KBD_INVALID_IOWAIT
439   ERROR_KBD_INVALID_HANDLE
445   ERROR_KBD_FOCUS_REQUIRED
447   ERROR_KBD_KEYBOARD_BUSY
464   ERROR_KBD_DETACHED
504   ERROR_KBD_EXTENDED_SG

xWPM
UShort
KbdSynch (fsWait)

The KbdSynch function synchronizes the keyboard subsystem to the keyboard device driver. This function blocks all other threads in a session until it returns from the subsystem to the router. fsWait contains 0 if you do not want to wait for access to the device driver. KbdSynch returns one of the following values:

    0   NO_ERROR
121   ERROR_SEM_TIMEOUT

xPM
UShort KbdXlate
(pkbdTrans, hkbd)

The KbdXlate function translates scan codes with shift states into ASCII characters. You might need to call this function several times to complete a translation because of accent key combinations or other complexities. pkbdTrans contains the address of the translation record structure. hkbd contains the keyboard handle. The translation record structure contains the following elements:

Offset	Length	Description
00h	2	See the KbdDDFlagWord call in the "Physical Keyboard Device Driver" section of the IBM OS/2 Technical Library Physical Device Driver Reference and Category 4 Functions 0x0074 and 0x0079 in Table 4-4.

Table 4-5   **Continued**

Function	Description		
	Offset	**Length**	**Description**
	02h	2	The translation flag bits include: translation complete (0) and reserved (1 through 15).
	04h	2	Translation state identification across calls. You can reset this entry to zero if you want to stop the current translation and start a new one.
	06h	2	Translation state identification across calls. You can reset this entry to zero if you want to stop the current translation and start a new one.

KbdXlate returns one of the following values:

0	NO_ERROR
439	ERROR_KBD_INVALID_HANDLE
445	ERROR_KBD_FOCUS_REQUIRED
447	ERROR_KBD_KEYBOARD_BUSY
464	ERROR_KBD_DETACHED
504	ERROR_KBD_EXTENDED_SG

MOU functions

The MOU (mouse) functions help you create, delete, move, and change the mouse pointer. They also allow you to retrieve various pieces of information like the mouse pointer position and the number of mouse buttons. Of course, the DOSDevIOCtl functions offer most of the same features. The big difference is the flexibility of the DOSDevIOCtl functions versus the improved reporting and ease of use of the MOU functions. The actual difference between the two sets of functions is inconsequential in most cases.

As with the KBD functions, OS/2 places restrictions on how and when you can use the MOU functions. There is at least one of the following three classifications assigned to each function. You can use FAPI functions in a family API application; a family API application runs equally well in DOS or OS/2. Presentation Manager will not allow you to use a xPM function within an application designed for that environment. However, you can use these functions in a windowed OS/2 character-mode session. A final restriction is that

xWPM functions cannot appear in windowed OS/2 character-mode sessions; you must restrict their use to full-screen sessions only.

The Borland compiler provides access to these functions through the BSESUB.H, BSEERR.H, and BSEDEV.H include files. The BSESUB.H file contains the function declarations. The BSEERR.H file contains all the error declarations. Finally, the BSEDEV.H file contains the constant declarations that you need to actually use the MOU functions. You might need to check the include files for your compiler to find references to these functions because most vendors do not document them. In some cases, the vendor uses a new name for the function. Fortunately, most vendors include a file with #defines that allow you to use the original names.

NOTE IBM did not choose to document these functions after version 1.3 of OS/2 because they are machine specific and IBM plans to port OS/2 to other platforms. The current OS/2 implementation encourages the developer to write to the less machine-specific Presentation Manager interface. You still can use all these functions within your current applications, but there is no guarantee that IBM will support them in future versions of OS/2. Use Presentation Manager specific functions whenever possible in your applications.

Table 4-6 contains a complete listing of the MOU functions. Remember, these are the calls supported by OS/2 versions 1.3 and above. Versions before 1.3 might or might not support all the listed calls. Each entry contains the function classification, calling syntax, complete description, and any appropriate errors. It does not include any compiler specific calls supported by the Borland (or any other) compiler.

MOU function listing

Table 4-6

Function	Description
xPM UShort MouClose (hmou)	The MouClose function closes the mouse device for the current session. hmou contains the mouse handle. MouClose returns one of the following values:

0	NO_ERROR
385	ERROR_MOUSE_NO_DEVICE
466	ERROR_MOU_DETACHED

Table 4-6   **Continued**

Function	Description
	501 ERROR_MOUSE_NO_CONSOLE 505 ERROR_MOU_EXTENDED_SG
xWPM UShort MouDeRegister (VOID)	The MouDeRegister function deregisters a mouse subsystem within a session. MouDeRegister returns one of the following values: 0 NO_ERROR 385 ERROR_MOUSE_NO_DEVICE 416 ERROR_MOUSE_DEREGISTER 466 ERROR_MOU_DETACHED 505 ERROR_MOU_EXTENDED_SG
xPM UShort MouDrawPtr (hmou)	The MouDrawPtr function notifies the mouse driver that a previously restricted area is free. This draws the pointer on the display. hmou contains the mouse handle. MouDrawPtr returns one of the following values: 0 NO_ERROR 385 ERROR_MOUSE_NO_DEVICE 466 ERROR_MOU_DETACHED 501 ERROR_MOUSE_NO_CONSOLE 505 ERROR_MOU_EXTENDED_SG
xPM UShort) MouFlushQue (hmou)	The MouFlushQue function empties the mouse event queue and monitor chain data for the session. hmou contains the mouse handle. MouFlushQue returns one of the following values: 0 NO_ERROR 385 ERROR_MOUSE_NO_DEVICE 466 ERROR_MOU_DETACHED 501 ERROR_MOUSE_NO_CONSOLE 505 ERROR_MOU_EXTENDED_SG
xPM UShort MouGetDevStatus (pfsDevStatus, hmou)	The MouGetDevStatus function returns the status flags for the installed mouse device driver. pfsDevStatus contains a pointer to the device status flags. The status flag bits contain the following information: event queue busy with I/O when set (0), block read in progress when set (1), flush in progress when set (2), pointer draw routine disabled by unsupported mode when set (3), reserved (4 through 7), interrupt level pointer draw routine not called when set (8), mouse data returned in mickeys when set (9), and reserved (10 through 15). hmou contains the mouse handle. MouGetDevStatus returns one of the following values: 0 NO_ERROR 385 ERROR_MOUSE_NO_DEVICE 466 ERROR_MOU_DETACHED 501 ERROR_MOUSE_NO_CONSOLE 505 ERROR_MOU_EXTENDED_SG

Function	Description
xPM UShort MouGetEventMask (pfsEvents, hmou)	The MouGetEventMask function returns the event queue mask. pfsEvents contains a pointer to the events mask structure. The event mask bits contain: all mouse motion (0), motion with button 1 down (1), button 1 is down (2), motion with button 2 down (3), button 2 is down (4), motion with button 3 down (5), button 3 is down (6), and reserved (7 through 15). hmou contains the mouse handle. MouGetEventMask returns one of the following values: 0 NO_ERROR 385 ERROR_MOUSE_NO_DEVICE 466 ERROR_MOU_DETACHED 501 ERROR_MOUSE_NO_CONSOLE 505 ERROR_MOU_EXTENDED_SG
xPM UShort MouGetNumButtons (pcButtons, hmou)	The MouGetNumButtons function returns the number of buttons on the mouse. pcButtons contains the number of buttons (1 through 3). hmou contains the mouse handle. MouGetNumButtons returns one of the following values: 0 NO_ERROR 385 ERROR_MOUSE_NO_DEVICE 466 ERROR_MOU_DETACHED 501 ERROR_MOUSE_NO_CONSOLE 505 ERROR_MOU_EXTENDED_SG
xPM UShort MouGetNumMickeys (pcMickeys, hmou)	The MouGetNumMickeys function returns the number of mickeys in each centimeter for the installed mouse driver. pcMickeys contains the number of mickeys per centimeter. hmou contains the mouse handle. MouGetNumMickeys returns one of the following values: 0 NO_ERROR 385 ERROR_MOUSE_NO_DEVICE 466 ERROR_MOU_DETACHED 501 ERROR_MOUSE_NO_CONSOLE 505 ERROR_MOU_EXTENDED_SG
xPM UShort MouGetNumQueEl (qmouQi, hmou)	The MouGetNumQueEl function returns the number of mouse queue elements. qmouQi contains a pointer to the mouse queue status structure. This structure contains two fields: the number of event queue elements and the total number of elements available. hmou contains the mouse handle. MouGetNumQueEl returns one of the following values: 0 NO_ERROR 385 ERROR_MOUSE_NO_DEVICE 466 ERROR_MOU_DETACHED 501 ERROR_MOUSE_NO_CONSOLE 505 ERROR_MOU_EXTENDED_SG
xPM	The MouGetPtrPos function returns the mouse pointer coordinates.

Table 4-6   **Continued**

Function	Description
UShort MouGetPtrPos (pMouLoc, hmou)	pMouLoc contains the mouse location in two fields: row and column location in two fields: row and column. hmou contains the mouse handle. MouGetPtrPos returns one of the following values:

0	NO_ERROR
385	ERROR_MOUSE_NO_DEVICE
466	ERROR_MOU_DETACHED
501	ERROR_MOUSE_NO_CONSOLE
505	ERROR_MOU_EXTENDED_SG

Function	Description
xPM UShort MouGetPtrShape (pBuf, pmoupsInfo, hmou)	The MouGetPtrShape function returns the pointer shape for the session. pBuf contains a pointer to a buffer used to hold the pointer information. If the buffer size is too small, the total length field of the pointer shape structure contains the actual size required. pmoupsInfo contains a pointer to the pointer shape structure. hmou contains the mouse handle. The pointer shape structure contains the following elements:

Offset	Length	Description
00h	2	Total length of the pointer buffer in bytes. The value for text modes is always 4. Use the following equation in graphics mode: total length = height in pels × width in pels × bits per pel × 2 / 8.
02h	2	Number of columns in the mouse pointer shape.
04h	2	Number of rows in the mouse pointer shape.
06h	2	Column offset of the pointer hotspot within the mouse pointer shape.
08h	2	Row offset of the pointer hotspot within the mouse pointer shape.

MouGetPtrShape returns one of the following values:

0	NO_ERROR
385	ERROR_MOUSE_NO_DEVICE
387	ERROR_MOUSE_INV_PARAMS
466	ERROR_MOU_DETACHED
501	ERROR_MOUSE_NO_CONSOLE
505	ERROR_MOU_EXTENDED_SG

Function	Description
xPM UShort MouGetScaleFact (pmouScFactors,	The MouGetScaleFact function returns the mouse scaling factors. pmouScFactors contains a pointer to the control block structure. This structure contains two fields: row Scale and colScale with values between 1 and (32K – 1). hmou contains the mouse handle.

Function	Description
hmou)	MouGetScaleFact returns one of the following values:

0	NO_ERROR
385	ERROR_MOUSE_NO_DEVICE
466	ERROR_MOU_DETACHED
501	ERROR_MOUSE_NO_CONSOLE
505	ERROR_MOU_EXTENDED_SG

Function	Description
xWPM UShort MouInitReal (pszDriverName)	The MouInitReal function initializes mouse support for DOS sessions. pszDriverName contains the name of the DOS mouse device driver. You must include this device driver name in CONFIG.SYS at startup time. Only the Base Video Subsystem should use this call. MouInitReal returns one of the following values:

0	NO_ERROR
385	ERROR_MOUSE_NO_DEVICE
412	ERROR_MOUSE_SMG_ONLY
466	ERROR_MOU_DETACHED
501	ERROR_MOUSE_NO_CONSOLE
505	ERROR_MOU_EXTENDED_SG

Function	Description
xPM UShort MouOpen (pszDriverName, phmou)	The MouOpen function opens the mouse device for the current session. This initializes the mouse to a known state, but does not present the mouse pointer on screen. pszDriverName contains the ASCIIZ mouse device driver name. You must include this device driver name in CONFIG.SYS at startup time. Applications that use the default device driver should push a double word of zeros in place of the driver name address. phmou contains a pointer to the mouse handle. MouOpen returns one of the following values:

0	NO_ERROR
385	ERROR_MOUSE_NO_DEVICE
390	ERROR_MOUSE_INV_MODULE_PT
466	ERROR_MOU_DETACHED
501	ERROR_MOUSE_NO_CONSOLE
505	ERROR_MOU_EXTENDED_SG

Function	Description
xPM UShort MouReadEventQue (pmouevEvent, pfWait, hmou)	The MouReadEventQue function reads a mouse event from the FIFO queue and places it in the specified structure. pmouevEvent contains a pointer to the mouse event structure. pfWait contains 0 if you want to return immediately even if the queue does not contain data. hmou contains the mouse handle. The mouse event structure contains the following elements:

Offset	Length	Description
00h	2	The event mask bits contain: all mouse motion (0), motion with button 1 down (1), button 1 is down (2), motion with button 2 down (3), button 2 is down (4), motion with button 3 down (5), button 3 is down (6), and reserved (7 through 15). hmou contains the mouse handle.

389

Table 4-6   **Continued**

Function	Description		
	02h	4	Time stamp in milliseconds since the user started the system.
	06h	2	Mouse row position in absolute or relative coordinates.
	08h	2	Mouse column position in absolute or relative coordinates.

MouReadEventQue returns one of the following values:

0	NO_ERROR
385	ERROR_MOUSE_NO_DEVICE
387	ERROR_MOUSE_INV_PARMS
393	ERROR_MOUSE_NO_DATA
466	ERROR_MOU_DETACHED
501	ERROR_MOUSE_NO_CONSOLE
505	ERROR_MOU_EXTENDED_SG

xWPM
UShort
MouRegister
(pszModName,
pszEntryName,
flFuncs)

The MouRegister function registers a mouse subsystem within a session. Each session can have one open MouRegister. pszModName contains the dynamic link module name. pszEntryName contains the name of the routine that receives control when the application calls any of the registered functions. flFuncs contains a mask of bits that determine which functions the mouse routine handles. These function bits include: MouGetNumButtons (0), MouGetNumMickeys (1), MouGetDevStatus (2), MouGetNumQueEl (3), MouReadEventQue (4), MouGetScaleFact (5), MouGetEventMask (6), MouSetScaleFact (7), MouSetEventMask (8), reserved (9 and 10), MouOpen (11), MouClose (12), MouGetPtrShape (13), MouSetPtrShape (14), MouDrawPtr (15), MouRemovePtr (16), MouGetPtrPos (17), MouSetPtrPos (18), MouInitReal (19), MouSetDevStatus (20), reserved (21 through 31). MouRegister returns one of the following values:

0	NO_ERROR
385	ERROR_MOUSE_NO_DEVICE
413	ERROR_MOUSE_INVALID_ASCII
414	ERROR_MOUSE_INVALID_MASK
415	ERROR_MOUSE_REGISTER
466	ERROR_MOU_DETACHED
505	ERROR_MOU_EXTENDED_SG

xPM
UShort
MouRemovePtr
(pmourtRect, hmou)

The MouRemovePtr function prevents the mouse driver from drawing the mouse pointer in the specified area. This area becomes the collision area. OS/2 allows only one active collision area at a time. pmourtRect contains a pointer to the pointer shape collision structure. hmou contains the mouse handle. The pointer shape collision structure contains the following elements:

Function	Description

Description

Offset	Length	Description
00h	2	Upper-left row coordinate.
02h	2	Upper-left column coordinate.
04h	2	Lower-right row coordinate.
06h	2	Lower-right column coordinate.

MouRemovePtr returns one of the following values:

0	NO_ERROR
385	ERROR_MOUSE_NO_DEVICE
387	ERROR_MOUSE_INV_PARMS
466	ERROR_MOU_DETACHED
501	ERROR_MOUSE_NO_CONSOLE
505	ERROR_MOU_EXTENDED_SG

xPM
UShort
MouSetDevStatus
(pfsDevStatus,
hmou)

The MouSetDevStatus function sets the mouse device driver status flags. pfsDevStatus contains the status flags. These flags include: reserved (0 through 7), disable drawing operations for the drawing routine when set (8), return data in mickeys when set (9), and reserved (10 through 15). hmou contains the mouse handle. MouSetDevStatus returns one of the following values:

0	NO_ERROR
385	ERROR_MOUSE_NO_DEVICE
387	ERROR_MOUSE_INV_PARMS
466	ERROR_MOU_DETACHED
501	ERROR_MOUSE_NO_CONSOLE
505	ERROR_MOU_EXTENDED_SG

xPM
UShort
MouSetEventMask
(pfsEvents, hmou)

The MouSetEventMask function sets the mouse event mask for the current mouse driver. pfsEvents contains the event mask (see MouGetEventMask for further details). hmou contains the mouse handle. MouSetEventMask returns one of the following values:

0	NO_ERROR
385	ERROR_MOUSE_NO_DEVICE
466	ERROR_MOU_DETACHED
501	ERROR_MOUSE_NO_CONSOLE
505	ERROR_MOU_EXTENDED_SG

xPM
UShort MouSetPtrPos
(pMouLoc, hmou)

The MouSetPtrLoc function sets the mouse pointer position on screen. pMouLoc contains a pointer to a structure containing two fields: row (the new mouse pointer row) and column (the new mouse pointer column). This function does not affect any collision areas. hmou contains the mouse handle. MouSetPtrPos returns one of the following values:

0	NO_ERROR
385	ERROR_MOUSE_NO_DEVICE
387	ERROR_MOUSE_INV_PARMS

Table 4-6   **Continued**

Function	Description
	466 ERROR_MOU_DETACHED 501 ERROR_MOUSE_NO_CONSOLE 505 ERROR_MOU_EXTENDED_SG
xPM UShort MouSetPtrShape (pBuf, pmouPSInfo, hmou)	The MouSetPtrShape function sets the mouse pointer shape and size. It affects all applications within a session. pBuf contains the address of a buffer holding the AND XOR pointer masks. pmouPSInfo contains a pointer to the mouse pointer strucutre (see MouGetPtrShape for further details). hmou contains the mouse handle. MouSetPtrShape returns one of the following values: 0 NO_ERROR 385 ERROR_MOUSE_NO_DEVICE 387 ERROR_MOUSE_INV_PARMS 466 ERROR_MOU_DETACHED 501 ERROR_MOUSE_NO_CONSOLE 505 ERROR_MOU_EXTENDED_SG
xPM UShort MouSetScaleFact (pmouScFact, hmou)	The MouSetScaleFact function assigns new scaling factors to the current mouse driver. pmouScFact contains two fields:rowScale and colScale. Each field can contain a value from 0 to (32K–1). The default rowScale value is 16 mickeys for 8 pixels. The default colScale value is 8 mickeys for 8 pixels. hmou contains the mouse handle. MouSetScaleFact returns one of the following values: 0 NO_ERROR 385 ERROR_MOUSE_NO_DEVICE 387 ERROR_MOUSE_INV_PARMS 466 ERROR_MOU_DETACHED 501 ERROR_MOUSE_NO_CONSOLE 505 ERROR_MOU_EXTENDED_SG
xWPM UShort MouSynch (ioWait)	The MouSynch function synchronizes the mouse subsystem to the current mouse driver. ioWait determines if the function waits for access to the mouse driver. A value of 0 causes the function to return immediately. MouSynch returns one of the following values: 0 NO_ERROR 121 ERROR_SEM_TIMEOUT

Parallel/serial port API

CHAPTER 5

E VERYONE knows that you need to perform some amount of magic to make the serial port work efficiently and without error under OS/2. Few might realize that you can even do very much with the parallel port—especially when it comes to printers. (Of course, you need to do some work to make the parallel port function with file transfer software, but this is another issue.) OS/2 provides you with the capability to work with both types of ports and optimize their use in your applications. It does require a little more low-level work that you might want to perform, but the capability does exist.

This chapter assumes that you want to write a low-level routine that might or might not appear as part of an application. There is one section for each port type. The DOSDevIOCtl function is a low-level routine that assumes the reader requires very low-level access to the port. This usually happens when the developer needs to create a device driver or other ring 2 application. However, they are equally useful in standard applications.

Use of the DOSDevIOCtl function appears in chapter 4. Refer to that chapter for instructions on using this function before you try to use the material that appears in the following paragraphs. This function is very powerful, but it does sidestep many of the mechanisms that you normally would use within a windowed environment.

Parallel and serial port DOSDevIOCtl functions

OS/2 provides a number of default device driver functions that you can access using the DOSDevIOCtl function. The printer and serial port functions make up only a part of the things that you can access. Many texts refer to the printer functions as PRT (for print) calls. Likewise, the serial port calls use an ASYNC (asynchronous communication) prefix. Your specific computer configuration might provide even more than you see here. For example, parallel ports in newer machines provide bidirectional data transfer. Given the right kind of device driver, you could use this capability to create a file transfer program. Newer serial ports provide hardware buffers that you could use to improve communication program performance in some situations. The right

kind of device driver would make this activity much easier. As you can see, it pays to fully explore the capabilities of your system and those of others you create programs for.

The following paragraphs concentrate on the generic printer and serial port functions, but it always pays to search the vendor documentation and the INI files on your system. You might want to check the device drivers themselves for additional information (provided the software licensing agreement does not prevent this action). Some vendors might even sell a developer's kit or other form of formal documentation for their device driver.

The Borland compiler provides access to the PRT functions through the BSEDEV.H and BSEDOS.H include files. The BSEDEV.H file contains the entries that you need to actually use the DOSDevIOCtl function. The BSEDOS.H file contains the DOSDevIOCtl function declaration. Both files provide interesting bits of information. You might need to check the include files for your compiler to find references to these functions because most vendors do not document them. In some cases, the vendor uses a new name for the function. Fortunately, most vendors include a file with #defines that allow you to use the original names. Table 5-1 provides a complete list of the printer and serial port DOSDevIOCtl functions.

NOTE

OS/2 Version 1.0 and 1.1 device drivers do not understand generic IOCtl packets. As a result, the kernel does not pass the ulDataLengthMax, pDataLengthInOut, ulParmLengthMax, and pParmLengthInOut parameters to the device driver. You must mark device drivers level 2 or higher to support receipt of these fields.

DOSDevIOCtl printer and serial port generic functions

Table 5-1

Function	Name	Description
Parallel Port IOCtl Commands (Category 5)		
0x0042	Set Frame Control	This function sets the frame control. The parameter information includes command information (BYTE). This is a reserved field; set it to 0. The data information includes: characters per line (80 and 132) and lines per inch (6 and 8). This function returns the following error codes:

Table 5-1   **Continued**

Function	**Name**	**Description**
		0x0100 Completed successfully
		0x8102 Device not ready
		0x8103 Invalid command
		0x810A Write fault
0x0044	Set Infinite Retry	This function sets infinite retry. It is always enabled when there is a monitor registered for the physical Parallel Port device driver. A disable request returns a good return code when you have a monitor registered even though the function does not do anything. The parameter information includes command information (BYTE). This is a reserved field; set it to 0. The data information contains infinite retry field (0 for disable and 1 for enable) (BYTE). This function returns the following error codes.
		0x0100 Completed successfully
		0x8103 Invalid command
0x0046	Initialize Parallel Port	This function initializes the parallel port; setting it to a known state. The parameter information includes command information (BYTE). This is a reserved field; set it to 0. The data information includes a reserved field (BYTE). This function returns the following error codes.
		0x0100 Completed successfully
		0x810A Write fault
0x0048	Activate Font	This function activates a particular printer font. You need to know the font capabilities of your printer to use cartridge capability provided by this function. The parameter information includes command information (BYTE). This is a reserved field; set it to 0. The data information includes: code page (WORD) and font identification (WORD). Using a value of 0 for the code page and font identification sets the printer to its default code page and font. The valid range of code page values includes 0x0001 to 0xFFFF. The font identification range is 0x0001 to 0xFFFF. You can select a cartridge by sending the identification number appearing on the cartridge to the printer. The cartridge number must appear in the DEVINFO statement for the printer. This function returns the following error codes:
		0x0100 Completed successfully
		0x810A Write fault
		0xC102 Code page not available
		0xC103 No code page available (spooler not started)
		0xC104 Font ID not available

Function	Name	Description
		0xC109 Error caused by switcher error
		0xC10A Error caused by invalid printer name
		0xC10D Code page switcher uninitialized
		0xC10F SFN table full
		0xC113 DASD error reading font file
		0xC115 DASD error reading font file definition block
		0xC117 DASD error while writing spool file
		0xC118 Disk full error while writing spool file
		0xC119 Bad spool file handle
0x004D	Set Print Job Title	This function sets the print job title. ASCII strings longer than 126 characters get truncated to 125 characters plus the null character. The parameter information includes command information (BYTE). This is a reserved field; set it to 0. The data information includes: buffer length of the print job title (WORD) and the address of the ASCIIZ string containing the print job title (DWORD). This function returns the following error codes:
		0x0100 Completed successfully
		0x8113 Invalid parameter
0x004E	Set Parallel Port IRQ Timeout Value	This function sets the parallel IRQ timeout value. This is the length in time that the printer driver waits for a printer IRQ before it cancels the print job. The valid timeout range is 0 to 65,535 seconds. You also must issue a PrfWriteProfileString to update the OS2SYS.INI file when changing this value. The parameter information includes command information (BYTE). This is a reserved field; set it to 0. The data information includes the timeout value in seconds (WORD). This function returns the following error codes:
		0x0100 Completed successfully
		0x8113 Invalid parameter
0x0062	Query Frame Control	This function returns the current number of print columns and rows. The parameter information includes command information (BYTE). This is a reserved field; set it to 0. The data information includes: characters per line (80 and 132) and lines per inch (6 and 8). This function returns the following error code:
		0x0100 Completed successfully
0x0064	Query Infinite Retry	This function returns the infinite retry status. The parameter information includes command information (BYTE). This is a reserved field; set it to 0. The data information contains infinite retry field (0 for disable and 1 for enable) (BYTE). This function returns the following error code:
		0x0100 Completed successfully

Table 5-1   **Continued**

Function	Name	Description
0x0066	Query Parallel Port Status	This function returns the parallel port status. The parameter information includes command information (BYTE). This is a reserved field; set it to 0. The data information contains the port data field. The port data field includes the following bits: timeout (0), reserved (1 and 2), I/O error (3), selected (4), out-of-paper (5), acknowledge (6) and not busy (7). This function returns the following error code: 0x0100 Completed successfully
0x0069	Query Active Font	This function returns the active font identification and code page information. The parameter information includes command information (BYTE). This is a reserved field; set it to 0. The data information includes: code page (WORD) and font identification (WORD). The valid range of code page values includes 0x0001 to 0xFFFF. The font identification range is 0x0001 to 0xFFFF. This function returns the following error codes: 0x0100 Completed successfully 0xC103 No code page available (spooler not started) 0xC109 Error caused by switcher error 0xC10A Error caused by invalid printer name 0xC10D Code page switcher uninitialized 0xC110 Received request for SFN not in SFN table
0x006A	Verify Font	This function verifies the availability of a particular font identification and code page for the specified printer. The parameter information includes command information (BYTE). This is a reserved field; set it to 0. The data information includes: code page (WORD) and font identification (WORD). Using a value of 0 for the code page and font identification requests the printer's default code page and font; this combination is always available. The valid range of code page values includes 0x0001 to 0xFFFF. The font identification range is 0x0001 to 0xFFFF. You can select a cartridge by sending the identification number appearing on the cartridge to the printer. The cartridge number must appear in the DEVINFO statement for the printer. This function returns the following error codes: 0x0100 Completed successfully 0xC102 Code page not available 0xC103 No code page available (spooler not started) 0xC104 Font ID not available 0xC10A Error caused by invalid printer name 0xC10D Code page switcher uninitialized

Function	Name	Description
0x006E	Query Parallel Port IRQ Timeout Value	This function returns the parallel IRQ timeout value. This is the length in time that the printer driver waits for a printer IRQ before it cancels the print job. The valid timeout range is 0 to 65,535 seconds. The parameter information includes command information (BYTE). This is a reserved field; set it to 0. The data information includes the timeout value in seconds (WORD). This function returns the following error codes: 0x0100 Completed successfully 0x8113 Invalid parameter

Serial Port (RS232-C) IOCtl Commands (Category 1)

Function	Name	Description
0x0041	Set Bit Rate	This function sets the bit rate. An OPEN request packet will not change the value that you set with this function. The default bit rate is 1200 bps. You can use values from 2 bps to 19200 on conventional serial devices and from 10 bps to 57,600 bps on enhanced serial devices. The parameter information includes the bit rate (WORD). The hardware must support any bit rate you request up to 19,200 bps with a 0.01% margin of error (110 bps uses 0.026% and 2000 bps uses 0.69%). The device driver does not check the tolerance for bit rates above 19,200 bps. Use function 0x0061 to check the actual bit rate if you set the bit rate above 19,200 bps. There is no data information. This function returns a general failure if it does not succeed.
0x0042	Set Line Characteristics	This function sets the serial port parameters. An OPEN request packet will not change the characteristics that you set with this function. The physical device driver automatically zeros the data high bits if you set the word length to less than 8 bits. Your application must ensure that this does not conflict with any control sequence characters required to maintain flow control or other control sequences. The parameter information includes: number of data bits (BYTE), parity (BYTE), and stop bits (BYTE). The range of the data bits field is 5 to 8 data bits. The parity field contains the following information: no parity (00h), odd parity (01h), even parity (default) (02h), mark parity (03h), space parity (04h), and reserved (05h to FFh). The stop bits field contains the following values: 1 stop bit (00h), 1.5 stop bits (01h), 2 stop bits (02h), and reserved (03h to FFh). There is no data information. This function returns a general failure if it does not succeed.
0x0043	Extended Set Bit Rate	This function sets the bit rate in DWORDs to cover bit rates higher than 19,200 bps. It is an extension of function 0x0041. The parameter information includes: bit rate in bps (DWORD) and fraction (BYTE). The bit rate range for enhanced UARTs is 10 bps to 345,600 bps. Use function

Table 5-1   **Continued**

Function	**Name**	**Description**
		0x0063 to determine the maximum bit rate supported by the hardware.
		The fraction field allows you to set very precise bit rates (the default setting for this field is 0). Determine the value that you need for this field using the following equation: Output Bit Rate = Baud Clock / Scalar / Divisor Count; then multiply the fractional portion of Output Bit Rate × 256. The baud clock for an enhanced chip is 22.1184 MHz. The scalar value is 32. You can determine the divisor count using the following equation: Divisor Count = Baud Clock / Scalar / Binary Bit Rate. A shortcut for this whole procedure is to multiply the fractional portion of the desired baud rate by 256. For example, if you wanted to set the baud rate to 19,200.5 bps, then you would multiply 0.5 × 256 and set fraction to 128. The hardware must support any bit rate that you request up to 19,200 bps with a 0.01% margin of error (110 bps uses 0.026% and 2000 bps uses 0.69%). The device driver does not check the tolerance for bit rates above 19,200 bps. Use function 0x0063 to check the actual hit rate if you set the bit rate above 19,200 bps. There is no data information. This function returns a general failure if it does not succeed.
0x0044	Transmit Byte Immediate	This function transmits a byte immediately. The function fails if there is already a character in the physical device queue. You can determine if this condition exists using function 0x0064. The parameter information includes the character you want to transmit (BYTE). There is no data information. This function returns a general failure if it does not succeed.
0x0045	Set Break OFF	This function forces the physical device driver to stop generating a break signal. There is no parameter information. The data information includes a communications error word (WORD). The physical device driver returns this information if the call does not generate an error (see function 0x006D for full details). This function returns a general failure if it does not succeed.
0x0046	Set MODEM Control Signals	This function sets the MODEM control signals. The parameter information includes: MODEM control signals ON mask (BYTE) and MODEM control signals OFF mask (BYTE). Attempting to set the same bit in both masks always results in a general error. Both masks use the following bits: DTR (0), RTS (1), and reserved (2 through 7). You set a control signal on using a 1 in the ON mask. You set a control signal off using a 0 in the OFF mask. For example, to set DTR, you would use a value of 01h in the ON mask and FFh

Function	Name	Description
		in the OFF mask. To clear DTR, you would use a value of 00h in the ON mask and a value of FEh in the OFF mask. The data information includes a communications error word (WORD). The physical device driver returns this information if the call does not generate an error (see function 0x006D for full details). This function returns a general failure if it does not succeed.
0x0047	Behave as if XOFF Received	This function causes the physical device driver to act as if it received an XOFF character if you enable automatic transmit flow control. It causes a general failure error if the reception of the XOFF character causes the data transmission to stop. There is no parameter or data information. This function returns a general failure if it does not succeed.
0x0048	Behave as if XON Received	This function causes the physical device driver to act as if it received an XON character. There is no parameter or data information. This function returns a general failure if it does not succeed.
0x004B	Set Break On	This function sets break ON. If this does not result in a general failure, the physical device driver immediately generates a break signal. The transmit hardware does not receive any more data until you set break OFF. There is no parameter information. The data information includes a communications error word (WORD). The physical device driver returns this information if the call does not generate an error (see function 0x006D for full details). This function returns a general failure if it does not succeed.
0x0053	Set DCB Parameters	This function sets the device control block (DCB) information. The parameter information includes: zero-based write timeout processing interval in 0.01 second increments (WORD), zero-based read timeout processing interval in 0.01 second increments (WORD), Flags1 (BYTE), Flags2 (BYTE), Flags3 (BYTE), error-replacement character (BYTE), break-replacement character (BYTE), XON character (BYTE), and XOFF character (BYTE). Flags1 contains: DTR control (0 and 1), reserved (2), enable output handshaking using CTS (3), enable output handshaking using DSR (4), enable output handshaking using DCD (5), enable input sensitivity using DSR (6), and reserved (7). The DTR values include: disable (00b), enable (01b), input handshaking (10b), and invalid input (11b). Flags2 contains: enable automatic flow control (0), enable automatic receive flow control (1), reserved (2), enable error replacement character (3), enable break replacement character (4), enable receive flow control (5), and RTS control mode (6 and 7). The RTS values include: disable (00b), enable (01b), input handshaking (10b), and toggling on transmit (11b). Flags3 contains: enable write timeout

Table 5-1

Continued

Function	Name	Description
		processing (0), enable read timeout processing (1 and 2), extended hardware buffering (3 and 4), received trigger level (5 and 6), and transmit buffer load count (0 = 1 character and 1 = 16 characters). The read timeout processing values include: invalid input (00b), normal read timeout processing (01b), and no-wait read timeout processing (10b or 11b). The extended hardware buffering values include: not supported (00b), disabled (01b), enabled (10b), and automatic protocol override (11b). The received trigger level values include: 1 character (00b), 4 characters (01b), 8 characters (10b), and 14 characters (11b). There is no data information. This function returns a general failure if it does not succeed.
0x0054	Set Enhanced Enhanced Mode Parameters	This function sets the enhanced-mode parameters used by the enhanced UART on many machines. The physical device driver uses either the DMA or Enhanced FIFO mode as a default. In DMA mode, the DMA chip takes care of all transfers between memory and the port. Enhanced mode uses the full buffering capabilities of the extended hardware buffer. The parameter information includes: enhanced Flags1 (BYTE) and reserved (DWORD). Enhanced Flags1 bit structure contains: enhanced mode supported by hardware (0), enable enhanced mode (1), DMA receive operation request (2 and 3), DMA transmit operation request (4 and 5), receive operation in DMA mode (6), and transmit operation in DMA mode (7). The DMA receive operation request values include: disable (00b), enable (01b), dedicate a DMA channel to receive operation (10b), and reserved (11b). The DMA transmit operation values include: disable (00b), enable (01b), dedicate a DMA channel to transmit operation (10b), and reserved (11b). There is no data information. This function returns a general failure if it does not succeed.
0x0061	Query Bit Rate	This function returns the current bit rate setting. If the current bit rate is greater than the value a 1-WORD field can hold, then the physical device driver sets the bit rate to 1200 and returns that value. There is no parameter information. The data information includes the bit rate in bps (bits per second) (WORD). This function returns a general failure if it does not succeed.
0x0062	Query Line Characteristics	This function returns the current line characteristics. There is no parameter information. The data information includes: number of data bits (BYTE), parity (BYTE), stop bits (BYTE), and transmitting break. The range of the data bits field is 5 to 8 data bits. The parity field contains the following information: no parity (00h), odd parity (01h), even parity

Function	Name	Description
		(default) (02h), mark parity (03h), space parity (04h), and reserved (05h to FFh). The stop bits field contains the following values: 1 stop bit (00h), 1.5 stop bits (01h), 2 stop bits (02h), and reserved (03h to FFh). The function sets the transmitting break field to 0 if the physical device driver is not transmitting a break character. This function returns a general failure if it does not succeed.
0x0063	Extended Query Bit Rate	This function returns the bit rate in DWORDs to cover bit rates higher than 19,200 bps. It is an extension of function 0x0061. There is no parameter information. The data information includes: bit rate in bps (DWORD), fraction of current bit rate (BYTE), minimum bit rate supported in bps (DWORD), fraction of minimum bit rate supported (BYTE), maximum bit rate supported (DWORD), and fraction of maximum bit rate supported (BYTE). The bit rate range for enhanced UARTs is 10 bps to 345,600 bps. Factors including overall system overhead, the electrical characteristics of the hardware cables, and serial port type all affect the maximum bit rate supported value. This function returns a general failure if it does not succeed.
0x0064	Query COM Status	This function returns the communications port status. There is no parameter information. The data information includes the COM status byte (BYTE). This status byte includes the following information: transmit status (Tx) waiting for CTS turn on (0), Tx waiting for DSR turn on (1), Tx waiting for DCD turn on (2), Tx waiting because XOFF received (3), Tx waiting because XOFF transmitted (4), Tx waiting because physical device driver is transmitting break character (5), character waiting to transmit immediately (6), and receive status (Rx) waiting for DSR turn on (7). This function returns a general failure if it does not succeed.
0x0065	Query Transmit Data Status	This function returns the transmit data status. There is no parameter information. The data information includes the transmit status (BYTE). The transmit status field contains the following information: WRITE request packets in progress or queued (0), data in the physical device driver transmit queue (1), transmit hardware currently transmitting data (2), character waiting for immediate transmission (3), waiting to automatically transmit XON (4), waiting to automatically transmit XOFF (5), and undefined (6 and 7). This function returns a general failure if it does not succeed.
0x0066	Query MODEM Output Signals	This function returns the MODEM control output signals. There is no parameter information. The data information includes the MODEM control output signals (BYTE). This field contains the following information: DTR (0), RTS (1), and undefined (2 through 7). This function returns a general failure if it does not succeed.

Table 5-1   **Continued**

Function	Name	Description
0x0067	Query MODEM Input Signals	This function returns the current MODEM control input signals. There is no parameter information. The data information includes the MODEM control input signals (BYTE). This field contains the following information: undefined (0 through 3), CTS (4), DSR (5), RI (6), and DCD (7). This function returns a general failure if it does not succeed.
0x0068	Query Number of Characters in Receive Queue	This function returns the number of characters in the receive queue. There is no parameter packet information. The data information includes: number of characters queued (WORD) and size of receive queue (WORD). You cannot assume that there are no unsatisfied read requests if there are characters in the queue. The default queue size is 1K in PIO mode and 2K in DMA mode. This function returns a general failure if it does not succeed.
0x0069	Query Number of Characters in Transmit Queue	This function returns the number of characters in the transmit queue. There is no parameter packet information. The data information includes: number of characters queued (WORD) and size of transmit queue (WORD). You cannot assume that there are no unsatisfied write requests if there are characters in the queue. The default queue size is 128 bytes in PIO mode and 255 bytes in DMA mode. This function returns a general failure if it does not succeed.
0x006D	Query COM Error	This function retrieves the COM device error information, then clears the COM error information buffer. There is no parameter information. The data information includes the COM error word (COMERR) (WORD). The physical device driver sets COMERR when any of the events listed for the bit field occur. Only this function or an OPEN call can clear the COMERR buffer. This field contains the following information: receive queue overrun (0), receive hardware overrun (1), hardware detected parity error (2), hardware detected framing error (3), and undefined (4 through 15). This function returns a general failure if it does not succeed.
0x0072	Query COM Event Information	This function retrieves then clears the COM device event WORD. There is no parameter information. The data information includes the COM event word (WORD). The physical device driver sets the appropriate bits in the COM event word whenever one of the following events occur: character read from the COM device receive hardware and placed in the receive queue (0); serial port controller generated receive timeout interrupt during a receive request (1); last character in transmit queue set to the COM device transmit hardware (2); CTS changed state (3); DSR changed

Function	Name	Description
		state (4); DCD changed state (5); break detected (6); parity, framing, or receive hardware overrun (7); RI detected (8); and undefined (9 through 15). This function returns a general failure if it does not succeed.
0x0073	Query DCB Parameters	This function returns the device control block (DCB) information. There is no parameter information. The data information includes: zero-based write timeout processing interval in 0.01 second increments (WORD), zero-based read timeout processing interval in 0.01 second increments (WORD), Flags1 (BYTE), Flags2 (BYTE), Flags3 (BYTE), error-replacement character (BYTE), break-replacement character (BYTE), XON character (BYTE), and XOFF character (BYTE). Flags1 contains: DTR control (0 and 1), reserved (2), enable output handshaking using CTS (3), enable output handshaking using DSR (4), enable output handshaking using DCD (5), enable input sensitivity using DSR (6), and reserved (7). The DTR values include: disable (00b), enable (01b), input handshaking (10b), and invalid input (11b). Flags2 contains: enable automatic flow control (0), enable automatic receive flow control (1), reserved (2), enable error-replacement character (3), enable break-replacement character (4), enable receive flow control (5), and RTS control mode (6 and 7). The RTS values include: disable (00b), enable (01b), input handshaking (10b), and toggling on transmit (11b). Flags3 contains: enable write timeout processing (0), enable read timeout processing (1 and 2), extended hardware buffering (3 and 4), received trigger level (5 and 6), and transmit buffer load count (0 = 1 character and 1 = 16 characters). The read timeout processing values include: invalid input (00b), normal read timeout processing (01b), and no-wait read timeout processing (10b or 11b). The extended hardware buffering values include: not supported (00b), disabled (01b), enabled (10b), and automatic protocol override (11b). The received trigger level values include: 1 character (00b), 4 characters (01b), 8 characters (10b), and 14 characters (11b). This function returns a general failure if it does not succeed.
0x0074	Query Enhanced Mode Parameters	This function returns the enhanced mode parameters used by the enhanced UART on many machines. The physical device driver uses either the DMA or Enhanced FIFO mode as a default. In DMA mode, the DMA chip takes care of all transfers between memory and the port. Enhanced mode uses the full buffering capabilities of the extended hardware buffer. There is no parameter information. The data information includes: enhanced Flags1 (BYTE) and reserved (DWORD). Enhanced Flags1 bit structure contains: enhanced mode supported by hardware (0), enable enhanced mode (1), DMA receive operation request (2 and 3), DMA transmit operation request (4 and 5), receive operation in DMA mode (6), and transmit operation in DMA mode (7). The DMA

Table 5-1   **Continued**
_____

Function   Name   Description

(01b), dedicate a DMA channel to receive operation (10b),
and reserved (11b). The DMA transmit operation values
include: disable (00b), enable (01b), dedicate a DMA channel
to transmit operation (10b), and reserved (11b). This function
returns a general failure if it does not succeed.

Using Table 5-1 is quite simple. The previous paragraphs describe the
calling syntax for this function. You obtain hDevHandle using an open
call. The ulCategory entry appears in the heading for each group of
function calls. The ulFunction entry appears in the first column of the
table. The rest of the entries (pParmList, ulParmLengthMax,
pParmLengthInOut, pDataArea, ulDataLengthMax, and
pDataLengthInOut) appear in the function description in chapter 4. You
need to provide the specifics required to make these function work.

Testing your printer application completely might require you to know
a little about the parallel port itself. For example, wouldn't it be nice
if you could test out some of your error trapping routines without
spending too much time trying to get the printer to simulate the
failure? You can build a small jig called a loopback plug to partially
test your print application without wasting one sheet of paper. This is
a parallel port plug that is wired in such a way that it fools the
computer into thinking there is a printer attached to the machine. In
reality, all you are doing is simulating a printer. Likewise, by removing
one of the interconnection wires, you can simulate a printer failure.
This allows you to check the response of your printer with the least
potential for problems. Table 5-2 provides a complete listing of the
interconnections required to create a loopback plug. Each connection
has a signal name associated with it. All you need to do is disconnect
the required connect to test a potential printer problem.

Figure 5-1

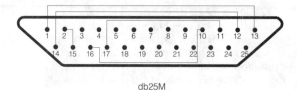

db25M

Parallel port pinouts.

Parallel port loopback plug connections   Table 5-2

From Connection	To Connection
11—Busy	17—Select input
10—Acknowledge printer	16—Initialize
12—Paper out	14—Autofeed
13—Select	01—Strobe
02—Data 0	15—Error

Many of the serial port functions listed in Table 5-1 use obscure looking acronyms. These acronyms come from the name of the signals that appear on the RS-232 port. Table 5-3 contains a complete list of all these acronyms along with their associated signal names.

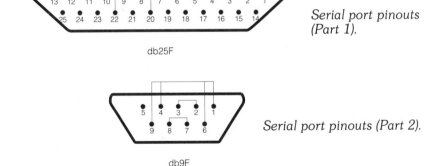

Figure 5-2

Serial port pinouts (Part 1).

Figure 5-3

Serial port pinouts (Part 2).

Table 5-3 provides you with more than just a few acronyms and definitions. You can use a loopback plug to test the functions of a serial port in much the same way as you can with a parallel port. The parallel port uses a male plug while the serial port uses a female plug, but the test concept is the same. Table 5-3 provides you with a complete list of interconnections required to make either a 9-pin or 25-pin serial loopback plug. You probably will want to make at least one of each type to ensure you have the right testing plug for all occasions.

You don't have to make these plugs yourself. There are many computer hardware supply stores that provide ready-made versions of

these useful plugs since technicians also use them to test the computer's hardware. You also can order the plugs from Performance Computer Diagnostics, 703 Grand Central Street, Clearwater, FL 34616, (813)443-1331.

Table 5-3

Serial port loopback plug connections

From Connection	To Connection
db9F Connector	
02—Received data (RD)	03—Transmitted data (TD)
07—Request to send (RTS)	08—Clear to send (CTS)
06—Data set ready (DSR) and 01—Carrier detect (CD)	04—Data terminal ready (DTR) and 09—Ring indicator (RI)
db25F Connector	
02—Received data (RD)	03—Transmitted data (TD)
04—Request to send (RTS)	05—Clear to send (CTS)
06—Data set ready (DSR) and 08—Carrier detect (CD)	20—Data terminal ready (DTR) and 22—Ring indicator (RI)

Disk API

WORKING with the OS/2 disk interface can get rather confusing for the average programmer. The operating system makes it easy to access a disk as long as you know the disk parameters and what type of access that you require. It seems like an easy thing to do until you consider that there are more disks on the market than anyone probably realizes. Each one uses a different set of parameters and some complicate matters by using disk translation to work with obsolete BIOS chips. Add to this maze the plethora of available controllers, and you get a puzzle of astronomical proportions. As you can see, figuring out what type of access you need and how to get it isn't as easy as it might first appear.

This chapter covers the three levels of support provided by OS/2 for disk operations. While it will not teach you everything there is to know about accessing hard disk drives, it does provide you with the OS/2 viewpoint. The first section tells you about the high-level disk specific functions provided by OS/2. The second section assumes the reader wants to create a Presentation Manager application. This is the section that covers OS/2's logical viewpoint of the disk. The third section is the disk operating system (or physical) level. Ring 2 and character-mode applications use this part of the API.

There are a number of "DOS" functions provided by OS/2. These functions usually provide you with high-level access that augments the access you gain using the WIN and GPI functions in chapter 3. (Remember, you can use a file as a device context in certain cases.) These functions appear in the first section of this chapter. Each description tells you about the function and how to use it. The descriptions also provide you with the ancillary information required to fully utilize the function in your applications.

OS/2 also provides disk access through the DOSDevIOCtrl function (I covered how you can use this flexible function to access other devices in the previous two chapters). Unlike the previous two chapters, the disk interface complicates matters by providing two levels of control: logical and physical.

⇨ DOSPhysicalDisk

The DOSPhysicalDisk function returns information about partitionable disks. The handle that you receive from the function allows you to access the drive using the DOSDevIOCtl function category 9 (logical disk access). You cannot use this handle for physical disk access. It uses the following syntax:

```
rc = DOSPhysicalDisk (ulFunction, pDataArea, ulDataLen,
    pParmList, ulParmLen)
```

The function provides only one return value (it does provide some return parameters discussed in the following paragraphs). rc contains a return code that tells you whether the function completed without error. It also contains an error code if it didn't. Table 6-1 provides a list of these error codes.

DOSPhysicalDisk function return codes   Table 6-1

Error number	Description
0	NO_ERROR
1	ERROR_INVALID_FUNCTION
87	ERROR_INVALID_PARAMETER

There are five parameters for this function. ulFunction contains a device specific function code in the range from 0 to 255. There are three tasks that you can perform with this function: obtain the total number of partitionable disks (INFO_COUNT_PARTITIONABLE_DISKS or a value of 1), get a handle to use with category 9 DOSDevIOCtl calls (INFO_GETIOCTLHANDLE or a value of 2), or release a handle used with category 9 DOSDevIOCtl calls (INFO_FREEIOCTLHANDLE or a value of 3). pDataArea contains address of the buffer used to hold the data information. Table 6-2 contains a complete listing of the data required for each task. ulDataLen contains the length of pDataArea in bytes (see Table 6-2 for valid lengths). A NULL value for pDataArea tells OS/2 that there is no data information defined for this call. OS/2 automatically ignores the ulDataLen parameter.

pParmList contains the address of the command-specific argument list. Table 6-3 contains a complete listing of the parameters required for each task. ulParmLen contains the length of pParmList in bytes. A NULL value for pParmList tells OS/2 that there is no parameter list defined for this call. OS/2 automatically ignores the ulParmLen parameter.

Table 6-2

DOSPhysicalDisk data values

Function	Data length	Description
1	2	Total number of partitionable disks in system.
2	2	Handle for the specified partitionable disk. You can use this handle with Category 9 IOCtl functions.
3	0	Always set the pointer to zero.

Table 6-3

DOSPhysicalDisk parameter values

Function	Data length	Description
1	0	Always set the pointer to zero.
2	Length of String	An ASCIIZ string that specifies the partitionable disk. In most cases, this parameter uses three bytes. You must include the following information: *DiskNumber:NULLbyte*.
3	2	The handle obtained in the data parameter of function 2.

⇨ DOSCancelLockRequest

The DOSCancelLockRequest function cancels the lock range request of an outstanding DOSSetFileLocks request. It cancels every request for that file. If two threads have waiting requests for a lock file range, then this function cancels both of them. This function uses the following calling syntax:

```
rc = DOSCancelLockRequest (hFileHandle, pLockRange)
```

Not all file-system drivers (FSDs) can cancel an outstanding lock request. This includes LANS that use a version of OS/2 prior to OS/2 version 2.00. It does not include the FAT or HPFS file systems.

The function provides only one return value. rc contains a return code that tells you whether the function completed without error. It also contains an error code if it didn't. Table 6-4 provides a list of these error codes.

DOSCancelLockRequest function return codes Table 6-4

Error number	Description
0	NO_ERROR
6	ERROR_INVALID_HANDLE
87	ERROR_INVALID_PARAMETER
173	ERROR_CANCEL_VIOLATION

This function uses two parameters. hFileHandle contains the file handle that you obtained using the DOSSetFileLocks function. pLockRange contains the address of a structure containing the following information: ulFileOffset (LONG) an offset to the beginning of the lock range and ulRangeLength (LONG) length of the range in bytes.

⇨ DOSClose

The DOSClose function closes a file, pipe, or device handle. You must issue a separate call for each handle that you create using the DOSDupHandle function before OS/2 updates the directory and writes information from the internal buffers to disk. OS/2 normally notifies the affected device before closing the handle. When you close all the handles on one end of a pipe, OS/2 considers the pipe broken. Closing the client end of a pipe disabled it until you call DOSDisConnectNPipe. Closing the server end of a pipe after you

close the client end automatically deallocates the pipe. This function uses the following calling syntax:

```
rc = DOSClose (hFileHandle)
```

The function provides only one return value. rc contains a return code that tells you whether the function completed without error. It also contains an error code if it didn't. Table 6-5 provides a list of these error codes.

Table 6-5

DOSClose function return codes

Error number	Description
0	NO_ERROR
2	ERROR_FILE_NOT_FOUND
5	ERROR_ACCESS_DENIED
6	ERROR_INVALID_HANDLE

This function uses one parameter. hFileHandle contains the file handle that you obtained using the DOSCreateNPipe, DOSCreatePipe, DOSDupHandle, or DOSOpen functions.

⇨ DOSCopy

The DOSCopy function copies the source file or directory to the specified destination. You cannot use wildcard characters in either the source or destination names. The source and destination can appear on different drives. You cannot replace a read-only file on the destination path using this function (this always results in an error). If you use a device name as a destination, then the source name must contain a file, not a directory.

The DOSCopy function does not always copy extended attributes (EAs) from the source to the destination. For example, it does not copy EAs if you want to append to an existing file. If the destination does not support EAs, then this function ends in an error. The

DOSCopy function takes the following actions when an I/O error occurs:

> ➤ If the source name is a directory, it deletes the file that it was in the process of copying from the target path.

> ➤ If the source name is a replacement file, it deletes the file from the target path.

> ➤ If the source name is a file that you want to append, it resizes the target file to its original size.

This function uses the following calling syntax:

```
rc = DOSCopy (pszSourceName, pszTargetName, ulOpCode)
```

The function provides only one return value. rc contains a return code that tells you whether the function completed without error. It also contains an error code if it didn't. Table 6-6 provides a list of these error codes.

DOSCopy function return codes

Table 6-6

Error number	Description
0	NO_ERROR
2	ERROR_FILE_NOT_FOUND
3	ERROR_PATH_NOT_FOUND
5	ERROR_ACCESS_DENIED
26	ERROR_NOT_DOS_DISK
32	ERROR_SHARING_VIOLATION
36	ERROR_SHARING_BUFFER_EXCEEDED
87	ERROR_INVALID_PARAMETER
108	ERROR_DRIVE_LOCKED
112	ERROR_DISK_FULL
206	ERROR_FILENAME_EXCED_RANGE
267	ERROR_DIRECTORY
282	ERROR_EAS_NOT_SUPPORTED
283	ERROR_NEED_EAS_NOT_FOUND

This function uses three parameters. pszSourceName contains the ASCIIZ name of the source file, subdirectory, or character devices. pszTargetName contains the ASCIIZ name of destination file, subdirectory, or character device. ulOpMode contains a DWORD bitmap that defines how OS/2 executes the DOSCopy function. Table 6-7 contains a complete description of these functions.

Table 6-7

DOSCopy function return codes

Bit	Description
0	Existing file disposition: 0 = Do not copy the source file if the name already exists on the destination. OS/2 returns an error for a single file copy when this condition exists. 1 = Copy the source file to the destination even if the filename already exists (DCPY_EXISTING).
1	Append the source file at the end of the destination file. 0 = Replace the destination file with the source file. 1 = Append the source file to the end of the destination file (DCPY_APPEND).
2	Discard the EAs if the source file contains EAs and the destination does not support them. 0 = Discard the EAs. 1 = Generate an error if the file system does not support EAs (DCPY_FAILEAS).
3-31	Reserved, always set to 0.

DOSCreateDir

The DOSCreateDir function creates a directory with the set of EAs specified by the application. If the path name contains nonexistent directories, then OS/2 does not create the desired subdirectory. Use the DOSQuerySysInfo maximum path length supported by the operating system. You cannot use blanks when creating a directory on a FAT file system drive. This function uses the following calling syntax:

```
rc = DOSCreateDir (pszDirName, pEABuf)
```

The function provides only one return value. rc contains a return code that tells you whether the function completed without error. It also contains an error code if it didn't. Table 6-8 provides a list of these error codes.

Error number[1]	Description
0	NO_ERROR
3	ERROR_PATH_NOT_FOUND
5	ERROR_ACCESS_DENIED
26	ERROR_NOT_DOS_DISK
87	ERROR_INVALID_PARAMETER
108	ERROR_DRIVE_LOCKED
206	ERROR_FILENAME_EXCED_RANGE
254	ERROR_INVALID_EA_NAME
255	ERROR_EA_LIST_INCONSISTENT

DOSCreateDir function return codes Table 6-8

[1] Some texts include the ERROR_EA_VALUE_UNSUPPORTABLE message. There is no standard error number associated with this message.

This function uses two parameters. pszPathName contains the ASCIIZ name of the directory that you want to create. You must not specify a path longer than the path supported by the operating system. pEABuf contains a pointer to the EA buffer (uses the EAOP2 data structure). If you specify a 0 value for pEABuf, then OS/2 creates a directory without extended attributes.

⇨ DOSDelete

The DOS delete function removes a filename from a directory. In most cases, you can recover the deleted file. You cannot use wildcard characters with this function. OS/2 will not allow you to delete read-only or shared files. Use the DOSSetFileInfo function to change the attribute of a read-only file before calling this function. The DOSDeleteDir function allows you to remove directories from the drive. This function uses the following calling syntax:

```
rc = DOSDelete (pszFileName)
```

The function provides only one return value. rc contains a return code that tells you whether the function completed without error. It also contains an error code if it didn't. Table 6-9 provides a list of these error codes.

Table 6-9   **DOSDelete function return codes**

Error number	Description
0	NO_ERROR
2	ERROR_FILE_NOT_FOUND
3	ERROR_PATH_NOT_FOUND
5	ERROR_ACCESS_DENIED
26	ERROR_NOT_DOS_DISK
32	ERROR_SHARING_VIOLATION
36	ERROR_SHARING_BUFFER_EXCEEDED
87	ERROR_INVALID_PARAMETER
206	ERROR_FILENAME_EXCED_RANGE

This function uses one parameter. pszFileName contains the ASCIIZ name of the file that you want to delete.

➾ DOSDeleteDir

The DOSDeleteDir function removes a directory from the disk drive. This function works only on empty directories (this includes hidden files). Use DOSDelete to remove the files from a directory. This function uses the following calling syntax:

```
rc = DOSDeleteDir (pszDirName)
```

The function provides only one return value. rc contains a return code that tells you whether the function completed without error. It also contains an error code if it didn't. Table 6-10 provides a list of these error codes.

DOSDeleteDir Function Return Codes Table 6-10

Error number	Description
0	NO_ERROR
2	ERROR_FILE_NOT_FOUND
3	ERROR_PATH_NOT_FOUND
5	ERROR_ACCESS_DENIED
16	ERROR_CURRENT_DIRECTORY
26	ERROR_NOT_DOS_DISK
87	ERROR_INVALID_PARAMETER
108	ERROR_DRIVE_LOCKED
206	ERROR_FILENAME_EXCED_RANGE

This function uses one parameter. pszDirName contains the ASCIIZ name of the directory that you want to delete.

 # DOSDupHandle

The DOSDupHandle function duplicates the handle of an open file. The new handle is tied to the old handle. For example, if you move the file pointer using one file handle, the pointer of the other handle moves with it. Issuing DOSClose for a handle does not close any of the duplicate handles. This function uses the following calling syntax:

```
rc = DOSDupHandle (hOldFileHandle, ppshfNewFileHandle)
```

The function provides only one return value. rc contains a return code that tells you whether the function completed without error. It also contains an error code if it didn't. Table 6-11 provides a list of these error codes.

Table 6-11	DOSDupHandle function return codes

Error number	Description
0	NO_ERROR
4	ERROR_TOO_MANY_OPEN_FILES
6	ERROR_INVALID_HANDLE
114	ERROR_INVALID_TARGET_HANDLE

This function uses two parameters. hOldFileHandle contains the handle that you want to duplicate. ppshfNewFileHandle contains a pointer to a DWORD that contains a description of how you want to duplicate the handle on input, and the new file handle on output. If ppshfNewFileHandle contains 0xFFFFFFFF on input, then OS/2 allocates a new handle and returns it. Using any other value assigns that handle number to the new handle. You can specify standard input (0x00000000), standard output (0x00000001), and standard error (0x00000002) as the value for the new handle.

⇨ DOSEditName

The DOSEditName changes the name of files and directories by transforming one ASCII string into another using wildcard filename characters for editing or search operations on the string. You normally use this function with functions like DOSMove and DOSCopy that do not allow the use of wildcard characters. This function works like any DOS wildcard filename function. If you specify the wildcard filename in the source string, then DOSEditName performs a search function. If you specify the wildcard filename in the edit string, then DOSEditName performs an edit function. This function uses the following calling syntax:

```
rc = DOSEditName (ulEditLevel, pszSourceString, pszEditString,
    pbTargetBuf, ulTargetBufLen)
```

The function provides only one return value (it does provide some return parameters discussed in the following paragraphs). rc contains a return code that tells you whether the function completed without error. It also contains an error code if it didn't. Table 6-12 provides a list of these error codes.

DOSEditName function return codes

Table 6-12

Error number	Description
0	NO_ERROR
87	ERROR_INVALID_PARAMETER
123	ERROR_INVALID_NAME

This function uses five parameters. usEditLevel contains the level of editing semantics to use in transforming the source string. A level of 1 uses the editing semantics of OS/2 version 1.2. pszSourceString contains the ASCIIZ string that you want to transform. pszEditString contains the ASCIIZ string that you want to use for editing. You can use wildcard characters in either pszSourceString or pszEditString. pbTargetBuf contains the output buffer for the resulting ASCIIZ string. ulTargetBufLen contains the length of pbTargetBuf in bytes.

 # DOSEnumAttrib

The DOSEnumAttrib function lists the EAs for a file or subdirectory. This includes the attribute name and length. You can use the structure that this function returns in pEnumBuf to calculate the buffer length required to store the entire EA structure returned by the DOSQueryPathInfo or DOSQueryFileInfo functions. Each field in the pEnumBuf structure contributes toward the overall length of the full EA (FEA) buffer. Each EA entry starts on a DWORD boundary. Table 6-13 provides the information that you need to calculate the buffer length. Simply add the entries together to obtain the overall length of the buffer. You could simplify this equation to 9 bytes + value of cbName + value of cbValue.

Table 6-13 **FEA buffer length entities**

Size	Description
4	oNextEntryOffset—Number of bytes to the beginning of the next EA data structure. Remember that each structure begins on a DWORD boundary. A value of 0 in this field indicates that this is the last data structure.
1	fEA
1	cbName
2	cbValue
Value of cbName	EA name
1	Terminating NULL in cbName
Value of cbValue	EA value

OS/2 allows you to cycle through the EA entries. To obtain the next EA entry, simply set the ulEntryNum value to its previous value plus the value of pEntryCnt. The DOSEnumAttribute function does not control EA ordering; it merely lists them for you.

You also need to consider the multitasking nature of OS/2 when enumerating the EAs. The value returned for EA 11 on one call might contain a different value on a second call. A DOSSetFileInfo or DOSSetPathInfo call could modify the entry during or after the time that you read it. Open the file using the deny-write attribute to prevent this from happening. Of course, this could result in a sharing violation should another process need to open the file. You do not need to worry about this when checking the EAs of a directory entry because two processes cannot share it. This function uses the following calling syntax:

```
rc = DOSEnumAttribute (ulRefType, pFileRef, ulEntryNum, pEnumBuf,
    ulEnumBufSize, pEnumCnt, ulInfoLevel)
```

The function provides only one return value (it does provide some return parameters discussed in the following paragraphs). rc contains a return code that tells you whether the function completed without error. It also contains an error code if it didn't. Table 6-14 provides a list of these error codes.

DOSEnumAttribute function return codes   Table 6-14

Error number	Description
0	NO_ERROR
3	ERROR_PATH_NOT_FOUND
5	ERROR_ACCESS_DENIED
6	ERROR_INVALID_HANDLE
8	ERROR_INVALID_PARAMETER
87	ERROR_INVALID_PARAMETER
111	ERROR_BUFFER_OVERFLOW
124	ERROR_INVALID_LEVEL
206	ERROR_FILENAME_EXCED_RANGE

This function uses seven parameters. ulRefType indicates whether pFileRef points to a handle or an ASCIIZ name. A value of 0 indicates a file handle, while a value of 1 indicates a file or subdirectory. pFileRef contains a pointer to the file handle or the ASCIIZ name of a file or subdirectory. ulEntryName contains the ordinal number of the EA entry that you want to retrieve. Never use a value of 0; 1 indicates the first EA entry. pEnumBuf contains a pointer to the buffer used to store the EA information. This entry uses a data structure of type DENA2. ulEnumBufSize contains the length of pEnumBuf (normally 9 bytes). pEnumBuf contains the number of EAs that you want returned on entry. Using a value of –1 returns all the EAs that pEnumBuf can hold. This parameter contains the actual number of EAs returned on exit. ulInfoLevel contains the level of information that you require. The only valid entry is ENUMEA_LEVEL_NO_VALUE (1), which indicates you require level 1 information.

⇨ DOSFindClose

The DOSFindClose function closes a find request handle, ending the current search. You cannot issue a DOSFindNext call after using this

function unless you issue a DOSFindFirst call first. This function uses the following calling syntax:

```
rc = DOSFindClose (hdirDirHandle)
```

The function provides only one return value. rc contains a return code that tells you whether the function completed without error. It also contains an error code if it didn't. Table 6-15 provides a list of these error codes.

Table 6-15

DOSCloseFind function return codes

Error number	Description
0	NO_ERROR
6	ERROR_INVALID_HANDLE

This function uses one parameter. hdirDirHandle contains the directory handle that you obtained using the DOSFindFirst function. This is the same handle you used to perform a directory search with the DOSFindNext function.

⇨ DOSFindFirst

The DOSFindFirst function finds the first of one or more file objects that match the file specification you supply. The file specification can include wildcard characters. This function returns the specified number of directory entries (if possible) and their matching EA information. You use the DOSFindNext function to continue the process of finding and returning directory entries. This function uses the following calling syntax:

```
rc = DOSFindFirst (pszFileName, pphdirDirHandle, ulAttribute,
    pResultBuf, ulResultBufLen, pSearchCount, ulFileInfoLevel)
```

The function provides only one return value (it does provide some return parameters discussed in the following paragraphs). rc contains a return code that tells you whether the function completed without error. It also contains an error code if it didn't. Table 6-16 provides a list of these error codes.

DOSFindFirst function return codes Table 6-16

Error number	Description
0	NO_ERROR
2	ERROR_FILE_NOT_FOUND
3	ERROR_PATH_NOT_FOUND
6	ERROR_INVALID_HANDLE
18	ERROR_NO_MORE_FILES
26	ERROR_NOT_DOS_DISK
87	ERROR_INVALID_PARAMETER
108	ERROR_DRIVE_LOCKED
111	ERROR_BUFFER_OVERFLOW
113	ERRO_NO_MORE_SEARCH_HANDLES
206	ERROR_FILENAME_EXCED_RANGE
208	ERROR_META_EXPANSION_TOO_LONG
254	ERROR_INVALID_EA_NAME
255	ERROR_EA_LIST_INCONSISTENT
275	ERROR_EAS_DIDN'T_FIT

This function uses seven parameters. pszFileName contains the
ASCIIZ filename or subdirectory that you want to find. You can use
wildcard characters with this parameter. pphdirDirHandle contains
the handle associated with the DOSFindFirst request. You can supply
the following values for this parameter: 0x00000000 (assign the
standard output handle) or 0xFFFFFFFF (allocate and return a search
handle). ulAttribute contains the file attribute values that you want to
find. These attribute bits include: FILE_READONLY (0),
FILE_HIDDEN (1), FILE_SYSTEM (2), reserved (3),
FILE_DIRECTORY (4), FILE_ARCHIVED (5), reserved (6 and 7),
MUST_HAVE_READONLY (8), MUST_HAVE_HIDDEN (9),
MUST_HAVE_SYSTEM (10), reserved (11),
MUST_HAVE_DIRECTORY (12), MUST_HAVE_ARCHIVED (13),
and reserved (14 through 31). You can use these bits individually or
in combination. The only attribute that you cannot specify is the
volume label attribute. Use the DOSQueryFSInfo function to obtain

this information. On entry, pResultBuf contains a pointer to the directory search structures for file object information levels 1 through 3. Use the value of ulFileInfoLevel to determine which search structure to use. The information returned in the buffer reflects the most recent call to DOSClose or DOSResetBuffer. ulResultBufLen contains the length of pResultBuf in bytes. pSearchCount contains the number of matching entries that you want on entry. On exit, this parameter contains the number of entries placed in pResultBuf. ulFileInfoLevel contains the level of information that you require. These levels include: FIL_STANDARD (level 1), FIL_QUERYEASIZE (level 2), and FIL_QUERYEASFROMLIST (level 3).

 # DOSFindNext

The DOSFindNext function performs subsequent searches for file or directory names using the handle obtained using the DOSFindFirst function. This function uses the following calling syntax:

```
rc = DOSFindNext (hdirDirHandle, pResultBuf, ulResultBufLen,
    pSearchCount)
```

The function provides only one return value (it does provide some return parameters discussed in the following paragraphs). rc contains a return code that tells you whether the function completed without error. It also contains an error code if it didn't. Table 6-17 provides a list of these error codes.

Table 6-17   **DOSFindNext function return codes**

Error number	Description
0	NO_ERROR
6	ERROR_INVALID_HANDLE
18	ERROR_NO_MORE_FILES
26	ERROR_NOT_DOS_DISK
87	ERROR_INVALID_PARAMETER
111	ERROR_BUFFER_OVERFLOW
275	ERROR_EAS_DIDN'T_FIT

This function uses four parameters. hdirDirHandle contains the directory handle. On entry, pResultBuf contains a pointer to the directory search structures for file object information levels 1 through 3. The information returned in the buffer reflects the most recent call to DOSClose or DOSResetBuffer. You normally use the same structure used for the DOSFindFirst call. ulResultBufLen contains the length of pResultBuf in bytes. pSearchCount contains the number of matching entries you want on entry. On exit, this parameter contains the number of entries placed in pResultBuf.

 # DOSForceDelete

The DOSForceDelete function permanently removes a filename from a directory. You cannot recover the file. OS/2 does not allow you to use wildcard characters with this function. In addition, this function will not delete read-only files or subdirectories. Use the DOSSetFileInfo function to change the attribute of read-only files. The DOSDeleteDir function allows you to delete directories. This function uses the following calling syntax:

```
rc = DOSForceDelete (pszFileName)
```

The function provides only one return value. rc contains a return code that tells you whether the function completed without error. It also contains an error code if it didn't. Table 6-18 provides a list of these error codes.

DOSForceDelete function return codes

Table 6-18

Error number	Description
0	NO_ERROR
2	ERROR_FILE_NOT_FOUND
3	ERROR_PATH_NOT_FOUND
5	ERROR_ACCESS_DENIED
26	ERROR_NOT_DOS_DISK
32	ERROR_SHARING_VIOLATION

427

Table 6-18   **Continued**

Error number	Description
36	ERROR_SHARING_BUFFER_EXCEEDED
87	ERROR_INVALID_PARAMETER
206	ERROR_FILENAME_EXCED_RANGE

This function uses one parameter. pszFileName contains the name of the file you want to delete.

⇨ DOSFSAttach

The DOSFSAttach function attaches or detaches a drive to or from a remote file system driver (FSD). You also can use it to attach or detach a pseudocharacter device name to or from a local or remote FSD. This function does not support the redirection of local drives. This function uses the following calling syntax:

```
rc = DOSFSAttach (pszDeviceName, pszFSDName, pDataBuffer,
    ulDataBufferLen, ulOpFlag)
```

The function provides only one return value (it does provide some return parameters discussed in the following paragraphs). rc contains a return code that tells you whether the function completed without error. It also contains an error code if it didn't. Table 6-19 provides a list of these error codes.

Table 6-19   **DOSFSAttach function return codes**

Error number	Description
0	NO_ERROR
8	ERROR_NOT_ENOUGH_MEMORY
15	ERROR_INVALID_DRIVE
124	ERROR_INVALID_LEVEL
252	ERROR_INVALID_FSD_NAME
253	ERROR_INVALID_PATH

This function uses five parameters. pszDeviceName contains the drive designation or a pseudocharacter device name when ulOpFlag equals 0 or 1. This parameter contains the name of a spooled device when ulOpFlag equals 2 or 3. A drive designation or spooled device name is an ASCIIZ string containing a drive letter and a colon. The file system does not see requests to a spooled device. A pseudocharacter device name consists of an ASCIIZ string with the filename subdirectory "\DEV\". The file system receives all requests for the pseudocharacter device name after successful attachment. pszFSDName contains the ASCIIZ name of the remote file system. Set this parameter to 0 when ulOpFlag equals 2 or 3. pDataBuffer contains a pointer to the user supplied FSD argument data area when ulOpFlag equals 0 or 1. The format of this data varies from driver to driver. The parameter contains the following information when ulOpFlag equals 2: hNmPipe (WORD), cbSpoolObj (BYTE), and szSpoolObj (ASCIIZ). Always set pDataBuffer to 0 when ulOpFlag equals 3. ulDataBufferLen contains the length of pDataBuffer in bytes. ulOpFlag determines which operation this function performs: attach (0), detach (1), spool attach (2), or spool detach (3).

 DOSFSCtl

The DOSFSCtl function provides an extended standard interface between an application and an FSD. This function uses the following calling syntax:

```
rc = DOSFSCtl (pDataArea, ulDataLengthMax, pDataLengthInOut,
    pParmList, ulParmLengthMax, pParmLengthInOut,
    ulFunctionCode, pszRouteName, hFileHandle, ulRouteMethod)
```

The function provides only one return value (it does provide some return parameters discussed in the following paragraphs). rc contains a return code that tells you whether the function completed without error. It also contains an error code if it didn't. Table 6-20 provides a list of these error codes.

Table 6-20   **DOSFSCtl function return codes**

Error number	Description
0	NO_ERROR
1	ERROR_INVALID_FUNCTION
6	ERROR_INVALID_HANDLE
87	ERROR_INVALID_PARAMETER
95	ERROR_INTERRUPT
111	ERROR_BUFFER_OVERFLOW
117	ERROR_INVALID_CATEGORY
124	ERROR_INVALID_LEVEL
252	ERROR_INVALID_FSD_NAME

This function uses ten parameters. pDataArea contains the data area address. ulDataLengthMax contains the length of pDataArea in bytes (the maximum length of the data returned by the FSD). pDataLengthInOut can contain a larger value than ulDataLengthMax on input, but not on output. pDataLengthInOut contains the length of the data passed to the FSD on input. It contains the length of the data passed by the FSD in pDataArea on output. If the function returns with an ERROR_BUFFER_OVERFLOW error, then this parameter contains the buffer length required to hold the FSD data. pParmList contains a command-specific parameter list. ulParmLengthMax contains the length of pParmList in bytes (the maximum data length that the FSD can return). pParmLength contains the length of the data sent to the FSD on input. It contains the length of the data returned by the FSD on output. If the function returns an ERROR_BUFFER_OVERFLOW error, then this parameter holds the buffer size required to hold the FSD data. ulFunctionCode contains an FSD specific function code. pszRouteName contains the ASCIIZ name of the FSD or the path name of a file or directory. hFileHandle contains a file or device specific handle. ulRouteMethod selects the request routing method: FSCTL_HANDLE (1) file handle directs routing and the FSD associated with the file handle receives the request, FSCTL_PATHNAME (2) path name directs routing and the FSD associated with the drive associated with the path name receives the request, and FSCTL_FSDNAME (3) FSD name directs routing.

 # DOSMove

The DOSMove function moves a file from one location to another on the same drive. It does not provide for inter-drive transfers. You also can use this function to change the filename. The DOSMove function does not allow you to use wildcard characters. There are other limitations that you need to observe when using this function:

➤ Attempts to move a parent directory to a position below one of its children always fails.

➤ Attributes always travel with the file to its new location.

➤ You cannot replace read-only files in the target directory.

➤ Always use the DOSQuerySysInfo function to determine the maximum path length allowed by the operating system.

You can use the DOSMove function to change the case of a file on a drive controlled by an FSD. This function uses the following calling syntax:

```
rc = DOSMove (pszOldPathName, pszNewPathName)
```

The function provides only one return value. rc contains a return code that tells you whether the function completed without error. It also contains an error code if it didn't. Table 6-21 provides a list of these error codes.

DOSMove function return codes Table 6-21

Error number	Description
0	NO_ERROR
2	ERROR_FILE_NOT_FOUND
3	ERROR_PATH_NOT_FOUND
5	ERROR_ACCESS_DENIED
17	ERROR_NOT_SAME_DEVICE
26	ERROR_NOT_DOS_DISK

Table 6-21   **Continued**

Error number	Description
32	ERROR_SHARING_VIOLATION
36	ERROR_SHARING_BUFFER_EXCEEDED
87	ERROR_INVALID_PARAMETER
108	ERROR_DRIVE_LOCKED
206	ERROR_FILENAME_EXCED_RANGE
250	ERROR_CIRCULARITY_REQUESTED
251	ERROR_DIRECTORY_IN_CDS

This function uses two parameters. pszOldPathName contains the name of the file or subdirectory that you want to move and/or rename. pszNewPathName contains the new file or subdirectory name (including the new path information).

DOSOpen

The DOSOpen function opens a new file, an existing file, or a replacement for an exiting file. It returns a handle that you can use to access the file and sets the read/write pointer to the first byte in the file. Use the DOSSetFilePtr function to change the position of the file pointer. You can provide EAs for an open file. This function uses the following calling syntax:

```
rc = DOSOpen (pszFileName, ppshfFileHandle, pActionTaken,
    ulFileSize, ulFileAttribute, ulOpenFlag, ulOpenMode, pEABuf)
```

The function provides only one return value (it does provide some return parameters discussed in the following paragraphs). rc contains a return code that tells you whether the function completed without error. It also contains an error code if it didn't. Table 6-22 provides a list of these error codes.

DOSOpen function return codes   Table 6-22

Error number	Description
0	NO_ERROR
2	ERROR_FILE_NOT_FOUND
3	ERROR_PATH_NOT_FOUND
4	ERROR_TOO_MANY_OPEN_FILES
5	ERROR_ACCESS_DENIED
12	ERROR_INVALID_ACCESS
26	ERROR_NOT_DOS_DISK
32	ERROR_SHARING_VIOLATION
36	ERROR_SHARING_BUFFER_EXCEEDED
82	ERROR_CANNOT_MAKE
87	ERROR_INVALID_PARAMETER
99	ERROR_DEVICE_IN_USE
108	ERROR_DRIVE_LOCKED
110	ERROR_OPEN_FAILED
112	ERROR_DISK_FULL
206	ERROR_FILENAME_EXCED_RANGE
231	ERROR_PIPE_BUSY

This function uses eight parameters. pszFileName contains the name of the file or device you want to open. ppshfFileHandle contains the file handle on exit. pEABuf contains the EA buffer which uses the EAOP2 structure. If you set this parameter to zero, the DOSOpen does not define any EAs for the file.

pActionTaken contains a value to define the action taken by the DOSOpen function that includes: FILE_EXISTED (1), FILE_CREATED (2), or FILE_TRUNCATED (3). This value has no meaning if the open fails. ulFileSize contains the new logical file size in bytes. The function ignores this parameter unless you create a new file or replace an existing one. You cannot create or replace a file with a zero length if the ulOpenMode parameter contains the read-only flag.

ulFileAttribute contains the file attribute bits: FILE_NORMAL or FILE_READONLY (0), FILE_HIDDEN (1), FILE_SYSTEM (2), reserved (3), FILE_DIRECTORY (4), FILE_ARCHIVED (5), and reserved (6 through 31). The function ignores this parameter unless you create a new file. You can use these bits individually or in combination.

ulOpenFlag contains flags that determine the action that DOSOpen takes depending on whether the file exists or not. The values for bits 0 through 3 include: OPEN_ACTION_REPLACE_IF_EXISTS, OPEN_ACTION_OPEN_IF_EXISTS, and OPEN_ACTION_FAIL_IF_EXITS. The values for bits 4 though 7 include: OPEN_ACTION_CREATE_IF_NEW and OPEN_ACTION_FAIL_IF_NEW. You must set bits 8 through 31 to zero.

ulOpenMode defines the open function mode. Bits 0 through 2 contain the access mode flags: OPEN_ACCESS_READONLY, OPEN_ACCESS_WRITEONLY, or OPEN_ACCESS_READWRITE. Bit 3 is reserved; always set it to zero. Bits 4 through 6 contain the share access mode flags: OPEN_SHARE_DENYREADWRITE, OPEN_SHARE_DENYWRITE, OPEN_SHARE_DENYREAD, or OPEN_SHARE_DENYNONE. Bit 7 contains the inheritance flag: a process created by DOSExecPrg inherits the flag (0) or flag private to the current process (1). Bits 8 through 10 contain the locality of reference flags: OPEN_FLAGS_NO_LOCALITY, OPEN_FLAGS_SEQUENTIAL, OPEN_FLAGS_RANDOM, or OPEN_FLAGS_RANDOMSEQUENTIAL. Bit 11 is reserved; set it to zero. Bit 12 contains the cache/no-cache flag (cache when set to 0). Bit 13 contains the fail errors flag: report through the system critical-error handler (0) or report directly to the caller (1). Bit 14 contains the write-through flag (write-through mode when set to 1). Bit 15 contains the direct open flag: open normally (0) or mounted volume to open for direct access (1). Bits 16 through 31 are reserved; set them to 0.

⇨ DOSQueryCurrentDir

The DOSQueryCurrentDir function returns the full path name of the current directory for the specified drive. Neither the drive letter nor

an initial backslash (\) appear as part of the returned string. This function uses the following calling syntax:

```
rc = DOSQueryCurrentDir (ulDriveNumber, pbDirPath, pDirPathLen)
```

The function provides only one return value (it does provide some return parameters discussed in the following paragraphs). rc contains a return code that tells you whether the function completed without error. It also contains an error code if it didn't. Table 6-23 provides a list of these error codes.

DOSQueryCurrentDir function return codes Table 6-23

Error number	Description
0	NO_ERROR
15	ERROR_INVALID_DRIVE
26	ERROR_NOT_DOS_DISK
108	ERROR_DRIVE_LOCKED
111	ERROR_BUFFER_OVERFLOW

This function uses three parameters. ulDriveNumber contains the drive number. Use a value of 0 for the current drive or a 1-based number for a specific drive. pbDirPath contains the fully qualified path name of the current directory. pDirPathLen contains the length of pbDirPath in bytes on input. If an error occurs, this parameter contains the buffer length required to hold the path information.

⇨ DOSQueryCurrentDisk

The DOSQueryCurrentDisk function returns the current default drive for the requesting process. This function uses the following calling syntax:

```
rc = DOSQueryCurrentDrive (pDriveNumber, pLogicalDriveMap)
```

The function provides only one return value (it does provide some return parameters discussed in the following paragraphs). rc contains

a return code that tells you the function completed without error (NO_ERROR). There are no error codes associated with this function.

This function uses two parameters. pDriveNumber contains the 1-based number of the default drive. For example, drive A equals 1. pLogicalDriveMap contains a bitmap where the system returns the logical drive map as a DWORD. This is a zero-based representation, with each drive consuming one bit (bits 26 through 31 always contain 0). A value of 1 in a specific drive location indicates that logical drive exists.

DOSQueryFHState

The DOSQueryFHState function returns the state of the specified file handle. You can use this function to return critical error handling control to the system when the application cannot handle it by turning off the fail/error bit and reissuing the failed I/O call. The Direct I/O flag provides physical access to the drive by bypassing the FSD. This function uses the following calling syntax:

```
rc = DOSQueryFHState (hFileHandle, pFileHandleState)
```

The function provides only one return value (it does provide some return parameters discussed in the following paragraphs). rc contains a return code that tells you whether the function completed without error. It also contains an error code if it didn't. Table 6-24 provides a list of these error codes.

Table 6-24   **DOSQueryFHState Function Return Codes**

Error number	Description
0	NO_ERROR
6	ERROR_INVALID_HANDLE
87	ERROR_INVALID_PARAMETER

This function uses two parameters. hFileHandle contains the file handle you want to query. pFileHandleState defines the file handle status. Bits 0 through 2 contain the access mode flags: OPEN_ACCESS_READONLY, OPEN_ACCESS_WRITEONLY, or OPEN_ACCESS_READWRITE. Bit 3 is reserved. Bits 4 through 6 contains the share access mode flags: OPEN_SHARE_DENYREADWRITE, OPEN_SHARE_DENYWRITE, OPEN_SHARE_DENYREAD, or OPEN_SHARE_DENYNONE. Bit 7 contains the inheritance flag: a process created by DOSExecPrg inherits the flag (0) or flag private to the current process (1). Bits 8 through 11 are reserved; set it to zero. Bit 12 contains the cache/no-cache flag (cache when set to 0). Bit 13 contains the fail errors flag: report through the system critical-error handler (0) or report directly to the caller (1). Bit 14 contains the write-through flag (write-through mode when set to 1). Bit 15 contains the direct open flag: open normally (0) or mounted volume to open for direct access (1).

DOSQueryFileInfo

The DOSQueryFileInfo function returns information about the specified file. It returns only the date and time information when requesting level 1 file information on a FAT drive. You must open the file with read access and a deny-write sharing mode using the DOSOpen function before calling this function to obtain information at the file information level. This function uses the following calling syntax:

```
rc = DOSQueryFileInfo (hFileHandle, ulFileInfoLevel,
    pFileInfoBuf, ulFileInfoBufSize)
```

The function provides only one return value (it does provide some return parameters discussed in the following paragraphs). rc contains a return code that tells you whether the function completed without error. It also contains an error code if it didn't. Table 6-25 provides a list of these error codes.

Table 6-25 **DOSQueryFHState Function Return Codes**

Error number	Description
0	NO_ERROR
5	ERROR_ACCESS_DENIED
6	ERROR_INVALID_HANDLE
111	ERROR_BUFFER_OVERFLOW
124	ERROR_INVALID_LEVEL
130	ERROR_DIRECT_ACCESS_HANDLE
254	ERROR_INVALID_EA_NAME
255	ERROR_EA_LIST_INCONSISTENT

This function uses four parameters. hFileHandle contains the file handle. ulFileInfoLevel contains the level of file information you want returned: FIL_STANDARD (level 1), FIL_QUERYEASIZE (level 2), or FIL_QUERYEASFROMLIST (level 3). pFileInfoBuf contains the address of the storage area for the file information. Each level of returned file information uses a different buffer: FILESTATUS3 (level 1), FILESTATUS4 (level 2), and EAOP2 (level 3). pFileInfoBufSize contains the length of pFileInfoBuf in bytes.

⇨ DOSQueryFSAttach

The DOSQueryFSAttach returns information about the attached file system. You also can use it to retrieve information about a character or pseudocharacter device attached to the file system. This function retrieves information about all block, character, and pseudocharacter devices. Because the subject of the information you request changes frequently, you might receive invalid information. There are two ways to use the information that you receive: to determine if the kernel recognizes the disk as one attached to its file system or to determine if the kernel attached its file system to the disk because the disk had no other FSDs attached. This function uses the following calling syntax:

```
rc = DOSQueryFSAttach (pszDeviceName, ulOrdinal, ulFSAInfoLevel,
    pDataBuffer, pDataBufferLen)
```

The function provides only one return value (it does provide some return parameters discussed in the following paragraphs). rc contains a return code that tells you whether the function completed without error. It also contains an error code if it didn't. Table 6-26 provides a list of these error codes.

DOSQueryFSAttach function return codes   Table 6-26

Error number	Description
0	NO_ERROR
15	ERROR_INVALID_DRIVE
111	ERROR_BUFFER_OVERFLOW
124	ERROR_INVALID_LEVEL
259	ERROR_NO_MORE_ITEMS

This function uses five parameters. pszDeviceName contains a drive designation or the name of a character or pseudocharacter device. A drive designation consists of an ASCIIZ string containing a drive letter followed by a colon. A character or pseudocharacter name consists of an ASCIIZ string continuing the filename and the subdirectory DEV. The function ignores this parameter for level 2 or 3 information (specified in ulFSAInfoLevel). ulOrdinal contains an index into the list of character devices, pseudocharacter devices, or drive designators. Use this parameter to step through the list. The ordinal number to item relationship is volatile; it can change from one call to the next. ulFSAInfoLevel contains the level of information returned in pDataBuffer: FSAIL_QUERYNAME (level 1), FSAIL_DEVNUMBER (level 2), or FSAIL_DRVNUMBER (level 3). pDataBuffer contains the returned information. This buffer contains the following fields: iType, cbName (which contains the item name length in bytes), cbFSDName (which contains the FSD name length in bytes), szName (which contains the ASCIIZ item name), szFSDName (which contains the ASCIIZ FSD name), and rgFSAData (which contains the FSD attach data). There are four different item

types returned in iType: FSAT_CHARDEV (1), FSAT_PSEUDODEV (2), FSAT_LOCALDRV (3), or FSAT_REMOTEDRV (4). pDataBufferLen contains the length of pDataBuffer on entry. It contains the actual data length on exit.

⇨ DOSQueryFSInfo

The DOSQueryFSInfo function returns information from the FSD. It does not return trailing volume label blanks. The maximum volume label length is 11 bytes. The volume serial number is a unique 32-bit number that the operating system uses to identify the disk or diskette volumes. This function uses the following calling syntax:

```
rc = DOSQueryCurrentDir (ulDriveNumber, ulFSInfoLevel,
    pFSInfoBuf, ulFSInfoBufSize)
```

The function provides only one return value (it does provide some return parameters discussed in the following paragraphs). rc contains a return code that tells you whether the function completed without error. It also contains an error code if it didn't. Table 6-27 provides a list of these error codes.

Table 6-27   **DOSQueryFSInfo function return codes**

Error number	Description
0	NO_ERROR
15	ERROR_INVALID_DRIVE
111	ERROR_BUFFER_OVERFLOW
124	ERROR_INVALID_LEVEL
125	ERROR_NO_VOLUME_LABEL

This function uses four parameters. ulDriveNumber contains the 1-based logical drive number. Using a value of 0 returns the information about the current drive. The attached FSD or FSD responsible for managing the drive's media type returns information about the specified drive. ulFSInfoLevel determines the level of information that the function returns: FSIL_ALLOC (level 1) or FSIL_VOLSER (level 2). pFSInfoBuf contains the information returned by the FSD. It includes the following fields for level 1 information: file system ID (ULONG), number of sectors per allocation unit (ULONG), number of allocation units (ULONG), number of available allocation units (ULONG), and number of bytes per sector (USHORT). It includes the following fields for level 2 information: volume serial number (ULONG), length of the volume label in bytes (BYTE), and the ASCIIZ volume label (CHAR). ulFSInfoBufSize contains the size of ulFSInfoBuf in bytes.

 DOSQueryHType

The DOSQueryHType function determines if a handle refers to a device or file. This function uses the following calling syntax:

```
rc = DOSQueryCurrentDir (hFileHandle, pHandleType, pFlagWord)
```

The function provides only one return value (it does provide some return parameters discussed in the following paragraphs). rc contains a return code that tells you whether the function completed without error. It also contains an error code if it didn't. Table 6-28 provides a list of these error codes.

DOSQueryHType function return codes   Table 6-28

Error number	Description
0	NO_ERROR
6	ERROR_INVALID_HANDLE

This function uses three parameters. hFileHandle contains the file handle. pHandleType contains the handle type bits on return: handle type (0 through 7), reserved (8 through 14), and network bit (0 for local or 1 for remote) (15). The handle types include: disk file (0), character device (1), and pipe (2). pFlagWord contains the address of the device driver attribute word if the handle type is a local character device.

DOSQueryPathInfo

The DOSQueryPathInfo function returns the file information for a file or subdirectory. You must open the file for read access with deny-write sharing mode before calling this function. This function uses the following calling syntax:

```
rc = DOSQueryPathInfo (pszPathName, ulPathInfoLevel,
    pPathInfoBuf, ulPathInfoBufSize)
```

The function provides only one return value (it does provide some return parameters discussed in the following paragraphs). rc contains a return code that tells you whether the function completed without error. It also contains an error code if it didn't. Table 6-29 provides a list of these error codes.

Table 6-29

DOSQueryPathInfo function return codes

Error number	Description
0	NO_ERROR
3	ERROR_PATH_NOT_FOUND
32	ERROR_SHARING_VIOLATION
111	ERROR_BUFFER_OVERFLOW
124	ERROR_INVALID_LEVEL
206	ERROR_FILENAME_EXCED_RANGE
254	ERROR_INVALID_EA_NAME
255	ERROR_EA_LIST_INCONSISTENT

This function uses four parameters. pszPathName contains the ASCIIZ full path name of the file or subdirectory. You can use wildcard characters when requesting level 5 information. ulPathInfoLevel contains the level of information you require: FIL_STANDARD (level 1), FIL_QUERYEASIZE (level 2), FIL_QUERYEASFROMLIST (level 3), reserved (level 4), and FIL_QUERYFULLNAME (level 5). pPathInfoBuf contains the path information. Each information level uses a different structure for this

information: FILESTATUS3 (level 1), FILESTATUS4 (level 2), EAOP2 (level 3), or fully qualified ASCIIZ name of pszPathName. ulPathInfoBufSize contains the size of pPathInfoBuf in bytes.

⇨ DOSQuerySysInfo

The DOSQuerySysInfo function returns the values of static system variables. You can request a single variable by setting the start index equal to the last index. Each variable is a DWORD value. The values you can retrieve include: QSV_MAX_PATH_LENGTH, QSV_MAX_TEXT_SESSIONS, QSV_MAX_PM_SESSIONS, QSV_MAX_VDM_SESSIONS, QSV_BOOT_DRIVE, QSV_DYN_PRI_VARIATION, QSV_MAX_WAIT, QSV_MIN_SLICE, QSV_MAX_SLICE, QSV_PAGE_SIZE, QSV_VERSION_MAJOR, QSV_VERSION_MINOR, QSV_VERSION_REVISION, QSV_MS_COUNT, QSV_TIME_LOW, QSV_TIME_HIGH, QSV_TOTPHYSMEM, QSV_TOTRESEMEM, QSV_TOTAVAILMEM, QSV_MAXPRMEM, QSV_MAXSHMEM, QSV_TIMER_INTERVAL, and QSV_MAX_COMP_LENGTH. This function uses the following calling syntax:

```
rc = DOSQueryCurrentDir (ulStartIndex, ulLastIndex, pDataBuf,
    ulDataBufLen)
```

The function provides only one return value (it does provide some return parameters discussed in the following paragraphs). rc contains a return code that tells you whether the function completed without error. It also contains an error code if it didn't. Table 6-30 provides a list of these error codes.

DOSQuerySysInfo function return codes   Table 6-30

Error number	Description
0	NO_ERROR
87	ERROR_INVALID_PARAMETER
111	ERROR_BUFFER_OVERFLOW

This function uses four parameters. ulStartIndex contains the value of the first system variable to return. ulLastIndex contains the value of the last system variable to return. pDataBuf contains a pointer to the buffer where OS/2 returns the variable values. pDataBufLen contains the length of pDataBuf in bytes.

DOSQueryVerify

The DOSQueryVerify function returns the write verification status. Write verification ensures that the data written to disk matches the original data in memory. This function uses the following calling syntax:

```
rc = DOSQueryVerify (pVerifySetting)
```

The function provides only one return value (it does provide some return parameters discussed in the following paragraphs). rc contains a return code that tells you that the function completed without error (NO_ERROR). There are no error codes associated with this function.

This function uses one parameter. pVerifySetting contains a pointer to the current verify setting. A value of 1 indicates the write verify is active.

DOSRead

The DOSRead function returns the specified number of bytes from a file, pipe, or device to a buffer. This function attempts to read the number of bytes requested but will not read beyond the end of file. A return value of 0 indicates that the read pointer is at the end of the file. OS/2 automatically moves the read pointer each time that you use this function. You also can use the DOSSetFilePtr function to move the read pointer.

This function also allows direct reads from an entire disk or diskette volume when you set the direct open flag to 1. Direct access bypasses the FSD. Always lock the volume before you read from it and unlock it when you finish. This function uses the following calling syntax:

```
rc = DOSRead (hFileHandle, pBufferArea, ulBufferLength,
     pBytesRead)
```

The function provides only one return value (it does provide some return parameters discussed in the following paragraphs). rc contains a return code that tells you whether the function completed without error. It also contains an error code if it didn't. Table 6-31 provides a list of these error codes.

DOSRead function return codes   Table 6-31

Error number	Description
0	NO_ERROR
5	ERROR_ACCESS_DENIED
6	ERROR_INVALID_HANDLE
26	ERROR_NOT_DOS_DISK
33	ERROR_LOCK_VIOLATION
109	ERROR_BROKEN_PIPE
234	ERROR_MORE_DATA

This function uses four parameters. hFileHandle contains the file handle you obtained using the DOSOpen function. pBufferArea contains the data read from the file, device, or pipe. ulBufferLength contains the length of pBufferArea in bytes. pBytesRead contains the number of bytes that the function actually returned.

⇨ DOSResetBuffer

The DOSResetBuffer function writes the buffers for the specified file to a device. Using this function on a file updates the file's directory entry as if you closed the file; however, the file remains open. Issuing this function for a pipe blocks the function at one end of the pipe until all the data gets written to the other end. This function uses the following calling syntax:

```
rc = DOSResetBuffer (hFileHandle)
```

The function provides only one return value (it does provide some return parameters discussed in the following paragraphs). rc contains a return code that tells you whether the function completed without error. It also contains an error code if it didn't. Table 6-32 provides a list of these error codes.

Table 6-32   **DOSResetBuffer function return codes**

Error number	Description
0	NO_ERROR
2	ERROR_FILE_NOT_FOUND
5	ERROR_ACCESS_DENIED
6	ERROR_INVALID_HANDLE

This function uses one parameter. hFileHandle contains the file handle whose buffers you want to write to disk. A value of 0xFFFF writes all the buffers for all file handles owned by the process to disk.

⇨ DOSScanEnv

The DOSScanEnv function searches an environment segment for the specified environment variable. The result pointer points at the data value of the variable if the search is successful. This function uses the following calling syntax:

```
rc = DOSScanEnv (pszEnvVarName, pszResultPointer)
```

The function provides only one return value (it does provide some return parameters discussed in the following paragraphs). rc contains a return code that tells you whether the function completed without error. It also contains an error code if it didn't. Table 6-33 provides a list of these error codes.

DOSScanEnv function return codes   Table 6-33

Error number	Description
0	NO_ERROR
203	ERROR_ENVVAR_NOT_FOUND

This function uses two parameters. pszEnvVarName contains the name of the environment variable that you want to retrieve. Do not include the trailing equals sign. pszResultPointer contains a pointer to the first character of the environment variable value.

 # DOSSearchPath

The DOSSearchPath function finds files residing along the specified paths. You can use the environment string or supply the path directly. This function uses the following calling syntax:

```
rc = DOSSearchPath (ulControl, pszPathRef, pszFileName,
    pbResultBuffer, ulResultBufferLen)
```

The function provides only one return value (it does provide some return parameters discussed in the following paragraphs). rc contains a return code that tells you whether the function completed without error. It also contains an error code if it didn't. Table 6-34 provides a list of these error codes.

DOSSearchPath function return codes   Table 6-34

Error number	Description
0	NO_ERROR
1	ERROR_INVALID_FUNCTION
2	ERROR_FILE_NOT_FOUND
87	ERROR_INVALID_PARAMETER
111	ERROR_BUFFER_OVERFLOW
203	ERROR_ENVVAR_NOT_FOUND

This function uses five parameters. ulControl determines the DOSSearchPath function behavior. The behavior bits include: SEARCH_CUR_DIRECTORY (0), SEARCH_ENVIRONMENT (1), SEARCH_IGNORENETERRS (2), and reserved (3 through 31). Each bit becomes active when set to one. pszPathRef contains a pointer to the search path. If ulControl bit 1 is one, then pszPathRef contains the name of an environment variable. Otherwise, it contains the actual search path. pszFileName contains the ASCIIZ filename. You can use wildcard characters for this parameter. If this parameter does not contain wildcard characters, then the function returns the filename as part of pbResultBuffer. This allows you to use the contents of pbResultBuffer directly in other functions. pbResultBuffer contains the full path name of the file. ulResultBufferLen contains the length of pbResultBuffer in bytes.

DOSSetCurrentDir

The DOSSetCurrentDir function sets the current directory. This function does not change the current directory if any members of the path do not exist. Only the directory of the current process changes. This function uses the following calling syntax:

```
rc = DOSSetCurrentDir (pszDirName)
```

The function provides only one return value. rc contains a return code that tells you whether the function completed without error. It also contains an error code if it didn't. Table 6-35 provides a list of these error codes.

Table 6-35

DOSSetCurrentDir function return codes

Error number	Description
0	NO_ERROR
2	ERROR_FILE_NOT_FOUND
3	ERROR_PATH_NOT_FOUND
5	ERROR_ACCESS_DENIED

Error number	Description
8	ERROR_NOT_ENOUGH_MEMORY
26	ERROR_NOT_DOS_DISK
87	ERROR_INVALID_PARAMETER
108	ERROR_DRIVE_LOCKED
206	ERROR_FILENAME_EXCED_RANGE

This function uses one parameter. pszDirName contains the ASCIIZ name of the directory path.

⇨ DOSSetDefaultDisk

The DOSSetDefaultDisk function sets the specified drive as the current drive. This function uses the following calling syntax:

```
rc = DOSSetDefaultDisk (ulDriveNumber)
```

The function provides only one return value. rc contains a return code that tells you whether the function completed without error. It also contains an error code if it didn't. Table 6-36 provides a list of these error codes.

DOSSetDefaultDisk function return codes   Table 6-36

Error number	Description
0	NO_ERROR
15	ERROR_INVALID_DRIVE

This function uses one parameter. ulDriveNumber contains a 1-based new default drive number.

⇨ DOSSetFHState

The DOSSetFHState function sets the state of the specified file handle. OS/2 does not guarantee that it will write data in any specific sector order for multiple sector writes. If you need to write data in a specific sector order, then use separate synchronous write operations for each sector. You can use this function to return critical error-handling control to the system when the application cannot handle it by turning off the fail/error bit and reissuing the failed I/O call. The Direct I/O flag provides physical access to the drive by bypassing the FSD. This function uses the following calling syntax:

```
rc = DOSSetFHState (hFileHandle, pFileHandleState)
```

The function provides only one return value (it does provide some return parameters discussed in the following paragraphs). rc contains a return code that tells you whether the function completed without error. It also contains an error code if it didn't. Table 6-37 provides a list of these error codes.

Table 6-37   **DOSQueryFHState function return codes**

Error number	Description
0	NO_ERROR
6	ERROR_INVALID_HANDLE
87	ERROR_INVALID_PARAMETER

This function uses two parameters. hFileHandle contains the file handle that you want to query. pFileHandleState defines the file handle status. Bits 0 through 6 are reserved. Bit 7 contains the inheritance flag: a process created by DOSExecPrg inherits the flag (0) or flag private to the current process (1). Bits 8 through 11 are reserved; set it to zero. Bit 12 contains the cache/no-cache flag (cache when set to 0). Bit 13 contains the fail errors flag: report through the system critical-error handler (0) or report directly to the caller (1). Bit 14 contains the write-through flag (write-through mode when set to 1). Bit 15 contains the direct open flag: open normally (0) or mounted volume to open for direct access (1).

 # DOSSetFileInfo

The DOSSetFileInfo function sets file information. It sets the date and time information only when setting level 1 file information on a FAT drive. Setting these parameters to 0 does not result in any change to the file data. You must open the file with read access and a deny-write sharing mode using the DOSOpen function before calling this function to obtain information at the file information level. This function uses the following calling syntax:

```
rc = DOSSetFileInfo (hFileHandle, ulFileInfoLevel, pFileInfoBuf,
    ulFileInfoBufSize)
```

The function provides only one return value (it does provide some return parameters discussed in the following paragraphs). rc contains a return code that tells you whether the function completed without error. It also contains an error code if it didn't. Table 6-38 provides a list of these error codes.

DOSSetFileInfo function return codes   Table 6-38

Error number	Description
0	NO_ERROR
1	ERROR_INVALID_FUNCTION
5	ERROR_ACCESS_DENIED
6	ERROR_INVALID_HANDLE
87	ERROR_INVALID_PARAMETER
122	ERROR_INSUFFICIENT_BUFFER
124	ERROR_INVALID_LEVEL
130	ERROR_DIRECT_ACCESS_HANDLE
254	ERROR_INVALID_EA_NAME
255	ERROR_EA_LIST_INCONSISTENT

This function uses four parameters. hFileHandle contains the file handle. ulFileInfoLevel contains the level of file information you want returned: FIL_STANDARD (level 1) or FIL_QUERYEASIZE (level 2). pFileInfoBuf contains the address of the storage area for the file information. Each level of returned file information uses a different buffer: FILESTATUS3 (level 1) and EAOP2 (level 2). pFileInfoBufSize contains the length of pFileInfoBuf in bytes.

⇨ DOSSetFileLocks

The DOSSetFileLocks function locks and/or unlocks a range of bytes in an open file. This function uses the following calling syntax:

```
rc = DOSSetFileLocks (hFileHandle, pUnlockRange, pLockRange,
    ulTimeOut, ulFlags)
```

The function provides only one return value. rc contains a return code that tells you whether the function completed without error. It also contains an error code if it didn't. Table 6-39 provides a list of these error codes.

Table 6-39   **DOSSetFileLocks function return codes**

Error number	Description
0	NO_ERROR
6	ERROR_INVALID_HANDLE
33	ERROR_LOCK_VIOLATION
36	ERROR_SHARING_BUFFER_EXCEEDED
87	ERROR_INVALID_PARAMETER
95	ERROR_INTERRUPT
174	ERROR_ATOMIC_LOCK_NOT_SUPPORTED
175	ERROR_READ_LOCKS_NOT_SUPPORTED

This function uses five parameters. hFileHandle contains the file handle. pUnlockRange contains the following fields: FileOffset

(LONG) and RangeLength (LONG). pLockRange contains the following fields: FileOffset (LONG) and RangeLength (LONG). ulTimeOut contains the maximum time that the process should wait for the locks in milliseconds. ulFlags determines the action this function takes. These bit values include: share when set to 1 (0), atomic locking when set to 1 (1), and reserved (2 through 31).

⇨ DOSSetFilePtr

The DOSSetFilePtr function moves the read/write pointer to the specified location. A positive distance value moves the pointer forward, while a negative value moves the pointer backward. You cannot use this function with a character device or pipe. This function uses the following calling syntax:

```
rc = DOSSetFilePtr (hFileHandle, lDistance, ulMoveType,
    pNewPointer)
```

The function provides only one return value (it does provide some return parameters discussed in the following paragraphs). rc contains a return code that tells you whether the function completed without error. It also contains an error code if it didn't. Table 6-40 provides a list of these error codes.

DOSSetFilePtr function return codes
Table 6-40

Error number	Description
0	NO_ERROR
1	ERROR_INVALID_FUNCTION
6	ERROR_INVALID_HANDLE
130	ERROR_DIRECT_ACCESS_HANDLE
131	ERROR_NEGATIVE_SEEK
132	ERROR_SEEK_ON_DEVICE

This function uses five parameters. hFileHandle contains the file handle. lDistance contains the distance to move the read/write

pointer in bytes. ulMoveType determines the location of the start position within the file: FILE_BEGIN (0), FILE_CURRENT (1), or FILE_END (2). pNewPointer contains the address of the read/write pointer location.

⇨ DOSSetFileSize

The DOSSetFileSize function changes the size of a file. You must open the file in a mode that allows write access before you issue this function. This function allows you to extend or truncate a file. OS/2 tries to allocate space in a contiguous or near contiguous space on the hard drive when you extend the file. This function uses the following calling syntax:

```
rc = DOSSetFileSize (hFileHandle, ulFileSize)
```

The function provides only one return value. rc contains a return code that tells you whether the function completed without error. It also contains an error code if it didn't. Table 6-41 provides a list of these error codes.

Table 6-41 **DOSSetFileSize function return codes**

Error number	Description
0	NO_ERROR
5	ERROR_ACCESS_DENIED
6	ERROR_INVALID_HANDLE
26	ERROR_NOT_DOS_DISK
33	ERROR_LOCK_VIOLATION
87	ERROR_INVALID_PARAMETER
112	ERROR_DISK_FULL

This function uses two parameters. hFileHandle contains the handle of the file that you want to change. ulFileSize contains the new file size in bytes.

⇨ DOSSetFSInfo

The DOSSetFSInfo function sets information for a file system device (FSD). It does not return trailing blanks in the volume label. You must open the volume in a mode that allows write access to use this function. This function uses the following calling syntax:

```
rc = DOSSetFSInfo (ulDriveNumber, ulFSInfoLevel, pFSInfoBuf,
    ulFSInfoBufSize)
```

The function provides only one return value. rc contains a return code that tells you whether the function completed without error. It also contains an error code if it didn't. Table 6-42 provides a list of these error codes.

DOSSetFSInfo function return codes   Table 6-42

Error number	Description
0	NO_ERROR
15	ERROR_INVALID_DRIVE
82	ERROR_CANNOT_MAKE
122	ERROR_INSUFFICIENT_BUFFER
123	ERROR_INVALID_NAME
124	ERROR_INVALID_LEVEL
154	ERROR_LABEL_TOO_LONG

This function uses four parameters. ulDriveNumber contains a 1-based number of the drive you want to change. A value of 0 uses the current drive. A value of 0xFFFF indicates that pFSInfoBuf contains the ASCIIZ path name of the FSD. ulFSInfoLevel contains the level of file information you want to set (2 is the only valid value). pFSInfoBuf contains the new file system information. The bytes in this parameter include: length of the volume label in bytes (1) and the ASCIIZ volume label name (2 through end of string). ulFSInfoBufSize contains the length of pFSInfoBuf in bytes.

⇨ DOSSetMaxFH

The DOSSetMaxFH function defines the maximum number of file handles that the calling process can use. The default setting is 20. This function preserves all open file handles when it increases the maximum number of file handles. This function uses the following calling syntax:

```
rc = DOSSetMaxFH (ulNumberHandles)
```

The function provides only one return value. rc contains a return code that tells you whether the function completed without error. It also contains an error code if it didn't. Table 6-43 provides a list of these error codes.

Table 6-43   **DOSSetMaxFH function return codes**

Error number	Description
0	NO_ERROR
8	ERROR_NOT_ENOUGH_MEMORY
87	ERROR_INVALID_PARAMETER

This function uses one parameter. ulNumberHandles contains the total number of handles your application requires.

⇨ DOSSetPathInfo

The DOSSetPathInfo function sets the information for a file or directory. You must open the file or directory object in exclusive write mode to use this function. Providing a value of 0 in the time and date field components leave those values unchanged. OS/2 modifies the last modification date and time if you change the extended attributes. This function uses the following calling syntax:

```
rc = DOSSetFileInfo (pszPathName, ulFileInfoLevel, pFileInfoBuf,
    ulFileInfoSize, ulPathInfoFlags)
```

The function provides only one return value. rc contains a return code that tells you whether the function completed without error. It also contains an error code if it didn't. Table 6-44 provides a list of these error codes.

DOSSetPathInfo function return codes
Table 6-44

Error number	Description
0	NO_ERROR
32	ERROR_SHARING_VIOLATION
87	ERROR_INVALID_PARAMETER
122	ERROR_INSUFFICIENT_BUFFER
124	ERROR_INVALID_LEVEL
206	ERROR_FILENAME_EXCED_RANGE
254	ERROR_INVALID_EA_NAME
255	ERROR_EA_LIST_INCONSISTENT

This function uses five parameters. pszPathName contains the ASCIIZ full path name of the file or directory that you want to modify. You cannot use wildcard characters with this function. ulFileInfoLevel determines the level of directory information you define: FIL_STANDARD (level 1) or FIL_QUERYEASIZE (level 2). pFileInfoBuf contains the new directory information. Each information level uses its own structure: FILESTATUS3 (level 1) or EAOP2 (level 2). ulFileInfoSize contains the length of pFileInfoBuf in bytes. ulPathInfoFlags controls how DOSSetFileInfo writes the data to disk. A value of DSPI_WRTTHRU sends the information to disk immediately.

DOSSetRelMaxFH

The DOSSetRelMax function changes the maximum number of file handles for the calling process. This function preserves all open file handles. As a result, OS/2 might defer or disregard a request to

reduce the number of file handles for the current process. This function uses the following calling syntax:

```
rc = DOSSetRelMaxFH (pReqCount, pCurMaxFH)
```

The function provides only one return value. rc contains a return code that tells you that the function completed without error. There are no error codes associated with this function.

This function uses two parameters. pReqCount contains the number of handles that you want to add the current number of handles. A negative value decreases the current handle count, while a positive number increases it. pCurMaxFH contains the new maximum number of file handles on exit.

DOSSetVerify

The DOSSetVerify function sets write verification. The operating systems verify all disk writes when you activate verification. This function uses the following calling syntax:

```
rc = DOSSetVerify (f32VerifySetting)
```

The function provides only one return value. rc contains a return code that tells you whether the function completed without error. It also contains an error code if it didn't. Table 6-45 provides a list of these error codes.

Table 6-45   **DOSSetVerify function return codes**

Error number	Description
0	NO_ERROR
118	ERROR_INVALID_VERIFY_SWITCH

This function uses one parameter. f32VerifySetting contains the state of the verify mode. A value of 1 activates verify mode.

 # DOSShutDown

The DOSShutDown function locks out all changes to file systems and writes the contents of the system buffers to disk in preparation for system shutdown. This function can take several minutes to complete depending on the contents of the system buffers. You cannot allocate memory once this function is issued. This means that you must allocate any required memory before issuing this function. This function uses the following calling syntax:

```
rc = DOSShutDown (ulReserved)
```

The function provides only one return value. rc contains a return code that tells you whether the function completed without error. It also contains an error code if it didn't. Table 6-46 provides a list of these error codes.

DOSShutdown function return codes

Table 6-46

Error number	Description
0	NO_ERROR
87	ERROR_INVALID_PARAMETER
274	ERROR_ALREADY_SHUTDOWN

This function uses one parameter. ulReserved is a reserved DWORD value; set it to 0.

DOSWrite

The DOSWrite function writes a specified number of bytes from a buffer to the specified file. It always begins writing at the current file pointer position. You can use the DOSSetFilePtr function to change the position of the file pointer prior to calling this function. OS/2 automatically updates the file pointer after it writes the data. This function automatically fails if you attempt to write to a read-only file

or if the target drive does not contain enough space. This function uses the following calling syntax:

```
rc = DOSWrite (hFileHandle, pBufferArea, ulBufferLength,
    pBytesWritten)
```

The function provides only one return value (it does provide some return parameters discussed in the following paragraphs). rc contains a return code that tells you whether the function completed without error. It also contains an error code if it didn't. Table 6-47 provides a list of these error codes.

Table 6-47   **DOSWrite function return codes**

Error number	Description
0	NO_ERROR
5	ERROR_ACCESS_DENIED
6	ERROR_INVALID_HANDLE
19	ERROR_WRITE_PROTECT
26	ERROR_NOT_DOS_DISK
29	ERROR_WRITE_FAULT
33	ERROR_LOCK_VIOLATION
109	ERROR_BROKEN_PIPE

This function uses four parameters. hFileHandle contains the file handle you obtained using the DOSOpen function. pBufferArea contains the address of a buffer that holds the information that you want to write. ulBufferLength contains the length of pBufferArea. pBytesWritten contains the actual number of bytes written to disk.

⇨ DOSDevIOCtl functions

You access both the physical and logical disk access methods provided by OS/2 using the DOSDevIOCtrl function that I originally outlined in chapter 4. You might want to refer to this chapter if you don't already

know how to use this function. Chapter 4 provides complete information on the call and parameter information required to use the DOSDevIOCtl function. Fortunately, each call to the function follows the same format; only the values of the parameters change from call to call. Each call can provide error information in addition to the generic error information provided in chapter 4.

As previously stated, there are three groups (types) of information required to use the DOSDevIOCtl function. The first group is the call definition. This should not change from implementation to implementation. Each vendor should define the calls using the same defines. If not, you probably will need to check the vendor-supplied header files and handle any differences yourself. One difference between disk access and other device access is that you use the DOSPhysicalDisk function (described at the beginning of this chapter) to obtain a handle for physical disk access. Do not use this function to get a handle for logical disk access.

The other two groups of information are the parameters required to use the function. Some texts call the first set of parameters the *parameter packet* and the second set the *data packet*. Other texts use different terms. This text uses the simple terminology *parameter information* and *data information* to differentiate the two sets of information. Make sure that you understand the difference so that you can cross reference the information in this book with any information provided by your compiler vendor. Because IBM does not provide in-depth documentation for this information in OS/2 versions 2.0 and above, you more than likely will see differences in terminology from vendor to vendor. In addition, your compiler vendor might add functions not directly addressed by the generic functions in this book. Always double-check the DOSDevIOCtl implementation used by your compiler vendor.

The following paragraphs concentrate on the generic logical and physical disk functions, but it always pays to search the hard disk vendor documentation and any INI files on your system. Most hard disks will not require INI files, but it never hurts to check. You might want to check the device drivers themselves for additional information (provided the software licensing agreement does not prevent this action). Some vendors might even sell a developer's kit

or other form of formal documentation for their device driver. Don't stop with the disk drive vendor either. Make sure that you check with the controller manufacturer as well. Some controllers provide advanced features that you can access only using the DOSDevIOCtl calls. For example, Adaptec controllers provide a special ASPI interface for tape drives connected to their SCSI controllers.

⇨ DSK functions

The DSK functions control logical access to the hard disk drive. Remember, the DOSDevIOCtl functions provide you with low-level access to the hard disk. You could just as easily use one of the many WIN or GPI functions within a PM application (a device context can be any device including the hard disk). The DOS functions described in the previous sections also provide a viable alternative to using these functions. The reason that you want to use DOSDevIOCtl is the need for lower-level access than you can get using these standard functions. On the other hand, the logical disk functions still provide a level of abstraction from the physical disk functions.

The Borland compiler provides access to the DSK functions through the BSEDEV.H and BSEDOS.H include files. Look in the BSEERR.H file for a complete list of error codes associated with these functions. The BSEDEV.H file contains the entries that you need to actually use the DOSDevIOCtl function. The BSEDOS.H file contains the DOSDevIOCtl function declaration. Both files provide interesting bits of information. You might need to check the include files for your compiler to find references to these functions because most vendors do not document them. In some cases, the vendor uses a new name for the function. Fortunately, most vendors include a file with #defines that allow you to use the original names. Table 6-48 provides a complete list of the logical disk DOSDevIOCtl functions.

NOTE OS/2 Version 1.0 and 1.1 device drivers do not understand generic IOCtl packets. As a result, the kernel does not pass the ulDataLengthMax, pDataLengthInOut, ulParmLengthMax, and pParmLengthInOut parameters to the device driver. You must mark device drivers level 2 or higher to support receipt of these fields.

DOSDevIOCtl logical disk generic functions

Table 6-48

Function	Name	Description
Logical Disk IOCtl Commands (Category 8)		
0x0000	Lock Drive	This function locks a drive. You use it to exclude another process from using the volume from I/O. It succeeds only if the only file handle open on the drive is the one that issues the lock drive call. The parameter information includes command information (BYTE). This is a reserved field, set it to 0. The data information includes a reserved field (BYTE).
0x0001	Unlock Drive	This function unlocks a drive previously locked using function 0x0000. The parameter information includes command information (BYTE). This is a reserved field, set it to 0. The data information includes a reserved field (BYTE).
0x0002	Redetermine Media	This function rebuilds the device parameters including the volume parameter block (VPB) used by the operating system to identify the drive. It accomplishes this by simulating a close of the current device handle and remounting the volume. This includes detaching the old FSD and attaching a new one. Always lock the volume using function 0x0000 before calling this function. The parameter information includes command information (BYTE). This is a reserved field, set it to 0. The data information includes a reserved field (BYTE).
0x0003	Set Logical Map	This function sets the next logical drive letter used to reference the drive. You can determine the last logical drive letter assigned to the physical drive using function 0x0021. The parameter information includes command information (BYTE). This is a reserved field, set it to 0. The data information includes a 1-based logical drive number on entry (BYTE). It contains the logical drive current mapped to the physical drive that uses the specified file handle on return. The parameter contains a zero if there is only one logical drive mapped onto this physical drive.
0x0004	Begin Format	This function mounts (attaches) the specified FSD to a logical disk volume. You normally use this function to force mount the FSD that formats the volume. The function automatically dismounts any current FSD. Using this function also sets a flag in the operating system kernel. The parameter information includes the ASCIIZ FSD name. A zero length string forces OS/2 to use the FAT file system. The data information includes command information (BYTE). This is a reserved field, set it to 0.

Table 6-48   **Continued**

Function	Name	Description
0x0020	Block Removable	This function determines if the media is removable or fixed. The parameter information includes: command information (BYTE) and drive unit (BYTE). The command information is a reserved field, set it to 0. The drive unit contains a 0-based drive number. The data information includes the data field (BYTE). A return value of 0 indicates removable media.
0x0021	Query Logical Map	This function returns the drive number last used to reference the logical drive. The parameter information includes command information (BYTE). This is a reserved field, set it to 0. The data information includes a 1-based logical drive number (BYTE). It returns zero if there is only one drive letter.
0x0043	Set Device Parameters	This function sets the drive parameters. The parameter information includes: command information (BYTE) and drive unit (BYTE). The first two bits of the command information determine what action this function takes: build BPB from the medium for all subsequent Build BPB functions (00b), change the default BPB for the device (01b), or change BPB for the medium to the specified BPB (10b). Set all other bits of this field to 0. The drive unit is a 0-based drive number. The data information includes: extended BPB for devices (31 BYTES), number of cylinders (WORD), device type (BYTE), and device attributes (WORD). The device type includes the following: 48 TPI diskette drive (0), 96 TPI diskette drive (1), 720K drive (2), 8-inch single density floppy (3), 8-inch double density floppy (4), fixed disk (5), tape drive (6), other (includes 1.44MB diskette) (7), R/W optical disk (8), and 2.88MB diskette (9). The device attribute bits include: removable media flag (0 = removable) (0) and changeline flag (1 = device supports changeline) (1). Set all other bits to 0. The extended BPB structure includes the following elements:

Length	Description
WORD	Bytes per sector
BYTE	Sectors per cluster
WORD	Reserved sectors
BYTE	Number of FATs
WORD	Root directory entries
WORD	Total sectors

Function	Name	Description

Length	Description
BYTE	Media descriptor
WORD	Sectors per FAT
WORD	Sectors per track
WORD	Number of heads
DWORD	Hidden sectors
DWORD	Large total sectors
6 BYTES	Reserved

Function	Name	Description
0x0044	Write Track	This function writes a track of information. The parameter information includes: command information (BYTE), head (WORD), cylinder (WORD), first sector (WORD), number of sectors (WORD), and track layout table (BYTES). The command information contains a 0 in bit 0 if the track layout consists of nonconsecutive sectors or does not start with sector 1. The data information contains the data packet buffer. This contains the information you want to write to the disk. The track layout table has the following format:

Length	Description
WORD	Sector number for sector 1
WORD	Sector size for sector 1
WORD	Sector number for sector 2 ...
WORD	Sector size for sector 2 ...
WORD	Sector number for sector N (one entry for each sector)
WORD	Sector size for sector N (one entry for each sector)

Function	Name	Description
0x0045	Format and Verify Track	This function formats and verifies the track contained in the track layout field. The controller performs the actual format based on the contents of this field. The parameter information includes: command information (BYTE), head (WORD), cylinder (WORD), number of tracks (WORD), number of sectors (WORD), and track layout table (BYTES). The command information contains a 0 in bit 0 if the track layout consists of nonconsecutive sectors or does not start with sector 1. The format track table is a series of four byte tuples. Each tuple contains the cylinder number, head number, sector ID, and bytes per sector. The bytes per sector values include: 128 (0), 256 (1), 512 (2), and 1024 (3). The data information contains the starting sector on entry (BYTE). It contains the first bad sector (if any) on return from a multi-track format.

Table 6-48

Continued

Function	Name	Description
0x0060	Query Media Sense	This function returns the media sense information. The parameter information includes command information (BYTE). This is a reserved field, set it to 0. The data information includes the media sense information (BYTE). This contains one of the following values: unable to determine media (0), 720K diskette (1), 1.44MB diskette (2), or 2.88MB diskette (3). This function returns the following error codes:

Error number	Description
0	NO_ERROR
1	ERROR_INVALID_FUNCTION
6	ERROR_INVALID_HANDLE
15	ERROR_INVALID_DRIVE
22	ERROR_BAD_COMMAND
31	ERROR_GEN_FAILURE
87	ERROR_INVALID_PARAMETER
115	ERROR_PROTECTION_VIOLATION
117	ERROR_INVALID_CATEGORY
119	ERROR_BAD_DRIVER_LEVEL
163	ERROR_UNCERTAIN_MEDIA
165	ERROR_MONITORS_NOT_SUPPORTED

Function	Name	Description
0x0063	Query Device Parameters	This function returns the parameters for the specified device. The parameter information includes: command information (BYTE) and drive unit (BYTE). The command information contains a 0 in bit 0, if you want the function to return the recommended BPB for the drive, or 1, if you want it to return the current BPB for the drive. The drive unit contains a 0-based drive number. The data information includes: extended BPB for device (see function 0x0043) (31 BYTES), number of cylinders (WORD), device type (BYTE), and device attributes (WORD). The device type includes the following: 48 TPI diskette drive (0), 96 TPI diskette drive (1), 720K drive (2), 8-inch single density floppy (3), 8-inch double density floppy (4), fixed disk (5), tape drive (6), other (includes 1.44MB diskette) (7), R/W optical disk (8), and 2.88MB diskette (9). The device attribute bits include: removable

Function	Name	Description
		media flag (0 = removable) (0) and changeline flag (1 = device supports changeline) (1).
0x0064	Read Track	This function reads a track of information. The parameter information includes: command information (BYTE), head (WORD), cylinder (WORD), first sector (WORD), number of sectors (WORD), and track layout table (BYTES). The command information contains a 0 in bit 0 if the track layout consists of nonconsecutive sectors or does not start with sector 1. Refer to function 0x0044 for the layout of the track layout table. The data information contains the data packet buffer. This contains the information you want to write to the disk.
0x0065	Verify Track	This function verifies a track of information. The parameter information includes: command information (BYTE), head (WORD), cylinder (WORD), first sector (WORD), number of sectors (WORD), and track layout table (BYTES). The command information contains a 0 in bit 0 if the track layout consists of nonconsecutive sectors or does not start with sector 1. Refer to function 0x0044 for the layout of the track layout table. There is no data information.

Using this table is quite simple. The previous paragraphs describe the calling syntax for this function. You obtain hDevHandle using an open call. The ulCategory entry appears in the heading for each group of function calls. The ulFunction entry appears in the first column of the table. The rest of the entries (pParmList, ulParmLengthMax, pParmLengthInOut, pDataArea, ulDataLengthMax, and pDataLengthInOut) appear in the function description in chapter 4. You need to provide the specifics required to make these functions work.

⇨ PDSK functions

The PDSK functions control physical access to the hard disk drive. This is different from logical access. There is only one physical drive. That one physical drive could contain many logical drives. A logical drive is not necessarily a partition. What it includes are all the drive letters that the machine supports. The physical drive is the base drive; the entire physical entity. This is an important distinction. When you use the function described in the following sections, you

are gaining access to the physical drive. This drive includes a lot more than simply data; it includes the partition and other information as well. As you can see, the PDSK functions provide a much lower level of disk access than any of the other functions discussed so far. They provide the lowest level of access you can get to the disk drive.

NOTE Always use the logical disk functions to access the drive whenever possible. The physical disk functions in this section of the chapter provide the lowest level access to the drive that you can achieve using OS/2 (short of writing your own device driver). Improper use of these functions could damage the drive and your data.

The Borland compiler provides access to the PDSK functions through the BSEDEV.H and BSEDOS.H include files. Look in the BSEERR.H file for a complete list of error codes associated with these functions. The BSEDEV.H file contains the entries that you need to actually use the DOSDevIOCtl function. The BSEDOS.H file contains the DOSDevIOCtl function declaration. Both files provide interesting bits of information. You might need to check the include files for your compiler to find references to these functions because most vendors do not document them. In some cases, the vendor uses a new name for the function. Fortunately, most vendors include a file with #defines that allow you to use the original names. Table 6-49 provides a complete list of the physical disk DOSDevIOCtl functions.

Table 6-49 **DOSDevIOCtl physical disk generic functions**

Function	Name	Description
Physical Disk IOCtl Commands (Category 9)		
0x0000	Lock Physical Drive	This function locks the physical drive. The parameter information includes command information (BYTE). This is a reserved field, set it to 0. The data information includes a reserved field (BYTE).
0x0001	Unlock Physical Drive	This function unlocks a physical drive previously locked using function 0x0000. The parameter information includes command information (BYTE). This is a reserved field, set it to 0. The data information includes a reserved field (BYTE).

Function	Name	Description
0x0044	Write Track	This function writes a track of information. The parameter information includes: command information (BYTE), head (WORD), cylinder (WORD), first sector (WORD), number of sectors (WORD), and track layout table (BYTES). The command information contains a 0 in bit 0 if the track layout consists of nonconsecutive sectors or does not start with sector 1. The data information contains the data packet buffer. This contains the information that you want to write to the disk. The track layout table has the following format:

Length	Description
WORD	Sector number for sector 1
WORD	Sector size for sector 1
WORD	Sector number for sector 2 ...
WORD	Sector size for sector 2 ...
WORD	Sector number for sector N (one entry for each sector)
WORD	Sector size for sector N (one entry for each sector)

Function	Name	Description
0x0063	Query Device Parameters	This function returns the parameters for the specified device. The parameter information includes the command information (BYTE). This is a reserved field, set it to 0. The data information includes: reserved field (WORD), number of cylinders (WORD), number of heads (WORD), number of sectors per track (WORD), reserved field (WORD), reserved field (WORD), reserved field (WORD), and reserved field (WORD).
0x0064	Read Track	This function reads a track of information. The parameter information includes: command information (BYTE), head (WORD), cylinder (WORD), first sector (WORD), number of sectors (WORD), and track layout table (BYTES). The command information contains a 0 in bit 0 if the track layout consists of nonconsecutive sectors or does not start with sector 1. Refer to function 0x0044 for the layout of the track layout table. The data information contains the data packet buffer. This contains the information that you want to write to the disk.
0x0065	Verify Track	This function verifies a track of information. The parameter information includes: command information (BYTE), head (WORD), cylinder (WORD), first sector (WORD), number of sectors (WORD), and track layout table (BYTES). The command information contains a 0 in bit 0 if the

Table 6-49   **Continued**

Function Name	Description
	track layout consists of nonconsecutive sectors or does not start with sector 1. Refer to function 0x0044 for the layout of the track layout table. There is no data information.

NOTE OS/2 Version 1.0 and 1.1 device drivers do not understand generic IOCtl packets. As a result, the kernel does not pass the ulDataLengthMax, pDataLengthInOut, ulParmLengthMax, and pParmLengthInOut parameters to the device driver. You must mark device drivers level 2 or higher to support receipt of these fields.

Using this table is quite simple. The previous paragraphs describe the calling syntax for this function. You obtain hDevHandle using an open call. The ulCategory entry appears in the heading for each group of function calls. The ulFunction entry appears in the first column of the table. The rest of the entries (pParmList, ulParmLengthMax, pParmLengthInOut, pDataArea, ulDataLengthMax, and pDataLengthInOut) appear in the function description in chapter 4. You need to provide the specifics required to make these functions work.

Multimedia API

VERSION 2.1 of OS/2 introduces multimedia extensions similar to those found in Windows NT and Windows 3.1 Users can attach sounds to specific events and use their computer to play CDs or MIDI files. This is the minimum that most users expect from their sound system. OS/2 adds the capability to work with full-motion video—a real bonus for the user. Fortunately for OS/2 users, you can fully exploit these new capabilities in an application without too much effort. This means that you can create a fully functional multimedia application without investing in additional toolkits or libraries.

This chapter covers the use of OS/2's multimedia extensions in REXX applications. It also looks at using these capabilities within a standard C application. Both types of programming use what OS/2 includes in the standard version without any additional tools. The last section of the chapter looks at what you could do with IBMs Multimedia Toolkit. This provides you with some ideas on what you can do with a standard installation versus a multimedia enhanced installation. In either case, OS/2 provides you with everything you need to exploit the multimedia environment.

The chapter takes a Presentation Manager application approach. It is very unlikely that anyone would want to write a character-mode multimedia application. After all, PM provides all the graphics capability that you need as a built-in feature. Why waste the effort required to duplicate this capability in a character-mode application? Most of the coding samples will concentrate on the sound board and CD-ROM drive because these are the two components most programmers need to include in their applications.

Understanding the Media Control Interface (MCI)

The media control interface (MCI) is a set of controls that you can use with most of the components of your multimedia system. Think of it as the remote control unit for your home stereo system. Every command is a button push on the remote control. This remote control actually takes the form of string commands, but it really helps

to think about it as a physical remote control device. You also need to look at the system connections much like your stereo system. Each device is a modular component that you mixed and matched with your computer system to create a multimedia environment.

The command structure for a string command is fairly simple. Every command can contain up to four components: command, object, keyword (or items), and wait. The command string appears as follows:

```
Command Object [Keywords/Items] [Wait]
```

Think about the remote control again. The command is the button that you push on the remote control. For example, you might push the play button. Some of the MCI commands are a little more esoteric than this. They include commands like acquire, capability, and info in addition to the more familiar commands like play.

The object part of the command string is the device you point at: videotape, videodisc, CDaudio, waveaudio, sequencer, or digitalaudio. There are a few additions to this as well. For example, you could point at a file instead of a device. MMPM/2 looks at the extension of the file to determine which device it belongs to. This might not work very well if you use nonstandard extensions for the filenames. MMPM/2 also provides the means for using a device name or an alias. A device name takes the form DevicetypeNN, where NN is a number starting with 01. You can use the device name option to poll a system and return the types of devices that OS/2 recognizes. This is especially useful when you have more than one of a specific device type or you are unsure of what devices the host machine supports. The alias option works with the open command. It allows you to reuse the device identifier later.

The two remaining parts of a command string are optional. A keyword modifies the command. For example, think of a multipurpose remote control for a moment. Some of the keys perform one task when used with one device and a totally different function when used with another device. The keywords work much this way. They modify the command and enhance its usefulness.

The wait part of a command string also is optional. It simply tells OS/2 to wait until it completes one command before it attempts to process the next one. Think of the havoc that would result if you tried to push several buttons on your remote control simultaneously. We all use our remote control buttons one at a time; waiting to see the effect of the button push before pushing the next one. The wait parameter of a command string allows OS/2 to do the same thing. You can obtain much faster reactions with multiple devices by issuing the commands in sequence without a wait added. This is why the wait parameter is a command string option.

Now that you have the basic idea of how to use a command string, it's time to look at what tasks the MCI allows you to perform. Table 7-1 provides a complete listing of the MCI commands. Notice that each command follows the format outlined in the previous paragraphs.

Table 7-1

MCI command reference

Command	Items	Description
Acquire	Exclusive—Obtains exclusive use of all resources associated with the object. OS/2 blocks other applications until you issue the release command.

Exclusive instance—Obtains exclusive use of only the resources required by your application. Other applications can use the device as long as such use does not interfere with your application.

Queue—Requests to use resources associated with an object. The function waits until an application finishes using the resources before returning. | This command provides access to a particular device. It allows you to gain use of the device exclusive or in conjunction with other applications. The default settings allow other applications to access the device. |
| Capability | This list contains the most common device items. Some devices provide other capabilities. The following items return TRUE if the device supports this capability: | This command provides information about the capabilities of a device. For example, you may want to know if a device can both playback and record. Use the DeviceNN where NN is a device number object with this command to individually poll each device on the |

Command	Items	Description

Command **Items** **Description**

Can record   Can save
Has audio   Uses files
Has video   Can lockeject
Can eject   Can setvolume
Can play

Compound device—Returns true if the device requires an element name.

Preroll type—Returns one of three values depending on the device's preroll type. Notified means the device preroll time is variable. Deterministic means that the device preroll time is fixed. None means the device does not support preroll.

Preroll time—Returns the device preroll time.

Device type—Returns one of the following: animation, ampmix, cdaudio, cdxa, digitalvideo, overlay, sequencer, videodisc, waveaudio, or other.

Message item—Returns true if the device supports the messages specified by item.

machine. This allows you to build a capabilities list for each machine before you attempt to implement various parts of your application. Always use the WAIT keyword with this function.

Close — There are no items associated with this command.

This command closes the device context and frees any resources. Use the same object to close as you used when opening the device context.

Connector — There are three actions that you can perform. All three usually require that you supply the number and/or type items.

Enable—This action starts the flow of information through the connector.

Disable—This action stops the flow of information through the connector.

Query—This action returns true if the connector is enabled or

This command enables, disables, or queries the status of device connectors.

Table 7-1   **Continued**

Command	Items	Description
	false if it is disabled.	
	You can use the following items to modify this command:	
	Number *connector_number*— The command assumes that you want to perform the action on the first connector unless you supply this item.	
	Type *connector_type*— Determines which type of connector you want to operate on. These types include: MIDI stream, CD stream, wave stream, XA stream, amp stream, headphones, speakers, microphone, line in, line out, video in, and video out.	
Info	There are no items associated with this command.	This command returns a string containing the product information associated with the object.
Load	Filename—Name of the file that you want to load into the device context. Using the NEW reserved filename opens an untitled file that you can save using the Save option of the File menu or the Save command (discussed later).	This command loads a new device element into a previously opened device context. Always use a PMREXX session to run digital video files.
Open	Shareable—Opens the device context as a shareable device. This allows other device contexts (usually applications) to use the device.	This command opens a device context using the specified object. It opens a value called the Device ID, which identifies the device context.
	Type *device_type*—Determines the compound device used to control a device element. If you don't specify a type, the MCI automatically determines the device type using the file's extension.	
	Alias *device_alias*—Defines an alternate name for the device.	

Command	Items	Description
	Use this alternate name in subsequent commands to identify a specific device context. The Open command uses this item as storage for the Device ID that it returns.	
Pause	There are no items associated with this command.	This command momentarily stops a device from playing. The actual difference between this command and the Stop command is device dependent. In most cases, the Pause command allows you to restart play at the position where you stopped. It also can reduce the device latency time.
Play	From *pos*—Determines the starting playing position. Omitting this item starts play at the current position.	This command starts playing the device or file.
	To *pos*—Determines the ending playing position. Omitting this item stops the device at the end of file or other media.	
Record	Insert—Allows you to add data to the device element starting at the specified or current position. This is the default setting on devices like hard disks that support data insertion. The command returns an error if the device does not support insertion.	This command starts data recording (if the device supports it). The default setting starts recording at the current position. Some devices like video tape do not support data insertion. This command defaults to data overwrite in this case.
	Overwrite—Allows you to replace the current data in the device element. This is the default setting on devices like video tape that do not support data insertion.	
	From *pos*—Determines the starting recording position. Omitting this item starts recording at the current position.	
	To *pos*—Determines the ending recording position. Omitting this item stops the device at the end of file or other media.	
Release	There are no items associated with this command.	This command releases the device context; telling MMPM/2 that you no

Table 7-1   **Continued**

Command	Items	Description
	Return resource—This keyword returns device control to the last application which lost it.	longer require the device. You do not necessarily lose device control when executing this command.
Resume	There are no items associated with this command.	This command resumes playing of a paused device. It keeps the previous settings in force.
Save	There are no items associated with this command.	This command saves the data associated with a device.
	You can specify a filename. This determines the name of the file used to store the information. MCI automatically uses the existing filename if you do not supply one. You can include a path with this parameter. MCI requires a filename for an untitled file.	
Seek	To *pos*—Determines the ending recording position. Omitting this item stops the device at the end of file or other media.	This command finds the specified position and stops the device.
	To start—Stops at the beginning of the media or file.	
	To end—Stops at the end of the media or file.	
Set	Audio [all ¦ left¦ right] [volume *percentage*] [on ¦ off] [over *milliseconds*]—There are four groups of audio settings. The first affects which channel you control. The second affects the volume level. The third turns the channel on or off. The fourth determines the amount of time required to enact the change.	This command establishes the device settings.
	Door closed—Retracts the tray and closes the door.	
	Door open—Opens the door and extends the tray.	

Command	Items	Description
	Door locked—Locks the door so that you cannot open it manually.	
	Door unlocked pos—Unlocks the door so that you can open it manually.	
	Master MIDI—Selects the MIDI sequencer as the synchronization source. MCI outputs the data in MIDI format. The IBM sequencer does not support this option.	
	Master none—Deselects all synchronization sources. The IBM sequencer does not support this option.	
	Master SMPTE—Selects the MIDI sequencer as the synchronization source. MCI outputs the data in SMPTE format. The IBM sequencer does not support this option.	
	Slave file—This is the default setting for the synchronization source. The MIDI sequencer uses a file for synchronization data.	
	Slave MIDI—Selects the MIDI file as the synchronization source. The MIDI sequencer uses this data with the incoming data. The sequencer recognizes synchronization data with the MIDI format. The IBM sequencer does not support this option.	
	Slave none—Deselects all sources of MIDI synchronization data.	
	Slave SMPTE—Selects the incoming MIDI data as the synchronization source. The sequencer recognizes synchronization data with the SMPTE format. The IBM sequencer does not support this option.	
	Time format milliseconds (or	

Table 7-1   **Continued**

Command	Items	Description
	ms)—Sets the time format to milliseconds.	
	Time format MMTIME—Sets the time format to MMTIME (3000 units per second).	
	Speed format percentage—Sets the speed format to percentage.	
	Speed format fps—Sets the speed format to frames per second (fps).	
	Video off—Turns the video output off.	
	Video on—Turns the video output on.	
Status	This command supports two item types: command and device specific. Common items include: length, mode, position, ready, time format, and volume. Device-specific items include: current track, length track *number*, number of tracks, position in track, position position track *number*, and speed format. The mode information includes: not ready, stopped, playing, seeking, recording, paused, or other. The volume setting returns the current volume as a string *left*:*right*. Each value is a percentage of the total volume.	This command returns the specified device status information.
Stop	These are no items associated with this command.	This command stops the device.

As you can see, the table contains fairly straightforward commands. You might not find some of them on your remote control at home, but they are essential to computer use of these devices. These additional commands are what make automatic device control using the computer possible. They also provide the level of flexibility required to create fully functional applications using REXX (the topic of the next section).

Using MCI with REXX

Some people might find it amusing to think that you could create a fully functional multimedia application with what amounts to a glorified batch language. Yet, REXX is a lot more than simply a batch language. Chapter 1 provides you with a full view of this rather flexible batch language. There is even talk of creating a REXX compiler (much like the batch file compilers used with DOS).

The important point to remember is that you can create a REXX multimedia application and not worry if the host machine contains a full multimedia suite. You can determine what capabilities the machine provides and program around any problem areas. You could do this with a standard language like C as well. The advantage to using REXX is that you need nothing more than a standard OS/2 installation.

Unfortunately, there are a few limitations to using REXX as your multimedia programming language. In most cases, you probably will find these limitations of little consequence unless you plan to create an application for musicians or other multimedia professionals. If your only goal is to create an application that plays existing files or perhaps interacts with a few common devices, REXX probably provides everything that you need. The following paragraphs outline the limitations of using REXX as a multimedia programming platform:

> MMPM/2 does not notify your REXX application when it loses or gains access to an MCI device, which means that you should open these devices exclusively. This prevents sharing by other applications and inconveniences the user a little.

> If you do decide to share the device with other applications, then place an Acquire Exclusive/Release Return command sequence around each of your MCI commands. This prevents another application from using the device while your application is using it. This also means that you must add error trapping because the Acquire Exclusive command will fail if another application is using the device.

➤ Opening a device in exclusive mode becomes a greater inconvenience if you hold it open for a long time. Make sure you release device control whenever possible to give other applications an opportunity to use the device.

➤ Try to create PMREXX applications instead of REXX applications. Many MCI commands require PM to work. For example, video image device and cut and paste commands fall into this category.

➤ The wait flag is the only way to maintain program synchronization. It is a lot less efficient than many of the methods available using standard languages.

➤ Using asynchronous device access requires additional programming on your part. REXX does not receive PM messages. This means that your application will not receive notification when a file or other media stops playing. Use the Status Mode command and a polling loop to get around this limitation.

➤ MCI does perform implicit opens. This means that you can play a file without opening a device. The only down side to this arrangement is that an implicit open always opens the device in shareable mode. This means that another application could interrupt you in the middle of playing a file.

As you can see, programming a multimedia application in REXX is no picnic, but you can do it. There is one more area that you need to learn about to complete the picture. MCI also includes several functions that provide the actual interface between REXX and MMPM/2. Remember, the previous section described commands. The commands are the MMPM/2 part of the picture. Table 7-2 provides a list of REXX functions that you use to work with MMPM/2.

Table 7-2 **REXX MCI functions**

Function	Description
CALL mciRxInit	This function initializes the MCI string interface to REXX. It does not require any parameters. It does return 0 for a successful completion.
CALL mciRxExit	This function terminates a REXX file containing MCI string commands. It does not require any parameters. It returns 0

Function	Description
	for successful completion. You must call this function to return allocated resources to the system.
ulDevID = mciRxGetDeviceID (sAlias)	This function returns the device identifier associated with an MCI device alias. ulDevID contains the same device identifier returned with the Open command. sAlias contains a string that identifies the device specified using a previous Open command.
rc1 = mciRxGetErrorString (rc2, 'sErrorStr')	This function returns the MCI error string that matches the specified error code. rc1 contains 0 for successful completion or an error code. rc2 contains the MCI return code. sErrorStr contains the error string. Notice that it appears within single quotes.
rc = mciRxSendString ('sCmdStr', 'sRetValue', sReserved1, sReserved2)	This function sends an MCI command string. See Table 7-1 for a complete list of these commands. rc contains 0 for successful completion or an error code. sCmdStr contains the MCI command string within single quotes. sRetValue contains the return value of the MCI command string. sReserved1 and sReserved2 are reserved parameters; set them to 0.

As you can see from the table, five simple commands are all you need to create a multimedia program using the commands in Table 7-1. There is one final REXX-specific reminder about the functions listed in Table 7-2: remember that you must register the mciRxInit function before you use it. Once you perform this task, you can use any other MCI REXX function or command string (listed in Table 7-1).

Now that you understand the basics, lets look at some actual example code. Figure 7-1 provides an example of how you can create a PMREXX application that uses a variety of multimedia devices to play files or other media. It also demonstrates one method that you can use for retrieving the installed base of multimedia devices on the host machine. Figure 7-2 shows the display provided by this application.

REXX MCI string programming demonstration source code.   Figure 7-1

```
/* REXX MCI String Programming Demonstration

This program demonstrates some of the tasks you can perform using the
multimedia capabilities provided with the MCI string capabilities provided
for REXX.  To use this application, you require the following equipment:
any sound board, a CD-ROM drive, and any other multimedia devices you
```

Figure 7-1 *Continued*

wish to test.
This is a PMREXX application. Simply type PMREXX PRG08-01 at the
OS/2 command line to run it. You can also add it to the desktop using
the program template.
Copyright 1993 - John Mueller and Tab Books
*/

/* Initialize the MCI string interface. */

CALL RXFUNCADD "mciRxInit", "MCIAPI", "mciRxInit"
CALL mciRxInit

/* Initialize the REXX utility functions. */

CALL RXFUNCADD "SysLoadFuncs", "RexxUtil", "SysLoadFuncs"
CALL SysLoadFuncs

/* Display the capabilities of this machine. */

CALL proddisp

/* If the user's machine has a wave audio device, ask if they want to play a file */

CALL waveplay

/* Exit the routine */

CALL mciRxExit
EXIT

proddisp: PROCEDURE

/* This procedure displays the capabilities of this machine by first
      checking to see if the device exists, then using the Capability command
      to display its capabilities.
*/

/* This section checks for video tape, then displays its capabilities. */

rc = mciRxSendString('INFO video tape product', 'sProdStr', '0', '0')
IF rc = 0 THEN SAY 'Video Tape -' sProdStr; ELSE SAY 'No Video Tape Installed'
rc = mciRxSendString('OPEN video tape alias checkdevice', 'sNullStr', '0', '0')
IF rc = 0 THEN CALL dispdevcap
rc = mciRxSendString('CLOSE checkdevice', 'sNullStr', '0', '0')
SAY

/* This section checks for video disk, the displays its capabilities. */

```
rc = mciRxSendString('INFO video disk product', 'sProdStr', '0', '0')
IF rc = 0 THEN SAY 'Video Disk -' sProdStr; ELSE SAY 'No Video Disk Installed'
rc = mciRxSendString('OPEN video disk alias checkdevice', 'sNullStr', '0', '0')
IF rc = 0 THEN CALL dispdevcap
rc = mciRxSendString('CLOSE checkdevice', 'sNullStr', '0', '0')
SAY

/* This section checks for CD audio, the displays its capabilities. */

rc = mciRxSendString('INFO cdaudio product', 'sProdStr', '0', '0')
IF rc = 0 THEN SAY 'CD Audio -' sProdStr; ELSE SAY 'No CD Audio Installed'
rc = mciRxSendString('OPEN cdaudio alias checkdevice', 'sNullStr', '0', '0')
IF rc = 0 THEN CALL dispdevcap
rc = mciRxSendString('CLOSE checkdevice', 'sNullStr', '0', '0')
SAY

/* This section checks for wave audio, then displays its capabilities. */

rc = mciRxSendString('INFO waveaudio product', 'sProdStr', '0', '0')
IF rc = 0 THEN SAY 'Wave Audio -' sProdStr; ELSE SAY 'No Wave Audio Installed'
rc = mciRxSendString('OPEN waveaudio alias checkdevice', 'sNullStr', '0', '0')
IF rc = 0 THEN CALL dispdevcap
rc = mciRxSendString('CLOSE checkdevice', 'sNullStr', '0', '0')
SAY

/* This section checks for sequencer, then displays its capabilities. */

rc = mciRxSendString('INFO sequencer product', 'sProdStr', '0', '0')
IF rc = 0 THEN SAY 'Sequencer -' sProdStr; ELSE SAY 'No Sequencer Installed'
rc = mciRxSendString('OPEN sequencer alias checkdevice', 'sNullStr', '0', '0')
IF rc = 0 THEN CALL dispdevcap
rc = mciRxSendString('CLOSE checkdevice', 'sNullStr', '0', '0')
SAY

/* This section checks for digital video, the displays its capabilities. */

rc = mciRxSendString('INFO digitalvideo product', 'sProdStr', '0', '0')
IF rc = 0 THEN SAY 'Digital Video -' sProdStr; ELSE SAY 'No Digital Video Installed'
rc = mciRxSendString('OPEN digitalvideo alias checkdevice', 'sNullStr', '0', '0')
IF rc = 0 THEN CALL dispdevcap
rc = mciRxSendString('CLOSE checkdevice', 'sNullStr', '0', '0')
SAY

/* Return to the calling procedure. */

RETURN

dispdevcap: PROCEDURE

/* This procedure actually displays the wave audio information. */
```

485

Figure 7-1   *Continued*

```
rc = mciRxSendString('CAPABILITY checkdevice can record WAIT', sProdCap1, 0, 0)
SAY 'Can Record:     ' sProdCap1
rc = mciRxSendString('CAPABILITY checkdevice has audio WAIT', sProdCap2, 0, 0)
SAY 'Has Audio:      ' sProdCap2
rc = mciRxSendString('CAPABILITY checkdevice has video WAIT', sProdCap3, 0, 0)
SAY 'Has Video:      ' sProdCap3
rc = mciRxSendString('CAPABILITY checkdevice can eject WAIT', sProdCap4, 0, 0)
SAY 'Can Eject:      ' sProdCap4
rc = mciRxSendString('CAPABILITY checkdevice can play WAIT', sProdCap5, 0, 0)
SAY 'Can Play:       ' sProdCap5
rc = mciRxSendString('CAPABILITY checkdevice can save WAIT', sProdCap6, 0, 0)
SAY 'Can Save:       ' sProdCap6
rc = mciRxSendString('CAPABILITY checkdevice compound device WAIT', sProdCap7, 0, 0)
SAY 'Compound Device: ' sProdCap7
rc = mciRxSendString('CAPABILITY checkdevice uses files WAIT', sProdCap8, 0, 0)
SAY 'Uses Files:     ' sProdCap8
rc = mciRxSendString('CAPABILITY checkdevice can lockeject WAIT', sProdCap9, 0, 0)
SAY 'Can Lockeject:   ' sProdCap9
rc = mciRxSendString('CAPABILITY checkdevice can setvolume WAIT', sProdCap10, 0, 0)
SAY 'Can Set Volume: ' sProdCap10
rc = mciRxSendString('CAPABILITY checkdevice preroll type WAIT', sProdCap11, 0, 0)
SAY 'Preroll Type:   ' sProdCap11
rc = mciRxSendString('CAPABILITY checkdevice preroll time WAIT', sProdCap12, 0, 0)
SAY 'Preroll Time:   ' sProdCap12
rc = mciRxSendString('CAPABILITY checkdevice device type WAIT', sProdCap13, 0, 0)
SAY 'Device Type:    ' sProdCap13

RETURN

waveplay: PROCEDURE

/* This procedure asks the user to enter the path and filename of a wave file.  It
   then plays the file for the user.
*/

/* Determine if device is available. */

rc = mciRxSendString('INFO waveaudio product', 'sProdStr', '0', '0')
IF rc  0 THEN RETURN

/* Determine if user wants to play a file. */

SAY 'Do you want to play a .WAV file? (YES or NO) '
PULL sAnswer
IF sAnswer = 'NO' THEN RETURN

/* Get the filename and create a file load string. */
SAY 'Enter the WAV path and filename: '
PULL sFileName
```

sLoadStr = 'LOAD waveaudio ' sFilename ' WAIT'

/* Open the device, load the file, play the file, and close the device. */

rc = mciRxSendString('OPEN waveaudio WAIT', 'sDevID', '0', '0')
rc = mciRxSendString(sLoadStr, 'sNullStr', '0', '0')
rc = mciRxSendString('PLAY waveaudio', 'sNullStr', '0', '0')
rc = mciRxSendString('CLOSE checkdevice', 'sNullStr', '0', '0')
Return

As you can see from Fig. 7-1, the actual procedure for using MCI strings in an application is quite simple. In most cases, you use the mciRxSendString function to output the commands required to make the application work. This is the technique used to obtain all the device specific information for the host machine. Notice that this application makes use of the alias capability provided by the REXX MCI string facility. This allows the application to use a single procedure to process each device, even though the devices normally use different names. The technique also allows the application to avoid using queues or other techniques to get the work accomplished. Using the alias capability can save you a lot of time and effort in creating your application. Avoid the pitfall of using an ambiguous name for the device alias. Notice that the name chosen in this case reflects the actual use of the alias within the application.

There are a few other tricks in this application. Notice the last procedure in the application. It uses the user input to build a load string for the application. This load string allows you to load the requested file without really knowing what it is in advance. You would need to add some error trapping to an actual application, but this sample shows you how to get started. Remember that you must pass strings in the mciRxSendString function; variables are either misinterpreted or result in an error. This means that you must always create a string before calling the function.

Figure 7-2 shows that the output from this application is fairly simple, but it does provide a lot of useful information. You normally would use this information to determine the host machine capabilities before you

Figure 7-2

```
┌─ PMREXX: prg08-01 ──────────────────────────────────── □ □ ─┐
│ File  Edit  Options  Action  Help                            │
├─────────────────────────────────────────────────────────────┤
│ Input: │                                                     │
├─────────────────────────────────────────────────────────────┤
│ Can Set Volume:    TRUE                                    ▲ │
│ Preroll Type:      1                                         │
│ Preroll Time:      0                                         │
│ Device Type:       Sequencer                                 │
│                                                              │
│ Digital Video - Software Motion Video                        │
│ Can Record:        FALSE                                     │
│ Has Audio:         TRUE                                      │
│ Has Video:         TRUE                                      │
│ Can Eject:         FALSE                                     │
│ Can Play:          TRUE                                      │
│ Can Save:          FALSE                                     │
│ Compound Device:   TRUE                                      │
│ Uses Files:        TRUE                                      │
│ Can Lockeject:     FALSE                                     │
│ Can Set Volume:    TRUE                                      │
│ Preroll Type:      3                                         │
│ Preroll Time:      0                                         │
│ Device Type:       Digitalvideo                              │
│                                                              │
│ Do you want to play a .WAV file? (YES or NO) YES             │
│                                                              │
│ Enter the WAV path and filename: D:\WIN\COOKOO.WAV         ▼ │
└─────────────────────────────────────────────────────────────┘
```

REXX MCI string programming demonstration output display.

attempted to perform some task. Using PMREXX allows you to create a better-looking display and perform a few additional tricks with your MCI applications. Always refer to the REXX limitations in the previous paragraphs before you commit to a REXX-specific application. Most MCI capabilities run better under PMREXX.

⇨ Understanding the Ultimedia Toolkit

The Ultimedia Toolkit is more than just another library, drawing tool, or utility application. It is a CD filled with many of the tools required to build a fully functional multimedia operating environment. This includes some of the more mundane activities like drawing graphics as well as some of the more exciting tasks like creating your own video. You don't have to be a programmer or a graphics artist to appreciate this toolkit (of course, it helps). These tools provide a lot of power without a lot of complexity.

From a programmer's perspective, the Ultimedia Toolkit provides some tools that you might never use. For example, few programmers will need the video capabilities of the product (at least in today's programming environment). On the other hand, all the viewers provided with this product allow you to build REXX or C applications that display information with a minimum of fuss. For instance, you could use the image viewer to display a BMP file while getting your REXX application initialized. Perfect Image/2 allows you to create detailed BMP and other video aids without resorting to the clunky editors many programmers try to use. You could even use the AVA/2 scripting language provided with Builder/2 to create a multimedia application without resorting to other programming languages. The AVA/2 scripting language provides the hooks you need to access your C applications or DLLs; allowing you to expand the capabilities of this product.

The Ultimedia Toolkit contains three components: Builder/2, Perfect Image/2, and Workplace/2. IBM also sells these three tools individually. Each product addresses a different need, so you can buy what you need without paying for what you don't want. The following paragraphs describe each tool in detail. You'll want to actually use them to see their full potential.

Builder/2

Builder/2 really is several tools in one. All the tools work together to create a fully functional multimedia author environment. This makes Builder/2 different from many of the products currently on the market. You actually can use this product to build applications, other products stop far short of this goal. Builder/2 contains the following elements:

➤ Scripting language and runtime environment to play the scripts.

➤ Interactive tool you can use to create scripts.

➤ Text/hex editor.

➤ Image, video, audio, and story browsing tools.

Each of these tools perform a different function. The AVA/2 scripting language helps you create multimedia programs. Like all programs, they consist of a set of computer instructions in human readable format. Unlike most programming languages, this one is specially designed for multimedia applications. You can easily expand this capability using C applications and DLLs.

Building a multimedia application requires you to use video and audio files. You can select from a variety of sources using Builder/2. The following list shows the graphics, video, and audio formats supported by this environment:

> AVC digital audio (AD, AU) (The Audio Visual Connection)

> AVC digital image (IM) (The Audio Visual Connection)

> DVI

> M-Motion Video (MOT)

> MIDI (MID)

> OS/2 1.3 and 2.x bitmaps (BMP)

> PCX

> Targa (TGA)

> TIF (Intel and Motorola)

> Wave (WAV)

> Windows 3.x bitmaps (BMP)

Builder/2 provides a wide variety of other items as well. For example, it provides a complete tutorial that you can use to learn the product. In addition, the menu-driven application builder allows you to create a multimedia presentation without knowing how to use the AVA/2 language. Figure 7-3 shows a picture of this front end. Notice that it provides boxes where you place the various elements of your presentation. While this interface will not allow you to fully utilize the power of Builder/2, it does make it a lot easier to learn the product. Contrast this with the text (command interface) shown in Fig. 7-4.

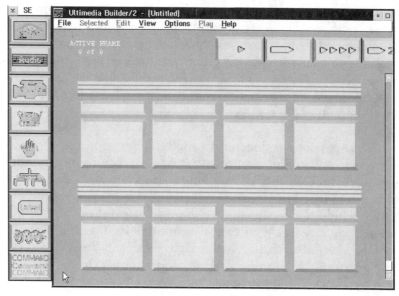

Figure 7-3

Ultimedia Builder/2 main window graphic display.

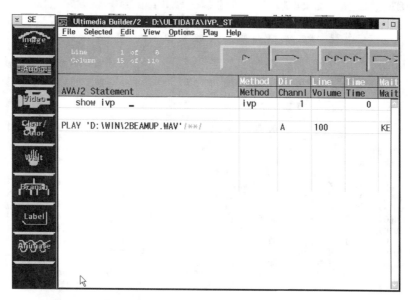

Figure 7-4

Ultimedia Builder/2 main window text display.

Builder/2 also provides five very useful utility programs. The main purpose for these utilities is to help you find the files that you need to create multimedia programs quickly and efficiently. None of the utilities are particularly exciting when you look at them individually. However, you probably will find them indispensable because of their quick load times. These utilities help you find what you need in the smallest amount of time possible.

The Text/Hex Browser doesn't do anything very special; it doesn't even provide any editing controls that you can use to modify a file. It does provide an easy way of checking a graphics file for damage or reading a text file. Theoretically, you could use it for a variety of purposes. Under DOS, the small memory footprint of this utility would provide a real reason to use it, but this isn't a very big problem under OS/2. Figure 7-5 shows the Text/Hex Browser. As you can see, it is very simple in design. Most programmers probably have something better in their arsenal, but this application could help when you least expect it.

Figure 7-5

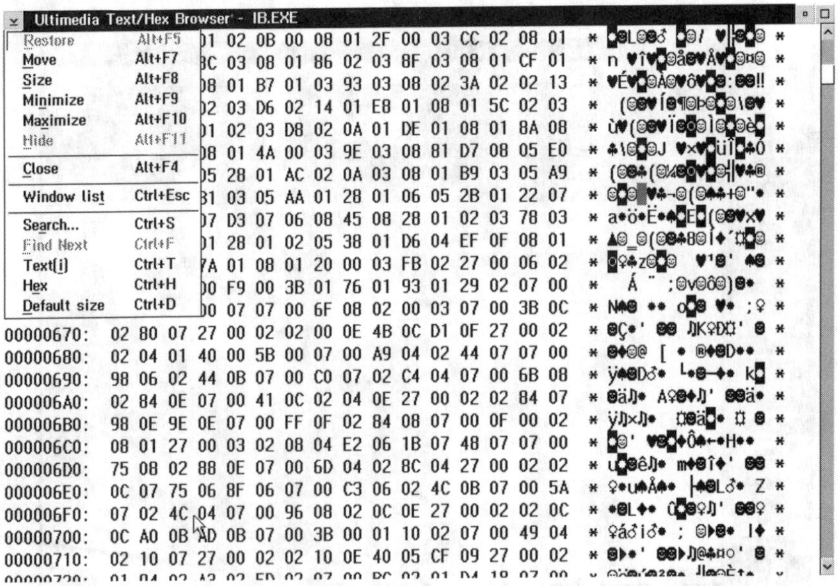

Ultimedia Text/Hex Browser.

The Text/Hex Browser does provide two extremely useful features that you might or might not have in your current viewer. First, nonprintable characters appear as their ASCII graphic equivalent. This can help you see file patterns that you could easily miss otherwise. It could help you locate extended ASCII characters as well. Second, the editor includes a search facility. This allows you to find what you need in the file quickly. Unfortunately, attempts to enter hexadecimal values didn't succeed. The search capability extends to ASCII characters only.

The Image Browser tool provides a simple way to quickly look at drawings or images. It supports all the file formats supported by Builder/2 so that you could use it as a means of performing a preliminary scan of your graphics files. You also could use it as the default viewing device for specific file extensions. One of the nice features of this little utility is that you can resize the image by simply moving the frame. Image Browser provides a display of the amount of expansion or compression as a percentage on the title bar. Figure 7-6 shows a typical Image Browser display. Notice there are no real controls or menus except those provided to every OS/2 application.

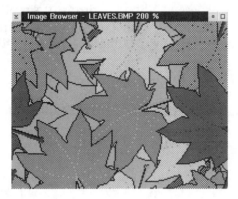

Figure 7-6

Ultimedia Image Browser.

The Video Browser allows you to look at AVS or DVI video files. It simply plays the contents of the file for you. There are no editing tools provided with this utility.

The Audio Browser looks like many of the WAV file players provided with various sound board products and with OS/2. There is one

unusual feature provided with this utility, you can use the two sliders to select the start and end time of the audio playback. This allows you to determine where you need to cut a large audio file to get the part that you need for your presentation. Figure 7-7 shows a typical Audio Browser dialog box. Notice that this utility does not provide any menus or other controls. This makes it perfect as an adjunct to a REXX application. You can simply call it from the command line with the name of the file that you want to play.

Figure 7-7

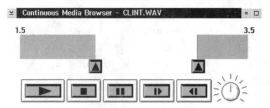

Ultimedia Continuous Media (WAVE) Browser.

The final utility provided with Builder/2 is the Story Browser. This utility provides quick text view of the commands in a Builder/2 file. Instead of waiting for the entire application to start, you can get an immediate view of a file using this utility. As with the Text/Hex Browser, this utility does not provide any editing controls; it simply lets you view the story file contents. It also provides the same search capability as the Text/Hex Browser. Figure 7-8 shows a typical Story Browser display.

Figure 7-8

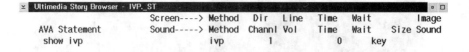

Ultimedia Story Browser.

 Perfect Image/2

Perfect Image/2 is an image-processing tool. This is different from a drawing tool in that Perfect Image/2 doesn't include any drawing tools. It simply processes graphics that you already have or accepts input from an input device like a video camera. It modifies these images much like you would by adding lenses or filters to a camera. The best part of this is that you can obtain very precise effects that you could not obtain using a camera. The following list tells you about the capabilities of Perfect Image/2:

➤ Displays a wide variety of image formats. This allows you to search for specific images. Perfect Image/2 provides better image display capabilities than the Image Browser provided with Builder/2.

➤ Converts a subset of the image formats it displays. This allows you to transfer images from one application to the next. You also can use it to convert the image to a format that works better with specific applications. (In some cases, using a different format actually can enhance an image's appearance due to the method the application uses to process it.)

➤ Adjusts, balances, and filters image colors. This is the same effect as adding a filter to your camera. This big difference is that you can do it with images other than the ones you retrieve from an input device. In addition, the effects that you achieve are much more precise than those you can obtain from a camera lens.

➤ Copy and paste images between applications or parts of images between screen locations. The big difference between this copy and paste and that provided by other applications is the types of things you can do to the image. This includes: copy and paste irregular images, fuzzy edge images, control transparency images, flip and rotate images, resize the image, and blend the image. All these processes allow you to modify the image's appearance without using drawing tools. This does not actually allow you to create a new image like a drawing tool would.

➤ Capture video images if you have a capture adapter. This allows you to create onscreen presentations using the same props that you would use for a person-to-person presentation. The big difference is that you can send this presentation to as many people as necessary by including a disk with your package.

➤ Display and modify TIF FAX image objects. This assumes that you have a FAX board in your machine and that the software recognizes the board. You could use this capability to enhance a FAX before sending it to upper management.

➤ Print the images that you display. This allows you to create a hardcopy for mailing or future reference. The print capability is not much better than the standard OS/2 print capability. However, this product does provide various printing levels that can greatly enhance image output, especially on a color printer.

➤ Limited editing features. There are no drawing features provided with Perfect Image/2, but you can increase or decrease image size, crop the image borders, and flip it horizontally or vertically. These transform functions can help you manipulate the image a little but really don't fall within the realm of image drawing. This only serves to point out the modification nature of Perfect Image/2.

Perfect Image/2 can retrieve and display a wide variety of graphic images. Even though there are many products on the market that can work with a wider variety of images, most of them are either data conversion or drawing programs. Remember that Perfect Image/2 is an image processor. This means that you can import an image, process it using various filters and effects, and export it to another application. The following list shows the graphic image formats this product supports:

➤ AVC (AD, AU, and IM) (The Audio Visual Connection)

➤ OS/2 1.3 and 2.x bitmaps (BMP)

➤ PCX

➤ Targa (TGA)

➤ TIF (Intel and Motorola)

➢ TIFF (single-bit FAX file)

➢ Windows 3.x bitmaps (BMP)

Many of these image formats support more than one bit-count range.
(The bit count determines how many colors the file can contain.)
Perfect Image/2 supports the following bit counts: 1-bit (FAX
format), 8-bit (256 colors), 16-bit RGB (64K colors), and 24-bit RGB
(16.7M colors). Notice that it does not support 16-color input. Use a
draw program like Paintbrush to convert the image from 16 colors to
256 colors. All of these bit counts correspond to the counts
supported by most display and color printer devices.

Perfect Image/2 provides an easy-to-use graphic interface and
toolbar. Figure 7-9 shows a typical Perfect Image/2 display. The File
menu contains the usual entries for opening and closing files. It also
contains two levels of image printing. One of the more interesting
options is Properties. This option displays a dialog box containing
the image parameters including: format, bit count, date and time
stamp, size, and on-disk storage requirements.

Figure 7-9

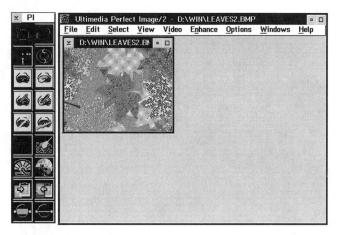

Ultimedia Perfect Image/2 Main Window.

The Edit menu contains the normal copy, paste, and undo entries. It
also allows you to size, crop, and flip the image. The Select menu
allows you to select the entire or specific parts of the image as well as

rotate it and perform other types of transforms. The View menu allows you to determine the quality of the display, amount of zoom, and whether Perfect Image/2 displays various masking elements. This Video display works with a video camera. It allows you to look at a live display, capture the current image, and select the video capture parameters. The Enhance menu contains all sorts of options that you can use to modify the appearance of a picture. This includes several types of filters, color adjustments, and blending. The Options menu helps you adjust Perfect Image/2 for optimal picture display. It includes options like the fuzz width used for blending and other modifications and the amount of picture transparency. The Windows and Help menus perform the same tasks that they do in most applications.

Figure 7-10 shows the toolbar that normally appears at the left side of the display. This provides the tools that you need to modify an image including: Select, Lasso, Node, Rotate, Mask area, Unmask area, Draw mask on, Draw mask off, Clear mask, Automask, Tool size, Blend, Adjust colors, Color balance, Copy, Paste, Zoom in, and Zoom out. Most of the tools are pretty self explanatory.

Figure 7-10

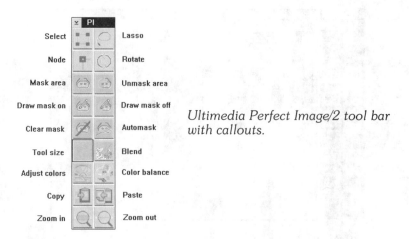

Ultimedia Perfect Image/2 tool bar with callouts.

Of special interest are the Select, Lasso, Node, and Rotate options. These four options allow you to perform specific transforms visually instead of relying on menu options. The various mask options allow you to apply filters to the image. The Color options determine how the masks affect the appearance of the image. The Zoom options

affect your perception of the image but do not affect the image itself. Finally, the Copy and Paste options work with the Select option to copy and paste all or part of the image. As you can see, Perfect Image/2 excels at image manipulation.

⇨ Workplace/2

Workplace/2 is an organization tool. If you have ever worked on a large programming project with a lot of icons, then you can appreciate the need for organization. Team projects require this organization even more. Ever try to get someone up to speed after the project gets started? It takes a lot of time and effort to do this—time that you could spend writing the application. Some people might view Workplace/2 as the graphic artist's or presentation expert's dream, but programmers can use it to organize their graphic files as well.

There are two unique tools provided with Workplace/2. These tools aren't tools in the normal sense of the word, they simply look like file folders. The installation program adds them to your Templates folder. Workplace/2 also contains the five browsers described in the Builder/2 section along with these unique tools.

The first folder is Light Table. The magic of this product lies in what the folder does for you. Instead of displaying the standard icon, these folders display the actual contents of the graphics files. Instead of having to guess what HAND.PCX contains, you could simply look at the file icon and see what it contains. Figure 7-11 shows a typical Light Table file.

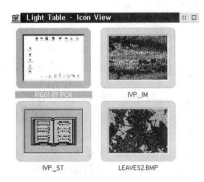

Figure 7-11

Ultimedia Workplace/2 Light Table.

Notice that each file icon (except the story file) contains a thumbnail sketch of its contents. The story file is an exception. Because this file contains a multimedia application, it contains the Story Browser icon. The same is true for audio and video files. They use a default icon instead of something unique. Double clicking on the file brings up one of the browsers discussed in the Builder/2 section of the chapter (unless you purposely associate the file with another application). In most cases, a browser will act a lot quicker and provide all the information that you need to know about the file until you actually use it. The counterpoint to this is that you might want to use it immediately instead of waiting until later.

NOTE   Most applications store PCX files in compressed format. You might need to run the MMIOINI.EXE program to install support for this format before Workplace/2 will display the contents of these files in a Light Table file. The same applies to many other graphic formats. If you experience difficulty getting the Light Table to read the file, then try installing support for it.

Opening the settings for a Light Table entry reveals another difference between it and a standard graphics file entry. There is a Reference page to the Notepad. Figure 7-12 shows a typical Reference page. Notice that this page contains the actual filename, a reference number, and a few other entries. The important entry is the Subject field. This is the entry that you use to help define the file. This information helps you locate the file later. In essence, it allows you to perform a database type search through your graphic files. What this means is that, if you need a hand icon, you can either search through your files one at a time or use the Workplace/2 query capability to find it almost instantly.

The database capability of Workplace/2 doesn't end here. You can specify additional data items by changing the Schema page of the Light Table folder's notebook. You can store the information in the file's EAs or in an external database. If you choose an external database, then the Light Table folder creates a link with an SQL database that stores the extra Reference page entries. (Workplace/2 can access dBASE IV, OS/2 Database Manager, or Oracle files.) Either choice allows you to create as many fields as you require to define a multimedia file. This flexibility means that you potentially

Figure 7-12

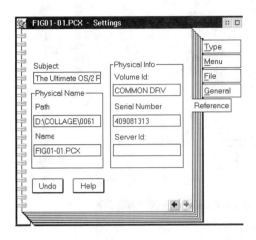

Multimedia File Reference dialog.

could create a database of enormous size. Some prior planning will help you keep the number of fields to a minimum. Remember that too much information is almost as bad as too little.

NOTE Select "Extended Attributes" in the Extended Attributes field of the Schema page of the Light Table notebook if you do not want to create a separate database to hold your search information. This highlights the EA Edit button that allows you to create new fields for your multimedia file Reference page. This also allows you to perform a Light Table Folder query without resorting to using a database manager to store your search data.

Whatever storage technique you choose, there are three steps in defining the schema of your multimedia storage. Figure 7-13 shows the three steps. The first step is to get the Schema page (upper left dialog box). The second step is to add one or more fields. You do this by selecting the Add button of the Schema Editor dialog box (upper right dialog box). Two other buttons allow you to delete or modify the entries that you create. The final step is adding the actual entry. This consists of filling out four fields. The Name field determines what you call the entry in queries. The Type field determines the type of information that this entry will contain. For example, a title would contain character information, while a job number would contain numeric information. The Size field determines how large the field is. You need to exercise some care with this entry because even a few characters or numbers can make a big difference in the size of the

Figure 7-13

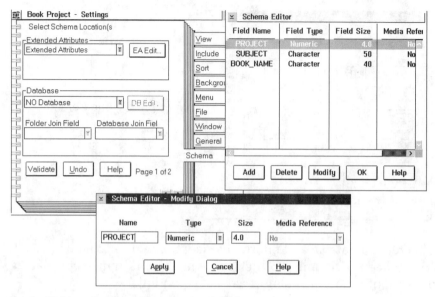

Light Table schema and associated dialogs.

EAs or database. Numeric information can contain integers as well as decimals. Simply separate the two entries by a comma. For example, 4,2 would create a numeric entry four characters long, two of which are decimals. The Media Reference entry determines if this is a media file link. You probably will set this entry to No more often than not.

Creating a query requires several steps, even if you simply want to scan the multimedia file EAs. It also requires some knowledge of SQL. The Workplace/2 documentation does contain some basic pointers, but it is far from complete. Learning SQL is a small price to pay for the flexibility that this system provides. The first step is to create another Query Sequence file. Once you accomplish this task, create one or more LT Query entries in the folder. You also need to create an LT Query Result entry. Figure 7-14 shows a typical single query folder.

Now that you have everything set up, it's time to enter all this additional information that you want to use for queries later. Open the Light Table folder that you plan to use for storage to the details view. You will see the standard entries when the view first opens. This

LT Query

LT Query Result

Figure 7-14

*Ultimedia Workplace/2
LTQuerySeq folder.*

includes items like the file size and the creation date. Scroll past this information, and you'll see the fields that you entered in the Schema page. There is one entry in the details page for each file that you add to it. All you need to do is point with the mouse to where the field and the file intersect. Press Alt and mouse button 1 at the same time. This will open the entry for editing. The Details view looks similar to the one shown in Fig. 7-15.

Figure 7-15

Icon	Title	PROJECT	SUBJECT	BOOK_NAME
	FIG01-01.PCX	0061	Organized PM Screen	Ultimate OS/2
	FIG01-02.PCX	0061	Borland C++ Main Installation Screen	
	FIG01-03.PCX	0061	Borland C++ Installation Options	
	FIG01-04.PCX	0061	PMATE Utility Screen	Ultimate OS/2

Light Table details view.

Once you finish entering all the data, you can start to perform queries on your multimedia files. Double click on the Query entry of the Query Sequence folder. The first dialog box that you see allows you to select a database type or the Light Table folder. The source that you choose depends on how you set up your schema. The query and the schema must match. It helps to keep the schema page of the Light Table folder open as you create the query.

Once you define a data source, you see the dialog box shown in Fig. 7-16. This is where your knowledge of SQL gets tested. Figure 7-16 shows the most common scenario. The SQL statement consists of three entries. The SELECT statement determines which fields the query displays. The FROM entry is important if you use a database to store the multimedia information. Simply type the location of the

Figure 7-16

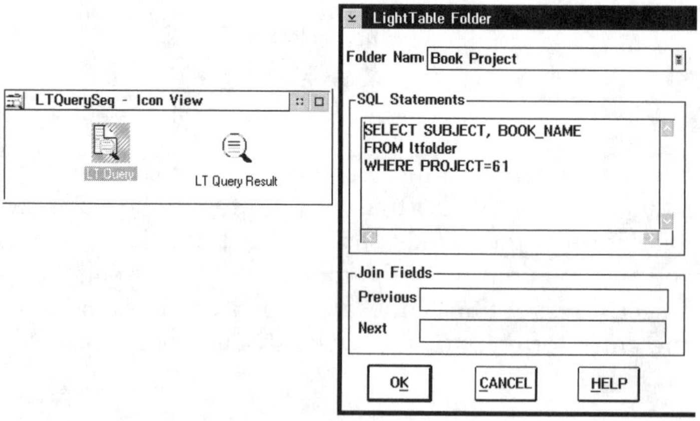

LTQuery dialog.

database file on disk. Make sure that you include a path and drive. If you use EAs to store your data, then put a dummy entry here. Workplace/2 automatically replaces this value with the optional Folder field shown at the top of the dialog box. The WHERE statement tells what search criteria you want to use. In this case, the query looks for all multimedia files associated with project number 61 and displays the BOOK_NAME and SUBJECT fields of the matching entries.

Once you complete the query, select OK to close the dialog box. This saves the query. Workplace/2 allows you to create multiple Query entries. The position of these entries within the Query Sequence folder is very important. Workplace/2 operates on each query in turn and uses the result of that query as the source of information for the next query. Using multiple queries allows you to modularize your search criteria, making it much more likely that you can use the individual queries later by recombining them. Of course, this is just an overview of the whole process.

There are three query specific options in the System menu of the Query Sequence folder. Run Query performs the SQL instructions in your Query entries and displays the result in the Query Result entry. You can use the Check Query option to check your SQL statements for errors before you attempt to run them. This is a very important

step, especially when you start learning to use Workplace/2. The Cancel Query option allows you to stop a long query before it completes. This is a handy option if you have a lot of data to search and think that one of the queries failed. It also allows you to get out of a query and quickly change the parameters.

Figure 7-17 shows the final result of using the query mechanism provided with Workplace/2. As you can see, it provides all the information that you requested in an easy to read format. The dialog box also allows you to save the query results for future use or change the results into a new Light Table that you can use to store the resulting multimedia files. There are other options that allow you to change the appearance of the display. For example, you can change the size of the icons to small or medium (the default size is large).

Figure 7-17

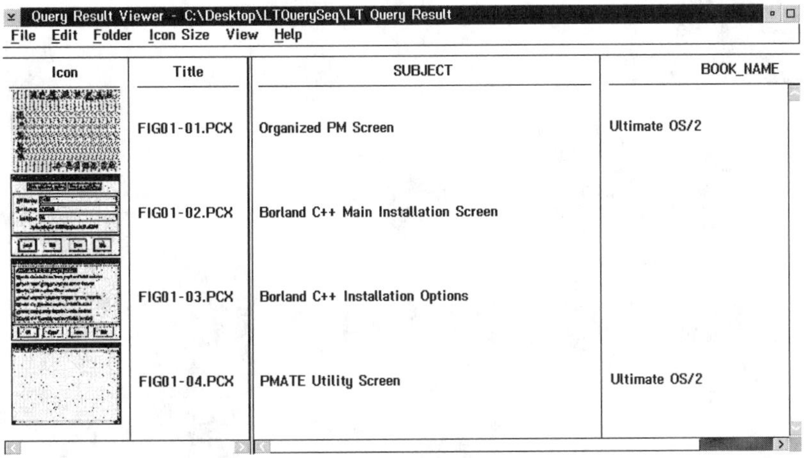

Icon	Title	SUBJECT	BOOK_NAME
	FIG01-01.PCX	Organized PM Screen	Ultimate OS/2
	FIG01-02.PCX	Borland C++ Main Installation Screen	
	FIG01-03.PCX	Borland C++ Installation Options	
	FIG01-04.PCX	PMATE Utility Screen	Ultimate OS/2

Query Result Viewer - C:\Desktop\LTQuerySeq\LT Query Result
File   Edit   Folder   Icon Size   View   Help

LTResult dialog.

As you can see, Workplace/2 is an extremely useful tool for managing your multimedia files. It doesn't matter if you're a graphic artist or a programmer, the needs are the same. The only real difference is the criteria used to search for these files. Workplace/2 provides more than sufficient flexibility to allow you to modify the storage and query criteria to meet your needs.

Memory management

EVEN though memory prices consistently decrease (despite a few ups and downs from time to time), no programmer can say that it's a quantity to waste on any machine. Few applications on the market today can say that they have sufficient memory to perform every task the user requires without also incorporating some form of memory management. (The only exception is utility applications that usually fall into this category anyway.) Whether memory management includes the dynamic allocation of variables or not is immaterial; there are many other forms of memory management that programmers might not even recognize as such. Any application that performs a significant amount of work will need memory management to get it done. This is old news to anyone who programmed in DOS. However, programming under OS/2 brings the programmer a new set of solutions and problems.

Even OS/2 participates in this very necessary activity. As previously stated, memory management includes a lot more than simply obtaining and freeing pieces of memory. It also includes a wide variety of alternatives. For example, your application could use virtual memory to extend its resources instead of obtaining and freeing memory. Assuming the user does not run out of hard disk space, you could easily double or triple available memory with little additional programming. Unfortunately, that memory increase involves a very real speed penalty. As you can see, memory management is not an easy issue to deal with.

This chapter takes a very low-level look at OS/2 memory management. It provides you with all the pieces required to create your own memory-management capabilities. Anyone creating an OS/2 program could benefit from the material in this chapter. It covers memory allocation, protection, virtual memory, and segmentation types. The chapter assumes that you want to create a general application—either character-mode OS/2 or something for the workplace shell. Even device driver and DLL writers need this type of information.

 # DOS functions

Memory management begins with the functions that you use to
control it. OS/2 provides many different functions that you can use
to obtain, free, share, and otherwise manage the memory used by
your application. The following sections provide you with the detailed
information required to use these functions. Each description consists
of the function, its calling syntax, a listing of any errors it returns,
and any other information you need to use it.

 # DOSAllocMem

The DOSAllocMem function allocates private memory within the
virtual address space. You can either reserve the memory or reserve
and commit it. OS/2 allocates the memory from the process' private
memory in multiples of 4K. Memory allocated and/or committed by
this function is swappable to disk. You can apply any required
protection to committed pages. OS/2 initially uses demand pages to
fulfill the memory allocation requirements. You cannot access
uncommitted pages. Execute and read accesses are the same when
using an 80386 processor. This function uses the following syntax:

```
rc = DOSAllocMem (pBaseAddress, ulObjectSize, ulAllocationFlags)
```

The function provides only one return value (it does provide some
return parameters discussed in the following paragraphs). rc contains
a return code that tells you if the function completed without error. It
also contains an error code if it didn't. Table 8-1 provides a list of
these error codes.

Table 8-1   **DOSAllocMem function return codes**

Error number	Description
0	NO_ERROR
8	ERROR_NOT_ENOUGH_MEMORY
87	ERROR_INVALID_PARAMETER
95	ERROR_INTERRUPT

There are three parameters for this function. pBaseAddress contains the base address of the allocated private memory object. ulObjectSize contains the size of the memory object that you want to create. OS/2 rounds this value up to the nearest 4K (page size boundary). ulAllocationFlags defines the allocation attributes and the access protection of the private memory object. You must set one of the following flags: PAG_READ, PAG_WRITE, or PAG_EXECUTE. All other flags are optional; set any unused bits to 0.

The allocation attributes include: PAG_COMMIT and OBJ_TILE. Use the PAG_COMMIT flag to automatically commit all pages in the allocated private memory. Use the OBJ_TILE flag if you need to allocate the memory within the first 512MB of virtual address space so that you can use 16-bit alias selectors to map the memory object.

The desired memory protection flags include: PAG_EXECUTE, PAG_READ, PAG_WRITE, and PAG_GUARD. The PAG_EXECUTE flag allows execute (essentially read) access to the private memory object. The PAG_READ flag allows the application to read the memory, but not write to it. The PAG_WRITE flag allows you to read and write the memory. The PAG_GUARD flag raises a "guard page entered" condition each time the application tries to access the affected memory.

DOSAllocSharedMem

The DOSAllocSharedMem function allocates a shared memory object within the virtual address space. This function maps the virtual address space of the calling process to the shared memory object. OS/2 reserves the shared memory address in the same location for every process. Giving the shared memory object a name allows other processes to gain access to it using DOSGetNamedSharedMem. You must include the \SHAREMEM\ prefix to name the shared memory object. You cannot specify named shared memory as giveable or gettable. However, unnamed memory can receive these attributes. OS/2 always rounds the memory allocation request up to the nearest 4K. OS/2 can move or swap committed memory. Execute and read accesses are equivalent when using an 80386 processor. This function uses the following syntax:

```
rc = DOSPhysicalDisk (pBaseAddress, pszName, ulObjectSize, ulFlags)
```

The function provides only one return value (it does provide some return parameters discussed in the following paragraphs). rc contains a return code that tells you if the function completed without error. It also contains an error code if it didn't. Table 8-2 provides a list of these error codes.

Table 8-2   **DOSAllocSharedMem function return codes**

Error number	Description
0	NO_ERROR
8	ERROR_NOT_ENOUGH_MEMORY
87	ERROR_INVALID_PARAMETER
95	ERROR_INTERRUPT
123	ERROR_INVALID_NAME
183	ERROR_ALREADY_EXISTS

There are four parameters for this function. pBaseAddress contains the base address of the allocated private memory object. pszName contains an optional ASCIIZ name for the shared memory object. Make sure you add the \SHAREMEM\ prefix to the name. ulObjectSize contains the size of the memory object that you want to create. OS/2 rounds this value up to the nearest 4K (page size boundary). ulAllocationFlags defines the allocation attributes and the access protection of the private memory object. You must set one of the following flags: PAG_READ, PAG_WRITE, or PAG_EXECUTE. All other flags are optional; set any unused bits to 0.

The allocation attributes include: PAG_COMMIT, OBJ_GIVEABLE, OBJ_GETTABLE, and OBJ_TILE. Use the PAG_COMMIT flag to automatically commit all pages in the allocated private memory. The OBJ_GIVEABLE flag marks the memory segment as one that you can give to another process using the DOSGiveSharedMem function. The OBJ_GETTABLE flag marks the memory segment as one that another process can access using the DOSGetSharedMem function. Use the OBJ_TILE flag if you need to allocate the memory within the first 512MB of virtual address space so that you can use 16-bit alias selectors to map the memory object.

The desired memory protection flags include: PAG_EXECUTE, PAG_READ, PAG_WRITE, and PAG_GUARD. The PAG_EXECUTE flag allows execute (essentially read) access to the private memory object. The PAG_READ flag allows the application to read the memory, but not write to it. The PAG_WRITE flag allows you to read and write the memory. The PAG_GUARD flag raises a "guard page entered" condition each time the application tries to access the affected memory.

⇨ DOSFreeMem

The DOSFreeMem function reduces the object count of a private or shared memory object by one. It also frees the memory object from the virtual address space of the process. OS/2 gives the released pages an access protection level of no access. The object does not get deleted until its object count is zero. More than one process can access the object; each access increments the object count. This function uses the following syntax:

```
rc = DOSFreeMem (pBaseAddress)
```

The function provides only one return value. rc contains a return code that tells you if the function completed without error. It also contains an error code if it didn't. Table 8-3 provides a list of these error codes.

DOSFreeMem function return codes   Table 8-3

Error number	Description
0	NO_ERROR
5	ERROR_ACCESS_DENIED
95	ERROR_INTERRUPT
487	ERROR_INVALID_ADDRESS

There is one parameter for this function. pBaseAddress contains the base virtual address of the private or shared memory that you want to release.

 # DOSGetNamedSharedMem

The DOSGetNamedSharedMem function obtains access to a named shared memory object. This provides access to the object within the virtual address space of the calling process. You must include the \SHAREMEM\ prefix with the shared memory name. The 80386 processor treats the execute and read access levels the same. Write access implies that you also gain read and execute access. The value of pBaseAddress returned by this function is the same value returned to the process that created the memory object. This function uses the following syntax:

```
rc = DOSGetNamedSharedMem (pBaseAddress, pszSharedMemName,
ulAttributeFlags)
```

The function provides only one return value (it does provide some return parameters discussed in the following paragraphs). rc contains a return code that tells you if the function completed without error. It also contains an error code if it didn't. Table 8-4 provides a list of these error codes.

Table 8-4   **DOSGetNamedSharedMem function return codes**

Error number	Description
0	NO_ERROR
2	ERROR_FILE_NOT_FOUND
8	ERROR_NOT_ENOUGH_MEMORY
87	ERROR_INVALID_PARAMETER
95	ERROR_INTERRUPT
123	ERROR_INVALID_NAME
212	ERROR_LOCKED

There are three parameters for this function. pBaseAddress contains the base address of the shared memory object on return. pszSharedMemName contains the name of the shared memory object. This is an ASCIIZ string in the form of an OS/2 filename.

Remember to include the \SHAREMEM\ prefix. ulAttributeFlags contains the level of access protection that you want to set for the shared memory object. You must set one of the following flags: PAG_READ, PAG_WRITE, or PAG_EXECUTE. All other flags are optional; set any unused bits to 0.

The shared memory object protection flags include: PAG_EXECUTE, PAG_READ, PAG_WRITE, and PAG_GUARD. The PAG_EXECUTE flag allows execute (essentially read) access to the private memory object. The PAG_READ flag allows the application to read the memory, but not write to it. The PAG_WRITE flag allows you to read and write the memory. The PAG_GUARD flag raises a "guard page entered" condition each time the application tries to access the affected memory.

⇨ OSGetSharedMem

The DOSGetSharedMem function obtains access to an unnamed shared memory object. It provides access to the allocated memory in the virtual address space of the process. You must use the same base address as the process that created the gettable shared memory object. Using some format of interprocess communication (IPC) accomplishes this task. Both processes use the same base address to access the gettable shared memory object. The calling function must use the same access protection for committed pages as the process that originally created the shared memory object. The 80386 processor treats the execute and read access levels the same. This function uses the following syntax:

```
rc = DOSGetSharedMem (pBaseAddress, ulAttributeFlags)
```

The function provides only one return value (it does provide some return parameters discussed in the following paragraphs). rc contains a return code that tells you if the function completed without error. It also contains an error code if it didn't. Table 8-5 provides a list of these error codes.

Table 8-5 **DOSGetSharedMem function return codes**

Error number	Description
0	NO_ERROR
5	ERROR_ACCESS_DENIED
8	ERROR_NOT_ENOUGH_MEMORY
87	ERROR_INVALID_PARAMETER
95	ERROR_INTERRUPT
212	ERROR_LOCKED

There are two parameters for this function. pBaseAddress contains the base address of the shared memory object. This is the address returned by the DOSAllocSharedMem function to the creating process. ulAttributeFlags contains the level of access protection that you want to set for the shared memory object. You must set one of the following flags: PAG_READ, PAG_WRITE, or PAG_EXECUTE. All other flags are optional; set any unused bits to 0.

The shared memory object protection flags include: PAG_EXECUTE, PAG_READ, PAG_WRITE, and PAG_GUARD. The PAG_EXECUTE flag allows execute (essentially read) access to the private memory object. The PAG_READ flag allows the application to read the memory, but not write to it. The PAG_WRITE flag allows you to read and write the memory. The PAG_GUARD flag raises a "guard page entered" condition each time the application tries to access the affected memory.

⇨ DOSGiveSharedMem

The DOSGiveSharedMem function gives another process access to a shared memory object. It provides access to the allocated memory in the virtual address space of the process (the same process performed by the DOSGetSharedMem function). Memory access uses the same base address as the process that created the giveable shared memory object. Use some format of interprocess communication (IPC) to exchange this information. The target function must use the same

access protection for committed pages as the process that originally created the shared memory object. The 80386 processor treats the execute and read access levels the same. This function uses the following syntax:

```
rc = DOSGiveSharedMem (pBaseAddress idProcessID, ulAttributeFlags)
```

The function provides only one return value (it does provide some return parameters discussed in the following paragraphs). rc contains a return code that tells you if the function completed without error. It also contains an error code if it didn't. Table 8-6 provides a list of these error codes.

DOSGiveSharedMem function return codes Table 8-6

Error number	Description
0	NO_ERROR
5	ERROR_ACCESS_DENIED
8	ERROR_NOT_ENOUGH_MEMORY
87	ERROR_INVALID_PARAMETER
95	ERROR_INTERRUPT
212	ERROR_LOCKED
303	ERROR_INVALID_PROCID
487	ERROR_INVALID_ADDRESS

There are three parameters for this function. pBaseAddress contains the base address of the shared memory object. This is the address returned by the DOSAllocSharedMem function to the creating process. idProcessID contains the target process identifier. This is the process that receives shared memory access. ulAttributeFlags contains the level of access protection that you want to set for the shared memory object. You must set one of the following flags: PAG_READ, PAG_WRITE, or PAG_EXECUTE. All other flags are optional; set any unused bits to 0.

The shared memory object protection flags include: PAG_EXECUTE, PAG_READ, PAG_WRITE, and PAG_GUARD. The PAG_EXECUTE flag allows execute (essentially read) access to the private memory object. The PAG_READ flag allows the application to read the memory, but not write to it. The PAG_WRITE flag allows you to read and write the memory. The PAG_GUARD flag raises a "guard page entered" condition each time the application tries to access the affected memory.

DOSQueryMem

The DOSQueryMem function returns information about a range of pages within the virtual address space of the specified process. The information returned includes the type and access protection of the pages. You can provide an address range outside a previously allocated memory object (this is the only function that allows this practice). If your request extends outside the range of a single memory object, then DOSQueryMem returns an error code, the region attributes, length of the page range that matches the attributes of the first page in the region. Use the pulRegionSize parameter to determine the actual range of pages with matching attributes. You can use this value to determine the range of pages that the function did not scan.

The function starts at the first page within the region and determines its state. It continues scanning pages until it scans the entire range, scans a page with a nonmatching attribute, or it encounters the first page of the next memory object (this allows you to determine the appearance of the virtual memory map including object boundaries). OS/2 considers a page region without the PAG_COMMIT or PAG_FREE allocation type as reserved; it has an access protection of no access. The 80386 processor treats the execute and read access levels the same. This function uses the following syntax:

```
rc = DOSQueryMem (pBaseAddress, pulRegionSize, pulAllocationFlags)
```

The function provides only one return value (it does provide some return parameters discussed in the following paragraphs). rc contains a return code that tells you if the function completed without error. It also contains an error code if it didn't. Table 8-7 provides a list of these error codes.

DOSQueryMem function return codes

Table 8-7

Error number	Description
0	NO_ERROR
87	ERROR_INVALID_PARAMETER
95	ERROR_INTERRUPT
487	ERROR_INVALID_ADDRESS

There are three parameters for this function. pBaseAddress contains the base address of the memory object that you want to query. pulRegionSize contains the size in bytes of the range of pages that you want to query on entry. OS/2 automatically rounds this value to an even 4K page size. On return, this parameter points to a variable that contains the actual size of the range of pages in bytes. pulAttributeFlags contains: allocation type and access protection level.

The allocation attributes include: PAG_COMMIT, PAG_FREE, PAG_SHARED, and PAG_BASE. The PAG_COMMIT flag indicates that OS/2 automatically commits all pages in the memory object region. The PAG_FREE flag indicates that the pages within the region are free. The PAG_SHARED flag indicates that pages are within a shared memory region. If this flag is not set, then the memory object exists within private memory. The PAG_BASE flag indicates the first page in an allocated memory object.

The access protection level flags include: PAG_EXECUTE, PAG_READ, PAG_WRITE, and PAG_GUARD. The PAG_EXECUTE flag allows execute (essentially read) access to the private memory object. The PAG_READ flag allows the application to read the memory, but not write to it. The PAG_WRITE flag allows you to read and write the memory. The PAG_GUARD flag raises a "guard page entered" condition each time the application tries to access the affected memory.

DOSSetMem

The DOSSetMem function commits or decommits a range of pages within a shared or private memory object. You also can use it to alter their access protection or create a sparse collection of committed pages within a memory object. Every page within a memory object is free, private or shared. You cannot use this function to commit or decommit a free page.

OS/2 allocates a committed page from backing storage (demand pages). Committing a reserved page within a shared memory object commits that page within each process that shares it. The first attempt to write to a committed page creates a page of zeros. You cannot decommit a committed page within shared memory. Decommitting a private page frees the backing storage and makes them inaccessible. OS/2 allows you to commit a decommitted page if there is sufficient backing storage.

Setting the protection on a range of previously committed pages changes their access protection. You can set the access protection only of committed pages. The PAG_GUARD access protection attribute provides the means for automatic stack checking. (You also can use it to separate other data structures when necessary.) Each time a process attempts to access a range of guard pages, OS/2 generates an access violation (page fault). This fault sets the access protection of the page and generates a condition that indicates a process entered the guard page. The 80386 processor treats the execute and read access levels the same. This function uses the following syntax:

```
rc = DOSSetMem (pBaseAddress, ulRegionSize, ulAttributeFlags)
```

The function provides only one return value (it does provide some return parameters discussed in the following paragraphs). rc contains a return code that tells you if the function completed without error. It also contains an error code if it didn't. Table 8-8 provides a list of these error codes.

DOSSetMem function return codes   Table 8-8

Error number	Description
0	NO_ERROR
5	ERROR_ACCESS_DENIED
8	ERROR_NOT_ENOUGH_MEMORY
87	ERROR_INVALID_PARAMETER
95	ERROR_INTERRUPT
212	ERROR_LOCKED
487	ERROR_INVALID_ADDRESS
32798	ERROR_CROSSES_OBJECT_BOUNDARY

There are three parameters for this function. pBaseAddress contains the base address of the memory object that you want to change. ulRegionSize contains the size in bytes of the range of pages that you want to change. OS/2 automatically rounds this value to an even 4K page size. ulAttributeFlags contains: commit type and access protection level.

The allocation attributes include: PAG_COMMIT and PAG_DECOMMIT. The PAG_COMMIT flag commits the specified range of pages in the memory object region. The PAG_DECOMMIT flag decommits the specified range of pages in the memory object. OS/2 will not change the commit type of the memory object unless you specify a commit type.

The access protection level flags include: PAG_EXECUTE, PAG_READ, PAG_WRITE, PAG_GUARD, PAG_DEFAULT, and PAG_DECOMMIT. The PAG_EXECUTE flag allows execute (essentially read) access to the private memory object. The PAG_READ flag allows the application to read the memory, but not write to it. The PAG_WRITE flag allows you to read and write the memory. The PAG_GUARD flag raises a "guard page entered" condition each time the application tries to access the affected memory. The PAG_DEFAULT flag sets the access protection to the level specified by the initial process during allocation. The

PAG_DECOMMIT flag decommits the specified memory object range. You must specify the PAG_READ, PAG_WRITE, or PAG_EXECUTE attributes if you do not set this bit. Set all other bits to 0.

⇨ DOSSubAllocMem

The DOSSubAllocMem function allocates a block of memory from a memory block previously initialized by the DOSSubSetMem function. OS/2 automatically rounds the allocation size up to the nearest 8 byte multiple. The maximum value for ulSize is 64 bytes less than the memory pool size set by DOSSubSetMem. This function uses the following syntax:

```
rc = DOSSubAllocMem (pOffset, pBlockOffset, ulSize)
```

The function provides only one return value (it does provide some return parameters discussed in the following paragraphs). rc contains a return code that tells you if the function completed without error. It also contains an error code if it didn't. Table 8-9 provides a list of these error codes.

Table 8-9   **DOSSubAllocMem function return codes**

Error number	Description
0	NO_ERROR
87	ERROR_INVALID_PARAMETER
311	ERROR_DOSSUB_NOMEM
532	ERROR_DOSSUB_CORRUPTED

There are three parameters for this function. pOffset contains the memory pool offset that you want to use to allocate the block. pBlockOffset contains the DWORD address of the allocated memory block on return. ulSize contains the size of the requested memory block in bytes.

 # DOSSubFreeMem

The DOSSubFreeMem function frees a block of memory previously allocated using the DOSSubAlloc function. OS/2 automatically rounds the allocation size up to the nearest 8 byte multiple. The maximum value for ulSize is 64 bytes less than the memory pool size set by DOSSubSetMem. This function uses the following syntax:

```
rc = DOSSubFreeMem (pOffset, pBlockOffset, ulSize)
```

The function provides only one return value (it does provide some return parameters discussed in the following paragraphs). rc contains a return code that tells you if the function completed without error. It also contains an error code if it didn't. Table 8-10 provides a list of these error codes.

DOSSubFreeMem function return   Table 8-10

Error number	Description
0	NO_ERROR
87	ERROR_INVALID_PARAMETER
312	ERROR_DOSSUB_OVERLAP
532	ERROR_DOSSUB_CORRUPTED

There are three parameters for this function. pOffset contains the memory pool offset that you want to use to free the block. pBlockOffset contains the DWORD address of the allocated memory block. This is the same value returned by the DOSSubAllocMem function. ulSize contains the size of the memory block to free in bytes.

DOSSubSetMem

The DOSSubSetMem function initializes a memory that you can use for suballocation. You also can use this function to increase the size of a previously allocated pool. Use one of the other memory

management functions to allocate a memory object before you call this function. Always call the DOSSubUnsetMem function to return the memory resources to OS/2 before you exit the application. Otherwise, these resources remain unusable until the next system boot.

There are a few other conditions that you must observe when using a memory pool. The minimum memory pool allocation is 72 bytes (64 bytes for memory management and 8 bytes for one memory block). Never use the DOSSetMem function on pages managed by a suballocation function. Every page spanned by the memory pool must have the same attributes to use suballocation management (read/write access is mandatory). This function uses the following syntax:

```
rc = DOSPhysicalDisk (pOffset, ulFlags, ulSize)
```

The function provides only one return value (it does provide some return parameters discussed in the following paragraphs). rc contains a return code that tells you if the function completed without error. It also contains an error code if it didn't. Table 8-11 provides a list of these error codes.

Table 8-11   **DOSSubSetMem function return codes**

Error number	Description
0	NO_ERROR
87	ERROR_INVALID_PARAMETER
310	ERROR_DOSSUB_SHRINK

There are three parameters for this function. pOffset contains the address of the memory pool that you want to use for suballocation. ulFlags describes the characteristics of the memory that you want to suballocate. ulSize contains the size of the memory pool in bytes. OS/2 automatically rounds this number to the nearest multiple of 8 bytes.

The suballocation characteristic bits include: DOSSUB_INIT (0), DOSSUB_GROW (1), DOSSUB_SPARSE_OBJ (2), and

DOSSUB_SERIALIZE (3). Set the DOSSUB_INIT flag to initialize the memory object for suballocation. Otherwise, OS/2 assumes that you want to attach a process to a previously initialized shared memory pool. Set the DOSSUB_GROW flag to increase the size of the memory pool. OS/2 ignores the DOSSUB_INIT flag if you set this flag. Set the DOSSUB_SPARSE_OBJ flag if you want a suballocation function to manage the commitment of pages spanned by the memory pool. Make sure there are no committed pages in the memory pool before using this flag. Always set this flag to its initial value before you issue a DOSSubSetMem grow request. Set the DOSSUB_SERIALIZE flag if you require serialized access to the memory pool. Always set this flag to its initial value before you issue a DOSSubSetMem grow request.

⇨ DOSSubUnsetMem

The DOSSubUnsetMem function ends the use of a memory pool. Using this function releases all resources used by the memory pool to general use. You must use this function before you free the memory object. This function uses the following syntax:

```
rc = DOSPhysicalDisk (pOffset)
```

The function provides only one return value. rc contains a return code that tells you if the function completed without error. It also contains an error code if it didn't. Table 8-12 provides a list of these error codes.

DOSSubUnsetMem function return codes Table 8-12

Error number	Description
0	NO_ERROR
532	ERROR_DOSSUB_CORRUPTED

There is one parameter for this function. pOffset contains the memory pool offset.

Memory protection

There are several forms of protection provided with OS/2. Most of this protection is built into the processor itself. OS/2 merely makes use of these capabilities to provide a robust memory environment. It's the interaction of OS/2 with the processor that provides the protection your applications enjoy. Other forms of memory protection come as a result of the way OS/2 manages tasks and threads. The user does not have to worry about these protection schemes very much, but the programmer should at least know how they work. Unless you program in assembler, it is very unlikely that you will ever need to control the memory protection directly. The type of application that you create usually determines the required protection level and most C compilers have the required information built-in.

One hardware-specific protection scheme used by OS/2 (and most advanced operating systems to varying degrees) is the layers of security built into the 80286 and above processors. Most of the Intel documentation refers to this protection as rings of security. The lower your access level, the more information you can access. Think of these rings of protection as the various levels of security implemented at any military base. Figure 8-1 provides you with a better idea of what these rings of security represent.

We can extend our military analogy to the hardware security used by OS/2 even further. The outer ring (3) is unclassified. Any application can access this level of information. Every application must access this level to run at all. This level provides access to the resources that every application requires to function properly. However, at this level, resources are strictly controlled. For example, an application running at this level cannot access the computer's video memory directly because that might corrupt the actions taken by another process. The same holds true for ports or any other direct hardware access. Consider this the police state level of the operating system, everything is censored.

You could consider the next ring (2) confidential. The operating system doesn't allow everyone access to this level, but it does allow a

Figure 8-1

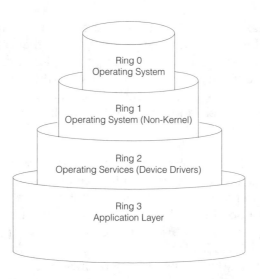

Ring 0 - This is the application layer. However, many OS/2 device drivers and DLL's operate at this level too. OS/2 (like the military) grants and application the lowest possible clearance to get the job done.

Ring 1 - OS/2 does not use this hardware ring, but it is available for specific tasks.

Ring 2 - This is the layer OS/2 uses for non-critical DLL's and device drivers. It provides a higher level of access than the application layer without exposing operating specific commands. It allows the kernel to maintain system control.

Ring 3 - Any OS/2 system files appear at this level. This provides the highest level of access that any application can obtain. Only kernel code appears at this level.

80x86 Processor protection rings.

select few applications to use it. OS/2 doesn't provide the application with access to anything that could hurt another application. It can't trust an application at this level that far. OS/2 usually places device drivers and DLLs at this layer. They both need better access to some of the low-level interfaces than an application does. For example, an application running at this level can access many of the PC's ports directly. On the other hand, it can't look at another processes' memory. This makes sense. A device driver has to know about the hardware to do its work. It doesn't need to know what another application is doing.

Consider the next security ring (1) as secret. It's so secret that OS/2 doesn't use it. Even though an application could theoretically run at this level from a hardware point of view, the operating system still has to cooperate. Other operating systems use this level for operating system components that are not part of the kernel. In other words, an application at this level can monitor other applications, but it doesn't directly interact with them.

The last level (0) is top secret. Only the operating system kernel and any applications directly attached to it have access to this level. The operating system has direct access to everything on the system; it is the application in control. This is the level where an application could not only damage itself, but also damage every other application on the system. This includes locking up the system. Unfortunately, it also includes more insidious forms of corruption. For example, an application at this level could corrupt memory, then write it out to the application's disk files, spreading the corruption even further. The next time that the user opened their application files she or he would see a big mess rather than a neat spreadsheet. As you can see, these layers of protection are essential to smooth operations within a multitasking environment.

Of course, memory protection doesn't stop there. It goes much further than that. Consider hardware protection as the first line of defense. A truly robust operating system needs more than that. It needs some form of monitoring capability that allows it to detect problems long before they trigger a hardware solution.

One of the ways that OS/2 detects application memory errors is the use of the flat memory addressing scheme described in the following paragraph. The application gets only one selector. To look at the memory used by another application, you need that application's selector. The minute that an application attempts to do this, OS/2 gets alerted and prevents the memory corruption. Using a flat addressing scheme frees OS/2 from a lot of overhead normally associated with monitoring memory accesses. Because each application gets only one selector, it becomes easier to simply look for an application using the wrong selector than to compare each memory access to a list of active selectors and then to the application that owns it.

⇨ Virtual memory

Virtual memory is one of those gray areas that many programmers
think that they understand, but few really do, especially from the
OS/2 point of view. The biggest advantage of virtual memory is that
it frees you from the physical memory constraints of the host
machine. The CPU under direction of the operating system uses the
hard drive to provide the additional memory that an application
requires in addition to the real memory on the machine. Using a
memory scheme of this nature means that you can no longer assume
that the piece of data that you accessed five minutes ago is where
you left it. The operating system moves memory between physical
memory and disk to accommodate changing application needs.
Because of this movement and the fact that several applications
probably share the physical memory on the host machine, you should
never assume anything about the memory that you use in an
application. Unlike DOS, you must allow OS/2 to manage the
memory for you. This is the reason that most of the DOS memory
functions only allocate or free memory. OS/2 takes care of every
other aspect of memory management for you.

OS/2 also uses the flat memory model of the 80386 and above
processors, which affects the way that you need to look at virtual
memory. Using the flat memory model is supposed to make OS/2
more portable to other systems. However, the big difference to the
programmer is that you no longer have to worry about the segmented
memory scheme that DOS used. Each OS/2 application has its own
0-based linear address space. Changing memory locations is a matter
of changing the offset, there are no segment considerations. This is
why OS/2 uses the term *memory object* when referring to a piece of
memory.

This isn't your only consideration when using virtual memory under
OS/2. Some programmers assume that you have the vast resources of
the 80386 and above processors at your disposal. According to the Intel
documentation for the 80386, you should have 4GB of address space
when using the flat memory model. In truth, virtual memory on an
OS/2 machine is limited to 512MB per application. Part of the reason
for this limitation is that OS/2 needs to maintain compatibility between

the 32-bit and 16-bit code combination that most applications use. This means that you still can build a very large application, but not one as large as the physical capabilities of the CPU.

Overall, OS/2 is a paged virtual memory system that uses the flat memory model. The paged part of this equation is the subject that gets many programmers into trouble. OS/2 uses 4K pages for memory allocation. The pages can reside on the hard disk or within physical memory. If your application requests a piece of memory that no longer resides in physical memory, then the CPU generates a page fault. OS/2 intercepts this fault, places your application on hold, retrieves the contents of that memory page from disk, makes any required changes to the memory request, and restarts your application. Your application never knows that this happened and even you wouldn't notice it except for the occasional application slow down that you see as OS/2 reads from disk. When OS/2 needs more physical memory to store pages that currently appear on disk, it uses a complicated scheme to determine which page it should read from memory to disk, it then replaces that page with the page the application requested from disk.

This means that OS/2 probably doesn't read your entire application from disk when you start it. This means that you need to consider this problem when creating your application. Try to keep routines that execute together in the same area of the application. This actually will reduce the number of page faults that your application will see and increase application speed by a small amount. OS/2 uses the term *process* for each application that executes under it.

Now that you have a good picture of memory under OS/2, there is one last item that you need to consider. OS/2 supports two types of data memory access: private and shared. You use private memory for most of an application's variables and internal processing. Shared memory comes into play when more than one process requires access to the same piece of memory. This is another memory protection feature of OS/2. You actually go through a special call to allow two processes to share a memory block. This allows you to send messages from one application to the next. It also allows both processes to receive the same input. OS/2 provides semaphores and other mechanisms that allow you to synchronize two applications. You also can send another application a standard message using the WIN function capabilities.

ASCII table

DEC	HEX		Character	DEC	HEX		Character
0	0		NULL (NUL)	16	10	►	Data link escape (DLE)
1	1	☺	Start of header (SOH)	17	11	◄	Device control 1 (DC1)
2	2	☻	Start of text (STX)	18	12	↕	Device control 2 (DC2)
3	3	♥	End of text (ETX)				
4	4	♦	End of transmission (EOT)	19	13	‼	Device control 3 (DC3)
5	5	♣	Enquire (ENQ)	20	14	¶	Device control 4 (DC4)
6	6	♠	Acknowledge (ACK)	21	15	§	Negative acknowledge (NAK)
7	7	•	Bell (BEL)				
8	8	◘	Backspace (BS)	22	16	▬	Synchronous idle (SYN)
9	9	○	Horizontal tab (HT)	23	17	↨	End of transmission block (ETB)
10	A	◙	Linefeed (LF)	24	18	↑	Cancel (CAN)
11	B	♂	Vertical tab (VT)	25	19	↓	End of medium (EM)
12	C	♀	Formfeed (FF)				
13	D	♪	Carriage return (CR)	26	1A	→	Substitute (SUB)
				27	1B	←	Escape (ESC)
14	E	♫	Shift out (SO)	28	1C	∟	File separator (FS)
15	F	☀	Shift in (SI)	29	1D	↔	Group separator (GS)

DEC	HEX	Character	DEC	HEX	Character
30	1E	▲ Record separator (RS)	49	31	1
31	1F	▼ Unit separator (US)	50	32	2
32	20	Space (SP)	51	33	3
33	21	!	52	34	4
34	22	"	53	35	5
35	23	#	54	36	6
36	24	$	55	37	7
37	25	%	56	38	8
38	26	&	57	39	9
39	27	'	58	3A	:
40	28	(	59	3B	;
41	29	)	60	3C	<
42	2A	*	61	3D	=
43	2B	+	62	3E	>
44	2C	,	63	3F	?
45	2D	-	64	40	@
46	2E	.	65	41	A
47	2F	/	66	42	B
48	30	0	67	43	C

DEC	HEX	Character	DEC	HEX	Character
68	44	D	87	57	W
69	45	E	88	58	X
70	46	F	90	5A	Z
71	47	G	91	5B	[
72	48	H	92	5C	\
73	49	I	93	5D	]
74	4A	J	94	5E	^
75	4B	K	95	5F	_
76	4C	L	96	60	`
77	4D	M	97	61	a
78	4E	N	98	62	b
79	4F	O	99	63	c
80	50	P	100	64	d
81	51	Q	101	65	e
82	52	R	102	66	f
83	53	S	103	67	g
84	54	T	104	68	h
85	55	U	105	69	i
86	56	V	106	6A	j

DEC	HEX	Character	DEC	HEX	Character
107	6B	k	126	7E	~
108	6C	l	127	7F	△ Delete (DEL)
109	6D	m	128	80	Ç
110	6E	n	129	81	ü
111	6F	o	130	82	é
112	70	p	131	83	â
113	71	q	132	84	ä
114	72	r	133	85	à
115	73	s	134	86	å
116	74	t	135	87	ç
117	75	u	136	88	ê
118	76	v	137	89	ë
119	77	w	138	8A	è
120	78	x	139	8B	ï
121	79	y	140	8C	î
122	7A	z	141	8D	ì
123	7B	{	142	8E	Ä
124	7C	¦	143	8F	Å
125	7D	}	144	90	É

DEC	HEX	Character	DEC	HEX	Character
145	91	æ	164	A4	ñ
146	92	Æ	165	A5	Ñ
147	93	ô	166	A6	ª
148	94	ö	167	A7	º
149	95	ò	168	A8	¿
150	96	û	169	A9	⌐
151	97	ù	170	AA	¬
152	98	ÿ	171	AB	½
153	99	Ö	172	AC	¼
154	9A	Ü	173	AD	¡
155	9B	¢	174	AE	«
156	9C	£	175	AF	»
157	9D	¥	176	B0	░
158	9E	₧	177	B1	▒
159	9F	■	178	B2	▓
160	A0	á	179	B3	│
161	A1	í	180	B4	┤
162	A2	ó	181	B5	╡
163	A3	ú	182	B6	╢

DEC	HEX	Character	DEC	HEX	Character
183	B7	╖	202	CA	╩
184	B8	╕	203	CB	╦
185	B9	╣	204	CC	╠
186	BA	║	205	CD	═
187	BB	╗	206	CE	╬
188	BC	╝	207	CF	╧
189	BD	╜	208	D0	╨
190	BE	╛	209	D1	╤
191	BF	┐	210	D2	╥
192	C0	└	211	D3	╙
193	C1	┴	212	D4	╘
194	C2	┬	213	D5	╒
195	C3	├	214	D6	╓
196	C4	─	215	D7	╫
197	C5	┼	216	D8	╪
198	C6	╞	217	D9	┘
199	C7	╟	218	DA	┌
200	C8	╚	219	DB	█
201	C9	╔	220	DC	▄

DEC	HEX	Character	DEC	HEX	Character
221	DD	▌	239	EF	∩
222	DE	▐	240	F0	≡
223	DF	▪	241	F1	±
224	E0	α	242	F2	≥
225	E1	β	243	F3	≤
226	E2	Γ	244	F4	⌠
227	E3	π	245	F5	⌡
228	E4	Σ	246	F6	÷
229	E5	σ	247	F7	≈
230	E6	μ	248	F8	°
231	E7	τ	249	F9	•
232	E8	Φ	250	FA	·
233	EA	Θ	251	FB	√
234	EB	Ω	252	FC	η
235	EC	δ	253	FD	²
236	ED	∞	254	FE	▪
237	ED	φ	255	FF	
238	EE	∈			

⇨ ASCII chart organized by type

All ASCII codes are given in decimals notation

Arrows

```
        24
        ↑

27←    →26

        ↓
        25
```

Single horizontal, single vertical line boxes

```
            196 194
218  ┌  –  ┬  ┐ 191
195 ├ 197 ┼ ┤ 180
179 │      │ │ 179
192 └  –  ┴  ┘ 217
            196 193
```

Single horizontal, double vertical box

```
            196 210
214 ╥  –  ╥ ╥ 183
199 ╟ 215 ╫ ╢ 182
186 ║      ║ ║ 186
211 ╨  –  ╨ ╜ 189
            196 207
```

Double horizontal, single vertical box

```
          205 209
213 ╒  =   ╤ ╕ 184
198 ╞ 216 ╪ ╡ 181
179 │      │ │ 179
212 ╘  =   ╧ ╛ 190
          205 207
```

Double horizontal, double vertical box

```
          205 203
201 ╔  =   ╦ ╗ 187
204 ╠ 206 ╬ ╣ 185
186 ║      ║ ║ 186
200 ╚  =   ╩ ╝ 188
          205 202
```

Foreign language characters

Ä	Å	â	ä	à	å	á	ª
142	143	131	132	133	134	160	166

Ç	ç
128	135

É	é	ê	ë
144	130	136	137

ï	î	ì	í
139	140	141	161

Ñ	ñ
165	164

Ö	ô	ö	ò	ó	º
153	147	148	149	162	167

Ü	ü	û	ù	ú
154	129	150	151	163

ÿ	Æ	æ	¿	¡
152	146	145	168	173

¢	£	¥	Pt	■
155	156	157	158	159

Mathematical symbols

½	¼	α	β	Γ	π	Σ
171	172	224	225	226	227	228

σ	µ	τ	φ	θ	Ω	δ
229	230	231	232	233	234	235

∞	Ø	∈	∩	≡	±	≥
236	237	238	239	240	241	242

≤	⌠	⌡	÷	≈	°	•
243	244	245	246	247	248	249

·	√	η	²
250	251	252	253

B

OS/2 error codes

THIS appendix provides a basic listing of the error codes that OS/2 returns for standard functions, allowing you to find unexpected error returns for specific functions. Even though the function listings in this book provide a list of *every* documented error code return, there are instances where you might receive an unexpected error number. Unfortunately, even this appendix might not provide a complete list of every error code returned by undocumented functions. In this case, a call to the technical support department of the vendor who wrote your compiler is in order. (Many of them do not bother to fully document each error; they simply provide a list of error numbers.) There are several groups of error codes. Each group represents a specific function type. The following paragraphs describe these error code groupings.

DOS, KBD, MOU, and VIO error codes

Table B-1 provides a complete listing of the error codes for the DOS, KBD, MOU, and VIO functions described in various chapters of this book. This table might or might not contain a complete list of error codes, because some of these functions contain undocumented features and some compiler vendors support their own special functions. IBM left many of the original error returns codes as reserved or undefined, leaving blanks for other vendors to use. In addition, there are instances where an unexpected action of the programmer's part can produce an unexpected return. The error code returned might not appear to match anything associated with the function that received it. In many cases, you can narrow this down to one of three causes: there was an unexpected hardware error, you supplied the wrong parameter type or information to the function, or the user performed some unexpected action.

NOTE The table does not provide descriptions for *every* error code. This usually occurs because the vendor documentation does not contain any description for the error code and no function uses it. In most cases, the definition column contains enough information for you to derive the meaning of the error within the context of the function that returned it.

Table B-1   **DOS, KBD, MOU, and VIO function error code summary**

Code	Definition	Description
0	NO_ERROR	No error, the function returned successfully.
1	ERROR_INVALID_FUNCTION	Invalid function number.
2	ERROR_FILE_NOT_FOUND	File not found.
3	ERROR_PATH_NOT_FOUND	Path not found.
4	ERROR_TOO_MANY_OPEN_FILES	Too many files open, increase the number of file handles.
5	ERROR_ACCESS_DENIED	Access denied. This might mean that the file is in use by another process or that it contains the wrong attributes.
6	ERROR_INVALID_HANDLE	Invalid handle.
7	ERROR_ARENA_TRASHED	Memory control blocks destroyed.
8	ERROR_NOT_ENOUGH_MEMORY	Insufficient memory, ask the user to close one or more applications to free memory. Alternatively, they could reduce the number of hard disk files to free space for the swap file.
9	ERROR_INVALID_BLOCK	Invalid memory block address.
10	ERROR_BAD_ENVIRONMENT	Invalid environment.
11	ERROR_BAD_FORMAT	Invalid format.
12	ERROR_INVALID_ACCESS	Invalid access code.
13	ERROR_INVALID_DATA	Invalid data. This could reference a corrupted memory block.
14	N/A	Reserved error code.
15	ERROR_INVALID_DRIVE	Invalid drive specified.
16	ERROR_CURRENT_DIRECTORY	Attempting to remove current directory. This can occur if you try to change the attributes of the current directory.
17	ERROR_NOT_SAME_DEVICE	A device context, handle, or other pointer no longer refers to the same device.
18	ERROR_NO_MORE_FILES	No more files to process.

Code	Definition	Description
19	ERROR_WRITE_PROTECT	Attempted to write to a write-protected (floppy) or nonwriteable (CD-ROM) disk.
20	ERROR_BAD_UNIT	Unknown unit. This can occur if the device experiences some type of failure or if the cable becomes disconnected.
21	ERROR_NOT_READY	Drive not ready. This often occurs when the user forgets to close the floppy drive door.
22	ERROR_BAD_COMMAND	Unknown command.
23	ERROR_CRC	Data error during a cyclic redundancy check. This usually refers to disk media.
24	ERROR_BAD_LENGTH	Invalid request structure length.
25	ERROR_SEEK	Seek error. This usually occurs during a disk or tape seek. A tape seek error simply might indicate an unformatted or corrupted tape.
26	ERROR_NOT_DOS_DISK	Unknown media type.
27	ERROR_SECTOR_NOT_FOUND	Sector not found. This usually refers to a disk error.
28	ERROR_OUT_OF_PAPER	Printer is out of paper.
29	ERROR_WRITE_FAULT	Write fault.
30	ERROR_READ_FAULT	Read fault.
31	ERROR_GEN_FAILURE	General failure. OS/2 could not return a specific error to describe the fault.
32	ERROR_SHARING_VIOLATION	Two processes tried to access a nonshareable file or other resource.
33	ERROR_LOCK_VIOLATION	Lock violation.
34	ERROR_WRONG_DISK	Invalid disk change. Usually occurs when the user changes the floppy in the middle of an operation.
35	ERROR_FCB_UNAVAILABLE	File control block (FCB) unavailable.
36	ERROR_SHARING_BUFFER_ EXCEEDED	Sharing buffer overflow.
37	ERROR_CODE_PAGE_MISMATCHED	Code page does not match.

543

Table B-1   **Continued**

Code	Definition	Description
38	ERROR_HANDLE_EOF	End of file (EOF) reached; there is no more data to process.
39	ERROR_HANDLE_DISK_FULL	Disk is full.
40–49	N/A	Reserved—Some libraries might return error codes in this area. Refer to your vendor documentation for specifics.
50	ERROR_NOT_SUPPORTED	Network request not supported.
51	ERROR_REM_NOT_LIST	Remote network node is not online. This error also occurs if the remote network experiences cabling or other hardware related problems.
52	ERROR_DUP_NAME	Duplicate network filename.
53	ERROR_BAD_NETPATH	Network path not found.
54	ERROR_NETWORK_BUSY	Network is busy. This error can occur during peak load periods as the result of certain hardware failures.
55	ERROR_DEV_NOT_EXIST	Device is not installed on the network, is not connected through a remote network, or experienced a failure.
56	ERROR_TOO_MANY_CMDS	Network command limit reached.
57	ERROR_ADAP_HDW_ERR	Network adapter hardware error or cable failure. This error can occur with a faulty terminator on ethernet networks.
58	ERROR_BAD_NET_RESP	Incorrect network response. Check the lines for noise.
59	ERROR_UNEXP_NET_ERR	Unexpected network error.
60	ERROR_BAD_REM_ADAP	The remote network adapter failed. This could indicate a faulty cable or terminator as well.
61	ERROR_PRINTQ_FULL	Network print queue is full.
62	ERROR_NO_SPOOL_SPACE	The print spool file is full. This usually happens when the hard drive gets full. Try reducing the number of files.

Code	Definition	Description
63	ERROR_PRINT_CANCELLED	The print spool file got deleted or corrupted. This can occur if someone renamed the file.
64	ERROR_NETNAME_DELETED	Network name deleted.
65	ERROR_NETWORK_ACCESS_DENIED	Network access denied. Check to see if all the drivers are loaded and the user logged in.
66	ERROR_BAD_DEV_TYPE	Invalid device type for a network.
67	ERROR_BAD_NET_NAME	Network name not found.
68	ERROR_TOO_MANY_NAMES	Network name limit exceeded.
69	ERROR_TOO_MANY_SESS	Network session limit exceeded.
70	ERROR_SHARING_PAUSED	Temporary pause in network.
71	ERROR_REQ_NOT_ACCEP	Network request denied. Make sure the user has appropriate access rights.
72	ERROR_REDIR_PAUSED	Pause in network print disk redirection.
73	ERROR_SBCS_ATT_WRITE_PROT	Attempted to write on a protected disk.
74	ERROR_SBCS_GENERAL_FAILURE	General failure, single-byte character set.
75–79	N/A	Reserved—Some libraries might return error codes in this area. Refer to your vendor documentation for specifics. Some vendors define error 75 as follows: ERROR_XGA_OUT_MEMORY. This indicates a display adapter out of memory condition.
80	ERROR_FILE_EXISTS	File exists.
81	ERROR_DUP_FCB	Duplicate file control block (FCB). Reserved for operating system use.
82	ERROR_CANNOT_MAKE	Cannot make directory entry.
83	ERROR_FAIL_I24	Failure on interrupt 24 (usually occurs during a disk failure).
84	ERROR_OUT_OF_STRUCTURES	Too many redirections.
85	ERROR_ALREADY_ASSIGNED	Duplicate redirection.

Table B-1   **Continued**

Code	Definition	Description
86	ERROR_INVALID_PASSWORD	User entered an invalid password.
87	ERROR_INVALID_PARAMETER	Function or process passed an invalid parameter.
88	ERROR_NET_WRITE_FAULT	Error writing to a network device.
89	ERROR_NO_PROC_SLOTS	No process slots available.
90	ERROR_NOT_FROZEN ERROR_SYS_COMP_NOT_LOADED	System failure. This could refer to a fatal hardware or software (operating system) failure.
91	ERR_TSTOVFL	Timer service table overflow.
92	ERR_TSTDUP	Timer service table duplicate.
93	ERROR_NO_ITEMS	No items to work on.
94	N/A	Reserved—Some libraries might return error codes in this area. Refer to your vendor documentation for specifics.
95	ERROR_INTERRUPT	Interrupted system call.
96–98	N/A	Reserved—Some libraries might return error codes in this area. Refer to your vendor documentation for specifics.
99	ERROR_DEVICE_IN_USE	Device in use by another process.
100	ERROR_TOO_MANY_SEMAPHORES	User/system open semaphore limit reached.
101	ERROR_EXCL_SEM_ALREADY_ OWNED	Exclusive semaphore already owned.
102	ERROR_SEM_IS_SET	The DOSCloseSemaphore function found the semaphore set.
103	ERROR_TOO_MANY_SEM_REQUESTS	Too many exclusive semaphore requests.
104	ERROR_INVALID_AT_INTERRUPT_ TIME	Operation invalid at interrupt time.
105	ERROR_SEM_OWNER_DIED	The previous owner of this semaphore terminated without freeing it.
106	ERROR_SEM_USER_LIMIT	Semaphore limited exceeded.

Code	Definition	Description
107	ERROR_DISK_CHANGE	The user either inserted the drive B disk into A or you need to ask them to insert the drive B disk into A. For example, during a diskcopy operation from drive A to drive A.
108	ERROR_DRIVE_LOCKED	Drive locked by another process.
109	ERROR_BROKEN_PIPE	There is no reader for this pipe. You cannot write to it.
110	ERROR_OPEN_FAILED	Open or create failed due to an explicit fail command.
111	ERROR_BUFFER_OVERFLOW	Buffer that was passed to the system call was too small to hold the return data. Allocate a larger buffer or change the value of any buffer length parameters passed during the call.
112	ERROR_DISK_FULL	The disk is full. Remove any unneeded files to make space.
113	ERROR_NO_MORE_SEARCH_ HANDLES	Cannot allocate another search structure and handle.
114	ERROR_INVALID_TARGET_HANDLE	Target handle in DOSDupHandle invalid. This usually means the target does not exist, you used the wrong handle, the handle got corrupted, the target experienced a failure, or the user affected the target in some way.
115	ERROR_PROTECTION_VIOLATION	Invalid user virtual address.
116	ERROR_VIOKBD_REQUEST	Error on display write or keyboard read. This is a general VIO and KBD function failure, OS/2 did not return anything more specific.
117	ERROR_INVALID_CATEGORY	The DOSDevIOCtl category is not defined. Refer to Table 5-2 for a list of valid categories.
118	ERROR_INVALID_VERIFY_SWITCH	Invalid value passed for verify flag.
119	ERROR_BAD_DRIVER_LEVEL	Level four driver not found.
120	ERROR_CALL_NOT_IMPLEMENTED	Invalid function called.
121	ERROR_SEM_TIMEOUT	Semaphore API function time-out occurred.

547

Table B-2   **Continued**

Code	Definition	Description
122	ERROR_INSUFFICIENT_BUFFER	Data buffer is too small. Allocate a larger data buffer or change the value of any buffer length parameters passed with the call.
123	ERROR_INVALID_NAME or HPFS_INVALID_VOLUME_CHAR	Illegal character or invalid file-system name.
124	ERROR_INVALID_LEVEL	Nonimplemented level for information retrieval or setting.
125	ERROR_NO_VOLUME_LABEL	No volume label found using the DOSQueryFSInfo function.
126	ERROR_MOD_NOT_FOUND	Module handle not found using getprocaddr or getmodhandle.
127	ERROR_PROC_NOT_FOUND	Procedure handle not found using getprocaddr.
128	ERROR_WAIT_NO_CHILDREN	The DOSWaitChild function finds no children.
129	ERROR_CHILD_NOT_COMPLETE	You did not terminate the DOSWaitChild function children.
130	ERROR_DIRECT_ACCESS_HANDLE	Handle operation invalid for direct disk-access handles.
131	ERROR_NEGATIVE_SEEK	Attempting to perform a seek using a negative offset.
132	ERROR_SEEK_ON_DEVICE	Application tried to perform a seek on a pipe or device.
133	ERROR_IS_JOIN_TARGET	Drive has previously joined drives.
134	ERROR_IS_JOINED	Drive is already joined.
135	ERROR_IS_SUBSTED	Drive is already substituted.
136	ERROR_NOT_JOINED	Cannot delete drive that is not joined.
137	ERROR_NOT_SUBSTED	Cannot delete drive that is not substituted.
138	ERROR_JOIN_TO_JOIN	Cannot join to a joined drive.
139	ERROR_SUBST_TO_SUBST	Cannot substitute to a substituted drive.
140	ERROR_JOIN_TO_SUBST	Cannot join to a substituted drive.

Code	Definition	Description
141	ERROR_SUBST_TO_JOIN	Cannot substitute to a joined drive.
142	ERROR_BUSY_DRIVE	Specified drive is busy.
143	ERROR_SAME_DRIVE	Cannot join or substitute a drive to a directory on the same drive.
144	ERROR_DIR_NOT_ROOT	Directory must be a subdirectory of the root. You cannot use the root directory.
145	ERROR_DIR_NOT_EMPTY	You must specify an empty directory to use the join command.
146	ERROR_IS_SUBST_PATH	The path that you specified is used in a substitute.
147	ERROR_IS_JOIN_PATH	The path that you specified is used in a join.
148	ERROR_PATH_BUSY	Another process is using the specified path.
149	ERROR_IS_SUBST_TARGET	Cannot join or substitute a drive that has a directory that is the target of a previous substitute.
150	ERROR_SYSTEM_TRACE	System trace error.
151	ERROR_INVALID_EVENT_COUNT	The DOSWaitMuxWaitSem function experienced an error.
152	ERROR_TOO_MANY_MUXWAITERS	System limit of 100 entries reached.
153	ERROR_INVALID_LIST_FORMAT	Invalid list format.
154	ERROR_LABEL_TOO_LONG or HPFS_VOL_LABEL_LONG	The volume label that you specified is too large.
155	ERROR_TOO_MANY_TCBS	Cannot create another TCB.
156	ERROR_SIGNAL_REFUSED	Signal refused.
157	ERROR_DISCARDED	The specified segment was discarded.
158	ERROR_NOT_LOCKED	The specified segment is not locked.
159	ERROR_BAD_THREADID_ADDR	Invalid thread-identity address.
160	ERROR_BAD_ARGUMENTS	Invalid environment pointer.
161	ERROR_BAD_PATHNAME	Invalid path name passed to exec.
162	ERROR_SIGNAL_PENDING	Signal already pending.
163	ERROR_UNCERTAIN_MEDIA	Error with interrupt 24 mapping. This usually occurs with a corrupted

Table B-1   **Continued**

Code	Definition	Description
		floppy or if the user attempts to perform a floppy disk operation without placing a disk in the drive.
164	ERROR_MAX_THRDS_REACHED	No more process slots.
165	ERROR_MONITORS_NOT_SUPPORTED	Error with interrupt 24 mapping. This usually occurs with a corrupted floppy or if the user attempts to perform a floppy disk operation without placing a disk in the drive.
166	ERROR_UNC_DRIVER_NOT_INSTALLED	This is the default redirection return code.
167	ERROR_LOCK_FAILED	Locking failed.
168	ERROR_SWAPIO_FAILED	Swap I/O failed.
169	ERROR_SWAPIN_FAILED	Swap in failed.
170	ERROR_BUSY	Segment is busy.
171–172	N/A	Reserved—Some libraries might return error codes in this area. Refer to your vendor documentation for specifics. Error 171 often returns an INT_TOO_LONG error.
173	ERROR_CANCEL_VIOLATION	A lock request is not outstanding for the specified file range or the file length is zero.
174	ERROR_ATOMIC_LOCK_NOT_SUPPORTED	The file-system driver (FSD) does not support atomic lock operations. OS/2 versions prior to 2.0 do not support atomic lock operations.
175	ERROR_READ_LOCKS_NOT_SUPPORTED	The file-system driver (FSD) does not support shared read locks.
176–179	N/A	Reserved—Some libraries might return error codes in this area. Refer to your vendor documentation for specifics.
180	ERROR_INVALID_SEGMENT_NUMBER	Invalid segment number.
181	ERROR_INVALID_CALLGATE	Invalid call gate.
182	ERROR_INVALID_ORDINAL	Invalid ordinal.

Code	Definition	Description
183	ERROR_ALREADY_EXISTS	Shared segment already exists.
184	ERROR_NO_CHILD_PROCESS	There is no child process to wait for.
185	ERROR_CHILD_ALIVE_NOWAIT	You specified NoWait and the child is alive.
186	ERROR_INVALID_FLAG_NUMBER	Invalid flag number.
187	ERROR_SEM_NOT_FOUND	Semaphore does not exist.
188	ERROR_INVALID_STARTING_ CODESEG	Invalid starting code segment or an incorrect END (label) directive.
189	ERROR_INVALID_STACKSEG	Invalid stack segment.
190	ERROR_INVALID_MODULETYPE	Invalid module type. You cannot use the specified dynamic-link library (DLL) as an application. Conversely, you cannot use the specified application as a DLL.
191	ERROR_INVALID_EXE_SIGNATURE	Invalid EXE signature (the characters at the beginning of an EXE file that define an OS/2 executable). If the first two letters of the file are MZ, then it is most likely a DOS application. Otherwise, it is another application type.
192	ERROR_EXE_MARKED_INVALID	The linker detected an error during EXE file creation and marked the EXE as invalid.
193	ERROR_BAD_EXE_FORMAT	Invalid EXE format. File is a DOS or other operating system application.
194	ERROR_ITERATED_DATA_EXCEEDS_ 64K	Iterated data exceeds 64K in length (one of the segments in the file exceeds 64K).
195	ERROR_INVALID_MINALLOCSIZE	Invalid minimum allocation size (one of the segments in the file is larger than the size that you specified).
196	ERROR_DYNLINK_FROM_INVALID_ RING	Dynamic link from invalid privilege level. A level 2 routine cannot link to dynamic-link libraries (DLLs). See the discussion in chapter 9 for further details.
197	ERROR_IOPL_NOT_ENABLED	Input/output privilege level (IOPL) not enabled. The user set the IOPL entry in CONFIG.SYS to NO.

Table B-1   **Continued**

Code	Definition	Description
198	ERROR_INVALID_SEGDPL	Invalid segment descriptor privilege level. You can use only levels 2 or 3.
199	ERROR_AUTODATASEG_EXCEEDS_ 64K.	Automatic data segment exceeds
200	ERROR_RING2SEG_MUST_BE_ MOVABLE	You must make a privilege level 2 segment movable. See chapter 9 for further details on privilege levels.
201	ERROR_RELOC_CHAIN_XEEDS_ SEGLIM	Relocation chain exceeds segment limit.
202	ERROR_INFLOOP_IN_RELOC_CHAIN	Infinite loop in relocation chain segment.
203	ERROR_ENVVAR_NOT_FOUND	Environment variable not found.
204	ERROR_NOT_CURRENT_CTRY	Not current country.
205	ERROR_NO_SIGNAL_SENT	The application did not send a signal. None of the processes in the command subtree has a signal handler.
206	ERROR_FILENAME_EXCED_RANGE	Filename is greater than 8 characters or extension is greater than 3 characters.
207	ERROR_RING2_STACK_IN_USE	Privilege level 2 stack is in use. Refer to chapter 9 for a discussion of privilege levels.
208	ERROR_META_EXPANSION_TOO_ LONG	Meta (global) expansion is too long.
209	ERROR_INVALID_SIGNAL_NUMBER	Invalid signal number.
210	ERROR_THREAD_1_INACTIVE	Inactive thread.
211	ERROR_INFO_NOT_AVAIL	There is no file system information available for this file. This could indicate a variety of problems including hard disk damage.
212	ERROR_LOCKED	Locked error.
213	ERROR_BAD_DYNALINK	Your application attempted to execute a nonfamily API (non-FAPI) function in DOS mode. See chapters 4 and 5 for the description of FAPI KBD, MOU, and VIO functions.

Code	Definition	Description
214	ERROR_TOO_MANY_MODULES	Too many modules.
215	ERROR_NESTING_NOT_ALLOWED	Nesting is not allowed.
216	ERROR_CANNOT_SHRINK	This is a nonstandard return value provided by some vendors. It usually indicates that you cannot reduce the size of a data construct.
217	ERROR_ZOMBIE_PROCESS	Zombie process. This usually signifies that the process died.
218	ERROR_STACK_IN_HIGH_MEMORY	The stack is located in high memory.
219	ERROR_INVALID_EXITROUTINE_RING	Invalid exit routine ring. See chapter 9 for details on protection rings.
220	ERROR_GETBUF_FAILED	Get buffer failed.
221	ERROR_FLUSHBUF_FAILED	Flush buffer failed.
222	ERROR_TRANSFER_TOO_LONG	Data transfer is too long.
223	ERROR_FORCENOSWAP_FAILED	This is a nonstandard return value provided by some vendors. It indicates that an attempt to force a no swap condition failed.
224	ERROR_SMG_NO_TARGET_WINDOW	You created the application window without using the FCF_TASKLIST style. It also could indicate that OS/2 could not create the window or already destroyed it.
228	ERROR_NO_CHILDREN	No child process.
229	ERROR_INVALID_SCREEN_GROUP	Invalid session.
230	ERROR_BAD_PIPE	Nonexistent pipe or invalid operation.
231	ERROR_PIPE_BUSY	Pipe is busy.
232	ERROR_NO_DATA	No data available on nonblocking read.
233	ERROR_PIPE_NOT_CONNECTED	Pipe was disconnected by server.
234	ERROR_MORE_DATA	There is more data available.
240	ERROR_VC_DISCONNECTED	Session was dropped due to errors.
250	ERROR_CIRCULARITY_REQUESTED	This error occurs when renaming a directory would cause circularity problems.
251	ERROR_DIRECTORY_IN_CDS	This error occurs when you try to

Table B-1   **Continued**

Code	Definition	Description
		rename a directory that is in use (usually by another process).
252	ERROR_INVALID_FSD_NAME	Your application tried to access a nonexistent file-system driver (FSD).
253	ERROR_INVALID_PATH	Invalid pseudo device.
254	ERROR_INVALID_EA_NAME	Invalid character in name. It also could indicate an invalid cbName.
255	ERROR_EA_LIST_INCONSISTENT	The EA list contents does not match its size or there are invalid EAs in the list.
256	ERROR_EA_LIST_TOO_LONG	FEAList is longer than 64K – 1 bytes.
257	ERROR_NO_META_MATCH	String does not match expression.
258	ERROR_FINDNOTIFY_TIMEOUT	This is a nonstandard error value provided by some vendors. It indicates that a find notify timed-out.
259	ERROR_NO_MORE_ITEMS	There are no more items for the DOSQueryFSAttach ordinal query.
260	ERROR_SEARCH_STRUC_REUSED	DOS mode find first or find next search structure reused.
261	ERROR_CHAR_NOT_FOUND	Character not found.
262	ERROR_TOO_MUCH_STACK	Stack request exceeds system limit.
263	ERROR_INVALID_ATTR	Invalid attribute.
264	ERROR_INVALID_STARTING_RING	Invalid starting ring. See chapter 9 for details on protection rings.
265	ERROR_INVALID_DLL_INIT_RING	Invalid DLL INIT (initialization) ring. See chapter 9 for details on protection rings.
266	ERROR_CANNOT_COPY	Cannot copy.
267	ERROR_DIRECTORY	DOSCopy experienced an error in DOSCall1.
268	ERROR_OPLOCKED_FILE	Oplocked file.
269	ERROR_OPLOCK_THREAD_EXISTS	Oplock thread exists.
270	ERROR_VOLUME_CHANGED	The volume changed. This usually happens when the user changes a floppy unexpectedly.

Code	Definition	Description
271	ERROR_FINDNOTIFY_HANDLE_ IN_USE	Reserved—Some libraries might return error codes in this area. Refer to your vendor documentation for specifics. Many vendors use this error to refer to a find notify handle error.
272	ERROR_FINDNOTIFY_HANDLE_ CLOSED	Reserved—Some libraries might return error codes in this area. Refer to your vendor documentation for specifics. Many vendors use this error to refer to a find notify handle error.
273	ERROR_NOTIFY_OBJECT_REMOVED	Reserved—Some libraries might return error codes in this area. Refer to your vendor documentation for specifics. Many vendors use this error to refer to a find notify object error.
274	ERROR_ALREADY_SHUTDOWN	The system already is shut down.
275	ERROR_EAS_DIDNT_FIT	The buffer that you provided was not large enough to hold the extended attributes (EAs). Allocate a larger buffer.
276	ERROR_EA_FILE_CORRUPT	The extended attribute (EA) file suffered damage. You usually can fix this problem using the CHKDSK utility.
277	ERROR_EA_TABLE_FULL	The extended attribute (EA) table is full.
278	ERROR_INVALID_EA_HANDLE	The extended attribute (EA) handle is invalid.
279	ERROR_NO_CLUSTER	No cluster. This usually indicates some type of disk error or invalid parameter values.
280	ERROR_CREATE_EA_FILE	Cannot create the extended attribute (EA) file.
281	ERROR_CANNOT_OPEN_EA_FILE	Cannot open the extended attribute (EA) file.
282	ERROR_EAS_NOT_SUPPORTED	Destination file system does not support extended attributes (EAs). This usually happens during a network drive access.

Table B-1   **Continued**

Code	Definition	Description
283	ERROR_NEED_EAS_FOUND	The destination file system does not support extended attributes (EAs) and the source file's EAs contain a need EA.
284	ERROR_DUPLICATE_HANDLE	The handle already exists.
285	ERROR_DUPLICATE_NAME	The name already exists.
286	ERROR_EMPTY_MUXWAIT	The list of semaphores in a muxwait semaphore is empty.
287	ERROR_MUTEX_OWNED	The calling thread owns one or more of the mutex semaphores in the list.
288	ERROR_NOT_OWNER	Caller does not own the semaphore.
289	ERROR_PARAM_TOO_SMALL	Parameter is not large enough to hold all the semaphore records in the muxwait semaphore.
290	ERROR_TOO_MANY_HANDLES	Number of handles limit reached.
291	ERROR_TOO_MANY_OPENS	There are too many files or semaphores open.
292	ERROR_WRONG_TYPE	Attempted to create the wrong type of semaphore.
293	ERROR_UNUSED_CODE	Code is not used.
294	ERROR_THREAD_NOT_TERMINATED	Thread was not terminated.
295	ERROR_INIT_ROUTINE_FAILED	Initialization routine failed.
296	ERROR_MODULE_IN_USE	Module in use.
297	ERROR_NOT_ENOUGH_WATCHPOINTS	There are not enough watchpoints.
298	ERROR_TOO_MANY_POSTS	An event semaphore reached its post count limit.
299	ERROR_ALREADY_POSTED	The event semaphore already is posted.
300	ERROR_ALREADY_RESET	The event semaphore already is reset.
301	ERROR_SEM_BUSY	The specified semaphore is busy.
302	N/A	Reserved—Some libraries might return error codes in this area. Refer

Code	Definition	Description
		to your vendor documentation for specifics.
303	ERROR_INVALID_PROCID	Invalid process identifier (PID).
304	ERROR_INVALID_PDELTA	Invalid priority delta.
305	ERROR_NOT_DESCENDANT	Not a descendent of this process.
306	ERROR_NOT_SESSION_MANAGER	Requester is not the session manager.
307	ERROR_INVALID_PCLASS	Invalid P class.
308	ERROR_INVALID_SCOPE	Invalid scope.
309	ERROR_INVALID_THREADID	Invalid thread identity (TID).
310	ERROR_DOSSUB_SHRINK	Cannot shrink the segment using the DOSSubSetMem function.
311	ERROR_DOSSUB_NOMEM	There is not enough memory to satisfy the DOSSubAllocMem function request.
312	ERROR_DOSSUB_OVERLAP	There is an overlap of the block that you want to free using DOSSubFreeMem with a block of allocated memory.
313	ERROR_DOSSUB_BADSIZE	Invalid size parameter for a DOSSubAllocMem or DOSSubFreeMem function call.
314	ERROR_DOSSUB_BADFLAG	Invalid flag parameter for a DOSSubSetMem function call.
315	ERROR_DOSSUB_BADSELECTOR	Invalid segment selector.
316	ERROR_MR_MSG_TOO_LONG or MGS_MR_MSG_TOO_LONG	Message too long for buffer. Allocate a larger buffer.
317	ERROR_MR_MID_NOT_FOUND	Message identity number not found.
318	ERROR_MR_UN_ACC_MSGF	Unable to access message file.
319	ERROR_MR_INV_MSGF_FORMAT	Invalid message file format.
320	ERROR_MR_INV_IVCOUNT	Invalid insertion variable count.
321	ERROR_MR_UN_PERFORM	Unable to perform function.
322	ERROR_TS_WAKEUP	Unable to wake up.
323	ERROR_TS_SEMHANDLE	Invalid system semaphore.
324	ERROR_TS_NOTIMER	No timers available.

Table B-1   **Continued**

Code	Definition	Description
326	ERROR_TS_HANDLE	Invalid timer handle.
327	ERROR_TS_DATETIME	Timer date or time is invalid.
328	ERROR_SYS_INTERNAL	Internal system error.
329	ERROR_QUE_CURRENT_NAME	The current queue name does not exist.
330	ERROR_QUE_PROC_NOT_OWNED	The current process does not own the specified queue.
331	ERROR_QUE_PROC_OWNED	The current process owns the specified queue.
332	ERROR_QUE_DUPLICATE	Duplicate queue name.
333	ERROR_QUE_ELEMENT_NOT_EXIST	The specified queue element does not exist.
334	ERROR_QUE_NO_MEMORY	There is not enough memory to meet queue requirements.
335	ERROR_QUE_INVALID_NAME	Invalid queue name.
336	ERROR_QUE_INVALID_PRIORITY	Invalid queue priority parameter.
337	ERROR_QUE_INVALID_HANDLE	Invalid queue handle.
338	ERROR_QUE_LINK_NOT_FOUND	Queue link not found.
339	ERROR_QUE_MEMORY_ERROR	Indicates a queue memory error. This usually happens when the memory gets corrupted. It also could indicate a hardware failure.
340	ERROR_QUE_PREV_AT_END	Previous queue element marked the end of the queue.
341	ERROR_QUE_PROC_NO_ACCESS	This process does not possess queue access.
342	ERROR_QUE_EMPTY	Queue is empty.
343	ERROR_QUE_NAME_NOT_EXIST	Queue name does not exist.
344	ERROR_QUE_NOT_INITIALIZED	Queue is not initialized.
345	ERROR_QUE_UNABLE_TO_ACCESS	Unable to access queues.
346	ERROR_QUE_UNABLE_TO_ADD	Unable to add new queue. This could indicate an insufficient memory condition.

Code	Definition	Description
347	ERROR_QUE_UNABLE_TO_INIT	Unable to initialize queues.
348	N/A	Reserved—Some libraries might return error codes in this area. Refer to your vendor documentation for specifics.
349	ERROR_VIO_INVALID_MASK	Invalid function replaced.
350	ERROR_VIO_PTR	Invalid parameter pointer.
351	ERROR_VIO_APTR	Invalid attribute pointer.
352	ERROR_VIO_RPTR	Invalid row pointer.
353	ERROR_VIO_CPTR	Invalid column pointer.
354	ERROR_VIO_LPTR	Invalid length pointer.
355	ERROR_VIO_MODE	Screen mode is not supported by the display adapter or the device driver.
356	ERROR_VIO_WIDTH	Invalid cursor width value.
357	ERROR_VIO_ATTR	Invalid cursor attribute value.
358	ERROR_VIO_ROW	Invalid row value.
359	ERROR_VIO_COL	Invalid column value.
360	ERROR_VIO_TOPROW	Invalid top row value.
361	ERROR_VIO_BOTROW	Invalid bottom row value.
362	ERROR_VIO_RIGHTCOL	Invalid right column value.
363	ERROR_VIO_LEFTCOL	Invalid left column value.
364	ERROR_SCS_CALL	The calling process is the not session manager.
365	ERROR_SCS_VALUE	Value is not for save or restore.
366	ERROR_VIO_WAIT_FLAG	Invalid wait flag setting.
367	ERROR_VIO_UNLOCK	Screen not previously locked.
368	ERROR_SGS_NOT_SESSION_MGR	The calling process is not the session manager.
369	ERROR_SMG_INVALID_SGID or ERROR_SMG_INVALID_SESSION_ID	Invalid session identity.
370	ERROR_SMG_NOSG or ERROR_SMG_NO_SESSIONS	No sessions available.
371	ERROR_SMG_GRP_NOT_FOUND or	Session not found. This could

Table B-1   **Continued**

Code	Definition	Description
	ERROR_SMG_SESSION_NOT_FOUND or SMG_SESSION_NOT_FOUND	indicate that the session terminated abnormally or that the session is not supported. For example, if the user did not install DOS or Windows support.
372	ERROR_SMG_SET_TITLE	You cannot change the title sent by the shell or parent.
373	ERROR_KBD_PARAMETER	Invalid keyboard parameter.
374	ERROR_KBD_NO_DEVICE	There is no keyboard attached to the system or the keyboard is faulty.
375	ERROR_KBD_INVALID_IOWAIT	Invalid I/O wait specified.
376	ERROR_KBD_INVALID_LENGTH	Invalid length for keyboard.
377	ERROR_KBD_INVALID_ECHO_MASK or KBD_INVALID_INPUT_MASK	Invalid echo mode mask.
378	ERROR_KBD_INVALID_INPUT_MASK	Invalid input mode mask.
379	ERROR_MON_INVALID_PARMS	Invalid DOSMon function parameters.
380	ERROR_MON_INVALID_DEVNAME	Invalid device name string.
381	ERROR_MON_INVALID_HANDLE	Invalid device handle.
382	ERROR_MON_BUFFER_TOO_SMALL	Monitor buffer is too small. Allocate a larger buffer.
383	ERROR_MON_BUFFER_EMPTY	Monitor buffer is empty.
384	ERROR_MON_DATA_TOO_LARGE	The data record is too large.
385	ERROR_MOUSE_NO_DEVICE	Mouse device is closed. This could indicate an invalid handle, an inoperative mouse, or lack of support from the operating system.
386	ERROR_MOUSE_INV_HANDLE	Mouse device is closed. This could indicate an invalid handle, an inoperative mouse, or lack of support from the operating system.
387	ERROR_MOUSE_INV_PARMS	Parameters invalid for the current display mode.
388	ERROR_MOUSE_CANT_RESET	The mouse driver cannot reset the mouse. This usually indicates a hardware problem.

Code	Definition	Description
389	ERROR_MOUSE_DISPLAY_PARMS	Parameters invalid for the current display mode.
390	ERROR_MOUSE_INV_MODULE	Mouse module is not valid.
391	ERROR_MOUSE_INV_ENTRY_PT	Mouse device driver entry point is not valid.
392	ERROR_MOUSE_INV_MASK	Function mask invalid.
393	NO_ERROR_MOUSE_NO_DATA	No valid mouse data.
394	NO_ERROR_MOUSE_PTR_DRAWN	The function drew the mouse pointer.
395	ERROR_INVALID_FREQUENCY	Invalid beep frequency.
396	ERROR_NLS_NO_COUNTRY_FILE or NO_COUNTRY_SYS	Cannot find the COUNTRY.SYS file.
397	ERROR_NLS_OPEN_FAILED or OPEN_COUNTRY_SYS	Cannot open the COUNTRY.SYS file.
398	ERROR_NLS_NO_CTRY_CODE or ERROR_NO_COUNTRY_OR_ CODEPAGE	Country code not found. This usually means that the country code does not exist in the current setup. Obtain updated system files.
399	ERROR_NLS_TABLE_TRUNCATED	The buffer that you provided is too small to hold the national language support (NLS) table. Allocate a larger buffer to retrieve the entire table.
400	ERROR_NLS_BAD_TYPE	The selected national language support (NLS) type does not exist.
401	ERROR_NLS_TYPE_NOT_FOUND or COUNTRY_NO_TYPE	The selected national language support (NLS) type does not appear in the file.
402	ERROR_VIO_SMG_ONLY	Only the session manager can issue this call.
403	ERROR_VIO_INVALID_ASCIIZ	Invalid ASCIIZ length.
404	ERROR_VIO_DEREGISTER	VIODeRegister function not allowed.
405	ERROR_VIO_NO_POPUP	You did not allocate a pop-up window.
406	ERROR_VIO_EXISTING_POPUP	The screen already contains a pop-up window.
407	ERROR_KBD_SMG_ONLY	Only the session manager can issue this call.

Table B-1   **Continued**

Code	Definition	Description
408	ERROR_KBD_INVALID_ASCIIZ	Invalid ASCIIZ length.
409	ERROR_KBD_INVALID_MASK	Invalid replacement mask.
410	ERROR_KBD_REGISTER	You cannot use KBDRegister here.
411	ERROR_KBD_DEREGISTER	You cannot use KBDDeRegister here.
412	ERROR_MOUSE_SMG_ONLY	Only the session manager can issue this call.
413	ERROR_MOUSE_INVALID_ASCIIZ	Invalid ASCIIZ length.
414	ERROR_MOUSE_INVALID_MASK	Invalid replacement mask.
415	ERROR_MOUSE_REGISTER	Mouse register not allowed.
416	ERROR_MOUSE_DEREGISTER	Mouse deregister not allowed.
417	ERROR_SMG_BAD_ACTION	Invalid action specified.
418	ERROR_SMG_INVALID_CALL	INIT called more than once. This also could indicate an invalid session identity.
419	ERROR_SCS_SG_NOTFOUND	New session number.
420	ERROR_SCS_NOT_SHELL	Only the shell can issue this call.
421	ERROR_VIO_INVALID_PARMS	Invalid parameters passed.
422	ERROR_VIO_FUNCTION_OWNED	Save and restore functions already owned by another process.
423	ERROR_VIO_RETURN	Nondestructive return. Any previous actions automatically undone.
424	ERROR_SCS_INVALID_FUNCTION	Caller invalid function.
425	ERROR_SCS_NOT_SESSION_MGR	Only the session manager can issue this call.
426	ERROR_VIO_REGISTER	VIO register not allowed.
427	ERROR_VIO_NO_MODE_THREAD	No mode restore thread in session.
428	ERROR_VIO_NO_SAVE_RESTORE_THD	No save or restore thread in session.
429	ERROR_VIO_IN_BG	You cannot issue this call while in the background.
430	ERROR_VIO_ILLEGAL_DURING_POPUP	You cannot issue this call during a pop-up.

Code	Definition	Description
431	ERROR_SMG_NOT_BASESHELL	Only the base shell can issue this call.
432	ERROR_SMG_BAD_STATUSREQ	Invalid status requested.
433	ERROR_QUE_INVALID_WAIT	NoWait parameter out of bounds (too high or low).
434	ERROR_VIO_LOCK	Error returned from Scroll Lock.
435	ERROR_MOUSE_INVALID_IOWAIT	Invalid parameters for IOWait.
436	ERROR_VIO_INVALID_HANDLE	Invalid VIO handle.
437	ERROR_VIO_ILLEGAL_DURING_LOCK	You cannot issue this call during screen lock.
438	ERROR_VIO_INVALID_LENGTH	Invalid VIO length.
439	ERROR_KBD_INVALID_HANDLE	Invalid KBD handle.
440	ERROR_KBD_NO_MORE_HANDLE	Ran out of handles.
441	ERROR_KBD_CANNOT_CREATE_KCB	Unable to create KCB.
442	ERROR_KBD_CODEPAGE_LOAD_INCOMPL	Unsuccessful code page load. This could indicate a damaged code page file or invalid parameters.
443	ERROR_KBD_INVALID_CODEPAGE_ID	Invalid code page identity.
444	ERROR_KBD_NO_CODEPAGE_SUPPORT	No code page support.
445	ERROR_KBD_FOCUS_REQUIRED	Keyboard focus required.
446	ERROR_KBD_FOCUS_ALREADY_ACTIVE	Calling thread has outstanding focus.
447	ERROR_KBD_KEYBOARD_BUSY	The keyboard is busy.
448	ERROR_KBD_INVALID_CODEPAGE	Invalid code page.
449	ERROR_KBD_UNABLE_TO_FOCUS	Focus attempt failed.
450	ERROR_SMG_SESSION_NON_SELECT	You cannot select this session.
451	ERROR_SMG_SESSION_NOT_FOREGRND	Parent or child session is not in the foreground.
452	ERROR_SMG_SESSION_NOT_PARENT	Calling process is not the parent of the requested child.
453	ERROR_SMG_INVALID_START_MODE	Invalid session start mode.
454	ERROR_SMG_INVALID_RELATED_OPT	Invalid session start related option.
455	ERROR_SMG_INVALID_BOND_OPTION	Invalid session bond option.

Table B-1   **Continued**

Code	Definition	Description
456	ERROR_SMG_INVALID_SELECT_OPT	Invalid session select option.
457	ERROR_SMG_START_IN_ BACKGROUND	Session started in background.
458	ERROR_SMG_INVALID_STOP_ OPTION/	Invalid session stop option.
459	ERROR_SMG_BAD_RESERVE	Reserved parameters are not zero.
460	ERROR_SMG_PROCESS_NOT_ PARENT	Session parent process already exists.
461	ERROR_SMG_INVALID_DATA_ LENGTH	Invalid data length.
462	ERROR_SMG_NOT_BOUND	Parent is not bound.
463	ERROR_SMG_RETRY_SUB_ALLOC	Retry request block allocation.
464	ERROR_KBD_DETACHED	A detached process identifier (PID) cannot issue this call.
465	ERROR_VIO_DETACHED	A detached process identifier (PID) cannot issue this call.
466	ERROR_MOU_DETACHED	A detached process identifier (PID) cannot issue this call.
467	ERROR_VIO_FONT	There is no font available to support the requested display mode.
468	ERROR_VIO_USER_FONT	User font is active.
469	ERROR_VIO_BAD_CP	Invalid code page specified.
470	ERROR_VIO_NO_CP	System displays do not support the specified code page.
471	ERROR_VIO_NA_CP	Current display does not support the specified code page.
472	ERROR_INVALID_CODE_PAGE	Invalid code page.
473	ERROR_CPLIST_TOO_SMALL	Code page list is too small.
474	ERROR_CP_NOT_MOVED	Code page was not moved.
475	ERROR_MODE_SWITCH_INIT	Mode switch initialization error. This could indicate a variety of problems including hardware failure or a bad device driver.
476	ERROR_CODE_PAGE_NOT_FOUND	Code page was not found.

Code	Definition	Description
477	ERROR_UNEXPECTED_SLOT_RETURNED	Internal error.
478	ERROR_SMG_INVALID_TRACE_OPTION	Invalid start session trace indicator.
479	ERROR_VIO_INTERNAL_RESOURCE	VIO internal resource error.
480	ERROR_VIO_SHELL_INIT	VIO shell initialization error.
481	ERROR_SMG_NO_HARD_ERRORS	No session manager hard errors.
482	ERROR_CP_SWITCH_INCOMPLETE	The DOSSetProcessCP function cannot set the KBD or VIO code page.
483	ERROR_VIO_TRANSPARENT_POPUP	Error during a VIO pop-up window.
484	ERROR_CRITSEC_OVERFLOW	Critical section overflow.
485	ERROR_CRITSEC_UNDERFLOW	Critical section underflow.
486	ERROR_VIO_BAD_RESERVE	Reserved parameter is not zero.
487	ERROR_INVALID_ADDRESS	Invalid physical address.
488	ERROR_ZERO_SELECTORS_REQUESTED	You must request at least one selector when using this function.
489	ERROR_NOT_ENOUGH_SELECTORS_AVA	There is not enough global descriptor table (GDT) space to satisfy the request.
490	ERROR_INVALID_SELECTOR	This is not a global descriptor table (GDT) selector.
491	ERROR_SMG_INVALID_PROGRAM_TYPE	Invalid program type.
492	ERROR_SMG_INVALID_PGM_CONTROL	Invalid program control.
493	ERROR_SMG_INVALID_INHERIT_OPT	Invalid inherit option.
494	ERROR_VIO_EXTENDED_SG	Invalid in PM session.
495	ERROR_VIO_NOT_PRES_MGR_SG	Only the session manager can issue this call.
496	ERROR_VIO_SHIELD_OWNED	Another process owns the VIO shield.
497	ERROR_VIO_NO_MORE_HANDLES	No more VIO handles.
498	ERROR_VIO_SEE_ERROR_LOG	Check the error log.
499	ERROR_VIO_ASSOCIATED_DC	The presentation space already is associated with a device context.

Table B-1   **Continued**

Code	Definition	Description
500	ERROR_KBD_NO_CONSOLE	There is no console associated with the keyboard.
501	ERROR_MOUSE_NO_CONSOLE	There is no console associated with the mouse.
502	ERROR_MOUSE_INVALID_HANDLE	Invalid mouse handle.
503	ERROR_SMG_INVALID_DEBUG_ PARMS	Invalid session manager debug parameters.
504	ERROR_KBD_EXTENDED_SG	Invalid in PM session.
505	ERROR_MOU_EXTENDED_SG	Invalid in PM session.
506	ERROR_SMG_INVALID_ICON_FILE	Invalid icon file.
507	ERROR_TRC_PID_NON_EXISTENT	The process identifier (PID) does not exist.
508	ERROR_TRC_COUNT_ACTIVE	
509	ERROR_TRC_SUSPENDED_BY_ COUNT	
510	ERROR_TRC_COUNT_INACTIVE	
511	ERROR_TRC_COUNT_REACHED	
512	ERROR_NO_MC_TRACE	
513	ERROR_MC_TRACE	
514	ERROR_TRC_COUNT_ZERO	
515	ERROR_SMG_TOO_MANY_DDS	
516	ERROR_SMG_INVALID_ NOTIFICATION	
517	ERROR_LF_INVALID_FUNCTION	
518	ERROR_LF_NOT_AVAIL	
519	ERROR_LF_SUSPENDED	
520	ERROR_LF_BUF_TOO_SMALL	
521	ERROR_LF_BUFFER_CORRUPTED	
521	ERROR_LF_BUFFER_FULL	
522	ERROR_LF_INVALID_DAEMON	
522	ERROR_LF_INVALID_RECORD	

Code	Definition	Description
523	ERROR_LF_INVALID_TEMPL	
523	ERROR_LF_INVALID_SERVICE	
524	ERROR_LF_GENERAL_FAILURE	
525	ERROR_LF_INVALID_ID	
526	ERROR_LF_INVALID_HANDLE	
527	ERROR_LF_NO_ID_AVAIL	
528	ERROR_LF_TEMPLATE_AREA_FULL	
529	ERROR_LF_ID_IN_USE	
530	ERROR_MOU_NOT_INITIALIZED	
531	ERROR_MOUINITREAL_DONE	
532	ERROR_DOSSUB_CORRUPTED	The suballocation memory pool previously initialized by DOSSubSetMem is corrupt.
533	ERROR_MOUSE_CALLER_NOT_ SUBSYS	
534	ERROR_ARITHMETIC_OVERFLOW	
535	ERROR_TMR_NO_DEVICE	
536	ERROR_TMR_INVALID_TIME	
537	ERROR_PVW_INVALID_ENTITY	
538	ERROR_PVW_INVALID_ENTITY_TYPE	
539	ERROR_PVW_INVALID_SPEC	
540	ERROR_PVW_INVALID_RANGE_TYPE	
541	ERROR_PVW_INVALID_COUNTER_ BLK	
542	ERROR_PVW_INVALID_TEXT_BLK	
543	ERROR_PRF_NOT_INITIALIZED	
544	ERROR_PRF_ALREADY_INITIALIZED	
545	ERROR_PRF_NOT_STARTED	
546	ERROR_PRF_ALREADY_STARTED	
547	ERROR_PRF_TIMER_OUT_OF_RANGE	
548	ERROR_PRF_TIMER_RESET	
549–638	N/A	Reserved—Some libraries might return error codes in this area. Refer to your vendor documentation for specifics.

Table B-1   **Continued**

Code	Definition	Description
639	ERROR_VDD_LOCK_USEAGE_DENIED	
640	ERROR_TIMEOUT	The semaphore timed out.
641	ERROR_VDM_DOWN	
642	ERROR_VDM_LIMIT	
643	ERROR_VDD_NOT_FOUND	OS/2 could not find the requested virtual device driver (VDD).
644	ERROR_INVALID_CALLER	An invalid caller used this function to open, close, or request a virtual device driver (VDD).
645	ERROR_PID_MISMATCH	
646	ERROR_INVALID_VDD_HANDLE	
647	ERROR_VLPT_NO_SPOOLER	
648	ERROR_VCOM_DEVICE_BUSY	
649	ERROR_VLPT_DEVICE_BUSY	
650	ERROR_NESTING_TOO_DEEP	Nesting level too deep.
651	ERROR_VDD_MISSING	
652–670	N/A	Reserved—Some libraries might return error codes in this area. Refer to your vendor documentation for specifics.
671	ERROR_BIDI_INVALID_LENGTH	
672	ERROR_BIDI_INVALID_INCREMENT	
673	ERROR_BIDI_INVALID_COMBINATION	
674	ERROR_BIDI_INVALID_RESERVED	
675	ERROR_BIDI_INVALID_EFFECT	
676	ERROR_BIDI_INVALID_CSDREC	
677	ERROR_BIDI_INVALID_CSDSTATE	
678	ERROR_BIDI_INVALID_LEVEL	
679	ERROR_BIDI_INVALID_TYPE_SUPPORT	
680	ERROR_BIDI_INVALID_ORIENTATION	
681	ERROR_BIDI_INVALID_NUM_SHAPE	

Code	Definition	Description
682	ERROR_BIDI_INVALID_CSD	
683	ERROR_BIDI_NO_SUPPORT	
684	NO_ERROR_BIDI_RW_INCOMPLETE	
685–690	N/A	Reserved—Some libraries might return error codes in this area. Refer to your vendor documentation for specifics.
691	ERROR_IMP_INVALID_PARM	
692	ERROR_IMP_INVALID_LENGTH	
693	MSG_HPFS_DISK_ERROR_WARN	
694–729	N/A	Reserved—Some libraries might return error codes in this area. Refer to your vendor documentation for specifics.
730	ERROR_MON_BAD_BUFFER	
731	ERROR_MODULE_CORRUPTED	
1477	ERROR_SM_OUTOF_SWAPFILE	
2055	ERROR_LF_TIMEOUT	
2057	ERROR_LF_SUSPEND_SUCCESS	
2058	ERROR_LF_RESUME_SUCCESS	
2059	ERROR_LF_REDIRECT_SUCCESS	
2060	ERROR_LF_REDIRECT_FAILURE	
32768	ERROR_SWAPPER_NOT_ACTIVE	
32769	ERROR_INVALID_SWAPID	
32770	ERROR_IOERR_SWAP_FILE	
32771	ERROR_SWAP_TABLE_FULL	
32772	ERROR_SWAP_FILE_FULL	
32773	ERROR_CANT_INIT_SWAPPER	
32774	ERROR_SWAPPER_ALREADY_INIT	
32775	ERROR_PMM_INSUFFICIENT_ MEMORY	
32776	ERROR_PMM_INVALID_FLAGS	
32777	ERROR_PMM_INVALID_ADDRESS	

Table B-1   Continued

Code	Definition	Description
32778	ERROR_PMM_LOCK_FAILED	
32779	ERROR_PMM_UNLOCK_FAILED	
32780	ERROR_PMM_MOVE_INCOMPLETE	
32781	ERROR_UCOM_DRIVE_RENAMED	
32782	ERROR_UCOM_FILENAME_ TRUNCATED	
32783	ERROR_UCOM_BUFFER_LENGTH	
32784	ERROR_MON_CHAIN_HANDLE	
32785	ERROR_MON_NOT_REGISTERED	
32786	ERROR_SMG_ALREADY_TOP	
32787	ERROR_PMM_ARENA_MODIFIED	
32788	ERROR_SMG_PRINTER_OPEN	
32789	ERROR_PMM_SET_FLAGS_FAILED	
32790	ERROR_INVALID_DOS_DD	
32791	ERROR_BLOCKED	
32792	ERROR_NOBLOCK	
32793	ERROR_INSTANCE_SHARED	
32794	ERROR_NO_OBJECT	
32795	ERROR_PARTIAL_ATTACH	
32796	ERROR_INCACHE	
32797	ERROR_SWAP_IO_PROBLEMS	
32798	ERROR_CROSSES_OBJECT_ BOUNDARY	The requested memory object crosses the boundary of another memory object.
32799	ERROR_LONGLOCK	
32800	ERROR_SHORTLOCK	
32801	ERROR_UVIRTLOCK	

Code	Definition	Description
32802	ERROR_ALIASLOCK	
32803	ERROR_ALIAS	
32804	ERROR_NO_MORE_HANDLES	
32805	ERROR_SCAN_TERMINATED	
32806	ERROR_TERMINATOR_NOT_FOUND	
32807	ERROR_NOT_DIRECT_CHILD	
32808	ERROR_DELAY_FREE	
32809	ERROR_GUARDPAGE	
32900	ERROR_SWAPERROR	
32901	ERROR_LDRERROR	
32902	ERROR_NOMEMORY	
32903	ERROR_NOACCESS	
32904	ERROR_NO_DLL_TERM	
65026	ERROR_CPSIO_CODE_PAGE_INVALID	
65027	ERROR_CPSIO_NO_SPOOLER	
65028	ERROR_CPSIO_FONT_ID_INVALID	
65033	ERROR_CPSIO_INTERNAL_ERROR	
65034	ERROR_CPSIO_INVALID_PTR_NAME	
65037	ERROR_CPSIO_NOT_ACTIVE	
65039	ERROR_CPSIO_PID_FULL	
65040	ERROR_CPSIO_PID_NOT_FOUND	
65043	ERROR_CPSIO_READ_CTL_SEQ	
65045	ERROR_CPSIO_READ_FNT_DEF	
65047	ERROR_CPSIO_WRITE_ERROR	
65048	ERROR_CPSIO_WRITE_FULL_ERROR	
65049	ERROR_CPSIO_WRITE_HANDLE_BAD	
65074	ERROR_CPSIO_SWIT_LOAD	
65077	ERROR_CPSIO_INV_COMMAND	
65078	ERROR_CPSIO_NO_FONT_SWIT	
65079	ERROR_ENTRY_IS_CALLGATE	The DLL procedure ordinal number refers to the call gate.

 # Presentation Manager error codes

Table B-2 contains a complete list of all the common Presentation Manager error codes. These error codes affect both the WIN and GPI functions as well as most of the other Presentation Manager specific function. They do not affect standard C functions or the messages associated with the WIN and GPI functions. In addition, most of these errors will not affect any object-oriented features of the compiler. Refer to your vendor documentation to obtain a complete list of common C and C++ function error codes.

Table B-2

Presentation Manager function error code summary

Code	Definition	Description
0x0000	PMERR_OK	There was no error, the function returned successfully.
0x1001	PMERR_INVALID_HWND	The process specified an invalid window handle.
0x1002	PMERR_INVALID_HMQ	The process specified an invalid message queue handle.
0x1003	PMERR_PARAMETER_OUT_OF_RANGE	The parameter value is out of range (exceeds its defined limit).
0x1004	PMERR_WINDOW_LOCK_UNDERFLOW	The process attempted to set the window use count below zero.
0x1005	PMERR_WINDOW_LOCK_OVERFLOW	The window use count overflowed.
0x1006	PMERR_BAD_WINDOW_LOCK_COUNT	The window use count is invalid.
0x1007	PMERR_WINDOW_NOT_LOCKED	The window specified in WINSendMsg was not locked.
0x1008	PMERR_INVALID_SELECTOR	The process attempted to pass an invalid selector.
0x1009	PMERR_CALL_FROM_WRONG_THREAD	
0x100A	PMERR_RESOURCE_NOT_FOUND	OS/2 could not find the specified resource identity.
0x100B	PMERR_INVALID_STRING_PARM	The string parameter is invalid.
0x100C	PMERR_INVALID_HHEAP	The process specified an invalid heap handle.

Code	Definition	Description
0x100D	PMERR_INVALID_HEAP_POINTER	OS/2 found an invalid heap pointer.
0x100E	PMERR_INVALID_HEAP_SIZE_PARM	OS/2 found invalid data within the heap.
0x100F	PMERR_INVALID_HEAP_SIZE	OS/2 found invalid data within the heap.
0x1010	PMERR_INVALID_HEAP_SIZE_WORD	OS/2 found invalid data within the heap.
0x1011	PMERR_HEAP_OUT_OF_MEMORY	An attempt to increase the heap size failed. This usually occurs due to lack of available memory.
0x1012	PMERR_HEAP_MAX_SIZE_REACHED	You cannot increase the heap size beyond the maximum size of 64K.
0x1013	PMERR_INVALID_HATOMTBL	The process specified an invalid atom table handle.
0x1014	PMERR_INVALID_ATOM	The specified atom does not exist in the atom table.
0x1015	PMERR_INVALID_ATOM_NAME	The process attempted to pass an invalid atom name string.
0x1016	PMERR_INVALID_INTEGER_ATOM	The specified atom is not a valid integer atom.
0x1017	PMERR_ATOM_NAME_NOT_FOUND	The specified atom name is not in the atom table.
0x1018	PMERR_QUEUE_TOO_LARGE	The requested queue size is too large.
0x1019	PMERR_INVALID_FLAG	The process set an invalid bit for a parameter. Always use predefined constants to avoid setting reserved bits.
0x101A	PMERR_INVALID_HACCEL	The process specified an invalid accelerator table handle.
0x101B	PMERR_INVALID_HPTR	The process specified an invalid pointer handle.
0x101C	PMERR_INVALID_HENUM	The process specified an invalid enumeration handle.
0x101D	PMERR_INVALID_SRC_CODEPAGE	The source code page parameter is invalid.
0x101E	PMERR_INVALID_DST_CODEPAGE	The destination code page parameter is invalid.

Table B-2   **Continued**

Code	Definition	Description
0x101f	PMERR_UNKNOWN_COMPONENT_ID	Unknown component identifier.
0x1020	PMERR_UNKNOWN_ERROR_CODE	Unknown error code.
0x1021	PMERR_SEVERITY_LEVELS	
0x1034	PMERR_INVALID_RESOURCE_FORMAT	OS/2 does not recognize the resource format.
0x1035	WINDBG_WINDOW_UNLOCK_WAIT	
0x1036	PMERR_NO_MSG_QUEUE	Your application failed to create a message queue to handle messages.
0x1037	PMERR_WIN_DEBUGMSG	
0x1038	PMERR_QUEUE_FULL	The specified queue is full.
0x1039	PMERR_LIBRARY_LOAD_FAILED	OS/2 could not load the specified dynamic link library (DLL).
0x103A	PMERR_PROCEDURE_LOAD_FAILED	OS/2 could not load the requested procedure.
0x103B	PMERR_LIBRARY_DELETE_FAILED	OS/2 could not delete the specified dynamic link library (DLL).
0x103C	PMERR_PROCEDURE_DELETE_FAILED	OS/2 could not delete the requested procedure.
0x103D	PMERR_ARRAY_TOO_LARGE	The array is too large.
0x103E	PMERR_ARRAY_TOO_SMALL	The array is too small.
0x103F	PMERR_DATATYPE_ENTRY_BAD_INDEX	Invalid datatype entry index.
0x1040	PMERR_DATATYPE_ENTRY_CTL_BAD	Invalid datatype entry control.
0x1041	PMERR_DATATYPE_ENTRY_CTL_MISS	The process did not provide a data type entry control.
0x1042	PMERR_DATATYPE_ENTRY_INVALID	The process did not provide a valid datatype entry.
0x1043	PMERR_DATATYPE_ENTRY_NOT_NUM	The process did not provide a numeric datatype entry.
0x1044	PMERR_DATATYPE_ENTRY_NOT_OFF	The process did not provide an offset datatype entry.
0x1045	PMERR_DATATYPE_INVALID	The process provided an invalid datatype.

Code	Definition	Description
0x1046	PMERR_DATATYPE_NOT_UNIQUE	The process must provide a unique datatype.
0x1047	PMERR_DATATYPE_TOO_LONG	The datatype is too large.
0x1048	PMERR_DATATYPE_TOO_SMALL	The datatype is too small.
0x1049	PMERR_DIRECTION_INVALID	
0x104A	PMERR_INVALID_HAB	The process specified an invalid anchor block handle.
0x104D	PMERR_INVALID_HSTRUCT	The process specified an invalid (NULL) structure handle.
0x104E	PMERR_LENGTH_TOO_SMALL	The process passed a parameter that did not contain enough information.
0x104F	PMERR_MSGID_TOO_SMALL	The process specified a message identifier that is too small.
0x1050	PMERR_NO_HANDLE_ALLOC	
0x1051	PMERR_NOT_IN_A_PM_SESSION	The process attempted to access a PM-only function even though it is not operating in a PM session.
0x1052	PMERR_MSG_QUEUE_ALREADY_EXISTS	The message queue already exists.
0x1055	PMERR_OLD_RESOURCE	
0x1101	PMERR_INVALID_PIB	The process passed an invalid PIB.
0x1102	PMERR_INSUFF_SPACE_TO_ADD	OS/2 could not extend the initialization file to add the required program or group. This might indicate a disk full condition.
0x1103	PMERR_INVALID_GROUP_HANDLE	The process specified an invalid program group handle.
0x1104	PMERR_DUPLICATE_TITLE	The program title that was specified in the PIBSTRUCT already exists within the same group.
0x1105	PMERR_INVALID_TITLE	The program or group title is too long or contains invalid characters.
0x1106	PMERR_INVALID_TARGET_HANDLE	The process specified an invalid program group handle.
0x1107	PMERR_HANDLE_NOT_IN_GROUP	
0x1108	PMERR_INVALID_PATH_STATEMENT	The process passed an invalid path statement.

Table B-2   **Continued**

Code	Definition	Description
0x1109	PMERR_NO_PROGRAM_FOUND	OS/2 could not find the specified program.
0x110A	PMERR_INVALID_BUFFER_SIZE	The specified buffer size is invalid.
0x110B	PMERR_BUFFER_TOO_SMALL	The buffer cannot hold the return data.
0x110C	PMERR_PL_INITIALISATION_FAIL	
0x110D	PMERR_CANT_DESTROY_SYS_GROUP	
0x110E	PMERR_INVALID_TYPE_CHANGE	The data type change is invalid.
0x110F	PMERR_INVALID_PROGRAM_HANDLE	The process specified an invalid program handle.
0x1110	PMERR_NOT_CURRENT_PL_VERSION	OS/2 found an unexpected data format in the initialization file.
0x1111	PMERR_INVALID_CIRCULAR_REF	
0x1112	PMERR_MEMORY_ALLOCATION_ERR	An error occurred during memory management.
0x1113	PMERR_MEMORY_DEALLOCATION_ ERR	An error occurred during memory management.
0x1114	PMERR_TASK_HEADER_TOO_BIG	The task header is too big.
0x1115	PMERR_INVALID_INI_FILE_HANDLE	The process specified an invalid initialization file handle.
0x1116	PMERR_MEMORY_SHARE	An error occurred during memory management.
0x1117	PMERR_OPEN_QUEUE	OS/2 could not open the queue. This usually occurs due to a lack of memory.
0x1118	PMERR_CREATE_QUEUE	OS/2 could not create the queue. This usually occurs due to a lack of memory.
0x1119	PMERR_WRITE_QUEUE	OS/2 experienced an error while writing to the queue.
0x111A	PMERR_READ_QUEUE	OS/2 could not read from the specified queue.
0x111B	PMERR_CALL_NOT_EXECUTED	
0x111C	PMERR_UNKNOWN_APIPKT	

Code	Definition	Description
0x111D	PMERR_INITHREAD_EXISTS	
0x111E	PMERR_CREATE_THREAD	
0x111F	PMERR_NO_HK_PROFILE_INSTALLED	
0x1120	PMERR_INVALID_DIRECTORY	The destination code page parameter is invalid.
0x1121	PMERR_WILDCARD_IN_FILENAME	The specified function does not support wildcards in the filename.
0x1122	PMERR_FILENAME_BUFFER_FULL	The filename buffer is full.
0x1123	PMERR_FILENAME_TOO_LONG	The filename does not conform to the 8,3 format for DOS disks.
0x1124	PMERR_INI_FILE_IS_SYS_OR_USER	OS/2 cannot close the user or system initialization file.
0x1125	PMERR_BROADCAST_PLMSG	
0x1126	PMERR_190_INIT_DONE	
0x1127	PMERR_HMOD_FOR_PMSHAPI	
0x1128	PMERR_SET_HK_PROFILE	
0x1129	PMERR_API_NOT_ALLOWED	
0x112A	PMERR_INI_STILL_OPEN	The initialization file still is open.
0x112B	PMERR_PROGDETAILS_NOT_IN_INI	The initialization file does not contain the requested program details.
0x112C	PMERR_PIBSTRUCT_NOT_IN_INI	
0x112D	PMERR_INVALID_DISKPROGDETAILS	OS/2 detected invalid program details in the initialization file.
0x112E	PMERR_PROGDETAILS_READ_FAILURE	OS/2 could not read the program details from the initialization file.
0x112F	PMERR_PROGDETAILS_WRITE_FAILURE	OS/2 could not write the program details to the initialization file.
0x1130	PMERR_PROGDETAILS_QSIZE_FAILURE	The specified queue was too small to hold the program details.
0x1131	PMERR_INVALID_PROGDETAILS	OS/2 detected invalid program details in the initialization file.
0x1132	PMERR_SHEPROFILEHOOK_NOT_FOUND	
0x1133	PMERR_190PLCONVERTED	

Table B-2   **Continued**

Code	Definition	Description
0x1134	PMERR_FAILED_TO_CONVERT_INI_PL	
0x1135	PMERR_PMSHAPI_NOT_INITIALISED	
0x1136	PMERR_INVALID_SHELL_API_ HOOK_ID	
0x1200	PMERR_DOS_ERROR	The DOS call returned an error. Refer to Table B-1 for a list of DOS call error codes.
0x1201	PMERR_NO_SPACE	OS/2 reached the limit of Window List entries while using the WINAddSwitchEntry function.
0x1202	PMERR_INVALID_SWITCH_HANDLE	The process specified an invalid Window List entry handle.
0x1203	PMERR_NO_HANDLE	The calling process did not supply a handle.
0x1204	PMERR_INVALID_PROCESS_ID	The process passed an invalid process identifier (PID).
0x1205	PMERR_NOT_SHELL	The requesting process is not the shell.
0x1206	PMERR_INVALID_WINDOW	The process provided an invalid frame window in a Window List call.
0x1207	PMERR_INVALID_POST_MSG	The process attempted to post an invalid message.
0x1208	PMERR_INVALID_PARAMETERS	The process passed one or more parameters with invalid data.
0x1209	PMERR_INVALID_PROGRAM_TYPE	OS/2 does not recognize the program type.
0x120A	PMERR_NOT_EXTENDED_FOCUS	
0x120B	PMERR_INVALID_SESSION_ID	The process passed an invalid session identifier. You must pass a value of 0 (for the application's own session) or the valid identifier of another session.
0x120C	PMERR_SMG_INVALID_ICON_FILE	The system manager could not use the specified icon file.
0x120D	PMERR_SMG_ICON_NOT_CREATED	The system manager icon was not created.

Code	Definition	Description
0x120E	PMERR_SHL_DEBUG	
0x1301	PMERR_OPENING_INI_FILE	OS/2 could not open the initialization file. This usually occurs due to a lack of disk space.
0x1302	PMERR_INI_FILE_CORRUPT	The initialization file is corrupt.
0x1303	PMERR_INVALID_PARM	The process passed a parameter with invalid data.
0x1304	PMERR_NOT_IN_IDX	OS/2 could not find the application name, key name, or program handle.
0x1305	PMERR_NO_ENTRIES_IN_GROUP	There are no group entries.
0x1306	PMERR_INI_WRITE_FAIL	OS/2 experienced an error writing the initialization file.
0x1307	PMERR_IDX_FULL	
0x1308	PMERR_INI_PROTECTED	OS/2 cannot update a read-only initialization file.
0x1309	PMERR_MEMORY_ALLOC	An error occurred during memory management.
0x130A	PMERR_INI_INIT_ALREADY_DONE	
0x130B	PMERR_INVALID_INTEGER	The specified parameter is not a valid integer.
0x130C	PMERR_INVALID_ASCIIZ	The profile string is not a valid zero-terminated string.
0x130D	PMERR_CAN_NOT_CALL_SPOOLER or PMERR_VALIDATION_REJECTED	An error occurred when the process tried to call the spooler validation routine. This error does not occur when the spooler is not installed.
0x1401	PMERR_WARNING_WINDOW_NOT_KILLED	OS/2 experienced an error while attempting to kill a window.
0x1402	PMERR_ERROR_INVALID_WINDOW	The specified window is invalid.
0x1403	PMERR_ALREADY_INITIALISED	
0x1405	PMERR_MSG_PROG_NO_MOU	There is no mouse attached to this machine, the device driver failed to load, or the mouse experienced a failure.
0x1406	PMERR_MSG_PROG_NON_RECOV	Nonrecoverable application error.
0x1407	PMERR_WINCONV_INVALID_PATH	

Table B-2   **Continued**

Code	Definition	Description
0x1408	PMERR_PI_NOT_INITIALISED	
0x1409	PMERR_PL_NOT_INITIALISED	
0x140A	PMERR_NO_TASK_MANAGER	The task manager is missing.
0x140B	PMERR_SAVE_NOT_IN_PROGRESS	There currently is no save in progress.
0x140C	PMERR_NO_STACK_SPACE	There is no stack space available.
0x140d	PMERR_INVALID_COLR_FIELD	The color field is invalid.
0x140e	PMERR_INVALID_COLR_VALUE	The color value is invalid.
0x140f	PMERR_COLR_WRITE	
0x1501	PMERR_TARGET_FILE_EXISTS	OS/2 could not overwrite the specified target file.
0x1502	PMERR_SOURCE_SAME_AS_TARGET	The direct manipulation source and target process are the same.
0x1503	PMERR_SOURCE_FILE_NOT_FOUND	OS/2 could not find the specified source file.
0x1504	PMERR_INVALID_NEW_PATH	The new path does not exist.
0x1505	PMERR_TARGET_FILE_NOT_FOUND	OS/2 could not find the specified target file.
0x1506	PMERR_INVALID_DRIVE_NUMBER	The specified drive does not exist.
0x1507	PMERR_NAME_TOO_LONG	The name string is too long.
0x1508	PMERR_NOT_ENOUGH_ROOM_ON_DISK	There is not enough disk storage space to complete the operation.
0x1509	PMERR_NOT_ENOUGH_MEM	There is not enough memory to complete the operation.
0x150B	PMERR_LOG_DRV_DOES_NOT_EXIST	The specified logical drive does not exist.
0x150C	PMERR_INVALID_DRIVE	The specified drive does not exist.
0x150D	PMERR_ACCESS_DENIED	The process did not allocate the memory block properly.
0x150E	PMERR_NO_FIRST_SLASH	
0x150F	PMERR_READ_ONLY_FILE	The process attempted to write to a read-only file.
0x151F	PMERR_GROUP_PROTECTED	

Code	Definition	Description
0x152F	PMERR_INVALID_PROGRAM_ CATEGORY	
0x1530	PMERR_INVALID_APPL	The process attempted to start an application with a type not recognized by the operating system.
0x1531	PMERR_CANNOT_START	You cannot start the session.
0x1532	PMERR_STARTED_IN_BACKGROUND	The application started a new process in the background.
0x1533	PMERR_INVALID_HAPP	The application handle passed to WINTerminateApp does not correspond to a valid session.
0x1534	PMERR_CANNOT_STOP	You cannot stop the session.
0x1601	PMERR_INTERNAL_ERROR_1	This is a Presentation Manager internal error. It usually indicates that a function failed due to circumstances outside application control.
0x1602	PMERR_INTERNAL_ERROR_2	This is a Presentation Manager internal error. It usually indicates that a function failed due to circumstances outside application control.
0x1603	PMERR_INTERNAL_ERROR_3	This is a Presentation Manager internal error. It usually indicates that a function failed due to circumstances outside application control.
0x1604	PMERR_INTERNAL_ERROR_4	This is a Presentation Manager internal error. It usually indicates that a function failed due to circumstances outside application control.
0x1605	PMERR_INTERNAL_ERROR_5	This is a Presentation Manager internal error. It usually indicates that a function failed due to circumstances outside application control.
0x1606	PMERR_INTERNAL_ERROR_6	This is a Presentation Manager internal error. It usually indicates that a function failed due to circumstances outside application control.

Table B-2   **Continued**

Code	Definition	Description
0x1607	PMERR_INTERNAL_ERROR_7	This is a Presentation Manager internal error. It usually indicates that a function failed due to circumstances outside application control.
0x1608	PMERR_INTERNAL_ERROR_8	This is a Presentation Manager internal error. It usually indicates that a function failed due to circumstances outside application control.
0x1609	PMERR_INTERNAL_ERROR_9	This is a Presentation Manager internal error. It usually indicates that a function failed due to circumstances outside application control.
0x160A	PMERR_INTERNAL_ERROR_10	This is a Presentation Manager internal error. It usually indicates that a function failed due to circumstances outside application control.
0x160B	PMERR_INTERNAL_ERROR_11	This is a Presentation Manager internal error. It usually indicates that a function failed due to circumstances outside application control.
0x160C	PMERR_INTERNAL_ERROR_12	This is a Presentation Manager internal error. It usually indicates that a function failed due to circumstances outside application control.
0x160D	PMERR_INTERNAL_ERROR_13	This is a Presentation Manager internal error. It usually indicates that a function failed due to circumstances outside application control.
0x160E	PMERR_INTERNAL_ERROR_14	This is a Presentation Manager internal error. It usually indicates that a function failed due to circumstances outside application control.
0x160F	PMERR_INTERNAL_ERROR_15	This is a Presentation Manager internal error. It usually indicates that a function failed due to circumstances outside application control.
0x1610	PMERR_INTERNAL_ERROR_16	This is a Presentation Manager internal error. It usually indicates that a function failed due to circumstances outside application control.

Code	Definition	Description
0x1611	PMERR_INTERNAL_ERROR_17	This is a Presentation Manager internal error. It usually indicates that a function failed due to circumstances outside application control.
0x1612	PMERR_INTERNAL_ERROR_18	This is a Presentation Manager internal error. It usually indicates that a function failed due to circumstances outside application control.
0x1613	PMERR_INTERNAL_ERROR_19	This is a Presentation Manager internal error. It usually indicates that a function failed due to circumstances outside application control.
0x1614	PMERR_INTERNAL_ERROR_20	This is a Presentation Manager internal error. It usually indicates that a function failed due to circumstances outside application control.
0x1615	PMERR_INTERNAL_ERROR_21	This is a Presentation Manager internal error. It usually indicates that a function failed due to circumstances outside application control.
0x1616	PMERR_INTERNAL_ERROR_22	This is a Presentation Manager internal error. It usually indicates that a function failed due to circumstances outside application control.
0x1617	PMERR_INTERNAL_ERROR_23	This is a Presentation Manager internal error. It usually indicates that a function failed due to circumstances outside application control.
0x1618	PMERR_INTERNAL_ERROR_24	This is a Presentation Manager internal error. It usually indicates that a function failed due to circumstances outside application control.
0x1619	PMERR_INTERNAL_ERROR_25	This is a Presentation Manager internal error. It usually indicates that a function failed due to circumstances outside application control.
0x161A	PMERR_INTERNAL_ERROR_26	This is a Presentation Manager internal error. It usually indicates that a function failed due to circumstances outside application control.
0x161B	PMERR_INTERNAL_ERROR_27	This is a Presentation Manager internal error. It usually indicates that a function failed due to circumstances outside application control.

Table B-2   **Continued**

Code	Definition	Description
0x161C	PMERR_INTERNAL_ERROR_28	This is a Presentation Manager internal error. It usually indicates that a function failed due to circumstances outside application control.
0x161D	PMERR_INTERNAL_ERROR_29	This is a Presentation Manager internal error. It usually indicates that a function failed due to circumstances outside application control.
0x1630	PMERR_INVALID_FREE_MESSAGE_ID	The process specified an invalid message identifier. OS/2 assumed the message parameter types are ULONG to complete the call.
0x1641	PMERR_FUNCTION_NOT_SUPPORTED	OS/2 does not support this function.
0x1642	PMERR_INVALID_ARRAY_COUNT	The array count is invalid; it is less than or equal to zero.
0x1643	PMERR_INVALID_LENGTH	The parameter length is invalid.
0x1644	PMERR_INVALID_BUNDLE_TYPE	The process attempted to pass an invalid bundle type.
0x1645	PMERR_INVALID_PARAMETER	The parameter value is invalid for its converted PM type. For example, you cannot convert a 4-byte value outside the range of −32,768 to +32,767 to a SHORT integer or a negative number to a ULONG or USHORT.
0x1646	PMERR_INVALID_NUMBER_OF_PARMS	The number of parameters is invalid.
0x1647	PMERR_GREATER_THAN_64K	The size of a data item or an array dimension exceeds 65,535 bytes.
0x1648	PMERR_INVALID_PARAMETER_TYPE	The parameter type is invalid for a bundle mask.
0x1649	PMERR_NEGATIVE_STRCOND_DIM	The process passed a negative array dimension as the data type length.
0x164A	PMERR_INVALID_NUMBER_OF_TYPES	The function call has an invalid number (zero) of types.
0x164B	PMERR_INCORRECT_HSTRUCT	The process provided a non-NULL structure handle that is invalid for one of the following reasons: it is not a data structure handle, it is the handle of an ERRINFO structure

Code	Definition	Description
		that it should not use on this call, or the process used a handle block returned by the bindings to the application for an in-line structure handle.
0x164C	PMERR_INVALID_ARRAY_SIZE	The control data type array size is invalid.
0x164D	PMERR_INVALID_CONTROL_ DATATYPE	The process specified an invalid control data type.
0x164E	PMERR_INCOMPLETE_CONTROL_SEQ	The control data type sequence is incomplete.
0x164F	PMERR_INVALID_DATATYPE	The process specified an invalid data type.
0x1650	PMERR_INCORRECT_DATATYPE	The process specified a data type that is incorrect for this function.
0x1651	PMERR_NOT_SELF_DESCRIBING_ DTYP	The data type is not self-describing.
0x1652	PMERR_INVALID_CTRL_SEQ_INDEX or PMERR_INVALID_CONTROL_SEQ_ INDEX	The parameter contains an invalid index in the control data type sequence. The index points to a nonexistent or nonnumeric entry.
0x1653	PMERR_INVALID_TYPE_FOR_LENGTH	The data type for a control length is invalid.
0x1654	PMERR_INVALID_TYPE_FOR_OFFSET	The data type for a control offset is invalid.
0x1655	PMERR_INVALID_TYPE_FOR_MPARAM	The message parameter type for a control MPARAM is invalid. You must use mparam1, mparam2, or mreply.
0x1656	PMERR_INVALID_MESSAGE_ID	The message identifier is invalid.
0x1657	PMERR_C_LENGTH_TOO_SMALL	The maximum length of the C structure is less than the total length required for the C component types.
0x1658	PMERR_APPL_STRUCTURE_TOO_ SMALL	The application buffer supplied by the process was smaller than the length required to complete the call.
0x1659	PMERR_INVALID_ERRORINFO_ HANDLE	The ERRINFO parameter is not the handle of an ERRINFO structure created by the WINGetErrorInfo function. This error usually occurs during a WINFreeErrorInfo call.

	Table B-2	Continued

Code	Definition	Description
0x165A	PMERR_INVALID_CHARACTER_INDEX	The character index is invalid during a WINNextChar or WINPrevChar call. It is always equal to 1 or the string length + 1.
0x2001	PMERR_ALREADY_IN_AREA	The process attempted to begin a new area even though an existing area bracket was open.
0x2002	PMERR_ALREADY_IN_ELEMENT	The process attempted to begin a new element even though an existing element bracket was open.
0x2003	PMERR_ALREADY_IN_PATH	The process attempted to begin a new path even though an existing path bracket was open.
0x2004	PMERR_ALREADY_IN_SEG	The process attempted to begin a new segment even though an existing segment bracket was open.
0x2005	PMERR_AREA_INCOMPLETE	This error occurs during one of three circumstances: the process opened, closed, or drew a segment. It issued the GPIAssociate function while an area bracket was opened. A drawn segment opened an area bracket and ended without closing it.
0x2006	PMERR_BASE_ERROR	An OS/2 base error occurred. You can access the error using the OffBinaryData field of the ERRINFO structure returned by the WINGetErrorInfo function.
0x2007	PMERR_BITBLT_LENGTH_EXCEEDED	The process exceeded the maximum BitBlt length.
0x2008	PMERR_BITMAP_IN_USE	The process tried to set a bitmap into a device context using GPISetBitMap when it already was selected into an existing device context. This error also occurs if the process attempts to tag a bitmap with a local pattern set identifier (setid) using GPISetBitMapID when it already was tagged with an existing setid.
0x2009	PMERR_BITMAP_IS_SELECTED	The process attempted to delete a bitmap when it was selected into a device context.

Code	Definition	Description
0x200A	PMERR_BITMAP_NOT_FOUND	The process attempted to use a bitmap that does not exist.
0x200B	PMERR_BITMAP_NOT_SELECTED	The process attempted to perform an operation on a presentation space associated with a memory device context that had no selected bitmap.
0x200C	PMERR_BOUNDS_OVERFLOW	OS/2 experienced an internal error during boundary data accumulation. This occurs if the coordinates or matrix transformation elements are invalid or too large.
0x200D	PMERR_CALLED_SEG_IS_CHAINED	The process tried to call a segment with a chained attribute set.
0x200E	PMERR_CALLED_SEG_IS_CURRENT	The process attempted to call a currently open segment.
0x200F	PMERR_CALLED_SEG_NOT_FOUND	The process attempted to call a nonexistent segment.
0x2010	PMERR_CANNOT_DELETE_ALL_DATA	
0x2011	PMERR_CANNOT_REPLACE_ELEMENT_0	
0x2012	PMERR_COL_TABLE_NOT_REALIZABLE	The process attempted to realize a color table that is not realizable.
0x2013	PMERR_COL_TABLE_NOT_REALIZED	The process tried to realize a color table on a device driver that does not support this function.
0x2014	PMERR_COORDINATE_OVERFLOW	OS/2 experienced an internal coordinate overflow. This occurs if the coordinates or the matrix transformation elements are invalid or too large.
0x2015	PMERR_CORR_FORMAT_MISMATCH	The coordinate format does not match the anticipated format.
0x2016	PMERR_DATA_TOO_LONG	The process attempted to transfer more than the 64,512 bytes allowed using GPIPutData, GPIGetData, or GPIElement.
0x2017	PMERR_DC_IS_ASSOCIATED	The process attempted to associate a presentation space with a device context that was already associated. This also occurs when the process attempts to destroy a device context without first disassociating it.

587

Table B-2 | Continued

Code	Definition	Description
0x2018	PMERR_DESC_STRING_TRUNCATED	The process provided a description string with GPIBeginElement that exceeded the maximum permitted length of 251 characters. OS/2 automatically truncated the string.
0x2019	PMERR_DEVICE_DRIVER_ERROR_1	This is a miscellaneous error number that OS/2 provides for user written device drivers. It usually does not have any significance.
0x201A	PMERR_DEVICE_DRIVER_ERROR_2	This is a miscellaneous error number that OS/2 provides for user written device drivers. It usually does not have any significance.
0x201B	PMERR_DEVICE_DRIVER_ERROR_3	This is a miscellaneous error number that OS/2 provides for user written device drivers. It usually does not have any significance.
0x201C	PMERR_DEVICE_DRIVER_ERROR_4	This is a miscellaneous error number that OS/2 provides for user written device drivers. It usually does not have any significance.
0x201D	PMERR_DEVICE_DRIVER_ERROR_5	This is a miscellaneous error number that OS/2 provides for user written device drivers. It usually does not have any significance.
0x201E	PMERR_DEVICE_DRIVER_ERROR_6	This is a miscellaneous error number that OS/2 provides for user written device drivers. It usually does not have any significance.
0x201F	PMERR_DEVICE_DRIVER_ERROR_7	This is a miscellaneous error number that OS/2 provides for user written device drivers. It usually does not have any significance.
0x2020	PMERR_DEVICE_DRIVER_ERROR_8	This is a miscellaneous error number that OS/2 provides for user written device drivers. It usually does not have any significance.
0x2021	PMERR_DEVICE_DRIVER_ERROR_9	This is a miscellaneous error number that OS/2 provides for user written device drivers. It usually does not have any significance.

Code	Definition	Description
0x2022	PMERR_DEVICE_DRIVER_ERROR_10	This is a miscellaneous error number that OS/2 provides for user written device drivers. It usually does not have any significance.
0x2023	PMERR_DEV_FUNC_NOT_INSTALLED	The presentation driver does not support the specified function.
0x2024	PMERR_DOSOPEN_FAILURE	The DOSOpen call did not successfully open the file even though it provided a good return code. This error usually happens during a GPILoadMetaFile or GPISaveMetaFile function call.
0x2025	PMERR_DOSREAD_FAILURE	The DOSRead call provided a good return code even though it did not read any more bytes from the file. This error usually occurs when the file contains more bytes to read and could indicate a hardware failure or the need to use the CHKDSK utility.
0x2026	PMERR_DRIVER_NOT_FOUND	OS/2 did not find the device driver specified for a DEVPostDeviceModes function call.
0x2027	PMERR_DUP_SEG	A metafile segment that the process wanted stored in the presentation space has the same segment identifier as an existing segment. This usually occurs during a GPIPlayMetaFile call with the drawing mode set to draw and retain or retain.
0x2028	PMERR_DYNAMIC_SEG_SEQ_ERROR	The internal state indicates that dynamic segment data still is visible after OS/2 processed all chained dynamic segments. The error usually occurs during a GPIDrawChain, GPIDrawForm, or GPIDrawSegment call processing with the removal of dynamic segments. This occurs if the process modifies or removes dynamically drawn segments (including called segments) from the chain while visible.
0x2029	PMERR_DYNAMIC_SEG_ZERO_INV	The process attempted to open a dynamic segment with a segment identifier or zero.

Table B-2   **Continued**

Code	Definition	Description
0x202A	PMERR_ELEMENT_INCOMPLETE	
0x202B	PMERR_ESC_CODE_NOT_SUPPORTED	The code the process provided for the DEVEscape call is not supported by the target device driver.
0x202C	PMERR_EXCEEDS_MAX_SEG_LENGTH	The system exceeded the maximum segment size during metafile creation or the generation of retained graphics.
0x202D	PMERR_FONT_AND_MODE_MISMATCH	The process attempted to draw characters using an incompatible character mode and character set. For example, the character specifies a vector/outline font when the mode calls for a image/raster font.
0x202E	PMERR_FONT_FILE_NOT_LOADED	The process attempted to unload a font file that it did not load.
0x202F	PMERR_FONT_NOT_LOADED	The process attempted to create a font that is not loaded.
0x2030	PMERR_FONT_TOO_BIG	The process attempted to load a font that is too large.
0x2031	PMERR_HARDWARE_INIT_FAILURE	OS/2 detected an error while initializing the hardware.
0x2032	PMERR_HBITMAP_BUSY	OS/2 detected an internal bitmap busy error. One thread locked the bitmap while another thread tried to access it.
0x2033	PMERR_HDC_BUSY	OS/2 detected an internal device context busy error. One thread locked the device context while another thread tried to access it.
0x2034	PMERR_HRGN_BUSY	OS/2 detected an internal region busy error. One thread locked the region while another thread tried to access it.
0x2035	PMERR_HUGE_FONTS_NOT_SUPPORTED	The process attempted to select a font larger than the 64K maximum size supported by the target device driver using the GPISetCharSet, GPISetAttrs, GPISetPatternSet, or GPISetMarkerSet functions.

Code	Definition	Description
0x2036	PMERR_ID_HAS_NO_BITMAP	There is no bitmap tagged with the setid specified for a GPIQueryBitmapHandle function call.
0x2037	PMERR_IMAGE_INCOMPLETE	The process attempted to select a bit map or perform a BitBlt operation using a bit map that has a format incompatible with the specified device context.
0x2038	PMERR_INCOMPAT_COLOR_FORMAT	The process attempted to select a color that has a format incompatible with the specified device context.
0x2039	PMERR_INCOMPAT_COLOR_OPTIONS	The process attempted to select a color option that is incompatible with the specified device context.
0x203A	PMERR_INCOMPATIBLE_BITMAP	The process attempted to select a bit map or perform a BitBlt operation using a bit map that has a format incompatible with the specified device context.
0x203B	PMERR_INCOMPATIBLE_METAFILE	The process attempted to associate a presentation space and a metafile that have incompatible page units, or size or coordinate format. This also can occur when the process attempts to play a metafile using the RES_RESET option (to reset the presentation space) to a presentation space associated with a metafile device context.
0x203C	PMERR_INCORRECT_DC_TYPE	The process attempted to perform a bitmap operation on a presentation space associated with a device context of a type that cannot support bitmap operations.
0x203D	PMERR_INSUFFICIENT_DISK_SPACE	The operation terminated due to insufficient disk space.
0x203E	PMERR_INSUFFICIENT_MEMORY	The operation terminated due to insufficient memory.
0x203F	PMERR_INV_ANGLE_PARM	The process provided an invalid angle parameter with the GPIPartialArc function.
0x2040	PMERR_INV_ARC_CONTROL	The process provided an invalid control parameter with the GPIFullArc function.

Table B-2   **Continued**

Code	Definition	Description
0x2041	PMERR_INV_AREA_CONTROL	The process provided an invalid options parameter with the GPIBeginArea function.
0x2042	PMERR_INV_ARC_POINTS	The process provided an invalid points parameter with the GPIFullArc function.
0x2043	PMERR_INV_ATTR_MODE	The process provided an invalid mode parameter with the GPISetAttrMode function.
0x2044	PMERR_INV_BACKGROUND_COL_ ATTR	The process specified an invalid background attribute value or the default value with the GPISetAttrs function instead of using the defaults mask.
0x2045	PMERR_INV_BACKGROUND_MIX_ ATTR	The process specified an invalid background attribute value or the default value with the GPISetAttrs function instead of using the defaults mask.
0x2046	PMERR_INV_BITBLT_MIX	The process provided an invalid lROP parameter with the GPIBitBlt or GPIWCBitBlt function.
0x2047	PMERR_INV_BITBLT_STYLE	The process provided an invalid options parameter with the GPIBitBlt or GPIWCBitBlt function.
0x2048	PMERR_INV_BITMAP_DIMENSION	The process provided an invalid dimension with the load bitmap function.
0x2049	PMERR_INV_BOX_CONTROL	The process provided an invalid control parameter with the GPIBox function.
0x204A	PMERR_INV_BOX_ROUNDING_PARM	The process provided an invalid corner rounding control parameter with the GPIBox function.
0x204B	PMERR_INV_CHAR_ANGLE_ATTR	The process set the default character angle attribute using the GPISetAttr function instead of using the defaults mask.

Code	Definition	Description
0x204C	PMERR_INV_CHAR_DIRECTION_ATTR	The process set the default character direction attribute using the GPISetAttr function instead of using the defaults mask.
0x204D	PMERR_INV_CHAR_MODE_ATTR	The process set the default character mode attribute using the GPISetAttr function instead of using the defaults mask.
0x204E	PMERR_INV_CHAR_POS_OPTIONS	The process provided an invalid options parameter with the GPICharStringPos or GPICharStringPosAt function.
0x204F	PMERR_INV_CHAR_SET_ATTR	The process provided an invalid character setid attribute or set the default value using the GPISetAttrs function instead of using the defaults mask.
0x2050	PMERR_INV_CHAR_SHEAR_ATTR	The process set the default character shear attribute using the GPISetAttr function instead of using the defaults mask.
0x2051	PMERR_INV_CLIP_PATH_OPTIONS	The process provided an invalid options parameter with the GPISetClipPath function.
0x2052	PMERR_INV_CODEPAGE	The process provided an invalid codepage parameter with the GPISetCP function.
0x2053	PMERR_INV_COLOR_ATTR	The process supplied an invalid color attribute value or set the default attribute value using GPISetAttrs instead of using the defaults mask.
0x2054	PMERR_INV_COLOR_DATA	The process provided invalid color table definition data with the GPICreateLogColorTable function.
0x2055	PMERR_INV_COLOR_FORMAT	The process provided an invalid format parameter with the GPICreateLogColorTable function.
0x2056	PMERR_INV_COLOR_INDEX	The process provided an invalid color index parameter with the GPIQueryRGBColor function.

Table B-2   **Continued**

Code	Definition	Description
0x2057	PMERR_INV_COLOR_OPTIONS	The process provided invalid color options parameter with the logical color table or color query function.
0x2058	PMERR_INV_COLOR_START_INDEX	The process provided an invalid starting index parameter with the logical color table or color query function.
0x2059	PMERR_INV_COORD_OFFSET	The process provided an invalid coordinate offset value.
0x205A	PMERR_INV_COORD_SPACE	The process provided an invalid source or target coordinate space parameter with the GPIConvert function.
0x205B	PMERR_INV_COORDINATE	The process provided an invalid coordinate value.
0x205C	PMERR_INV_CORRELATE_DEPTH	The process provided an invalid maxdepth parameter with the GPICorrelateSegment, GPICorrelateFrom, or GPICorrelateChain function.
0x205D	PMERR_INV_CORRELATE_TYPE	The process provided an invalid type parameter with the GPICorrelateSegment, GPICorrelateFrom, or GPICorrelateChain function.
0x205E	PMERR_INV_CURSOR_BITMAP	The process provided an invalid pointer with the WINSetPointer function.
0x205F	PMERR_INV_DC_DATA	The process provided an invalid data parameter with the DEVOpenDC function.
0x2060	PMERR_INV_DC_TYPE	The process provided an invalid type parameter with the DEVOpenDC function, or it issued a function that is invalid for a OD_METAFILE_ NOQUERY device context.
0x2061	PMERR_INV_DEVICE_NAME	The process provided an invalid devicename parameter with the DEVPostDeviceModes function.

Code	Definition	Description
0x2062	PMERR_INV_DEV_MODES_OPTIONS	The process provided an invalid options parameter with the DEVPostDeviceModes function.
0x2063	PMERR_INV_DRAW_CONTROL	The process specified an invalid control parameter with the GPISetDrawControl function.
0x2064	PMERR_INV_DRAW_VALUE	The process specified an invalid value parameter with the GPISetDrawControl function.
0x2065	PMERR_INV_DRAWING_MODE	The process specified an invalid mode parameter with the GPISetDrawControl function with draw and retain or draw set.
0x2066	PMERR_INV_DRIVER_DATA	The process specified invalid driver data.
0x2067	PMERR_INV_DRIVER_NAME	The process specified an uninstalled device driver name.
0x2068	PMERR_INV_DRAW_BORDER_OPTION	The process specified an invalid option parameter with the WINDrawBorder function.
0x2069	PMERR_INV_EDIT_MODE	The process provided an invalid mode parameter with the GPISetEditMode function.
0x206A	PMERR_INV_ELEMENT_OFFSET	The process provided an invalid offset parameter with the GPIQueryElement function.
0x206B	PMERR_INV_ELEMENT_POINTER	The process attempted to issue a GPIPutData call without setting the element pointer to point at the last element.
0x206C	PMERR_INV_END_PATH_OPTIONS	The process attempted to create or delete a path out of context of the path bracket.
0x206D	PMERR_INV_ESC_CODE	The process provided an invalid code parameter with the DEVEscape function.
0x206E	PMERR_INV_ESCAPE_DATA	The process provided an invalid data parameter with the DEVEscape function.
0x206F	PMERR_INV_EXTENDED_LCID	The process specified an invalid local identifier.

Code	Definition	Description
0x2070	PMERR_INV_FILL_PATH_OPTIONS	The process provided an invalid options parameter with the GPIFillPath function.
0x2071	PMERR_INV_FIRST_CHAR	The process provided an invalid firstchar parameter with the GPIQueryWidthTable function.
0x2072	PMERR_INV_FONT_ATTRS	The process provided an invalid attribute parameter with the GPICreateLogFont function.
0x2073	PMERR_INV_FONT_FILE_DATA	The GPILoadFonts, GPILoadPublicFonts, GPIQueryFontFileDescriptions, or GPIQueryFullFontFileDescs font file contains invalid data.
0x2074	PMERR_INV_FOR_THIS_DC_TYPE	The process issued a GPIRemoveDynamics or GPIDrawDynamics call to a presentation space associated with a metafile device context.
0x2075	PMERR_INV_FORMAT_CONTROL	
0x2076	PMERR_INV_FORMS_CODE	The process provided an invalid forms code parameter with the DEVQueryHardcopyCaps function.
0x2077	PMERR_INV_FONTDEF	The process specified an invalid font definition.
0x2078	PMERR_INV_GEOM_LINE_WIDTH_ATTR	The process specified an invalid geometric line width attribute value.
0x2079	PMERR_INV_GETDATA_CONTROL	The process specified an invalid format parameter with the GPIGetData function.
0x207A	PMERR_INV_GRAPHICS_FIELD	The process provided an invalid field parameter with the GPISetGraphicsField function.
0x207B	PMERR_INV_HBITMAP	The process specified an invalid bitmap handle.
0x207C	PMERR_INV_HDC	The process specified an invalid device context handle or micro presentation space handle.

Code	Definition	Description
0x207D	PMERR_INV_HJOURNAL	
0x207E	PMERR_INV_HMF	The process specified an invalid metafile handle.
0x207F	PMERR_INV_HPS	The process specified an invalid presentation space handle.
0x2080	PMERR_INV_HRGN	The process specified an invalid region handle.
0x2081	PMERR_INV_ID	The process provided an invalid lPSid parameter with the GPIRestorePS function.
0x2082	PMERR_INV_IMAGE_DATA_LENGTH	The process provided an invalid lLength parameter with the GPIImage function. There is mismatch between the image size and data length (lLength).
0x2083	PMERR_INV_IMAGE_DIMENSION	The process provided an invalid psizlImageSize parameter with the GPIImage function.
0x2084	PMERR_INV_IMAGE_FORMAT	The process provided an invalid lFormat parameter with the GPIImage function.
0x2085	PMERR_INV_IN_AREA	The process attempted to issue a function that is invalid within an area bracket. You usually can detect this while the actual drawing mode is draw or draw and retain or during segment drawing or correlation functions.
0x2086	PMERR_INV_IN_CALLED_SEG	
0x2087	PMERR_INV_IN_CURRENT_EDIT_MODE	The process attempted to issue a function that is invalid when using the current editing mode.
0x2088	PMERR_INV_IN_DRAW_MODE	The process attempted to issue a function that is invalid in draw mode.
0x2089	PMERR_INV_IN_ELEMENT	The process attempted to issue a function that is invalid within an element bracket.
0x208A	PMERR_INV_IN_IMAGE	The process attempted to issue a function that is invalid within an element bracket.

Table B-2   **Continued**

Code	Definition	Description
0x208B	PMERR_INV_IN_PATH	The process attempted to issue a function that is invalid within a path bracket.
0x208C	PMERR_INV_IN_RETAIN_MODE	The process attempted to issue a function (for example a query) that is invalid when the actual drawing mode is not draw or draw and retain.
0x208D	PMERR_INV_IN_SEG	The process attempted to issue a function that is invalid within a segment bracket.
0x208E	PMERR_INV_IN_VECTOR_SYMBOL	OS/2 detected an invalid order inside a vector symbol definition while drawing a vector (outline) font.
0x208F	PMERR_INV_INFO_TABLE	The process specified an invalid bitmap information table with a bitmap operation.
0x2090	PMERR_INV_JOURNAL_OPTION	
0x2091	PMERR_INV_KERNING_FLAGS	
0x2092	PMERR_INV_LENGTH_OR_COUNT	The process specified an invalid length or count parameter.
0x2093	PMERR_INV_LINE_END_ATTR	The process specified an invalid line end attribute value.
0x2094	PMERR_INV_LINE_JOIN_ATTR	The process specified an invalid line join attribute value.
0x2095	PMERR_INV_LINE_TYPE_ATTR	The process specified an invalid line type attribute value or the default value using the GPISetAttrs function instead of using the defaults mask.
0x2096	PMERR_INV_LINE_WIDTH_ATTR	The process specified an invalid line width attribute value or the default value using the GPISetAttrs function instead of using the defaults mask.
0x2097	PMERR_INV_LOGICAL_ADDRESS	The process specified an invalid device logical address.
0x2098	PMERR_INV_MARKER_BOX_ATTR	The process specified an invalid marker box attribute value.

Code	Definition	Description
0x2099	PMERR_INV_MARKER_SET_ATTR	The process specified an invalid marker set attribute value or the default value using the GPISetAttrs function instead of using the defaults mask.
0x209A	PMERR_INV_MARKER_SYMBOL_ATTR	The process specified an invalid marker symbol attribute value or the default value using the GPISetAttrs function instead of using the defaults mask.
0x209B	PMERR_INV_MATRIX_ELEMENT	The process specified an invalid transformation matrix element.
0x209C	PMERR_INV_MAX_HITS	The process provided an invalid maxhits parameter with the GPICorrelateSegment, GPICorrelateForm, or GPICorrelateChain function.
0x209D	PMERR_INV_METAFILE	The process provided an invalid metafile with the GPIPlayMetaFile function.
0x209E	PMERR_INV_METAFILE_LENGTH	The process specified an invalid length parameter with the GPISetMetaFileBits or GPIQueryMetaFileBits function.
0x209F	PMERR_INV_METAFILE_OFFSET	The process specified an invalid length parameter with the GPISetMetaFileBits or GPIQueryMetaFileBits function.
0x20A0	PMERR_INV_MICROPS_DRAW_ CONTROL	The process provided a draw control parameter with GPISetDrawControl that is invalid within a micro presentation space.
0x20A1	PMERR_INV_MICROPS_FUNCTION	The process attempted to issue a function that is invalid in a micro presentation space.
0x20A2	PMERR_INV_MICROPS_ORDER	The process attempted to play a metafile containing orders that are invalid within a micro presentation space.
0x20A3	PMERR_INV_MIX_ATTR	The process specified an invalid mix attribute value or the default value using the GPISetAttrs function instead of using the defaults mask.

599

Table B-2   **Continued**

Code	Definition	Description
0x20A4	PMERR_INV_MODE_FOR_OPEN_DYN	The process attempted to open a segment with the ATTR_DYNAMIC segment set while the drawing mode was set to DM_DRAW or DM_DRAWANDRETAIN.
0x20A5	PMERR_INV_MODE_FOR_REOPEN_SEG	The process attempted to reopen an existing segment while the draw mode was set to DM_DRAW or DM_DRAWANDRETAIN.
0x20A6	PMERR_INV_MODIFY_PATH_MODE	The process provided an invalid mode parameter with the GPIModifyPath function.
0x20A7	PMERR_INV_MULTIPLIER	The process provided an invalid multiplier parameter with the GPIPartialArc or GPIFullArc function.
0x20A8	PMERR_INV_NESTED_FIGURES	OS/2 detected nested figures within a path definition.
0x20A9	PMERR_INV_OR_INCOMPAT_OPTIONS	The process provided an invalid or incompatible (with micro presentation space) options parameter with the GPICreatePS or GPISetPS function.
0x20AA	PMERR_INV_ORDER_LENGTH	The process provided an invalid order length during GPIPutData or segment drawing.
0x20AB	PMERR_INV_ORDERING_PARM	The process provided an invalid ordering parameter with the GPISetSegmentPriority function.
0x20AC	PMERR_INV_OUTSIDE_DRAW_MODE	The process attempted to issue a GPISavePS or GPIRestorePS call or an output-only function (for example, GPIPaintRegion) from GPIPlayMetaFile without setting the drawing mode to DM_DRAW.
0x20AD	PMERR_INV_PAGE_VIEWPORT	The process provided an invalid viewport parameter with the GPISetPageViewport function.
0x20AE	PMERR_INV_PATH_ID	The process provided an invalid options parameter with the GPIOutlinePath function.

Code	Definition	Description
0x20AF	PMERR_INV_PATH_MODE	The process specified an invalid path identifier parameter.
0x20B0	PMERR_INV_PATTERN_ATTR	The process specified an invalid pattern symbol attribute value or the default value using the GPISetAttrs function instead of using the defaults mask.
0x20B1	PMERR_INV_PATTERN_REF_PT_ATTR	The specified provided an invalid attribute value.
0x20B2	PMERR_INV_PATTERN_SET_ATTR	The process specified an invalid pattern set attribute value or the default value using the GPISetAttrs function instead of using the defaults mask.
0x20B3	PMERR_INV_PATTERN_SET_FONT	The process attempted to use an unsuitable font as a pattern set.
0x20B4	PMERR_INV_PICK_APERTURE_OPTION	The process provided an invalid options parameter with the GPISetPickApertureSize function.
0x20B5	PMERR_INV_PICK_APERTURE_POSN	The process specified an invalid pick aperture position.
0x20B6	PMERR_INV_PICK_APERTURE_SIZE	The process provided an invalid pick aperture size parameter with the GPISetPickApertureSize function.
0x20B7	PMERR_INV_PICK_NUMBER	
0x20B8	PMERR_INV_PLAY_METAFILE_OPTION	The process provided an invalid option parameter with the GPIPlayMetaFile function.
0x20B9	PMERR_INV_PRIMITIVE_TYPE	The process provided an invalid primitive type parameter with the GPISetAttrs or GPIQueryAttrs function.
0x20BA	PMERR_INV_PS_SIZE	The process provided an invalid size parameter with the GPICreatePS or GPISetPS function.
0x20BB	PMERR_INV_PUTDATA_FORMAT	The process provided an invalid format parameter with the GPIPutData function.
0x20BC	PMERR_INV_QUERY_ELEMENT_NO	The process provided an invalid start parameter with the DEVQueryCaps function.

Table B-2   **Continued**

Code	Definition	Description
0x20BD	PMERR_INV_RECT	The process specified an invalid rectangle parameter.
0x20BE	PMERR_INV_REGION_CONTROL	The process provided an invalid control parameter with the GPIQueryRegionRects function.
0x20BF	PMERR_INV_REGION_MIX_MODE	The process provided an invalid mode parameter with the GPICombineRegion function.
0x20C0	PMERR_INV_REPLACE_MODE_FUNC	The process attempted to issue a GPIPutData call with the editing mode set to SEGEM_REPLACE.
0x20C1	PMERR_INV_RESERVED_FIELD	The process specified an invalid reserved field.
0x20C2	PMERR_INV_RESET_OPTIONS	The process provided an invalid options parameter with the GPIResetPS function.
0x20C3	PMERR_INV_RGBCOLOR	The process provided an invalid RGB color parameter with the GPIQueryNearestColor or GPIQueryColor function.
0x20C4	PMERR_INV_SCAN_START	The process provided an invalid scan start parameter with a bitmap function.
0x20C5	PMERR_INV_SEG_ATTR	The process provided an invalid attribute parameter with the GPISetSegmentAttrs, GPIQuerySegmentAttrs, GPISetInitialSegmentAttrs, or GPIQueryInitialSegementAttrs function.
0x20C6	PMERR_INV_SEG_ATTR_VALUE	The process provided an invalid attribute value parameter with the GPISetSegmentAttrs or GPISetInitialSegmentAttrs function.
0x20C7	PMERR_INV_SEG_CH_LENGTH	The process specified an invalid chained segment length.
0x20C8	PMERR_INV_SEG_NAME	The process specified an invalid segment identifier.
0x20C9	PMERR_INV_SEG_OFFSET	The process provided an invalid offset parameter with the GPIPutData function.

Code	Definition	Description
0x20CA	PMERR_INV_SETID	The process specified an invalid setid.
0x20CB	PMERR_INV_SETID_TYPE	The process specified an invalid setid type.
0x20CC	PMERR_INV_SET_VIEWPORT_OPTION	
0x20CD	PMERR_INV_SHARPNESS_PARM	The process provided an invalid sharpness parameter with the GPIPolyFilletSharp function.
0x20CE	PMERR_INV_SOURCE_OFFSET	The process specified an invalid source offset.
0x20CF	PMERR_INV_STOP_DRAW_VALUE	The process provided an invalid value parameter with the GPISetStopDraw function.
0x20D0	PMERR_INV_TRANSFORM_TYPE	The process provided an invalid options parameter with the transform matrix function.
0x20D1	PMERR_INV_USAGE_PARM	The process provided an invalid options parameter with the GPICreateBitmap function.
0x20D2	PMERR_INV_VIEWING_LIMITS	The process provided an invalid limits parameter with the GPISetViewingLimits function.
0x20D3	PMERR_JFILE_BUSY	
0x20D4	PMERR_JNL_FUNC_DATA_TOO_LONG	
0x20D5	PMERR_KERNING_NOT_SUPPORTED	The process requested kerning on a GPICreateLogFont call to a presentation space associated with a device context that does not support kerning.
0x20D6	PMERR_LABEL_NOT_FOUND	The specified element label does not exist.
0x20D7	PMERR_MATRIX_OVERFLOW	OS/2 detected an internal overflow error during matrix multiplication. This occurs if the coordinates or matrix transformation elements are invalid or too large.
0x20D8	PMERR_METAFILE_INTERNAL_ERROR	OS/2 detected an internal inconsistency during metafile unlock processing.
0x20D9	PMERR_METAFILE_IN_USE	A thread tried to access a metafile in use by another thread.

Table B-2

Continued

Code	Definition	Description
0x20DA	PMERR_METAFILE_LIMIT_EXCEEDED	The process exceeded the maximum permitted metafile size during recording.
0x20DB	PMERR_NAME_STACK_FULL	The name stack is full.
0x20DC	PMERR_NOT_CREATED_BY_ DEVOPENDC	The process attempted to destroy a device context using DEVCloseDC that it did not create using DEVOpenDC.
0x20DD	PMERR_NOT_IN_AREA	The process attempted to end an area using the GPIEndArea function or during segment drawing while not in an area bracket.
0x20DE	PMERR_NOT_IN_DRAW_MODE	The process attempted to issue the GPISavePS or GPIRestorePS function while the drawing mode was set to DM_DRAW.
0x20DF	PMERR_NOT_IN_ELEMENT	The process attempted to end an element using the GPIEndElement function or during segment drawing while not in an element bracket.
0x20E0	PMERR_NOT_IN_IMAGE	The process attempted to end an image during segment drawing even though it was not in an image bracket.
0x20E1	PMERR_NOT_IN_PATH	The process attempted to end a path using the GPIEndPath function or during segment drawing while not in a path bracket.
0x20E2	PMERR_NOT_IN_RETAIN_MODE	The process attempted to issue a segment editing element function that is invalid when the actual drawing mode is not set to retain.
0x20E3	PMERR_NOT_IN_SEG	The process attempted to end a segment using the GPIEndSegment function while not in a segment bracket.
0x20E4	PMERR_NO_BITMAP_SELECTED	The process attempted to operate on a memory device context that has no bitmap selected.
0x20E5	PMERR_NO_CURRENT_ELEMENT	The process attempted to issue a GPIQueryElement or GPIQueryElementType call even though there is no open element.

Code	Definition	Description
0x20E6	PMERR_NO_CURRENT_SEG	The process attempted to issue a GPIQueryElement or GPIQueryElementType call even though there is no open segment.
0x20E7	PMERR_NO_METAFILE_RECORD_HANDLE	OS/2 could not find the metafile record handle during metafile recording, or the process did not issue a DEVEscape (DEVESC_STARTDOC) call when drawing to a OD_QUEUED device context with a pszDataType field of PM_Q_STD.
0x20E8	PMERR_ORDER_TOO_BIG	OS/2 exceeded an internal size limit while converting orders from short to long format during GPIPutData processing. It could mean that an order was too long to convert.
0x20E9	PMERR_OTHER_SET_ID_REFS	OS/2 could not unload the specified font because another process still is referencing the setid.
0x20EA	PMERR_OVERRAN_SEG	
0x20EB	PMERR_OWN_SET_ID_REFS	
0x20EC	PMERR_PATH_INCOMPLETE	The process attempted to open or close a segment either directly or during segment drawing. This error also could occur if the process issued a GPIAssociate while there is an open path bracket.
0x20ED	PMERR_PATH_LIMIT_EXCEEDED	OS/2 exceeded an internal size limit during path or area processing.
0x20EE	PMERR_PATH_UNKNOWN	The process attempted to perform a path function using a nonexistent path.
0x20EF	PMERR_PEL_IS_CLIPPED	The process attempted to query a clipped PEL using the GPIQueryPel function.
0x20F0	PMERR_PEL_NOT_AVAILABLE	The process attempted to query a pel that did not exist using the GPIQueryPel function. This could occur with a memory device context with no selected bitmap.
0x20F1	PMERR_PRIMITIVE_STACK_EMPTY	The primitive stack is empty.

Table B-2   **Continued**

Code	Definition	Description
0x20F2	PMERR_PROLOG_ERROR	
0x20F3	PMERR_PROLOG_SEG_ATTR_NOT_SET	OS/2 detected a prolog error during drawing. It uses segment prologs internally within retained segments and metafiles. This error also occurs when OS/2 issues an End Prolog order outside a prolog.
0x20F4	PMERR_PS_BUSY	The process attempted to access the presentation space from more than one thread simultaneously.
0x20F5	PMERR_PS_IS_ASSOCIATED	The process attempted to destroy a presentation or associate a presentation space that still is associated with a device context.
0x20F6	PMERR_RAM_JNL_FILE_TOO_SMALL	
0x20F7	PMERR_REALIZE_NOT_SUPPORTED	The process attempted to create a realizable logical color table on a device driver that does not support this function.
0x20F8	PMERR_REGION_IS_CLIP_REGION	The process attempted to perform a region operation on a region that is selected as a clip region.
0x20F9	PMERR_RESOURCE_DEPLETION	An internal resource depletion error occurred.
0x20FA	PMERR_SEG_AND_REFSEG_ARE_ SAME	The process passed the same identifier for the segid and refsegid when calling the GPISetSegmentPriority function.
0x20FB	PMERR_SEG_CALL_RECURSIVE	OS/2 detected a recursive condition in a segment call.
0x20FC	PMERR_SEG_CALL_STACK_EMPTY	OS/2 detected an empty call stack condition while attempting to a pop function during GPIPop or segment drawing.
0x20FD	PMERR_SEG_CALL_STACK_FULL	OS/2 detected a stack full condition when attempting to call a segment using the GPICallSegmentMatrix function, attempting to preserve an attribute, or during segment drawing.

Code	Definition	Description
0x20FE	PMERR_SEG_IS_CURRENT	The process attempted to issue a GPIGetData call for a currently open segment.
0x20FF	PMERR_SEG_NOT_CHAINED	The process attempted to issue a GPIDrawFrom, GPICorrelateFrom, or GPIQuerySegmentPriority call for an unchained segment.
0x2100	PMERR_SEG_NOT_FOUND	The specified segment identifier does not exist.
0x2101	PMERR_SEG_STORE_LIMIT_EXCEEDED	The process exceeded the maximum permitted segment store size limit.
0x2102	PMERR_SETID_IN_USE	The process attempted to specify a setid that already was in use as the currently selected character, marker, or pattern set.
0x2103	PMERR_SETID_NOT_FOUND	The process attempted to delete a nonexistent setid.
0x2104	PMERR_STARTDOC_NOT_ISSUED	The process attempted to request to write spooled output without issuing a STARTDOC first.
0x2105	PMERR_STOP_DRAW_OCCURRED	OS/2 stopped segment drawing or GPIPlayMetaFile prematurely in response to a GPISetStopDraw request.
0x2106	PMERR_TOO_MANY_METAFILES_IN_USE	A process exceeded the maximum number of metafiles.
0x2107	PMERR_TRUNCATED_ORDER	OS/2 detected an incomplete order during segment processing.
0x2108	PMERR_UNCHAINED_SEG_ZERO_INV	The process attempted to open a segment using segment identifier zero and did not specify the ATTR_CHAINED attribute.
0x2109	PMERR_UNSUPPORTED_ATTR	Unsupported attribute.
0x210A	PMERR_UNSUPPORTED_ATTR_VALUE	Unsupported attribute value.
0x210B	PMERR_ENDDOC_NOT_ISSUED	The process attempted to close spooled output without first issuing an ENDDOC.
0x210C	PMERR_PS_NOT_ASSOCIATED	The process attempted to access a presentation space that is not associated with a device context.

Table B-2   **Continued**

Code	Definition	Description
0x210D	PMERR_INV_FLOOD_FILL_OPTIONS	The process provided invalid flood fill parameters.
0x210E	PMERR_INV_FACENAME	The process provided an invalid font family name to the GPIQueryFaceString function.
0x210F	PMERR_PALETTE_SELECTED	You cannot perform a palette operation in a presentation space while the palette is selected.
0x2110	PMERR_NO_PALETTE_SELECTED	An attempt to realize a palette failed because the process did not previously select a palette into the presentation space.
0x2111	PMERR_INV_HPAL	The process specified an invalid color palette handle.
0x2112	PMERR_PALETTE_BUSY	The process attempted to reset the owner of a palette while it was busy.
0x2113	PMERR_START_POINT_CLIPPED	The specified flood file starting point is outside the current clipping path or region.
0x2114	PMERR_NO_FILL	OS/2 did not perform a flood fill for one of two reasons: the starting point color was the same as the input color when the process requested a boundary fill, or the starting point color was not the same as the input color when the process requested a surface fill.
0x2115	PMERR_INV_FACENAMEDESC	The process provided an invalid face name description.
0x2116	PMERR_INV_BITMAP_DATA	The process provided an invalid bitmap.
0x2117	PMERR_INV_CHAR_ALIGN_ATTR	The process provided an invalid text alignment attribute with the GPISetTextAlignment function.
0x2118	PMERR_INV_HFONT	The process specified an invalid font handle.
0x2119	PMERR_HFONT_IS_SELECTED	The process tried to change the owner of a font or delete it when it currently is selected.

Code	Definition	Description
0x4001	PMERR_SPL_DRIVER_ERROR	The spooler cannot find and the application has not supplied the specified Presentation Manager device driver.
0x4002	PMERR_SPL_DEVICE_ERROR	The spooler experience an error.
0x4003	PMERR_SPL_DEVICE_NOT_INSTALLED	The spooler device is not installed.
0x4004	PMERR_SPL_QUEUE_ERROR	No spooler queue supplied or found.
0x4005	PMERR_SPL_INV_HSPL	The spooler handle is invalid.
0x4006	PMERR_SPL_NO_DISK_SPACE	There is not enough free disk space.
0x4007	PMERR_SPL_NO_MEMORY	There is not enough free memory.
0x4008	PMERR_SPL_PRINT_ABORT	The spooler already aborted the job.
0x4009	PMERR_SPL_SPOOLER_NOT_INSTALLED	The spooler is not installed.
0x400A	PMERR_SPL_INV_FORMS_CODE	The job form code is invalid.
0x400B	PMERR_SPL_INV_PRIORITY	The job priority is invalid.
0x400C	PMERR_SPL_NO_FREE_JOB_ID	There is no free job id available.
0x400D	PMERR_SPL_NO_DATA	No data supplied or found.
0x400E	PMERR_SPL_INV_TOKEN	The token is invalid.
0x400F	PMERR_SPL_INV_DATATYPE	The spool file data type is invalid.
0x4010	PMERR_SPL_PROCESSOR_ERROR	No spooler queue processor supplied or found.
0x4011	PMERR_SPL_INV_JOB_ID	The job id is invalid.
0x4012	PMERR_SPL_JOB_NOT_PRINTING	The print job is not printing.
0x4013	PMERR_SPL_JOB_PRINTING	The print job already is printing.
0x4014	PMERR_SPL_QUEUE_ALREADY_EXISTS	The spooler queue already exists.
0x4015	PMERR_SPL_INV_QUEUE_NAME	The spooler queue name is invalid.
0x4016	PMERR_SPL_QUEUE_NOT_EMPTY	The spooler queue contains print jobs.
0x4017	PMERR_SPL_DEVICE_ALREADY_EXISTS	The specified spooler device already exists.
0x4018	PMERR_SPL_DEVICE_LIMIT_REACHED	The spooler has reached its limit on the number of devices.
0x4019	PMERR_SPL_STATUS_STRING_TRUNC	The spooler truncated the print job status string.

609

Table B-2   **Continued**

Code	Definition	Description
0x401A	PMERR_SPL_INV_LENGTH_OR_COUNT	The length or count is invalid.
0x401B	PMERR_SPL_FILE_NOT_FOUND	Unable to find the specified file.
0x401C	PMERR_SPL_CANNOT_OPEN_FILE	The spooler could not open the specified file.
0x401D	PMERR_SPL_DRIVER_NOT_INSTALLED	The Presentation Manger device driver has not been installed.
0x401E	PMERR_SPL_INV_PROCESSOR_DATTYPE	The data type is invalid for the spooler queue processor.
0x401F	PMERR_SPL_INV_DRIVER_DATATYPE	The data type is not valid for a Presentation Manager device driver.
0x4020	PMERR_SPL_PROCESSOR_NOT_INST	There is no spool queue processor installed.
0x4021	PMERR_SPL_NO_SUCH_LOG_ADDRESS	The logical address does not exist. It is not defined within the initialization file.
0x4022	PMERR_SPL_PRINTER_NOT_FOUND	The spooler could not find the printer definition.
0x4023	PMERR_SPL_DD_NOT_FOUND	The spooler could not find the Presentation Manager printer device driver definition.
0x4024	PMERR_SPL_QUEUE_NOT_FOUND	OS/2 could not find the spooler queue definition.
0x4025	PMERR_SPL_MANY_QUEUES_ASSOC	There is more than one queue associated with the printer.
0x4026	PMERR_SPL_NO_QUEUES_ASSOCIATED	There is not queue associated with the printer.
0x4027	PMERR_SPL_INI_FILE_ERROR	The spooler experienced an error accessing the initialization file.
0x4028	PMERR_SPL_NO_DEFAULT_QUEUE	There is no default spooler queue for the printer.
0x4029	PMERR_SPL_NO_CURRENT_FORMS_CODE	The Presentation Manager device driver does not have a defined forms code.
0x402A	PMERR_SPL_NOT_AUTHORISED	The calling process is not authorized to perform this operation.
0x402B	PMERR_SPL_TEMP_NETWORK_ERROR	The spooler experienced a temporary network error.

Using CodeView

APPENDIX C

THIS chapter does not present a complete explanation of all CodeView functions and operations. It does provide a complete and concise overview of CodeView options, command line semantics, and general commands. In most cases, this provides all you need to use CodeView to debug your application. There are three versions of CodeView supplied with most versions of Microsoft programming languages. One version works with DOS, the second works with Windows, and the third works with OS/2. (Some current Microsoft products do not provide the protected mode version of CodeView required for OS/2. In most cases, you can obtain OS/2 support by using an older version of the same product.) Figure C-1 shows a typical CodeView display. Table C-1 describes each item labeled on Fig. C-1.

Figure C-1

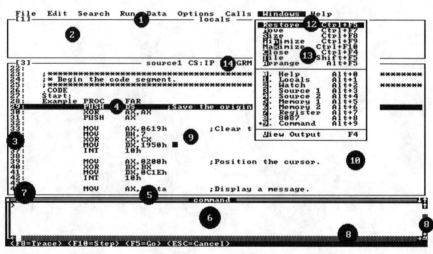

CodeView display breakdown.

Table C-1

The CodeView display elements

Element	Description
1	Menu Bar—Contains a list of Main menu items. When you select one of the menu items, CodeView displays a submenu with lists of commands that you can perform.
2	Local Window (optional)—Contains a list of variables local to the current scope. You also can set this window to display variables local to other scopes.

614

Element	Description
3	Code Lines—Codeview numbers each line of code within a file sequentially. Each external file that is called within a program uses its own numbering starting at one. Codeview highlights the numbers of lines selected as breakpoints.
4	Current Location Line—Shows the line of code that CodeView will execute next. This line is not always visible because you can scroll throughout the current file.
5	Window/Dialog Box Border—There are several elements to this border. The horizontal and vertical scroll bars allow you to scroll the display to show other areas of information contained in the dialog box or window. The double line in the lower right corner of the border allows you to size the dialog box or window. The right-most arrow shown in the upper left corner of the border allows you to maximize the dialog box or window. The left-most arrow in the upper left corner allows you to minimize the dialog box or window. The box in the upper left corner of the board allows you to close the dialog box or window. Finally, you can move the dialog box or window by grabbing the title bar in the middle of upper line.
6	Command Window—Use this window to enter commands that you want CodeView to perform. You can scroll through this window to review the results of previous commands.
7	Cursor—Shows the location within the Dialog or Display Windows that Codeview allows you to enter commands. Entry always begins at the location directly under the cursor.
8	Scroll Bars—Allows you to scroll through the contents of the Dialog or Display windows using a mouse. The highlighted area shows the current location of the cursor within the window. The arrows determine the direction of scrolling.
9	Mouse Pointer—Shows the current location of the mouse. CodeView displays the mouse pointer only if you have a mouse installed.
10	Source Window—Shows the program code loaded into CodeView for debugging. You can display the code in one of three modes. Source mode shows the program code as you wrote it. Assembly-language mode displays the code as the compiler converted it for the processor. Mixed mode shows both the source code and assembly language equivalent.
11 (Not Shown)	Register Window (optional)—The register window shows the current status of the 80x86 or 8088 processor registers. You can toggle this window open or closed by pressing F2. A special 80386 mode allows you to view all the registers associated with the 80386 processor. The operand address at the bottom of the display shows the physical location of an operand (variable) in memory.
12	Menu Highlight—Highlights the current menu selection. You change the highlight by pressing the Up or Down arrows.
13	Menu—Contains selections relating to the category displayed on the Menu Bar. You can select a menu by pressing Alt, then the highlighted letter of the menu on the Menu Bar.

Table C-1   **Continued**

Element	Description
14	Program Name—Displays the name of the file loaded into memory. If you used the CodeView switches while compiling and linking your code, the Program Name changes as you go between library and other source code modules.
15 (Not Shown)	Dialog Box—Appears in the center of the display when you select a menu item requiring a response. The Dialog Box disappears when you type an answer and press Enter.
16 (Not Shown)	Message Box—Appears in the center of the display when an error occurs or when CodeView needs to warn you about some condition. The Message Box disappears when you correct the error condition and press Enter.
17 (Not Shown)	Watch Window (optional)—Contains a list of selected variables and expressions and their current status. CodeView displays this window whenever you define a variable or expression to monitor.
18 (Not Shown)	Memory Window (optional)—Displays the contents of memory at a specific location. You can use more than one memory window to display more than one area of memory. The memory window also allows you to change the contents of memory.
19 (Not Shown)	8087 Window (optional)—Displays the contents of the math coprocessor registers or the software emulator.
20 (Not Shown)	Help Window (optional)—Displays the current help topic.

 # Operation

This chapter looks at only the OS/2 version of the CodeView product. You can use many of the same switches with the Windows and DOS versions of the product. To access the OS/2 version of CodeView, simply type CV; to access the Windows version, type CVW. The following examples show you the command line format for using CodeView:

```
CV[W] [options] executable_filename [arguments]
CV[W] @File executable_filename [arguments]
```

The CodeView option descriptions appear in the next section. The executable filename is any legitimate source code filename. The arguments are command line parameters to the executable file.

⇨ Options

The following options affect the way CodeView reacts to the system hardware and programs. All of these options are appropriate when using either the DOS or Windows version. (Each command line parameter shows which version it works with.)

The /2 option
CV, CVW
The /2 option permits using two monitors. The default monitor displays the program, while the other monitor displays CodeView information.

The /8 option
CVW
The /8 option applies to only the Windows version of CodeView (CVW). This option allows you to use an 8514 display as the primary monitor and a VGA display as the secondary monitor. The primary monitor displays the application as it runs; the secondary monitor displays the source code.

The /43 option
CV, CVW
The /43 option enables the 43 line display mode of EGA equipped computers.

The /50 option
CV, CVW
The /50 option enables the 50 line display mode of VGA equipped computers.

The /B option
CV, CVW
This option disables color presentation when using a two-color monitor with a CGA card.

The /C *commands* option
CV, CVW
Use this option to execute the command in the commands field automatically upon CodeView start-up.

The /F option
CV
Use this option to enable screen flipping. CodeView flips between two display pages in the graphic memory to display both CodeView and program screens. This option is faster than the screen swapping mode required for monochrome displays. CodeView disables this option when using two displays.

The /G option
CV, CVW
Use this option to suppress snow on some CGA displays.

The /I *number* option
CV, CVW
This option forces CodeView to handle both NMI and 8259 interrupt trapping when used with the /I0 setting. The /I1 and /I settings force CodeView to ignore both NMIs and 8259 interrupts. Use this option on computers that are not 100% IBM compatible.

The /LDLL and /LEXE options
CVW
Use this option to load an application or DLL when debugging Windows code. CodeView does not load debugging information for an external library or application when you load the application you want to debug. Using this switch forces CodeView to load the external module and search it for symbolic information.

The /M option
CV, CVW
This option disables mouse support.

The /N option
CV, CVW
This option forces CodeView to handle NMI interrupt trapping when used with the /N0 setting. The /N1 and /N settings force CodeView to ignore NMIs. Use this option on computers that are not 100% IBM compatible.

The /S option
CV
The /S option enables screen swapping. Use this option with a monochrome adapter, a non-IBM CGA/EGA adapter, or a program that uses multiple video pages. This option works slower than the standard screen flipping mode explained earlier. Do not use this option when using two displays.

The /TSF option
CV, CVW
Use the Toggle State File (TSF) option to toggle the reading of CodeView's state and color files. The Statefileread entry in the CodeView section of the TOOLS.INI file determines whether the toggle forces CodeView to read or not read the files. The option works as an exclusive OR with the Statefileread entry. If you specify one or the other, then CodeView reads the state and color files. If you specify both or neither, then CodeView does not read the state and color files.

The /X and /Y options
CVW
Use this option to specify the starting X and Y coordinates of the CodeView window within Windows. Once CodeView starts you cannot change the Window location or size.

⇨ Commands and controls

The following commands and control keys include all the keyboard commands used to control various aspects of the debugger display

and program control. It also includes all commands entered at the prompt that affect program execution and control.

The 8087 (7) command

This command tells CodeView to display the contents of the 8087/80287 chip registers in the dialog window as shown in Fig. C-2. It also works with 8087 emulator libraries.

Figure C-2

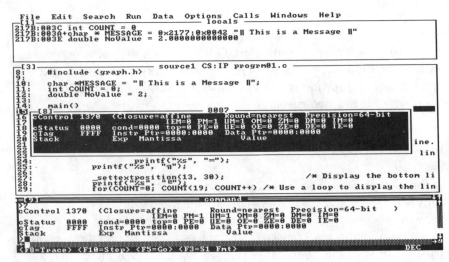

CodeView 80x87 support window.

Alt–*menu_letter*

Pressing Alt–*menu_letter* brings up any of the menu entries at the top of the display. For example, pressing Alt–H displays the Help menu shown in Fig. C-3. The only menu item that doesn't always display a list of items is the Call menu. If you press Alt–C and nothing happens, then you are in the main procedure of the program; it isn't performing a subroutine.

Alt–*number*

Pressing Alt–*number* displays the specified window on screen. For example, pressing Alt–8 displays the 8087 window. Table C-2 provides a complete listing of the Windows you can display in CodeView.

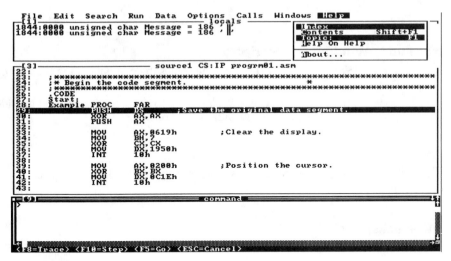

Figure C-3

CodeView Help menu.

The CodeView windows

Table C-2

Number	Window	Description
0	Help	This window contains the current help topic. (If you haven't used the window before, help automatically displays the Microsoft Advisor index.) Use the options on the Help menu to change topics using an index or context sensitive search.
1	Local	Displays the local variables. Change the contents of the Locals window using the *Locals Options* entry of the Options menu.
2	Watch	Displays any watch entries that you create using the options on the Data menu.
3	Source 1	Displays the source contained in the Source 1 window. You can modify the appearance of this display using the *Source 1 Window* entry of the Options menu.
4	Source 2	Displays the source contained in the Source 2 window. You can modify the appearance of this display using the *Source 2 Window* entry of the Options menu.
5	Memory 1	Displays the source contained in the Memory 1 window. You can modify the appearance of this display using the *Memory 1 Window* entry of the Options menu.
6	Memory 2	Displays the source contained in the Memory 2 window. You can modify the appearance of this display using the *Memory 2 Window* entry of the Options menu.
7	Register	The Register window shows the contents of the 80x86 processor registers.

Table C-2   **Continued**

Number	Window	Description
8	8087	The 8087 window shows the contents of the 80x87 coprocessor registers.
9	Command	This window allows you to enter commands that provide CodeView with instructions.

Alt–/
The Alt–/ key combination allows you to repeat the last find you initiated.

Alt–Backspace
Use the Alt–Backspace key combination to undo your last edit.

Alt–F4
Use this key combination to exit CodeView when you finish debugging your application.

Alt–F5
The Arrange function (Alt–F5) allows you to arrange all the windows on the display so that none of the windows overlap. For example, if you start CodeView in the default combination and display the Register windows, then pressing Alt–F5 will place the Register window on the left side of the display and reduce the sizes of the Local, Source 1, and Command windows appropriately.

Assemble
Syntax   A [*address*]
The Assemble command converts 8088, 8086, 80286, 80386, and 80486 mnemonics to executable code. The optional address field specifies where to place the code; otherwise, assembly begins at the current address.

Breakpoint Clear
Syntax   BC [*list*¦*]
The Breakpoint Clear command removes a single breakpoint (specified by list) or all breakpoints (specified by an asterisk).

Breakpoint Disable
Syntax BD [*list*|*]
The Breakpoint Disable command to disable one or all breakpoints. the list field specifies which breakpoints to disable. An asterisk disables all breakpoints.

Breakpoint Enable
Syntax BE [*list*|*]
The Breakpoint Enable command selectively enables the breakpoints specified by list. Using an asterisk with this command enables all breakpoints.

Breakpoint List
Syntax BL
The Breakpoint List command displays a listing of both enabled and disabled breakpoints.

Breakpoint Set
Syntax BP [*address*] [*passcount*] ["*commands*"]
The Breakpoint Set command places a breakpoint at the specified address. If the programmer does not specify an address, the breakpoint appears at the current program execution line. The *passcount* field provides a means of ignoring the breakpoint for the number of times specified. CodeView executes the commands entered in the "*commands*" field every time it encounters the breakpoint.

Ctrl–\
You can use this key combination to search for the highlighted text. Simply highlight the text that you want to search for, then press Ctrl–\.

Ctrl–C
Pressing Ctrl–C halts program execution. The Ctrl–Break key combination performs the same function.

Ctrl–F4
Use this key combination to close the currently active window.

Ctrl–F5

CodeView allows you to maximize windows to see more of the contents of a window or minimize them so they don't take any screen real-estate. The Ctrl–F5 key combination allows you to restore the window to its previous condition.

Ctrl–F7

You can move the active window by pressing the Ctrl–F7 key combination and moving it with the arrow keys.

Ctrl–F8

You can change the size of the active window by pressing the Ctrl–F8 key combination, then pressing the arrow keys.

Ctrl–F9

Instead of closing the active window when you get done with it, you can minimize it to an icon using the Ctrl–F9 (minimize) key combination. This allows you to access the window quickly without resorting to using the Window menu. Figure C-4 shows a typical display setup for quick window access using a mouse.

Figure C-4

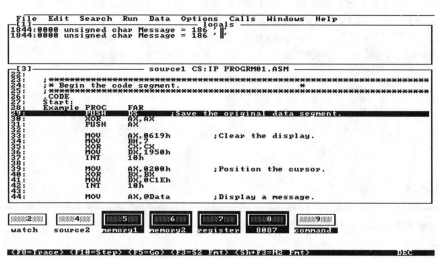

Arranging the CodeView display for maximum use.

Ctrl–F10

The maximize key combination fills the entire display area with the contents of the active window. You can use it when you need to see more information.

Ctrl–Ins

You can copy any highlighted text to a clipboard using the Ctrl–Ins key combination. Simply highlight the text you want to copy and press Ctrl–Ins.

Ctrl–U

The Ctrl–U key combination performs the same function as pressing Alt–D, then D. CodeView displays a listing of the current watchpoints, as shown in Fig. C-5. Selecting one of the watchpoints and pressing Enter deletes it.

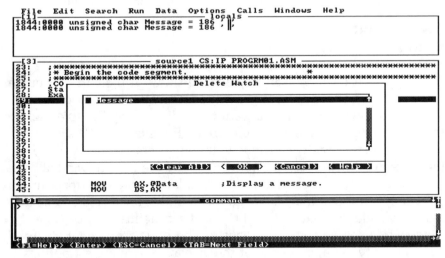

Figure C-5

CodeView Delete Watch dialog box.

Ctrl–W

Use the Ctrl–W key combination to invoke the Add Watch option of the Watch menu (Fig. C-6). It performs the same function as pressing

Figure C-6

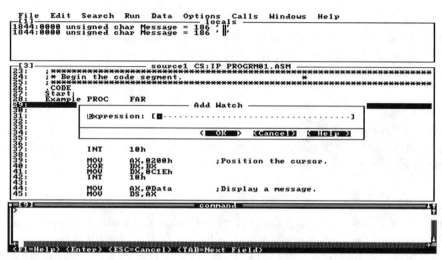

CodeView Add Watch dialog box.

Alt–D, then A. This option causes CodeView to display the contents of the selected variable or expression during program execution.

Display Mode Selection

Syntax S[*display*[*mode*]] [/*option*]

This command allows you to display and modify the current state of the display. Using S by itself displays the status of the current Source Code window. The *display* argument contains the number of the Source Code window that you want to modify. Using S*display* selects the window number specified by *display*. For example, S1 would select the first source code window. If you do not specify a window, then CodeView assumes you want to modify the current window. The *mode* argument defines what type of display to create: + for source code only, – for assembly language only, and & for mixed source and assembly code. For example, S1+ would set the first source code window to a source code only display. The *option* argument allows you to modify the appearance of the display. There are six options: show addresses (A), show machine code (B), upper case instructions (C), mixed mode order—source line (L), show symbolic name (S), and trace on (T). To turn an option on, simply follow it with a plus sign. For example, to show addresses in source code window one, you would type S1 /A+ in the Command window. To turn an option off, simply type a minus sign.

Display Expression
Syntax   ? *expression* [,*format*]
Use the Display Expression command to display any valid CodeView expression. The *expression* field contains the expression to evaluate. The optional format field specifies the display format.

Down arrow
The down arrow moves the cursor down one line in the display or dialog box.

Dump
Syntax   D [*type*] [*address* ¦ *range*]
The Dump command displays data contained in the area specified by address in both hexadecimal and ASCII formats. Using D by itself produces a display of the data pointed to by DS:0000 or the data after the previous display. The range field specifies a starting and ending address to display. Using a segment override allows display of data not pointed to by the DS register. Adding a dump type specifier changes the default dump display. The following examples show all the different forms of dump:

```
D     CS:0    50    ;Dumps the data pointed to by the CS
                    ;register from offset 0 to 50.
DA    CS:0    50    ;Dumps the same data in ASCII format.
DB    CS:0    50    ;Dumps the same data in byte format.
DD    CS:0    50    ;Dumps the same data in double word format.
DI    CS:0    50    ;Dumps the same data in integer format.
DIU   CS:0    50    ;Dumps the same data in unsigned integer format.
DIX   CS:0    50    ;Dumps the same data in hexadecimal integer format.
DL    CS:0    50    ;Dumps the same data in long real format.
DLU   CS:0    50    ;Dumps the same data in unsigned long real format.
DLX   CS:0    50    ;Dumps the same data in hexadecimal long real
                    ;format.
DR    CS:0    50    ;Dumps the same data in real format.
DRL   CS:0    50    ;Dumps the same data in long real format.
DRT   CS:0    50    ;Dumps the same data in 10-byte real format.
DW    CS:0    50    ;Dumps the same data in word format.
```

End

Moves the cursor to the end of the command buffer in the dialog window or source file/program instructions in the display window.

Enter

Syntax   E [*type*] *address* [*list*]

Use the Enter command to change the contents of memory. There is one non-optional field associated with this command. CodeView will treat the E as execute unless the *address* field contains a valid address. As with other commands, this command assumes the segment address of the DS register unless the address field contains a segment override. The *list* field contains the data CodeView enters at that address. If the *list* field is empty, CodeView presents an area for entering the data. The *type* field determines the size of data entered into memory. The following examples show how to use this command:

```
E    0001   22      ;Enter data in the default type.
EA   0001   "HI"    ;Enter ASCII.
EB   0001   44      ;Enter a byte.
ED   0001   44      ;Enter a double word.
EI   0001   -12     ;Enter an integer.
EIU  0001   12      ;Enter an unsigned integer.
EIX  0001   12      ;Enter a hexadecimal integer.
EL   0001   12      ;Enter a long real.
ELU  0001   12      ;Enter an unsigned long real.
ELX  0001   12      ;Enter a hexadecimal long real.
EW   0001   ADOC    ;Enter a word.
```

Examine Symbols

Syntax   X*scope* [*context*] [*regular_expression*]

The Examine Symbols command displays symbolic information about a program, as shown in Fig. C-7. There are six different *scopes* that you can specify with this command: lexical, function, module, executable, public, and global. To specify a scope, simply type its first letter. Use the asterisk to tell CodeView that you want to look at all scopes. The *context* specifies where you want CodeView to look. It follows the format:

{[*function*], [*module*], [DLL/EXE]} [*object*]

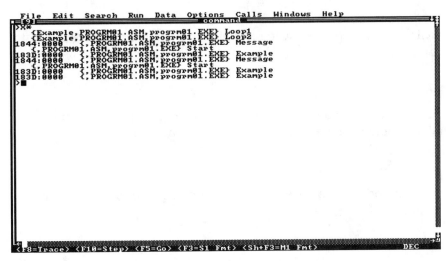

Figure C-7

Using the CodeView Command window.

The *regular_expression* entry allows you to look for specific entries. There are several wildcard operators associated with this argument. The period matches any single character. The carot matches any text at the beginning of the line. The dollar sign matches text at the end of the line. The asterisk matches zero or more repetitions of the characters preceding it. Finally, text appearing within square brackets has special significance. Using a carot in front of a set of characters matches everything but those characters. Using a dash matches all ASCII characters within the range specified by the characters before and after the dash. For example, [A - C] would match all symbols beginning with letters from A to C.

Execute
Syntax   E
The Execute command, which is renamed Animate in newer versions of CodeView, performs the same function as the Go command in slow motion. This allows the observer to see the changing of the contents of the CPU registers, and any watched variables or expressions.

F1
Displays the online Help menu.

F2

Switches the display between showing/not showing the CPU register contents.

F3

Use this key to change the output display between source code, mixed source code and assembly, and assembly only.

F4

This key toggles the display between the debugger and program outputs.

F5

Performs the same function as the Go command. The program executes until CodeView encounters a breakpoint or the file ends.

F6

Toggles the cursor between the displayed windows.

F7

This option is active when the cursor is in the display window. If the line pointed to by the cursor represents code and CodeView does not encounter another breakpoint or the end of the executable file, then the program executes to the cursor line.

F8

Use this key to execute a Trace command.

F9

This key tells CodeView to add a breakpoint to the line pointed to by the cursor.

F10

Pressing this key executes a program step command. CodeView steps over any calls or interrupts to the next displayed instruction.

Go
Syntax   G *break_address*
The Go command continuously executes program instructions until it encounters the address specified by *break_address*, a preset breakpoint, a Ctrl–C or Ctrl–Break, or the end of the executable file.

Graphic Display
Syntax   ?? *variable*[,C]
The Graphic Display command provides an enhanced view of structured variables. The *variable* field states which variable to observe. The optional C entry allows an ASCII display of single byte entries. The graphic display is similar in nature to the Watch command.

Help
Syntax   H
Use this command to obtain help on various topics. It performs the same function as the F1 key.

Home
Pressing the Home key moves the cursor to the beginning of the command buffer in the dialog window or source file/program instructions in the display window.

Input and Output Redirection
Syntax   =*device_name*
The Input and Output command changes both the default input and output to the device specified by device name. The following example shows commands specifically used during input/output redirection:

```
T>REDIR.TXT          ;Redirect the output.
* This is a Comment.  ;Add a comment to the file.
<INFILE.TXT          ;Redirect the input.
:                    ;Short command processing delay.
:::::                ;Longer command processing delay.
"                    ;Pause until the programmer
                     ;presses a key.
```

Input Redirection
Syntax *device_name*
The Input Redirection command changes default input from the console to the specified device name.

Memory Compare
Syntax MC *range address*
Use the Memory Compare command to compare two memory ranges. It replaces the Compare command found in previous versions of CodeView. The *range* argument contains the range of memory you want to compare. The range consists of a starting and ending address. The *address* argument contains the address of the second area of memory that you want to compare with the selected range.

Memory Dump
Syntax*MD
See the Dump command for a description of the Memory Dump command.

Memory Enter
Syntax*ME
See the Enter command for a description of the Memory Enter command.

Memory Fill
Syntax MF *range value_list*
The Memory Fill command replaces the Fill command used in previous versions of CodeView. The *range* argument contains a starting and ending address value. It specifies the range of memory that you want to fill. The *value_list* argument contains a list of values you want to place in the selected range. You can use the Memory window to monitor the results of using the Memory Fill command. Figure C-8 shows how you can use the Memory window to monitor the results of using Memory Fill command.

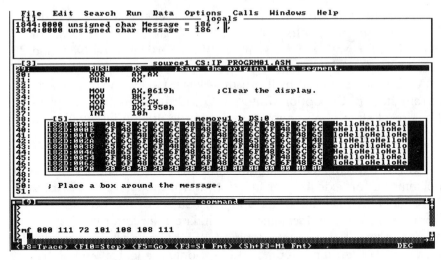

Figure C-8

Using the CodeView Memory window.

Memory Move
Syntax MM *range address*
The Memory Move command replaces the Move command used in previous versions of CodeView. The *range* argument contains the starting and ending address of the range of memory you want to move. The *address* argument contains the starting address where you want to move the data.

Memory Search
Syntax MS *range list*
Use the Memory Search command to look for specific items in a range of memory. It replaces the Search command used in previous versions of CodeView. The *range* argument contains the starting and ending address range of memory you want to search. The *list* argument contains the data you want to search for.

Option
Syntax O [*option*] [+ | –]
The Option command changes the default condition of items appearing on the options menu. Valid options for the *option* field

include: A for status bar, F for flip/swap screens, B for bytes coded, C for case-sensitive, H for horizontal scroll bar, L for show symbol address, N for Native, S for symbols, V for vertical scroll bars, and 3 for 386 mode. Adding a plus sign to the end of the option turns it on, and a minus sign turns it off; otherwise, CodeView displays the current state of the option. Entering O with no arguments displays the current state of all options. For example, typing OL would show the state of the Show Symbol Address option.

The Show Symbol Address option contains several suboptions including: L for lexical, F for function, M for module, E for EXE, and G for global. Unlike the other options, you set or reset these suboptions simply by including or excluding their letter on the command line. For example, typing OLFMEG sets all the options to on. On the other hand, typing OLG set only the lexical and global scoping to on.

Output Redirection
Syntax   [T] >[>] *device_name*
The output redirection command changes the default output to the device specified by *device_name*. The optional T prefix allows simultaneous output to both display and device. Using the second greater-than symbol allows CodeView to append the new output to the end of an old file.

PgDn
PgDn moves the cursor one page down the command buffer in the dialog window or source file/program instructions in the display window.

PgUp
PgUp moves the cursor one page up the command buffer in the dialog window or source file/program instructions in the display window.

Port Import
Syntax   I *port*
This command tells CodeView to import data from the specified port. It displays the data in the current default radix.

Restart
Syntax L *arguments*
The Restart command returns the CPU registers and program variables to the conditions encountered on program entry. CodeView passes any parameters placed in the *arguments* field to the program as command line variables.

Screen Exchange
Syntax \ [*time*]
This command performs the same function as pressing the F4 key. Use it to see executing program output. The *time* field operates only with the protected mode version. The protected mode version screen returns to the debugging display automatically. The optional *time* field sets the amount of time that elapses before the screen returns to the debugging display.

Search Source File
Syntax / [*regular_expression*]
The Search Source File command is similar in nature to the Search Memory command. Instead of searching memory, CodeView searches a source file for the specified regular expression. CodeView then places the cursor where it found the expression.

Shell Escape
Syntax ! [*commands*]
Use the Shell Escape command to suspend debugging temporarily to execute a DOS command. When no command appears in the commands field, CodeView executes a copy of the command processor; otherwise, it executes the command.

Shift–F1
Pressing Shift–F1 displays the help table of contents. This allows you to search for any topic contained in the help files.

Shift–F5
Tiling the windows displayed on screen allows you to display your windows in a little more logical sequence than the arrange option. Unfortunately, this arrangement doesn't always provide the best view of the information the window contains. Figure C-9 shows a typical tiled setup. Simply press Shift–F5 to obtain this feature.

Port Output
Syntax   O *port byte*
Use the Port Output command to output the value specifiec
byte field to the specified *port*.

Program Step
Syntax   P *count*
The Program Step command executes a program step. If it
encounters a procedure, routine, or interrupt, it executes all
to the next executable step in the displayed procedure. The
step command normally executes once; specifying a value in
executes it that number of times.

Quit
Syntax   Q
The Quit command closes all program files and returns the
programmer to the DOS prompt.

Radix
Syntax   N [*radix_number*]
Use the Radix command to change the default base used to (
numeric data. Entering N with no argument displays the curr
radix. Valid radix arguments are 8 for octal, 10 for decimal, :
for hexadecimal.

Register
Syntax   R [*register_name*] [=[*expression*]]
Use this command without any parameters to display the cor
all registers. When using an 80386-equipped machine, Code
displays all 32-bit registers.

CodeView displays the current value of the register and asks :
new value when the *register_name* field contains a valid regis
name but the *expression* field is blank. It automatically replac
designated register with an expression when one is supplied.

Redraw
Syntax   @
The Redraw command redraws the CodeView display.

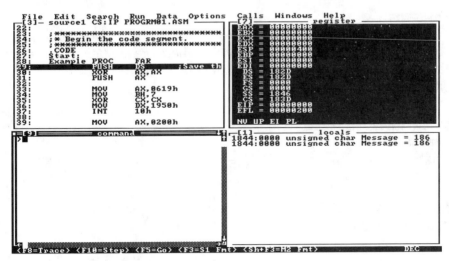

Figure C-9

Using the CodeView Register window.

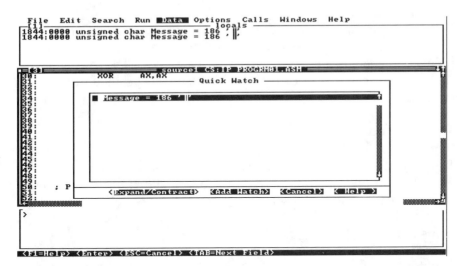

Figure C-10

The CodeView Quick Watch dialog box.

Shift–F9

Pressing Shift–F9 is the fastest way to create a new watch data structure to the Watch window. Simply highlight a variable or other entity and press Shift–F9. CodeView displays a dialog box that asks how you want the variable added to the Watch window, as shown in Fig. C-10.

Shift–Ins

Use the Shift–Ins key combination to paste the contents of the clipboard to the current cursor position. There are limitations on pasting text. For example, you cannot copy the contents of the clipboard to the Source 1 or Source 2 windows.

Stack Trace
Syntax K

The Stack Trace command displays a list of calls made by a program during program execution.

Tab Set
Syntax # *number*

Use the Tab Set command to change the spacing between tabs.

Trace
Syntax T [*count*]

The Trace command causes CodeView to execute one line of code. If the code calls another procedure/routine or interrupt, CodeView shows that code as the next executable instruction. The Trace command executes once or the number of times specified by the optional *count* field.

Trace Speed
Syntax T S|M|F

The Trace Speed command determines how fast the trace animation runs. The S option pauses ½ second between steps, the M option ¼ second. There is no delay when you use the F option.

Unassemble
Syntax U [*address*|*range*]

Use the Unassemble command to produce an unassembled listing of an executable file. Unless the command includes an address, CodeView displays one screen of unassembled data starting at the address pointed to by CS:IP. When the command includes a range of addresses, CodeView unassembles code from the starting to ending address.

Up arrow

Moves the cursor up one line in the display or dialog box.

Use Language

Syntax USE *language_name*

The Use Language command allows you to change the language evaluator that CodeView uses during debugging. The default setting is AUTO, which tells CodeView to automatically select the correct evaluator.

View Memory

Syntax VM [*window*] [*type*] [*address*] [*options*]

The View Memory command allows you to view memory in various formats using either of two Memory windows. The *window* argument allows you to specify a particular window. The *type* argument determines how CodeView formats the window. You can choose any of the following formats: A for ASCII characters, B for byte, I for integer, IU for unsigned integer, IX for hexadecimal integer, L for long real, LU for unsigned long real, LX for hexadecimal long real, R for real, RL for long real, and RT for 10-byte real. The *address* argument specifies the starting address of the display. There are several options associated with this command. The /R[+¦–] option enables or disables the display of raw data. The /L[+¦–] option enables or disables automatic (live) display updates. The /F[*¦*length*] determines the length of the displayed items. If you use the asterisk, then CodeView displays as many items as will fit in the Memory window. Using the *length* argument allows you to specify a fixed number of characters from 1 to 125.

View Source

Syntax VS [*display* [*mode*]] [*/option*]

The View Source command provides the same functionality as the Display Mode Selection Command described earlier.

Add Watch

Syntax W? *expression*[, *format*]

Use the Add Watch command to add an expression to the watch list. The *expression* argument contains the name of a variable or other expression. The *format* argument contains the format that you want

to use to display the expression. For example, you could type W?
Message,S at the Command window to add a variable called
Message using the string format.

Delete Watch
Syntax   WC *number*¦*

The Delete Watch command allows you to remove either one or all of
the watch expressions from the Watch window. Specifying a
particular number removes one expression. Using the asterisk
removes all the expressions from the Watch window.

Watch List
Syntax   WL

The Watch List command displays a list of the current watch
expressions along with their watch number.

Expressions, symbols, constants, strings, and display formats

The following sections describe the expressions, symbols, constants,
strings, and display formats used in CodeView.

Expressions

The expressions used in MASM coincide with the same expressions
used in C. However, MASM does not use some of the symbols used in
C. Table C-3 presents only the symbols used in MASM and their
order of precedence.

Table C-3   **The CodeView Assembly language expressions**

Precedence	Operators
1	() [] -> .
2	! ~$-^1$ (type) ++ -- *^{2} &^{3} sizeof

Precedence	Operators
3	$*^2$ / % :
4	+ $-^1$
5	< > <= >=
6	== !=
7	&&
8	0
9	= += -= *= /= %=
10	BY (byte) WO (word) DW (double word)

[1] The precedence 2 minus sign is the unary (number value) operator. The precedence 4 minus sign is the binary (subtraction) operator.

[2] The precedence 2 asterisk represents the pointer operator. The precedence 3 asterisk is the multiplication operator.

[3] The ampersand at precedence 2 is the address-of operator. CodeView does not support the ampersand as a bitwise AND operator.

Symbols

Symbols represent variables, registers, segment addresses, offset addresses, or full 32-bit addresses. CodeView accepts requests for information about any valid register, address, global variable, or variable in the current procedure.

Constants

A constant is any integer number that CodeView uses as part of a command. The default radix that CodeView uses with assembly language programs is hexadecimal. To change the radix, use either the radix command described earlier to change the radix or use a radix override in front of the number permanently. The form of a number with a radix override is:

override + number

as shown here:

```
16    ;This represents 16 in the default radix.
O16   ;This represents 16 octal.
```

On16   ;This represents 16 decimal
Ox16   ;This represents 16 hexadecimal

 # Strings

A string consists of characters delimited by double quotes. CodeView uses strings as part of some commands (for instance searches). The following example shows the difference between a string and nonstring:

"This is a string."
This is not a string.

Display formats

CodeView provides a set of nine display format extensions to various commands. Table C-4 provides a list of these extensions and their meanings.

Table C-4   **The CodeView display format specifiers**

Char.	Output format
d	Signed Decimal Integer
i	Signed Decimal Integer
u	Unsigned Decimal Integer
o	Unsigned Octal Integer
f	Signed Floating Point Decimal Value (6 Places)
e or E	Signed Floating Point Decimal Value Using Scientific Notation (6 Places)
g or G	Either F or E Format (whichever is more compact)
c	Single Character
s	Characters Printed to the First Null Character

Note: Using the capitalized version of a format specifier results in uppercase letters in the output.

⇨ Restrictions

The use of the CodeView debugger requires you to observe the following six restrictions on program type:

➢ CodeView can debug programs with include files. You cannot see the contents of the include file.

➢ You cannot use the standard EXEPAC utility or any LINK pack options on files used with CodeView. You can use the CVPACK utility to reduce executable file size.

➢ The programs cannot alter the environment. CodeView discards any changes to the environment when it exits.

➢ Some programs might experience problems if they directly access the Program Segment Prefix (PSP). CodeView preprocesses the PSP the same way C programs do.

In addition to the previous restrictions, the protected mode version of CodeView has the following two restrictions:

➢ Only one copy of CodeView can run at a time.

➢ If you don't use the /2 option when debugging and the program calls dynamic link library functions outside the API, then CodeView cannot access the program's environment, drive, or directory.

Index

ROM page select, 150
SSV transfer register, 153-154
subsystem status/control register, 149-150
TMS34010 file B functions, 160-161
virtual memory control, 203
virtual memory interrupt status, 203
XGA, 201
Release command, 477-478
REM command, 5
REP command, 72
REPE command, 72
REPNE command, 72
REPNZ command, 72
REPZ command, 72
Resume command, 478
RET command, 69
RETI instruction, 175
RETS N instruction, 175
RETURN command, 20
REV instruction, 175
REVERSE function, 31
REXX, 6-47
  command files, 6-9
  commands, 15-22
  control structures, 10-14
  functions, 22-42
  macro language, 9-42
  programming, 43-47
  using MCI with, 481-488
RIGHT function, 31
RL instruction, 175
RMO instruction, 191
ROL command, 66
ROR command, 66
RSM command, 99
RXFUNCADD function, 31
RXFUNCDROP function, 31
RXFUNCQUERY function, 31
RXMESSAGEBOX function, 42-43
RXQUEUE function, 31-32

S

SAHF command, 70

SAL command, 66
SAR command, 66
Save command, 478
SAY command, 20
SBB command, 65
SCASB command, 72-73
SCASD command, 93
SCASW command, 73
security, memory protection, 524-526
SEED_FILL instruction, 191
SEED_PATNFILL instruction, 191
Seek command, 478
segment start address (SSA), 163
SELECT..WHEN..OTHERWISE, 14
SELECT_FONT instruction, 191
serial ports, 393-408
  loopback plug connections, 408
  pinouts, 407
Set command, 478-480
SETA command, 90
SETAE command, 90
SETB command, 90
SETBE command, 90-91
SETC command, 91
SETC instruction, 175
SETE command, 91
SETF instruction, 175
SETG command, 91
SETGE command, 91
SETINGE command, 92
SETL command, 91
SETLE command, 91
SetLocal command, 5
SETNA command, 91
SETNAE command, 91SETNB command, 91
SETNBE command, 91
SETNC command, 91
SETNE command, 91
SETNG command, 91
SETNL command, 92
SETNLE command, 92
SETNO command, 92
SETNP command, 92
SETNS command, 92

About the Author

John Mueller is the Technical Editor for *Data Based Advisor* magazine. He also works on their CompuServe forum as one of the Sysops and is always in search of new information. (You can reach him on CompuServe at 75300,576). John has writing in his blood, having produced 18 books and many more articles to date. The topics range from networking to artificial intelligence and from database management to heads down programming.

When John isn't working at the computer, you can find him in his workshop. He's an avid woodworker and candle maker. On any given afternoon you can find him working at a lathe or putting the finishing touches on a bookcase. One of his favorite projects is making candle sticks and the candles to go with them.